CRACKNELL'S STATUTES

Land:
THE LAW OF REAL PROPERTY

Sixth Edition

D G CRACKNELL
LLB, of the Middle Temple, Barrister

OLD BAILEY PRESS

OLD BAILEY PRESS
at Holborn College, Woolwich Road,
Charlton, London, SE7 8LN

First published 1997
Sixth edition 2005

ISBN 1 85836 585 6

British Library Cataloguing-in-Publication.

A CIP Catalogue record for this book is available from the
British Library.

Printed and bound in Great Britain.

CONTENTS

Preface	vii
Alphabetical Table of Statutes	ix
Fires Prevention (Metropolis) Act 1774	1
Prescription Act 1832	2–4
Wills Act 1837	5–6
Common Law Procedure Act 1852	7–8
Bodies Corporate (Joint Tenancy) Act 1899	9
Law of Property Act 1922	10–12
Settled Land Act 1925	13–76
Trustee Act 1925	77–83
Law of Property Act 1925	84–157
Administration of Estates Act 1925	158–164
Law of Property (Amendment) Act 1926	165
Landlord and Tenant Act 1927	166–169
Law of Property (Amendment) Act 1929	170
Law of Property (Entailed Interests) Act 1932	171
Leasehold Property (Repairs) Act 1938	172–174
Settled Land and Trustee Acts (Court's General Powers) Act 1943	175–176
Landlord and Tenant Act 1954	177–183
Rights of Light Act 1959	184–187
Married Women's Property Act 1964	188
Perpetuities and Accumulations Act 1964	189–195
Law of Property (Joint Tenants) Act 1964	196
Commons Registration Act 1965	197–200
Misrepresentation Act 1967	201–202
Leasehold Reform Act 1967	203–209

Contents

Law of Property Act 1969   210–212

Administration of Justice Act 1970   213–214

Defective Premises Act 1972   215–216

Land Charges Act 1972   217–227

Administration of Justice Act 1973   228–229

Matrimonial Causes Act 1973   230–231

Consumer Credit Act 1974   232–234

Local Land Charges Act 1975   235–240

Race Relations Act 1976   241–243

Rent Act 1977   244–261

Protection from Eviction Act 1977   262–267

Criminal Law Act 1977   268–272

Charging Orders Act 1979   273–274

Limitation Act 1980   275–286

Supreme Court Act 1981   287–288

Civil Aviation Act 1982   289–290

County Courts Act 1984   291–294

Matrimonial and Family Proceedings Act 1984   295

Housing Act 1985   296–301

Landlord and Tenant Act 1985   302–310

Agricultural Holdings Act 1986   311–317

Reverter of Sites Act 1987   318–323

Landlord and Tenant Act 1988   324–326

Housing Act 1988   327–361

Law of Property (Miscellaneous Provisions) Act 1989   362–364

Local Government and Housing Act 1989   365–366

Town and County Planning Act 1990   367–372

Planning (Listed Buildings and Conservation Areas) Act 1990   373–374

Water Resources Act 1991   375–378

Access to Neighbouring Land Act 1992   379–383

Charities Act 1993   384–385

Leasehold Reform, Housing and Urban Development Act 1993   386–392

Contents

Law of Property (Miscellaneous Provisions) Act 1994   393–401

Agricultural Tenancies Act 1995   402–412

Landlord and Tenants (Covenants) Act 1995   413–434

Disability Discrimination Act 1995   435–439

Treasure Act 1996   440–444

Party Wall etc Act 1996   445–458

Trusts of Land and Appointment of Trustees Act 1996   459–475

Family Law Act 1996   476–502

Housing Act 1996   503–523

Trustee Act 2000   524–526

Land Registration Act 2002   527–569

Commonhold and Leasehold Reform Act 2002   570–606

Gender Recognition Act 2004   607–608

Civil Partnership Act 2004   609–611

Index   613–620

PREFACE

WHILE the 1925 property legislation remains the cornerstone of English land law, many other statutes contain rules of vital importance. The extent and complexity of these rules – particularly in the field of landlord and tenant – make it impossible to include every provision of every Act. Nevertheless, the statutes covered, in whole or in part, all in their present form, are those to which students will need to refer, if only to obtain a clear indication of the general purpose and framework of the legislation.

Changes – insertions, substitutions and repeals – in force on 1 May 2005 have been taken into account. The source of any changes is noted at the end of a particular statute.

However, relevant provisions of the Civil Partnership Act 2004, and amendments made by them, have been included since it is known that they will come into force on 5 December 2005. Certain provisions of the Housing Act 2004 have also been covered and note has been made in the text where they are not yet in force.

Observations and suggestions as to material to include in, or omit from, the next edition would be gratefully received and carefully considered.

ALPHABETICAL TABLE OF STATUTES

Access to Neighbouring Land Act 1992
379–383
    s1   *379–380*
    s3   *380–382*
    s4   *382*
    s5   *382*
    s8   *383*

Administration of Estates Act 1925
158–164
    s1   *158*
    s2   *158–159*
    s3   *159*
    s9   *159–160*
    s33   *160–161*
    s35   *161*
    s36   *161–163*
    s55   *163–164*

Administration of Justice Act 1970
213–214
    s36   *213*
    s39   *213–214*

Administration of Justice Act 1973
    s8   *228–229*

Agricultural Holdings Act 1986   *311–317*
    s1   *311*
    s2   *312*
    s3   *312*
    s4   *313*
    s5   *313*
    s10   *313–314*
    s16   *314–315*
    s17   *315*
    s18   *315*
    s23   *315–316*
    s24   *316*
    s96   *316–317*

Agricultural Tenancies Act 1995
402–412

Agricultural Tenancies Act 1995 (*contd.*)
    s1   *402–403*
    s2   *403*
    s4   *403–404*
    s5   *404–405*
    s8   *405–406*
    s9   *406*
    s10   *406*
    s12   *406–407*
    s13   *407*
    s14   *407*
    s15   *407*
    s16   *407–408*
    s17   *408*
    s18   *408*
    s19   *408*
    s20   *409*
    s21   *409*
    s22   *409*
    s27   *410*
    s30   *410*
    s32   *410*
    s33   *410*
    s34   *411*
    s37   *411*
    s38   *411–412*
    s41   *412*

Bodies Corporate (Joint Tenancy) Act 1899
    s1   *9*

Charging Orders Act 1979   *273–274*
    s1   *273*
    s2   *273–274*
    s3   *274*
    s6   *274*

Charities Act 1993   *384–385*

Charities Act 1993 (*contd.*)
s35 *384*
s36 *384–385*
Civil Aviation Act 1982 *289–290*
s76 *289*
s105 *290*
Civil Partnership Act 2004 *609–611*
s1 *609*
s65 *609–610*
s66 *610*
s67 *610–611*
s68 *611*
Common Law Procedure Act 1852 *7–8*
s210 *7*
s211 *7–8*
s212 *8*
Commonhold and Leasehold Reform Act
2002 *570–606*
s1 *570*
s2 *570–571*
s3 *571*
s4 *571*
s7 *571–572*
s9 *572–573*
s10 *573*
s11 *573*
s12 *573*
s13 *574*
s14 *574*
s15 *574–575*
s16 *575*
s17 *575–576*
s18 *576*
s19 *576*
s20 *576–577*
s21 *577–578*
s22 *578*
s25 *578–579*
s26 *579*
s27 *579*
s28 *579*
s29 *580*
s31 *580–581*
s32 *581*
s33 *581*

Commonhold and Leasehold Reform Act
2002 (*contd.*)
s34 *581*
s35 *581–582*
s37 *582*
s57 *582*
s61 *582–583*
s63 *583*
s66 *583*
s67 *583*
s69 *583–584*
s71 *584*
s72 *584–585*
s73 *585*
s74 *585–586*
s75 *586*
s76 *586–587*
s77 *587–588*
s78 *588–589*
s79 *589–590*
s84 *590–591*
s95 *591*
s96 *591–592*
s97 *592*
s100 *592–593*
s101 *593*
s102 *593*
s109 *593–594*
s112 *594–595*
s164 *595–596*
s166 *596–597*
s167 *597–598*
s168 *598–599*
s169 *599–600*
s173 *600*
s175 *600–601*
s179 *601*
Schedule 1 *601–602*
Schedule 2 *602–603*
Schedule 6 *603–605*
Schedule 7 *605–606*
Commons Registration Act 1965
197–200
s1 *197*
s8 *197–198*

Commons Registration Act 1965 (*contd.*)
    s9   *198*
    s10   *198*
    s12   *198*
    s16   *198–199*
    s21   *199*
    s22   *199–200*
Consumer Credit Act 1974   *232–234*
    s8   *232*
    s9   *232*
    s94   *232*
    s137   *232–233*
    s138   *233*
    s139   *233–234*
    s140   *234*
County Courts Act 1984   *291–294*
    s138   *291–293*
    s139   *293*
    s140   *293–294*
Criminal Law Act 1977   *268–272*
    s6   *268–269*
    s7   *269*
    s12   *269–270*
    s12A   *270–272*

Defective Premises Act 1972   *215–216*
    s4   *215–216*
    s6   *216*
Disability Discrimination Act 1995
435–439
    s18A   *435*
    s18B   *436*
    s22   *436–437*
    s23   *437–438*
    s24   *438–439*
    s25   *439*

Family Law Act 1996   *476–502*
    s30   *476–477*
    s31   *477–479*
    s32   *479*
    s33   *479–481*
    s34   *481*
    s35   *481–483*
    s36   *483–485*

Family Law Act 1996 (*contd.*)
    s37   *486*
    s38   *486–487*
    s39   *487–488*
    s40   *488*
    s41   *489*
    s42   *489*
    s43   *489*
    s44   *489–490*
    s45   *490*
    s46   *490–491*
    s47   *491*
    s49   *491*
    s53   *491*
    s54   *491–492*
    s55   *492*
    s56   *492–493*
    s62   *493–494*
    s63   *494–496*
    Schedule 7   *496–502*
    Schedule 9   *502*
Fires Prevention (Metropolis) Act 1774
    1–2
    s83   *1*
    s86   *1*

Gender Recognition Act 2004   *607–608*
    s1   *607*
    s15   *607*
    s16   *607*
    s17   *607–608*
    s18   *608*

Housing Act 1985   *296–301*
    s79   *296*
    s80   *296–297*
    s81   *297*
    s82   *297*
    s82A   *297–298*
    s118   *298*
    s119   *299*
    s120   *299*
    s121   *299*
    s121A   *299*
    s183   *299–300*

Housing Act 1985 (*contd.*)
  s610   *300*
  Schedule 5   *300–301*
Housing Act 1988   *327–361*
  s1   *327–328*
  s2   *328*
  s3   *328–329*
  s4   *329*
  s5   *329–330*
  s6   *331–332*
  s6A   *332–333*
  s7   *333–334*
  s15   *334–335*
  s16   *335*
  s19A   *335*
  s20   *335–336*
  s20A   *336–337*
  s20B   *338*
  s21   *338–339*
  s27   *340–342*
  s34   *342–343*
  s35   *343–345*
  s36   *345–346*
  s37   *346–347*
  s38   *347–348*
  Schedule 1   *349–353*
  Schedule 2   *353–358*
  Schedule 2A   *359–361*
Housing Act 1996   *503–523*
  s1   *503*
  s2   *503–505*
  s8   *505*
  s9   *506–506*
  s10   *506*
  s16   *506–508*
  s17   *508*
  s37   *508*
  s38   *508*
  s63   *509*
  s81   *510–511*
  s124   *511–512*
  s125   *512–513*
  s125A   *513*
  s125B   *513–514*

Housing Act 1996 (*contd.*)
  s126   *514*
  s127   *514*
  s128   *514*
  s131   *515*
  s132   *515*
  s133   *515–516*
  s134   *516–517*
  s138   *517*
  s139   *517*
  s140   *517*
  s143A   *517–518*
  s143B   *518*
  s143D   *518*
  s143H   *519*
  s143K   *519*
  s143O   *519–520*
  s143P   *520*
  s153A   *520–521*
  s153B   *521*
  s153E   *521–522*
  s229   *522*
  s230   *522–523*

Land Charges Act 1972   *217–227*
  s1   *217–218*
  s2   *218–220*
  s3   *220*
  s4   *220–221*
  s5   *221–222*
  s6   *222*
  s7   *223*
  s8   *223*
  s9   *223*
  s10   *223–224*
  s11   *224*
  s12   *224*
  s13   *224–225*
  s14   *225*
  s17   *225–226*
  Schedule 1   *226*
  Schedule 2   *226*
Land Registration Act 2002   *527–569*
  s1   *527*

Land Registration Act 2002 (*contd.*)

s2	*527*
s3	*528*
s4	*528–530*
s6	*530*
s7	*530–531*
s8	*531*
s9	*531–532*
s10	*532*
s11	*532–533*
s12	*533–534*
s14	*534*
s15	*534–535*
s16	*535*
s17	*535*
s18	*535–536*
s19	*536*
s22	*536*
s23	*536–537*
s24	*537*
s25	*537*
s26	*537*
s27	*537–538*
s28	*538*
s29	*538–539*
s30	*539*
s32	*539–540*
s33	*540*
s34	*540*
s35	*541*
s36	*541*
s37	*541*
s38	*542*
s40	*542*
s41	*542*
s42	*543*
s43	*543–544*
s44	*544*
s45	*544*
s46	*544–545*
s47	*545*
s48	*545*
s49	*545–546*
s50	*546*

Land Registration Act 2002 (*contd.*)

s51	*546*
s52	*546*
s53	*546*
s54	*547*
s55	*547*
s56	*547*
s57	*547*
s58	*547*
s59	*547*
s60	*548*
s61	*548*
s62	*548–549*
s63	*549*
s64	*549*
s65	*549*
s66	*550*
s67	*550*
s70	*550–551*
s71	*551*
s72	*551–552*
s73	*552*
s74	*552*
s77	*552–553*
s78	*553*
s85	*553*
s86	*553–554*
s87	*554*
s88	*554*
s89	*554–555*
s96	*555*
s97	*555*
s98	*555–556*
s99	*556*
s100	*556–557*
s107	*557*
s108	*557*
s111	*557–558*
s112	*558*
s115	*558*
s116	*558*
s117	*558*
s120	*559*
s127	*559*

Land Registration Act 2002 (*contd.*)
s129   *559*
s130   *559–560*
s131   *560*
s132   *560–561*
Schedule 1   *561–562*
Schedule 2   *562–563*
Schedule 3   *564–565*
Schedule 6   *565–569*
Landlord and Tenant Act 1927   *166–169*
s18   *166–167*
s19   *167–169*
Landlord and Tenant Act 1954   *177–183*
s23   *177–178*
s24   *178–179*
s24A   *179*
s25   *179–180*
s28   *180*
s33   *180*
s34   *180–181*
s35   *181–182*
s43   *182*
s51   *182–183*
s53   *183*
Landlord and Tenant Act 1985   *302–310*
s8   *302–303*
s9   *303*
s10   *303–304*
s11   *304–305*
s12   *305–306*
s13   *306*
s14   *306–307*
s15   *307*
s16   *307*
s17   *308*
s18   *308*
s19   *308–309*
s32   *309*
s36   *309*
s37   *309–310*
s38   *310*
Landlord and Tenant Act 1988   *324–326*
s1   *324–325*
s3   *325–326*

Landlord and Tenant Act 1988 (*contd.*)
s4   *326*
s5   *326*
Landlord and Tenant (Covenants) Act 1995
413–434
s1   *413*
s2   *413–414*
s3   *414–415*
s4   *415*
s5   *415*
s6   *416*
s7   *416–417*
s8   *417*
s9   *417–418*
s10   *418–419*
s11   *419–420*
s12   *420–421*
s13   *421–422*
s15   *422*
s16   *422–424*
s17   *424–425*
s18   *426*
s19   *426–428*
s20   *428–429*
s21   *429–430*
s23   *430*
s24   *430–431*
s25   *431–432*
s26   *432*
s28   *432–433*
s29   *434*
s30   *434*
s31   *434*
Law of Property Act 1922   *10–12*
s145   *10*
s190   *10*
Fifteenth Schedule   *10–12*
Law of Property Act 1925   *84–157*
s1   *84–85*
s2   *85–87*
s3   *87*
s4   *87–88*
s5   *88*
s6   *88*
s7   *88–89*

Law of Property Act 1925 (*contd.*)

s8	*89*
s9	*89–90*
s12	*90*
s13	*90*
s14	*90*
s15	*90*
s20	*90*
s21	*91*
s22	*91*
s24	*91*
s27	*91–92*
s31	*92*
s33	*92*
s34	*93*
s36	*93–94*
s37	*94*
s38	*94*
s39	*94*
s51	*94–95*
s52	*95*
s53	*95*
s54	*95–96*
s55	*96*
s56	*96*
s57	*96*
s59	*96*
s60	*96–97*
s61	*97*
s62	*97–98*
s63	*98*
s65	*98–99*
s67	*99*
s68	*99*
s72	*99*
s77	*99–101*
s78	*101*
s79	*101*
s80	*101–102*
s81	*102*
s82	*103*
s83	*103*
s84	*103–106*
s85	*106–107*

Law of Property Act 1925 (*contd.*)

s86	*107*
s87	*108*
s88	*108–109*
s89	*109–110*
s90	*111*
s91	*111–112*
s92	*112*
s93	*112*
s94	*112–113*
s95	*113*
s96	*113–114*
s97	*114*
s98	*114*
s99	*114–117*
s100	*117–119*
s101	*119–120*
s102	*120*
s103	*121*
s104	*121*
s105	*121–122*
s106	*122*
s107	*122*
s108	*122–123*
s109	*123–124*
s110	*124–125*
s111	*125*
s113	*125–126*
s114	*126*
s115	*126–127*
s116	*128*
s117	*128*
s119	*128–129*
s120	*129*
s130	*129*
s132	*129–130*
s134	*130*
s135	*130*
s137	*130–132*
s139	*132*
s140	*132–133*
s141	*133*
s142	*133–134*
s143	*134*
s144	*135*

Law of Property Act 1925 (*contd.*)
s146	*135–137*
s147	*137*
s148	*138*
s149	*138–139*
s150	*139–140*
s152	*140–141*
s153	*141–143*
s154	*143*
s155	*143*
s156	*143*
s157	*144*
s158	*144*
s159	*144–145*
s161	*145*
s162	*145–146*
s164	*146*
s165	*147*
s166	*147*
s173	*147*
s174	*147–148*
s184	*148*
s185	*148*
s186	*148*
s187	*148*
s193	*148–149*
s194	*149–150*
s198	*150*
s199	*150–151*
s200	*151–152*
s201	*152*
s205	*152–155*
First Schedule	*155–156*
Second Schedule	*156–157*

Law of Property Act 1969   *210–212*
s23	*210*
s24	*210*
s25	*211–212*

Law of Property (Amendment) Act 1926
s1	*165*

Law of Property (Amendment) Act 1929
s1	*170*

Law of Property (Entailed Interests) Act 1932
s2	*171*

Law of Property (Joint Tenants) Act 1964 *196*
s1	*196*
s3	*196*

Law of Property (Miscellaneous Provisions) Act 1989   *362–364*
s1	*362–363*
s2	*363–364*

Law of Property (Miscellaneous Provisions) Act 1994   *393–401*
s1	*393*
s2	*393–394*
s3	*394–395*
s4	*395*
s5	*395–396*
s6	*396*
s7	*396*
s8	*396–397*
s9	*397*
s10	*397*
s11	*397–398*
s12	*398–399*
s13	*399*
s14	*399*
s15	*399–400*
s16	*400*
s17	*400*
s18	*400–401*
s20	*401*
s21	*401*
s23	*401*

Leasehold Property (Repairs) Act 1938 *172–174*
s1	*172–173*
s2	*173*
s3	*173*
s6	*173*
s7	*174*

Leasehold Reform Act 1967   *203–209*
s1	*203–206*
s1A	*206*
s1AA	*206–207*
s1B	*207*
s2	*207–208*
s3	*208*

Leasehold Reform Act 1967 (*contd.*)
   s4   *208*
   s4A   *208–209*
Leasehold Reform, Housing and Urban
  Development Act 1993   *386–392*
   s1   *386–387*
   s2   *387–388*
   s3   *388*
   s4   *388–389*
   s4A   *389*
   s4B   *389–390*
   s5   *390*
   s7   *390–391*
   s39   *391–392*
Limitation Act 1980   *275–286*
   s1   *275*
   s5   *275*
   s15   *275–276*
   s16   *276*
   s17   *276*
   s18   *276–277*
   s19   *277*
   s19A   *277*
   s20   *277–278*
   s28   *279*
   s29   *279–280*
   s30   *280*
   s31   *280–281*
   s32   *281–282*
   s36   *282*
   s38   *283–284*
   Schedule 1   *284–286*
Local Government and Housing Act 1989
  365–366
   s186   *365*
   Schedule 10   *366*
Local Land Charges Act 1975   *235–240*
   s1   *235–236*
   s2   *236*
   s3   *236–237*
   s4   *237*
   s6   *237*
   s7   *238*
   s10   *238–240*
   s11   *240*

Local Land Charges Act 1975 (*contd.*)
   s12   *240*
   s13   *240*

Married Women's Property Act 1964
   s1   *188*
Matrimonial and Family Proceedings Act
  1984
   s22   *295*
Matrimonial Causes Act 1973   *230–231*
   s24   *230*
   s24A   *231*
Misrepresentation Act 1967   *201–202*
   s1   *201*
   s2   *201*
   s3   *202*

Party Wall etc Act 1996   *445–458*
   s1   *445–446*
   s2   *446–448*
   s3   *448*
   s4   *449*
   s5   *449*
   s6   *449–451*
   s7   *451*
   s8   *451–452*
   s9   *452*
   s10   *452–453*
   s11   *453–455*
   s12   *455*
   s13   *455–456*
   s14   *456*
   s16   *456*
   s17   *456*
   s19   *456–457*
   s20   *457–458*
   s21   *458*
Perpetuities and Accumulations Act 1964
  189–195
   s1   *189*
   s2   *189–190*
   s3   *190–191*
   s4   *191–192*
   s5   *192*
   s6   *192*

Perpetuities and Accumulations Act 1964
(*contd.*)
s7   *192–193*
s8   *193*
s9   *193*
s10   *193–194*
s11   *194*
s12   *194*
s13   *194*
s14   *195*
s15   *195*

Planning (Listed Buildings and
Conservation Areas) Act 1990
373–374
s1   *373*
s72   *373*
s87   *374*

Prescription Act 1832   *2–4*
s1   *2*
s2   *2–3*
s3   *3*
s4   *3*
s5   *3*
s6   *4*
s7   *4*
s8   *4*

Protection from Eviction Act 1977
262–267
s1   *262–263*
s2   *263*
s3   *263–264*
s3A   *264–265*
s5   *265–266*
s8   *266–267*

Race Relations Act 1976   *241–243*
s21   *241*
s22   *241–242*
s23   *242*
s24   *242–243*
s78   *243*

Rent Act 1977   *244–261*
s1   *244*
s2   *244*
s3   *245*

Rent Act 1977 (*contd.*)
s4   *245–246*
s5   *246–247*
s5A   *247–248*
s6   *248*
s7   *248*
s8   *248*
s9   *249*
s10   *249*
s11   *249*
s12   *249–250*
s14   *250*
s15   *250–251*
s16   *251*
s18   *251*
s24   *251*
s26   *251*
s98   *252*
s119 *252*
s123 *253*
s128 *253*
Schedule 15   *253–261*

Reverter of Sites Act 1987   *318–323*
s1   *318–319*
s2   *319–321*
s3   *321–322*
s6   *322*
s7   *322–323*

Rights of Light Act 1959   *184–186*
s2   *184–185*
s3   *185–186*
s7   *186*

Settled Land Act 1925   *13–76*
s1   *13–14*
s2   *14*
s3   *14–15*
s4   *15*
s5   *15–16*
s6   *16*
s7   *16–17*
s8   *17*
s9   *18*
s10   *18–19*

Settled Land Act 1925 (*contd.*)

s11	*19–20*
s12	*20*
s13	*20–21*
s14	*21*
s16	*21–23*
s17	*23*
s18	*24*
s19	*24–25*
s20	*25–26*
s21	*26–27*
s22	*27*
s23	*27–28*
s24	*28*
s25	*28*
s26	*29*
s30	*30*
s33	*30–31*
s34	*31*
s35	*31–32*
s36	*32*
s38	*33*
s39	*33–34*
s40	*34*
s41	*34*
s42	*34–35*
s43	*35*
s44	*35–36*
s45	*36*
s46	*36–37*
s47	*37*
s48	*37*
s49	*38*
s50	*38–39*
s51	*39*
s52	*39–40*
s53	*40*
s54	*41*
s55	*41–42*
s56	*42*
s57	*43*
s58	*43–44*
s59	*44*
s60	*44–45*

Settled Land Act 1925 (*contd.*)

s61	*45*
s62	*45*
s63	*46*
s64	*46*
s65	*46*
s66	*46–47*
s67	*47*
s68	*47–48*
s69	*48*
s70	*48*
s71	*48–49*
s72	*49–50*
s73	*50–52*
s74	*52*
s75	*52–53*
s75A	*53*
s77	*54*
s79	*54*
s83	*54*
s84	*55–56*
s85	*56*
s86	*56*
s87	*56*
s88	*56–57*
s89	*57–58*
s90	*58–59*
s92	*59*
s93	*59*
s94	*59*
s95	*60*
s97	*60*
s98	*60–61*
s99	*61*
s101	*61*
s102	*62–63*
s104	*63–65*
s105	*65*
s106	*65–66*
s107	*66*
s108	*66–67*
s109	*67*
s110	*67–69*
s111	*69*
s112	*69–70*

Settled Land Act 1925 (*contd.*)
    s117   *70–73*
    Third Schedule   *73–74*
Settled Land and Trustee Acts (Court's
    General Powers) Act 1943
    s1   *175–176*
Supreme Court Act 1981   *287–288*
    s37   *287*
    s38   *287–288*
    s39   *288*

Town and Country Planning Act 1990
    367–372
    s55   *367–369*
    s57   *369*
    s58   *369–370*
    s59   *370*
    s62   *370*
    s70   *370–371*
    s70A   *371*
    s106   *371–372*
    s242   *372*
    s328   *372*
Treasure Act 1996   *440–444*
    s1   *440*
    s2   *440*
    s3   *441*
    s4   *441*
    s5   *441–442*
    s6   *442*
    s7   *442*
    s8   *442–443*
    s9   *443*
    s10   *443–444*
    s11   *444*
    s12   *444*
    s15   *444*
Trustee Act 1925   *77–83*
    s12   *77*
    s13   *77*
    s16   *78*
    s17   *78*
    s34   *78*
    s35   *79*
    s40   *79–80*

Trustee Act 1925 (*contd.*)
    s44   *80–81*
    s64   *81–82*
    s67   *82*
    s68   *82–83*
    s69   *83*
Trustee Act 2000   *524–526*
    s1   *524*
    s2   *524*
    s8   *524*
    s9   *525*
    s10   *525*
    s35   *525*
    Schedule 1   *525–526*
Trusts of Land and Appointment of
    Trustees Act 1996   *459–475*
    s1   *459*
    s2   *459–460*
    s3   *460*
    s4   *460*
    s5   *460*
    s6   *461*
    s7   *461–462*
    s8   *462*
    s9   *462–463*
    s9A   *463–464*
    s10   *464*
    s11   *464–465*
    s12   *465*
    s13   *465–466*
    s14   *466*
    s15   *466–467*
    s16   *467–468*
    s17   *468*
    s18   *468–469*
    s19   *469*
    s20   *469–470*
    s21   *470–471*
    s22   *471*
    s23   *471*
    s24   *471–472*
    s25   *472*
    s26   *472*
    Schedule 1   *472–474*
    Schedule 2   *474–475*

Water Resources Act 1991   *375–378*
    s24   *375*
    s27   *376*
    s27A   *376*
    s72   *376–377*
    s221   *377–378*

Wills Act 1837   *5–6*
    s3   *5*
    s23   *5*
    s26   *5*
    s27   *6*
    s28   *6*

FIRES PREVENTION (METROPOLIS) ACT 1774
(14 Geo 3 c 78)

83 Money insured on houses burnt: how to be applied

And in order to deter and hinder ill-minded persons from wilfully setting their house or houses or other buildings on fire with a view of gaining to themselves the insurance money, whereby the lives and fortunes of many families may be lost or endangered: Be it further enacted by the authority aforesaid, that it shall and may be lawful to and for the respective governors or directors of the several insurance offices for insuring houses or other buildings against loss by fire, and they are hereby authorised and required, upon the request of any person or persons interested in or intitled unto any house or houses or other buildings which may hereafter be burnt down, demolished or damaged by fire, or upon any grounds of suspicion that the owner or owners, occupier or occupiers, or other person or persons who shall have insured such house or houses or other buildings have been guilty of fraud, or of wilfully setting their house or houses or other buildings on fire, to cause the insurance money to be laid out and expended, as far as the same will go, towards rebuilding, reinstating or repairing such house or houses or other buildings so burnt down, demolished or damaged by fire, unless the party or parties claiming such insurance money shall, within sixty days next after his, her or their claim is adjusted, give a sufficient security to the governors or directors of the insurance office where such house or houses or other buildings are insured, that the same insurance money shall be laid out and expended as aforesaid, or unless the said insurance money shall be in that time settled and disposed of to and amongst all the contending parties, to the satisfaction and approbation of such governors or directors of such insurance office respectively.

86 No action to lie against a person where the fire accidentally begins

And no action, suit or process whatever shall be had, maintained or prosecuted against any person in whose house, chamber, stable, barn or other building, or on whose estate any fire shall accidentally begin, nor shall any recompence be made by such person for any damage suffered thereby, any law, usage or custom to the contrary notwithstanding: provided that no contract or agreement made between landlord and tenant shall be hereby defeated or made void.

As amended by the Statute Law Revision Acts 1888, 1948 and 1958.

PRESCRIPTION ACT 1832
(2 & 3 Will 4 c 71)

1   Claims to right of common and other profits à prendre, (except tithes, etc), not to be defeated after thirty years enjoyment by merely showing the commencement of the right – after sixty years enjoyment the right to be absolute, unless shown to be had by consent or agreement

No claim which may be lawfully made at the common law, by custom, prescription, or grant, to any right of common or other profit or benefit to be taken and enjoyed from or upon any land of our sovereign lord the King, or any land being parcel of the duchy of Lancaster or of the duchy of Cornwall, or of any ecclesiastical or lay person, or body corporate, except such matters and things as are herein specially provided for, and except tithes, rent, and services, shall, where such right, profit, or benefit shall have been actually taken and enjoyed by any person claiming right thereto without interruption for the full period of thirty years, be defeated or destroyed by showing only that such right, profit, or benefit was first taken or enjoyed at any time prior to such period of thirty years, but nevertheless such claim may be defeated in any other way by which the same is now liable to be defeated; and when such right, profit, or benefit shall have been so taken and enjoyed as aforesaid for the full period of sixty years, the right thereto shall be deemed absolute and indefeasible, unless it shall appear that the same was taken and enjoyed by some consent or agreement expressly made or given for that purpose by deed or writing.

2   In claims of rights of way or other easements the periods to be twenty years and forty years

No claim which may be lawfully made at the common law, by custom, prescription, or grant, to any way or other easement, or to any watercourse, or the use of any water, to be enjoyed or derived upon, over, or from any land or water of our said lord the King, or being parcel of the duchy of Lancaster or of the duchy of Cornwall, or being the property of any ecclesiastical or lay person, or body corporate, when such way or other matter as herein last before mentioned shall have been actually enjoyed by any person claiming right thereto without interruption for the full period of twenty years, shall be defeated or destroyed by showing only that such way or other matter was first enjoyed at any time prior to such period of twenty years, but nevertheless such claim may be defeated in any other way by which the same is now liable to be defeated; and where such way or other matter as herein last before mentioned shall have been so enjoyed as aforesaid for the full period of forty years, the right thereto shall be deemed absolute and indefeasible, unless it shall appear that the same was enjoyed by some consent or agreement expressly given or made for that purpose by deed or writing.

3 Right to the use of light enjoyed for twenty years, indefeasible, unless shown to have been by consent

When the access and use of light to and for any dwelling house, workshop, or other building shall have been actually enjoyed therewith for the full period of twenty years without interruption, the right thereto shall be deemed absolute and indefeasible, any local usage or custom to the contrary notwithstanding, unless it shall appear that the same was enjoyed by some consent or agreement expressly made or given for that purpose by deed or writing.

4 The periods to be those next before the suit or action – what shall constitute an interruption

Each of the respective periods of years herein-before mentioned shall be deemed and taken to be the period next before some suit or action wherein the claim or matter to which such period may relate shall have been or shall be brought into question; and no act or other matter shall be deemed to be an interruption, within the meaning of this statute, unless the same shall have been or shall be submitted to or acquiesced in for one year after the party interrupted shall have had or shall have notice thereof, and of the person making or authorising the same to be made.

5 What claimant may allege

In all actions upon the case and other pleadings, wherein the party claiming may now by law allege his right generally, without averring the existence of such right from time immemorial, such general allegation shall still be deemed sufficient, and if the same shall be denied, all and every the matters in this Act mentioned and provided, which shall be applicable to the case, shall be admissible in evidence to sustain or rebut such allegation; and in all pleadings to actions of trespass, and in all other pleadings wherein before the passing of this Act it would have been necessary to allege the right to have existed from time immemorial, it shall be sufficient to allege the enjoyment thereof as of right by the occupiers of the tenement in respect whereof the same is claimed for and during such of the periods mentioned in this Act as may be applicable to the case, and without claiming in the name or right of the owner of the fee, as is now usually done; and if the other party shall intend to rely on any proviso, exception, incapacity, disability, contract, agreement, or other matter herein-before mentioned, or on any cause or matter of fact or of law not inconsistent with the simple fact of enjoyment, the same shall be specially alleged and set forth in answer to the allegation of the party claiming, and shall not be received in evidence on any general traverse or denial of such allegation.

6 Restricting the presumption to be allowed in support of claims herein provided for

In the several cases mentioned in and provided for by this Act, no presumption shall be allowed or made in favour or support of any claim, upon proof of the exercise or enjoyment of the right or matter claimed for any less period of time or number of years than for such period or number mentioned in this Act as may be applicable to the case and to the nature of the claim.

7 Proviso where any person capable of resisting a claim is an infant, etc

Provided also, that the time during which any person otherwise capable of resisting any claim to any of the matters before mentioned shall have been or shall be an infant, idiot, non compos mentis, feme covert, or tenant for life, or during which any action or suit shall have been pending, and which shall have been diligently prosecuted, until abated by the death of any party or parties thereto, shall be excluded in the computation of the periods herein-before mentioned, except only in cases where the right or claim is hereby declared to be absolute and indefeasible.

8 What time to be excluded in computing the term of forty years appointed by this Act

Provided always, that when any land or water upon, over or from which any such way or other convenient watercourse or use of water shall have been or shall be enjoyed or derived hath been or shall be held under or by virtue of any term of life, or any term of years exceeding three years from the granting thereof, the time of the enjoyment of any such way or other matter as herein last before mentioned, during the continuance of such term, shall be excluded in the computation of the said period of forty years, in case the claim shall within three years next after the end or sooner determination of such term be resisted by any person entitled to any reversion expectant on the determination thereof.

As amended by the Statute Law Revision (No 2) Act 1888; Statute Law Revision Act 1890.

WILLS ACT 1837
(7 Will 4 & 1 Vict c 26)

3 All property may be disposed of by will

It shall be lawful for every person to devise, bequeath, or dispose of, by his will executed in manner herein-after required, all real estate and all personal estate which he shall be entitled to, either at law or in equity, at the time of his death, and which, if not so devised, bequeathed, and disposed of, would devolve upon his executor or administrator; and the power hereby given shall extend to all contingent, executory or other future interests in any real or personal estate, whether the testator may or may not be ascertained as the person or one of the persons in whom the same respectively may become vested, and whether he may be entitled thereto under the instrument by which the same respectively were created, or under any disposition thereof by deed or will; and also to all rights of entry for conditions broken, and other rights of entry; and also to such of the same estates, interests, and rights respectively, and other real and personal estate, as the testator may be entitled to at the time of his death, notwithstanding that he may become entitled to the same subsequently to the execution of his will.

23 A devise not to be rendered inoperative by any subsequent conveyance or act

No conveyance or other act made or done subsequently to the execution of a will of or relating to any real or personal estate therein comprised, except an act by which such will shall be revoked as aforesaid, shall prevent the operation of the will with respect to such estate or interest in such real or personal estate as the testator shall have power to dispose of by will at the time of his death.

26 A general devise of the testator's lands shall include leasehold as well as freehold lands, in the absence of a contrary intention

A devise of the land of the testator, or of the land of the testator in any place or in the occupation of any person mentioned in his will, or otherwise described in a general manner, and any other general devise which would describe a leasehold estate if the testator had no freehold estate which could be described by it, shall be construed to include the leasehold estates of the testator, or his leasehold estates, or any of them, to which such description shall extend, as the case may be, as well as freehold estates, unless a contrary intention shall appear by the will.

27 A general gift of realty or personalty shall include property over which the testator has a general power of appointment

A general devise of the real estate of the testator, or of the real estate of the testator in any place or in the occupation of any person mentioned in his will, or otherwise described in a general manner, shall be construed to include any real estate, or any real estate to which such description shall extend (as the case may be), which he may have power to appoint in any manner he may think proper, and shall operate as an execution of such power, unless a contrary intention shall appear by the will; and in like manner a bequest of the personal estate of the testator, or any bequest of personal property described in a general manner, shall be construed to include any personal estate, or any personal estate to which such description shall extend (as the case may be), which he may have power to appoint in any manner he may think proper, and shall operate as an execution of such power, unless a contrary intention shall appear by the will.

28 A devise of real estate without any words of limitation shall pass the fee, etc

Where any real estate shall be devised to any person without any words of limitation, such devise shall be construed to pass the fee simple, or other the whole estate or interest which the testator had power to dispose of by will in such real estate, unless a contrary intention shall appear by the will.

As amended by the Statute Law Revision (No 2) Act 1888; Statute Law (Repeals) Act 1969.

COMMON LAW PROCEDURE ACT 1852
(15 & 16 Vict c 76)

210 Proceedings in ejectment by landlord for nonpayment of rent

In all cases between landlord and tenant, as often as it shall happen that one half year's rent shall be in arrear, and the landlord or lessor, to whom the same is due, hath right by law to re-enter for the nonpayment thereof, such landlord or lessor shall and may, without any formal demand or re-entry, serve a writ in ejectment for the recovery of the demised premises, which service shall stand in the place and stead of a demand and re-entry; and in case of judgment against the defendant for non-appearance, if it shall be made appear to the court where the said action is depending, by affidavit, or be proved upon the trial in case the defendant appears, that half a year's rent was due before the said writ was served, and that no sufficient distress was to be found on the demised premises, countervailing the arrears then due, and that the lessor had power to re-enter, then and in every such case the lessor shall recover judgment and execution, in the same manner as if the rent in arrear had been legally demanded, and a re-entry made; and in case the lessee or his assignee, or other person claiming or deriving under the said lease, shall permit and suffer judgment to be had and recovered on such trial in ejectment, and execution to be executed thereon, without paying the rent and arrears, together with full costs, and without proceeding for relief in equity within six months after such execution executed, then and in such case the said lessee, his assignee, and all other persons claiming and deriving under the said lease, shall be barred and foreclosed from all relief or remedy in law or equity, other than by bringing error for reversal of such judgment, in case the same shall be erroneous, and the said landlord or lessor shall from thenceforth hold the said demised premises discharged from such lease; provided that nothing herein contained shall extend to bar the right of any mortgagee of such lease, or any part thereof, who shall not be in possession, so as such mortgagee shall and do, within six months after such judgment obtained and execution executed pay all rent in arrear, and all costs and damages sustained by such lessor or person entitled to the remainder or reversion as aforesaid, and perform all the covenants and agreements which, on the part and behalf of the first lessee, are and ought to be performed.

211 Lessee proceeding in equity not to have injunction or relief without payment of rent and costs

In case the said lessee, his assignee, or other person claiming any right, title, or interest, in law or equity, of, in, or to the said lease, shall, within the time aforesaid, proceed for relief in any court of equity, such person shall not have or continue any injunction against the proceedings at law on such ejectment, unless he does or shall, within forty days next after a full and perfect answer shall be made by the claimant in such ejectment, bring into court, and lodge with the proper officer such sum and sums of money as the lessor or landlord shall in his answer swear to be due and in arrear over and above all just allowances, and also the costs taxed in the said suit, there to remain till the hearing of the cause, or to be paid out to the lessor or landlord on good security, subject to the decree of the court; and in case such proceedings for relief in equity shall be taken within the time aforesaid, and after execution is executed, the lessor or landlord shall be accountable only for so much and no more as he shall really and bona fide, without fraud, deceit, or wilful neglect, make of the demised premises from the time of his entering into the actual possession thereof; and if what shall be so made by the lessor or landlord happen to be less than the rent reserved on the said lease, then the said lessee or his assignee, before he shall be restored to his possession, shall pay such lessor or landlord what the money so by him made fell short of the reserved rent for the time such lessor or landlord held the said lands.

212 Tenant paying all rent, with costs, proceedings to cease

If the tenant or his assignee do or shall, at any time before the trial in such ejectment, pay or tender to the lessor or landlord, his executors or administrators, or his or their attorney in that cause, or pay into the court where the same cause is depending, all the rent and arrears, together with the costs, then and in such case all further proceedings on the said ejectment shall cease and be discontinued; and if such lessee, his executors, administrators, or assigns, shall, upon such proceedings as aforesaid, be relieved in equity, he and they shall have, hold, and enjoy the demised lands, according to the lease thereof made, without any new lease.

As amended by the Statute Law Revision Act 1892.

BODIES CORPORATE (JOINT TENANCY) ACT 1899
(62 & 63 Vict c 20)

1   Power for corporations to hold property as joint tenants

(1) A body corporate shall be capable of acquiring and holding any real or personal property in joint tenancy in the same manner as if it were an individual; and where a body corporate and an individual, or two or more bodies corporate, become entitled to any such property under circumstances or by virtue of any instrument which would, if the body corporate had been an individual, have created a joint tenancy, they shall be entitled to the property as joint tenants:

Provided that the acquisition and holding of property by a body corporate in joint tenancy shall be subject to the like conditions and restrictions as attach to the acquisition and holding of property to a body corporate in severalty.

(2) Where a body corporate is joint tenant of any property, then on its dissolution the property shall devolve on the other joint tenant.

LAW OF PROPERTY ACT 1922
(12 & 13 Geo 5 c 16)

145 Conversion of perpetually renewable leaseholds

For the purpose of converting perpetually renewable leases and underleases (not being an interest in perpetually renewable copyhold land enfranchised by Part V of this Act, but including a perpetually renewable underlease derived out of an interest in perpetually renewable copyhold land) into long terms, for preventing the creation of perpetually renewable leasehold interests and for providing for the interests of the persons affected, the provisions contained in the Fifteenth Schedule to this Act shall have effect.

190 Special definitions applicable to Part VII

In Part VII of this Act –

...

(iii) 'A perpetually renewable lease or underlease' means a lease or underlease the holder of which is entitled to enforce (whether or not subject to the fulfilment of any condition) the perpetual renewal thereof, and includes a lease or underlease for a life or lives or for a term of years, whether determinable with life or lives or not, which is perpetually renewable as aforesaid, but does not include copyhold land held for a life or lives or for years, whether or not determinable with life, where the tenant had before the commencement of this Act a right of perpetual renewal subject or not to the fulfilment of any condition;

(iv) 'Underlease', unless the context otherwise requires, includes a subterm created out of a derivative leasehold interest.

FIFTEENTH SCHEDULE

PROVISIONS RELATING TO PERPETUALLY RENEWABLE LEASES AND UNDERLEASES

1. *Conversion of perpetually renewable leases into long terms*

(1) Land comprised in a perpetually renewable lease which was subsisting at the commencement of this Act shall, by virtue of this Act, vest in the person who at such commencement was entitled to such lease, for a term of two thousand years, to be calculated from the date at which the existing term or interest commenced, at the rent and subject to the lessees' covenants and conditions (if any) which under the

lease would have been payable or enforceable during the subsistence of such term or interest.

(2) The rent, covenants and conditions (if any) shall (subject to the express provisions of this Act to the contrary) be payable and enforceable during the subsistence of the term created by this Act; and that term shall take effect in substitution for the term or interest created by the lease, and be subject to the like power of re-entry (if any) and other provisions which affected the term or interest created by the lease, but without any right of renewal. ...

5. *Dispositions purporting to create perpetually renewable leaseholds*

A grant, after the commencement of this Act, of a term, subterm, or other leasehold interest with a covenant or obligation for perpetual renewal, which would have been valid if this Part of this Act had not been passed, shall (subject to the express provisions of this Act) take effect as a demise for a term of two thousand years or in the case of a subdemise for a term less in duration by one day than the term out of which it is derived, to commence from the date fixed for the commencement of the term, subterm, or other interest, and in every case free from any obligation for renewal or for payment of any fines, fees, costs, or other money in respect of renewal. ...

10. *Powers and covenants implied in leases and underleases affected*

(1) Every lease or underlease which, by virtue of this Part of this Act, takes effect for a term of two thousand years or for a derivative term of two thousand years less one or more days (as the case may require) shall be deemed to contain –

(i) A power (exerciseable only with the consent of the person, if any, interested in any derivative interest which might be prejudicially affected) for the lessee or underlessee by giving notice in writing to the lessor at least ten days before the lease or underlease would (but for this Act) have expired if it had not been renewed after the commencement of this Act, to determine the lease or underlease at the date on which (but for this Act) it would have expired if it had not been renewed as aforesaid; also a like power (exerciseable with the like consent if any) to determine subsequently by notice as aforesaid the lease or underlease at the time at which, if this Act had not been passed and all renewals had in the meantime been made in due course, the lease or underlease would have expired if it had not been further renewed after the date of the notice:

Provided that if any such notice be given all uncommuted additional rent attributable to a fine or other money which, if this Act had not been passed, would have been payable on a renewal made after the date of the notice, shall cease or not become payable:

(ii) A covenant by the lessee or underlessee to register every assignment or devolution of the term or subterm, including all probates or letters of administration affecting the same, with the lessor or his solicitor or agent, within six months from the date of the assignment, devolution, or grant of probate or letters of administration, and to pay a fee of one guinea (which shall be accepted in satisfaction of all costs) in respect of each registration; and the covenant so deemed to be contained shall be in substitution for any express covenant to register with the lessor or his solicitor or agent, assignments or devolutions of the term or subterm, and to pay fees or costs in respect of such registration:

(iii) A covenant by the lessee or underlessee within one year from the commencement of this Act to produce his lease or underlease or sufficient evidence thereof (including an assignment of part of the land comprised in the lease or underlease) with any particulars required to show that a perpetual right of renewal was subsisting at the commencement of this Act, to the lessor or his solicitor or agent, who shall, subject to the payment of his costs, if the right of renewal is admitted or proved, endorse notice of that fact on the lease, underlease, assignment, or copy thereof, at the expense of the lessee or underlessee; and such endorsement signed by or on behalf of the lessor shall, in favour of a purchaser, be sufficient evidence that the right of renewal was subsisting as aforesaid, either in respect of the whole or part of the land as the case may require:

and the power of re-entry (if any) contained in the lease or underlease shall apply and extend to the breach of every covenant deemed to be contained as aforesaid.

(2) If any dispute arises respecting the date on which a notice is authorised to be served by this section, or whether or not a lease or underlease or assignment or a copy thereof ought to be endorsed as aforesaid, the matter shall be submitted to the Secretary of State for determination in the manner provided by this Act. ...

As amended by the Ministry of Agriculture, Fisheries and Food (Dissolution) Order 2002, art 5(1), Schedule 1, para 1.

SETTLED LAND ACT 1925
(15 Geo 5 c 18)

PART I

GENERAL PRELIMINARY PROVISIONS

1   What constitutes a settlement

(1) Any deed, will, agreement for a settlement or other agreement, Act of Parliament. or other instrument, or any number of instruments, whether made or passed before or after, or partly before and partly after, the commencement of this Act, under or by virtue of which instrument or instruments any land, after the commencement of this Act, stands for the time being –

(i) limited in trust for any persons by way of succession; or

(ii) limited in trust for any person in possession –

(a) for an entailed interest whether or not capable of being barred or defeated;

(b) for an estate in fee simple or for a term of years absolute subject to an executory limitation, gift, or disposition over on failure of his issue or in any other event;

(c) for a base or determinable fee (other than a fee which is a fee simple absolute by virtue of section 7 of the Law of Property Act 1925) or any corresponding interest in leasehold land;

(d) being an infant, for an estate in fee simple or for a term of years absolute; or

(iii) limited in trust for any person for an estate in fee simple or for a term of years absolute contingently on the happening of any event; or

(v) charged, whether voluntarily or in consideration of marriage or by way of family arrangement, and whether immediately or after an interval, with the payment of any rentcharge for the life of any person, or any less period, or of any capital, annual, or periodical sums for the portions, advancement, maintenance, or otherwise for the benefit of any persons, with or without any term of years for securing or raising the same;

creates or is for the purposes of this Act a settlement and is in this Act referred to as a settlement, or as the settlement, as the case requires: provided that, where land is the subject of a compound settlement, references in this Act to the settlement shall be construed as meaning such compound settlement, unless the context otherwise requires.

(2) Where an infant is beneficially entitled to land for an estate in fee simple or for a term of years absolute and by reason of an intestacy or otherwise there is no instrument under which the interest of the infant arises or is acquired, a settlement shall be deemed to have been made by the intestate, or by the person whose interest the infant has acquired.

(3) An infant shall be deemed to be entitled in possession notwithstanding any subsisting right of dower (not assigned by metes and bounds) affecting the land, and such a right of dower shall be deemed to be an interest comprised in the subject of the settlement and coming to the dowress under or by virtue of the settlement. Where dower has been assigned by metes and bounds, the letters of administration or probate granted in respect of the estate of the husband of the dowress shall be deemed a settlement made by the husband.

(4) An estate or interest not disposed of by a settlement and remaining in or reverting to the settlor, or any person deriving title under him, is for the purposes of this Act an estate or interest comprised in the subject of the settlement and coming to the settlor or such person under or by virtue of the settlement.

(5) Where –

    (a) a settlement creates an entailed interest which is incapable of being barred or defeated, or a base or determinable fee, whether or not the reversion or right of reverter is in the Crown, or any corresponding interest in leasehold land; or

    (b) the subject of a settlement is an entailed interest, or a base or determinable fee, whether or not the reversion or right of reverter is in the Crown, or any corresponding interest in leasehold land;

the reversion or right of reverter upon the cesser of the interest so created or settled shall be deemed to be an interest comprised in the subject of the settlement, and limited by the settlement.

(6) Subsections (4) and (5) of this section bind the Crown.

(7) This section does not apply to land held upon trust for sale.

2   What is settled land

Land not held upon trust for sale which is or is deemed to be the subject of a settlement is for the purposes of this Act settled land, and is in relation to the settlement referred to in this Act as the settled land.

3   Duration of settlements

Land which has been subject to a settlement which is a settlement for the purposes of this Act shall be deemed for the purposes of this Act to remain and be settled land, and the settlement shall be deemed to be a subsisting settlement for the purposes of this Act so long as –

(a) any limitation, charge, or power of charging under the settlement subsists, or is capable of being exercised; or

(b) the person who, if of full age, would be entitled as beneficial owner to have that land vested in him for a legal estate is an infant.

4   Authorised method of settling land inter vivos

(1) Every settlement of a legal estate in land inter vivos shall, save as in this Act otherwise provided, be effected by two deeds, namely, a vesting deed and a trust instrument and if effected in any other way shall not operate to transfer or create a legal estate.

(2) By the vesting deed the land shall be conveyed to the tenant for life or statutory owner (and if more than one as joint tenants) for the legal estate the subject of the intended settlement: provided that, where such legal estate is already vested in the tenant for life or statutory owner, it shall be sufficient, without any other conveyance, if the vesting deed declares that the land is vested in him for that estate.

(3) The trust instrument shall –

(a) declare the trusts affecting the settled land;

(b) appoint or constitute trustees of the settlement;

(c) contain the power, if any, to appoint new trustees of the settlement;

(d) set out, either expressly or by reference, any powers intended to be conferred by the settlement in extension of those conferred by this Act;

(e) bear any ad valorem stamp duty which may be payable (whether by virtue of the vesting deed or otherwise) in respect of the settlement.

5   Contents of vesting deeds

(1) Every vesting deed for giving effect to a settlement or for conveying settled land to a tenant for life or statutory owner during the subsistence of the settlement (in this Act referred to as a 'principal vesting deed') shall contain the following statements and particulars, namely –

(a) A description, either specific or general, of the settled land;

(b) A statement that the settled land is vested in the person or persons to whom it is conveyed or in whom it is declared to be vested upon the trusts from time to time affecting the settled land;

(c) The names of the persons who are the trustees of the settlement;

(d) Any additional or larger powers conferred by the trust instrument relating to the settled land which by virtue of this Act operate and are exercisable as if conferred by this Act on a tenant for life;

(e) The name of any person for the time being entitled under the trust instrument to appoint new trustees of the settlement.

(2) The statements or particulars required by this section may be incorporated by

reference to an existing vesting instrument, and, where there is a settlement subsisting at the commencement of this Act, by reference to that settlement and to any instrument whereby land has been conveyed to the uses or upon the trusts of that settlement, but not (save as last aforesaid) by reference to a trust instrument nor by reference to a disentailing deed.

(3) A principal vesting deed shall not be invalidated by reason only of any error in any of the statements or particulars by this Act required to be contained therein.

6   Procedure in the case of settlements by will

Where a settlement is created by the will of an estate owner who dies after the commencement of this Act –

    (a) the will is for the purposes of this Act a trust instrument; and

    (b) the personal representatives of the testator shall hold the settled land on trust, if and when required so to do, to convey it to the person who, under the will, or by virtue of this Act, is the tenant for life or statutory owner, and, if more than one, as joint tenants.

7   Procedure on change of ownership

(1) If, on the death of a tenant for life or statutory owner, or of the survivor of two or more tenants for life or statutory owners, in whom the settled land was vested, the land remains settled land, his personal representatives shall hold the settled land on trust, if and when required so to do, to convey it to the person who under the trust instrument or by virtue of this Act becomes the tenant for life or statutory owner and, if more than one, as joint tenants.

(2) If a person by reason of attaining full age becomes a tenant for life for the purposes of this Act of settled land, he shall be entitled to require the trustees of the settlement, personal representatives, or other persons in whom the settled land is vested, to convey the land to him.

(3) If a person who, when of full age, will together with another person or other persons constitute the tenant for life for the purposes of this Act of settled land attains that age, he shall be entitled to require the tenant for life, trustees of the settlement, personal representatives or other persons in whom the settled land is vested to convey the land to him and the other person or persons who together with him constitute the tenant for life as joint tenants.

(4) If by reason of forfeiture, surrender, or otherwise the estate owner of any settled land ceases to have the statutory powers of a tenant for life and the land remains settled land, he shall be bound forthwith to convey the settled land to the person who under the trust instrument, or by virtue of this Act, becomes the tenant for life or statutory owner and, if more than one, as joint tenants.

(5) If any person of full age becomes absolutely entitled to the settled land (whether beneficially, or as personal representative, or as trustee of land, or otherwise) free from all limitations, powers, and charges taking effect under the settlement, he

shall be entitled to require the trustees of the settlement, personal representatives, or other persons in whom the settled land is vested, to convey the land to him, and if more persons than one being of full age become so entitled to the settled land they shall be entitled to require such persons as aforesaid to convey the land to them as joint tenants.

8   Mode and costs of conveyance, and saving of rights of personal representatives and equitable chargees

(1) A conveyance by personal representatives under either of the last two preceding sections may be made by an assent in writing signed by them which shall operate as a conveyance.

(2) Every conveyance under either of the last two preceding sections shall be made at the cost of the trust estate.

(3) The obligations to convey settled land imposed by the last two preceding sections are subject and without prejudice –

(a) where the settlement is created by a will, to the rights and powers of the personal representatives for purposes of administration; and

(b) in any case, to the person on whom the obligation is imposed being satisfied that provision has been or will be made for the payment of any unpaid death duties in respect of the land or any interest therein for which he is accountable, and any interest and costs in respect of such duties, or that he is otherwise effectually indemnified against such duties, interest and costs.

(4) Where the land is or remains settled land a conveyance under either of the last two preceding sections shall –

(a) if by deed, be a principal vesting deed; and

(b) if by an assent, be a vesting assent, which shall contain the like statements and particulars as are required by this Act in the case of a principal vesting deed.

(5) Nothing contained in either of the last two preceding sections affects the right of personal representatives to transfer or create such legal estates to take effect in priority to a conveyance under either of those sections as may be required for giving effect to the obligations imposed on them by statute.

(6) A conveyance under either of the last two preceding sections, if made by deed, may contain a reservation to the person conveying of a term of years absolute in the land conveyed, upon trusts for indemnifying him against any unpaid death duties in respect of the land conveyed or any interest therein, and any interest and costs in respect of such duties.

(7) Nothing contained in either of the last two preceding sections affects any right which a person entitled to an equitable charge for securing money actually raised, and affecting the whole estate the subject of the settlement, may have to require effect to be given thereto by a legal mortgage, before the execution of a conveyance under either of those sections.

9   Procedure in the case of settlements and of instruments deemed to be trust instruments

(1) Each of the following settlements or instruments shall for the purposes of this Act be deemed to be a trust instrument, and any reference to a trust instrument contained in this Act shall apply thereto, namely –

(i) An instrument executed, or, in case of a will, coming into operation, after the commencement of this Act which by virtue of this Act is deemed to be a settlement;

(ii) A settlement which by virtue of this Act is deemed to have been made by any person after the commencement of this Act;

(iii) An instrument inter vivos intended to create a settlement of a legal estate in land which is executed after the commencement of this Act, and does not comply with the requirements of this Act with respect to the method of effecting such a settlement; and

(iv) A settlement made after the commencement of this Act (including a settlement by the will of a person who dies after such commencement) of any of the following interests –

(a) an equitable interest in land which is capable, when in possession, of subsisting at law; or

(b) an entailed interest; or

(c) a base or determinable fee or any corresponding interest in leasehold land,

but only if and when the interest settled takes effect free from all equitable interests and powers under every prior settlement (if any).

(2) As soon as practicable after a settlement, or an instrument which for the purposes of this Act is deemed to be a trust instrument, takes effect as such, the trustees of the settlement may, and on the request of the tenant for life or statutory owner shall, execute a principal vesting deed, containing the proper statements and particulars, declaring that the legal estate in the settled land shall vest or is vested in the person or persons therein named, being the tenant for life or statutory owner, and including themselves if they are the statutory owners, and such deed shall, unless the legal estate is already so vested, operate to convey or vest the legal estate in the settled land to or in the person or persons aforesaid and, if more than one, as joint tenants.

(3) If there are no trustees of the settlement, then (in default of a person able and willing to appoint such trustees) an application under this Act shall be made to the court for the appointment of such trustees.

(4) The provisions of the last preceding section with reference to a conveyance shall apply, so far as they are applicable, to a principal vesting deed under this section.

10   Procedure on acquisition of land to be made subject to a settlement

(1) Where after the commencement of this Act land is acquired with capital money

arising under this Act or in exchange for settled land, or a rentcharge is reserved on a grant of settled land, the land shall be conveyed to, and the rentcharge shall by virtue of this Act become vested in, the tenant for life or statutory owner, and such conveyance or grant is in this Act referred to as a subsidiary vesting deed: Provided that, where an instrument is subsisting at the commencement of this Act, or is made or comes into operation after such commencement, by virtue of which any money or securities are liable under this Act, or the Acts which it replaces, or under a trust or direction contained in the instrument, to be invested in the purchase of land to be conveyed so as to become settled land, but at the commencement of this Act, or when such instrument is made or comes into operation after such commencement, as the case may be, there is no land in respect of which a principal vesting deed is capable of being executed, the first deed after the commencement of this Act by which any land is acquired as aforesaid shall be a principal vesting deed and shall be framed accordingly.

(2) A subsidiary vesting deed executed on the acquisition of land to be made subject to a settlement shall contain the following statements and particulars, namely –

(a) particulars of the last or only principal vesting instrument affecting land subject to the settlement;

(b) a statement that the land conveyed is to be held upon and subject to the same trusts and powers as the land comprised in such last or only principal vesting instrument;

(c) the names of the persons who are the trustees of the settlement;

(d) the name of any person for the time being entitled to appoint new trustees of the settlement.

(3) A subsidiary vesting deed reserving a rentcharge on a grant of settled land shall contain the following statements and particulars –

(a) a statement that the rentcharge is vested in the grantor and is subject to the settlement which, immediately before the grant, was subsisting with respect to the land out of which it was reserved;

(b) particulars of the last or only principal vesting instrument affecting such land.

(4) A subsidiary vesting deed shall not be invalidated by reason only of any error in any of the statements or particulars by this Act required to be contained therein.

(5) The acquisition of the land shall not operate to increase or multiply charges or powers of charging.

11   As to contracts for the settlement of land

(1) A contract made or other liability created or arising after the commencement of this Act for the settlement of land –

(i) by or on the part of an estate owner; or

(ii) by a person entitled to –

> (a) an equitable interest which is capable when in possession of subsisting at law; or
>
> (b) an entailed interest; or
>
> (c) a base or determinable fee or any corresponding interest in leasehold land;

shall, but in cases under paragraph (ii) only if and when the interest of the person entitled takes effect free from all equitable interests and powers under every prior settlement, if any, be deemed an estate contract within the meaning of the Land Charges Act 1925 and may be registered as a land charge accordingly, and effect shall be given thereto by a vesting deed and a trust instrument in accordance with this Act.

(2) A contract made or other liability created or arising before the commencement of this Act to make a settlement of land shall be deemed to be sufficiently complied with if effect is given thereto by a vesting deed and a trust instrument in accordance with this Act.

12   Power to make vesting orders as to settled land

(1) If –

> (a) any person who is bound under this Part of this Act to execute a conveyance, vesting deed or vesting assent or in whom settled land is wrongly vested refuses or neglects to execute the requisite conveyance, vesting deed or vesting assent within one month after demand in writing; or
>
> (b) any such person is outside the United Kingdom, or cannot be found, or it is not known whether he is alive or dead; or
>
> (c) for any reason the court is satisfied that the conveyance, vesting deed or vesting assent cannot be executed, or cannot be executed without undue delay or expense;

the court may, on the application of any person interested, make an order vesting the settled land in the tenant for life or statutory owner or person, if any, of full age absolutely entitled (whether beneficially or as personal representative or trustee of land or otherwise), and, if the land remains settled land, the provisions of this Act relating to a principal vesting deed or a subsidiary vesting deed, as the case may be, shall apply to any order so made and every such order shall contain the like statements and particulars.

(2) No stamp duty shall be payable in respect of a vesting order made in place of a vesting or other assent.

13   Dispositions not to take effect until vesting instrument is made

Where a tenant for life or statutory owner has become entitled to have a principal vesting deed or a vesting assent executed in his favour, then until a vesting instrument is executed or made pursuant to this Act in respect of the settled land, any purported disposition thereof inter vivos by any person, other than a personal representative (not being a disposition which he has power to make in right of his equitable interests or powers under a trust instrument), shall not take effect except in favour of a purchaser of a legal estate without notice of such tenant for life or statutory owner having become so entitled as aforesaid but, save as aforesaid, shall operate only as a contract for valuable consideration to carry out the transaction after the requisite vesting instrument has been executed or made, and a purchaser of a legal estate shall not be concerned with such disposition unless the contract is registered as a land charge. Nothing in this section affects the creation or transfer of a legal estate by virtue of an order of the court or the Minister or other competent authority.

14   Forfeiture and stamps

(1) Any vesting effected under the powers conferred by this Act in relation to settled land shall not operate as a breach of a covenant or condition against alienation or give rise to a forfeiture.

(2) Nothing in this Act shall operate to impose any stamp duty on a vesting or other assent.

16   Enforcement of equitable interests and powers against estate owner

(1) All equitable interests and powers in or over settled land (whether created before or after the date of any vesting instrument affecting the legal estate) shall be enforceable against the estate owner in whom the settled land is vested (but in the case of personal representatives without prejudice to their rights and powers for purposes of administration) in manner following (that is to say) –

(i) The estate owner shall stand possessed of the settled land and the income thereof upon such trusts and subject to such powers and provisions as may be requisite for giving effect to the equitable interests and powers affecting the settled land or the income thereof of which he has notice according to their respective priorities;

(ii) Where any person of full age becomes entitled to require a legal estate in the settled land to be vested in him in priority to the settlement, by reason of a right of reverter, statutory or otherwise, or an equitable right of entry taking effect, or on the ground that his interest ought no longer to be capable of being over-reached under the powers of this Act, the estate owner shall be bound, if so requested in writing, to transfer or create such legal estate as may be required for giving legal effect to the rights of the person so entitled;

(iii) Where –

(a) any principal sum is required to be raised on the security of the settled land, by virtue of any trust, or by reason of the exercise of an equitable power affecting the settled land, or by any person or persons who under the settlement is or are entitled or together entitled to or has or have a general power of appointment over the settled land, whether subject to any equitable charges or powers of charging subsisting under the settlement or not; or

(b) the settled land is subject to any equitable charge for securing money actually raised and affecting the whole estate the subject of the settlement;

the estate owner shall be bound, if so requested in writing, to create such legal estate or charge by way of legal mortgage as may be required for raising the money or giving legal effect to the equitable charge:

Provided that so long as the settlement remains subsisting, any legal estate or charge by way of legal mortgage so created shall take effect and shall be expressed to take effect subject to any equitable charges or powers of charging subsisting under the settlement which have priority to the interests or powers of the person or persons by or on behalf of whom the money is required to be raised or legal effect is required to be given to the equitable charge, unless the persons entitled to the prior charges or entitled to exercise the powers consent in writing to the same being postponed, but it shall not be necessary for such consent to be expressed in the instrument creating such legal estate or charge by way of legal mortgage.

(2) Where a mortgage or charge is expressed to be made by an estate owner pursuant to this section, then, in favour of the mortgagee or chargee and persons deriving title under him, the same shall take effect in priority to all the trusts of the settlement and all equitable interests and powers subsisting or to arise under the settlement except those to which it is expressly made subject, and shall so take effect, whether the mortgagee or chargee has notice of any such trusts, interests, or powers, or not, and the mortgagee or chargee shall not be concerned to see that a case had arisen to authorise the mortgage or charge, or that no more money than was granted was raised.

(3) Nothing contained in paragraph (iii) of subsection (1) of this section affects the power conferred by this Act on a tenant for life of raising money by mortgage or of directing capital money to be supplied in discharge of incumbrances.

(4) Effect may be given by means of a legal mortgage to an agreement for a mortgage, or a charge or lien, whether or not arising by operation of law, if the agreement charge or lien ought to have priority over the settlement.

(5) Save as hereinbefore expressly provided, no legal estate shall, so long as the settlement is subsisting, be transferred or created by the estate owner for giving effect to any equitable interest or power under the settlement.

(6) If a question arises or a doubt is entertained whether any and what legal estate ought to be transferred or created pursuant to this section, an application may be made to the court for directions as hereinafter provided.

(7) If an estate owner refuses or neglects for one month after demand in writing to transfer or create any such legal estate, or if by reason of his being outside the United Kingdom, or being unable to be found, or by reason of the dissolution of a corporation, or for any other reason, the court is satisfied that the transaction cannot otherwise be effected, or cannot be effected without undue delay or expense, the court may, on the application of any person interested, make a vesting order transferring or creating the requisite legal estate.

(8) This section does not affect a purchaser of a legal estate taking free from any equitable interest or power.

17   Deed of discharge on termination of settlement

(1) Where the estate owner of any settled land holds the land free from all equitable interests and powers under a trust instrument, the persons who in the last or only principal vesting instrument or the last or only endorsement on or annex thereto are declared to be the trustees of the settlement or the survivors of them shall, save as hereinafter mentioned, be bound to execute, at the cost of the trust estate, a deed declaring that they are discharged from the trust so far as regards that land: Provided that, if the trustees have notice of any derivative settlement, trust of land or equitable charge affecting such land, they shall not execute a deed of discharge until –

    (a) in the case of a derivative settlement, or trust of land, a vesting instrument or a conveyance has been executed or made for giving effect thereto; and

    (b) in the case of an equitable charge, they are satisfied that the charge is or will be secured by a legal mortgage, or is protected by registration as a land charge, or by deposit of the documents of title, or that the owner thereof consents to the execution of the deed of discharge.

Where the land is affected by a derivative settlement or trust of land, the deed of discharge shall contain a statement that the land is settled land by virtue of such vesting instrument as aforesaid and the trust instrument therein referred to, or is subject to a trust of land by virtue of such conveyance as aforesaid, as the case may require.

(2) If, in the circumstances mentioned in subsection (1) of this section and when the conditions therein mentioned have been complied with, the trustees of a settlement on being requested to execute a deed of discharge –

    (a) by the estate owner; or

    (b) by a person interested under, or by the trustees of, a derivative settlement; or

    (c) by the trustees of land;

refuse to do so, or if for any reason the discharge cannot be effected without undue delay or expense, the estate owner, person interested, or trustees may apply to the court for an order discharging the first mentioned trustees as respects the whole or any part of the settled land, and the court may make such order as it may think fit.

(3) Where a deed or order of discharge contains no statement to the contrary, a purchaser of a legal estate in the land to which the deed or order relates shall be entitled to assume that the land has ceased to be settled land, and is not subject to a trust of land.

18 Restrictions on dispositions of settled land where trustees have not been discharged

(1) Where land is the subject of a vesting instrument and the trustees of the settlement have not been discharged under this Act, then –

(a) any disposition by the tenant for life or statutory owner of the land, other than a disposition authorised by this Act or any other statute, or made in pursuance of any additional or larger powers mentioned in the vesting instrument, shall be void, except for the purpose of conveying or creating such equitable interests as he has power, in right of his equitable interests and powers under the trust instrument, to convey or create; and

(b) if any capital money is payable in respect of a transaction, a conveyance to a purchaser of the land shall only take effect under this Act if the capital money is paid to or by the direction of the trustees of the settlement or into court; and

(c) notwithstanding anything to the contrary in the vesting instrument, or the trust instrument, capital money shall not, except where the trustee is a trust corporation, be paid to or by the direction of fewer persons than two as trustees of the settlement.

(2) The restrictions imposed by this section do not affect –

(a) the right of a personal representative in whom the settled land may be vested to convey or deal with the land for the purposes of administration;

(b) the right of a person of full age who has become absolutely entitled (whether beneficially or as trustee of land or personal representative or otherwise) to the settled land, free from all limitations, powers, and charges taking effect under the trust instrument, to require the land to be conveyed to him;

(c) the power of the tenant for life, statutory owner, or personal representative in whom the settled land is vested to transfer or create such legal estates, to take effect in priority to the settlement, as may be required for giving effect to any obligations imposed on him by statute, but where any capital money is raised or received in respect of the transaction the money shall be paid to or by the direction of the trustees of the settlement or in accordance with an order of the court.

19 Who is tenant for life

(1) The person of full age who is for the time being beneficially entitled under a settlement to possession of settled land for his life is for the purposes of this Act the tenant for life of that land and the tenant for life under that settlement.

(2) If in any case there are two or more persons of full age so entitled as joint tenants, they together constitute the tenant for life for the purposes of this Act.

(3) If in any case there are two or more persons so entitled as joint tenants and they are not all of full age, such one or more of them as is or are for the time being of full age is or (if more than one) together constitute the tenant for life for the

purposes of this Act, but this subsection does not affect the beneficial interests of such of them as are not for the time being of full age.

(4) A person being tenant for life within the foregoing definitions shall be deemed to be such notwithstanding that, under the settlement or otherwise, the settled land, or his estate or interest therein, is incumbered or charged in any manner or to any extent, and notwithstanding any assignment by operation of law or otherwise of his estate or interest under the settlement, whether before or after it came into possession, other than an assurance which extinguishes that estate or interest.

20 Other limited owners having powers of tenant for life

(1) Each of the following persons being of full age shall, when his estate or interest is in possession, have the powers of a tenant for life under this Act, (namely) –

(i) A tenant in tail, including a tenant in tail after possibility of issue extinct, and a tenant in tail who is by Act of Parliament reinstated from barring or defeating his estate tail, and although the reversion is in the Crown, but not including such a tenant in tail where the land in respect whereof he is so restrained was purchased with money provided by Parliament in consideration of public services;

(ii) A person entitled to land for an estate in fee simple or for a term of years absolute with or subject to, in any of such cases, an executory limitation, gift, or disposition over on failure of his issue or in any other event;

(iii) A person entitled to a base or determinable fee, although the reversion or right of reverter is in the Crown, or to any corresponding interest in leasehold land;

(iv) A tenant for years determinable on life, not holding merely under a lease at a rent;

(v) A tenant for the life of another, not holding merely under a lease at a rent;

(vi) A tenant for his own or any other life, or for years determinable on life, whose estate is liable to cease in any event during that life, whether by expiration of the estate, or by conditional limitation, or otherwise, or to be defeated by an executory limitation, gift, or disposition over, or is subject to a trust for accumulation of income for any purpose;

(vii) A tenant by the curtesy;

(viii) A person entitled to the income of land under a trust or direction for payment thereof to him during his own or any other life, whether or not subject to expenses of management or to a trust for accumulation of income for any purpose, or until sale of the land, or until forfeiture, cesser or determination by any means of his interest therein, unless the land is subject to a trust of land;

(ix) A person beneficially entitled to land for an estate in fee simple or for a term of years absolute subject to any estates, interests, charges, or powers of charging, subsisting or capable of being exercised under a settlement.

(2) In every such case as is mentioned in subsection (1) of this section, the provisions of this Act referring to a tenant for life, either as conferring powers on him or

otherwise, shall extend to each of the persons aforesaid, and any reference in this Act to death as regards a tenant for life shall, where necessary, be deemed to refer to the determination by death or otherwise of the estate or interest of the person on whom the powers of a tenant for life are conferred by this section.

(3) For the purposes of this Act the estate or interest of a tenant by the curtesy shall be deemed to be an estate or interest arising under a settlement made by his wife.

(4) Where the reversion or right of reverter or other reversionary right is in the Crown, the exercise by a person on whom the powers of a tenant for life are conferred by this section of his powers under this Act, binds the Crown.

21   Absolute owners subject to certain interests to have the powers of tenant for life

(1) Where a person of full age is beneficially entitled in possession to a legal estate subject to any equitable interests or powers, then, for the purpose of overreaching such interests or powers, he may, notwithstanding any stipulation to the contrary, by deed (which shall have effect as a principal vesting deed within the meaning of this Act) declare that the legal estate is vested in him on trust to give effect to all equitable interests and powers affecting the legal estate, and that deed shall be executed by two or more individuals approved or appointed by the court or a trust corporation, who shall be stated to be the trustees of the settlement for the purposes of this Act. Thereupon so long as any of the equitable interests and powers are subsisting the following provisions shall have effect –

(a) The person so entitled as aforesaid and each of his successors in title being an estate owner shall have the powers of a tenant for life and the land shall be deemed to be settled land;

(b) The instrument (if any) under which his estate arises or is acquired, and the instrument (if any) under which the equitable interests or powers are subsisting or capable of taking effect shall be deemed to be the trust instrument: provided that where there is no such instrument as last aforesaid then a deed (which shall take effect as a trust instrument) shall be executed contemporaneously with the vesting deed, and shall declare the trusts affecting the land;

(c) The persons stated in the principal vesting deed to be the trustees of the settlement for the purposes of this Act shall also be the trustees of the trust instrument for those purposes; and

(d) Capital money arising on any disposition of the land shall be paid to or by the direction of the trustees of the settlement or into court, and shall be applicable towards discharging or providing for payment in due order of any principal money payable in respect of such interests or charges as are overreached by such disposition, and until so applied shall be invested or applied as capital money under the trust instrument, and the resultant profits shall be applied as the income of such capital money, and be liable for keeping down in due order any annual or periodical sum which may be overreached by the disposition.

(2) The following equitable interests and powers are excepted from the operation of subsection (1) of this section, namely –

(i) an equitable interest protected by a deposit of documents relating to the legal estate affected;

(ii) the benefit of a covenant or agreement restrictive of the user of land;

(iii) an easement, liberty or privilege over or affecting land and being merely an equitable interest;

(iv) the benefit of a contract to convey or create a legal estate, including a contract conferring either expressly or by statutory implication a valid option of purchase, a right of pre-emption, or any other like right;

(v) any equitable interest protected by registration under the Land Charges Act 1925 other than –

(a) an annuity within the meaning of Part II of that Act;

(b) a limited owner's charge or a general equitable charge within the meaning of that Act.

(3) Subject to the powers conferred by this Act on a tenant for life, nothing contained in this section shall deprive an equitable chargee of any of his rights or of his remedies for enforcing those rights.

22   Provisions applicable where interest in settled land is restored

(1) Where by a disentailing assurance settled land is expressed to be limited (whether subject or not to any estates, interests, charges or powers expressly created or conferred thereby) upon the trusts subsisting with respect thereto immediately before the execution of such disentailing assurance, or any of such trusts, then, for the purposes of this Act and otherwise, a person entitled to any estate or interest in the settled land under any such previously subsisting trust is entitled thereto after the execution of such disentailing assurance as of his former estate or interest.

(2) Where by a resettlement of settled land any estate or interest therein is expressed to be limited to any person (whether subject or not to any estate, interest, charge or power expressly created or conferred by the resettlement) in restoration or confirmation of his estate or interest under a prior settlement, then, for the purposes of this Act and otherwise, that person is entitled to the estate or interest so restored or confirmed as of his former estate or interest, and in addition to the powers exercisable by him in respect of his former estate or interest, he is capable of exercising all such further powers as he could have exercised by virtue of the resettlement, if his estate or interest under the prior settlement had not been so restored or confirmed, but he had been entitled under the resettlement only.

23   Powers of trustees, etc, when there is no tenant for life

(1) Where under a settlement there is no tenant for life nor, independently of this section, a person having by virtue of this Act the powers of a tenant for life then –

(a) any person of full age on whom such powers are by the settlement expressed to be conferred; and

(b) in any other case the trustees of the settlement;

shall have the powers of a tenant for life under this Act.

(2) This section applies to trustees of settlements of land purchased with money provided by Parliament in consideration of public services where the tenant in tail is restrained from barring or defeating his estate tail, except that, if the tenant in tail is of full age and capacity, the powers shall not be exercised without his consent, but a purchaser shall not be concerned to see or inquire whether such consent has been given.

24   As to a tenant for life who has parted with his interest

(1) If it is shown to the satisfaction of the court that a tenant for life, who has by reason of bankruptcy, assignment, incumbrance, or otherwise ceased in the opinion of the court to have a substantial interest in his estate or interest in the settled land or any part thereof, has unreasonably refused to exercise any of the powers conferred on him by this Act, or consents to an order under this section, the court may, on the application of any person interested in the settled land or the part thereof affected, make an order authorising the trustees of the settlement, to exercise in the name and on behalf of the tenant for life, any of the powers of a tenant for life under this Act, in relation to the settled land or the part thereof affected, either generally and in such manner and for such period as the court may think fit, or in a particular instance, and the court may by the order direct that any documents of title in the possession of the tenant for life relating to the settled land be delivered to the trustees of the settlement.

(2) While any such order is in force, the tenant for life shall not, in relation to the settled land or the part thereof affected, exercise any of the powers thereby authorised to be exercised in his name and on his behalf, but no person dealing with the tenant for life shall be affected by any such order, unless the order is for the time being registered as an order affecting land.

(3) An order may be made under this section at any time after the estate or interest of the tenant for life under the settlement has taken effect in possession, and notwithstanding that he disposed thereof when it was an estate or interest in remainder or reversion.

25   Married woman, how to be affected

(1) The foregoing provisions of this Act apply to a married woman of full age, whether or not she is entitled to her estate or interest for her separate use or as her separate property, and she, without her husband, may exercise the powers of a tenant for life under this Act.

26   Infants, how to be affected

(1) Where an infant is beneficially entitled in possession to land for an estate in fee simple or for a term of years absolute or would if of full age be a tenant for life of or have the powers of a tenant for life over settled land, then, during the minority of the infant –

> (a) if the settled land is vested in a personal representative, the personal representative, until a principal vesting instrument has been executed pursuant to the provisions of this Act; and

> (b) in every other case, the trustees of the settlement;

shall have, in reference to the settled land and capital money, all the powers conferred by this Act and the settlement on a tenant for life, and on the trustees of the settlement.

(2) If the settled land is vested in a personal representative, then, if and when during the minority the infant, if of full age, would have been entitled to have the legal estate in the settled land conveyed to or otherwise vested in him pursuant to the provisions of this Act, a principal vesting instrument shall, if the trustees of the settlement so require, be executed, at the cost of the trust estate, for vesting the legal estate in themselves, and in the meantime the personal representatives shall, during the minority, give effect to the direction of the trustees of the settlement, and shall not be concerned with the propriety of any conveyance directed to be made by those trustees if the conveyance appears to be a proper conveyance under the powers conferred by this Act or by the settlement, and the capital money, if any, arising under the conveyance is paid to or by the direction of the trustees of the settlement or into court, but a purchaser dealing with the personal representative and paying the capital money, if any, to him shall not be concerned to see that the money is paid to trustees of the settlement or into court, or to inquire whether the personal representative is liable to give effect to any such directions, or whether any such directions have been given.

(3) Subsection (2) of this section applies whether the infant becomes entitled before or after the commencement of this Act, and has effect during successive minorities until a person of full age becomes entitled to require the settled land to be vested in him.

(4) This section does not apply where an infant is beneficially entitled in possession to land for an estate in fee simple or for a term of years absolute jointly with a person of full age (for which case provision is made in the Law of Property Act 1925), but it applies to two or more infants entitled as aforesaid jointly, until one of them attains full age.

(5) This section does not apply where an infant would, if of full age, constitute the tenant for life or have the powers of a tenant for life together with another person of full age, but it applies to two or more infants who would, if all of them were of full age, together constitute the tenant for life or have the power of a tenant for life, until one of them attains full age.

(6) Nothing in this section affects prejudicially any beneficial interest of an infant.

30 Who are trustees for purposes of Act

(1) Subject to the provisions of this Act, the following persons are trustees of a settlement for the purposes of this Act, and are in this Act referred to as the 'trustees of the settlement' or 'trustees of a settlement', namely –

(i) the persons, if any, who are for the time being under the settlement, trustees with power of sale of the settled land (subject or not to the consent of any person), or with power of consent to or approval of the exercise of such a power of sale, or if there are no such persons; then

(ii) the persons, if any, for the time being, who are by the settlement declared to be trustees thereof for the purposes of the Settled Land Acts 1882 to 1890 or any of them, or this Act, or if there are no such persons; then

(iii) the persons, if any, who are for the time being under the settlement trustees with a power or duty to sell any other land comprised in the settlement and subject to the same limitations as the land to be sold or otherwise dealt with, or with power of consent to or approval of the exercise of such a power of sale, or, if there are no such persons; then

(iv) the persons, if any, who are for the time being under the settlement trustees with a future power or duty to sell the settled land, or with power of consent to or approval of the exercise of such a future power of sale, and whether the power or duty takes effect in all events or not, or, if there are no such persons; then

(v) the persons, if any, appointed by deed to be trustees of the settlement by all the persons who at the date of the deed were together able, by virtue of their beneficial interests or by the exercise of an equitable power, to dispose of the settled land in equity for the whole estate the subject of the settlement.

(2) Paragraphs (i) (iii) and (iv) of the last preceding subsection take effect in like manner as if the powers therein referred to had not by this Act been made exercisable by the tenant for life or statutory owner.

(3) Where a settlement is created by will, or a settlement has arisen by the effect of an intestacy, and apart from this subsection there would be no trustees for the purposes of this Act of such settlement, then the personal representatives of the deceased shall, until other trustees are appointed, be by virtue of this Act the trustees of the settlement, but where there is a sole personal representative, not being a trust corporation, it shall be obligatory on him to appoint an additional trustee to act with him for the purposes of this Act, and the provisions of the Trustee Act 1925 relating to the appointment of new trustees and the vesting of trust property shall apply accordingly.

33 Continuance of trustees in office, and as to certain compound settlements

(1) Where any persons have been appointed or constituted trustees of a settlement, whether by an order of the court or otherwise, or have by reason of a power or duty to sell, or by reason of a power of consent to, or approval of, the exercise of a power

of sale, or by compound virtue of this Act, or otherwise at any time become trustees of a settlement for the purposes of the Settled Land Acts 1882 to 1890 or this Act, then those persons or their successors in office shall remain and be trustees of the settlement as long as that settlement is subsisting or deemed to be subsisting for the purposes of this Act. In this subsection 'successors in office' means the persons who, by appointment or otherwise, have become trustees for the purposes aforesaid
...

34   Appointment of trustees by court

(1) If at any time there are no trustees of a settlement, or where in any other case it is expedient, for the purposes of this Act, that new trustees of a settlement be appointed, the court may, if it thinks fit, on the application of the tenant for life, statutory owner, or of any other person having, under the settlement, an estate or interest in the settled land, in possession, remainder or otherwise, or, in the case of an infant, of his testamentary or other guardian or next friend, appoint fit persons to be trustees of the settlement.

(2) The persons so appointed, and the survivors and survivor of them, while continuing to be trustees or trustee, and, until the appointment of new trustees, the personal representatives or representative for the time being of the last surviving or continuing trustee, shall become and be the trustees or trustee of the settlement.

35   Procedure on appointment of new trustees

(1) Whenever a new trustee for the purposes of this Act is appointed of a trust instrument or a trustee thereof for the purposes aforesaid is discharged from the trust without a new trustee being appointed, a deed shall be executed supplemental to the last or only principal vesting instrument containing a declaration that the persons therein named, being the persons who after such appointment or discharge, as the case may be, are the trustees of the trust instrument for the purposes aforesaid, are the trustees of the settlement for those purposes; and a memorandum shall be endorsed on or annexed to the last or only principal vesting entitlement in accordance with the Trustee Act 1925.

(2) Every such deed as aforesaid shall, if the trustee was appointed or discharged by the court, be executed by such person as the court may direct, and, in any other case, shall be executed by –

(i) the person if any, named in the principal vesting instrument as the person for the time being entitled to appoint new trustees of the settlement, or if no person is so named, or the person is dead or unable or unwilling to act, the persons who if the principal vesting instrument had been the only instrument constituting the settlement would have had power to appoint new trustees thereof;

(ii) the persons named in the deed of declaration as the trustees of the settlement; and

(iii) any trustee who is discharged as aforesaid or retires.

(3) A statement contained in any such deed of declaration as is mentioned in this section to the effect that the person named in the principal vesting instrument as the person for the time being entitled to appoint new trustees of the settlement is unable or unwilling to act, or that a trustee has remained outside the United Kingdom for more than twelve months, or refuses or is unfit to act, or is incapable of acting, shall in favour of a purchaser of a legal estate be conclusive evidence of the matter stated.

36   Undivided shares to take effect behind a trust of land

(1) If and when, after the commencement of this Act, settled land is held in trust for persons entitled in possession under a trust instrument in undivided shares, the trustees of the settlement (if the settled land is not already vested in them) may require the estate owner in whom the settled land is vested (but in the case of a personal representative subject to his rights and powers for purposes of administration), at the cost of the trust estate, to convey the land to them, or assent to the land vesting in them as joint tenants, and in the meantime the land shall be held on the same trusts as would have been applicable thereto if it had been so conveyed to or vested in the trustees.

(2) If and when the settled land so held in trust in undivided shares is or becomes vested in the trustees of the settlement, the land shall be held by them (subject to any incumbrances affecting the settled land which are secured by a legal mortgage, but freed from any incumbrances affecting the undivided shares or not secured as aforesaid, and from any interests, powers and charges subsisting under the trust instrument which have priority to the trust for the persons entitled to the undivided shares) in trust for the persons interested in the land.

(3) If the estate owner refuses or neglects for one month after demand in writing to convey the settled land so held in trust in undivided shares in manner aforesaid, or if by reason of his being outside the United Kingdom or being unable to be found, or by reason of the dissolution of a corporation, or for any other reason, the court is satisfied that the conveyance cannot otherwise be made, or cannot be made without undue delay or expense, the court may, on the application of the trustees of the settlement, make an order vesting the settled land in them in trust for the persons interested in the land.

(4) An undivided share in land shall not be capable of being created except under a trust instrument or under the Law of Property Act 1925 and shall then only take effect behind a trust of land.

(5) Nothing in this section affects the priority inter se of any incumbrances whether affecting the entirety of the land or an undivided share.

(6) In subsections (2) and (3) of this section references to the persons interested in the land include persons interested as trustees or personal representatives (as well as persons beneficially interested). ...

PART II

POWERS OF A TENANT FOR LIFE

38   Powers of sale and exchange

A tenant for life –

(i) May sell the settled land, or any part thereof, or any easement, right or privilege of any kind over or in relation to the land; and

(iii) May make an exchange of the settled land, or any part thereof, or of any easement, right, or privilege of any kind, whether or not newly created, over or in relation to the settled land, or any part thereof, for other land, or for any easement, right or privilege of any kind, whether or not newly created, over or in relation to other land, including an exchange in consideration of money paid for equality of exchange.

39   Regulations respecting sales

(1) Save as hereinafter provided every sale shall be made for the best consideration in money that can reasonably be obtained.

(2) A sale may be made in consideration wholly or partially of a perpetual rent, or a terminable rent consisting of principal and interest combined, payable yearly or half yearly to be secured upon the land sold, or the land to which the easement, right or privilege sold is to be annexed in enjoyment or an adequate part thereof. In the case of a terminable rent, the conveyance shall distinguish the part attributable to principal and that attributable to interest, and the part attributable to principal shall be capital money arising under this Act: provided that, unless the part of the terminable rent attributable to interest varies according to the amount of the principal repaid, the trustees of the settlement shall, during the subsistence of the rent, accumulate the profits from the capital money by investing them and any resulting profits under the general power of investment in section 3 of the Trustee Act 2000 and shall add the accumulations to capital.

(3) The rent to be reserved on any such sale shall be the best rent that can reasonably be obtained, regard being had to any money paid as part of the consideration, or laid out, or to be laid out, for the benefit of the settled land, and generally to the circumstances of the case, but a peppercorn rent, or a nominal or other rent less than the rent ultimately payable, may be made payable during any period not exceeding five years from the date of the conveyance.

(4) Where a sale is made in consideration of a rent, the following provisions shall have effect –

(i) The conveyance shall contain a covenant by the purchaser for payment of the rent, and the statutory powers and remedies for the recovery of the rent shall apply;

(ii) A duplicate of the conveyance shall be executed by the purchaser and delivered to the tenant for life or statutory owner, of which execution and delivery the execution of the conveyance by the tenant for life or statutory owner shall be sufficient evidence;

(iii) A statement, contained in the conveyance or in an indorsement thereon, signed by the tenant for life or statutory owner, respecting any matter of fact or of calculation under this Act in relation to the sale, shall, in favour of the purchaser and of those claiming under him, be sufficient evidence of the matter stated. ...

(6) A sale may be made in one lot or in several lots, and either by auction or by private contract, and may be made subject to any stipulations respecting title, or evidence of title, or other things.

(7) On a sale the tenant for life may fix reserve biddings and may buy in at an auction.

40   Regulations respecting exchanges

(1) Save as in this Part of this Act provided, every exchange shall be made for the best consideration in land or in land and money that can reasonably be obtained.

(2) An exchange may be made subject to any stipulations respecting title, or evidence of title, or other things.

(3) Settled land in England or Wales shall not be given in exchange for land out of England and Wales.

41   Power to lease for ordinary or building or mining or forestry purposes

A tenant for life may lease the settled land, or any part thereof, or any easement, right, or privilege of any kind over or in relation to the land, for any purpose whatever, whether involving waste or not, for any term not exceeding –

(i) In case of a building lease, nine hundred and ninety-nine years;

(ii) In case of a mining lease, one hundred years;

(iii) In case of a forestry lease, nine hundred and ninety-nine years;

(iv) In case of any other lease, fifty years.

42   Regulations respecting leases generally

(1) Save as hereinafter provided, every lease –

(i) shall be by deed, and be made to take effect in possession not later than twelve months after its date, or in reversion after an existing lease having not more than seven years to run at the date of the new lease;

(ii) shall reserve the best rent that can reasonably be obtained, regard being had to any fine taken, and to any money laid out or to be laid out for the benefit of the settled land, and generally to the circumstances of the case;

(iii) shall contain a covenant by the lessee for payment of the rent, and a condition of re-entry on the rent not being paid within a time therein specified not exceeding thirty days.

(2) A counterpart of every lease shall be executed by the lessee and delivered to the tenant for life or statutory owner, of which execution and delivery the execution of the lease by the tenant for life or statutory owner shall be sufficient evidence.

(3) A statement, contained in a lease or in an indorsement thereon, signed by the tenant for life or statutory owner, respecting any matter of fact or of calculation under this Act in relation to the lease, shall, in favour of the lessee and of those claiming under him, be sufficient evidence of the matter stated.

(4) A fine received on the grant of a lease under any power conferred by this Act shall be deemed to be capital money arising under this Act.

(5) A lease at the best rent that can be reasonably obtained without fine, and whereby the lessee is not exempted from punishment for waste, may be made –

(i) Where the term does not exceed twenty-one years –

(a) without any notice of an intention to make the lease having been given under this Act; and

(b) notwithstanding that there are no trustees of the settlement; and

(ii) Where the term does not extend beyond three years from the date of the writing, by any writing under hand only containing an agreement instead of a covenant by the lessee for payment of rent.

43 Leasing powers for special objects

The leasing power of a tenant for life extends to the making of –

(i) a lease for giving effect (in such manner and so far as the law permits) to a covenant of renewal, performance whereof could be enforced against the owner for the time being of the settled land; and

(ii) a lease for confirming, as far as may be, a previous lease being void or voidable, but so that every lease, as and when confirmed, shall be such a lease as might at the date of the original lease have been lawfully granted under this Act or otherwise, as the case may require.

44 Regulations respecting building leases

(1) Every building lease shall be made partly in consideration of the lessee, or some person by whose direction the lease is granted, or some other person, having erected or agreeing to erect buildings, new or additional, or having improved or repaired or agreeing to improve or repair buildings, or having executed or agreeing to execute on the land leased, an improvement authorised by this Act for or in connection with building purposes.

(2) A peppercorn rent or a nominal or other rent less than the rent ultimately payable, may be made payable for the first five years or any less part of the term.

(3) Where the land is contracted to be leased in lots, the entire amount of rent to be ultimately payable may be apportioned among the lots in any manner: provided that –

(i) the annual rent reserved by any lease shall not be less than 50p; and

(ii) the total amount of the rents reserved on all leases for the time being granted shall not be less than the total amount of the rents which, in order that leases may be in conformity with this Act, ought to be reserved in respect of the whole land for the time being leased; and

(iii) the rent reserved by any lease shall not exceed one-fifth part of the full annual value of the land comprised in that lease with the buildings thereon when completed.

45   Regulations respecting mining leases

(1) In a mining lease –

(i) the rent may be made to be ascertainable by or to vary according to the acreage worked, or by or according to the quantities of any mineral or substance gotten, made merchantable, converted, carried away, or disposed of, in or from the settled land, or any other land, or by or according to any facilities given in that behalf; and

(ii) the rent may also be made to vary according to the price of the minerals or substances gotten, or any of them, and such price may be the saleable value, or the price or value appearing in any trade or market or other price list or return from time to time, or may be the marketable value as ascertained in any manner prescribed by the lease (including a reference to arbitration), or may be an average of any such prices or values taken during a specified period; and

(iii) a fixed or minimum rent may be made payable, with or without power for the lessee, in case the rent, according to acreage or quantity or otherwise, in any specified period does not produce an amount equal to the fixed or minimum rent, to make up the deficiency in any subsequent specified period, free of rent other than the fixed or minimum rent.

(2) A lease may be made partly in consideration of the lessee having executed, or agreeing to execute, on the land leased an improvement authorised by this Act, for or in connexion with mining purposes.

46   Variation of building or mining lease according to circumstances of district

(1) Where it is shown to the court with respect to the district in which any settled land is situate, either –

(i) that it is the custom for land therein to be leased for building or mining purposes for a longer term or on other conditions than the term or conditions specified in that behalf in this Act; or

(ii) that it is difficult to make leases for building or mining purposes of land therein, except for a longer term or on other conditions than the term and conditions specified in that behalf in this Act;

the court may, if it thinks fit, authorise generally the tenant for life or statutory owner to make time to time leases of or affecting the settled land in that district, or parts thereof for any term or on any conditions as in the order of the court expressed, or may, if it thinks fit, authorise the tenant for life or statutory owner to make any such lease in any particular case.

(2) Thereupon the tenant for life or statutory owner, and, subject to any direction in the order of the court to the contrary, each of his successors in title being a tenant for life or statutory owner, may make in any case, or in the particular case, a lease of the settled land, or part thereof, in conformity with the order.

47   Capitalisation of part of mining rent

Under a mining lease, whether the mines or minerals leased are already opened or in work or not, unless a contrary intention is expressed in the settlement there shall be from time to time set aside, as capital money arising under this Act, part of the rent as follows, namely – where the tenant for life or statutory owner is impeachable for waste in respect of minerals, three fourth parts of the rent, and otherwise one fourth part thereof, and in every such case the residue of the rent shall go as rents and profits.

48   Regulations respecting forestry leases

(1) In the case of a forestry lease –

(i) a peppercorn rent or a nominal or other rent less than the rent ultimately payable, may be made payable for the first ten years or any less part of the term;

(ii) the rent may be made to be ascertainable by, or to vary according to the value of the timber on the land comprised in the lease, or the produce thereof, which may during any year be cut, converted, carried away, or otherwise disposed of;

(iii) a fixed or minimum rent may be made payable, with or without power for the lessee, in case the rent according to value in any specified period does not produce an amount equal to the fixed or minimum rent, to make up the deficiency in any subsequent specified period, free of rent other than the fixed or minimum rent; and

(iv) any other provisions may be made for the sharing of the proceeds or profits of the user of the land between the reversioner and the Forestry Commissioners.

(2) In this section the expression 'timber' includes all forest products.

49 Powers on dispositions to impose restrictions and make reservations and stipulations

(1) On a sale or other disposition or dealing under the powers of this Act –

(a) any easement, right, or privilege of any kind may be reserved or granted over or in relation to the settled land or any part thereof or other land, including the land disposed of, and in the case of an exchange, the land taken in exchange; and

(b) any restriction with respect to building on or other user of land, or with respect to mines and minerals, or with respect to or for the purpose of the more beneficial working thereof, or with respect to any other thing, may be imposed and made binding, as far as the law permits, by covenant, condition or otherwise, on the tenant for life or statutory owner and the settled land or any part thereof, or on the other party and any land disposed of to him; and

(c) the whole or any part of any capital or annual sum (and in the case of an annual sum whether temporary or perpetual) charged on or payable out of the land disposed of, or any part thereof, and other land subject to the settlement, may as between the tenant for life or statutory owner and his successors in title, and the other party and persons deriving title under or in succession to him (but without prejudice to the rights of the person entitled to such capital or annual sum) be charged exclusively on the land disposed of, or any part thereof, or such other land as aforesaid, or any part thereof, in exoneration of the rest of the land on or out of which such capital or annual sum is charged or payable.

(2) A sale of land may be made subject to a stipulation that all or any of the timber and other trees, pollards, tellers, underwood, saplings and plantations on the land sold (in this section referred to as 'timber') or any articles attached to the land (in this section referred to as 'fixtures') shall be taken by the purchaser at a valuation, and the amount of the valuation shall form part of the price of the land, and shall be capital money accordingly.

(3) Where on a sale the consideration attributable to any timber or fixtures is by mistake paid to a tenant for life or other person not entitled to receive it, then, if such person or the purchaser or the persons deriving title under either of them subsequently pay the aforesaid consideration, with such interest, if any, thereon as the court may direct, to the trustees of the settlement or other persons entitled thereto or into court, the court may, on the application of the purchaser or the persons deriving title under him, declare that the disposition is to take effect as if the whole of the consideration had at the date thereof been duly paid to the trustees of the settlement or other persons entitled to receive the same. The person, not entitled to receive the same, to whom the consideration is paid, and his estate and effects shall remain liable to make good any loss attributable to the mistake.

50 Separate dealing with surface and minerals, with or without wayleaves, etc

A sale, exchange, lease or other authorised disposition, may be made either of land, with or without an exception or reservation of all or any of the mines and minerals therein, or of any mines and minerals, and in any such case with or without a grant or reservation of powers of working, wayleaves or rights of way, rights of water and drainage, and other powers, easements, rights, and privileges for or incident to or connected with mining purposes, in relation to the settled land, or any part thereof, or any other land.

51   Power to grant options

(1) A tenant for life may at any time, either with or without consideration, grant by writing an option to purchase or take a lease of the settled land, or any part thereof, or any easement, right, or privilege over or in relation to the same at a price or rent fixed at the time of the granting of the option.

(2) Every such option shall be made exercisable within an agreed number of years not exceeding ten.

(3) The price or rent shall be the best which, having regard to all the circumstances, can reasonably be obtained and either –

(a) may be a specified sum of money or rent, or at a specified rate according to the superficial area of the land with respect to which the option is exercised, or the frontage thereof or otherwise; or

(b) in the case of an option to purchase contained in a lease or agreement for a lease, may be a stated number of years' purchase of the highest rent reserved by the lease or agreement; or

(c) if the option is exercisable as regards part of the land comprised in the lease or agreement, may be a proportionate part of such highest rent;

and any aggregate price or rent may be made to be apportionable in any manner, or according to any system, or by reference to arbitration.

(4) An option to take a mining lease may be coupled with the grant of a licence to search for and prove any mines or minerals under the settled land, or any part thereof, pending the exercise of the option.

(5) The consideration for the grant of the option shall be capital money arising under this Act.

52   Surrenders and regrants

(1) A tenant for life may accept, with or without consideration, a surrender of any lease of settled land, whether made under this Act or not, or a regrant of any land granted in fee simple, whether under this Act or not, in respect of the whole land leased or granted, or any part thereof, with or without an exception of all or any of the mines and minerals therein, or in respect of mines and minerals, or any of them, and with or without an exception of any easement, right or privilege of any land over or in relation to the land surrendered or regranted.

(2) On a surrender of a lease, or a regrant of land granted in fee simple, in respect of part only of the land or mines and minerals leased or granted, the rent or rentcharge may be apportioned.

(3) On a surrender or regrant, the tenant for life may in relation to the land or mines and minerals surrendered or regranted, or of any part thereof, make a new or other lease, or grant in fee simple, or new or other leases, or grants in fee simple, in lots.

(4) A new or other lease, or grant in fee simple, may comprise additional land or mines and minerals, and may reserve any apportioned or other rent or rentcharge.

(5) On a surrender or regrant, and the making of a new or other lease, whether for the same or for any extended or other term, or of a new or other grant in fee simple, and whether or not subject to the same or to any other covenants, provisions, or conditions, the value of the lessee's or grantee's interest in the lease surrendered, or the land regranted, may be taken into account in the determination of the amount of the rent or rentcharge to be reserved, and of any fine or consideration in money to be taken, and of the nature of the covenants, provisions, and conditions to be inserted in the new or other lease, or grant in fee simple.

(6) Every new or other lease, or grant in fee simple, shall be in conformity with this Act.

(7) All money, not being rent or a rentcharge, received on the exercise by the tenant for life of the powers conferred by this section, shall, unless the court, on an application made within six months after the receipt thereof or within such further time as the court may in special circumstances allow, otherwise directs, be capital money arising under this Act.

(8) A regrant shall be made to the tenant for life or statutory owner, and shall be deemed a subsidiary vesting deed, and the statements and particulars required in the case of subsidiary vesting deeds shall be inserted therein.

(9) In this section 'land granted in fee simple' means land so granted with or subject to a reservation thereout of a perpetual or terminable rentcharge which is or forms part of the settled land, and 'grant in fee simple' has a corresponding meaning.

53   Acceptance of leases

(1) A tenant for life may accept a lease of any land, or of any mines and minerals or of any easement, right, or privilege, convenient to be held or worked with or annexed in enjoyment to the settled land, or any part thereof, for such period, and upon such terms and conditions, as the tenant for life thinks fit: Provided that no fine shall be paid out of capital money in respect of such lease.

(2) The lease shall be granted to the tenant for life or statutory owner, and shall be deemed a subsidiary vesting deed, and the statements and particulars required in the case of subsidiary vesting deeds shall either be inserted therein or endorsed thereon.

(3) The lease may contain an option to purchase the reversion expectant on the term thereby granted.

54 Power to grant water rights to statutory bodies

(1) For the development, improvement, or general benefit of the settled land, or any part thereof, a tenant for life may make a grant in fee simple or absolutely, or a lease for any term of years absolute, for a nominal price or rent, or for less than the best price or rent that can reasonably be obtained, or gratuitously, to any statutory authority, of any water or streams or springs of water in, upon, or under the settled land, and of any rights of taking, using, enjoying and conveying water, and of laying, constructing, maintaining, and repairing mains, pipes, reservoirs, dams, weirs and other works of any kind proper for the supply and distribution of water, and of any part of the settled land required as a site for any of the aforesaid works, and of any easement, right or privilege over or in relation to the settled land or any part thereof in connexion with any of the aforesaid works.

(2) This section does not authorise the creation of any greater rights than could have been created by a person absolutely entitled for his own benefit to the settled land affected.

(3) In this section 'statutory authority' means an authority or company for the time being empowered by any Act of Parliament, public general, or local or private, or by any order or certificate having the force of an Act of Parliament, to provide with a supply of water any town, parish or place in which the settled land or any part thereof is situated.

(4) All money, not being rent, received on the exercise of any power conferred by this section shall be capital money arising under this Act.

55 Power to grant land for public and charitable purposes

(1) For the development, improvement, or general benefit of the settled land, or any part thereof, a tenant for life may make a grant in fee simple, or absolutely, or a lease for any term of years absolute, for a nominal price or rent, or for less than the best price or rent that can reasonably be obtained, or gratuitously, of any part of the settled land, with or without any easement, right or privilege over or in relation to the settled land or any part thereof, for all or any one or more of the following purposes, namely –

(i) For the site, or the extension of any existing site, of a place of religious worship, residence for a minister of religion, school house, town hall, market house, public library, public baths, museum, hospital, infirmary, or other public building, literary or scientific institution, drill hall, working-men's club, parish room, reading room or village institute, with or without in any case any yard, garden, or other ground to be held with any such building; or

(ii) For the construction, enlargement, or improvement of any railway, canal, road (public or private), dock, sea-wall, embankment, drain, watercourse, or reservoir; or

(iii) For any other public or charitable purpose in connection with the settled land, or any part thereof, or tending to the benefit of the persons residing, or for whom dwellings may be erected, on the settled land, or any part thereof.

Not more than one acre shall in any particular case be conveyed for any purpose mentioned in paragraphs (i) and (iii) of this subsection, nor more than five acres for any purpose mentioned in paragraph (ii) of this subsection, unless the full consideration be paid or reserved in respect of the excess.

(2) All money, not being rent, received on the exercise of any power conferred by this section shall be capital money arising under this Act.

56 Dedication for streets, open spaces, etc

(1) On or after or in connexion with a sale or grant for building purposes, or a building lease, or the development as a building estate of the settled land, or any part thereof, or at any other reasonable time, the tenant for life, for the general benefit of the residents on the settled land, or on any part thereof –

(i) may cause or require any parts of the settled land to be appropriated and laid out for streets, roads, paths, squares, gardens, or other open spaces, for the use, gratuitously or on payment, of the public or of individuals, with sewers, drains, watercourses, fencing, paving, or other works necessary or proper in connexion therewith; and

(ii) may provide that the parts so appropriated shall be conveyed to or vested in the trustees of the settlement, or other trustees, or any company or public body, on trusts or subject to provisions for securing the continued appropriation thereof to the purposes aforesaid, and the continued repair or maintenance of streets and other places and works aforesaid, with or without provision for appointment of new trustees when required; and

(iii) may execute any general or other deed necessary or proper for giving effect to the provisions of this section (which deed may be inrolled in the Central Office of the Supreme Court), and thereby declare the mode, terms, and conditions of the appropriation, and the manner in which and the persons by whom the benefit thereof is to be enjoyed, and the nature and extent of the privileges and conveniences granted.

(2) In regard to the dedication of land for the public purposes aforesaid, a tenant for life shall be in the same position as if he were an absolute owner.

(3) A tenant for life shall have power –

(a) to enter into any agreement for the recompense to be made for any part of the settled land which is required for the widening of a highway under the Highways Act 1980 or otherwise;

(b) to consent to the diversion of any highway over the settled land under the Highways Act 1980 or otherwise;

and any agreement or consent so made or given shall be as valid and effectual, for all purposes, as if made or given by an absolute owner of the settled land.

(4) All money, not being rent, received on the exercise of any power conferred by this section shall be capital money arising under this Act.

57 Provision of land for small dwellings, small holdings and dwellings for working classes

(1) Where land is sold, or given in exchange or leased –

(a) for the purpose of the erection on such land of small dwellings; or

(b) to the council of a county or county borough for the purposes of small holdings;

the sale, exchange, or lease may, notwithstanding anything contained in this Act, be made for such consideration in money, or land, or in land and money, or may reserve such rent, as having regard to the said purposes and to all the circumstances of the case, is the best that can reasonably be obtained, notwithstanding that a better consideration or rent might have been obtained if the land were sold, exchanged, or leased, for another purpose.

(2) Notwithstanding anything contained in, and in addition to the other powers conferred by this Act, a tenant for life may at any time –

(a) for the purpose of the erection of dwellings for the working classes, or the provision of gardens to be held therewith; or

(b) for the purpose of the Small Holdings and Allotments Acts 1908 to 1919;

make a grant in fee simple or absolutely, or a lease for any term of years absolute of any part of the settled land, with or without any easement, right or privilege of any kind over or in relation to the settled land or any part thereof, for a nominal price or rent, or for less than the best price or rent that can reasonably be obtained or gratuitously: provided that, except under an order of the court, not more than two acres in the case of land situate in an urban district, or ten acres in the case of land situate in a rural district, in any one parish shall be granted or leased under the powers conferred by this subsection, unless the full consideration be paid or reserved in respect of the excess.

(3) All money, not being rent, received on the exercise of any power conferred by this section shall be capital money arising under this Act.

58 Power to compromise claims and release restrictions, etc

(1) A tenant for life may with the consent in writing of the trustees of the settlement, either with or without giving or taking any consideration in money or otherwise, compromise, compound, abandon, submit to arbitration, or otherwise settle any claim, dispute, or question whatsoever relating to the settled land, or any part thereof, including in particular claims, disputes or questions as to boundaries, the ownership of mines and minerals, rights and powers of working mines and minerals, local laws and customs relative to the working of mines and minerals and other matters, easements, and restrictive covenants, and for any of those purposes may enter into, give, execute, and do such agreements, assurances, releases, and other things as the tenant for life may, with such consent as aforesaid, think proper.

(2) A tenant for life may, with the consent in writing of the trustees of the settlement, at any time, by deed or writing, either with or without consideration in

money or otherwise, release, waive, or modify, or agree to release, waive, or modify, any covenant, agreement, or restriction imposed on any other land for the benefit of the settled land, or any part thereof, or release, or agree to release, any other land from any easement, right or privilege, including a right of pre-emption, affecting the same for the benefit of the settled land, or any part thereof …

59 Power to vary leases and grants and to give licences and consents

(1) A tenant for life may, at any time, by deed, either with or without consideration in money or otherwise, vary, release, waive or modify, either absolutely or otherwise, the terms of any lease whenever made of the settled land or any part thereof, or any covenants or conditions contained in any grant in fee simple whenever made of land with or subject to a reservation thereout of a rent which is or forms part of the settled land, and in either case in respect of the whole or any part of the land comprised in any such lease or grant, but so that every such lease or grant shall, after such variation, release, waiver or modification as aforesaid, be such a lease or grant as might then have been lawfully made under this Act if the lease had been surrendered, or the land comprised in the grant had never been so comprised, or had been regranted.

(2) Where land is or has been disposed of subject to any covenant requiring the licence, consent, or approval of the covenantee or his successors in title as to –

(a) the user of the land in any manner; or

(b) the erection construction or alteration of or addition to buildings or works of any description on the land; or

(c) the plans or elevations of any proposed buildings or other works on the land; or

(d) any other act, matter, or thing relating to the land, or any buildings or works thereon; or

(e) any assignment, underletting or parting with the possession of all or any part of the property comprised in any lease affecting the settled land;

and the covenant enures for the benefit of settled land (including, where the disposition is a lease, the reversion expectant on the determination thereof), the licence, consent or approval may be given by the tenant for life of the settled land affected.

60 Power to apportion rents

(1) A tenant for life may, at any time, by deed, either with or without consideration in money or otherwise, agree for the apportionment of any rent reserved or created by any such lease or grant as mentioned in the last preceding section, or any rent being or forming part of the settled land, so that the apportioned parts of such rent shall thenceforth be payable exclusively out of or in respect of such respective portions of the land subject thereto as may be thought proper, and also agree that any covenants, agreements, powers, or remedies for securing such rent and any other covenants or agreements by the lessee or grantee and any conditions shall

also be apportioned and made applicable exclusively to the respective portions of the land out of or in respect of which the apportioned parts of such rent shall thenceforth be payable.

(2) Where the settled land, or any part thereof, is held or derived under a lease, or under a grant reserving rent, or subject to covenants, agreements or conditions, whether such lease or grant comprises other land or not, the tenant for life may at any time by deed, with or without giving or taking any consideration in money or otherwise, procure the variation, release, waiver, or modification, either absolutely or otherwise, of the terms, covenants, agreements, or conditions contained in such lease or grant, in respect of the whole or any part of the settled land comprised therein, including the apportionment of any rent, covenants, agreements, conditions, and provisions reserved, or created by, or contained in, such lease or grant.

(3) This section applies to leases or grants made either before or after the commencement of this Act.

61   Provisions as to consideration

(1) All money, not being rent, payable by the tenant for life in respect of any transaction to which any of the three last preceding sections relates shall be paid out of capital money arising under this Act, and all money, not being rent, received on the exercise by the tenant for life of the powers conferred by any of those sections, shall, unless the court, on an application made within six months after the receipt thereof or within such further time as the court may in special circumstances allow, otherwise directs, be capital money arising under this Act.

(2) For the purpose of the three last preceding sections 'consideration in money or otherwise' means –

(a) a capital sum of money or a rent;

(b) land being freehold or leasehold for any term of years whereof not less than sixty years shall be unexpired;

(c) any easement, right or privilege over or in relation to the settled land, or any part thereof, or any other land;

(d) the benefit of any restrictive covenant or condition; and

(e) the release of the settled land, or any part thereof, or any other land, from any easement, right or privilege, including a right of pre-exemption, or from the burden of any restrictive covenant or condition affecting the same.

62   Special provisions as to manorial incidents, etc

(4) In reference to the conversion of a perpetually renewable lease or underlease into a long term, a tenant for life may enter into such agreements and do such acts and things as the lessor or lessee or underlessee, as the case may require, is, by any enactment authorised to enter into or do.

63 Power to complete predecessor's contracts

A tenant for life may make any disposition which is necessary or proper for giving effect to a contract entered into by a predecessor in title, and which if made by that predecessor would have been valid as against his successors in title.

64 General power for the tenant for life to effect any transaction under an order of the court

(1) Any transaction affecting or concerning the settled land, or any part thereof, or any other land (not being a transaction otherwise authorised by this Act, or by the settlement) which in the opinion of the court would be for the benefit of the settled land, or any part thereof, or the persons interested under the settlement, may, under an order of the court, be effected by a tenant for life, if it is one which could have been validly effected by an absolute owner.

(2) In this section 'transaction' includes any sale, exchange, assurance, grant, lease, surrender, reconveyance, release, reservation, or other disposition, and any purchase or other acquisition, and any covenant, contract, or option, and any application of capital money and any compromise or other dealing, or arrangement; and 'effected' has the meaning appropriate to the particular transaction; and the references to land include references to restrictions and burdens affecting land.

65 Power to dispose of mansion

(1) The powers of disposing of settled land conferred by this Act on a tenant for life may be exercised as respects the principal mansion house, if any, on any settled land, and the pleasure grounds and park and lands, if any, usually occupied therewith: provided that those powers shall not be exercised without the consent of the trustees of the settlement or an order of the court –

   (a) if the settlement is a settlement made or coming into operation before the commencement of this Act and the settlement does not expressly provide to the contrary; or

   (b) if the settlement is a settlement made or coming into operation after the commencement of this Act and the settlement expressly provides that these powers or any of them shall not be exercised without such consent or order.

(2) Where a house is usually occupied as a farmhouse, or where the site of any house and the pleasure grounds and park and lands, if any, usually occupied therewith do not together exceed twenty-five acres in extent, the house is not to be deemed a principal mansion house within the meaning of this section, and may accordingly be disposed of in like manner as any other part of the settled land.

66 Cutting and sale of timber, and capitalisation of part of proceeds

(1) Where a tenant for life is impeachable for waste in respect of timber, and there is on the settled land timber ripe and fit for cutting, the tenant for life, on obtaining the consent of the trustees of the settlement or an order of the court, may cut and sell that timber, or any part thereof.

(2) Three fourth parts of the net proceeds of the sale shall be set aside as and be capital money arising under this Act, and the other fourth part shall go as rents and profits.

67   Sale and purchase of heirlooms under order of court

(1) Where personal chattels are settled so as to devolve with settled land, or to devolve therewith as nearly as may be in accordance with the law or practice in force at the date of the settlement, or are settled together with land, or upon trusts declared by reference to the trusts affecting land, a tenant for life of the land may sell the chattels or any of them.

(2) The money arising by the sale shall be capital money arising under this Act, and shall be paid, invested, or applied and otherwise dealt with in like manner in all respects as by this Act directed with respect to other capital money arising under this Act, or may be invested in the purchase of other chattels of the same or any other nature, which, when purchased, shall be settled and held on the same trusts, and shall devolve in the same manner as the chattels sold.

(3) A sale or purchase of chattels under this section shall not be made without an order of the court.

(4) Any reference in any enactment to personal chattels settled as heirlooms shall extend to any chattels to which this section applies.

68   Provision enabling dealings with tenant for life

(1) In the manner mentioned and subject to the provisions contained in this section –

   (a) a sale, grant, lease, mortgage, charge or other disposition of settled land, or of any easement, right, or privilege over the same may be made to the tenant for life; or

   (b) capital money may be advanced on mortgage to him; or

   (c) a purchase may be made from him of land to be made subject to the limitations of the settlement; or

   (d) an exchange may be made with him of settled land for other land; and

   (e) any such disposition, advance, purchase, or exchange as aforesaid may be made to, from, or with any persons of whom the tenant for life is one.

(2) In every such case the trustees of the settlement shall, in addition to their powers as trustees, have all the powers of a tenant for life in reference to negotiating and completing the transaction, and shall have power to enforce any covenants by the tenant for life, or, where the tenant for life is himself one of the trustees, then the other or others of them shall have such power, and the said powers of a tenant for life may be exercised by the trustees of the settlement in the name and on behalf of the tenant for life.

(3) This section applies, notwithstanding that the tenant for life is one of the

trustees of the settlement, or that an order has been made authorising the trustees to act on his behalf, or that he is suffering from mental disorder but does not apply to dealings with any body of persons which includes a trustee of the settlement, not being the tenant for life, unless the transaction is either previously or subsequently approved by the court.

69   Shifting of incumbrances

Where there is an incumbrance affecting any part of the settled land (whether capable of being over-reached on the exercise by the tenant for life of his powers under this Act or not), the tenant for life, with the consent of the incumbrancer, may charge that incumbrance on any other part of the settled land, or on all or any part of the capital money or securities representing capital money subject or to become subject to the settlement, whether already charged therewith or not, in exoneration of the first mentioned part, and, by a legal mortgage, or otherwise, make provision accordingly.

70   Power to vary provisions of an incumbrance and to charge by way of additional security

(1) Where an incumbrance affects any part of the settled land, the tenant for life may, with the consent of the incumbrancer, vary the rate of interest charged and any of the other provisions of the instrument, if any, creating the incumbrance, and with the like consent charge that incumbrance on any part of the settled land, whether already charged therewith or not, or on all or any part of the capital money or securities representing capital money subject or to become subject to the settlement, by way of additional security, or of consolidation of securities, and by a legal mortgage or otherwise, make provision accordingly.

(2) 'Incumbrance' in this section includes any annual sum payable during a life or lives or during a term of years absolute or determinable, but in any such case an additional security shall be effected so as only to create a charge or security similar to the original charge or security.

71   Power to raise money by mortgage

(1) Where money is required for any of the following purposes namely –

(i) Discharging an incumbrance on the settled land or part thereof;

(ii) Paying for any improvement authorised by this Act or by the settlement;

(iii) Equality of exchange; ...

(vii) Commuting any additional rent made payable on the conversion of a perpetually renewable leasehold interest into a long term;

(viii) Satisfying any claims for compensation on the conversion of a perpetually renewable leasehold interest into a long term by any officer, solicitor, or other agent of the lessor in respect of fees or remuneration which would have been payable by the lessee or under-lessee on any renewal;

(ix) Payment of the costs of any transaction authorised by this section or either of the two last preceding sections;

the tenant for life may raise the money so required, on the security of the settled land, or of any part thereof, by a legal mortgage, and the money so raised shall be capital money for that purpose, and may be paid or applied accordingly.

(2) 'Incumbrance' in this section does not include any annual sum payable only during a life or lives or during a term of years absolute or determinable.

(3) The restrictions imposed by this Part of this Act on the leasing powers of a tenant for life do not apply in relation to a mortgage term created under this Act.

72   Completion of transactions by conveyance

(1) On a sale, exchange, lease, mortgage, charge, or other disposition, the tenant for life may, as regards land sold, given in exchange, leased, mortgaged, charged, or otherwise disposed of, or intended so to be, or as regards easements or other rights or privileges sold, given in exchange, leased, mortgaged, or otherwise disposed of, or intended so to be, effect the transaction by deed to the extent of the estate or interest vested or declared to be vested in him by the last or only vesting instrument affecting the settled land or any less estate or interest, in the manner requisite for giving effect to the sale, exchange, lease, mortgage, charge, or other disposition, but so that a mortgage shall be effected by the creation of a term of years absolute in the settled land or by charge by way of legal mortgage, and not otherwise.

(2) Such a deed, to the extent and in the manner to and in which it is expressed or intended to operate and can operate under this Act, is effectual to pass the land conveyed, or the easements, rights, privileges or other interests created, discharged from all the limitations, powers, and provisions of the settlement, and from all estates, interests, and charges subsisting or to arise thereunder, but subject to and with the exception of –

(i) all legal estates and charges by way of legal mortgage having priority to the settlement; and

(ii) all legal estates and charges by way of legal mortgage which have been conveyed or created for securing money actually raised at the date of the deed; and

(iii) all leases and grants at fee-farm rents or otherwise, and all grants of easements, rights of common, or other rights or privileges which –

(a) were before the date of the deed granted or made for value in money or money's worth, or agreed so to be, by the tenant for life or statutory owner, or by any of his predecessors in title, or any trustees for them, under the settlement, or under any statutory power, or are at that date otherwise binding on the successors in title of the tenant for life or statutory owner; and

(b) are at the date of the deed protected by registration under the Land Charges Act, 1925, if capable of registration thereunder.

(3) Notwithstanding registration under the Land Charges Act 1925 of –

(a) an annuity within the meaning of Part II of that Act;

(b) a limited owner's charge or a general equitable charge within the meaning of that Act;

a disposition under this Act operates to overreach such annuity or charge which shall, according to its priority, take effect as if limited by the settlement.

(4) Where a lease is by this Act authorised to be made by writing under hand only, such writing shall have the same operation under this section as if it had been a deed.

PART III

INVESTMENT OR OTHER APPLICATION OF CAPITAL MONEY

73   Modes of investment or application

(1) Capital money arising under this Act, subject to payment of claims properly payable thereout and to the application thereof for any special authorised object for which the capital money was raised, shall, when received, be invested or otherwise applied wholly in one, or partly in one and partly in another or others, of the following modes (namely) –

(i) In investment in securities either under the general power of invetment in section 3 of the Trustee Act 2000 or under a power to invest conferred on the trustees of the settlement by the settlement;

(ii) In discharge, purchase, or redemption of incumbrances affecting the whole estate the subject of the settlement, or of rentcharge in lieu of tithe, Crown rent, chief rent, or quit rent, charged on or payable out of the settled land, or of any charge in respect of an improvement created on a holding under the Agricultural Holdings Act 1986 or any similar previous enactment;

(iii) In payment for any improvement authorised by this Act;

(iv) In payment as for an improvement authorised by this Act of any money expended and costs incurred by a landlord under or in pursuance of the Agricultural Holdings Act 1986 or any similar previous enactment, or under custom or agreement or otherwise, in or about the execution of any improvement comprised in Schedule 7 to the said Agricultural Holdings Act;

(v) In payment for equality of exchange of settled land; ...

(ix) In commuting any additional rent made payable on the conversion of a perpetually renewable leasehold interest into a long term, and in satisfying any claim for compensation on such conversion by any officer, solicitor, or other agent of the lessor in respect of fees or remuneration which would have been payable by the lessee or under-lessee on any renewal;

(x) In purchase of the freehold reversion in fee of any part of the settled land, being leasehold land held for years;

(xi) In purchase of land in fee simple, or of leasehold land held for sixty years or more unexpired at the time of purchase, subject or not to any exception or reservation of or in respect of mines or minerals therein, or of or in respect of rights or powers relative to the working of mines or minerals therein, or in other land;

(xii) In purchase either in fee simple, or for a term of sixty years or more, of mines and minerals convenient to be held or worked with the settled land, or of any easement, right, or privilege convenient to be held with the settled land for mining or other purposes;

(xiii) In redemption of an improvement rentcharge, that is to say, a rentcharge (temporary or permanent) created, whether before or after the commencement of this Act, in pursuance of any act of Parliament, with the object of paying off any money advanced for defraying the expenses of an improvement of any kind authorised by Part I of the Third Schedule to this Act;

(xiv) In the purchase, with the leave of the court, of any leasehold interest where the immediate reversion is settled land, so as to merge the leasehold interest (unless the court otherwise directs) in the reversion, and notwithstanding that the leasehold interest may have less than sixty years to run;

(xv) In payment of the costs and expenses of all plans, surveys, and schemes, including schemes under the Town Planning Act 1925 or any similar previous enactment, made with a view to, or in connexion with the improvement or development of the settled land, or any part thereof, or the exercise of any statutory powers, and of all negotiations entered into by the tenant for life with a view to the exercise of any of the said powers, notwithstanding that such negotiations may prove abortive, and in payment of the costs and expenses of opposing any such proposed scheme as aforesaid affecting the settled land, whether or not the scheme is made;

(xvii) In payment to a local or other authority of such sum as may be agreed in consideration of such authority taking over and becoming liable to repair a private road on the settled land or a road for the maintenance whereof a tenant for life is liable ratione tenurae;

(xviii) In financing any person who may have agreed to take a lease or grant for building purposes of the settled land, or any part thereof, by making advances to him in the usual manner on the security of an equitable mortgage of his building agreement;

(xix) In payment to any person becoming absolutely entitled or empowered to give an absolute discharge;

(xx) In payment of costs, charges, and expenses of or incidental to the exercise of any of the powers, or the execution of any of the provisions of this Act including the costs and expenses incidental to any of the matters referred to in this section;

(xxi) In any other mode authorised by the settlement with respect to money produced by the sale of the settled land

(2) Notwithstanding anything in this section capital money arising under this Act

from settled land in England or Wales shall not be applied in the purchase of land out of England and Wales, unless the settlement expressly authorises the same.

74   Power to acquire land subject to certain incumbrances

(1) Land may be acquired on a purchase or exchange to be made subject to a settlement, notwithstanding that the land is subject to any Crown rent, quit rent, chief rent, or other incident of tenure, or to any easement, right or privilege, or to any restrictive covenant, or to any liability to maintain or repair walls, fences, sea-walls, river banks, dykes, roads, streets, sewers, or drains, or to any improvement rentcharge which is capable under this Act of being redeemed out of capital money ...

75   Regulations respecting investment, devolution and income of securities, etc

(1) Capital money arising under this Act shall, in order to its being invested or applied as aforesaid, be paid either to the trustees of the settlement or into court at the option of the tenant for life, and shall be invested or applied by the trustees, or under the direction of the court, as the case may be, accordingly.

(2) Subject to Part IV of the Trustee Act 2000, to section 75A of this Act and to the following provisions of this section –

 (a) the investment or other application by the trustees shall be made according to the discretion of the trustees, but subject to any consent required or direction given by the settlement with respect to the investment or other application by the trustees of trust money of the settlement, and

 (b) any investment shall be in the names or under the control of the trustees.

(3) The investment or other application under the direction of the court shall be made on the application of the tenant for life, or of the trustees.

(4) The trustees, in exercising their power to invest or apply capital money, shall –

 (a) so far as is practicable, consult the tenant for life; and

 (b) so far as consistent with the general interest of the settlement, give effect to his wishes.

(4A) Any investment or other application of capital money under the direction of the court shall not during the subsistence of the beneficial interest of the tenant for life be altered without his consent.

(4B) The trustees may not under section 11 of the Trustee Act 2000 authorise a person to exercise their functions with respect to the investment or application of capital money on terms that prevent them from complying with subsection (4) of this section.

(4C) A person who is authorised under section 11 of the Trustee Act 2000 to exercise any of their functions with respect to the investment or application of capital money is not subject to subsection (4) of this section.

(5) Capital money arising under this Act while remaining uninvested or unapplied, and securities on which an investment of any such capital money is made shall for all purposes of disposition, transmission and devolution be treated as land, and shall be held for and go to the same persons successively, in the same manner and for and on the same estates, interests, and trusts, as the land wherefrom the money arises would, if not disposed of, have been held and have gone under the settlement.

(6) The income of those securities shall be paid or applied as the income of that land, if not disposed of, would have been payable or applicable under the settlement.

(7) Those securities may be converted into money, which shall be capital money arising under this Act.

(8) All or any part of any capital money paid into court may, if the court thinks fit, be at any time paid out to the trustees of the settlement.

75A Power to accept charge as security for part payment for land sold

(1) Where –

(a) land subject to the settlement is sold by the tenant for life or statutory owner, for an estate in fee simple or a term having at least five hundred years to run, and

(b) the proceeds of sale are liable to be invested,

the tenant for life or statutory owner may, with the consent of the trustees of the settlement, contract that the payment of any part, not exceeding two-thirds, of the purchase money shall be secured by a charge by way of legal mortgage of the land sold, with or without the security of any other property.

(2) If any buildings are comprised in the property secured by the charge, the charge must contain a covenant by the mortgagor to keep them insured for their full value against loss or damage due to any event.

(3) A person exercising the power under subsection (1) of this section, or giving consent for the purposes of that subsection –

(a) is not required to comply with section 5 of the Trustee Act 2000 before giving his consent, and

(b) is not liable for any loss incurred merely because the security is insufficient at the date of the charge.

(4) The power under subsection (1) of this section is exercisable subject to the consent of any person whose consent to a change of investment is required by the instrument, if any, creating the trust.

(5) Where the sale referred to in subsection (1) of this section is made under the order of the court, the power under that subsection applies only if and as far as the court may by order direct.

77   Application of money in hands of trustees under powers of settlement

Where –

(a) under any instrument coming into operation either before or after the commencement of this Act money is in the hands of trustees, and is liable to be laid out in the purchase of land to be made subject to the trusts declared by that instrument; or

(b) under any instrument coming into operation after the commencement of this Act money or securities or the proceeds of sale of any property is or are held by trustees on trusts creating entailed interests therein;

then, in addition to such powers of dealing therewith as the trustees have independently of this Act, they may, at the option of the tenant for life, invest or apply the money securities or proceeds as if they were capital money arising under this Act.

79   Application of money paid for lease or reversion

Where capital money arising under this Act is purchase-money paid in respect of –

(a) a lease for years; or

(b) any other estate or interest in land less than the fee simple; or

(c) a reversion dependent on any such lease, estate, or interest;

the trustees of the settlement or the court, as the case may be, and in the case of the court on the application of any party interested in that money, may, notwithstanding anything in this Act, require and cause the same to be laid out, invested, accumulated, and paid in such manner as, in the judgment of the trustees or of the court, as the case may be, will give to the parties interested in that money the like benefit therefrom as they might lawfully have had from the lease, estate, interest, or reversion in respect whereof the money was paid, or as near thereto as may be.

PART IV

IMPROVEMENTS

83   Description of improvements authorised by Act

Improvements authorised by this Act are the making or execution on, or in connexion with, and for the benefit of settled land, of any of the works mentioned in the Third Schedule to this Act, or of any works for any of the purposes mentioned in that Schedule, and any operation incident to or necessary or proper in the execution of any of those works, or necessary or proper for carrying into effect any of those purposes, or for securing the full benefit of any of those works or purposes.

84 Mode of application of capital money

(1) Capital money arising under this Act may be applied in or towards payment for any improvement authorised by this Act or by the settlement, without any scheme for the execution of the improvement being first submitted for approval to, or approved by, the trustees of the settlement or the court.

(2) Where the capital money to be expended is in the hands of the trustees of the settlement, they may apply that money in or towards payment for the whole or any part of any work or operation comprised in the improvement on –

(i) a certificate to be furnished by a competent engineer or able practical surveyor employed independently of the tenant for life, certifying that the work or operation comprised in the improvement or some specific part thereof, has been properly executed, and what amount is properly payable in respect thereof, which certificate shall be conclusive in favour of the trustees as an authority and discharge for any payment made by them in pursuance thereof; or

(ii) an order of the court directing or authorising the trustees so to apply a specified portion of the capital money:

Provided that –

(a) In the case of improvements not authorised by Part I of the Third Schedule to this Act or by the settlement, the trustees may, if they think fit, and shall if so directed by the court, before they make any such application of capital money require that that money, or any part thereof, shall be repaid to them out of the income of the settled land by not more than fifty half-yearly instalments, the first of such instalments to be paid or to be deemed to have become payable at the expiration of six months from the date when the work or operation, in payment for which the money is to be applied, was completed;

(b) No capital money shall be applied by the trustees in payment for improvements not authorised by Parts I and II of the Third Schedule to this Act, or by the settlement, except subject to provision for the repayment thereof being made in manner mentioned in the preceding paragraph of this proviso.

(3) Where the capital money to be expended is in court, the court may, if it thinks fit, on a report or certificate of the Secretary of State, or of a competent engineer or able practical surveyor approved by the court, or on such other evidence as the court may think sufficient, make such order and give such directions as it thinks fit for the application of the money, or any part thereof, in or towards payment for the whole or any part of any work or operation comprised in the improvement.

(4) Where the court authorises capital money to be applied in payment for any improvement or intended improvement not authorised by Part I of the Third Schedule to this Act or by the settlement, the court, as a condition of making the order, may in any case require that the capital money or any part thereof, and shall as respects an improvement mentioned in Part III of that Schedule (unless the improvement is authorised by the settlement), require that the whole of the capital money shall be repaid to the trustees of the settlement out of the income of the

settled land by a fixed number of periodical instalments to be paid at the times appointed by the court, and may require that any incumbrancer of the estate or interest of the tenant for life shall be served with notice of the proceedings.

(5) All money received by the trustees of the settlement in respect of any instalments under this section shall be held by them as capital money arising from freehold land under the settlement, unless the court otherwise directs.

85 Creation of rentcharges to discharge instalments

(1) When the tenant for life is required by the trustees to repay by instalments the capital money expended, or any part thereof, the tenant for life is by this section authorised to create out of the settled land, or any part thereof, a yearly rentcharge in favour of the trustees of the settlement sufficient in amount to discharge the said half-yearly instalments.

(2) Where an order is made requiring repayment by instalments, the settled land shall stand charged with the payment to the trustees of the settlement of a yearly rentcharge sufficient in amount to discharge the periodical instalments, and the rentcharge shall accrue from day to day, and be payable at the times appointed for payment of the periodical instalments, and shall have effect as if limited by the settlement prior to the estate of the tenant for life, and the trustees of the settlement shall have all statutory and other powers for recovery thereof.

(3) A rentcharge created by or under this section shall not be redeemed out of capital money, but may be overreached in like manner as if the same were limited by the settlement, and shall cease if and when the land affected by the improvement ceases to be settled or is sold or exchanged, but if part of the land so affected remains subject to the settlement the rentcharge shall remain in force in regard to the settled land.

86 Concurrence in improvements

The tenant for life may join or concur with any other person interested in executing any improvement authorised by this Act, or in contributing to the cost thereof.

87 Court may order payment for improvements executed

The court may, in any case where it appears proper, make an order directing or authorising capital money to be applied in or towards payment for any improvement authorised by the Settled Land Acts 1882 to 1890, or this Act, notwithstanding that a scheme was not, before the execution of the improvement, submitted for approval, as required by the Settled Land Act 1882, to the trustees of the settlement or to the court, and notwithstanding that no capital money is immediately available for the purpose.

88 Obligation on tenant for life and successors to maintain, insure, etc

(1) The tenant for life, and each of his successors in title having under the trust

instrument a limited estate or interest only in the settled land, shall, during such period, if any, as the Secretary of State by certificate in any case prescribes, maintain and repair, at his own expense, every improvement executed under the foregoing provisions of this Act or the enactments replaced thereby, and where a building or work in its nature insurable against damage by fire is comprised in the improvement, shall at his own expense insure and keep insured the improvement in such amount, if any, as the Secretary of State by certificate in any case prescribes.

(2) The tenant for life, or any of his successors as aforesaid, shall not cut down or knowingly permit to be cut down, except in proper thinning, any trees planted as an improvement under the foregoing provisions of this Act, or under the enactments replaced by those provisions.

(3) The tenant for life, and each of his successors as aforesaid, shall from time to time, if required by the Secretary of State on or without the application of any person having under the trust instrument any estate or interest in the settled land in possession, remainder, or otherwise, report to the Secretary of State the state of every improvement executed under this Act, and the fact and particulars of fire insurance, if any.

(4) The Secretary of State may vary any certificate made by him under this section in such manner or to such extent as circumstances appear to him to require, but not so as to increase the liabilities of the tenant for life, or any of his successors as aforesaid.

(5) If the tenant for life, or any of his successors as aforesaid, fails in any respect to comply with the requisitions of this section, or does any act in contravention thereof, any person having, under the trust instrument, any estate or interest in the settled land in possession, remainder, or reversion, shall have a right of action, in respect of that default or act, against the tenant for life; and the estate of the tenant for life, after his death, shall be liable to make good to the persons entitled under the trust instrument any damages occasioned by that default or act.

(6) Where in connexion with any improvement an improvement rentcharge, as hereinbefore defined, has been created, and that rentcharge has been redeemed out of capital money, this section shall apply to the improvement as if it had been an improvement executed under this Act.

89   Protection as regards waste in execution and repair of improvements

The tenant for life, and each of his successors in title having, under the trust instrument, a limited estate or interest only in the settled land, and all persons employed by or under contract with the tenant for life or any such successor, may from time to time enter on the settled land, and, without impeachment of waste by any remainderman or reversioner, thereon execute any improvement authorised by this Act, or inspect, maintain, and repair the same, and for the purposes thereof do, make, and use on the settled land, all acts, works, and conveniences proper for the execution, maintenance, repair, and use thereof, and get and work freestone, limestone, clay, sand, and other substances, and make tramways and other ways, and burn and make bricks, tiles, and other things, and cut down and use timber and other trees not planted or left standing for shelter or ornament.

PART V

MISCELLANEOUS PROVISIONS

90 Power for tenant for life to enter into contracts

(1) A tenant for life –

(i) may contract to make any sale, exchange, mortgage, charge or other disposition authorised by this Act; and

(ii) may vary or rescind, with or without consideration, the contract in the like cases and manner in which, if he were absolute owner of the settled land, he might lawfully vary or rescind the same, but so that the contract as varied be in conformity with this Act; and

(iii) may contract to make any lease, and in making the lease may vary the terms, with or without consideration, but so that the lease be in conformity with this Act; and

(iv) may accept a surrender of a contract for a lease or a grant in fee simple at a rent, in like manner and on the like terms in and on which he might accept a surrender of a lease or a regrant, and thereupon may make a new or other contract for or relative to a lease or leases, or a grant or grants in fee simple at a rent, in like manner and on the like terms in and on which he might make a new or other lease or grant, or new or other leases or grants, where a lease or a grant in fee simple at a rent had been executed; and

(v) may enter into a contract for or relating to the execution of any improvement authorised by this Act, and may vary or rescind any such contract, and

(vi) may, in any other case, enter into a contract to do any act for carrying into effect any of the purposes of this Act, and may vary or rescind any such contract.

(2) Every contract, including a contract arising by reason of the exercise of an option, shall be binding on and shall enure for the benefit of the settled land, and shall be enforceable against and by every successor in title for the time being of the tenant for life, or statutory owner, and may be carried into effect by any such successor, but so that it may be varied or rescinded by any such successor, in the like case and manner, if any, as if it had been made by himself.

(3) The court may, on the application of the tenant for life, or statutory owner, or of any such successor as aforesaid, or of any person interested in any contract, give directions respecting the enforcing, carrying into effect, varying, or rescinding thereof.

(4) A preliminary contract under this Act for or relating to a lease, and a contract

conferring an option, shall not form part of the title or evidence of the title of any person to the lease, or to the benefit thereof, or to the land the subject of the option.

(5) All money, not being rent, received on the exercise by the tenant for life or statutory owner of the powers conferred by subsection (1) of this section, shall, unless the court on an application made within six months after the receipt of the money, or within such further time as the court may in special circumstances allow, otherwise directs, be capital money arising under this Act.

92 Proceedings for protection or recovery of land settled or claimed as settled

The court may, if it thinks fit, approve of any action, defence, petition to Parliament, parliamentary opposition, or other proceeding taken or proposed to be taken for the protection of settled land, or of any action or proceeding taken or proposed to be taken for the recovery of land being or alleged to be subject to a settlement, and may direct that any costs, charges, or expenses incurred or to be incurred in relation thereto, or any part thereof, be paid out of property subject to the settlement.

93 Reference of questions to court

If a question arises or a doubt is entertained –

(a) respecting the exercise or intended exercise of any of the powers conferred by this Act, or any enactment replaced by this Act, or the settlement, or any matter relating thereto; or

(b) as to the person in whose favour a vesting deed or assent ought to be executed, or as to the contents thereof; or

(c) otherwise in relation to property subject to a settlement;

the tenant for life or statutory owner, or the trustees of the settlement, or any other person interested under the settlement, may apply to the court for its decision or directions thereon, or for the sanction of the court to any conditional contract, and the court may make such order or give such directions respecting the matter as the court thinks fit.

PART VI

GENERAL PROVISIONS AS TO TRUSTEES

94 Number of trustees to act

(1) Notwithstanding anything in this Act, capital money arising under this Act shall not be paid to fewer than two persons as trustees of a settlement, unless the trustee is a trust corporation.

(2) Subject as aforesaid the provisions of this Act referring to the trustees of a settlement apply to the surviving or continuing trustees or trustee of the settlement for the time being.

95   Trustees' receipts

The receipt or direction in writing of or by the trustees of the settlement, or where a sole trustee is a trust corporation, of or by that trustee, or of or by the personal representatives of the last surviving or continuing trustee, for or relating to any money or securities, paid or transferred to or by the direction of the trustees, trustee, or representatives, as the case may be, effectually discharges the payer or transferor therefrom, and from being bound to see to the application or being answerable for any loss or misapplication thereof, and, in case of a mortgagee or other person advancing money, from being concerned to see that any money advanced by him is wanted for any purpose of this Act, or that no more than is wanted is raised.

97   Protection of trustees generally

The trustees of a settlement, or any of them –

(a) are not liable for giving any consent, or for not making, bringing, taking, or doing any such application, action, proceeding, or thing, as they might make, bring, take, or do; and

(b) in case of a purchase of land with capital money arising under this Act, or of an exchange, lease, or other disposition, are not liable for adopting any contract made by the tenant for life or statutory owner, or bound to inquire as to the propriety of the purchase, exchange, lease, or other disposition, or answerable as regards any price, consideration, or fine; and

(c) are not liable to see to or answerable for the investigation of the title, or answerable for a conveyance of land, if the conveyance purports to convey the land in the proper mode; and

(d) are not liable in respect of purchase-money paid by them by the direction of the tenant for life or statutory owner to any person joining in the conveyance as a conveying party, or as giving a receipt for the purchase-money, or in any other character, or in respect of any other money paid by them by the direction of the tenant for life or statutory owner on the purchase, exchange, lease, or other disposition.

98   Protection of trustees in particular cases

(3) The trustees of the settlement shall not be liable in any way on account of any vesting instrument or other documents of title relating to the settled land, other than securities for capital money, being placed in the possession of the tenant for life or statutory owner: Provided that where, if the settlement were not disclosed, it would appear that the tenant for life had a general power of appointment over, or was absolutely and beneficially entitled to the settled land, the trustees of the settlement shall, before they deliver the documents to him, require that notice of the last or only principal vesting instrument be written on one of the documents under which the tenant for life acquired his title, and may, if the documents are not in their possession, require such notice to be written as aforesaid, but, in the

latter case, they shall not be liable in any way for not requiring the notice to be written.

(4) This section applies to dealings and matters effected before as well as after the commencement of this Act.

99 Indemnities to personal representatives and others

Personal representatives, trustees, or other persons who have in good faith, pursuant to this Act, executed a vesting deed, assent, or other conveyance of the settled land, or a deed of discharge of trustees, shall be absolutely discharged from all liability in respect of the equitable interests and powers taking effect under the settlement, and shall be entitled to be kept indemnified at the cost of the trust estate from all liabilities affecting the settled land, but the person to whom the settled land is conveyed (not being a purchaser taking free therefrom) shall hold the settled land upon the trusts, if any, affecting the same.

101 Notice to trustees

(1) Save as otherwise expressly provided by this Act, a tenant for life or statutory owner, when intending to make a sale, exchange, lease, mortgage, or charge or to grant an option –

> (a) shall give notice of his intention in that behalf to each of the trustees of the settlement, by posting registered letters, containing the notice, addressed to the trustees severally, each at his usual or last known place of abode in the United Kingdom; and
>
> (b) shall give a like notice to the solicitor for the trustees, if any such solicitor is known to the tenant for life or statutory owner, by posting a registered letter, containing the notice, addressed to the solicitor at his place of business in the United Kingdom;

every letter under this section being posted not less than one month before the making or granting by the tenant for life or statutory owner of the sale, exchange, lease, mortgage, charge, or option, or of a contract for the same: provided that a notice under this section shall not be valid unless at the date thereof the trustee is a trust corporation, or the number of trustees is not less than two.

(2) The notice required by this section of intention to make a sale, exchange, or lease, or to grant an option, may be notice of a general intention in that behalf.

(3) The tenant for life or statutory owner is, upon request by a trustee of the settlement, to furnish to him such particulars and information as may reasonably be required by him from time to time with reference to sales, exchanges, or leases effected, or in progress, or immediately intended.

(4) Any trustee, by writing under his hand, may waive notice either in any particular case, or generally, and may accept less than one month's notice.

(5) A person dealing in good faith with the tenant for life is not concerned to inquire respecting the giving of any such notice as is required by this section.

102 Management of land during minority or pending contingency

(1) If and as long as any person who is entitled to a beneficial interest in possession affecting land is an infant, the trustees appointed for this purpose by the settlement, or if there are none so appointed, then the trustees of the settlement, unless the settlement or the order of the court whereby they or their predecessors in office were appointed to be such trustees expressly provides to the contrary, or if there are none, then any persons appointed as trustees for this purpose by the court on the application of a guardian or next friend of the infant, may enter into and continue in possession of the land on behalf of the infant, and in every such case the subsequent provisions of this section shall apply.

(2) The trustees shall manage or superintend the management of the land, with full power –

(a) to fell timber or cut underwood from time to time in the usual course for sale, or for repairs or otherwise; and

(b) to erect, pull down, rebuild, and repair houses, and other buildings and erections; and

(c) to continue the working of mines, minerals, and quarries which have usually been worked; and

(d) to drain or otherwise improve the land or any part thereof; and

(e) to insure against risks of loss or damage due to any event under section 19 of the Trustee Act 1925; and

(f) to make allowances to and arrangements with tenants and others; and

(g) to determine tenancies, and to accept surrenders of leases and tenancies; and

(h) generally to deal with the land in a proper and due course of management;

but so that, where the infant is impeachable for waste, the trustees shall not commit waste, and shall cut timber on the same terms only, and subject to the same restrictions on and subject to which the infant could, if of full age, cut the same.

(3) The trustees may from time to time, out of the income of the land, including the produce of the sale of timber and underwood, pay the expenses incurred in the management, or in the exercise of any power conferred by this section, or otherwise in relation to the land, and all outgoings not payable by any tenant or other person, and shall keep down any annual sum, and the interest of any principal sum, charged on the land.

(4) This section has effect subject to an express appointment by the settlement, or the court, of trustees for the purposes of this section or of any enactment replaced by this section.

(5) Where any person is contingently entitled to land, this section shall, subject to any prior interests or charges affecting that land, apply until his interest vests, or, if his interest vests during his minority, until he attains the age of eighteen years.

This subsection applies only where a person becomes contingently entitled under an instrument coming into operation after the commencement of this Act.

(6) This section applies only if and as far as a contrary intention is not expressed in the instrument, if any, under which the interest of the infant or person contingently entitled as aforesaid arises, and has effect subject to the terms of that instrument and to the provisions therein contained.

PART VII

RESTRICTIONS, SAVINGS, AND PROTECTION OF PURCHASERS

104 Powers not assignable, and contract not to exercise powers void

(1) The powers under this Act of a tenant for life are not capable of assignment or release, and do not pass to a person as being, by operation of law or otherwise, an assignee of a tenant for life, and remain exercisable by the tenant for life after and notwithstanding any assignment, by operation of law or otherwise, of his estate or interest under the settlement. This subsection applies notwithstanding that the estate or interest of the tenant for life under the settlement was not in possession when the assignment was made or took effect by operation of law.

(2) A contract by a tenant for life not to exercise his powers under this Act or any of them shall be void.

(3) Where an assignment for value of the estate or interest of the tenant for life was made before the commencement of this Act, this section shall operate without prejudice to the rights of the assignee, and in that case the assignee's rights shall not be affected without his consent, except that –

   (a) unless the assignee is actually in possession of the settled land or the part thereof affected, his consent shall not be requisite for the making of leases thereof by the tenant for life or statutory owner, provided the leases are made at the best rent that can reasonably be obtained, without fine, and in other respects are in conformity with this Act; and

   (b) the consent of the assignee shall not be required to an investment of capital money for the time being affected by the assignment in securities.

(4) Where such an assignment for value is made or comes into operation after the commencement of this Act, the consent of the assignee shall not be requisite for the exercise by the tenant for life of any of the powers conferred by this Act: Provided that –

   (a) the assignee shall be entitled to the same or the like estate or interest in or charge on the land, money, or securities for the time being representing the land, money, or securities comprised in the assignment, as he had by virtue of the assignment in the last-mentioned land, money, or securities; and

   (b) if the assignment so provides, or if it takes effect by operation of the law of bankruptcy, and after notice thereof to the trustees of the settlement, the consent of the assignee shall be required to an investment of capital money for the time being affected by the assignment in investments other than securities, and to any application of such capital money; and

(c) notice of the intended transaction shall, unless the assignment otherwise provides, be given to the assignee, but a purchaser shall not be concerned to see or inquire whether such notice has been given.

(5) Where such an assignment for value was made before the commencement of this Act, then on the exercise by the tenant for life after such commencement of any of the powers conferred by this Act –

(a) a purchaser shall not be concerned to see or inquire whether the consent of the assignee has been obtained; and

(b) the provisions of paragraph (a) of the last subsection shall apply for the benefit of the assignee.

(6) A trustee or personal representative who is an assignee for value shall have power to consent to the exercise by the tenant for life of his powers under this Act, or to any such investment or application of capital money as aforesaid, and to bind by such consent all persons interested in the trust estate, or the estate of the testator or intestate.

(7) If by the original assignment, or by any subsequent disposition, the estate or interest assigned or created by the original assignment, or any part thereof, or any derivative interest is settled on persons in succession, whether subject to any prior charge or not, and there is no trustee or personal representative in whom the entirety of the estate or interest so settled is vested, then the person for the time being entitled in possession under the limitations of that settlement, whether as trustee or beneficiary, or who would, if of full age, be so entitled, and notwithstanding any charge or incumbrance subsisting or to arise under such settlement, shall have power to consent to the exercise by the tenant for life of his powers under this Act, or to any such investment or application of capital money as aforesaid, and to bind by such consent all persons interested or to become interested under such settlement.

(8) Where an assignee for value, or any person who has power to consent as aforesaid under this section, is an infant, the consent may be given on his behalf by his parents or parent or testamentary or other guardian in the order named.

(9) The court shall have power to authorise any person interested under any assignment to consent to the exercise by the tenant for life of his powers under this Act, or to any such investment or application of capital money as aforesaid, on behalf of himself and all other persons interested, or who may become interested under such assignment.

(10) An assignment by operation of the law of bankruptcy, where the assignment comes into operation after the commencement of this Act, shall be deemed to be an assignment for value for the purposes of this section.

(11) An instrument whereby a tenant for life, in consideration of marriage or as part or by way of any family arrangement, not being a security for payment of money

advanced, makes an assignment of or creates a charge upon his estate or interest under the settlement is to be deemed one of the instruments creating the settlement, and not an assignment for value for the purposes of this section: provided that this subsection shall not have effect with respect to any disposition made before the eighteenth day of August, eighteen hundred and ninety, if inconsistent with the nature or terms of the disposition.

(12) This section extends to assignments made or coming into operation before or after the commencement of this Act, and in this section 'assignment' includes assignment by way of mortgage, and any partial or qualified assignment, and any charge or incumbrance, 'assignee' has a corresponding meaning, and 'assignee for value' includes persons deriving title under the original assignee.

105 Effect of surrender of life estate to the next remainderman

(1) Where the estate or interest of a tenant for life under the settlement has been or is absolutely assured with intent to extinguish the same, either before or after the commencement of this Act, to the person next entitled in remainder or reversion under the settlement, then the statutory powers of the tenant for life under this Act shall, in reference to the property affected by the assurance, and notwithstanding the provisions of the last preceding section, cease to be exercisable by him, and the statutory powers shall thenceforth become exercisable as if he were dead, but without prejudice to any incumbrance affecting the estate or interest assured, and to the rights to which any incumbrancer would have been entitled if those powers had remained exercisable by the tenant for life. This subsection applies whether or not any term of years or charge intervenes, or the estate of the remainder-man or reversioner is liable to be defeated, and whether or not the estate or interest of the tenant for life under the settlement was in possession at the date of the asssurance. This subsection does not prejudice anything done by the tenant for life before the commencement of this Act, in exercise of any power operating under the Settled Land Acts 1882 to 1890 or, unless the assurance provides to the contrary, operate to accelerate any such intervening term of years or charge as aforesaid.

(2) In this section 'assurance' means any surrender, conveyance, assignment or appointment under a power (whether vested in any person solely, or jointly in two or more persons) which operates in equity to extinguish the estate or interest of the tenant for life, and 'assured' has a corresponding meaning.

106 Prohibition or limitation against exercise of powers void, and provision against forfeiture

(1) If in a settlement, will, assurance, or other instrument executed or made before or after, or partly before and partly after, the commencement of this Act a provision is inserted –

> (a) purporting or attempting, by way of direction, declaration, or otherwise, to forbid a tenant for life or statutory owner to exercise any power under this Act, or his right to require the settled land to be vested in him; or

(b) attempting, or tending, or intended, by a limitation, gift, or disposition over of settled land, or by a limitation, gift, or disposition of other real or any personal property, or by the imposition of any condition, or by forfeiture, or in any other manner whatever, to prohibit or prevent him from exercising, or to induce him to abstain from exercising, or to put him into a position inconsistent with his exercising, any power under this Act, or his right to require the settled land to be vested in him;

that provision, as far as it purports, or attempts, or tends, or is intended to have, or would or might have, the operation aforesaid, shall be deemed to be void.

(2) For the purposes of this section an estate or interest limited to continue so long only as a person abstains from exercising any such power or right as aforesaid shall be and take effect as an estate or interest to continue for the period for which it would continue if that person were to abstain from exercising the power or right, discharged from liability to determination or cesser by or on his exercising the same.

(3) Notwithstanding anything in a settlement, the exercise by the tenant for life or statutory owner of any power under this Act shall not occasion a forfeiture.

107 Tenant for life trustee for all parties interested

(1) A tenant for life or statutory owner shall, in exercising any power under this Act, have regard to the interests of all parties entitled under the settlement, and shall, in relation to the exercise thereof by him, be deemed to be in the position and to have the duties and liabilities of a trustee for those parties.

(1A) The following provisions apply to the tenant for life as they apply to the trustees of the settlement –

(a) sections 11, 13 to 15 and 21 to 23 of the Trustee Act 2000 (power to employ agents subject to certain restrictions),

(b) section 32 of that Act (remuneration and expenses of agents, etc),

(c) section 19 of the Trustee Act 1925 (power to insure), and

(d) in so far as they relate to the provisions mentioned in paragraphs (a) and (c), Part I of, and Schedule 1 to, the Trustee Act 2000 (the duty of care).

(2) The provision by a tenant for life or statutory owner, at his own expense, of dwellings available for the working classes on any settled land shall not be deemed to be an injury to any interest in reversion or remainder in that land, but such provision shall not be made by a tenant for life or statutory owner without the previous approval in writing of the trustees of the settlement.

108 Saving for and exercise of other powers

(1) Nothing in this Act shall take away, abridge, or prejudicially affect any power for the time being subsisting under a settlement, or by statute or otherwise, exercisable by a tenant for life, or (save as hereinafter provided) by trustees with his consent, or

on his request, or by his direction, or otherwise, and the powers given by this Act are cumulative.

(2) In case of conflict between the provisions of a settlement and the provisions of this Act, relative to any matter in respect whereof the tenant for life or statutory owner exercises or contracts or intends to exercise any power under this Act, the provisions of this Act shall prevail; and, notwithstanding anything in the settlement, any power (not being merely a power of revocation or appointment) relating to the settled land thereby conferred on the trustees of the settlement or other persons exercisable for any purpose, whether or not provided for in this Act, shall, after the commencement of this Act, be exercisable by the tenant for life or statutory owner as if it were an additional power conferred on the tenant for life within the next following section of this Act and not otherwise.

(3) If a question arises or a doubt is entertained respecting any matter within this section, the tenant for life or statutory owner, or the trustees of the settlement, or any other person interested, under the settlement may apply to the court for its decision thereon, and the court may make such order respecting the matter as the court thinks fit.

109 Saving for additional or larger powers under settlement

(1) Nothing in this Act precludes a settlor from conferring on the tenant for life, or (save as provided by the last preceding section) on the trustees of the settlement, any powers additional to or larger than those conferred by this Act.

(2) Any additional or larger powers so conferred shall, as far as may be, notwithstanding anything in this Act, operate and be exercisable in the like manner, and with all the like incidents, effects, and consequences, as if they were conferred by this Act, and, if relating to the settled land, as if they were conferred by this Act on a tenant for life.

110 Protection of purchasers, etc

(1) On a sale, exchange, lease, mortgage, charge, or other disposition, a purchaser dealing in good faith with a tenant for life or statutory owner shall, as against all parties entitled under the settlement, be conclusively taken to have given the best price, consideration, or rent, as the case may require, that could reasonably be obtained by the tenant for life or statutory owner, and to have complied with all the requisitions of this Act.

(2) A purchaser of a legal estate in settled land shall not, except as hereby expressly provided, be bound or entitled to call for the production of the trust instrument or any information concerning that instrument or any ad valorem stamp duty thereon, and whether or not he has notice of its contents he shall, save as hereinafter provided, be bound and entitled if the last or only principal vesting instrument contains the statements and particulars required by this Act to assume that –

> (a) the person in whom the land is by the said instrument vested or declared to be vested in the tenant for life or statutory owner and has all the powers of a

tenant for life under this Act, including such additional or larger powers, if any, as are therein mentioned;

(b) the persons by the said instrument stated to be the trustees of the settlement, or their successors appearing to be duly appointed, are the properly constituted trustees of the settlement;

(c) the statements and particulars required by this Act and contained (expressly or by reference) in the said instrument were correct at the date thereof;

(d) the statements contained in any deed executed in accordance with this Act declaring who are the trustees of the settlement for the purposes of this Act are correct;

(e) the statements contained in any deed of discharge, executed in accordance with this Act, are correct:

Provided that, as regards the first vesting instrument executed for the purpose of giving effect to –

(a) a settlement subsisting at the commencement of this Act; or

(b) an instrument which by virtue of this Act is deemed to be a settlement; or

(c) a settlement which by virtue of this Act is deemed to have been made by any person after the commencement of this Act; or

(d) an instrument inter vivos intended to create a settlement of a legal estate in land which is executed after the commencement of this Act and does not comply with the requirements of this Act with respect to the method of effecting such a settlement;

a purchaser shall be concerned to see –

(i) that the land disposed of to him is comprised in such settlement or instrument;

(ii) that the person in whom the settled land is by such vesting instrument vested, or declared to be vested, is the person in whom it ought to be vested as tenant for life or statutory owner;

(iii) that the persons thereby stated to be the trustees of the settlement are the properly constituted trustees of the settlement.

(3) A purchaser of a legal estate in settled land from a personal representative shall be entitled to act on the following assumptions –

(i) If the capital money, if any, payable in respect of the transaction is paid to the personal representative, that such representative is acting under his statutory or other powers and requires the money for purposes of administration;

(ii) If such capital money is, by the direction of the personal representative, paid to persons who are stated to be the trustees of a settlement, that such persons are the duly constituted trustees of the settlement for the purposes of this Act, and that the personal representative is acting under his statutory powers during a minority;

(iii) In any other case, that the personal representative is acting under his statutory or other powers.

(4) Where no capital money arises under a transaction, a disposition by a tenant for life or statutory owner shall, in favour of a purchaser of a legal estate, have effect under this Act notwithstanding that at the date of the transaction there are no trustees of the settlement.

(5) If a conveyance of or an assent relating to land formerly subject to a vesting instrument does not state who are the trustees of the settlement for the purposes of this Act, a purchaser of a legal estate shall be bound and entitled to act on the assumption that the person in whom the land was thereby vested was entitled to the land free from all limitations, powers, and charges taking effect under that settlement, absolutely and beneficially, or, if so expressed in the conveyance or assent, as personal representative, or trustee of land or otherwise, and that every statement of fact in such conveyance or assent is correct.

111   Purchaser of beneficial interest of tenant for life to have remedies of a legal owner

Where –

(a) at the commencement of this Act the legal beneficial interest of a tenant for life under a settlement is vested in a purchaser; or

(b) after the commencement of this Act a tenant for life conveys or deals with his beneficial interest in possession in favour of a purchaser, and the interest so conveyed or created would, but for the restrictions imposed by statute on the creation of legal estates, have been a legal interest;

the purchaser shall (without prejudice to the powers conferred by this Act on the tenant for life) have and may exercise all the same rights and remedies as he would have had or have been entitled to exercise if the interest had remained or been a legal interest and the reversion, if any, on any leases or tenancies derived out of the settled land had been vested in him: provided that, where the conveyance or dealing is effected after the commencement of this Act, the purchaser shall not be entitled to the possession of the documents of title relating to the settled land, but shall have the same rights with respect thereto as if the tenant for life had given to him a statutory acknowledgement of his right to production and delivery of copies thereof, and a statutory undertaking for the safe custody thereof. The tenant for life shall not deliver any such documents to a purchaser of his beneficial interest, who is not also a purchaser of the whole of the settled land to which such documents relate.

112   Exercise of powers; limitation of provisions, etc

(1) Where a power of sale, exchange, leasing, mortgaging, charging, or other power is exercised by a tenant for life, or statutory owner or by the trustees of a settlement, he and they may respectively execute, make, and do all deeds, instruments, and things necessary or proper in that behalf.

(2) Where any provision in this Act refers to sale, purchase, exchange, mortgaging, charging, leasing, or other disposition or dealing, or to any power, consent, payment, receipt, deed, assurance, contract, expenses, act, or transaction, it shall (unless the contrary appears) be construed as extending only to sales, purchases, exchanges, mortgages, charges, leases, dispositions, dealings, powers, consents, payments, receipts, deeds, assurances, contracts, expenses, acts, and transactions under this Act.

PART IX

SUPPLEMENTARY PROVISIONS

117 Definitions

(1) In this Act, unless the context otherwise requires, the following expressions have the meanings hereby assigned to them respectively, that is to say –

(i) 'Building purposes' include the erecting and the improving of, and the adding to, and the repairing of buildings; and a 'building lease' is a lease for any building purposes or purposes connected therewith;

(ii) 'Capital money arising under this Act' means capital money arising under the powers and provisions of this Act or the Acts replaced by this Act, and receivable for the trusts and purposes of the settlement and includes securities representing capital money;

(iii) 'Death duty' means estate duty and every other duty leviable or payable on death;

(iv) 'Determinable fee' means a fee determinable whether by limitation or condition;

(v) 'Disposition' and 'conveyance' include a mortgage, charge by way of legal mortgage, lease, assent, vesting declaration, vesting instrument, disclaimer, release and every other assurance of property or of an interest therein by any instrument, except a will, and 'dispose of' and 'convey' have corresponding meanings;

(vi) 'Dower' includes 'freebench';

(vii) 'Hereditaments' mean real property which on an intestacy might before the commencement of this Act have devolved on an heir;

(viii) 'Instrument' does not include a statute unless the statute creates a settlement;

(ix) 'Land' includes land of any tenure, and mines and minerals whether or not held apart from the surface, buildings or parts of buildings (whether the division is horizontal, vertical or made in any other way) and other corporeal hereditaments; also a manor, an advowson, and a rent and other incorporeal hereditaments, and an easement, right, privilege, or benefit in, over, or derived from land, and any estate or interest in land, but does not (except in the phrase 'trust of land') include an undivided share in land;

(x) 'Lease' includes an agreement for a lease, and 'forestry lease' means a lease to the Forestry Commissioners for any purpose for which they are authorised to acquire land by the Forestry Act, 1919;

(xi) 'Legal mortgage' means a mortgage by demise or sub-demise or a charge by way of legal mortgage, and 'legal mortgagee' has a corresponding meaning; 'legal estate' means an estate interest or charge in or over land (subsisting or created at law) which is by statute authorised to subsist or to be created at law; and 'equitable interests' mean all other interests and charges in or over land or in the proceeds of sale thereof; an equitable interest 'capable of subsisting at law' means such an equitable interest as could validly subsist at law, if clothed with the legal estate; and 'estate owner' means the owner of a legal estate;

(xii) 'Limitation' includes a trust, and 'trust' includes an implied or constructive trust;

(xiv) 'Manor' includes lordship, and reputed manor or lordship; and 'manorial incident' has the same meaning as in the Law of Property Act 1922;

(xv) 'Mines and minerals' mean mines and minerals whether already opened or in work or not, and include all minerals and substances in, on, or under the land, obtainable by underground or by surface working; and 'mining purposes' include the sinking and searching for, winning, working, getting, making merchantable, smelting or otherwise converting or working for the purposes of any manufacture, carrying away, and disposing of mines and minerals, in or under the settled land, or any other land, and the erection of buildings, and the execution of engineering and other works suitable for those purposes; and a 'mining lease' is a lease for any mining purposes or purposes connected therewith, and includes a grant or licence for any mining purposes;

(xvii) 'Notice' includes constructive notice;

(xviii) 'Personal representative' means the executor, original or by representation, or administrator, for the time being of a deceased person, and where there are special personal representatives for the purposes of settled land means those personal representatives;

(xix) 'Possession' includes receipt of rents and profits, or the right to receive the same, if any; and 'income' includes rents and profits;

(xx) 'Property' includes any thing in action, and any interest in real or personal property;

(xxi) 'Purchaser' means a purchaser in good faith for value, and includes a lessee, mortgagee or other person who in good faith acquires an interest in settled land for value; and in reference to a legal estate includes a chargee by way of legal mortgage;

(xxii) 'Rent' includes yearly or other rent, and toll, duty, royalty, or other reservation, by the acre, or the ton, or otherwise; and, in relation to rent, 'payment' includes delivery; and 'fine' includes premium or fore-gift, and any payment, consideration, or benefit in the nature of a fine, premium, or fore-gift;

(xxiii) 'Securities' include stocks, funds, and shares;

(xxiv) 'Settled land' includes land which is deemed to be settled land; 'settlement' includes an instrument or instruments which under this Act or the Acts which it replaces is or are deemed to be or which together constitute a settlement, and a settlement which is deemed to have been made by any person or to be subsisting for the purposes of this Act; 'a settlement subsisting at the commencement of this Act' includes a settlement created by virtue of this Act immediately on the commencement thereof; and 'trustees of the settlement' mean the trustees thereof for the purposes of this Act howsoever appointed or constituted;

(xxv) 'Small dwellings 'mean dwelling-houses of a rateable value not exceeding one hundred pounds per annum;

(xxvi) 'Statutory owner' means the trustees of the settlement or other persons who, during a minority, or at any other time when there is no tenant for life, have the powers of a tenant for life under this Act, but does not include the trustees of the settlement, where by virtue of an order of the court or otherwise the trustees have power to convey the settled land in the name of the tenant for life;

(xxvii) 'Steward' includes deputy steward, or other proper officer, of a manor;

(xxviii) 'Tenant for life' includes a person (not being a statutory owner) who has the powers of a tenant for life under this Act, and also (where the context requires) one of two or more persons who together constitute the tenant for life, or have the powers of a tenant for life; and 'tenant in tail' includes a person entitled to an entailed interest in any property; and 'entailed interest' has the same meaning as in the Law of Property Act 1925;

(xxix) A 'term of years absolute' means a term of years, taking effect either in possession or in reversion, with or without impeachment for waste, whether at a rent or not and whether subject or not to another legal estate, and whether certain or liable to determination by notice, re-entry, operation of law, or by a provision for cesser on redemption, or in any other event (other than the dropping of a life, or the determination of a determinable life interest), but does not include any term of years determinable with life or lives or with the cesser of a determinable life interest, nor, if created after the commencement of this Act, a term of years which is not expressed to take effect in possession within twenty-one years after the creation thereof where required by statute to take effect within that period; and in this definition the expression 'term of years' includes a term for less than a year, or for a year or years and a fraction of a year or from year to year;

(xxx) 'Trust corporation' means the Public Trustee or a corporation either appointed by the court in any particular case to be a trustee or entitled by rules made under subsection (3) of section four of the Public Trustee Act 1906 to act as custodian trustee, and 'trust for sale' has the same meaning as in the Law of Property Act 1925;

(xxxi) In relation to settled land 'vesting deed' or 'vesting order' means the instrument whereby settled land is conveyed to or vested or declared to be vested in a tenant for life or statutory owner; 'vesting assent' means the instrument whereby a personal representative, after the death of a tenant for life or statutory owner, or the survivor of two or more tenants for life or statutory owners, vests settled land in a person entitled as tenant for life or statutory owner; 'vesting instrument' means a vesting deed, a vesting assent or, where the land affected remains settled land, a vesting order; 'principal vesting instrument' includes any vesting instrument other than a subsidiary vesting deed; and 'trust instrument' means the instrument whereby the trusts of the settled land are declared, and includes any two or more such instruments and a settlement or instrument which is deemed to be a trust instrument;

(xxxii) 'United Kingdom' means Great Britain and Northern Ireland;

(xxxiii) 'Will' includes codicil.

(1A) Any reference in this Act to money, securities or proceeds of sale being paid or transferred into court shall be construed as referring to the money, securities or proceeds being paid or transferred into the Supreme Court or any other court that has jurisdiction, and any reference in this Act to the court, in a context referring to the investment or application of money, securities or proceeds of sale paid or transferred into court, shall be construed, in the case of money, securities or proceeds paid or transferred into the Supreme Court, as referring to the High Court, and, in the case of money, securities or proceeds paid or transferred into another court, as referring to that other court.

(2) Where an equitable interest in or power over property arises by statute or operation of law, references to the 'creation' of an interest or power include any interest or power so arising.

(3) References to registration under the Land Charges Act 1925 apply to any registration made under any statute which is by the Land Charges Act 1925 to have effect as if the registration had been made under that Act.

THIRD SCHEDULE

PART I

IMPROVEMENTS, THE COSTS OF WHICH ARE NOT LIABLE TO BE REPLACED BY INSTALMENTS

(i) Drainage, including the straightening, widening, or deepening of drains, streams, and watercourses:

(ii) Bridges:

(iii) Irrigation; warping:

(iv) Drains, pipes, and machinery for supply and distribution of sewage as manure:

(v) Embanking or weiring from a river or lake, or from the sea, or a tidal water:

(vi) Groynes; sea walls; defences against water:

(vii) Inclosing; straightening of fences; re-division of fields

(viii) Reclamation; dry warping:

(ix) Farm roads; private roads; roads or streets in villages or towns:

(x) Clearing; trenching; planting:

(xi) Cottages for labourers, farm-servants, and artisans, employed on the settled land or not:

(xii) Farmhouses, offices, and outbuildings, and other buildings for farm purposes:

(xiii) Saw-mills, scutch-mills, and other mills, water-wheels, engine-houses, and kilns, which will increase the value of the settled land for agricultural purposes or as woodland or otherwise:

(xiv) Reservoirs, tanks, conduits, watercourses, pipes, wells, ponds, shafts, dams, weirs, sluices, and other works and machinery for supply and distribution of water for agricultural, manufacturing, or other purposes, or for domestic or other consumption:

(xv) Tramways; railways; canals; docks:

(xvi) Jetties, piers, and landing places on rivers, lakes, the sea, or tidal waters, for facilitating transport of persons and of agricultural stock and produce, and of manure and other things required for agricultural purposes, and of minerals, and of things required for mining purposes:

(xvii) Markets and market-places:

(xviii) Streets, roads, paths, squares, gardens, or other open spaces for the use, gratuitously or on payment, of the public or of individuals, or for dedication to the public, the same being necessary or proper in connexion with the conversion of land into building land:

(xix) Sewers, drains, watercourses, pipe-making, fencing, paving, brick-making, tile-making, and other works necessary or proper in connexion with any of the objects aforesaid:

(xx) Trial pits for mines, and other preliminary works necessary or proper in connection with development of mines:

(xxi) Reconstruction, enlargement, or improvement of any of those works:

(xxii) The provision of small dwellings, either by means of building new buildings or by means of the reconstruction, enlargement, or improvement of existing buildings, if that provision of small dwellings is, in the opinion of the court, not injurious to the settled land or is agreed to by the tenant for life and the trustees of the settlement:

(xxiii) Additions to or alterations in buildings reasonably necessary or proper to enable the same to be let:

(xxiv) Erection of buildings in substitution for buildings within an urban sanitary district taken by a local or other public authority, or for buildings taken under compulsory powers, but so that no more money be expended than the amount received for the buildings taken and the site thereof:

(xxv) The rebuilding of the principal mansion house on the settled land: Provided that the sum to be applied under this head shall not exceed one-half of the annual rental of the settled land.

PART II

IMPROVEMENTS, THE COSTS OF WHICH THE TRUSTEES OF THE SETTLEMENT OR THE COURT MAY REQUIRE TO BE REPLACED BY INSTALMENTS

(i) Residential houses for land or mineral agents, managers, clerks, bailiffs, woodmen, gamekeepers and other persons employed on the settled land, or in connection with the management or development thereof:

(ii) Any offices, workshops and other buildings of a permanent nature required in connection with the management or development of the settled land or any part thereof:

(iii) The erection and building of dwelling houses, shops, buildings for religious, educational, literary, scientific, or public purposes, market places, market houses, places of amusement and entertainment, gasworks, electric light or power works, or any other works necessary or proper in connexion with the development of the settled land, or any part thereof as a building estate:

(iv) Restoration or reconstruction of buildings damaged or destroyed by dry rot:

(v) Structural additions to or alterations in buildings reasonably required, whether the buildings are intended to be let or not, or are already let:

(vi) Boring for water and other preliminary works in connection therewith

PART III

IMPROVEMENTS, THE COSTS OF WHICH THE TRUSTEES OF THE SETTLEMENT AND THE COURT MUST REQUIRE TO BE REPLACED BY INSTALMENTS

(i) Heating, hydraulic or electric power apparatus for buildings, and engines, pumps, lifts, rams, boilers, flues, and other works required or used in connexion therewith:

(ii) Engine houses, engines, gasometers, dynamos, accumulators, cables, pipes, wiring, switchboards, plant and other works required for the installation of electric, gas, or other artificial light, in connexion with any principal mansion house, or other house or buildings; but not electric lamps, gas fittings, or decorative fittings required in any such house or building:

(iii) Steam rollers, traction engines, motor lorries and moveable machinery for farming or other purposes.

As amended by the Law of Property (Amendment) Act 1926, ss6, 7, Schedule; Law of Property

(Entailed Interests) Act 1932, s1(1); Settled Land and Trustee Acts (Court's General Powers) Act 1943, s2; Finance Act 1949, s52, Schedule II, Pt IV; Married Women (Restraint upon Anticipation) Act 1949, s1(4), Schedule 2; Transfer of Functions (Ministry of Food) Order 1955; Highways Act 1959, s312(2), Schedule 25; Mental Health Act 1959, s149, Schedule 7, Pt I, Schedule 8, Pt I; Charities Act 1960, s48(2), Schedule 7, Pts I, II; Finance Act 1963, s73(8)(b),Schedule 11, Pt VI; Administration of Justice Act 1965, s17(1), Schedule 1; Family Law Reform Act 1969, ss1(3), 11(a), Schedule 1; Statute Law (Repeals) Act 1969; Decimal Currency Act 1969, s10(1); Highways Act 1980, s343(2), Schedule 24, para 2; Agricultural Holdings Act 1986, s100, Schedule 14, para 11; Trusts of Land and Appointment of Trustees Act 1996, s25(1), (2), Schedule 3, para 2, Schedule 4; Statute Law (Repeals) Act 1998, s1(1), Schedule 1, Pt II; Trustee Act 2000, s40(1), Schedule 2, Pt II, paras 7–11, 13, 15–17; Ministry of Agriculture, Fisheries and Food (Dissolution) Order 2002, art 5(1), (2), Schedule 1, paras 2, 3, Schedule 2.

TRUSTEE ACT 1925
(15 & 16 Geo 5 c 19)

GENERAL POWERS OF TRUSTEES AND PERSONAL REPRESENTATIVES

12   Power of trustees for sale to sell by auction, etc

(1) Where a trustee has a duty or power to sell property, he may sell or concur with any other person in selling all or any part of the property, either subject to prior charges or not, and either together or in lots, by public auction or by private contract, subject to any such conditions respecting title or evidence of title or other matter as the trustee thinks fit, with power to vary any contract for sale, and to buy in at any auction, or to rescind any contract for sale and to re-sell, without being answerable for any loss.

(2) A duty or power to sell or dispose of land includes a duty or power to sell or dispose of part thereof, whether the division is horizontal, vertical or made in any other way.

(3) This section does not enable an express power to sell settled land to be exercised where the power is not vested in the tenant for life or statutory owner.

13   Power to sell subject to depreciatory conditions

(1) No sale made by a trustee shall be impeached by any beneficiary upon the ground that any of the conditions subject to which the sale was made may have been unnecessarily depreciatory, unless it also appears that the consideration for the sale was thereby rendered inadequate.

(2) No sale made by a trustee shall, after the execution of the conveyance, be impeached as against the purchaser upon the ground that any of the conditions subject to which the sale was made may have been unnecessarily depreciatory, unless it appears that the purchaser was acting in collusion with the trustee at the time when the contract for sale was made.

(3) No purchaser, upon any sale made by the trustee, shall be at liberty to make any objection against the title upon any of the grounds aforesaid.

(4) This section applies to sales made before or after the commencement of this Act.

16   Power to raise money by sale, mortgage, etc

(1) Where trustees are authorised by the instrument, if any, creating the trust or by law to pay or apply capital money subject to the trust for any purpose or in any manner, they shall have and shall be deemed always to have had power to raise the money required by sale, conversion, calling in, or mortgage of all or any part of the trust property for the time being in possession.

(2) This section applies notwithstanding anything to the contrary contained in the instrument, if any, creating the trust, but does not apply to trustees of property held for charitable purposes, or to trustees of a settlement for the purposes of the Settled Land Act 1925, not being also the statutory owners.

17   Protection to purchasers and mortgagees dealing with trustees

No purchaser or mortgagee, paying or advancing money on a sale or mortgage purporting to be made under any trust or power vested in trustees, shall be concerned to see that such money is wanted, or that no more than is wanted is raised, or otherwise as to the application thereof.

PART III

APPOINTMENT AND DISCHARGE OF TRUSTEES

34   Limitation of the number of trustees

(1) Where, at the commencement of this Act, there are more than four trustees of a settlement of land, or more than four trustees holding land on trust for sale, no new trustees shall (except where as a result of the appointment the number is reduced to four or less) be capable of being appointed until the number is reduced to less than four, and thereafter the number shall not be increased beyond four.

(2) In the case of settlements and dispositions creating trusts of land made or coming into operation after the commencement of this Act –

   (a) the number of trustees thereof shall not in any case exceed four, and where more than four persons are named as such trustees, the four first named (who are able and willing to act) shall alone be the trustees, and the other persons named shall not be trustees unless appointed on the occurrence of a vacancy;

   (b) the number of the trustees shall not be increased beyond four.

(3) This section only applies to settlements and dispositions of land, and the restrictions imposed on the number of trustees do not apply –

   (a) in the case of land vested in trustees for charitable, ecclesiastical, or public purposes; or

   (b) where the net proceeds of the sale of the land are held for like purposes; or

   (c) to the trustees of a term of years absolute limited by a settlement on trusts for raising money, or of a like term created under the statutory remedies relating to annual sums charged on land.

35 Appointments of trustees of settlements and trustees of land

(1) Appointments of new trustees of land and of new trustees of any trust of the proceeds of sale of the land shall, subject to any order of the court, be effected by separate instruments, but in such manner as to secure that the same persons become trustees of land and trustees of the trust of the proceeds of sale.

(2) Where new trustees of a settlement are appointed, a memorandum of the names and addresses of the persons who are for the time being the trustees thereof for the purposes of the Settled Land Act 1925 shall be endorsed on or annexed to the last or only principal vesting instrument by or on behalf of the trustees of the settlement, and such vesting instrument shall, for that purpose, be produced by the person having the possession thereof to the trustees of the settlement when so required.

(3) Where new trustees of land are appointed, a memorandum of the persons who are for the time being the trustees of the land shall be endorsed on or annexed to the conveyance by which the land was vested in trustees of land; and that conveyance shall be produced to the persons who are for the time being the trustees of the land by the person in possession of it in order for that to be done when the trustees require its production.

(4) This section applies only to settlements and dispositions of land.

40 Vesting of trust property in new or continuing trustees

(1) Where by a deed a new trustee is appointed to perform any trust, then –

(a) if the deed contains a declaration by the appointer to the effect that any estate or interest in any land subject to the trust, or in any chattel so subject, or the right to recover or receive any debt or other thing in action so subject, shall vest in the persons who by virtue of the deed become or are the trustees for performing the trust, the deed shall operate, without any conveyance or assignment, to vest in those persons as joint tenants and for the purposes of the trust the estate interest or right to which the declaration relates; and

(b) if the deed is made after the commencement of this Act and does not contain such a declaration, the deed shall, subject to any express provision to the contrary therein contained, operate as if it had contained such a declaration by the appointer extending to all the estates interests and rights with respect to which a declaration could have been made.

(2) Where by a deed a retiring trustee is discharged under section 39 of this Act or section 19 of the Trusts of Land and Appointment of Trustees Act 1996 without a new trustee being appointed, then –

(a) if the deed contains such a declaration as aforesaid by the retiring and continuing trustees, and by the other persons, if any, empowered to appoint trustees, the deed shall, without any conveyance or assignment, operate to vest in the continuing trustees alone, as joint tenants, and for the purposes of the trust, the estate, interest, or right of which the declaration relates; and

(b) if the deed is made after the commencement of this Act and does not contain such a declaration, the deed shall, subject to any express provision to the contrary therein contained, operate as if it had contained such a declaration by such persons as aforesaid extending to all the estates, interests and rights with respect to which a declaration could have been made.

(3) An express vesting declaration, whether made before or after the commencement of this Act, shall, notwithstanding that the estate, interest or right to be vested is not expressly referred to, and provided that the other statutory requirements were or are complied with, operate and be deemed always to have operated (but without prejudice to any express provision to the contrary contained in the deed of appointment or discharge) to vest in the persons respectively referred to in subsections (1) and (2) of this section, as the case may require, such estates, interests and rights are as capable of being and ought to be vested in those persons.

(4) This section does not extend –

(a) to land conveyed by way of mortgage for securing money subject to the trust, except land conveyed on trust for securing debentures or debenture stock;

(b) to land held under a lease which contains any covenant, condition or agreement against assignment or disposing of the land without licence or consent, unless, prior to the execution of the deed containing expressly or impliedly the vesting declaration, the requisite licence or consent has been obtained, or unless, by virtue of any statute or rule of law, the vesting declaration, express or implied, would not operate as a breach of covenant or give rise to a forfeiture;

(c) to any share, stock, annuity or property which is only transferable in books kept by a company or other body, or in manner directed by or under an Act of Parliament.

In this subsection 'lease' includes an underlease and an agreement for a lease or underlease.

(5) For purposes of registration of the deed in any registry, the person or persons making the declaration expressly or impliedly shall be deemed the conveying party or parties, and the conveyance shall be deemed to be made by him or them under a power conferred by this Act.

(6) This section applies to deeds of appointment and discharge executed on or after the first day of January, eighteen hundred and eighty-two.

44 Vesting orders of land

In any of the following cases, namely –

(i) Where the court appoints or has appointed a trustee, or where a trustee has been appointed out of court under any statutory or express power;

(ii) Where a trustee entitled to or possessed of any land or interest therein, whether by way of mortgage or otherwise, or entitled to a contingent right therein, either solely or jointly with any other person –

(a) is under disability; or

(b) is out of the jurisdiction of the High Court; or

(c) cannot be found, or, being a corporation, has been dissolved;

(iii) Where it is uncertain who was the survivor of two or more trustees jointly entitled to or possessed of any interest in land;

(iv) Where it is uncertain whether the last trustee known to have been entitled to or possessed of any interest in land is living or dead;

(v) Where there is no personal representative of a deceased trustee who was entitled to or possessed of any interest in land, or where it is uncertain who is the personal representative of a deceased trustee who was entitled to or possessed of any interest in land;

(vi) Where a trustee jointly or solely entitled to or possessed of any interest in land, or entitled to a contingent right therein, has been required, by or on behalf of a person entitled to require a conveyance of the land or interest or a release of the right, to convey the land or interest or to release the right, and has wilfully refused or neglected to convey the land or interest or release the right for twenty-eight days after the date of the requirement;

(vii) Where land or any interest therein is vested in a trustee whether by way of mortgage or otherwise, and it appears to the court to be expedient;

the court may make an order (in this Act called a vesting order) vesting the land or interest therein in any such person in any such manner and for any such estate or interest as the court may direct, or releasing or disposing of the contingent right to such person as the court may direct: Provided that –

(a) Where the order is consequential on the appointment of a trustee the land or interest therein shall be vested for such estate as the court may direct in the persons who on the appointment are the trustees; and

(b) Where the order relates to a trustee entitled or formerly entitled jointly with another person, and such trustee is under disability or out of the jurisdiction of the High Court or cannot be found, or being a corporation has been dissolved, the land interest or right shall be vested in such other person who remains entitled, either alone or with any other person the court may appoint.

PART V

GENERAL PROVISIONS

64 Application of Act to Settled Land Act trustees

(1) All the powers and provisions contained in this Act with reference to the appointment of new trustees, and the discharge and retirement of trustees, apply to and include trustees for the purposes of the Settled Land Act 1925, and trustees for the purpose of the management of land during a minority, whether such trustees are appointed by the court or by the settlement, or under provisions contained in any instrument.

(2) Where, either before or after the commencement of this Act, trustees of a settlement have been appointed by the court for the purposes of the Settled Land Acts 1882 to 1890, or of the Settled Land Act 1925, then, after the commencement of this Act –

(a) the person or persons nominated for the purpose of appointing new trustees by the instrument, if any, creating the settlement, though no trustees for the purposes of the said Acts were thereby appointed; or

(b) if there is no such person, or no such person able and willing to act, the surviving or continuing trustees or trustee for the time being for the purposes of the said Acts or the personal representatives of the last surviving or continuing trustee for those purposes,

shall have the powers conferred by this Act to appoint new or additional trustees of the settlement for the purposes of the said Acts.

(3) Appointments of new trustees for the purposes of the said Acts made or expressed to be made before the commencement of this Act by the trustees or trustee or personal representatives referred to in paragraph (b) of the last preceding subsection or by the persons referred to in paragraph (a) of that subsection are, without prejudice to any order of the court made before such commencement, hereby confirmed.

67   Jurisdiction of the 'court'

(1) In this Act 'the court' means the High Court or the county court, where those courts respectively have jurisdiction.

(2) The procedure under this Act in county courts shall be in accordance with the Acts and rules regulating the procedure of those courts.

68   Definitions

(1) In this Act, unless the context otherwise requires, the following expressions have the meanings hereby assigned to them respectively, that is to say – ...

(6) 'Land' includes land of any tenure, and mines and minerals, where or not severed from the surface, buildings or parts of buildings, whether the division is horizontal, vertical or made in any other way, and other corporeal hereditaments; also a manor, an advowson, and a rent and other incorporeal hereditaments, and an easement, right, privilege, or benefit in, over, or derived from land; and in this definition 'mines and minerals' include any strata or seam of minerals or substances in or under any land, and powers of working and getting the same; and 'hereditaments' mean real property which under an intestacy occurring before the commencement of this Act might have devolved on an heir;

(7) 'Mortgage' and 'mortgagee' include a charge or chargee by way of legal mortgage, and relate to every estate and interest regarded in equity as merely a security for money, and every person deriving title under the original mortgagee; ...

(11) 'Property' includes real and personal property, and any estate share and interest in any property, real or personal, and any debt, and any thing in action, and any other right or interest, whether in possession or not; ...

(15) 'Tenant for life', 'statutory owner', 'settled land', 'settlement', 'trust instrument', 'trustees of the settlement', 'term of years absolute' and 'vesting instrument' have the same meanings as in the Settled Land Act 1925, and 'entailed interest' has the same meaning as in the Law of Property Act 1925; ...

(17) 'Trust' does not include the duties incident to an estate conveyed by way of mortgage, but with this exception the expressions 'trust' and 'trustee' extend to implied and constructive trusts, and to cases where the trustee has a beneficial interest in the trust property, and to the duties incident to the office of a personal representative, and 'trustee', where the context admits, includes a personal representative, and 'new trustee' includes an additional trustee;

(18) 'Trust corporation' means the Public Trustee or a corporation either appointed by the court in any particular case to be a trustee, or entitled by rules made under subsection (3) of section four of the Public Trustee Act 1906, to act as custodian trustee;

(19) 'Trust for sale' in relation to land means an immediate trust for sale, whether or not exercisable at the request or with the consent of any person;

(20) 'United Kingdom' means Great Britain and Northern Ireland.

(2) Any reference in this Act to paying money or securities into court shall be construed as referring to paying the money or transferring or depositing the securities into or in the Supreme Court or into or in any other court that has jurisdiction, and any reference in this Act to payment of money or securities into court shall be construed –

(a) with reference to an order of the High Court, as referring to payment of the money or transfer or deposit of the securities into or in the Supreme Court; and

(b) with reference to an order of any other court, as referring to payment of the money or transfer or deposit of the securities into or in that court.

69 Application of Act

(1) This Act, except where otherwise expressly provided, applies to trusts including, so far as this Act applies thereto, executorship and administrationships constituted or created either before or after the commencement of this Act.

(2) The powers conferred by this Act on trustees are in addition to the powers conferred by the instrument, if any, creating the trust, but those powers, unless otherwise stated, apply if and so far only as a contrary intention is not expressed in the instrument, if any, creating the trust, and have effect subject to the terms of that instrument.

As amended by the Mental Health Act 1959, s149(2), Schedule 8, Pt I; Courts Act 1971, s56, Schedule 11, Pt II; Trusts of Land and Appointment of Trustees Act 1996, s25(1), (2), Schedule 3, para 3, Schedule 4.

LAW OF PROPERTY ACT 1925
(15 Geo 5 c 20)

GENERAL PRINCIPLES AS TO LEGAL ESTATES, EQUITABLE INTERESTS AND POWERS

1 Legal estates and equitable interests

(1) The only estates in land which are capable of subsisting or of being conveyed or created at law are –

    (a) An estate in fee simple absolute in possession;

    (b) A term of years absolute.

(2) The only interests or charges in or over land which are capable of subsisting or of being conveyed or created at law are –

    (a) An easement, right, or privilege in or over land for an interest equivalent to an estate in fee simple absolute in possession or a term of years absolute;

    (b) A rentcharge in possession issuing out of or charged on land being either perpetual or for a term of years absolute;

    (c) A charge by way of legal mortgage;

    (d) Any other similar charge on land which is not created by an instrument;

    (e) Rights of entry exercisable over or in respect of a legal term of years absolute, or annexed, for any purpose, to a legal rentcharge.

(3) All other estates, interests, and charges in or over land take effect as equitable interests.

(4) The estates, interests, and charges which under this section are authorised to subsist or to be conveyed or created at law are (when subsisting or conveyed or created at law) in this Act referred to as 'legal estates', and have the same incidents as legal estates subsisting at the commencement of this Act; and the owner of a legal estate is referred to as 'an estate owner' and his legal estate is referred to as his estate.

(5) A legal estate may subsist concurrently with or subject to any other legal estate in the same land in like manner as it could have done before the commencement of this Act.

(6) A legal estate is not capable of subsisting or of being created in an undivided share in land or of being held by an infant.

(7) Every power of appointment over, or power to convey or charge land or any interest therein, whether created by a statute or other instrument or implied by law, and whether created before or after the commencement of this Act (not being a power vested in a legal mortgagee or an estate owner in right of his estate and exercisable by him or by another person in his name and on his behalf), operates only in equity.

(8) Estates, interests, and charges in or over land which are not legal estates are in this Act referred to as 'equitable interests', and powers which by this Act are to operate in equity only are in this Act referred to as 'equitable powers'.

(9) The provisions in any statute or other instrument requiring land to be conveyed to uses shall take effect as directions that the land shall (subject to creating or reserving thereout any legal estate authorised by this Act which may be required) be conveyed to a person of full age upon the requisite trusts.

(10) The repeal of the Statute of Uses (as amended) does not affect the operation thereof in regard to dealings taking effect before the commencement of this Act.

2   Conveyances overreaching certain equitable interests and powers

(1) A conveyance to a purchaser of a legal estate in land shall overreach any equitable interest or power affecting that estate, whether or not he has notice thereof, if –

(i) the conveyance is made under the powers conferred by the Settled Land Act 1925, or any additional powers conferred by a settlement, and the equitable interest or power is capable of being overreached thereby, and the statutory requirements respecting the payment of capital money arising under the settlement are complied with;

(ii) the conveyance is made by trustees of land and the equitable interest or power is at the date of the conveyance capable of being overreached by such trustees under the provisions of subsection (2) of this section or independently of that subsection, and the requirements of section 27 of this Act respecting the payment of capital money arising on such a conveyance are complied with;

(iii) the conveyance is made by a mortgagee or personal representative in the exercise of his paramount powers, and the equitable interest or power is capable of being overreached by such conveyance, and any capital money arising from the transaction is paid to the mortgagee or personal representative;

(iv) the conveyance is made under an order of the court and the equitable interest or power is bound by such order, and any capital money arising from the transaction is paid into, or in accordance with the order of, the court.

(1A) An equitable interest in land subject to a trust of land which remains in, or is to revert to, the settlor shall (subject to any contrary intention) be overreached by the conveyance if it would be so overreached were it an interest under the trust.

(2) Where the legal estate affected is subject to a trust of land, then if at the date of a conveyance made after the commencement of this Act by the trustees, the trustees (whether original or substituted) are either –

(a) two or more individuals approved or appointed by the court or the successors in office of the individuals so approved or appointed; or

(b) a trust corporation,

any equitable interest or power having priority to the trust shall, notwithstanding any stipulation to the contrary, be overreached by the conveyance, and shall, according to its priority, take effect as if created or arising by means of a primary trust affecting the proceeds of sale and the income of the land until sale.

(3) The following equitable interests and powers are excepted from the operation of subsection (2) of this section, namely –

(i) Any equitable interest protected by a deposit of documents relating to the legal estate affected;

(ii) The benefit of any covenant or agreement restrictive of the user of land;

(iii) Any easement, liberty, or privilege over or affecting land and being merely an equitable interest (in this Act referred to as an 'equitable easement');

(iv) The benefit of any contract (in this Act referred to as an 'estate contract') to convey or create a legal estate, including a contract conferring either expressly or by statutory implication a valid option to purchase, a right of pre-emption, or any other like right;

(v) Any equitable interest protected by registration under the Land Charges Act 1925, other than –

(a) an annuity within the meaning of Part II of that Act;

(b) a limited owner's charge or a general equitable charge within the meaning of that Act.

(4) Subject to the protection afforded by this section to the purchaser of a legal estate, nothing contained in this section shall deprive a person entitled to an equitable charge of any of his rights or remedies for enforcing the same.

(5) So far as regards the following interests, created before the commencement of this Act (which accordingly are not within the provisions of the Land Charges Act 1925), namely –

(a) the benefit of any covenant or agreement restrictive of the user of the land;

(b) any equitable easement;

(c) the interest under a puisne mortgage within the meaning of the Land Charges Act 1925, unless and until acquired under a transfer made after the commencement of this Act;

(d) the benefit of an estate contract, unless and until the same is acquired under a conveyance made after the commencement of this Act;

a purchaser of a legal estate shall only take subject thereto if he has notice thereof, and the same are not overreached under the provisions contained or in the manner referred to in this section.

3   Manner of giving effect to equitable interests and powers

(1) All equitable interests and powers in or over land shall be enforceable against the estate owner of the legal estate affected in manner following (that is to say) –

(a) Where the legal estate affected is settled land, the tenant for life or statutory owner shall be bound to give effect to the equitable interests and powers in manner provided by the Settled Land Act 1925;

(c) In any other case, the estate owner shall be bound to give effect to the equitable interests and powers affecting his estate of which he has notice according to their respective priorities. This provision does not affect the priority or powers of a legal mortgagee, or the powers of personal representatives for purposes of administration.

(3) Where, by reason of an equitable right of entry taking effect, or for any other reason, a person becomes entitled to require a legal estate to be vested in him, then and in any such case the estate owner whose estate is affected shall be bound to convey or create such legal estate as the case may require.

(4) If any question arises whether any and what legal estate ought to be transferred or created as aforesaid, any person interested may apply to the court for directions in the manner provided by this Act.

(5) If the estate owners refuse or neglect for one month after demand to transfer or create any such legal estate, or if by reason of their being out of the United Kingdom or being unable to be found, or by reason of the dissolution of a corporation, or for any other reason, the court is satisfied that the transaction cannot otherwise be effected, or cannot be effected without undue delay or expense, the court may, on the application of any person interested, make a vesting order transferring or creating a legal estate in the manner provided by this Act.

(6) This section does not affect a purchaser of a legal estate taking free from an equitable interest or power. ...

4   Creation and disposition of equitable interests

(1) Interests in land validly created or arising after the commencement of this Act, which are not capable of subsisting as legal estates, shall take effect as equitable interests, and, save as otherwise expressly provided by statute, interests in land which under the Statute of Uses or otherwise could before the commencement of this Act have been created as legal interests, shall be capable of being created as equitable interests: provided that, after the commencement of this Act (and save as hereinafter expressly enacted), an equitable interest in land shall only be capable of being validly created in any case in which an equivalent equitable interest in property real or personal could have been validly created before such commencement.

(2) All rights and interests in land may be disposed of, including –

(a) a contingent, executory or future equitable interest in any land, or a possibility coupled with an interest in any land, whether or not the object of the gift or limitation of such interest or possibility be ascertained;

(b) a right of entry, into or upon land whether immediate or future, and whether vested or contingent.

(3) All rights of entry affecting a legal estate which are exercisable on condition broken or for any other reason may after the commencement of this Act, be made exercisable by any person and the persons deriving title under him, but, in regard to an estate in fee simple (not being a rentcharge held for a legal estate) only within the period authorised by the rule relating to perpetuities.

5 Satisfied terms, whether created out of freehold or leasehold land to cease

(1) Where the purposes of a term of years created or limited at any time out of freehold land, become satisfied either before or after the commencement of this Act (whether or not that term either by express declaration or by construction of law becomes attendant upon the freehold reversion) it shall merge in the reversion expectant thereon and shall cease accordingly.

(2) Where the purposes of a term of years created or limited, at any time, out of leasehold land, become satisfied after the commencement of this Act, that term shall merge in the reversion expectant thereon and shall cease accordingly.

(3) Where the purposes are satisfied only as respects part of the land comprised in a term, this section shall have effect as if a separate term had been created in regard to that part of the land.

6 Saving of lessors' and lessees' covenants

(1) Nothing in this Part of this Act affects prejudicially the right to enforce any lessor's or lessee's covenants, agreements or conditions (including a valid option to purchase or right of pre-emption over the reversion), contained in any such instrument as is in this section mentioned, the benefit or burden of which runs with the reversion of the term.

(2) This section applies where the covenant, agreement or condition is contained in any instrument –

(a) creating a term of years absolute, or

(b) varying the rights of the lessor or lessee under the instrument creating the term.

7 Saving of certain legal estates and statutory powers

(1) A fee simple which, by virtue of the Lands Clauses Acts or any similar statute, is liable to be divested, is for the purposes of this Act a fee simple absolute, and

remains liable to be divested as if this Act had not been passed and a fee simple subject to a legal or equitable right of entry or re-entry is for the purposes of this Act a fee simple absolute.

(2) A fee simple vested in a corporation which is liable to determine by reason of the dissolution of the corporation is, for the purposes of this Act, a fee simple absolute.

(3) The provisions of –

(b) the Friendly Societies Act 1896, in regard to land to which that Act applies;

(c) any other statutes conferring special facilities or prescribing special modes (whether by way of registered memorial or otherwise) for disposing of or acquiring land, or providing for the vesting (by conveyance or otherwise) of the land in trustees or any person, or the holder for the time being of an office or any corporation sole or aggregate (including the Crown);

shall remain in full force.

(4) Where any such power for disposing of or creating a legal estate is exercisable by a person who is not the estate owner, the power shall, when practicable, be exercised in the name and on behalf of the estate owner.

8   Saving of certain legal powers to lease

(1) All leases or tenancies at a rent for a term of years absolute authorised to be granted by a mortgagor or mortgagee or by the Settled Land Act 1925, or any other statute (whether or not extended by any instrument) may be granted in the name and on behalf of the estate owner by the person empowered to grant the same, whether being an estate owner or not, with the same effect and priority as if this Part of this Act had not been passed; but this section does not (except as respects the usual qualified covenant for quiet enjoyment) authorise any person granting a lease in the name of an estate owner to impose any personal liability on him.

(2) Where a rentcharge is held for a legal estate, the owner thereof may under the statutory power or under any corresponding power, create a legal term of years absolute for securing or compelling payment of the same; but in other cases terms created under any such power shall, unless and until the estate owner of the land charged gives legal effect to the transaction, take effect only as equitable interests.

9   Vesting orders and dispositions of legal estates operating as conveyances by an estate owner

(1) Every such order, declaration, or conveyance as is hereinafter mentioned, namely –

(a) every vesting order made by any court or other competent authority;

(b) every vesting declaration (express or implied) under any statutory power;

(c) every vesting instrument made by the trustees of a settlement or other persons under the provisions of the Settled Land Act 1925;

(d) every conveyance by a person appointed for the purpose under an order of the court or authorised under any statutory power to convey in the name or on behalf of an estate owner;

(e) every conveyance made under any power reserved or conferred by this Act,

which is made or executed for the purpose of vesting, conveying, or creating a legal estate, shall operate to convey or create the legal estate disposed of in like manner as if the same had been a conveyance executed by the estate owner of the legal estate to which the order, declaration, vesting instrument, or conveyance relates.

(2) Where the order, declaration, or conveyance is made in favour of a purchaser, the provisions of this Act relating to a conveyance of a legal estate to a purchaser shall apply thereto.

(3) The provisions of the Trustee Act 1925 relating to vesting orders and orders appointing a person to convey shall apply to all vesting orders authorised to be made by this Part of this Act.

12   Limitation and Prescription Acts

Nothing in this Part of this Act affects the operation of any statute, or of the general law for the limitation of actions or proceedings relating to land or with reference to the acquisition of easements or rights over or in respect of land.

13   Effect of possession of documents

This Act shall not prejudicially affect the right of interest of any person arising out of or consequent on the possession by him of any documents relating to a legal estate in land, nor affect any question arising out of or consequent upon any omission to obtain or any other absence of possession by any person of any documents relating to a legal estate in land.

14   Interests of persons in possession

This Part of this Act shall not prejudicially affect the interest of any person in possession or in actual occupation of land to which he may be entitled in right of such possession or occupation.

15   Presumption that parties are of full age

The persons expressed to be parties to any conveyance shall, until the contrary is proved, be presumed to be of full age at the date thereof.

20   Infants not to be appointed trustees

The appointment of an infant to be a trustee in relation to any settlement or trust shall be void, but without prejudice to the power to appoint a new trustee to fill the vacancy.

21   Receipts by married infants

A married infant shall have power to give valid receipts for all income (including statutory accumulations of income made during the minority) to which the infant may be entitled in like manner as if the infant were of full age.

22   Conveyances on behalf of persons suffering from mental disorder and as to land held by them in trust

(1) Where a legal estate in land (whether settled or not) is vested in a person suffering from mental disorder, either solely or jointly with any other person or persons, his receiver or (if no receiver is acting for him) any person authorised in that behalf shall, under an order of the authority having jurisdiction under Part VII of the Mental Health Act 1983, or of the court, or under any statutory power, make or concur in making all requisite dispositions for conveying or creating a legal estate in his name and on his behalf.

(2) If land subject to a trust of land is vested, either solely or jointly with any other person or persons, in a person who is incapable, by reason of mental disorder, of exercising his functions as trustee, a new trustee shall be appointed in the place of that person, or he shall be otherwise discharged from the trust, before the legal estate is dealt with by the trustees.

(3) Subsection (2) of this section does not prevent a legal estate being dealt with without the appointment of a new trustee, or the discharge of the incapable trustee, at a time when the donee of an enduring power (within the meaning of the Enduring Powers of Attorney Act 1985) is entitled to act for the incapable trustee in the dealing.

24   Appointment of trustees of land

(1) The persons having power to appoint new trustees of land shall be bound to appoint the same persons (if any) who are for the time being trustees of any trust of the proceeds of sale of the land.

(2) A purchaser shall not be concerned to see that subsection (1) of this section has been complied with.

(3) This section applies whether the trust of land and the trust of proceeds of sale are created, or arise, before or after the commencement of this Act.

27   Purchaser not to be concerned with the trusts of the proceeds of sale which are to be paid to two or more trustees or to a trust corporation

(1) A purchaser of a legal estate from trustees of land shall not be concerned with the trusts affecting the land, the net income of the land or the proceeds of sale of the land whether or not those trusts are declared by the same instrument as that by which the trust of land is created.

(2) Notwithstanding anything to the contrary in the instrument (if any) creating a trust of land or in any trust affecting the net proceeds of sale of the land if it is sold, the proceeds of sale or other capital money shall not be paid to or applied by the direction of fewer than two persons as trustees, except where the trustee is a trust corporation, but this subsection does not affect the right of a sole personal representative as such to give valid receipts for, or direct the application of, proceeds of sale or other capital money, nor, except where capital money arises on the transaction, render it necessary to have more than one trustee.

31   Trust of mortgaged property where right of redemption is barred

(1) Where any property, vested in trustees by way of security, becomes, by virtue of the statutes of limitation, or of an order for foreclosure or otherwise, discharged from the right of redemption, it shall be held by them in trust –

(a) to apply the income from the property in the same manner as interest paid on the mortgage debt would have been applicable; and

(b) if the property is sold, to apply the net proceeds of sale, after payment of costs and expenses, in the same manner as repayment of the mortgage debt would have been applicable.

(2) Subsection (1) of this section operates without prejudice to any rule of law relating to the apportionment of capital and income between tenant for life and remainderman.

(4) Where –

(a) the mortgage money is capital money for the purposes of the Settled Land Act 1925;

(b) land other than any forming the whole or part of the property mentioned in subsection (1) of this section is, or is deemed to be, subject to the settlement; and

(c) the tenant for life or statutory owner requires the trustees to execute with respect to land forming the whole or part of that property a vesting deed such as would have been required in relation to the land if it had been acquired on a purchase with capital money,

the trustees shall execute such a vesting deed.

(5) This section applied whether the right of redemption was discharged before or after the first day of January, nineteen hundred and twelve, but has effect without prejudice to any dealings or arrangements made before that date.

33   Application of Part I to personal representatives

The provisions of this Part of this Act relating to trustees of land apply to personal representatives holding land in trust, but without prejudice to their rights and powers for purposes of administration.

34   Effect of future dispositions to tenants in common

(1) An undivided share in land shall not be capable of being created except as provided by the Settled Land Act 1925, or as hereinafter mentioned.

(2) Where, after the commencement of this Act, land is expressed to be conveyed to any persons in undivided shares and those persons are of full age, the conveyance shall (notwithstanding anything to the contrary in this Act) operate as if the land had been expressed to be conveyed to the grantees, or, if there are more than four grantees, to the four first named in the conveyance, as joint tenants in trust for the persons interested in the land: Provided that, where the conveyance is made by way of mortgage the land shall vest in the grantees or such four of them as aforesaid for a term of years absolute (as provided by this Act) as joint tenants subject to cesser on redemption in like manner as if the mortgage money had belonged to them on a joint account, but without prejudice to the beneficial interests in the mortgage money and interest.

(3) A devise bequest or testamentary appointment, coming into operation after the commencement of this Act, of land to two or more persons in undivided shares shall operate as a devise bequest or appointment of the land to the personal representative of the testator, (but without prejudice to the rights and powers of the personal representatives for purposes of administration) in trust for the persons interested in the land.

(3A) In subsections (2) and (3) of this section references to the persons interested in the land include persons interested as trustees or personal representatives (as well as persons beneficially interested).

36   Joint tenancies

(1) Where a legal estate (not being settled land) is beneficially limited to or held in trust for any persons as joint tenants, the same shall be held in trust, in like manner as if the persons beneficially entitled were tenants in common, but not so as to sever their joint tenancy in equity.

(2) No severance of a joint tenancy of a legal estate, so as to create a tenancy in common in land, shall be permissible, whether by operation of law or otherwise, but this subsection does not affect the right of a joint tenant to release his interest to the other joint tenants, or the right to sever a joint tenancy in an equitable interest whether or not the legal estate is vested in the joint tenants: provided that, where a legal estate (not being settled land) is vested in joint tenants beneficially, and any tenant desires to sever the joint tenancy in equity, he shall give to the other joint tenants a notice in writing of such desire or do such other acts or things as would, in the case of personal estate, have been effectual to sever the tenancy in equity, and thereupon the land shall be held in trust on terms which would have been requisite for giving effect to the beneficial interests if there had been an actual severance. Nothing in this Act affects the right of a survivor of joint tenants, who is solely and beneficially interested, to deal with his legal estate as if it were not held in trust.

(3) Without prejudice to the right of a joint tenant to release his interest to the other joint tenants no severance of a mortgage term or trust estate, so as to create a tenancy in common, shall be permissible.

37 Rights of husband and wife

A husband and wife shall, for all purposes of acquisition of any interest in property, under a disposition made or coming into operation after the commencement of this Act, be treated as two persons.

38 Party structures

(1) Where under a disposition or other arrangement which, if a holding in undivided shares had been permissible, would have created a tenancy in common, a wall or other structure is or is expressed to be made a party wall or structure, that structure shall be and remains severed vertically as between the respective owners, and the owner of each part shall have such rights to support and user over the rest of the structure as may be requisite for conferring rights corresponding to those which would have subsisted if a valid tenancy in common had been created.

(2) Any person interested may, in case of dispute, apply to the court for an order declaring the rights and interests under this section of the persons interested in any such party structure, and the court may make such order as it thinks fit.

39 Transitional provisions in First Schedule

For the purpose of effecting the transition from the law existing prior to the commencement of the Law of Property Act 1922 to the law enacted by that Act (as amended), the provisions set out in the First Schedule to this Act shall have effect –

(1) for converting existing legal estates, interests and charges not capable under the said Act of taking effect as legal interests into equitable interests;

(2) for discharging, getting in or vesting outstanding legal estates;

(3) for making provisions with respect to legal estates vested in infants;

(4) for subjecting land held in undivided shares to trusts;

(5) for dealing with party structures and open spaces held in common;

(7) for converting existing freehold mortgages into mortgages by demise;

(8) for converting existing leasehold mortgages into mortgages by sub-demise.

PART II

CONTRACTS, CONVEYANCES AND OTHER INSTRUMENTS

51 Lands lie in grant only

(1) All lands and all interests therein lie in grant and are incapable of being conveyed by livery or livery and seisin, or by feoffment, or by bargain and sale;

and a conveyance of an interest in land may operate to pass the possession or right to possession thereof, without actual entry, but subject to all prior rights thereto.

(2) The use of the word grant is not necessary to convey land or to create any interest therein.

52   Conveyances to be by deed

(1) All conveyances of land or of any interest therein are void for the purpose of conveying or creating a legal estate unless made by deed.

(2) This section does not apply to –

(a) assents by a personal representative;

(b) disclaimers made in accordance with sections 178 to 180 or section 315 to 319 of the Insolvency Act 1986 or not required to be evidenced in writing;

(c) surrenders by operation of law, including surrenders which may, by law, be effected without writing;

(d) leases or tenancies or other assurances not required by law to be made in writing;

(e) receipts other than those falling within section 115 below;

(f) vesting orders of the court or other competent authority;

(g) conveyances taking effect by operation of law.

53   Instruments required to be in writing

(1) Subject to the provisions hereinafter contained with respect to the creation of interests in land by parol –

(a) no interest in land can be created or disposed of except by writing signed by the person creating or conveying the same, or by his agent thereunto lawfully authorised in writing, or by will, or by operation of law;

(b) a declaration of trust respecting any land or any interest therein must be manifested and proved by some writing signed by some person who is able to declare such trust or by his will;

(c) a disposition of an equitable interest or trust subsisting at the time of the disposition, must be in writing signed by the person disposing of the same, or by his agent thereunto lawfully authorised in writing or by will.

(2) This section does not affect the creation or operation of resulting, implied or constructive trusts.

54   Creation of interests in land by parol

(1) All interests in land created by parol and not put in writing and signed by the persons so creating the same, or by their agents thereunto lawfully authorised in writing, have, notwithstanding any consideration having been given for the same, the force and effect of interests at will only.

(2) Nothing in the foregoing provisions of this Part of this Act shall affect the creation by parol of leases taking effect in possession for a term not exceeding three years (whether or not the lessee is given power to extend the term) at the best rent which can be reasonably obtained without taking a fine.

55   Savings in regard to last two sections

Nothing in the last two foregoing sections shall –

(a) invalidate dispositions by will; or

(b) affect any interest validly created before the commencement of this Act; or

(c) affect the right to acquire an interest in land by virtue of taking possession; or

(d) affect the operation of the law relating to part performance.

56   Persons taking who are not parties and as to indentures

(1) A person may take an immediate or other interest in land or other property, or the benefit of any condition, right of entry, covenant or agreement over or respecting land or other property, although he may not be named as a party to the conveyance or other instrument.

(2) A deed between parties, to effect its objects, has the effect of an indenture though not indented or expressed to be an indenture.

57   Description of deeds

Any deed, whether or not being an indenture, may be described (at the commencement thereof or otherwise) as a deed simply, or as a conveyance, deed of exchange, vesting deed, trust instrument, settlement, mortgage, charge, transfer of mortgage, appointment, lease or otherwise according to the nature of the transaction intended to be effected.

59   Conditions and certain covenants not implied

(1) An exchange or other conveyance of land made by deed after the first day of October, eighteen hundred and forty-five, does not imply any condition in law.

(2) The word 'give' or 'grant' does not, in a deed made after the date last aforesaid, imply any covenant in law, save where otherwise provided by statute.

60   Abolition of technicalities in regard to conveyances and deeds

(1) A conveyance of freehold land to any person without words of limitation, or any equivalent expression, shall pass to the grantee the fee simple or other the whole interest which the grantor had power to convey in such land, unless a contrary intention appears in the conveyance.

(2) A conveyance of freehold land to a corporation sole by his corporate designation

without the word 'successors' shall pass to the corporation the fee simple or other the whole interest which the grantor had power to convey in such land, unless a contrary intention appears in the conveyance.

(3) In a voluntary conveyance a resulting trust for the grantor shall not be implied merely by reason that the property is not expressed to be conveyed for the use or benefit of the grantee.

(4) The foregoing provisions of this section apply only to conveyances and deeds executed after the commencement of this Act: Provided that in a deed executed after the thirty-first day of December, eighteen hundred and eighty-one, it is sufficient –

(a) In the limitation of an estate in fee simple, to use the words 'in fee simple', without the word 'heirs'.

61   Construction of expressions used in deeds and other instruments

In all deeds, contracts, wills, orders and other instruments executed, made or coming into operation after the commencement of this Act, unless the context otherwise requires –

(a) 'Month' means calendar month;

(b) 'Person' includes a corporation;

(c) The singular includes the plural and vice versa;

(d) The masculine includes the feminine and vice versa.

62   General words implied in conveyances

(1) A conveyance of land shall be deemed to include and shall by virtue of this Act operate to convey, with the land, all buildings, erections, fixtures, commons, hedges, ditches, fences, ways, waters, water-courses, liberties, privileges, easements, rights and advantages whatsoever, appertaining or reputed to appertain to the land, or any part thereof, or, at the time of conveyance, demised, occupied, or enjoyed with, or reputed or known as part or parcel of or appurtenant to the land or any part thereof.

(2) A conveyance of land, having houses or other buildings thereon, shall be deemed to include and shall by virtue of this Act operate to convey, with the land, houses, or other buildings, all outhouses, erections, fixtures, cellars, areas, courts, courtyards, cisterns, sewers, gutters, drains, ways, passages, lights, watercourses, liberties, privileges, easements, rights, and advantages whatsoever, appertaining or reputed to appertain to the land, houses, or other buildings conveyed, or any of them, or any part thereof, or, at the time of conveyance, demised, occupied, or enjoyed with, or reputed or known as part or parcel of or appurtenant to, the land, houses, or other buildings conveyed, or any of them, or any part thereof.

(3) A conveyance of a manor shall be deemed to include and shall by virtue of this Act operate to convey, with the manor, all pastures, feedings, wastes, warrens, commons, mines, minerals, quarries, furzes, trees, woods, underwoods, coppices, and the ground and soil thereof, fishings, fisheries, fowlings, courts leet, courts

baron, and other courts, view of frankpledge and all that to view of frankpledge doth belong, mills, mulctures, customs, tolls, duties, reliefs, heriots, fines, sums of money, amerciaments, waifs, estrays, chief-rents, quitrents, rentscharge, rents seck, rents of assize, fee farm rents, services, royalties jurisdictions, franchises, liberties, privileges, easements, profits, advantages, rights, emoluments, and hereditaments whatsoever, to the manor appertaining or reputed to appertain, or, at the time of conveyance, demised, occupied, or enjoyed with the same, or reputed or known as part, parcel or member thereof. For the purpose of this subsection the right to compensation for manorial incidents on the extinguishment thereof shall be deemed to be a right appertaining to the manor.

(4) This section applies only if and as far as a contrary intention is not expressed in the conveyance, and has effect subject to the terms of the conveyance and to the provisions therein contained.

(5) This section shall not be construed as giving to any person a better title to any property, right, or thing in this section mentioned than the title which the conveyance gives to him to the land or manor expressed to be conveyed, or as conveying to him any property, right, or thing in this section mentioned, further or otherwise than as the same could have been conveyed to him by the conveying parties.

(6) This section applies to conveyances made after the thirty-first day of December, eighteen hundred and eighty-one.

63 All estate clause implied

(1) Every conveyance is effectual to pass all the estate, right, title, interest, claim, and demand which the conveying parties respectively have, in, to, or on the property conveyed, or expressed or intended so to be, or which they respectively have power to convey in, to, or on the same.

(2) This section applies only if and as far as a contrary intention is not expressed in the conveyance, and has effect subject to the terms of the conveyance and to the provisions therein contained.

(3) This section applies to conveyances made after the thirty-first day of December, eighteen hundred and eighty-one.

65 Reservation of legal estates

(1) A reservation of a legal estate shall operate at law without any execution of the conveyance by the grantee of the legal estate out of which the reservation is made, or any regrant by him, so as to create the legal estate reserved, and so as to vest the same in possession in the person (whether being the grantor or not) for whose benefit the reservation is made.

(2) A conveyance of a legal estate expressed to be made subject to another legal estate not in existence immediately before the date of the conveyance, shall operate as a reservation, unless a contrary intention appears.

(3) This section applies only to reservations made after the commencement of this Act.

67 Receipt in deed sufficient

(1) A receipt for consideration money or securities in the body of a deed shall be a sufficient discharge for the same to the person paying or delivering the same, without any further receipt for the same being indorsed on the deed ...

68 Receipt in deed or indorsed evidence

(1) A receipt for consideration money or other consideration in the body of a deed or indorsed thereon shall, in favour of a subsequent purchaser, not having notice that the money or other consideration thereby acknowledged to be received was not in fact paid or given, wholly or in part, be sufficient evidence of the payment or giving of the whole amount thereof ...

72 Conveyances by a person to himself, etc

(1) In conveyances made after the twelfth day of August, eighteen hundred and fifty-nine, personal property, including chattels real, may be conveyed by a person to himself jointly with another person by the like means by which it might be conveyed by him to another person.

(2) In conveyances made after the thirty-first day of December, eighteen hundred and eighty-one, freehold land, or a thing in action, may be conveyed by a person to himself jointly with another person, by the like means by which it might be conveyed by him to another person; and may, in like manner, be conveyed by a husband to his wife, and by a wife to her husband, alone or jointly with another person.

(3) After the commencement of this Act a person may convey land to or vest land in himself.

(4) Two or more persons (whether or not being trustees or personal representatives) may convey, and shall be deemed always to have been capable of conveying, any property vested in them to any one or more of themselves in like manner as they could have conveyed such property to a third party; provided that if the persons in whose favour the conveyance is made are, by reason of any fiduciary relationship or otherwise, precluded from validly carrying out the transaction, the conveyance shall be liable to be set aside.

77 Implied covenants in conveyances subject to rents

(1) In addition to the covenants implied under Part I of the Law of Property (Miscellaneous Provisions) Act 1994, there shall in the several cases in this section mentioned, be deemed to be included and implied, a covenant to the effect in this section stated, by and with such persons as are hereinafter mentioned, that is to say –

(A) In a conveyance for valuable consideration, other than a mortgage, of the entirety of the land affected by a rentcharge, a covenant by the grantee or joint and several covenants by the grantees, if more than one, with the conveying parties and with each of them, if more than one, in the terms set out in Part VII of the Second Schedule to this Act. Where a rentcharge has been apportioned in respect of any land, with the consent of the owner of the rentcharge, the covenants in this paragraph shall be implied in the conveyance of that land in like manner as if the apportioned rentcharge were the rentcharge referred to, and the document creating the rentcharge related solely to that land:

(B) In a conveyance for valuable consideration, other than a mortgage, of part of land affected by a rentcharge, subject to a part of that rentcharge which has been or is by that conveyance apportioned (but in either case without the consent of the owner of the rentcharge) in respect of the land conveyed –

   (i) A covenant by the grantee of the land or joint and several covenants by the grantees, if more than one, with the conveying parties and with each of them, if more than one, in the terms set out in paragraph (i) of Part VIII of the Second Schedule to this Act;

   (ii) A covenant by a person who conveys or is expressed to convey as beneficial owner, or joint and several covenants by the persons who so convey or are expressed to so convey, if at the date of the conveyance any part of the land affected by such rentcharge is retained, with the grantees of the land and with each of them (if more than one) in the terms set out in paragraph (ii) of Part VIII of the Second Schedule to this Act.

(2) Where in a conveyance for valuable consideration, other than a mortgage, part of land affected by a rentcharge is, without the consent of the owner of the rentcharge, expressed to be conveyed subject to or charged with the entire rent, paragraph (B)(i) of subsection (1) of this section shall apply as if, in paragraph (i) of Part VIII of the Second Schedule to this Act –

   (a) any reference to the apportioned rent were to the entire rent; and

   (b) the words '(other than the covenant to pay the entire rent)' were omitted.

(2A) Where in a conveyance for valuable consideration, other than a mortgage, part of land affected by a rentcharge is, without the consent of the owner of the rentcharge, expressed to be conveyed discharged or exonerated from the entire rent, paragraph (B)(ii) of subsection (1) of this section shall apply as if, in paragraph (ii) of Part VIII of the Second Schedule to this Act –

   (a) any reference to the balance of the rent were to the entire rent; and

   (b) the words 'other than the covenant to pay the entire rent,' were omitted.

(3) In this section 'conveyance' does not include a demise by way of lease at a rent.

(4) Any covenant which would be implied under this section by reason of a person conveying or being expressed to convey as beneficial owner may, by express reference to this section, be implied, with or without variation, in a conveyance, whether or not for valuable consideration, by a person who conveys or is expressed

to convey as settlor, or as trustee, or as mortgagee, or as personal representative of a deceased person, or under an order of the court.

(5) The benefit of a covenant implied as aforesaid shall be annexed and incident to, and shall go with, the estate or interest of the implied covenantee, and shall be capable of being enforced by every person in whom that estate or interest is, for the whole or any part thereof, from time to time vested.

(6) A covenant implied as aforesaid may be varied or extended by deed, and, as so varied or extended, shall, as far as may be, operate in the like manner, and with all the like incidents, effects and consequences, as if such variations or extensions were directed in this section to be implied.

(7) In particular any covenant implied under this section may be extended by providing that –

   (a) the land conveyed; or

   (b) the part of the land affected by the rentcharge which remains vested in the covenantor;

shall, as the case may require, stand charged with the payment of all money which may become payable under the implied covenant. ...

78 Benefit of covenants relating to land

(1) A covenant relating to any land of the covenantee shall be deemed to be made with the covenantee and his successors in title and the persons deriving title under him or them, and shall have effect as if such successors and other persons were expressed. For the purposes of this subsection in connexion with covenants restrictive of the user of land 'successors in title' shall be deemed to include the owners and occupiers for the time being of the land of the covenantee intended to be benefited. ...

79 Burden of covenants relating to land

(1) A covenant relating to any land of a covenantor or capable of being bound by him, shall, unless a contrary intention is expressed, be deemed to be made by the covenantor on behalf of himself his successors in title and the persons deriving title under him or them, and, subject as aforesaid, shall have effect as if such successors and other persons were expressed. This subsection extends to a covenant to do some act relating to the land, notwithstanding that the subject-matter may not be in existence when the covenant is made.

(2) For the purposes of this section in connexion with covenants restrictive of the user of land 'successors in title' shall be deemed to include the owners and occupiers for the time being of such land. ...

80 Covenants binding land

(1) A covenant and a bond and an obligation or contract made under seal after 31st

December 1881 but before the coming into force of section 1 of the Law of Property (Miscellaneous Provisions) Act 1989 or executed as a deed in accordance with that section after its coming into force, binds the real estate as well as the personal estate of the person making the same if and so far as a contrary intention is not expressed in the covenant, bond, obligation, or contract. This subsection extends to a covenant implied by virtue of this Act.

(2) Every covenant running with the land, whether entered into before or after the commencement of this Act, shall take effect in accordance with any statutory enactment affecting the devolution of the land, and accordingly the benefit or burden of every such covenant shall vest in or bind the persons who by virtue of any such enactment or otherwise succeed to the title of the covenantee or the covenantor, as the case may be.

(3) The benefit of a covenant relating to land entered into after the commencement of this Act may be made to run with the land without the use of any technical expression if the covenant is of such a nature that the benefit could have been made to run with the land before the commencement of this Act.

(4) For the purposes of this section, a covenant runs with the land when the benefit or burden of it, whether at law or in equity, passes to the successors in title of the covenantee or the covenantor, as the case may be.

81   Effect of covenant with two or more jointly

(1) A covenant, and a contract under seal, and a bond or obligation under seal, made with two or more jointly, to pay money or to make a conveyance, or to do any other act, to them or for their benefit, shall be deemed to include, and shall, by virtue of this Act, imply, an obligation to do the act to, or for the benefit of, the survivor or survivors of them, and to, or for the benefit of, any other person to whom the right to sue on the covenant, contract, bond, or obligation devolves, and where made after the commencement of this Act shall be construed as being also made with each of them.

(2) This section extends to a covenant implied by virtue of this Act.

(3) This section applies only if and as far as a contrary intention is not expressed in the covenant, contract, bond, or obligation, and has effect subject to the covenant, contract, bond, or obligation, and to the provisions therein contained.

(4) Except as otherwise expressly provided, this section applies to a covenant, contract, bond, or obligation made or implied after the thirty-first day of December, eighteen hundred and eighty-one.

(5) In its application to instruments made after the coming into force of section 1 of the Law of Property (Miscellaneous Provisions) Act 1989 subsection (1) above shall have effect as if for the words 'under seal, and a bond or obligation under seal,' there were substituted the words 'bond or obligation executed as a deed in accordance with section 1 of the Law of Property (Miscellaneous Provisions) Act 1989'.

82 Covenants and agreements entered into by a person with himself and another or others

(1) Any covenant, whether express or implied, or agreement entered into by a person with himself and one or more other persons shall be construed and be capable of being enforced in like manner as if the covenant or agreement had been entered into with the other person or persons alone.

(2) This section applies to covenants or agreements entered into before or after the commencement of this Act, and to covenants implied by statute in the case of a person who conveys or is expressed to convey to himself and one or more other persons, but without prejudice to any order of the court made before such commencement.

83 Construction of implied covenants

In the construction of a covenant or proviso, or other provision, implied in a deed or assent by virtue of this Act, words importing the singular or plural number, or the masculine gender, shall be read as also importing the plural or singular number, or as extending to females, as the case may require.

84 Power to discharge or modify restrictive covenants affecting land

(1) The Lands Tribunal shall (without prejudice to any concurrent jurisdiction of the court) have power from time to time, on the application of any person interested in any freehold land affected by any restriction arising under covenant or otherwise as to the user thereof or the building thereon, by order wholly or partially to discharge or modify any such restriction on being satisfied –

   (a) that by reason of changes in the character of the property or the neighbourhood or other circumstances of the case which the Lands Tribunal may deem material, the restriction ought to be deemed obsolete; or

   (aa) that (in a case falling within subsection (1A) below) the continued existence thereof would impede some reasonable user of the land for public or private purposes or, as the case may be, would unless modified so impede such user; or

   (b) that the persons of full age and capacity for the time being or from time to time entitled to the benefit of the restriction, whether in respect of estates in fee simple or any lesser estates or interests in the property to which the benefit of the restriction is annexed, have agreed, either expressly or by implication, by their acts or omissions, to the same being discharged or modified; or

   (c) that the proposed discharge or modification will not injure the persons entitled to the benefit of the restriction;

and an order discharging or modifying a restriction under this subsection may direct the applicant to pay to any person entitled to the benefit of the restriction such sum by way of consideration as the Tribunal may think it just to award under one, but not both, of the following heads, that is to say, either –

(i) a sum to make up for any loss or disadvantage suffered by that person in consequence of the discharge or modification; or

(ii) a sum to make up for any effect which the restriction had, at the time when it was imposed, in reducing the consideration then received for the land affected by it.

(1A) Subsection (1)(aa) above authorises the discharge or modification of a restriction by reference to its impeding some reasonable user of land in any case in which the Lands Tribunal is satisfied that the restriction, in impeding that user, either –

(a) does not secure to persons entitled to the benefit of it any practical benefits of substantial value or advantage to them; or

(b) is contrary to the public interest;

and that money will be an adequate compensation for the loss or disadvantage (if any) which any such person will suffer from the discharge or modification.

(1B) In determining whether a case is one falling within subsection (1A) above, and in determining whether (in any such case or otherwise) a restriction ought to be discharged or modified, the Lands Tribunal shall take into account the development plan and any declared or ascertainable pattern for the grant or refusal of planning permissions in the relevant areas, as well as the period at which and context in which the restriction was created or imposed and any other material circumstances.

(1C) It is hereby declared that the power conferred by this section to modify a restriction includes power to add such further provisions restricting the user of or the building on the land affected as appear to the Lands Tribunal to be reasonable in view of the relaxation of the existing provisions, and as may be accepted by the applicant; and the Lands Tribunal may accordingly refuse to modify a restriction without some such addition.

(2) The court shall have power on the application of any person interested –

(a) to declare whether or not in any particular case any freehold land is, or would in any given event be, affected by a restriction imposed by any instrument; or

(b) to declare what, upon the true construction of any instrument purporting to impose a restriction, is the nature and extent of the restriction thereby imposed and whether the same is, or would in any given event be, enforceable and if so by whom.

Neither subsections (7) and (11) of this section nor, unless the contrary is expressed, any later enactment providing for this section not to apply to any restrictions shall affect the operation of this subsection or the operation for purposes of this subsection of any other provisions of this section.

(3) The Lands Tribunal shall, before making any order under this section, direct such enquiries, if any, to be made of any government department or local authority, and such notices, if any, whether by way of advertisement or otherwise, to be given to such of the persons who appear to be entitled to the benefit of the restriction

intended to be discharged, modified, or dealt with as, having regard to any enquiries, notices or other proceedings previously made, given or taken, the Lands Tribunal may think fit.

(3A) On an application to the Lands Tribunal under this section the Lands Tribunal shall give any necessary directions as to the persons who are or are not to be admitted (as appearing to be entitled to the benefit of the restriction) to oppose the application, and no appeal shall lie against any such direction; but rules under the Lands Tribunal Act 1949 shall make provision whereby, in cases in which there arises on such an application (whether or not in connection with the admission of persons to oppose) any such question as is referred to in subsection (2)(a) or (b) of this section, the proceedings on the application can and, if the rules so provide, shall be suspended to enable the decision of the court to be obtained on that question by an application under that subsection, or by means of a case stated by the Lands Tribunal, or otherwise, as may be provided by those rules or by rules of court.

(5) Any order made under this section shall be binding on all persons, whether ascertained or of full age or capacity or not, then entitled or thereafter capable of becoming entitled to the benefit of any restriction, which is thereby discharged, modified or dealt with, and whether such persons are parties to the proceedings or have been served with notice or not.

(6) An order may be made under this section notwithstanding that any instrument which is alleged to impose the restriction intended to be discharged, modified, or dealt with, may not have been produced to the court or the Lands Tribunal, and the court or the Lands Tribunal may act on such evidence of that instrument as it may think sufficient.

(7) This section applies to restrictions whether subsisting at the commencement of this Act or imposed thereafter, but this section does not apply where the restriction was imposed on the occasion of a disposition made gratuitously or for a nominal consideration for public purposes.

(8) This section applies whether the land affected by the restrictions is registered or not.

(9) Where any proceedings by action or otherwise are taken to enforce a restrictive covenant, any person against whom the proceedings are taken, may in such proceedings apply to the court for an order giving leave to apply to the Lands Tribunal under this section, and staying the proceedings in the meantime.

(11) This section does not apply to restrictions imposed by the Commissioners of Works under any statutory power for the protection of any Royal Park or Garden or to restrictions of a like character imposed upon the occasion of any enfranchisement effected before the commencement of this Act in any manor vested in His Majesty in right of the Crown or the Duchy of Lancaster, nor (subject to subsection (11A) below) to restrictions created or imposed –

   (a) for naval, military or air force purposes,

   (b) for civil aviation purposes under the powers of the Air Navigation Act 1920, of section 19 or 23 of the Civil Aviation Act 1949 or of section 30 or 41 of the Civil Aviation Act 1982.

(11A) Subsection (11) of this section –

(a) shall exclude the application of this section to a restriction falling within subsection (11)(a), and not created or imposed in connection with the use of any land as an aerodrome, only so long as the restriction is enforceable by or on behalf of the Crown; and

(b) shall exclude the application of this section to a restriction falling within subsection (11)(b), or created or imposed in connection with the use of any land as an aerodrome, only so long as the restriction is enforceable by or on behalf of the Crown or any public or international authority.

(12) Where a term of more than forty years is created in land (whether before or after the commencement of this Act) this section shall, after the expiration of twenty-five years of the term, apply to restrictions, affecting such leasehold land in like manner as it would have applied had the land been freehold: Provided that this subsection shall not apply to mining leases.

PART III

MORTGAGES, RENTCHARGES, AND POWERS OF ATTORNEY

85 Mode of mortgaging freeholds

(1) A mortgage of an estate in fee simple shall only be capable of being effected at law either by a demise for a term of years absolute, subject to a provision for cesser on redemption, or by a charge by deed expressed to be by way of legal mortgage: Provided that a first mortgagee shall have the same right to the possession of documents as if his security included the fee simple.

(2) Any purported conveyance of an estate in fee simple by way of mortgage made after the commencement of this Act shall (to the extent of the estate of the mortgagor) operate as a demise of the land to the mortgagee for a term of years absolute, without impeachment for waste, but subject to cesser on redemption, in manner following, namely –

(a) A first or only mortgagee shall take a term of three thousand years from the date of the mortgage:

(b) A second or subsequent mortgagee shall take a term (commencing from the date of the mortgage) one day longer than the term vested in the first or other mortgagee whose security ranks immediately before that of such second or subsequent mortgagee:

and, in this subsection, any such purported conveyance as aforesaid includes an absolute conveyance with a deed of defeasance and any other assurance which, but for this subsection, would operate in effect to vest the fee simple in a mortgagee subject to redemption.

(3) Subsection (2) does not apply to registered land, but, subject to that, this section applies whether or not the land is registered land and whether or not the mortgage is expressed to be made by way of trust for sale or otherwise.

(4) Without prejudice to the provisions of this Act respecting legal and equitable powers, every power to mortgage or to lend money on mortgage of an estate in fee simple shall be construed as a power to mortgage the estate for a term of years absolute, without impeachment for waste, or by a charge by way of legal mortgage or to lend on such security.

86 Mode of mortgaging leaseholds

(1) A mortgage of a term of years absolute shall only be capable of being effected at law either by a subdemise for a term of years absolute, less by one day at least than the term vested in the mortgagor, and subject to a provision for cesser on redemption, or by a charge by deed expressed to be by way of legal mortgage; and where a licence to subdemise by way of mortgage is required, such licence shall not be unreasonably refused: Provided that a first mortgagee shall have the same right to the possession of documents as if his security had been effected by assignment.

(2) Any purported assignment of a term of years absolute by way of mortgage made after the commencement of this Act shall (to the extent of the estate of the mortgagor) operate as a subdemise of the leasehold land to the mortgagee for a term of years absolute, but subject to cesser on redemption, in manner following, namely –

(a) The term to be taken by a first or only mortgagee shall be ten days less than the term expressed to be assigned:

(b) The term to be taken by a second or subsequent mortgagee shall be one day longer than the term vested in the first or other mortgagee whose security ranks immediately before that of the second or subsequent mortgagee, if the length of the last mentioned term permits, and in any case for a term less by one day at least than the term expressed to be assigned:

and, in this subsection, any such purported assignment as aforesaid includes an absolute assignment with a deed of defeasance and any other assurance which, but for this subsection, would operate in effect to vest the term of the mortgagor in a mortgagee subject to redemption.

(3) Subsection (2) does not apply to registered land, but, subject to that, this section applies whether or not the land is registered land and whether or not the mortgage is made by way of sub-mortgage of a term of years absolute, or is expressed to be by way of trust for sale or otherwise.

(4) Without prejudice to the provisions of this Act respecting legal and equitable powers, every power to mortgage for or to lend money on mortgage of a term of years absolute by way of assignment shall be construed as a power to mortgage the term by subdemise for a term of years absolute or by a charge by way of legal mortgage, or to lend on such security.

87 Charges by way of legal mortgage

(1) Where a legal mortgage of land is created by a charge by deed expressed to be by way of legal mortgage, the mortgagee shall have the same protection, powers and remedies (including the right to take proceedings to obtain possession from the occupiers and the persons in receipt of rents and profits, or any of them) as if –

(a) where the mortgage is a mortgage of an estate in fee simple, a mortgage term for three thousand years without impeachment of waste had been thereby created in favour of the mortgagee; and

(b) where the mortgage is a mortgage of a term of years absolute, a sub-term less by one day than the term vested in the mortgagor had been thereby created in favour of the mortgagee.

(2) Where an estate vested in a mortgagee immediately before the commencement of this Act has by virtue of this Act been converted into a term of years absolute or sub-term, the mortgagee may, by a declaration in writing to that effect signed by him, convert the mortgage into a charge by way of legal mortgage, and in that case the mortgage term shall be extinguished in the inheritance or in the head term as the case may be, and the mortgagee shall have the same protection, powers and remedies (including the right to take proceedings to obtain possession from the occupiers and the persons in receipt of rents and profits or any of them) as if the mortgage term or sub-term had remained subsisting. The power conferred by this subsection may be exercised by a mortgagee notwithstanding that he is a trustee or personal representative.

(3) Such declaration shall not affect the priority of the mortgagee or his right to retain possession of documents, nor affect his title to or right over any fixtures or chattels personal comprised in the mortgage.

(4) Subsection (1) of this section shall not be taken to be affected by section 23(1)(a) of the Land Registration Act 2002 (under which owner's powers in relation to a registered estate do not include power to mortgage by demise or sub-demise).

88 Realisation of freehold mortgages

(1) Where an estate in fee simple has been mortgaged by the creation of a term of years absolute limited thereout or by a charge by way of legal mortgage and the mortgagee sells under his statutory or express power of sale –

(a) the conveyance by him shall operate to vest in the purchaser the fee simple in the land conveyed subject to any legal mortgage having priority to the mortgage in right of which the sale is made and to any money thereby secured, and thereupon;

(b) the mortgage term or the charge by way of legal mortgage and any subsequent mortgage term or charges shall merge or be extinguished as respects the land conveyed;

and such conveyance may, as respects the fee simple, be made in the name of the estate owner in whom it is vested.

(2) Where any such mortgagee obtains an order for foreclosure absolute, the order shall operate to vest the fee simple in him (subject to any legal mortgage having priority to the mortgage in right of which the foreclosure is obtained and to any money thereby secured), and thereupon the mortgage term, if any, shall thereby be merged in the fee simple, and any subsequent mortgage term or charge by way of legal mortgage bound by the order shall thereupon be extinguished.

(3) Where any such mortgagee acquires a title under the Limitation Acts, he, or the persons deriving title under him, may enlarge the mortgage term into a fee simple under the statutory power for that purpose discharged from any legal mortgage affected by the title so acquired, or in the case of a chargee by way of legal mortgage may by deed declare that the fee simple is vested in him discharged as aforesaid, and the same shall vest accordingly.

(4) Where the mortgage includes fixtures or chattels personal any statutory power of sale and any right to foreclose or take possession shall extend to the absolute or other interest therein affected by the charge.

(5) In the case of a sub-mortgage by subdemise of a long term (less a nominal period) itself limited out of an estate in fee simple, the foregoing provisions of this section shall operate as if the derivative term, if any, created by the sub-mortgage had been limited out of the fee simple, and so as to enlarge the principal term and extinguish the derivative term created by the sub-mortgage as aforesaid, and to enable the sub-mortgagee to convey the fee simple or acquire it by foreclosure, enlargement, or otherwise as aforesaid.

(6) This section applies to a mortgage whether created before or after the commencement of this Act, and to a mortgage term created by this Act, but does not operate to confer a better title to the fee simple than would have been acquired if the same had been conveyed by the mortgage (being a valid mortgage) and the restrictions imposed by this Act in regard to the effect and creation of mortgages were not in force, and all prior mortgages (if any) not being merely equitable charges had been created by demise or by charge by way of legal mortgage.

89   Realisation of leasehold mortgages

(1) Where a term of years absolute has been mortgaged by the creation of another term of years absolute limited thereout or by a charge by way of legal mortgage and the mortgagee sells under his statutory or express power of sale, –

  (a) the conveyance by him shall operate to convey to the purchaser not only the mortgage term, if any, but also (unless expressly excepted with the leave of the court) the leasehold reversion affected by the mortgage, subject to any legal mortgage having priority to the mortgage in right of which the sale is made and to any money thereby secured, and thereupon

  (b) the mortgage term, or the charge by way of legal mortgage and any subsequent mortgage term or charge, shall merge in such leasehold reversion or be extinguished unless excepted as aforesaid;

and such conveyance may, as respects the leasehold reversion, be made in the name of the estate owner in whom it is vested. Where a licence to assign is required on a sale by a mortgagee, such licence shall not be unreasonably refused.

(2) Where any such mortgagee obtains an order for foreclosure absolute, the order shall, unless it otherwise provides, operate (without giving rise to a forfeiture for want of a licence to assign) to vest the leasehold reversion affected by the mortgage and any subsequent mortgage term in him, subject to any legal mortgage having priority to the mortgage in right of which the foreclosure is obtained and to any money thereby secured, and thereupon the mortgage term and any subsequent mortgage term or charge by way of legal mortgage bound by the order shall, subject to any express provision to the contrary contained in the order, merge in such leasehold reversion or be extinguished.

(3) Where any such mortgagee acquires a title under the Limitation Acts, he, or the persons deriving title under him, may by deed declare that the leasehold reversion affected by the mortgage and any mortgage term affected by the title so acquired shall vest in him, free from any right of redemption which is barred, and the same shall (without giving rise to a forfeiture for want of a licence to assign) vest accordingly, and thereupon the mortgage term, if any, and any other mortgage term or charge by way of legal mortgage affected by the title so acquired shall, subject to any express provision to the contrary contained in the deed, merge in such leasehold reversion or be extinguished.

(4) Where the mortgage includes fixtures or chattels personal, any statutory power of sale and any right to foreclose or take possession shall extend to the absolute or other interest therein affected by the charge.

(5) In the case of a sub-mortgage by subdemise of a term (less a nominal period) itself limited out of a leasehold reversion, the foregoing provisions of this section shall operate as if the derivative term created by the sub-mortgage had been limited out of the leasehold reversion, and so as (subject as aforesaid) to merge the principal mortgage term therein as well as the derivative term created by the sub-mortgage and to enable the sub-mortgagee to convey the leasehold reversion or acquire it by foreclosure, vesting, or otherwise as aforesaid.

(6) This section takes effect without prejudice to any incumbrance or trust affecting the leasehold reversion which has priority over the mortgage in right of which the sale, foreclosure, or title is made or acquired, and applies to a mortgage whether executed before or after the commencement of this Act, and to a mortgage term created by this Act, but does not apply where the mortgage term does not comprise the whole of the land included in the leasehold reversion unless the rent (if any) payable in respect of that reversion has been apportioned as respects the land affected, or the rent is of no money value or no rent is reserved, and unless the lessee's covenants and conditions (if any) have been apportioned, either expressly or by implication, as respects the land affected. In this subsection references to an apportionment include an equitable apportionment made without the consent of the lessor ...

90   Realisation of equitable charges by the court

(1) Where an order for sale is made by the court in reference to an equitable mortgage on land (not secured by a legal term of years absolute or by a charge by way of legal mortgage) the court may, in favour of a purchaser, make a vesting order conveying the land or may appoint a person to convey the land or create and vest in the mortgagee a legal term of years absolute to enable him to carry out the sale, as the case may require, in like manner as if the mortgage had been created by deed by way of legal mortgage pursuant to this Act, but without prejudice to any incumbrance having priority to the equitable mortgage unless the incumbrancer consents to the sale.

(2) This section applies to equitable mortgages made or arising before or after the commencement of this Act, but not to a mortgage which has been over-reached under the powers conferred by this Act or otherwise ...

91   Sale of mortgaged property in action for redemption or foreclosure

(1) Any person entitled to redeem mortgaged property may have a judgment or order for sale instead of for redemption in an action brought by him either for redemption alone, or for sale alone, or for sale or redemption in the alternative.

(2) In any action, whether for foreclosure, or for redemption, or for sale, or for the raising and payment in any manner of mortgage money, the court, on the request of the mortgagee, or of any person interested either in the mortgage money or in the right of redemption, and, notwithstanding that –

   (a) any other person dissents; or

   (b) the mortgagee or any person so interested does not appear in the action;

and without allowing any time for redemption or for payment of any mortgage money, may direct a sale of the mortgaged property, on such terms as it thinks fit, including the deposit in court of a reasonable sum fixed by the court to meet the expenses of sale and to secure performance of the terms.

(3) But, in an action brought by a person interested in the right of redemption and seeking a sale, the court may, on the application of any defendant, direct the plaintiff to give such security for costs as the court thinks fit, and may give the conduct of the sale to any defendant, and may give such directions as it thinks fit respecting the costs of the defendants or any of them.

(4) In any case within this section the court may, if it thinks fit, direct a sale without previously determining the priorities of incumbrancers.

(5) This section applies to actions brought either before or after the commencement of this Act.

(6) In this section 'mortgaged property' includes the estate or interest which a mortgagee would have had power to convey if the statutory power of sale were applicable.

(7) For the purposes of this section the court may, in favour of a purchaser, make a

vesting order conveying the mortgaged property, or appoint a person to do so, subject or not to any incumbrance, as the court may think fit; or, in the case of an equitable mortgage, may create and vest a mortgage term in the mortgagee to enable him to carry out the sale as if the mortgage had been made by deed by way of legal mortgage ...

92   Power to authorise land and minerals to be dealt with separately

(1) Where a mortgagee's power of sale in regard to land has become exercisable but does not extend to the purposes mentioned in this section, the court may, on his application, authorise him and the persons deriving title under him to dispose –

(a) of the land, with an exception or reservation of all or any mines and minerals, and with or without rights and powers of or incidental to the working, getting or carrying away of minerals; or

(b) of all or any mines and minerals, with or without the said rights or powers separately from the land;

and thenceforth the powers so conferred shall have effect as if the same were contained in the mortgage ...

93   Restriction on consolidation of mortgages

(1) A mortgagor seeking to redeem any one mortgage is entitled to do so without paying any money due under any separate mortgage made by him, or by any person through whom he claims, solely on property other than that comprised in the mortgage which he seeks to redeem. This subsection applies only if and as far as a contrary intention is not expressed in the mortgage deeds or one of them.

(2) This section does not apply where all the mortgages were made before the first day of January, eighteen hundred and eighty-two.

(3) Save as aforesaid, nothing in this Act, in reference to mortgages, affects any right of consolidation or renders inoperative a stipulation in relation to any mortgage made before or after the commencement of this Act reserving a right to consolidate.

94   Tacking and further advances

(1) After the commencement of this Act, a prior mortgagee shall have a right to make further advances to rank in priority to subsequent mortgages (whether legal or equitable) –

(a) if an arrangement has been made to that effect with the subsequent mortgagees; or

(b) if he had no notice of such subsequent mortgages at the time when the further advance was made by him; or

(c) whether or not he had such notice as aforesaid, where the mortgage imposes an obligation on him to make such further advances.

This subsection applies whether or not the prior mortgage was made expressly for securing further advances.

(2) In relation to the making of further advances after the commencement of this Act a mortgagee shall not be deemed to have notice of a mortgage merely by reason that it was registered as a land charge, if it was not so registered at the time when the original mortgage was created or when the last search (if any) by or on behalf of the mortgagee was made, whichever last happened. This subsection only applies where the prior mortgage was made expressly for securing a current account or other further advances.

(3) Save in regard to the making of further advances as aforesaid, the right to tack is hereby abolished: Provided that nothing in this Act shall affect any priority acquired before the commencement of this Act by tacking, or in respect of further advances made without notice of a subsequent incumbrance or by arrangement with the subsequent incumbrancer.

(4) This section applies to mortgages of land made before or after the commencement of this Act, but not to charges on registered land.

95 Obligation to transfer instead of reconveying, and as to right to take possession

(1) Where a mortgagor is entitled to redeem, then subject to compliance with the terms on compliance with which he would be entitled to require a reconveyance or surrender, he shall be entitled to require the mortgagee, instead of reconveying or surrendering, to assign the mortgage debt and convey the mortgaged property to any third person, as the mortgagor directs; and the mortgagee shall be bound to assign and convey accordingly.

(2) The rights conferred by this section belong to and are capable of being enforced by each incumbrancer, or by the mortgagor, notwithstanding any intermediate incumbrance; but a requisition of an incumbrancer prevails over a requisition of the mortgagor, and, as between incumbrancers, a requisition of a prior incumbrancer prevails over a requisition of a subsequent incumbrancer.

(3) The foregoing provisions of this section do not apply in the case of a mortgagee being or having been in possession.

(4) Nothing in this Act affects prejudicially the right of a mortgagee of land whether or not his charge is secured by a legal term of years absolute to take possession of the land, but the taking of possession by the mortgagee does not convert any legal estate of the mortgagor into an equitable interest.

(5) This section applies to mortgages made either before or after the commencement of this Act, and takes effect notwithstanding any stipulation to the contrary.

96 Regulations respecting inspection, production and delivery of documents, and priorities

(1) A mortgagor, as long as his right to redeem subsists, shall be entitled from time

to time, at reasonable times, on his request, and at his own cost, and on payment of the mortgagee's costs and expenses in this behalf, to inspect and make copies or abstracts of or extracts from the documents of title relating to the mortgaged property in the custody or power of the mortgagee. This subsection applies to mortgages made after the thirty-first day of December, eighteen hundred and eighty-one, and takes effect notwithstanding any stipulation to the contrary.

(2) A mortgagee, whose mortgage is surrendered or otherwise extinguished, shall not be liable on account of delivering documents of title in his possession to the person not having the best right thereto, unless he has notice of the right or claim of a person having a better right, whether by virtue of a right to require a surrender or reconveyance or otherwise. In this subsection notice does not include notice implied by reason of registration under the Land Charges Act 1925.

97   Priorities as between puisne mortgages

Every mortgage affecting a legal estate in land made after the commencement of this Act, whether legal or equitable (not being a mortgage protected by the deposit of documents relating to the legal estate affected) shall rank according to its date of registration as a land charge pursuant to the Land Charges Act 1925. This section does not apply to mortgages or charges to which the Land Charges Act 1972 does not apply by virtue of section 14(3) of that Act (which excludes certain land charges created by instruments necessitating registration under the Land Registration Act 2002), or to mortgages or charges of registered land.

98   Actions for possession by mortgagors

(1) A mortgagor for the time being entitled to the possession or receipt of the rents and profits of any land, as to which the mortgagee has not given notice of his intention to take possession or to enter into the receipt of the rents and profits thereof, may sue for such possession, or for the recovery of such rents or profits, or to prevent or recover damages in respect of any trespass or other wrong relative thereto, in his own name only, unless the cause of action arises upon a lease or other contract made by him jointly with any other person.

(2) This section does not prejudice the power of a mortgagor independently of this section to take proceedings in his own name only, either in right of any legal estate vested in him or otherwise.

(3) This section applies whether the mortgage was made before or after the commencement of this Act.

99   Leasing powers of mortgagor and mortgagee in possession

(1) A mortgagor of land while in possession shall, as against every incumbrancer, have power to make from time to time any such lease of the mortgaged land, or any part thereof, as is by this section authorised.

(2) A mortgagee of land while in possession shall, as against all prior

incumbrancers, if any, and as against the mortgagor, have power to make from time to time any such lease as aforesaid.

(3) The leases which this section authorises are –

(i) agricultural or occupation leases for any term not exceeding twenty-one years, or, in the case of a mortgage made after the commencement of this Act, fifty years; and

(ii) building leases for any term not exceeding ninety-nine years, or, in the case of a mortgage made after the commencement of this Act, nine hundred and ninety-nine years.

(4) Every person making a lease under this section may execute and do all assurances and things necessary or proper in that behalf.

(5) Every such lease shall be made to take effect in possession not later than twelve months after its date.

(6) Every such lease shall reserve the best rent that can reasonably be obtained, regard being had to the circumstances of the case, but without any fine being taken.

(7) Every such lease shall contain a covenant by the lessee for payment of the rent, and a condition of re-entry on the rent not being paid within a time therein specified not exceeding thirty days.

(8) A counterpart of every such lease shall be executed by the lessee and delivered to the lessor, of which execution and delivery the execution of the lease by the lessor shall, in favour of the lessee and all persons deriving title under him, be sufficient evidence.

(9) Every such building lease shall be made in consideration of the lessee, or some person by whose direction the lease is granted, having erected, or agreeing to erect within not more than five years from the date of the lease, buildings, new or additional, or having improved or repaired buildings, or agreeing to improve or repair buildings within that time, or having executed, or agreeing to execute within that time, on the land leased, an improvement for or in connexion with building purposes.

(10) In any such building lease a peppercorn rent, or a nominal or other rent less than the rent ultimately payable, may be made payable for the first five years, or any less part of the term.

(11) In case of a lease by the mortgagor, he shall, within one month after making the lease, deliver to the mortgagee, or, where there are more than one, to the mortgagee first in priority, a counterpart of the lease duly executed by the lessee, but the lessee shall not be concerned to see that this provision is complied with.

(12) A contract to make or accept a lease under this section may be enforced by or against every person on whom the lease if granted would be binding.

(13) Subject to subsection (13A) below, this section applies only if and as far as contrary intention is not expressed by the mortgagor and mortgagee in the

mortgage deed, or otherwise in writing, and has effect subject to the terms of the mortgage deed or of any such writing and to the provisions therein contained.

(13A) Subsection (13) of this section –

(a) shall not enable the application of any provision of this section to be excluded or restricted in relation to any mortgage of agricultural land made after 1st March 1948 but before 1st September 1995, and

(b) shall not enable the power to grant a lease of an agricultural holding to which, by virtue of section 4 of the Agricultural Tenancies Act 1995, the Agricultural Holdings Act 1986 will apply, to be excluded or restricted in relation to any mortgage of agricultural land made on or after 1st September 1995.

(13B) In subsection (13A) of this section –

'agricultural holding' has the same meaning as in the Agricultural Holdings Act 1986; and

'agricultural land' has the same meaning as in the Agriculture Act 1947.

(14) The mortgagor and mortgagee may, by agreement in writing, whether or not contained in the mortgage deed, reserve to or confer on the mortgagor or the mortgagee, or both, any further or other powers of leasing or having reference to leasing; and any further or other powers so reserved or conferred shall be exercisable, as far as may be, as if they were conferred by this Act, and with all the like incidents, effects, and consequences: Provided that the powers so reserved or conferred shall not prejudicially affect the rights of any mortgagee interested under any other mortgage subsisting at the date of the agreement, unless that mortgagee joins in or adopts the agreement.

(15) Nothing in this Act shall be construed to enable a mortgagor or mortgagee to make a lease for any longer term or on any other conditions than such as could have been granted or imposed by the mortgagor, with the concurrence of all the incumbrancers, if this Act and the enactments replaced by this section had not been passed: Provided that, in the case of a mortgage of leasehold land, a lease granted under this section shall reserve a reversion of not less than one day.

(16) Subject as aforesaid, this section applies to any mortgage made after the thirty-first day of December, eighteen hundred and eighty-one, but the provisions thereof, or any of them, may, by agreement in writing made after that date between mortgagor and mortgagee, be applied to a mortgage made before that date, so nevertheless that any such agreement shall not prejudicially affect any right or interest of any mortgagee not joining in or adopting the agreement.

(17) The provisions of this section referring to a lease shall be construed to extend and apply, as far as circumstances admit, to any letting, and to an agreement, whether in writing or not, for leasing or letting.

(18) For the purposes of this section 'mortgagor' does not include any incumbrancer deriving title under the original mortgagor.

(19) The powers of leasing conferred by this section shall, after a receiver of the income of the mortgaged property or any part thereof has been appointed by a mortgagee under his statutory power, and so long as the receiver acts, be exercisable by such mortgagee instead of by the mortgagor, as respects any land affected by the receivership, in like manner as if such mortgagee were in possession of the land, and the mortgagee may, by writing, delegate any of such powers to the receiver.

100 Powers of mortgagor and mortgagee in possession to accept surrenders of leases

(1) For the purpose only of enabling a lease authorised under the last preceding section, or under any agreement made pursuant to that section, or by the mortgage deed (in this section referred to as an authorised lease) to be granted, a mortgagor of land while in possession shall, as against every incumbrancer, have, by virtue of this Act, power to accept from time to time a surrender of any lease of the mortgaged land or any part thereof comprised in the lease, with or without an exception of or in respect of all or any of the mines and minerals therein, and, on a surrender of the lease so far as it comprises part only of the land or mines and minerals leased, the rent may be apportioned.

(2) For the same purpose, a mortgagee of land while in possession shall, as against all prior or other incumbrancers, if any, and as against the mortgagor, have, by virtue of this Act, power to accept from time to time any such surrender as aforesaid.

(3) On a surrender of part only of the land or mines and minerals leased, the original lease may be varied, provided that the lease when varied would have been valid as an authorised lease if granted by the person accepting the surrender; and, on a surrender and the making of a new or other lease, whether for the same or for any extended or other term, and whether subject or not to the same or to any other covenants, provisions, or conditions, the value of the lessee's interest in the lease surrendered may, subject to the provisions of this section, be taken into account in the determination of the amount of the rent to be reserved, and of the nature of the covenants, provisions, and conditions to be inserted in the new or other lease.

(4) Where any consideration for the surrender, other than an agreement to accept an authorised lease, is given by or on behalf of the lessee to or on behalf of the person accepting the surrender, nothing in this section authorises a surrender to a mortgagor without the consent of the incumbrancers, or authorises a surrender to a second or subsequent incumbrancer without the consent of every prior incumbrancer.

(5) No surrender shall, by virtue of this section, be rendered valid unless –

    (a) An authorised lease is granted of the whole of the land or mines and minerals comprised in the surrender to take effect in possession immediately or within one month after the date of the surrender; and

    (b) The term certain or other interest granted by the new lease is not less in duration than the unexpired term or interest which would have been subsisting under the original lease if that lease had not been surrendered; and

(c) Where the whole of the land mines and minerals originally leased has been surrendered, the rent reserved by the new lease is not less than the rent which would have been payable under the original lease if it had not been surrendered; or where part only of the land or mines and minerals has been surrendered, the aggregate rents respectively remaining payable or reserved under the original lease and new lease are not less than the rent which would have been payable under the original lease if no partial surrender had been accepted.

(6) A contract to make or accept a surrender under this section may be enforced by or against every person on whom the surrender, if completed, would be binding.

(7) This section applies only if and as far as a contrary intention is not expressed by the mortgagor and mortgagee in the mortgage deed, or otherwise in writing, and shall have effect subject to the terms of the mortgage deed or of any such writing and to the provisions therein contained.

(8) This section applies to a mortgage made after the thirty-first day of December, nineteen hundred and eleven, but the provisions of this section, or any of them, may, by agreement in writing made after that date, between mortgagor and mortgagee, be applied to a mortgage made before that date, so nevertheless that any such agreement shall not prejudicially affect any right or interest of any mortgagee not joining in or adopting the agreement.

(9) The provisions of this section referring to a lease shall be construed to extend and apply, as far as circumstances admit, to any letting, and to any agreement, whether in writing or not, for leasing or letting.

(10) The mortgagor and mortgagee may, by agreement in writing, whether or not contained in the mortgage deed, reserve or confer on the mortgagor or mortgagee, or both, any further or other powers relating to the surrender of leases; and any further or other powers so conferred or reserved shall be exercisable, as far as may be, as if they were conferred by this Act, and with all the like incidents, effects and consequences: Provided that the powers so reserved or conferred shall not prejudicially affect the rights of any mortgagee interested under any other mortgage subsisting at the date of the agreement, unless that mortgagee joins in or adopts the agreement.

(11) Nothing in this section operates to enable a mortgagor or mortgagee to accept a surrender which could not have been accepted by the mortgagor with the concurrence of all the incumbrancers if this Act and the enactments replaced by this section had not been passed.

(12) For the purposes of this section 'mortgagor' does not include an incumbrancer deriving title under the original mortgagor.

(13) The powers of accepting surrenders conferred by this section shall, after a receiver of the income of the mortgaged property or any part thereof has been appointed by the mortgagee, under the statutory power, and so long as the receiver

acts, be exercisable by such mortgagee instead of by the mortgagor, as respects any land affected by the receivership, in like manner as if such mortgagee were in possession of the land; and the mortgagee may, by writing, delegate any of such powers to the receiver.

101 Powers incident to estate or interest of mortgagee

(1) A mortgagee, where the mortgage is made by deed, shall, by virtue of this Act, have the following powers, to the like extent as if they had been in terms conferred by the mortgage deed, but not further (namely) –

(i) A power, when the mortgage money had become due, to sell, or to concur with any other person in selling, the mortgaged property, or any part thereof, either subject to prior charges or not, and either together or in lots, by public auction or by private contract, subject to such conditions respecting title, or evidence of title, or other matter, as the mortgagee thinks fit, with power to vary any contract for sale, and to buy in at an auction, or to rescind any contract for sale, and to re-sell; without being answerable for any loss occasioned thereby; and

(ii) A power, at any time after the date of the mortgage deed, to insure and keep insured against loss or damage by fire any building, or any effects or property of an insurable nature, whether affixed to the freehold or not, being or forming part of the property which or an estate or interest wherein is mortgaged, and the premiums paid for any such insurance shall be a charge on the mortgaged property or estate or interest, in addition to the mortgage money, and with the same priority, and with interest at the same rate, as the mortgage money; and

(iii) A power, when the mortgage money has become due, to appoint a receiver of the income of the mortgaged property, or any part thereof; or, if the mortgaged property consists of an interest in income, or of a rentcharge or an annual or other periodical sum, a receiver of that property or any part thereof; and

(iv) A power, while the mortgagee is in possession, to cut and sell timber and other trees ripe for cutting, and not planted or left standing for shelter or ornament, or to contract for any such cutting and sale, to be completed within any time not exceeding twelve months from the making of the contract.

(1A) Subsection 1(i) is subject to section 21 of the Commonhold and Leasehold Reform Act 2002 (no disposition of part-units).

(2) Where the mortgage deed is executed after the thirty-first day of December, nineteen hundred and eleven, the power of sale aforesaid includes the following powers as incident thereto (namely) –

(i) A power to impose or reserve or make binding, as far as the law permits, by covenant, condition, or otherwise, on the unsold part of the mortgaged property or any part thereof, or on the purchaser and any property sold, any restriction or reservation with respect to building on or other user of land, or with respect to mines and minerals, or for the purpose of the more beneficial working thereof, or with respect to any other thing:

(ii) A power to sell the mortgaged property, or any part thereof, or all or any mines and minerals apart from the surface:

(a) With or without a grant or reservation of rights of way, rights of water, easements, rights, and privileges for or connected with building or other purposes in relation to the property remaining in mortgage or any part thereof, or to any property sold: and

(b) With or without an exception or reservation of all or any of the mines and minerals in or under the mortgaged property, and with or without a grant or reservation of powers of working, wayleaves, or rights of way, rights of water and drainage and other powers, easements, rights and privileges for or connected with mining purposes in relation to the property remaining unsold or any part thereof, or to any property sold: and

(c) With or without covenants by the purchaser to expend money on the land sold.

(3) The provisions of this Act relating to the foregoing powers, comprised either in this section, or in any other section regulating the exercise of those powers, may be varied or extended by the mortgage deed, and, as so varied or extended, shall, as far as may be, operate in the like manner and with all the like incidents, effects, and consequences, as if such variations or extensions were contained in this Act.

(4) This section applies only if and as far as a contrary intention is not expressed in the mortgage deed, and has effect subject to the terms of the mortgage deed and to the provisions therein contained.

(5) Save as otherwise provided, this section applies where the mortgage deed is executed after the thirty-first day of December, eighteen hundred and eighty-one.

(6) The power of sale conferred by this section includes such power of selling the estate in fee simple or any leasehold reversion as is conferred by the provisions of this Act relating to the realisation of mortgages.

102 Provisions as to mortgages of undivided shares in land

(1) A person who was before the commencement of this Act a mortgagee of an undivided share in land shall have the same power to sell his interest under the trust to which the land is subject, as, independently of this Act, he would have had in regard to the share in the land; and shall also have a right to require the trustees in whom the land is vested to account to him for the income attributable to that share or to appoint a receiver to receive the same from such trustees corresponding to the right which, independently of this Act, he would have had to take possession or to appoint a receiver of the rents and profits attributable to the same share.

(2) The powers conferred by this section are exercisable by the persons deriving title under such mortgagee.

103 Regulation of exercise of power of sale

A mortgagee shall not exercise the power of sale conferred by this Act unless and until –

(i) Notice requiring payment of the mortgage money has been served on the mortgagor or one of two or more mortgagors, and default has been made in payment of the mortgage money, or of part thereof, for three months after such service; or

(ii) Some interest under the mortgage is in arrear and unpaid for two months after becoming due; or

(iii) There has been a breach of some provision contained in the mortgage deed or in this Act, or in an enactment replaced by this Act, and on the part of the mortgagor, or of some person concurring in making the mortgage, to be observed or performed, other than and besides a covenant for payment of the mortgage money or interest thereon.

104 Conveyance on sale

(1) A mortgagee exercising the power of sale conferred by this Act shall have power, by deed, to convey the property sold, for such estate and interest therein as he is by this Act authorised to sell or convey or may be the subject of the mortgage, freed from all estates, interests, and rights to which the mortgage has priority, but subject to all estates, interests, and rights which have priority to the mortgage.

(2) Where a conveyance is made in exercise of the power of sale conferred by this Act, or any enactment replaced by this Act, the title of the purchaser shall not be impeachable on the ground –

(a) that no case had arisen to authorise the sale; or

(b) that due notice was not given; or

(c) where the mortgage is made after the commencement of this Act, that leave of the court, when so required, was not obtained; or

(d) whether the mortgage was made before or after such commencement, that the power was otherwise improperly or irregularly exercised;

and a purchaser is not, either before or on conveyance, concerned to see or inquire whether a case has arisen to authorise the sale, or due notice has been given, or the power is otherwise properly and regularly exercised; but any person damnified by an unauthorised, or improper, or irregular exercise of the power shall have his remedy in damages against the person exercising the power.

(3) A conveyance on sale by a mortgagee, made after the commencement of this Act, shall be deemed to have been made in exercise of the power of sale conferred by this Act unless a contrary intention appears.

105 Application of proceeds of sale

The money which is received by the mortgagee, arising from the sale, after discharge of prior incumbrances to which the sale is not made subject, if any, or after payment into court under this Act of a sum to meet any prior incumbrance, shall be held by him in trust to be applied by him, first, in payment of all costs, charges, and expenses properly incurred by him as incident to the sale or any attempted sale, or otherwise; and secondly, in discharge of the mortgage money, interest, and costs, and other money, if any, due under the mortgage; and the residue of the money so received shall be paid to the person entitled to the mortgaged property, or authorised to give receipts for the proceeds of the sale thereof.

106 Provisions as to exercise of power of sale

(1) The power of sale conferred by this Act may be exercised by any person for the time being entitled to receive and give a discharge for the mortgage money.

(2) The power of sale conferred by this Act does not affect the right of foreclosure.

(3) The mortgagee shall not be answerable for any involuntary loss happening in or about the exercise or execution of the power of sale conferred by this Act, or of any trust connected therewith, or, where the mortgage is executed after the thirty-first day of December, nineteen hundred and eleven, of any power or provision contained in the mortgage deed.

(4) At any time after the power of sale conferred by this Act has become exercisable, the person entitled to exercise the power may demand and recover from any person, other than a person having in the mortgaged property an estate, interest, or right in priority to the mortgage, all the deeds and documents relating to the property, or to the title thereto, which a purchaser under the power of sale would be entitled to demand and recover from him.

107 Mortgagee's receipts, discharges, etc

(1) The receipt in writing of a mortgagee shall be a sufficient discharge for any money arising under the power of sale conferred by this Act, or for any money or securities comprised in his mortgage, or arising thereunder; and a person paying or transferring the same to the mortgagee shall not be concerned to inquire whether any money remains due under the mortgage.

(2) Money received by a mortgagee under his mortgage or from the proceeds of securities comprised in his mortgage shall be applied in like manner as in this Act directed respecting money received by him arising from a sale under the power of sale conferred by this Act, but with this variation, that the costs, charges, and expenses payable shall include the costs, charges and expenses properly incurred of recovering and receiving the money or securities, and of conversion of securities into money, instead of those incident to sale.

108 Amount and application of insurance money

(1) The amount of an insurance effected by a mortgagee against loss or damage by

fire under the power in that behalf conferred by this Act shall not exceed the amount specified in the mortgage deed, or, if no amount is therein specified, two third parts of the amount that would be required, in case of total destruction, to restore the property insured.

(2) An insurance shall not, under the power conferred by this Act, be effected by a mortgagee in any of the following cases (namely):

(i) Where there is a declaration in the mortgage deed that no insurance is required:

(ii) Where an insurance is kept up by or on behalf of the mortgagor in accordance with the mortgage deed:

(iii) Where the mortgage deed contains no stipulation respecting insurance, and an insurance is kept up by or on behalf of the mortgagor with the consent of the mortgagee to the amount to which the mortgagee is by this Act authorised to insure.

(3) All money received on an insurance of mortgaged property against loss or damage by fire or otherwise effected under this Act, or any enactment replaced by this Act, or on an insurance for the maintenance of which the mortgagor is liable under the mortgage deed, shall, if the mortgagee so requires, be applied by the mortgagor in making good the loss or damage in respect of which the money is received.

(4) Without prejudice to any obligation to the contrary imposed by law, or by special contract, a mortgagee may require that all money received on an insurance of mortgaged property against loss or damage by fire or otherwise effected under this Act, or any enactment replaced by this Act, or on an insurance for the maintenance of which the mortgagor is liable under the mortgage deed, be applied in or towards the discharge of the mortgage money.

109 Appointment, powers, remuneration and duties of receiver

(1) A mortgagee entitled to appoint a receiver under the power in that behalf conferred by this Act shall not appoint a receiver until he has become entitled to exercise the power of sale conferred by this Act, but may then, by writing under his hand, appoint such person as he thinks fit to be receiver.

(2) A receiver appointed under the powers conferred by this Act, or any enactment replaced by this Act, shall be deemed to be the agent of the mortgagor; and the mortgagor shall be solely responsible for the receiver's acts or defaults unless the mortgage deed otherwise provides.

(3) The receiver shall have power to demand and recover all the income of which he is appointed receiver, by action, distress, or otherwise, in the name either of the mortgagor or of the mortgagee, to the full extent of the estate or interest which the mortgagor could dispose of, and to give effectual receipts accordingly for the same, and to exercise any powers which may have been delegated to him by the mortgagee pursuant to this Act.

(4) A person paying money to the receiver shall not be concerned to inquire whether any case has happened to authorise the receiver to act.

(5) The receiver may be removed, and a new receiver may be appointed, from time to time by the mortgagee by writing under his hand.

(6) The receiver shall be entitled to retain out of any money received by him, for his remuneration, and in satisfaction of all costs, charges, and expenses incurred by him as receiver, a commission at such rate, not exceeding five per centum on the gross amount of all money received, as is specified in his appointment, and if no rate is so specified, then at the rate of five per centum on that gross amount, or at such other rate as the court thinks fit to allow, on application made by him for that purpose.

(7) The receiver shall, if so directed in writing by the mortgagee, insure to the extent, if any, to which the mortgagee might have insured and keep insured against loss or damage by fire, out of the money received by him, any building, effects, or property comprised in the mortgage, whether affixed to the freehold or not, being of an insurable nature.

(8) Subject to the provisions of this Act as to the application of insurance money, the receiver shall apply all money received by him as follows, namely:

(i) In discharge of all rents, taxes, rates, and outgoings whatever affecting the mortgaged property; and

(ii) In keeping down all annual sums or other payments, and the interest on all principal sums, having priority to the mortgage in right whereof he is receiver; and

(iii) In payment of his commission, and of the premiums on fire, life, or other insurances, if any, properly payable under the mortgage deed or under this Act, and the cost of executing necessary or proper repairs directed in writing by the mortgagee; and

(iv) In payment of the interest accruing due in respect of any principal money due under the mortgage; and

(v) In or towards discharge of the principal money if so directed in writing by the mortgagee;

and shall pay the residue, if any, of the money received by him to the person who, but for the possession of the receiver, would have been entitled to receive the income of which he is appointed receiver, or who is otherwise entitled to the mortgaged property.

110 Effect of bankruptcy of the mortgagor on the power to sell or appoint a receiver

(1) Where the statutory or express power for a mortgagee either to sell or to appoint a receiver is made exercisable by reason of the mortgagor being adjudged a bankrupt, such power shall not be exercised only on account of the adjudication, without the leave of the court.

(2) This section applies only where the mortgage deed is executed after the commencement of this Act.

111 Effect of advance on joint account

(1) Where –

(a) in a mortgage, or an obligation for payment of money, or a transfer of a mortgage or of such an obligation, the sum, or any part of the sum, advanced or owing is expressed to be advanced by or owing to more persons than one out of money, or as money, belonging to them on a joint account; or

(b) a mortgage, or such an obligation, or such a transfer is made to more persons than one, jointly;

the mortgage money, or other money or money's worth, for the time being due to those persons on the mortgage or obligation, shall, as between them and the mortgagor or obligor, be deemed to be and remain money or money's worth belonging to those persons on a joint account; and the receipt in writing of the survivors of last survivor of them, or of the personal representative of the last survivor, shall be a complete discharge for all money or money's worth for the time being due, notwithstanding any notice to the payer of a severance of the joint account.

(2) This section applies if and so far as a contrary intention is not expressed in the mortgage, obligation, or transfer, and has effect subject to the terms of the mortgage, obligation, or transfer, and to the provisions therein contained.

(3) This section applies to any mortgage obligation or transfer made after the thirty-first day of December, eighteen hundred and eighty-one.

113 Notice of trusts affecting mortgage debts

(1) A person dealing in good faith with a mortgagee, or with the mortgagor if the mortgage has been discharged released or postponed as to the whole or any part of the mortgaged property, shall not be concerned with any trust at any time affecting the mortgage money or the income thereof, whether or not he has notice of the trust, and may assume unless the contrary is expressly stated in the instruments relating to the mortgage –

(a) that the mortgagees (if more than one) are or were entitled to the mortgage money on a joint account; and

(b) that the mortgagee has or had power to give valid receipts for the purchase money or mortgage money and the income thereof (including any arrears of interest) and to release or postpone the priority of the mortgage debt or any part thereof or to deal with the same or the mortgaged property or any part thereof;

without investigating the equitable title to the mortgage debt or the appointment or discharge of trustees in reference thereto.

(2) This section applies to mortgages made before or after the commencement of this Act, but only as respects dealings effected after such commencement.

(3) This section does not affect the liability of any person in whom the mortgage debt is vested for the purposes of any trust to give effect to that trust.

114 Transfers of mortgages

(1) A deed executed by a mortgagee purporting to transfer his mortgage or the benefit thereof shall, unless a contrary intention is therein expressed, and subject to any provisions therein contained, operate to transfer to the transferee –

(a) the right to demand, sue for, recover, and give receipts for, the mortgage money or the unpaid part thereof, and the interest then due, if any, and thenceforth to become due thereon; and

(b) the benefit of all securities for the same, and the benefit of and the right to sue on all covenants with the mortgagee, and the right to exercise all powers of the mortgagee; and

(c) all the estate and interest in the mortgaged property then vested in the mortgagee subject to redemption or cesser, but as to such estate and interest subject to the right of redemption then subsisting.

(2) In this section 'transferee' includes his personal representatives and assigns.

(3) A transfer of mortgage may be made in the form contained in the Third Schedule to this Act with such variations and additions, if any, as the circumstances may require.

(4) This section applies, whether the mortgage transferred was made before or after the commencement of this Act, but applies only to transfers made after the commencement of this Act.

(5) This section does not extend to a transfer of a bill of sale of chattels by way of security.

115 Reconveyances of mortgages by endorsed receipts

(1) A receipt endorsed on, written at the foot of, or annexed to, a mortgage for all money thereby secured, which states the name of the person who pays the money and is executed by the chargee by way of legal mortgage or the person in whom the mortgaged property is vested and who is legally entitled to give a receipt for the mortgage money shall operate, without any reconveyance, surrender, or release –

(a) Where a mortgage takes effect by demise or subdemise, as a surrender of the term, so as to determine the term or merge the same in the reversion immediately expectant thereon;

(b) Where the mortgage does not take effect by demise or subdemise, as a reconveyance thereof to the extent of the interest which is the subject matter of the mortgage, to the person who immediately before the execution of the receipt was entitled to the equity of redemption;

and in either case, as a discharge of the mortgaged property from all principal money and interest secured by, and from all claims under the mortgage, but without prejudice to any term or other interest which is paramount to the estate or interest of the mortgagee or other person in whom the mortgaged property was vested.

(2) Provided that, where by the receipt the money appears to have been paid by a person who is not entitled to the immediate equity of redemption, the receipt shall operate as if the benefit of the mortgage had by deed been transferred to him; unless –

   (a) it is otherwise expressly provided; or

   (b) the mortgage is paid off out of capital money, or other money in the hands of a personal representative or trustee properly applicable for the discharge of the mortgage, and it is not expressly provided that the receipt is to operate as a transfer.

(3) Nothing in this section confers on a mortgagor a right to keep alive a mortgage paid off by him, so as to affect prejudicially any subsequent incumbrancer; and where there is no right to keep the mortgage alive, the receipt does not operate as a transfer.

(4) This section does not affect the right of any person to require a reassignment, surrender, release, or transfer to be executed in lieu of a receipt.

(5) A receipt may be given in the form contained in the Third Schedule to this Act, with such variations and additions, if any, as may be deemed expedient.

(6) In a receipt given under this section the same covenants shall be implied as if the person who executes the receipt had by deed been expressed to convey the property as mortgagee, subject to any interest which is paramount to the mortgage.

(7) Where the mortgage consists of a mortgage and a further charge or of more than one deed, it shall be sufficient for the purposes of this section, if the receipt refers either to all the deeds whereby the mortgage money is secured or to the aggregate amount of the mortgage money thereby secured and for the time being owing, and is endorsed on, written at the foot of, or annexed to, one of the mortgage deeds.

(8) This section applies to the discharge of a charge by way of legal mortgage, and to the discharge of a mortgage, whether made by way of statutory mortgage or not, executed before or after the commencement of this Act, but only as respects discharges effected after such commencement.

(9) The provisions of this section relating to the operation of a receipt shall (in substitution for the like statutory provisions relating to receipts given by or on behalf of a building society) apply to the discharge of a mortgage made to any such society, provided that the receipts is executed in the manner required by the statute relating to the society.

(10) This section does not apply to the discharge of a registered charge (within the meaning of the Land Registration Act 2002).

(11) In this section 'mortgaged property' means the property remaining subject to the mortgage at the date of the receipt.

116 Cesser of mortgage terms

Without prejudice to the right of a tenant for life or other person having only a limited interest in the equity of redemption to require a mortgage to be kept alive by transfer or otherwise, a mortgage term shall, when the money secured by the mortgage has been discharged, become a satisfied term and shall cease.

117 Forms of statutory legal charges

(1) As a special form of charge by way of legal mortgage, a mortgage of freehold or leasehold land may be made by a deed expressed to be made by way of statutory mortgage, being in one of the forms (Nos 1 or 4) set out in the Fourth Schedule to this Act, with such variations and additions, if any, as circumstances may require, and if so made the provisions of this section shall apply thereto.

(2) There shall be deemed to be included, and there shall by virtue of this Act be implied, in such a mortgage deed –

First, a covenant with the mortgagee by the person therein expressed to charge as mortgagor to the effect following, namely:

That the mortgagor will, on the stated day, pay to the mortgagee the stated mortgage money, with interest thereon in the meantime at the stated rate, and will thereafter, if and as long as the mortgage money or any part thereof remains unpaid, pay to the mortgagee (as well after as before any judgment is obtained under the mortgage) interest thereon, or on the unpaid part thereof, at the stated rate, by equal half-yearly payments the first thereof to be made at the end of six months from the day stated for payment of the mortgage money:

Secondly, a provision to the following effect (namely):

That if the mortgagor on the stated day pays to the mortgagee the stated mortgage money, with interest thereon in the meantime at the stated rate, the mortgagee at any time thereafter, at the request and cost of the mortgagor, shall discharge the mortgaged property or transfer the benefit of the mortgage as the mortgagor may direct.

This subsection applies to a mortgage deed made under section twenty-six of the Conveyancing Act 1881, with a substitution of a reference to 'the person therein expressed to convey as mortgagor' for the reference in this subsection to 'the person therein expressed to charge as mortgagor'.

119 Implied covenants, joint and several

In a deed of statutory mortgage, or of statutory transfer of mortgage, where more persons than one are expressed to convey or charge as mortgagors, or to join as covenantors, the implied covenant on their part shall be deemed to be a joint and several covenant by them; and where there are more mortgagees or more transferees than one, the implied covenant with them shall be deemed to be a covenant with them jointly, unless the amount secured is expressed to be secured to them in shares or distinct sums, in which latter case the implied covenant with them shall be deemed to be a covenant with each severally in respect of the share or distinct sum secured to him.

120 Form of discharge of statutory mortgage or charge

A statutory mortgage may be surrendered or discharged by a receipt in the form (No 5) set out in the Fourth Schedule to this Act with such variations and additions, if any, as circumstances may require.

PART IV

EQUITABLE INTERESTS AND THINGS IN ACTION

130 Entailed interests in real and personal property

(4) In default of and subject to the execution of a disentailing assurance or the exercise of the testamentary power conferred by this Act, an entailed interest (to the extent of the property affected) shall devolve as an equitable interest, from time to time, upon the persons who would have been successively entitled thereto as the heirs of the body (either generally or of a particular class) of the tenant in tail or other person, or as tenant by the curtesy, if the entailed interest had, before the commencement of this Act, been limited in respect of freehold land governed by the general law in force immediately before such commencement, and such law had remained unaffected.

(5) Where personal chattels are settled without reference to settled land on trusts creating entailed interests therein, the trustees, with the consent of the usufructuary for the time being if of full age, may sell the chattels or any of them, and the net proceeds of any such sale shall be held in trust for and shall go to the same persons successively, in the same manner and for the same interests, as the chattels sold would have been held and gone if they had not been sold, and the income of investments representing such proceeds of sale shall be applied accordingly.

(7) In this Act where the context so admits 'entailed interest' includes an estate tail (now made to take effect as an equitable interest) created before the commencement of this Act.

132 As to heirs taking by purchase

(1) A limitation of real or personal property in favour of the heir, either general or special, of a deceased person which, if limited in respect of freehold land before the commencement of this Act, would have conferred on the heir an estate in the land by purchase, shall operate to confer a corresponding equitable interest in the property on the person who would, if the general law in force immediately before such commencement had remained unaffected, have answered the description of the heir, either general or special, of the deceased in respect of his freehold land,

either at the death of the deceased or at the time named in the limitation, as the case may require.

(2) This section applies whether the deceased person dies before or after the commencement of this Act, but only applies to limitations or trusts created by an instrument coming into operation after such commencement.

134 Restriction on executory limitations

(1) Where there is a person entitled to –

(a) an equitable interest in land for an estate in fee simple or for any less interest not being an entailed interest, or

(b) any interest in other property, not being an entailed interest,

with an executory limitation over on default or failure of all or any of his issue, whether within or at any specified period or time or not, that executory limitation shall be or become void and incapable of taking effect, if and as soon as there is living any issue who has attained the age of eighteen years of the class on default or failure whereof the limitation over was to take effect.

(2) This section applies where the executory limitation is contained in an instrument coming into operation after the thirty-first day of December, eighteen hundred and eighty-two, save that, as regards instruments coming into operation before the commencement of this Act, it only applies to limitations of land for an estate in fee, or for a term of years absolute or determinable on life, or for a term of life.

135 Equitable waste

An equitable interest for life without impeachment of waste does not confer upon the tenant for life any right to commit waste of the description known as equitable waste, unless an intention to confer such right expressly appears by the instrument creating such equitable interest.

137 Dealings with life interests, reversions and other equitable interests

(1) The law applicable to dealings with equitable things in action which regulates the priority of competing interests therein, shall, as respects dealings with equitable interests in land, capital money, and securities representing capital money effected after the commencement of this Act, apply to and regulate the priority of competing interests therein. This subsection applies whether or not the money or securities are in court.

(2) (i) In the case of a dealing with an equitable interest in settled land, capital money or securities representing capital money, the persons to be served with notice of the dealing shall be the trustees of the settlement; and where the equitable interest is created by a derivative or subsidiary settlement, the persons to be served with notice shall be the trustees of that settlement.

(ii) In the case of a dealing with an equitable interest in land subject to a trust of land, or the proceeds of sale of such land, the persons to be served with notice shall be the trustees.

(iii) In any other case the person to be served with notice of a dealing with an equitable interest in land shall be the estate owner of the land affected.

The persons on whom notice is served pursuant to this subsection shall be affected thereby in the same manner as if they had been trustees of personal property out of which the equitable interest was created or arose. This subsection does not apply where the money or securities are in court.

(3) A notice, otherwise than in writing, given to, or received by, a trustee after the commencement of this Act as respects any dealing with an equitable interest in real or personal property, shall not affect the priority of competing claims of purchasers in that equitable interest.

(4) Where, as respects any dealing with an equitable interest in real or personal property –

(a) the trustees are not persons to whom a valid notice of the dealing can be given; or

(b) there are no trustees to whom a notice can be given; or

(c) for any other reason a valid notice cannot be served, or cannot be served without unreasonable cost or delay;

a purchaser may at his own cost require that –

(i) a memorandum of the dealing be endorsed, written on or permanently annexed to the instrument creating the trust;

(ii) the instrument be produced to him by the person having the possession or custody thereof to prove that a sufficient memorandum has been placed thereon or annexed thereto.

Such memorandum shall, as respects priorities, operate in like manner as if notice in writing of the dealing had been given to trustees duly qualified to receive the notice at the time when the memorandum is placed on or annexed to the instrument creating the trust.

(5) Where the property affected is settled land, the memorandum shall be placed on or annexed to the trust instrument and not the vesting instrument. Where the property affected is land subject to a trust of land, the memorandum shall be placed on or annexed to the instrument whereby the equitable interest is created.

(6) Where the trust is created by statute or by operation of law, or in any other case where there is no instrument whereby the trusts are declared, the instrument under which the equitable interest is acquired or which is evidence of the devolution thereof shall, for the purposes of this section, be deemed the instrument creating the trust. In particular, where the trust arises by reason of an intestacy, the letters of administration or probate in force when the dealing was effected shall be deemed such instrument.

(7) Nothing in this section affects any priority acquired before the commencement of this Act.

(8) Where a notice in writing of a dealing with an equitable interest in real or personal property has been served on a trustee under this section, the trustees from time to time of the property affected shall be entitled to the custody of the notice, and the notice shall be delivered to them by any person who for the time being may have the custody thereof; and subject to the payment of costs, any person interested in the equitable interest may require production of the notice.

(9) The liability of the estate owner of the legal estate affected to produce documents and furnish information to persons entitled to equitable interests therein shall correspond to the liability of a trustee for sale to produce documents and furnish information to persons entitled to equitable interests in the proceeds of sale or the land.

(10) This section does not apply until a trust has been created, and in this section 'dealing' includes a disposition by operation of law.

PART V

LEASES AND TENANCIES

139 Effect of extinguishment of reversion

(1) Where a reversion expectant on a lease of land is surrendered or merged, the estate or interest which as against the lessee for the time being confers the next vested right to the land, shall be deemed the reversion for the purpose of preserving the same incidents and obligations as would have affected the original reversion had there been no surrender or merger thereof …

140 Apportionment of conditions on severance

(1) Notwithstanding the severance by conveyance, surrender, or otherwise of the reversionary estate in any land comprised in a lease, and notwithstanding the avoidance or cesser in any other manner of the term granted by a lease as to part only of the land comprised therein, every condition or right of re-entry, and every other condition contained in the lease, shall be apportioned, and shall remain annexed to the severed parts of the reversionary estate as severed, and shall be in force with respect to the term whereon each severed part is reversionary, or the term in the part of the land as to which the term has not been surrendered, or has not be avoided or has not otherwise ceased, in like manner as if the land comprised in each severed part, or the land as to which the term remains subsisting, as the case may be, had alone originally been comprised in the lease.

(2) In this section 'right of re-entry' includes a right to determine the lease by notice to quit or otherwise; but where the notice is served by a person entitled to a severed part of the reversion so that it extends to part only of the land demised, the lessee may within one month determine the lease in regard to the rest of the

land by giving to the owner of the reversionary estate therein a counter notice expiring at the same time as the original notice.

(3) This section applies to leases made before or after the commencement of this Act and whether the severance of the reversionary estate or the partial avoidance or cesser of the term was effected before or after such commencement: Provided that, where the lease was made before the first day of January eighteen hundred and eighty-two nothing in this section shall affect the operation of a severance of the reversionary estate or partial avoidance or cesser of the term which was effected before the commencement of this Act.

141 Rent and benefit of lessee's covenants to run with the reversion

(1) Rent reserved by a lease, and the benefit of every covenant or provision therein contained, having reference to the subject-matter thereof, and on the lessee's part to be observed or performed, and every condition of re-entry and other condition therein contained, shall be annexed and incident to and shall go with the reversionary estate in the land, or in any part thereof, immediately expectant on the term granted by the lease, notwithstanding severance of that reversionary estate, and without prejudice to any liability affecting a covenantor or his estate.

(2) Any such rent, covenant or provision shall be capable of being recovered, received, enforced, and taken advantage of, by the person from time to time entitled, subject to the term, to the income of the whole or any part, as the case may require, of the land leased.

(3) Where that person becomes entitled by conveyance or otherwise, such rent, covenant or provision may be recovered, received, enforced or taken advantage of by him notwithstanding that he becomes so entitled after the condition of re-entry or forfeiture has become enforceable, but this subsection does not render enforceable any condition of re-entry or other condition waived or released before such person becomes entitled as aforesaid.

(4) This section applies to leases made before or after the commencement of this Act, but does not affect the operation of –

(a) any severance of the reversionary estate; or

(b) any acquisition by conveyance or otherwise of the right to receive or enforce any rent covenant or provision;

effected before the commencement of this Act.

142 Obligation of lessor's covenants to run with reversion

(1) The obligation under a condition or of a covenant entered into by a lessor with reference to the subject-matter of the lease shall, if and as far as the lessor has power to bind the reversionary estate immediately expectant on the term granted by the lease, be annexed and incident to and shall go with that reversionary estate, or the several parts thereof, notwithstanding severance of that reversionary estate, and may be taken advantage of and enforced by the person in whom the term is

from time to time vested by conveyance, devolution in law, or otherwise; and, if and as far as the lessor has power to bind the person from time to time entitled to that reversionary estate, the obligation aforesaid may be taken advantage of and enforced against any person so entitled.

(2) This section applies to leases made before or after the commence-ment of this Act, whether the severance of the reversionary estate was effected before or after such commencement: provided that, where the lease was made before the first day of January eighteen hundred and eighty-two, nothing in this section shall affect the operation of any severance of the reversionary estate effected before such commencement. This section takes effect without prejudice to any liability affecting a covenantor or his estate.

143 Effect of licences granted to lessees

(1) Where a licence is granted to a lessee to do any act, the licence, unless otherwise expressed, extends only –

(a) to the permission actually given; or

(b) to the specific breach of any provision or covenant referred to; or

(c) to any other matter thereby specifically authorised to be done;

and the licence does not prevent any proceedings for any subsequent breach unless otherwise specified in the licence.

(2) Notwithstanding any such licence –

(a) All rights under covenants and powers of re-entry contained in the lease remain in full force and are available as against any subsequent breach of covenant, condition or other matter not specifically authorised or waived, in the same manner as if no licence had been granted; and

(b) The condition or right of entry remains in force in all respects as if the licence had not been granted, save in respect of the particular matter authorised to be done.

(3) Where in any lease there is a power or condition of re-entry on the lessee assigning, subletting or doing any other specified act without a licence, and a licence is granted –

(a) to any one or two or more lessees to do any act, or to deal with his equitable share or interest; or

(b) to any lessee, or to any one of two or more lessees to assign or underlet part only of the property, or to do any act in respect of part only of the property;

the licence does not operate to extinguish the right of entry in case of any breach of covenant or condition by the co-lessees of the other shares or interests in the property, or by the lessee or lessees of the rest of the property (as the case may be) in respect of such shares or interests or remaining property, but the right of entry remains in force in respect of the shares, interests or property not the subject of the licence. This subsection does not authorise the grant after the commencement of this Act of a licence to create an undivided share in a legal estate ...

144 No fine to be exacted for licence to assign

In all leases containing a covenant, condition, or agreement against assigning, underletting, or parting with the possession, or disposing of the land or property leased without licence or consent, such covenant, condition, or agreement shall, unless the lease contains an express provision to the contrary, be deemed to be subject to a proviso to the effect that no fine or sum of money in the nature of a fine shall be payable for or in respect of such licence or consent; but this proviso does not preclude the right to require the payment of a reasonable sum in respect of any legal or other expense incurred in relation to such licence or consent.

146 Restrictions on and relief against forfeiture of leases and under-leases

(1) A right of re-entry or forfeiture under any proviso or stipulation in a lease for a breach of any covenant or condition in the lease shall not be enforceable, by action or otherwise, unless and until the lessor serves on the lessee a notice –

(a) specifying the particular breach complained of; and

(b) if the breach is capable of remedy, requiring the lessee to remedy the breach; and

(c) in any case, requiring the lessee to make compensation in money for the breach;

and the lessee fails, within a reasonable time thereafter, to remedy the breach, if it is capable of remedy, and to make reasonable compensation in money, to the satisfaction of the lessor, for the breach.

(2) Where a lessor is proceeding, by action or otherwise, to enforce such a right of re-entry or forfeiture, the lessee may, in the lessor's action, if any, or in any action brought by himself, apply to the court for relief; and the court may grant or refuse relief, as the court, having regard to the proceedings and conduct of the parties under the foregoing provisions of this section, and to all the other circumstances, thinks fit; and in case of relief may grant it on such terms, if any, as to costs, expenses, damages, compensation, penalty, or otherwise, including the granting of an injunction to restrain any like breach in the future, as the court, in the circumstances of each case, thinks fit.

(3) A lessor shall be entitled to recover as a debt due to him from a lessee, and in addition to damages (if any), all reasonable costs and expenses properly incurred by the lessor in the employment of a solicitor and surveyor or valuer, or otherwise, in reference to any breach giving rise to a right of re-entry or forfeiture which, at the request of the lessee, is waived by the lessor, or from which the lessee is relieved, under the provisions of this Act.

(4) Where a lessor is proceeding by action or otherwise to enforce a right of re-entry or forfeiture under any covenant, proviso, or stipulation in a lease, or for non-payment of rent, the court may, on application by any person claiming as under-lessee any estate or interest in the property comprised in the lease or any part thereof, either in the lessor's action (if any) or in any action brought by such

person for that purpose, make an order vesting, for the whole term of the lease or any less term, the property comprised in the lease or any part thereof in any person entitled as under-lessee to any estate or interest in such property upon such conditions as to execution of any deed or other document, payment of rent, costs, expenses, damages, compensation, giving security, or otherwise, as the court in the circumstances of each case may think fit, but in no case shall any such under-lessee be entitled to require a lease to be granted to him for any longer term than he had under his original sub-lease.

(5) For the purposes of this section –

(a) 'Lease' includes an original or derivative under-lease; also an agreement for a lease where the lessee has become entitled to have his lease granted; also a grant at a fee farm rent, or securing a rent by condition;

(b) 'Lessee' includes an original or derivative under-lease, and the persons deriving title under a lessee; also a grantee under any such grant as aforesaid and the persons deriving title under him;

(c) 'Lessor' includes an original or derivative under-lessor, and the persons deriving title under a lessor; also a person making such grant as aforesaid and the persons deriving title under him;

(d) 'Under-lease' includes an agreement for an underlease where the under-lessee has become entitled to have his underlease granted;

(e) 'Under-lessee' includes any person deriving title under an under-lessee.

(6) This section applies although the proviso or stipulation under which the right of re-entry or forfeiture accrues is inserted in the lease in pursuance of the directions of any Act of Parliament.

(7) For the purposes of this section a lease limited to continue as long only as the lessee abstains from committing a breach of covenant shall be and take effect as a lease to continue for any longer term for which it could subsist, but determinable by a proviso for re-entry on such a breach.

(8) This section does not extend –

(i) To a covenant or condition against assigning, underletting, parting with the possession, or disposing of the land leased where the breach occurred before the commencement of this Act; or

(ii) In the case of a mining lease, to a covenant or condition for allowing the lessor to have access to or inspect books, accounts, records, weighing machines or other things, or to enter or inspect the mine or the workings thereof.

(9) This section does not apply to a condition for forfeiture on the bankruptcy of the lessee or on taking in execution of the lessee's interest if contained in a lease of –

(a) Agricultural or pastoral land;

(b) Mines or minerals;

(c) A house used or intended to be used as a public-house or beershop;

(d) A house let as a dwelling-house, with the use of any furniture, books, works of art, or other chattels not being in the nature of fixtures;

(e) Any property with respect to which the personal qualifications of the tenant are of importance for the preservation of the value or character of the property, or on the ground of neighbourhood to the lessor, or to any person holding under him.

(10) Where a condition of forfeiture on the bankruptcy of the lessee or on taking in execution of the lessee's interest is contained in any lease, other than a lease of any of the classes mentioned in the last subsection, then –

(a) if the lessee's interest is sold within one year from the bankruptcy or taking in execution, this section applies to the forfeiture condition aforesaid;

(b) if the lessee's interest is not sold before the expiration of that year, this section only applies to the forfeiture condition aforesaid during the first year from the date of the bankruptcy or taking in execution.

(11) This section does not, save as otherwise mentioned, affect the law relating to re-entry or forfeiture or relief in case of non-payment of rent.

(12) This section has effect notwithstanding any stipulation to the contrary. ...

147 Relief against notice to effect decorative repairs

(1) After a notice is served on a lessee relating to the internal decorative repairs to a house or other building, he may apply to the court for relief, and if, having regard to all the circumstances of the case (including in particular the length of the lessee's term or interest remaining unexpired), the court is satisfied that the notice is unreasonable, it may, by order, wholly or partially relieve the lessee from liability for such repairs.

(2) This section does not apply –

(i) where the liability arises under an express covenant or agreement to put the property in a decorative state of repair and the covenant or agreement has never been performed;

(ii) to any matter necessary or proper –

(a) for putting or keeping the property in a sanitary condition, or

(b) for the maintenance or preservation of the structure;

(iii) to any statutory liability to keep a house in all respects reasonably fit for human habitation;

(iv) to any covenant or stipulation to yield up the house or other building in a specified state of repair at the end of the term.

(3) In this section 'lease' includes an underlease and an agreement for a lease, and 'lessee' has a corresponding meaning and includes any person liable to effect the repairs.

(4) This section applies whether the notice is served before or after the commencement of this Act, and has effect notwithstanding any stipulation to the contrary ...

148 Waiver of a covenant in a lease

(1) Where any actual waiver by a lessor or the persons deriving title under him of the benefit of any covenant or condition in any lease is proved to have taken place in any particular instance, such waiver shall not be deemed to extend to any instance, or to any breach of covenant or condition save that to which such waiver specially relates, nor operate as a general waiver of the benefit of any such covenant or condition.

(2) This section applies unless a contrary intention appears ...

149 Abolition of interesse termini, and as to reversionary leases and leases for lives

(1) The doctrine of interesse termini is hereby abolished.

(2) As from the commencement of this Act all terms of years absolute shall, whether the interest is created before or after such commencement, be capable of taking effect at law or in equity, according to the estate interest or powers of the grantor, from the date fixed for commencement of the term, without actual entry.

(3) A term, at a rent or granted in consideration of a fine, limited after the commencement of this Act to take effect more than twenty-one years from the date of the instrument purporting to create it, shall be void, and any contract made after such commencement to create such a term shall likewise be void; but this subsection does not apply to any term taking effect in equity under a settlement, or created out of an equitable interest under a settlement, or under an equitable power for mortgage, indemnity or other like purposes.

(4) Nothing in subsections (1) and (2) of this section prejudicially affects the right of any person to recover any rent or to enforce or take advantage of any covenants or conditions, or, as respects terms or interests created before the commencement of this Act, operates to vary any statutory or other obligations imposed in respect of such terms or interests.

(5) Nothing in this Act affects the rule of law that a legal term, whether or not being a mortgage term, may be created to take effect in reversion expectant on a longer term, which rule is hereby confirmed.

(6) Any lease or underlease, at a rent, or in consideration of a fine, for life or lives or for any term of years determinable with life or lives, or on the marriage of the lessee or on the formation of a civil partnership between the lessee and another person, or any contract therefor, made before or after the commencement of this Act, or created by virtue of Part V of the Law of Property Act 1922, shall take effect as a lease, underlease or contract therefor, for a term of ninety years determinable after (as the case may be) the death or marriage of, or the formation of a civil partnership by, the original lessee or the survivor of the original lessees, by at least one month's notice in writing given to determine the same on one of the quarter days applicable to the tenancy, either by the lessor or the persons deriving title under him, to the person entitled to the leasehold interest, or if no such person is in existence by affixing the same to the premises, or by the lessee or other persons

in whom the leasehold interest is vested to the lessor or the persons deriving title under him: Provided that –

(a) this subsection shall not apply to any term taking effect in equity under a settlement or created out of an equitable interest under a settlement for mortgage, indemnity, or other like purposes;

(b) the person in whom the leasehold interest is vested by virtue of Part V of the Law of Property Act 1922 shall, for the purposes of this subsection, be deemed an original lessee;

(c) if the lease, underlease, or contract therefor is made determinable on the dropping of the lives of persons other than or besides the lessees, then the notice shall be capable of being served after the death of any person or of the survivor of any persons (whether or not including the lessees) on the cesser of whose life or lives the lease, underlease, or contract is made determinable, instead of after the death of the original lessee or of the survivor of the original lessees;

(d) if there are no quarter days specially applicable to the tenancy, notice may be given to determine the tenancy on one of the usual quarter days.

(7) Subsection (8) applies where a lease, underlease or contract –

(a) relates to commonhold land, and

(b) would take effect by virtue of subsection (6) as a lease, underlease or contract of the kind mentioned in that subsection.

(8) The lease, underlease or contract shall be treated as if it purported to be a lease, underlease or contract of the kind referred to in subsection (7)(b) (and sections 17 and 18 of the Commonhold and Leasehold Reform Act 2002 (residential and non-residential leases) shall apply accordingly).

150 Surrender of a lease, without prejudice to underleases with a view to the grant of a new lease

(1) A lease may be surrendered with a view to the acceptance of a new lease in place thereof, without a surrender of any under-lease derived thereout.

(2) A new lease may be granted and accepted, in place of any lease so surrendered, without any such surrender of an under-lease as aforesaid, and the new lease operates as if all under-leases derived out of the surrendered lease had been surrendered before the surrender of that lease was effected.

(3) The lessee under the new lease and any person deriving title under him is entitled to the same rights and remedies in respect of the rent reserved by and the covenants, agreements and conditions contained in any under-lease as if the original lease had not been surrendered but was or remained vested in him.

(4) Each under-lessee and any person deriving title under him is entitled to hold and enjoy the land comprised in his under-lease (subject to the payment of any rent reserved by and to the observance of the covenants agreements and conditions

contained in the under-lease) as if the lease out of which the under-lease was derived had not been surrendered.

(5) The lessor granting the new lease and any person deriving title under him is entitled to the same remedies, by distress or entry in and upon the land comprised in any such under-lease for rent reserved by or for breach of any covenant, agreement or condition contained in the new lease (so far only as the rents reserved by or the covenants, agreements or conditions contained in the new lease do not exceed or impose greater burdens than those reserved by or contained in the original lease out of which the under-lease is derived) as he would have had –

(a) If the original lease had remained on foot; or

(b) If a new under-lease derived out of the new lease had been granted to the under-lessee or a person deriving title under him;

as the case may require.

(6) This section does not affect the powers of the court to give relief against forfeiture.

152 Leases invalidated by reason of non-compliance with terms of powers under which they are granted

(1) Where in the intended exercise of any power of leasing, whether conferred by an Act of Parliament or any other instrument, a lease (in this section referred to as an invalid lease) is granted, which by reason of any failure to comply with the terms of the power is invalid, then –

(a) as against the person entitled after the determination of the interest of the grantor to the reversion; or

(b) as against any other person who, subject to any lease properly granted under the power, would have been entitled to the land comprised in the lease;

the lease, if it was made in good faith, and the lessee has entered thereunder, shall take effect in equity as a contract for the grant, at the request of the lessee, of a valid lease under the power, of like effect as the invalid lease, subject to such variations as may be necessary in order to comply with the terms of the power: Provided that a lessee under an invalid lease shall not, by virtue of any such implied contract, be entitled to obtain a variation of the lease if the other persons who would have been bound by the contract are willing and able to confirm the lease without variation.

(2) Where a lease granted in the intended exercise of such a power is invalid by reason of the grantor not having power to grant the lease at the date thereof, but the grantor's interest in the land comprised therein continues after the time when he might, in the exercise of the power, have properly granted a lease in the like terms, the lease shall take effect as a valid lease in like manner as if it had been granted at that time.

(3) Where during the continuance of the possession taken under an invalid lease the person for the time being entitled, subject to such possession, to the land comprised

therein or to the rents and profits thereof, is able to confirm the lease without variation, the lessee, or other person who would have been bound by the lease had it been valid, shall, at the request of the person so able to confirm the lease, be bound to accept a confirmation thereof, and thereupon the lease shall have effect and be deemed to have had effect as a valid lease from the grant thereof. Confirmation under this subsection may be by a memorandum in writing signed by or on behalf of the persons respectively confirming and accepting the confirmation of the lease.

(4) Where a receipt or a memorandum in writing confirming an invalid lease is, upon or before the acceptance of rent thereunder, signed by or on behalf of the person accepting the rent, that acceptance shall, as against that person, be deemed to be a confirmation of the lease.

(5) The foregoing provisions of this section do not affect prejudicially –

(a) any right of action or other right or remedy to which, but for those provisions or any enactment replaced by those provisions, the lessee named in an invalid lease would or might have been entitled under any covenant on the part of the grantor for title or quiet enjoyment contained therein or implied thereby; or

(b) any right of re-entry or other right or remedy to which, but for those provisions or any enactment replaced thereby, the grantor or other person for the time being entitled to the reversion expectant on the termination of the lease, would or might have been entitled by reason of any breach of the covenants, conditions or provisions contained in the lease and binding on the lessee.

(6) Where a valid power of leasing is vested in or may be exercised by a person who grants a lease which, by reason of the determination of the interest of the grantor or otherwise, cannot have effect and continuance according to the terms thereof independently of the power, the lease shall for the purposes of this section be deemed to have been granted in the intended exercise of the power although the power is not referred to in the lease.

(7) This section does not apply to a lease of land held on charitable, ecclesiastical or public trusts.

(8) This section takes effect without prejudice to the provision in this Act for the grant of leases in the name and on behalf of the estate owner of the land affected.

153 Enlargement of residue of long terms into fee simple estates

(1) Where a residue unexpired of not less than two hundred years of a term, which, as originally created, was for not less than three hundred years, is subsisting in land, whether being the whole land originally comprised in the term, or part only thereof, –

(a) without any trust or right of redemption affecting the term in favour of the freeholder, or other person entitled in reversion expectant on the term; and

(b) without any rent, or with merely a peppercorn rent or other rent having no money value, incident to the reversion, or having had a rent, not being merely a peppercorn rent or other rent having no money value, originally so incident, which subsequently has been released or has become barred by lapse of time, or has in any other way ceased to be payable;

the term may be enlarged into a fee simple in the manner, and subject to the restrictions in this section provided.

(2) This section applies to and includes every such term as aforesaid whenever created, whether or not having the freehold as the immediate reversion thereon; but does not apply to –

(i) Any term liable to be determined by re-entry for condition broken; or

(ii) Any term created by subdemise out of a superior term, itself incapable of being enlarged into fee simple.

(3) This section extends to mortgage terms, where the right of redemption is barred.

(4) A rent not exceeding the yearly sum of one pound which has not been collected or paid for a continuous period of twenty years or upwards shall, for the purposes of this section, be deemed to have ceased to be payable.

(5) Where a rent incident to a reversion expectant on a term to which this section applies is deemed to have ceased to be payable for the purposes aforesaid, no claim for such rent or for any arrears thereof shall be capable of being enforced.

(6) Each of the following persons, namely –

(i) Any person beneficially entitled in right of the term, whether subject to any incumbrance or not, to possession of any land comprised in the term, and, in the case of a married woman without the concurrence of her husband, whether or not she is entitled for her separate use or as her separate property;

(ii) Any person being in receipt of income as trustee, in right of the term, or having the term vested in him as a trustee of land, whether subject to any incumbrance or not;

(iii) Any person in whom, as personal representative of any deceased person, the term is vested, whether subject to any incumbrance or not;

shall, so far as regards the land to which he is entitled, or in which he is interested in right of the term, in any such character as aforesaid, have power by deed to declare to the effect that, from and after the execution of the deed, the term shall be enlarged into a fee simple.

(7) Thereupon, by virtue of the deed and of this Act, the term shall become and be enlarged accordingly, and the person in whom the term was previously vested shall acquire and have in the land a fee simple instead of the term.

(8) The estate in fee simple so acquired by enlargement shall be subject to all the same trusts, powers, executory limitations over, rights, and equities, and to all the same covenants and provisions relating to user and enjoyment, and to all the same obligations of every kind, as the term would have been subject to if it had not been so enlarged.

(9) But where –

(a) any land so held for the residue of a term has been settled in trust by reference to other land, being freehold land, so as to go along with that other land, or, in the case of settlements coming into operation before the commencement of this Act, so as to go along with that other land as far as the law permits; and

(b) at the time of enlargement, the ultimate beneficial interest in the term, whether subject to any subsisting particular estate or not, has not become absolutely and indefeasibly vested in any person, free from charges or powers of charging created by a settlement;

the estate in fee simple acquired as aforesaid shall, without prejudice to any conveyance for value previously made by a person having a contingent or defeasible interest in the term, be liable to be, and shall be, conveyed by means of a subsidiary vesting instrument and settled in like manner as the other land, being freehold land, aforesaid, and until so conveyed and settled shall devolve beneficially as if it had been so conveyed and settled.

(10) The estate in fee simple so acquired shall, whether the term was originally created without impeachment of waste or not, include the fee simple in all mines and minerals which at the time of enlargement have not been severed in right or in fact, or have not been severed or reserved by an inclosure Act or award.

154 Application of Part V to existing leases

This part of this Act, except where otherwise expressly provided, applies to leases created before or after the commencement of this Act, and 'lease' includes an under-lease or other tenancy.

PART VI

POWERS

155 Release of powers simply collateral

A person to whom any power, whether coupled with an interest or not, is given may by deed release, or contract not to exercise, the power.

156 Disclaimer of power

(1) A person to whom any power, whether coupled with an interest or not, is given may by deed disclaim the power, and, after disclaimer, shall not be capable of exercising or joining in the exercise of the power.

(2) On such disclaimer, the power may be exercised by the other person or persons or the survivor or survivors of the other persons, to whom the power is given, unless the contrary is expressed in the instrument creating the power.

157 Protection of purchasers claiming under certain void appointments

(1) An instrument purporting to exercise a power of appointment over property, which, in default of and subject to any appointment, is held in trust for the class or number of persons of whom the appointee is one, shall not (save as hereinafter provided) be void on the ground of fraud on the power as against a purchaser in good faith: Provided that, if the interest appointed exceeds, in amount or value, the interest in such property to which immediately before the execution of the instrument the appointee was presumptively entitled under the trust in default of appointment, having regard to any advances made in his favour and to any hotchpot provision, the protection afforded by this section to a purchaser shall not extend to such excess.

(2) In this section 'a purchaser in good faith' means a person dealing with an appointee of the age of not less than twenty-five years for valuable consideration in money or money's worth, and without notice of the fraud, or of any circumstances from which, if reasonable inquiries had been made, the fraud might have been discovered.

(3) Persons deriving title under any purchaser entitled to the benefit of this section shall be entitled to the like benefit ...

158 Validation of appointments where objects are excluded or take illusory shares

(1) No appointment made in exercise of any power to appoint any property among two or more objects shall be invalid on the ground that –

(a) an unsubstantial, illusory, or nominal share only is appointed to or left unappointed to devolve upon any one or more of the objects of the power; or

(b) any object of the power is thereby altogether excluded;

but every such appointment shall be valid notwithstanding that any one or more of the objects is not thereby, or in default of appointment, to take any share in the property.

(2) This section does not affect any provision in the instrument creating the power which declares the amount of any share from which any object of the power is not to be excluded ...

159 Execution of powers not testamentary

(1) A deed executed in the presence of and attested by two or more witnesses (in the manner in which deeds are ordinarily executed and attested) is so far as respects the execution and attestation thereof, a valid execution of a power of appointment by deed or by any instrument in writing, not testamentary, notwithstanding that it is expressly required that a deed or instrument in writing, made in exercise of the power, is to be executed or attested with some additional or other form of execution or attestation or solemnity.

(2) This section does not operate to defeat any direction in the instrument creating the power that –

(a) the consent of any particular person is to be necessary to a valid execution;

(b) in order to give validity to any appointment, any act is to be performed having no relation to the mode of executing and attesting the instrument.

(3) This section does not prevent the donee of a power from executing it in accordance with the power by writing, or otherwise than by an instrument executed and attested as a deed; and where a power is so executed this section does not apply ...

PART VII

PERPETUITIES AND ACCUMULATIONS

161 Abolition of the double possibility rule

(1) The rule of law prohibiting the limitation, after a life interest to an unborn person, of an interest in land to the unborn child or other issue of an unborn person is hereby abolished, but without prejudice to any other rule relating to perpetuities.

(2) This section only applies to limitations or trusts created by an instrument coming into operation after the commencement of this Act.

162 Restrictions on the perpetuity rule

(1) For removing doubts, it is hereby declared that the rule of law relating to perpetuities does not apply and shall be deemed never to have applied –

(a) To any power to distrain on or to take possession of land or the income thereof given by way of indemnity against a rent, whether charged upon or payable in respect of any part of that land or not; or

(b) To any rentcharge created only as an indemnity against another rentcharge, although the indemnity rentcharge may only arise or become payable on breach of a condition or stipulation; or

(c) To any power, whether exercisable on breach of a condition or stipulation or not, to retain or withhold payment of any instalment of a rentcharge as an indemnity against another rentcharge; or

(d) To any grant, exception, or reservation of any right of entry on, or user of, the surface of land or of any easements, rights, or privileges over or under land for the purpose of –

(i) winning, working, inspecting, measuring, converting, manufacturing, carrying away, and disposing of mines and minerals;

(ii) inspecting, grubbing up, felling and carrying away timber and other trees, and the tops and lops thereof;

(iii) executing repairs, alterations, or additions to any adjoining land, or the buildings and erections thereon;

(iv) constructing, laying down, altering, repairing, renewing, cleansing, and maintaining sewers, watercourses, cesspools, gutters, drains, water-pipes, gas-pipes, electric wires or cables or other like works.

(2) This section applies to instruments coming into operation before or after the commencement of this Act.

164 General restrictions on accumulation of income

(1) No person may by any instrument or otherwise settle or dispose of any property in such manner that the income thereof shall, save as hereinafter mentioned, be wholly or partially accumulated for any longer period than one of the following, namely –

(a) the life of the grantor or settlor; or

(b) a term of twenty-one years from the death of the grantor, settlor or testator; or

(c) the duration of the minority or respective minorities of any person or persons living or en ventre sa mère at the death of the grantor, settlor or testator; or

(d) the duration of the minority or respective minorities only of any person or persons who under the limitations of the instrument directing the accumulations would, for the time being, if of full age, be entitled to the income directed to be accumulated.

In every case where any accumulation is directed otherwise than as aforesaid, the direction shall (save as hereinafter mentioned) be void; and the income of the property directed to be accumulated shall, so long as the same is directed to be accumulated contrary to this section, go to and be received by the person or persons who would have been entitled thereto if such accumulation had not been directed.

(2) This section does not extend to any provision –

(i) for payment of the debts of any grantor, settlor, testator or other person;

(ii) for raising portions for –

(a) any child, children or remoter issue of any grantor, settlor or testator; or

(b) any child, children or remoter issue of a person taking any interest under any settlement or other disposition directing the accumulations or to whom any interest is thereby limited;

(iii) respecting the accumulation of the produce of timber or wood;

and accordingly such provisions may be made as if no statutory restrictions on accumulation of income had been imposed.

(3) The restrictions imposed by this section apply to instruments made on or after the twenty-eighth day of July, eighteen hundred, but in the case of wills only where the testator was living and of testamentary capacity after the end of one year from that date.

165 Qualification of restrictions on accumulation

Where accumulations of surplus income are made during a minority under any statutory power or under the general law, the period for which such accumulations are made is not (whether the trust was created or the accumulations were made before or after the commencement of this Act) to be taken into account in determining the periods for which accumulations are permitted to be made by the last preceding section, and accordingly an express trust for accumulation for any other permitted period shall not be deemed to have been invalidated or become invalid, by reason of accumulations also having been made as aforesaid during such minority.

166 Restriction on accumulation for the purchase of land

(1) No person may settle or dispose of any property in such manner that the income thereof shall be wholly or partially accumulated for the purchase of land only, for any longer period than the duration of the minority or respective minorities of any person or persons who, under the limitations of the instrument directing the accumulation, would for the time being, if of full age, be entitled to the income so directed to be accumulated.

(2) This section does not, nor do the enactments which it replaces, apply to accumulations to be held as capital money for the purposes of the Settled Land Act 1925, or the enactments replaced by that Act, whether or not the accumulations are primarily liable to be laid out in the purchase of land.

(3) This section applies to settlements and dispositions made after the twenty-seventh day of June eighteen hundred and ninety-two.

PART IX

VOIDABLE DISPOSITIONS

173 Voluntary disposition of land how far voidable as against purchasers

(1) Every voluntary disposition of land made with intent to defraud a subsequent purchaser is voidable at the instance of that purchaser.

(2) For the purposes of this section, no voluntary disposition, whenever made, shall be deemed to have been made with intent to defraud by reason only that a subsequent conveyance for valuable consideration was made, if such subsequent conveyance was made after the twenty-eighth day of June, eighteen hundred and ninety-three.

174 Acquisitions of reversions at an under value

(1) No acquisition made in good faith, without fraud or unfair dealing, of any reversionary interest in real or personal property, for money or money's worth, shall

be liable to be opened or set aside merely on the ground of under value. In this subsection 'reversionary interest' includes an expectancy or possibility.

(2) This section does not affect the jurisdiction of the court to set aside or modify unconscionable bargains.

PART XI

MISCELLANEOUS

184 Presumption of survivorship in regard to claims to property

In all cases where, after the commencement of this Act, two or more persons have died in circumstances rendering it uncertain which of them survived the other or others, such deaths shall (subject to any order of the court), for all purposes affecting the title to property, be presumed to have occurred in order of seniority, and accordingly the younger shall be deemed to have survived the elder.

185 Merger

There is no merger by operation of law only of any estate the beneficial interest in which would not be deemed to be merged or extinguished in equity.

186 Rights of pre-emption capable of release

All statutory and other rights of pre-emption affecting a legal estate shall be and be deemed always to have been capable of release, and unless released shall remain in force as equitable interests only.

187 Legal easements

(1) Where an easement, right or privilege for a legal estate is created, it shall enure for the benefit of the land to which it is intended to be annexed.

(2) Nothing in this Act affects the right of a person to acquire, hold or exercise an easement, right or privilege over or in relation to land for a legal estate in common with any other person, or the power of creating or conveying such an easement right or privilege.

193 Rights of the public over commons and waste lands

(1) Members of the public shall, subject as hereinafter provided, have rights of access for air and exercise to any land which is a metropolitan common within the meaning of the Metropolitan Commons Acts 1866 to 1898, or manorial waste, or a common, which is wholly or partly situated within an area which immediately before 1st April 1974 was a borough or urban district, and to any land which at the commencement of this Act is subject to rights of common and to which this section may from time to time be applied in manner hereinafter provided: Provided that –

(a) such rights of access shall be subject to any Act, scheme, or provisional order for the regulation of the land, and to any byelaw, regulation or order made thereunder or under any statutory authority; and

(b) the Minister shall, on the application of any person entitled as lord of the manor or otherwise to the soil of the land, or entitled to any commonable rights affecting the land, impose such limitations on and conditions as to the exercise of the rights of access or as to the extent of the land to be affected as, in the opinion of the Minister, are necessary or desirable for preventing any estate, right or interest of a profitable or beneficial nature in, over, or affecting the land from being injuriously affected, for conserving flora, fauna or geological or physiographical features of the land, or for protecting any object of historical interest and, where any such limitations or conditions are so imposed, the rights of access shall be subject thereto; and

(c) such rights of access shall not include any right to draw or drive upon the land a carriage, cart, caravan, truck, or other vehicle, or to camp or light any fire thereon; and

(d) the rights of access shall cease to apply –

(i) to any land over which the commonable rights are extinguished under any statutory provision;

(ii) to any land over which the commonable rights are otherwise extinguished if the council of the county, county borough or metropolitan district in which the land is situated by resolution assent to its exclusion from the operation of this section, and the resolution is approved by the Minister.

(3) Where limitations or conditions are imposed by the Minister under this section, they shall be published by such person and in such manner as the Minister may direct.

(4) Any person who, without lawful authority, draws or drives upon any land to which this section applies any carriage, cart, caravan, truck, or other vehicle, or camps or lights any fire thereon, or who fails to observe any limitation or condition imposed by the Minister under this section in respect of any such land, shall be liable on summary conviction to a fine ... for each offence.

(5) Nothing in this section shall prejudice or affect the right of any person to get and remove mines or minerals or to let down the surface of the manorial waste or common.

(6) This section does not apply to any common or manorial waste which is for the time being held for Naval, Military or Air Force purposes and in respect of which rights of common have been extinguished or cannot be exercised.

194 Restrictions on inclosure of commons

(1) The erection of any building or fence, or the construction of any other work, whereby access to land to which this section applies is prevented or impeded, shall not be lawful unless the consent of the Minister thereto is obtained, and in giving or withholding his consent the Minister shall have regard to the same considerations

and shall, if necessary, hold the same inquiries as are directed by the Commons Act 1876 to be taken into consideration and held by the Minister before forming an opinion whether an application under the Inclosure Acts 1845 to 1882 shall be acceded to or not.

(2) Where any building or fence is erected, or any other work constructed without such consent as is required by this section, the county court within whose jurisdiction the land is situated, shall, on an application being made by the council of any county or county borough or district concerned, or by the lord of the manor or any other person interested in the common, have power to make an order for the removal of the work, and the restoration of the land to the condition in which it was before the work was erected or constructed, but any such order shall be subject to the like appeal as an order made under section thirty of the Commons Act 1876.

(3) This section applies to any land which at the commencement of this Act is subject to rights of common: provided that this section shall cease to apply –

(a) to any land over which the rights of common are extinguished under any statutory provision;

(b) to any land over which the rights of common are otherwise extinguished, if the council of the county, county borough or metropolitan district in which the land is situated by resolution assent to its exclusion from the operation of this section and the resolution is approved by the Minister.

(4) This section does not apply to any building or fence erected or work constructed if specially authorised by Act of Parliament, or in pursuance of an Act of Parliament or Order having the force of an Act, or if lawfully erected or constructed in connexion with the taking or working of minerals in or under any land to which the section is otherwise applicable, or to any electronic communications apparatus installed for the purposes of an electronic communications code network.

198   Registration ... to be notice

(1) The registration of any instrument or matter in any register kept under the Land Charges Act 1972 or any local land charges register shall be deemed to constitute actual notice of such instrument or matter, and if the fact of such registration, to all persons and for all purposes connected with the land affected, as from the date of registration or other prescribed date and so long as the registration continues in force.

(2) This section operates without prejudice to the provisions of this Act respecting the making of further advances by a mortgagee, and applies only to instruments and matters required or authorised to be registered in any such register.

199   Restrictions on constructive notice

(1) A purchaser shall not be prejudicially affected by notice of –

(i) any instrument or matter capable of registration under the provisions of the Land Charges Act 1925, or any enactment which it replaces, which is void or not enforceable as against him under that Act or enactment, by reason of the non-registration thereof;

(ii) any other instrument or matter or any fact or thing unless –

(a) it is within his own knowledge, or would have come to his knowledge if such inquiries and inspections had been made as ought reasonably to have been made by him; or

(b) in the same transaction with respect to which a question of notice to the purchaser arises, it has come to the knowledge of his counsel, as such, or of his solicitor or other agent, as such, or would have come to the knowledge of his solicitor or other agent, as such, if such inquiries and inspections had been made as ought reasonably to have been made by the solicitor or other agent.

(2) Paragraph (ii) of the last subsection shall not exempt a purchaser from any liability under, or any obligation to perform or observe, any covenant, condition, provision, or restriction contained in any instrument under which his title is derived, mediately or immediately; and such liability or obligation may be enforced in the same manner and to the same extent as if that paragraph had not been enacted.

(3) A purchaser shall not by reason of anything in this section be affected by notice in any case where he would not have been so affected if this section had not been enacted.

(4) This section applies to purchases made either before or after the commencement of this Act.

200 Notice of restrictive covenants and easements

(1) Where land having a common title with other land is disposed of to a purchaser (other than a lessee or a mortgagee) who does not hold or obtain possession of the documents forming the common title, such purchaser, notwithstanding any stipulation to the contrary, may require that a memorandum giving notice of any provision contained in the disposition to him restrictive of user of, or giving rights over, any other land comprised in the common title, shall, where practicable, be written or indorsed on, or, where impracticable, be permanently annexed to some one document selected by the purchaser but retained in the possession or power of the person who makes the disposition, and being or forming part of the common title.

(2) The title of any person omitting to require an indorsement to be made or a memorandum to be annexed shall not, by reason only of this enactment, be prejudiced or affected by the omission.

(3) This section does not apply to dispositions of registered land.

(4) Nothing in this section affects the obligation to register a land charge in respect of –

(a) any restrictive covenant or agreement affecting freehold land; or

(b) any estate contract; or

(c) any equitable easement, liberty or privilege.

PART XII

CONSTRUCTION, JURISDICTION, AND GENERAL PROVISIONS

201 Provisions of Act to apply to incorporeal hereditaments

(1) The provisions of this Act relating to freehold land apply to manors, reputed manors, lordships, advowsons, perpetual rentcharges, and other incorporeal hereditaments, subject only to the qualifications necessarily arising by reason of the inherent nature of the hereditament affected.

(2) This Act does not affect the special restrictions imposed on dealings with advowsons by the Benefices Act 1898, or any other statute or measure, nor affect the limitation of, or authorise any dispositions to be made of, a title or dignity of honour which in its nature is inalienable.

205 General definitions

(1) In this Act unless the context otherwise requires, the following expressions have the meanings hereby assigned to them respectively, that is to say –

...

(ii) 'Conveyance' includes a mortgage, charge, lease, assent, vesting declaration, vesting instrument, disclaimer, release and every other assurance of property or of an interest therein by any instrument, except a will; 'convey' has a corresponding meaning; and 'disposition' includes a conveyance and also a devise, bequest, or an appointment of property contained in a will; and 'dispose of' has a corresponding meaning;

(iii) 'Building purposes' include the erecting and improving of, and the adding to, and the repairing of buildings; and a 'building lease' is a lease for building purposes or purposes connected therewith;

(iv) 'Death duty' means estate duty and every other duty leviable or payable on a death;

(v) 'Estate owner' means the owner of a legal estate, but an infant is not capable of being an estate owner;

(vi) 'Gazette' means the London Gazette;

(vii) 'Incumbrance' includes a legal or equitable mortgage and a trust for securing money, and a lien, and a charge of a portion, annuity, or other capital or annual sum; and 'incumbrancer' has a meaning corresponding with that of incumbrance, and includes every person entitled to the benefit of an incumbrance, or to require payment or discharge thereof;

(viii) 'Instrument' does not include a statute, unless the statute creates a settlement;

(ix) 'Land' includes land of any tenure, and mines and minerals, whether or not held apart from the surface, buildings or parts of buildings (whether the division is horizontal, vertical or made in any other way) and other corporeal hereditaments; also a manor, an advowson, and a rent and other incorporeal hereditaments, and an easement, right, privilege, or benefit in, over, or derived from land; and 'mines and minerals' include any strata or seam of minerals or substances in or under any land, and powers of working and getting the same; and 'manor' includes a lordship, and reputed manor or lordship; and 'hereditament' means any real property which on an intestacy occurring before the commencement of this Act might have devolved upon an heir;

(x) 'Legal estates' mean the estate, interests and charges, in or over land (subsisting or created at law) which are by this Act authorised to subsist or to be created as legal estates; 'equitable interests' mean all the other interests and charges in or over land; an equitable interest 'capable of subsisting as a legal estate' means such as could validly subsist or be created as a legal estate under this Act;

(xi) 'Legal powers' include the powers vested in a chargee by way of legal mortgage or in an estate owner under which a legal estate can be transferred or created; and 'equitable powers' mean all the powers in or over land under which equitable interests or powers only can be transferred or created;

(xii) 'Limitation Acts' mean the Real Property Limitation Acts 1833, 1837 and 1874, and 'limitation' includes a trust;

(xiii) 'Mental disorder' has the meaning assigned to it by section 1 of the Mental Health Act 1983 and 'receiver' in relation to a person suffering from mental disorder, means a receiver appointed for that person under Part VIII of the Mental Health Act 1959 or Part VII of the said Act of 1983;

(xiv) A 'mining lease' means a lease for mining purposes, that is, the searching for, winning, working, getting, making merchantable, carrying away, or disposing of mines and minerals, or purposes connected therewith, and includes a grant or licence for mining purposes;

(xv) 'Minister' means the Minister of Agriculture, Fisheries and Food;

(xvi) 'Mortgage' includes any charge or lien on any property for securing money or money's worth; 'legal mortgage' means a mortgage by demise or subdemise or a charge by way of legal mortgage and 'legal mortgagee' has a corresponding meaning; 'mortgage money' means money or money's worth secured by a mortgage; 'mortgagor' includes any person from time to time deriving title under the original mortgagor or entitled to redeem a mortgage according to his estate interest or right in the mortgaged property; 'mortgagee' includes a chargee by way of legal mortgage and any person from time to time deriving title under the original mortgagee; and 'mortgagee in possession' is, for the purposes of this Act, a mortgagee who, in right of the mortgage, has entered into and is in possession of the mortgaged property; and 'right of redemption' includes an option to repurchase only if the option in effect creates a right of redemption;

(xvii) 'Notice' includes constructive notice;

(xviii) 'Personal representative' means the executor, original or by representation, or administrator for the time being of a deceased person, and as regards any liability for the payment of death duties includes any person who takes possession of or intermeddles with the property of a deceased person without the authority of the personal representatives or the court;

(xix) 'Possession' includes receipts of rents and profits or the right to receive the same, if any; and 'income' includes rents and profits;

(xx) 'Property' includes any thing in action, and any interest in real or personal property;

(xxi) 'Purchaser' means a purchaser in good faith for valuable consideration and includes a lessee, mortgagee or other person who for valuable consideration acquires an interest in property except that in Part I of this Act and elsewhere where so expressly provided 'purchaser' only means a person who acquires an interest in or charge on property for money or money's worth; and in reference to a legal estate includes a chargee by way of legal mortgage; and where the context so requires 'purchaser' includes an intending purchaser; 'purchase' has a meaning corresponding with that of 'purchaser'; and 'valuable consideration' includes marriage, and the formation of a civil partnership, but does not include a nominal consideration in money;

(xxii) 'Registered land' has the same meaning as in the Land Registration Act 2002;

(xxiii) 'Rent' includes a rent service or a rentcharge, or other rent, toll, duty, royalty, or annual or periodical payment in money or money's worth, reserved or issuing out of or charged upon land, but does not include mortgage interest; 'rentcharge' includes a fee farm rent; 'fine' includes a premium or foregift and any payment, consideration, or benefit in the nature of a fine, premium or foregift; 'lessor' includes an underlessor and a person deriving title under a lessor or underlessor; and 'lessee' includes an underlessee and a person deriving title under a lessee or underlessee, and 'lease' includes an underlease or other tenancy;

(xxiv) 'Sale' includes an extinguishment of manorial incidents, but in other respects means a sale properly so called;

(xxv) 'Securities' include stocks, funds and shares;

(xxvi) 'Tenant for life', 'statutory owner', 'settled land', 'settlement', 'vesting deed', 'subsidiary vesting deed', 'vesting order', 'vesting instrument', 'trust instrument', 'capital money', and 'trustees of the settlement' have the same meaning as in the Settled Land Act 1925;

(xxvii) 'Term of years absolute' means a term of years (taking effect either in possession or in reversion whether or not at a rent) with or without impeachment for waste, subject or not to another legal estate, and either certain or liable to determination by notice, re-entry, operation of law, or by a provision for cesser on redemption, or in any other event (other than the dropping of a life, or the determination of a determinable life interest); but does not include any term of years determinable with life or lives or with the cesser of a determinable life interest, nor, if created after the commencement of this Act, a term of years which is not expressed to take effect in possession within twenty-one years after the creation thereof where required by this Act to take effect within that period; and in this definition the expression 'term of years' includes a term for less than a year, or for a year or years and a fraction of a year or from year to year;

(xxviii) 'Trust Corporation' means the Public Trustee or a corporation either appointed by the court in any particular case to be a trustee or entitled by rules made under subsection (3) of section four of the Public Trustee Act 1906 to act as custodian trustee;

(xxix) 'Trust for sale', in relation to land, means an immediate trust for sale, whether or not exercisable at the request or with the consent of any person; 'trustees for sale' mean the persons (including a personal representative) holding land on trust for sale;

(xxx) 'United Kingdom' means Great Britain and Northern Ireland;

(xxxi) 'Will' includes codicil.

(1A) Any reference in this Act to money being paid into court shall be construed as referring to the money being paid into the Supreme Court or any other court that has jurisdiction, and any reference in this Act to the court, in a context referring to the investment or application of money paid into court, shall be construed, in the case of money paid into the Supreme Court, as referring to the High Court, and in the case of money paid into another court, as referring to that other court.

(2) Where an equitable interest in or power over property arises by statute or operation of law, references to the creation of an interest or power include references to any interest or power so arising.

(3) References to registration under the Land Charges Act 1925 apply to any registration made under any other statute which is by the Land Charges Act 1925 to have effect as if the registration had been made under that Act.

FIRST SCHEDULE

TRANSITIONAL PROVISIONS

PART I

CONVERSION OF CERTAIN EXISTING LEGAL ESTATES INTO EQUITABLE INTERESTS

All estates, interests and charges in or over land, including fees determinable whether by limitation or condition, which immediately before the commencement of this Act were estates, interests or charges, subsisting at law, or capable of taking effect as such, but which by virtue of Part I of this Act are not capable of taking effect as legal estates, shall as from the commencement of this Act be converted into equitable interests, and shall not fail by reason of being so converted into equitable interests either in the land or in the proceeds of sale thereof, nor shall the priority of any such estate, charge or interest over other equitable interests be affected ...

PART III

PROVISIONS AS TO LEGAL ESTATE VESTED IN INFANT

1. Where immediately before the commencement of this Act a legal estate in land is vested in one or more infants beneficially, or where immediately after the commencement of this Act a legal estate in land would by virtue of this Act have become vested in one or more infants beneficially if he or they had been of full age, the legal estate shall vest in the manner provided by the Settled Land Act 1925 ...

PART V

PROVISIONS AS TO PARTY STRUCTURES AND OPEN SPACES

1. Where, immediately before the commencement of this Act, a party wall or other party structure is held in undivided shares, the ownership thereof shall be deemed to be severed vertically as between the respective owners, and the owner of each part shall have such rights to support and of user over the rest of the structure as may be requisite for conferring rights corresponding to those subsisting at the commencement of this Act ...

SECOND SCHEDULE

IMPLIED COVENANTS

PART VIII

COVENANT IMPLIED IN A CONVEYANCE FOR VALUABLE CONSIDERATION, OTHER THAN A MORTGAGE, OR PART OF LAND AFFECTED BY A RENTCHARGE, SUBJECT TO A PART (NOT LEGALLY APPORTIONED) OF THAT RENTCHARGE

(i) That the grantees, or the persons deriving title under them, will at all times, from the date of the conveyance or other date therein stated, pay the apportioned rent and observe and perform all the covenants (other than the covenant to pay the entire rent) and conditions contained in the deed or other document creating the rentcharge, so far as the same relate to the land conveyed:

And also will at all times, from the date aforesaid, save harmless and keep indemnified the conveyancing parties and their respective estates and effects, from and against all proceedings, costs, claims and expenses on account of any omission to pay the said apportioned rent, or any breach of any of the said covenants and conditions, so far as the same relate as aforesaid.

(ii) That the conveyancing parties, or the persons deriving title under them, will at all times, from the date of the conveyance or other date therein stated, pay the balance of the rentcharge (after deducting the apportioned rent aforesaid, and any other rents similarly apportioned in respect of land not retained), and observe and perform all the covenants, other than the covenant to pay the entire rent, and conditions contained in the deed or other document creating the rentcharge, so far as the same relate to the land not included in the conveyance and remaining vested in the covenantors:

And also will at all times, from the date aforesaid, save harmless and keep indemnified the grantees and their estates and effects, from and against all proceedings, costs, claims and expenses on account of any omission to pay the aforesaid balance of the rentcharge, or any breach of any of the said covenants and conditions so far as they relate as aforesaid.

NB Where at the commencement of the Trusts of Land and Appointment of Trustees Act 1996 (ie, at 1 January 1997) any land was held on trust for sale, or on the statutory trusts, by virtue of Schedule 1 to the Law of Property Act 1925 (transitional provisions), it is after that commencement held in trust for the persons interested in the land: 1996 Act, s5, Schedule 2, para 7.

As amended by the Law of Property (Amendment) Act 1926, s7, Schedule; Law of Property (Entailed Interests) Act 1932, s1; Tithe Act 1936, s48(3), Schedule 9; Criminal Justice Act 1948, s83, Schedule 10; Married Women (Restraint upon Anticipation) Act 1949, s1, Schedule 2; Finance Act 1949, s52(9), (10), Schedule 11, Pt IV; Mental Health Act 1959, s149(1), (2), Schedule 7, Pt I, Schedule 8, Pt I; Finance Act 1963, s73(8)(b), Schedule 14, Pt IV; Industrial and Provident Societies Act 1965, s77(1), Schedule 5; Administration of Justice Act 1965, ss17, 18, Schedule 1; Family Law Reform Act 1969, ss1(3), 28(3), Schedule 1; Law of Property Act 1969, s28(1), Schedule 3; Finance Act 1971, s64, Schedule 14, Pt VI; Friendly Societies Act 1971, s14(2), Schedule 3; Land Charges Act 1972, s18, Schedule 3, para 1; Local Government Act 1972, ss189(4), 272(1), Schedule 30; Local Land Charges Act 1975, s17(2), Schedule 1; Civil Aviation Act 1982, s109, Schedule 15, para 1; Mental Health Act 1983, s148, Schedule 4, para 5(a), (b); County Courts Act 1984, s148(1), Schedule 2, Pt II, paras 2, 3(2); Local Government Act 1985, s16, Schedule 8, para 10(5); Insolvency Act 1985, s235(3), Schedule 10, Pt III; Insolvency Act 1986, s439(2), Schedule 14; Reverter of Sites Act 1987, s8(2), (3), Schedule; Law of Property (Miscellaneous Provisions) Act 1989, s1(8), Schedule 1, paras 2, 4; High Court and County Courts Jurisdiction Order 1991, art 2(8), Schedule; Local Government (Wales) Act 1994, s66(6), Schedule 16, para 7; Law of Property (Miscellaneous Provisions) Act 1994, s21(1), Schedule 1, para 1; Agricultural Tenancies Act 1995, s31(1)–(3); Landlord and Tenant (Covenants) Act 1995, s14(a), Schedules 1, 2; Trusts of Land and Appointment of Trustees Act 1996, ss5, 25(1), (2), Schedule 2, paras 1–4, Schedule 3, para 4, Schedule 4; Trustee Delegation Act 1999, s9(1); Countryside and Rights of Way Act 2000, ss46(1)(a), (3), 102, Schedule 4, para 1, Schedule 16, Pt I; Land Registration Act 2002, ss133, 135, Schedule 11, para 2(1), (5)–(11), (13), Schedule 13; Commonhold and Leasehold Reform Act 2002, s68, Schedule 5, paras 2, 3; Communications Act 2003, s406(1), Schedule 17, para 3; Statute Law (Repeals) Act 2004, s1(1), Schedule 1, Pt 12; Civil Partnership Act 2004, ss80, 261(1), Schedule 8, para 1, Schedule 27, para 7.

ADMINISTRATION OF ESTATES ACT 1925
(15 & 16 Geo 5 c 23)

PART I

DEVOLUTION OF REAL ESTATE

1 Devolution of real estate on personal representative

(1) Real estate to which a deceased person was entitled for an interest not ceasing on his death shall on his death, and notwithstanding any testamentary disposition thereof, devolve from time to time on the personal representative of the deceased, in like manner as before the commencement of this Act chattels real devolved on the personal representative from time to time of a deceased person.

(2) The personal representatives for the time being of a deceased person are deemed in law his heirs and assigns within the meaning of all trusts and powers.

(3) The personal representatives shall be the representatives of the deceased in regard to his real estate to which he was entitled for an interest not ceasing on his death as well as in regard to his personal estate.

2 Application to real estate of law affecting chattels real

(1) Subject to the provisions of this Act, all enactments and rules of law, and all jurisdiction of any court with respect to the appointment of administrators or to probate or letters of administration, or to dealings before probate in the case of chattels real, and with respect to costs and other matters in the administration of personal estate, in force before the commencement of this Act, and all powers, duties, rights, equities, obligations, and liabilities of a personal representative in force at the commencement of this Act with respect to chattels real, shall apply and attach to the personal representative and shall have effect with respect to real estate vested in him, and in particular all such powers of disposition and dealing as were before the commencement of this Act exercisable as respects chattels real by the survivor or survivors of two or more personal representatives, as well as by a single personal representative, or as by all the personal representatives together, shall be exercisable by the personal representatives or representative of the deceased with respect to his real estate.

(2) Where as respects real estate there are two or more personal representatives, a conveyance of real estate devolving under this Part of this Act or a contract for such a conveyance shall not be made without the concurrence therein of all such

representatives or an order of the court, but where probate is granted to one or some of two or more persons named as executors, whether or not power is reserved to the other or others to prove, any conveyance of the real estate or contract for such a conveyance may be made by the proving executor or executors for the time being, without an order of the court, and shall be as effectual as if all the persons named as executors had concurred therein.

(3) Without prejudice to the rights and powers of a personal representative, the appointment of a personal representative in regard to real estate shall not, save as hereinafter provide, affect –

(a) any rule as to marshalling or as to administration of assets;

(b) the beneficial interest in real estate under any testamentary disposition;

(c) any mode of dealing with any beneficial interest in real estate, or the proceeds of sale thereof;

(d) the right of any person claiming to be interested in the real estate to take proceedings for the protection or recovery thereof against any person other than the personal representative.

3   Interpretation of Part I

(1) In this Part of this Act 'real estate' includes –

(i) chattels real, and land in possession, remainder, or reversion, and every interest in or over land to which a deceased person was entitled at the time of his death; and

(ii) real estate held on trust (including settled land) or by way of mortgage or security, but not money secured or charged on land.

(2) A testator shall be deemed to have been entitled at his death to any interest in real estate passing under any gift contained in his will which operates as an appointment under a general power to appoint by will, or operates under the testamentary power conferred by statute to dispose of an entailed interest.

(3) An entailed interest of a deceased person shall (unless disposed of under the testamentary power conferred by statute) be deemed an interest ceasing on his death, but any further or other interest of the deceased in the same property in remainder or reversion which is capable of being disposed of by his will shall not be deemed to be an interest so ceasing.

(4) The interest of a deceased person under a joint tenancy where another tenant survives the deceased is an interest ceasing on his death.

9   Vesting of estate in Public Trustee where intestacy of lack of executors

(1) Where a person dies intestate, his real and personal estate shall vest in the Public Trustee until the grant of administration.

(2) Where a testator dies and –

(a) at the time of his death there is no executor with power to obtain probate of the will, or

(b) at any time before probate of the will is granted there ceases to be any executor with power to obtain probate,

the real and personal estate of which he disposes by the will shall vest in the Public Trustee until the grant of representation.

(3) The vesting of real or personal estate in the Public Trustee by virtue of this section does not confer on him any beneficial interest in, or impose on him any duty, obligation or liability in respect of, the property.

33 Trust for sale

(1) On the death of a person intestate as to any real or personal estate, that estate shall be held in trust by his personal representatives with the power to sell it.

(2) The personal representatives shall pay out of –

(a) the ready money of the deceased (so far as not disposed of by his will, if any); and

(b) any net money arising from disposing of any other part of his estate (after payment of costs),

all such funeral, testamentary and administration expenses, debts and other liabilities as are properly payable thereout having regard to the rules of administration contained in this Part of this Act, and out of the residue of the said money the personal representative shall set aside a fund sufficient to provide for any pecuniary legacies bequeathed by the will (if any) of the deceased.

(3) During the minority of any beneficiary or the subsistence of any life interest and pending the distribution of the whole or any part of the estate of the deceased, the personal representatives may invest the residue of the said money, or so much thereof as may not have been distributed under the Trustee Act 2000.

(4) The residue of the said money and any investments for the time being representing the same, and any part of the estate of the deceased which remains unsold and is not required for the administration purposes aforesaid, is in this Act referred to as 'the residuary estate of the intestate'.

(5) The income (including net rents and profits of real estate and chattels real after payment of rates, taxes, rent, costs of insurance, repairs and other outgoings properly attributable to income) of so much of the real and personal estate of the deceased as may not be disposed of by his will, if any, or may not be required for the administration purposes aforesaid, may, however such estate is invested, as from the death of the deceased, be treated and applied as income, and for that purpose any necessary apportionment may be made between tenant for life and remainderman.

(6) Nothing in this section affects the rights of any creditor of the deceased or the rights of the Crown in respect of death duties.

(7) Where the deceased leaves a will, this section has effect subject to the provisions contained in the will.

35 Charges on property of deceased to be paid primarily out of the property charged

(1) Where a person dies possessed of, or entitled to, or, under a general power of appointment (including the statutory power to dispose of entailed interest) by his will disposes of, an interest in property, which at the time of his death is charged with the payment of money, whether by way of legal mortgage, equitable charge or otherwise (including a lien for unpaid purchase money), and the deceased has not by will deed or other document signified a contrary or other intention, the interest so charged shall, as between the different persons claiming through the deceased, be primarily liable for the payment of the charge; and every part of the said interest, according to its value, shall bear a proportionate part of the charge on the whole thereof.

(2) Such contrary or other intention shall not be deemed to be signified –

(a) by a general direction for the payment of debts or of all the debts of the testator out of his personal estate, or his residuary real and personal estate, or his residuary real estate; or

(b) by a charge of debts upon any such estate;

unless such intention is further signified by words expressly or by necessary implication referring to all or some part of the charge.

(3) Nothing in this section affects the right of a person entitled to the charge to obtain payment or satisfaction thereof either out of the other assets of the deceased or otherwise.

36 Effect of assent or conveyance by personal representative

(1) A personal representative may assent to the vesting, in any person who (whether by devise, bequest, devolution, appropriation or otherwise) may be entitled thereto, either beneficially or as a trustee or personal representative, of any estate or interest in real estate to which the testator or intestate was entitled or over which he exercised a general power of appointment by his will, including the statutory power to dispose of entailed interests, and which devolved upon the personal representative.

(2) The assent shall operate to vest in that person the estate or interest to which the assent relates, and, unless a contrary intention appears, the assent shall relate back to the death of the deceased.

(4) An assent to the vesting of a legal estate shall be in writing, signed by the personal representative, and shall name the person in whose favour it is given and shall operate to vest in that person the legal estate to which it relates; and an assent not in writing or not in favour of a named person shall not be effectual to pass a legal estate.

(5) Any person in whose favour an assent or conveyance of a legal estate is made by a personal representative may require that notice of the assent or conveyance be written or endorsed on or permanently annexed to the probate or letters of administration, at the cost of the estate of the deceased, and that the probate or letters of administration be produced, at the like cost, to prove that the notice has been placed thereon or annexed thereto.

(6) A statement in writing by a personal representative that he has not given or made an assent or conveyance in respect of a legal estate, shall, in favour of a purchaser, but without prejudice to any previous disposition made in favour of another purchaser deriving title mediately or immediately under the personal representative, be sufficient evidence that an assent or conveyance has not been given or made in respect of the legal estate to which the statement relates, unless notice of a previous assent or conveyance affecting that estate has been placed on or annexed to the probate or administration.

A conveyance by a personal representative of a legal estate to a purchaser accepted in the faith of such a statement shall (without prejudice as aforesaid and unless notice of a previous assent or conveyance affecting that estate has been placed on or annexed to the probate or administration) operate to transfer or create the legal estate expressed to be conveyed in like manner as if no previous assent or conveyance had been made by the personal representative.

A personal representative making a false statement, in regard to any such matter, shall be liable in like manner as if the statement had been contained in a statutory declaration.

(7) An assent or conveyance by a personal representative in respect of a legal estate shall, in favour of a purchaser, unless notice of a previous assent or conveyance affecting that legal estate has been placed on or annexed to the probate or administration, be taken as sufficient evidence that the person in whose favour the assent or conveyance is given or made is the person entitled to have the legal estate conveyed to him, and upon the proper trusts, if any, but shall not otherwise prejudicially affect the claim of any person rightfully entitled to the estate vested or conveyed or any charge thereon.

(8) A conveyance of a legal estate by a personal representative to a purchaser shall not be invalidated by reason only that the purchaser may have notice that all the debts, liabilities, funeral, and testamentary or administration expenses, duties and legacies of the deceased have been discharged or provided for.

(9) An assent or conveyance given or made by a personal representative shall not, except in favour of a purchaser of a legal estate, prejudice the right of the personal representative or any other person to recover the estate or interest to which the assent or conveyance relates, or to be indemnified out of such estate or interest against any duties, debt or liability to which such estate or interest would have been subject if there had not been any assent or conveyance.

(10) A personal representative may, as a condition of giving an assent or making a conveyance, require security for the discharge of any such duties, debt, or liability,

but shall not be entitled to postpone the giving of an assent merely by reason of the subsistence of any such duties, debt or liability if reasonable arrangements have been made for discharging the same; and an assent may be given subject to any legal estate or charge by way of legal mortgage.

(11) This section shall not operate to impose any stamp duty in respect of an assent, and in this section 'purchaser' means a purchaser for money or money's worth.

(12) This section applies to assents and conveyances made after the commencement of this Act, whether the testator or intestate died before or after such commencement.

PART V

SUPPLEMENTAL

55 Definitions

In this Act, unless the context otherwise requires, the following expressions have the meanings hereby assigned to them respectively, that is to say –

(1) (i) 'Administration' means, with reference to the real and personal estate of a deceased person, letters of administration, whether general or limited, or with the will annexed or otherwise;

(ii) 'Administrator' means a person to whom administration is granted; ...

(v) 'Income' includes rents and profits;

(vi) 'Intestate' includes a person who leaves a will but dies intestate as to some beneficial interest in his real or personal estate;

(via) 'Land' has the same meaning as in the Law of Property Act 1925;

(vii) 'Legal estates' mean the estates' charges and interests in or over land (subsisting or created at law) which are by statute authorised to subsist or to be created at law; and 'equitable interests' mean all other interests and charges in or over land; ...

(ix) 'Pecuniary legacy' includes an annuity, a general legacy, a demonstrative legacy so far as it is not discharged out of the designated property, and any other general direction by a testator for the payment of money, including all death duties free from which any devise, bequest, or payment is made to take effect;

(x) 'Personal chattels' mean carriages, horses, stable furniture and effects (not used for business purposes), motor cars and accessories (not used for business purposes), garden effects, domestic animals, plate, plated articles, linen, china, glass, books, pictures, prints, furniture, jewellery, articles of household or personal use or ornament, musical and scientific instruments and apparatus, wines, liquors and consumable stores, but do not include any chattels used at the death of the intestate for business purposes nor money or securities for money.

(xi) 'Personal representative' means the executor, original or by representation, or administrator for the time being of a deceased person, and as regards any liability for the payment of death duties includes any person who takes possession of or intermeddles with the property of a deceased person without the authority of the personal representatives or the court, and 'executor' includes a person deemed to be appointed executor as respects settled land; ...

(xviii) 'Purchaser' means a lessee, mortgagee or other person who in good faith acquires an interest in property for valuable consideration, also an intending purchaser and 'valuable consideration' includes marriage and formation of a civil partnership, but does not include a nominal consideration in money;

(xix) 'Real estate' save as provided in Part IV of this Act means real estate, including chattels real, which by virtue of Part I of this Act devolves on the personal representative of a deceased person; ...

(xxiv) 'Tenants for life', 'statutory owner', 'settled land', 'settlement', 'trustees of the settlement', 'term of years absolute', 'death duties', and 'legal mortgage', have the same meanings as in the Settled Land Act 1925, and 'entailed interest' and 'charge by way of legal mortgage' have the same meanings as in the Law of Property Act 1925; ...

(xxviii) 'Will' includes codicil.

(2) References to a child or issue living at the death of any person include a child or issue en ventre sa mère at the death.

(3) References to the estate of a deceased person include property over which the deceased exercises a general power of appointment (including the statutory power to dispose of entailed interests) by his will.

As amended by the Law of Property (Miscellaneous Provisions) Act 1994, ss14(1), 16(1), 21(2), Schedule 2; Trusts of Land and Appointment of Trustees Act 1996, ss5, 25(1), Schedule 2, para 5, Schedule 3, para 6, Schedule 4; Trustee Act 2000, s40(1), Schedule 2, Pt II, para 27; Civil Partnership Act 2004, s71, Schedule 4, Pt 2, para 12.

LAW OF PROPERTY (AMENDMENT) ACT 1926
(16 & 17 Geo 5 c 11)

1   Conveyance of legal estates subject to certain interests

(1) Nothing in the Settled Land Act 1925 shall prevent a person on whom the powers of a tenant for life are conferred by paragraph (ix) of subsection (1) of section twenty of that Act from conveying or creating a legal estate subject to a prior interest as if the land had not been settled land.

(2) In any of the following cases, namely –

   (a) where a legal estate has been conveyed or created under subsection one of this section, or under section sixteen of the Settled Land Act 1925, subject to any prior interest, or

   (b) where before the first day of January, nineteen hundred and twenty-six, land has been conveyed to a purchaser for money or money's worth subject to any prior interest whether or not on the purchase the land was expressed to be exonerated from, or the grantor agreed to indemnify the purchaser against, such prior interest,

the estate owner for the time being of the land subject to such prior interest may, notwithstanding any provision contained in the Settled Land Act 1925, but without prejudice to any power whereby such prior interest is capable of being overreached, convey or create a legal estate subject to such prior interest as if the instrument creating the prior interest was not an instrument or one of the instruments constituting a settlement of the land.

(3) In this section 'interest' means an estate, interest, charge or power of charging subsisting, or capable of arising or of being exercised, under a settlement, and, where a prior interest arises under the exercise of a power, 'instrument' includes both the instrument conferring the power and the instrument exercising it.

LANDLORD AND TENANT ACT 1927
(17 & 18 Geo 5 c 36)

18   Provisions as to covenants to repair

(1) Damages for a breach of a covenant or agreement to keep or put premises in repair during the currency of a lease, or to leave or put premises in repair at the termination of a lease, whether such covenant or agreement is expressed or implied, and whether general or specific, shall in no case exceed the amount (if any) by which the value of the reversion (whether immediate or not) in the premises is diminished owing to the breach of such covenant or agreement as aforesaid; and in particular no damage shall be recovered for a breach of any such covenant or agreement to leave or put premises in repair at the termination of a lease, if it is shown that the premises, in whatever state of repair they might be, would at or shortly after the termination of the tenancy have been or be pulled down, or such structural alterations made therein as would render valueless the repairs covered by the covenant or agreement.

(2) A right of re-entry or forfeiture for a breach of any such covenant or agreement as aforesaid shall not be enforceable, by action or otherwise, unless the lessor proves that the fact that such a notice as is required by section one hundred and forty-six of the Law of Property Act 1925 has been served on the lessee was known either –

(a) to the lessee; or

(b) to an under-lessee holding under an under-lease which reserved a nominal reversion only to the lessee; or

(c) to the person who last paid the rent due under the lease either on his own behalf or as agent for the lessee or under-lessee;

and that a time reasonably sufficient to enable the repairs to be executed had elapsed since the time when the fact of the service of the notice came to the knowledge of any such person.

Where a notice has been sent by registered post addressed to a person at his last known place of abode in the United Kingdom, then, for the purposes of this subsection, that person shall be deemed, unless the contrary is proved, to have had knowledge of the fact that the notice had been served as from the time at which the letter would have been delivered in the ordinary course of post.

This subsection shall be construed as one with section one hundred and forty-six of the Law of Property Act 1925.

(3) This section applies whether the lease was created before or after the commencement of this Act.

19 Provisions as to covenants not to assign, etc without licence or consent

(1) In all leases whether made before or after the commencement of this Act containing a covenant condition or agreement against assigning, underletting, charging or parting with the possession of demised premises or any part thereof without licence or consent, such covenant condition or agreement shall, notwithstanding any express provision to the contrary, be deemed to be subject –

(a) to a proviso to the effect that such licence or consent is not to be unreasonably withheld, but this proviso does not preclude the right of the landlord to require payment of a reasonable sum in respect of any legal or other expenses incurred in connection with such licence or consent; and

(b) (if the lease is for more than forty years, and is made in consideration wholly or partially of the erection, or the substantial improvement, addition or alteration of buildings, and the lessor is not a Government department or local or public authority, or a statutory or public utility company) to a proviso to the effect that in the case of any assignment, under-letting, charging or parting with the possession (whether by the holders of the lease or any under-tenant whether immediate or not) effected more than seven years before the end of the term no consent or licence shall be required, if notice in writing of the transaction is given to the lessor within six months after the transaction is effected.

(1A) Where the landlord and the tenant under a qualifying lease have entered into an agreement specifying for the purposes of this subsection –

(a) any circumstances in which the landlord may withhold his licence or consent to an assignment of the demised premises or any part of them, or

(b) any conditions subject to which any such licnece or consent may be granted,

then the landlord –

(i) shall not be regarded as unreasonably withholding his licence or consent to any such assignment if he withholds it on the ground (and it is the case) that any such circumstances exist, and

(ii) if he gives any such licence or consent subject to any such conditions, shall not be regarded as giving it subject to unreasonable conditions;

and section 1 of the Landlord and Tenant Act 1988 (qualified duty to consent to assignment etc) shall have effect subject to the provisions of this subsection.

(1B) Subsection (1A) of this section applies to such an agreement as is mentioned in that subsection –

(a) whether it is contained in the lease or not, and

(b) whether it is made at the time when the lease is granted or at any other time falling before the application for the landlord's licence or consent is made.

(1C) Subsection (1A) shall not, however, apply to any such agreement to the extent that the circumstances or conditions specified in it are framed by reference to any matter falling to be determined by the landlord or by any other person for the purposes of the agreement, unless under the terms of the agreement –

(a) that person's power to determine that matter is required to be exercised reasonably, or

(b) the tenant is given an unrestricted right to have any such determination reviewed by a person independent of both landlord and tenant whose identity is ascertainable by reference to the agreement,

and in the latter case the agreement provides for the determination made by any such independent person on the review to be conclusive as to the matter in question.

(1D) In its application to a qualifying lease, subsection (1)(b) of this section shall not have effect in relation to any assignment of the lease.

(1E) In subsections (1A) and (1D) of this section –

(a) 'qualifying lease' means any lease which is a new tenancy for the purposes of section 1 of the Landlord and Tenant (Covenants) Act 1995 other than a residential lease, namely a lease by which a building or part of a building is let wholly or mainly as a single private residence; and

(b) references to assignment include parting with possession on assignment.

(2) In all leases whether made before or after the commencement of this Act containing a covenant condition or agreement against the making of improvements without licence or consent, such covenant condition or agreement shall be deemed, notwithstanding any express provision to the contrary, to the subject to a proviso that such licence or consent is not to be unreasonably withheld; but this proviso does not preclude the right to require as a condition of such licence or consent the payment of a reasonable sum in respect of any damage to or diminution in the value of the premises or any neighbouring premises belonging to the landlord, and of any legal or other expenses properly incurred in connection with such licence or consent nor, in the case of an improvement which does not add to the letting value of the holding, does it preclude the right to require as a condition of such licence or consent, where such a requirement would be reasonable, an undertaking on the part of the tenant to reinstate the premises in the condition in which they were before the improvement was executed.

(3) In all leases whether made before or after the commencement of this Act containing a covenant condition or agreement against the alteration of the user of the demised premises, without licence or consent, such covenant condition or agreement shall, if the alteration does not involve any structural alteration of the premises, be deemed, notwithstanding any express provision to the contrary, to be subject to a proviso that no fine or sum of money in the nature of a fine, whether by way of increase of rent or otherwise, shall be payable for or in respect of such licence or consent; but this proviso does not preclude the right of the landlord to require payment of a reasonable sum in respect of any damage to or diminution in

the value of the premises or any neighbouring premises belonging to him and of any legal or other expenses incurred in connection with such licence or consent.

Where a dispute as to the reasonableness of any such sum has been determined by a court of competent jurisdiction, the landlord shall be bound to grant the licence or consent on payment of the sum so determined to be reasonable.

(4) This section shall not apply to leases of agricultural holdings within the meaning of the Agricultural Holdings Act 1986 which are leases in relation to which that Act applies, or to farm business tenancies within the meaning of the Agricultural Tenancies Act 1995, and paragraph (b) of subsection (1), subsection (2) and subsection (3) of this section shall not apply to mining leases.

As amended by the Agricultural Holdings Act 1986, s100, Schedule 14, para 15; Agricultural Tenancies Act 1995, s40, Schedule, para 5; Landlord and Tenant (Covenants) Act 1995, s22.

LAW OF PROPERTY (AMENDMENT) ACT 1929

(19 & 20 Geo 5 c 9)

1 Relief of under-lessees against breach of covenant

Nothing in subsection (8), subsection (9) or subsection (10) of section one hundred and forty-six of the Law of Property Act 1925 (which relates to restrictions on and relief against forfeiture of leases and under-leases) shall affect the provisions of subsection (4) of the said section.

LAW OF PROPERTY (ENTAILED INTERESTS) ACT 1932
(22 & 23 Geo 5 c 27)

2   Definition of rentcharge

For removing doubt it is hereby declared that a rentcharge (not being a rentcharge limited to take effect in remainder after or expectant on the failure or determination of some other interest) is a rentcharge in possession within the meaning of paragraph (b) of subsection (2) of section one of the Law of Property Act 1925, notwithstanding that the payments in respect thereof are limited to commence or accrue at some time subsequent to its creation.

LEASEHOLD PROPERTY (REPAIRS) ACT 1938
(1 & 2 Geo 6 c 34)

1   Restriction on enforcement of repairing covenants in long leases of small houses

(1) Where a lessor serves on a lessee under subsection (1) of section one hundred and forty-six of the Law of Property Act 1925, a notice that relates to a breach of a covenant or agreement to keep or put in repair during the currency of the lease all or any of the property comprised in the lease, and at the date of the service of the notice three years or more of the term of the lease remain unexpired, the lessee may within twenty-eight days from that date serve on the lessor a counter-notice to the effect that he claims the benefit of this Act.

(2) A right to damages for a breach of such a covenant as aforesaid shall not be enforceable by action commenced at any time at which three years or more of the term of the lease remain unexpired unless the lessor has served on the lessee not less than one month before the commencement of the action such a notice as is specified in subsection (1) of section one hundred and forty-six of the Law of Property Act 1925, and where a notice is served under this subsection, the lessee may, within twenty-eight days from the date of the service thereof, serve on the lessor a counter-notice to the effect that he claims the benefit of this Act.

(3) Where a counter-notice is served by a lessee under this section, then, notwithstanding anything in any enactment or rule of law, no proceedings, by action or otherwise, shall be taken by the lessor for the enforcement of any right of re-entry or forfeiture under any proviso or stipulation in the lease for breach of the covenant or agreement in question, or for damages for breach thereof, otherwise than with the leave of the court.

(4) A notice served under subsection (1) of section one hundred and forty-six of the Law of Property Act 1925, in the circumstances specified in subsection (1) of this section, and a notice served under subsection (2) of this section shall not be valid unless it contains a statement, in characters not less conspicuous than those used in any other part of the notice, to the effect that the lessee is entitled under this Act to serve on the lessor a counter-notice claiming the benefit of this Act, and a statement in the like characters specifying the time within which, and the manner in which, under this Act a counter-notice may be served and specifying the name and address for service of the lessor.

(5) Leave for the purposes of this section shall not be given unless the lessor proves –

(a) that the immediate remedying of the breach in question is requisite for preventing substantial diminution in the value of his reversion, or that the value thereof has been substantially diminished by the breach;

(b) that the immediate remedying of the breach is required for giving effect in relation to the premises to the purposes of any enactment, or of any byelaw or other provision having effect under an enactment, or for giving effect to any order of a court or requirement of any authority under any enactment or any such byelaw or other provision as aforesaid;

(c) in a case in which the lessee is not in occupation of the whole of the premises as respects which the covenant or agreement is proposed to be enforced, that the immediate remedying of the breach is required in the interests of the occupier of those premises or of part thereof;

(d) that the breach can be immediately remedied at an expense that is relatively small in comparison with the much greater expense that would probably be occasioned by postponement of the necessary work; or

(e) special circumstances which in the opinion of the court, render it just and equitable that leave should be given.

(6) The court may, in granting or in refusing leave for the purposes of this section, impose such terms and conditions on the lessor or on the lessee as it may think fit.

2   Restriction on right to recover expenses of survey, etc

A lessor on whom a counter-notice is served under the preceding section shall not be entitled to the benefit of subsection (3) of section one hundred and forty-six of the Law of Property Act 1925, (which relates to costs and expenses incurred by a lessor in reference to breaches of covenant), so far as regards any costs or expenses incurred in reference to the breach in question, unless he makes an application for leave for the purposes of the preceding section, and on such an application the court shall have power to direct whether and to what extent the lessor is to be entitled to the benefit thereof.

3   Saving for obligation to repair on taking possession

This Act shall not apply to a breach of a covenant or agreement in so far as it imposes on the lessee an obligation to put premises in repair that is to be performed upon the lessee taking possession of the premises or within a reasonable time thereafter.

6   Court having jurisdiction under this Act

(1) In this Act the expression 'the court' means the county court, except in a case in which any proceedings by action for which leave may be given would have to be taken in a court other than the county court, and means in the said excepted case that other court.

7   Application of certain provisions of Law of Property Act 1925

(1) In this Act the expressions 'lessor', 'lessee' and 'lease' have the meanings assigned to them respectively by sections one hundred and forty-six and one hundred and fifty-four of the Law of Property Act 1925, except that they do not include any reference to such a grant as is mentioned in the said section one hundred and forty-six, or to the person making, or to the grantee under such a grant, or to persons deriving title under such a person; and 'lease' means a lease for a term of seven years or more, not being a lease of an agricultural holding within the meaning of the Agricultural Holdings Act 1986 which is a lease in relation to which that Act applies and not being a farm business tenancy within the meaning of the Agricultural Tenancies Act 1995.

(2) The provisions of section one hundred and ninety-six of the said Act (which relate to the service of notices) shall extend to notices and counter-notices required or authorised by this Act.

As amended by the Landlord and Tenant Act 1954, s51(1), (2), (5); Agricultural Holdings Act 1986, s100, Schedule 14, para 17; Agricultural Tenancies Act 1995, s40, Schedule, para 8.

SETTLED LAND AND TRUSTEE ACTS (COURT'S GENERAL POWERS) ACT 1943
(6 & 7 Geo 6 c 25)

1   Extension of powers under 15 Geo 5 c 18, s64 and c 19, s57

(1) The jurisdiction of the court under section 64 of the Settled Land Act 1925 (which confers power on a tenant for life to effect under an order of the court any transaction, including an application of capital money), and, so far as regards trustees of land, the jurisdiction of the court under section 57 of the Trustee Act 1925 (under which the court may make an order conferring on trustees power to effect any transaction, including an expenditure of money, and may direct in what manner money to be expended is to be paid as between capital and income) shall include power, in the circumstances specified in subsection (2) of this section, to make an order authorising any expense of action taken or proposed in or for the management of settled land or of land subject to a trust of land, as the case may be, to be treated as a capital outgoing, notwithstanding that in other circumstances that expense could not properly have been so treated.

(2) The said circumstances are that the court is satisfied –

(a) that the action taken or proposed was or would be for the benefit of the persons entitled under the settlement, or under the trust of land, as the case may be, generally; and either

(b) that the available income from all sources of a person who, as being beneficially entitled to possession or receipt of rents and profits of the land or to reside in a house comprised therein, might otherwise have been expected to bear the expense of the action taken or proposed has been so reduced as to render him unable to bear the expense thereof, or unable to bear it without undue hardship; or

(c) in a case in which there is no such person as aforesaid, that the income available for meeting that expense has become insufficient.

(3) In determining whether to make such an order as aforesaid the court shall have regard to all the circumstances of the case, including the extent of the obligations, whether legally enforceable or not and whether or not relating to the land, of the person referred to in paragraph (b) of the last preceding subsection, the extent to which other persons entitled under the settlement or trust of land are likely to benefit from the action taken or proposed or from the relief which would accrue to that person from the making of the order, and the extent to which the making of the

order would be likely to involve a loss to any other person so entitled without his receiving any corresponding benefit.

(4) Such an order as aforesaid may be made notwithstanding that the action in question was taken, or the expense thereof discharged, before the passing of this Act or before the application for the order, and the court may direct such adjustments of accounts and such repayments to be made as may appear to the court to be requisite for giving full effect to the purposes of any such order.

(5) In this section –

the expression 'management' includes all the acts referred to in subsection (2) of section 102 of the Settled Land Act 1925, and references in this section to expense of management include references to the expense of the employment of a solicitor, accountant, surveyor, or other person in an advisory or supervisory capacity.

As amended by the Emergency Laws (Miscellaneous Provisions) Act 1953, ss9, 14, Schedule 3; Trusts of Land and Appointment of Trustees Act 1996, s25(1), Schedule 3, para 8.

LANDLORD AND TENANT ACT 1954
(2 & 3 Eliz 2 c 56)

PART II

SECURITY OF TENURE FOR BUSINESS, PROFESSIONAL AND OTHER TENANTS

23   Tenancies to which Part II applies

(1) Subject to the provisions of this Act, this Part of this Act applies to any tenancy where the property comprised in the tenancy is or includes premises which are occupied by the tenant and are so occupied for the purposes of a business carried on by him or for those and other purposes.

(1A) Occupation or the carrying on of a business –

(a) by a company in which the tenant has a controlling interest; or

(b) where the tenant is a company, by a person with a controlling interest in the company,

shall be treated for the purposes of this section as equivalent to occupation or, as the case may be, the carrying on of a business by the tenant.

(1B) Accordingly references (however expressed) in this Part of this Act to the business of, or to use, occupation or enjoyment by, the tenant shall be construed as including references to the business of, or to use, occupation or enjoyment by, a company falling within subsection (1A)(a) above or a person falling within subsection (1A)(b) above.

(2) In this Part of this Act the expression 'business' includes a trade, profession or employment and includes any activity carried on by a body of persons, whether corporate or unincorporate.

(3) In the following provisions of this Part of this Act the expression 'the holding', in relation to a tenancy to which this Part of this Act applies, means the property comprised in the tenancy, there being excluded any part thereof which is occupied neither by the tenant nor by a person employed by the tenant and so employed for the purposes of a business by reason of which the tenancy is one to which this Part of this Act applies.

(4) Where the tenant is carrying on a business, in all or any part of the property comprised in a tenancy, in breach of a prohibition (however expressed) of use for business purposes which subsists under the terms of the tenancy and extends to the

whole of that property, this Part of this Act shall not apply to the tenancy unless the immediate landlord or his predecessor in title has consented to the breach or the immediate landlord has acquiesced therein.

In this subsection the reference to a prohibition of use for business purposes does not include a prohibition of use for the purposes of a specified business, or of use for purposes of any but a specified business, but save as aforesaid includes a prohibition of use for the purposes of some one or more only of the classes of business specified in the definition of that expression in subsection (2) of this section.

24 Continuation of tenancies to which Part II applies and grant of new tenancies

(1) A tenancy to which this Part of this Act applies shall not come to an end unless terminated in accordance with the provisions of this Part of this Act; and, subject to the following provisions of this Act either the tenant or the landlord under such a tenancy may apply to the court for an order for the grant of a new tenancy –

(a) if the landlord has given notice under section 25 of this Act to terminate the tenancy, or

(b) if the tenant has made a request for a new tenancy in accordance with section twenty-six of this Act.

(2) The last foregoing subsection shall not prevent the coming to an end of a tenancy by notice to quit given by the tenant, by surrender or forfeiture, or by the forfeiture of a superior tenancy unless –

(a) in the case of a notice to quit, the notice was given before the tenant had been in occupation in right of the tenancy for one month.

(2A) Neither the tenant nor the landlord may make an application under subsection (1) above if the other has made such an application and the application has been served.

(2B) Neither the tenant nor the landlord may make such an application if the landlord has made an application under section 29(2) of this Act and the application has been served.

(2C) The landlord may not withdraw an application under subsection (1) above unless the tenant consents to its withdrawal.

(3) Notwithstanding anything in subsection (1) of this section –

(a) where a tenancy to which this Part of this Act applies ceases to be such a tenancy, it shall not come to an end by reason only of the cesser, but if it was granted for a term of years certain and has been continued by subsection (1) of this section then (without prejudice to the termination thereof in accordance with any terms of the tenancy) it may be terminated by not less than three nor more than six months' notice in writing given by the landlord to the tenant;

(b) where, at a time when a tenancy is not one to which this Part of this Act applies, the landlord gives notice to quit, the operation of the notice shall not be affected by reason that the tenancy becomes one to which this Part of this Act applies after the giving of the notice.

24A Applications for determination of interim rent while tenancy continues

(1) Subject to subsection (2) below, if –

(a) the landlord of a tenancy to which this Part of this Act applies has given notice under section 25 of this Act to terminate the tenancy; or

(b) the tenant of such a tenancy has made a request for a new tenancy in accordance with section 26 of this Act,

either of them may make an application to the court to determine a rent (an 'interim rent') which the tenant is to pay while the tenancy ('the relevant tenancy') continues by virtue of section 24 of this Act and the court may order payment of an interim rent in accordance with section 24C or 24D of this Act.

(2) Neither the tenant nor the landlord may make an application under subsection (1) above if the other has made such an application and has not withdrawn it.

(3) No application shall be entertained under subsection (1) above if it is made more than six months after the termination of the relevant tenancy.

25 Termination of tenancy by the landlord

(1) The landlord may terminate a tenancy to which this Part of this Act applies by a notice given to the tenant in the prescribed form specifying the date at which the tenancy is to come to an end (hereinafter referred to as 'the date of termination'): Provided that this subsection has effect subject to the provisions of section 29B(4) of this Act and the provisions of Part IV of this Act as to the interim continuation of tenancies pending the disposal of applications to the court.

(2) Subject to the provisions of the next following subsection, a notice under this section shall not have effect unless it is given not more than twelve nor less than six months before the date of termination specified therein.

(3) In the case of a tenancy which apart from this Act could have been brought to an end by notice to quit given by the landlord –

(a) the date of termination specified in a notice under this section shall not be earlier than the earliest date on which apart from this Part of this Act the tenancy could have been brought to an end by notice to quit given by the landlord on the date of the giving of the notice under this section; and

(b) where apart from this Part of this Act more than six months' notice to quit would have been required to bring the tenancy to and end, the last foregoing subsection shall have effect with the substitution for twelve months of a period six months longer than the length of notice to quit which would have been required as aforesaid.

(4) In the case of any other tenancy, a notice under this section shall not specify a date of termination earlier than the date on which apart from this Part of this Act the tenancy would have come to an end by effluxion of time.

(6) A notice under this section shall not have effect unless it states whether the landlord is opposed to the grant of a new tenancy to the tenant.

(7) A notice under this section which states that the landlord is opposed to the grant of a new tenancy to the tenant shall not have effect unless it also specifies one or more of the grounds specified in section 30(1) of this Act as the ground or grounds for his opposition.

(8) A notice under this section which states that the landlord is opposed to the grant of a new tenancy to the tenant shall not have effect unless it sets out the landlord's proposals as to –

(a) the property to be comprised in the new tenancy (being either the whole or part of the property comprised in the current tenancy);

(b) the rent to be payable under the new tenancy; and

(c) the other terms of the new tenancy.

28   Renewal of tenancies by agreement

Where the landlord and tenant agree for the grant to the tenant of a future tenancy of the holding, or of the holding with other land, on terms and from a date specified in the agreement, the current tenancy shall continue until that date but no longer, and shall not be a tenancy to which this Part of this Act applies.

33   Duration of new tenancy

Where on an application under this Part of this Act the court makes an order for the grant of a new tenancy, the new tenancy shall be such tenancy as may be agreed between the landlord and the tenant, or, in default of such an agreement, shall be such a tenancy as may be determined by the court to be reasonable in all the circumstances, being, if it is a tenancy for a term of years certain, a tenancy for a term not exceeding fifteen years, and shall begin on the coming to an end of the current tenancy.

34   Rent under new tenancy

(1) The rent payable under a tenancy granted by order of the court under this Part of this Act shall be such as may be agreed between the landlord and the tenant or as, in default of such agreement, may be determined by the court to be that at which, having regard to the terms of the tenancy (other than those relating to rent), the holding might reasonably be expected to be let in the open market by a willing lessor, there being disregarded –

(a) any effect on rent of the fact that the tenant has or his predecessors in title have been in occupation of the holding,

(b) any goodwill attached to the holding by reason of the carrying on thereat of the business of the tenant (whether by him or by a predecessor of his in that business),

(c) any effect on rent of an improvement to which this paragraph applies;

(d) in the case of a holding comprising licensed premises, any addition to its value attributable to the licence, if it appears to the court that having regard to the terms of the current tenancy and any other relevant circumstances the benefit of the licence belongs to the tenant.

(2) Paragraph (c) of the foregoing subsection applies to any improvement carried out by a person who at the time it was carried out was the tenant, but only if it was carried out otherwise than in pursuance of an obligation to his immediate landlord, and either it was carried out during the current tenancy or the following conditions are satisfied, that is to say, –

(a) that it was completed not more than twenty-one years before the application to the court was made; and

(b) that the holding or any part of it affected by the improvement has at all times since the completion of the improvement been comprised in tenancies of the description specified in section 23(1) of this Act; and

(c) that at the termination of each of those tenancies the tenant did not quit.

(2A) If this Part of this Act applies by virtue of section 23(1A) of this Act, the reference in subsection (1)(d) above to the tenant shall be construed as including –

(a) a company in which the tenant has a controlling interest, or

(b) where the tenant is a company, a person with a controlling interest in the company.

(3) Where the rent is determined by the court the court may, if it thinks fit, further determine that the terms of the tenancy shall include such provision for varying the rent as may be specified in the determination.

(4) It is hereby declared that the matters which are to be taken into account by the court in determining the rent include any effect on rent of the operation of the provisions of the Landlord and Tenant (Covenants) Act 1995.

35 Other terms of new tenancy

(1) The terms of a tenancy granted by order of the court under this Part of this Act (other than terms as to the duration thereof and as to the rent payable thereunder), including, where different persons own interest which fulfil the conditions specified in section 44(1) of this Act in different parts of it, terms as to the apportionment of the rent, shall be such as may be agreed between the landlord and the tenant or as, in default of such agreement, may be determined by the court; and in determining those terms the court shall have regard to the terms of the current tenancy and to all relevant circumstances.

(2) In subsection (1) of this section the reference to all relevant circumstances

includes (without prejudice to the gnerality of that reference) a reference to the operation of the provisions of the Landlord and Tenant (Covenants) Act 1995.

43   Tenancies excluded from Part II

(1) This Part of this Act does not apply –

(a) to a tenancy of an agricultural holding which is a tenancy in relation to which the Agricultural Holdings Act 1986 applies or a tenancy which would be a tenancy of an agricultural holding in relation to which that Act applied if subsection (3) of section 2 of that Act did not have effect or, in a case where approval was given under subsection (1) of that section, if that approval had not been given;

(aa) to a farm business tenancy;

(b) to a tenancy created by a mining lease.

(2) This Part of this Act does not apply to a tenancy granted by reason that the tenant was the holder of an office, appointment or employment from the grantor thereof and continuing only so long as the tenant holds the office, appointment or employment, or terminable by the grantor on the tenant's ceasing to hold it, or coming to an end at a time fixed by reference to the time at which the tenant ceases to hold it: Provided that this subsection shall not have effect in relation to a tenancy granted after the commencement of this Act unless the tenancy was granted by an instrument in writing which expressed the purpose for which the tenancy was granted.

(3) This Part of this Act does not apply to a tenancy granted for a term certain not exceeding six months unless –

(a) the tenancy contains provision for renewing the term or for extending it beyond six months from its beginning; or

(b) the tenant has been in occupation for a period which, together with any period during which any predecessor in the carrying on of the business carried on by the tenant was in occupation, exceeds twelve months.

PART IV

MISCELLANEOUS AND SUPPLEMENTARY

51   Extension of Leasehold Property (Repairs) Act 1938

(1) The Leasehold Property (Repairs) Act 1938 (which restricts the enforcement of repairing covenants in long leases of small houses) shall extend to every tenancy (whether of a house or of other property, and without regard to rateable value) where the following conditions are fulfilled, that is to say –

(a) that the tenancy was granted for a term of years certain of not less than seven years;

(b) that three years or more of the term remain unexpired at the date of the service of the notice of dilapidations or, as the case may be, at the date of commencement of the action for damages; and

(c) that the tenancy is neither a tenancy of an agricultural holding in relation to which the Agricultural Holdings Act 1986 applies nor a farm business tenancy [as defined in section 1 of the Agricultural Tenancies Act 1995]. ...

(6) In this section the expression 'notice of dilapidations' means a notice under subsection (1) of section one hundred and forty-six of the Law of Property Act 1925.

53   Jurisdiction of county court where lessor refuses licence or consent

(1) Where a landlord withholds his licence or consent –

(a) to an assignment of the tenancy or a subletting, charging or parting with the possession of the demised property or any part thereof, or

(b) to the making of an improvement on the demised property or any part thereof, or

(c) to a change in the use of the demised property or any part thereof, or to the making of a specified use of that property,

and the High Court has jurisdiction to make a declaration that the licence or consent was unreasonably withheld, then without prejudice to the jurisdiction of the High Court the county court shall have the like jurisdiction whatever the net annual value for rating of the demised property is taken to be for the purposes of the County Courts Act 1984 and notwithstanding that the tenant does not seek any relief other than the declaration.

(2) Where on the making of an application to the county court for such a declaration the court is satisfied that the licence or consent was unreasonably withheld, the court shall make a declaration accordingly.

(3) The foregoing provisions of this section shall have effect whether the tenancy in question was created before or after the commencement of this Act and whether the refusal of the licence or consent occurred before or after the commencement of this Act.

(4) Nothing in this section shall be construed as conferring jurisdiction on the county court to grant any relief other than such a declaration as aforesaid.

As amended by the Agricultural Act 1958, s8(1), Schedule 1, Pt I, para 29; Law of Property Act 1969, ss1(1), 3(1), (2), 2, 4(1), 12; County Courts Act 1984, s148(1), Schedule, Pt V, para 23; Agricultural Holdings Act 1986, s100, Schedule 14, para 21; Landlord and Tenant (Licensed Premises) Act 1990, ss1, 2(a); Agricultural Tenancies Act 1995, s40, Schedule, paras 10–12; Landlord and Tenant (Covenants) Act 1995, s30(1), Schedule 1, paras 3, 4; Regulatory Reform (Business Tenancies) (England and Wales) Order 2003, arts 2–4, 9, 11, 15, 18, 26, 27(3), 28(2), Schedule 6.

RIGHTS OF LIGHT ACT 1959
(7 & 8 Eliz 2 c 56)

2   Registration of notice in lieu of obstruction of access of light

(1) For the purpose of preventing the access and use of light from being taken to be enjoyed without interruption, any person who is an owner of land (in this and the next following section referred to as 'the servient land') over which light passes to a dwelling-house, workshop or other building (in this and then next following section referred to as 'the dominant building') may apply to the local authority in whose area the dominant building is situated for the registration of a notice under this section.

(2) An application for the registration of a notice under this section shall be in the prescribed form and shall –

(a) identify the servient land and the dominant building in the prescribed manner, and

(b) state that the registration of a notice in pursuance of the application is intended to be equivalent to the obstruction of the access of light to the dominant building across the servient land which would be caused by the erection, in such position on the servient land as may be specified in the application, of an opaque structure of such dimensions specified.

(3) Any such application shall be accompanied by one or other of the following certificates issued by the Lands Tribunal, that is to say –

(a) a certificate certifying that adequate notice of the proposed application has been given to all persons who, in the circumstances existing at the time when the certificate is issued, appear to the Lands Tribunal to be persons likely to be affected by the registration of a notice in pursuance of the application;

(b) a certificate certifying that, in the opinion of the Lands Tribunal, the case is one of exceptional urgency, and that accordingly a notice should be registered forthwith as a temporary notice for such period as may be specified in the certificate.

(4) Where application is duly made to a local authority for the registration of a notice under this section, it shall be the duty of that authority to register the notice in the appropriate local land charges register, and –

(a) any notice so registered under this section shall be a local land charge; but

—— 184 ——

(b) section 5(1) and (2) and section 10 of the Local Land Charges Act 1975 shall not apply in relation thereto.

(5) Provision shall be made by rules under section three of the Lands Tribunal Act 1949, for regulating proceedings before the Lands Tribunal with respect to the issue of certificates for the purposes of this section, and, subject to the approval of the Treasury, the fees chargeable in respect of those proceedings; and, without prejudice to the generality of subsection (6) of that section, any such rules made for the purposes of this section shall include provision –

(a) for requiring applicants for certificates under paragraph (a) of subsection (3) of this section to give such notices, whether by way of advertisement or otherwise, and to produce such documents and provide such information, as may be determined by or under the rules;

(b) for determining the period to be specified in a certificate issued under paragraph (b) of subsection (3) of this section; and

(c) in connection with any certificate issued under the said paragraph (b), for enabling a further certificate to be issued in accordance (subject to the necessary modifications) with paragraph (a) of subsection (3) of this section.

3   Effect of registered notice and proceedings relating thereto

(1) Where, in pursuance of an application made in accordance with the last preceding section, a notice is registered thereunder, then, for the purpose of determining whether any person is entitled (by virtue of the Prescription Act 1832, or otherwise) to a right to the access of light to the dominant building across the servient land, the access of light to that building across that land shall be treated as obstructed to the same extent, and with the like consequences, as if an opaque structure, of the dimensions specified in the application –

(a) had, on the date of registration of the notice, been erected in the position on the servient land specified in the application, and had been so erected by the person who made the application, and

(b) had remained in that position during the period for which the notice has effect and had been removed at the end of that period.

(2) For the purposes of this section a notice registered under the last preceding section shall be taken to have effect until either –

(a) the registration is cancelled, or

(b) the period of one year beginning with the date of registration of the notice expires, or

(c) in the case of a notice registered in pursuance of an application accompanied by a certificate issued under paragraph (b) of subsection (3) of the last preceding section, the period specified in the certificate expires without such a further certificate as is mentioned in paragraph (c) of subsection (5) of that section having before the end of that period been lodged with the local authority,

and shall cease to have effect on the occurrence of any one of those events.

(3) Subject to the following provisions of this section, any person who, if such a structure as is mentioned in subsection (1) of this section had been erected as therein mentioned, would have had a right of action in any court in respect of that structure, on the grounds that he was entitled to a right to the access of light to the dominant building across the servient land, and that the said right was infringed by that structure, shall have the like right of action in that court in respect of the registration of a notice under the last preceding section: Provided that an action shall not be begun by virtue of this subsection after the notice in question has ceased to have effect.

(4) Where, at any time during the period for which a notice registered under the last preceding section has effect, the circumstances are such that, if the access of light to the dominant building had been enjoyed continuously from a date one year earlier than the date on which the enjoyment thereof in fact began, a person would have had a right of action in any court by virtue of the last preceding subsection in respect of the registration of the notice, that person shall have the like right of action in that court by virtue of this subsection in respect of the registration of the notice.

(5) The remedies available to the plaintiff in an action brought by virtue of subsection (3) or subsection (4) of this section (apart from any order as to costs) shall be such declaration as the court may consider appropriate in the circumstances, and an order directing the registration of the notice to be cancelled or varied, as the court may determine.

(6) For the purposes of section four of the Prescription Act 1832 (under which a period of enjoyment of any of the rights to which that Act applies is not to be treated as interrupted except by a matter submitted to or acquiesced in for one year after notice thereof) –

    (a) as from the date of registration of a notice under the last preceding section, all persons interested in the dominant building or any part thereof shall be deemed to have notice of the registration thereof and of the person on whose application it was registered;

    (b) until such time as an action is brought by virtue of subsection (3) or subsection (4) of this section in respect of the registration of a notice under the last preceding section, all persons interested in the dominant building or any part thereof shall be deemed to acquiesce in the obstruction which, in accordance with subsection (1) of this section, is to be treated as resulting from the registration of the notice;

    (c) as from the date on which such an action is brought, no person shall be treated as submitting to or acquiescing in that obstruction;

Provided that if, in any such action, the court decides against the claim of the plaintiff, the court may direct that the preceding provisions of this subsection shall apply in relation to the notice as if that action had not been brought.

7   Interpretation

(1) In this Act, except in so far as the context otherwise requires, the following expressions have the meanings hereby assigned to them respectively, that is to say:

'action' includes a counterclaim, and any reference to the plaintiff in an action shall be construed accordingly;

'local authority', in relation to land in a district or a London borough, means the council of the district or borough, and, in relation to land in the City of London, means the Common Council of the City;

'owner', in relation to any land, means a person who is the estate owner in respect of the fee simple thereof, or is entitled to a tenancy thereof (within the meaning of the Landlord and Tenant Act 1954) for a term of years certain of which, at the time in question, not less than seven years remain unexpired, or is a mortgagee in possession (within the meaning of the Law of Property Act 1925) where the interest mortgaged is either the fee simple of the land or such a tenancy thereof; ...

(2) References in this Act to any enactment shall, except where the context otherwise requires, be construed as references to that enactment as amended by or under any other enactment.

As amended by the Local London Charges Act 1975, s17(2), Schedule 1.

MARRIED WOMEN'S PROPERTY ACT 1964

(1964 c 19)

1   Money and property derived from housekeeping allowance

If any question arises as to the right of a husband or wife to money derived from any allowance made by the husband for the expenses of the matrimonial home or for similar purposes, or to any property acquired out of such money, the money or property shall, in the absence of any agreement between them to the contrary, be treated as belonging to the husband and the wife in equal shares.

PERPETUITIES AND ACCUMULATIONS ACT 1964

(1964 c 55)

1   Power to specify perpetuity period

(1) Subject to section 9(2) of this Act and subsection (2) below, where the instrument by which any disposition is made so provides, the perpetuity period applicable to the disposition under the rule against perpetuities, instead of being of any other duration, shall be of a duration equal to such number of years not exceeding eighty as is specified in that behalf in the instrument.

(2) Subsection (1) above shall not have effect where the disposition is made in exercise of a special power of appointment, but where a period is specified under that subsection in the instrument creating such a power the period shall apply in relation to any disposition under the power as it applies in relation to the power itself.

2   Presumptions and evidence as to future parenthood

(1) Where in any proceedings there arises on the rule against perpetuities a question which turns on the ability of a person to have a child at some future time, then –

(a) subject to paragraph (b) below, it shall be presumed that a male can have a child at the age of fourteen years or over, but not under that age, and that a female can have a child at the age of twelve years or over, but not under that age or over the age of fifty-five years; but

(b) in the case of a living person evidence may be given to show that he or she will or will not be able to have a child at the time in question.

(2) Where any such question is decided by treating a person as unable to have a child at a particular time, and he or she does so, the High Court may make such order as it thinks fit for placing the persons interested in the property comprised in the disposition, so far as may be just, in the position they would have held if the question had not been so decided.

(3) Subject to subsection (2) above, where any such question is decided in relation to a disposition by treating a person as able or unable to have a child at a particular time, then he or she shall be so treated for the purpose of any question which may

arise on the rule against perpetuities in relation to the same disposition in any subsequent proceedings.

(4) In the foregoing provisions of this section references to having a child are references to begetting or giving birth to a child, but those provisions (except subsection (1)(b)) shall apply in relation to the possibility that a person will at any time have a child by adoption, legitimation or other means as they apply to his or her ability at that time to beget or give birth to a child.

3 Uncertainty as to remoteness

(1) Where, apart from the provisions of this section and sections 4 and 5 of this Act, a disposition would be void on the ground that the interest disposed of might not become vested until too remote a time, the disposition shall be treated, until such time (if any) as it becomes established that the vesting must occur, if at all, after the end of the perpetuity period, as if the disposition were not subject to the rule against perpetuities; and its becoming so established shall not affect the validity of anything previously done in relation to the interest disposed of by way of advancement, application of intermediate income or otherwise.

(2) Where, apart from the said provisions, a disposition consisting of the conferring of a general power of appointment would be void on the ground that the power might not become exercisable until too remote a time, the disposition shall be treated, until such time (if any) as it becomes established that the power will not be exercisable within the perpetuity period, as if the disposition were not subject to the rule against perpetuities.

(3) Where, apart from the said provisions, a disposition consisting of the conferring of any power, option or other right would be void on the ground that the right might be exercised at too remote a time, the disposition shall be treated as regards any exercise of the right within the perpetuity period as if it were not subject to the rule against perpetuities and, subject to the said provisions, shall be treated as void for remoteness only if, and so far as, the right is not fully exercised within that period.

(4) Where this section applies to a disposition and the duration of the perpetuity period is not determined by virtue of section 1 or 9(2) of this Act, it shall be determined as follows:

(a) where any persons falling within subsection (5) below are individuals in being and ascertainable at the commencement of the perpetuity period the duration of the period shall be determined by reference to their lives and no others, but so that the lives of any description of persons falling within paragraph (b) or (c) of that subsection shall be disregarded if the number of persons of that description is such as to render it impracticable to ascertain the date of birth of the survivor;

(b) where there are no lives under paragraph (a) above the period shall be twenty-one years.

(5) The said persons are as follows:

(a) the person by whom the disposition was made;

(b) a person to whom or in whose favour the disposition was made, that is to say –

> (i) in the case of a disposition to a class of persons, any member or potential member of that class;

> (ii) in the case of an individual disposition to a person taking only on certain conditions being satisfied, any person as to whom some of the conditions are satisfied and the remainder may in time be satisfied;

> (iii) in the case of a special power of appointment exercisable in favour of members of a class, any member or potential member of the class;

> (iv) in the case of a special power of appointment exercisable in favour of one person only, that person or, where the object of the power is ascertainable only on certain conditions being satisfied, any person as to whom some of the conditions are satisfied and the remainder may in time be satisfied;

> (v) in the case of any power, option or other right, the person on whom the right is conferred;

(c) a person having a child or grandchild within sub-paragraphs (i) to (iv) of paragraph (b) above, or any of whose children or grandchildren, if subsequently born, would by virtue of his or her descent fall within those sub-paragraphs;

(d) any person on the failure or determination of whose prior interest the disposition is limited to take effect.

4   Reduction of age and exclusion of class members to avoid remoteness

(1) Where a disposition is limited by reference to the attainment by any person or persons of a specified age exceeding twenty-one years, and it is apparent at the time the disposition is made or becomes apparent at a subsequent time –

> (a) that the disposition would, apart from this section, be void for remoteness, but

> (b) that it would not be so void if the specified age had been twenty-one years,

the disposition shall be treated for all purposes as if, instead of being limited by reference to the age in fact specified, it had been limited by reference to the age nearest to that age which would, if specified instead, have prevented the disposition from being so void.

(2) Where in the case of any disposition different ages exceeding twenty-one years are specified in relation to different persons –

> (a) the reference in paragraph (b) of subsection (1) above to the specified age shall be construed as a reference to all the specified ages, and

> (b) that subsection shall operate to reduce each such age so far as is necessary to save the disposition from being void for remoteness.

(3) Where the inclusion of any persons, being potential members of a class or unborn

persons who at birth would become members or potential members of the class, prevents the foregoing provisions of this section from operating to save a disposition from being void for remoteness, those persons shall thenceforth be deemed for all the purposes of the disposition to be excluded from the class, and the said provisions shall thereupon have effect accordingly.

(4) Where, in the case of a disposition to which subsection (3) above does not apply, it is apparent at the time the disposition is made or becomes apparent at a subsequent time that, apart from this subsection, the inclusion of any persons, being potential members of a class or unborn persons who at birth would become members or potential members of the class, would cause the disposition to be treated as void for remoteness, those persons shall, unless their exclusion would exhaust the class, thenceforth be deemed for all the purposes of the disposition to be excluded from the class.

(5) Where this section has effect in relation to a disposition to which section 3 above applies, the operation of this section shall not effect the validity of anything previously done in relation to the interest disposed of by way of advancement, application of intermediate income or otherwise ...

(7) For the avoidance of doubt it is hereby declared that a question arising under section 3 of this Act or subsection (1)(a) above of whether a disposition would be void apart from this section is to be determined as if subsection (6) above [repealed s163 of the Law of Property Act 1925] had been a separate section of this Act.

5   Condition relating to death of surviving spouse

Where a disposition is limited by reference to the time of death of the survivor of a person in being at the commencement of the perpetuity period and any spouse of that person, and that time has not arrived at the end of the perpetuity period, the disposition shall be treated for all purposes, where to do so would save it from being void for remoteness, as if it had instead been limited by reference to the time immediately before the end of that period.

6   Saving and acceleration of expectant interests

A disposition shall not be treated as void for remoteness by reason only that the interest disposed of is ulterior to and dependent upon an interest under a disposition which is so void, and the vesting of an interest shall not be prevented from being accelerated on the failure of a prior interest by reason only that the failure arises because of remoteness.

7   Powers of appointment

For the purposes of the rule against perpetuities, a power of appointment shall be treated as a special power unless –

(a) in the instrument creating the power it is expressed to be exercisable by one person only, and

(b) it could, at all times during its currency when that person is of full age and capacity, be exercised by him so as immediately to transfer to himself the whole of the interest governed by the power without the consent of any other person or compliance with any other condition, not being a formal condition relating only to the mode of exercise of the power:

Provided that for the purpose of determining whether a disposition made under a power of appointment exercisable by will only is void for remoteness, the power shall be treated as a general power where it would have fallen to be so treated if exercisable by deed.

8   Administrative powers of trustees

(1) The rule against perpetuities shall not operate to invalidate a power conferred on trustees or other persons to sell, lease, exchange or otherwise dispose of any property for full consideration, or to do any other act in the administration (as opposed to the distribution) of any property, and shall not prevent the payment to trustees or other persons of reasonable remuneration for their services.

(2) Subsection (1) above shall apply for the purposes of enabling a power to be exercised at any time after the commencement of this Act notwithstanding that the power is conferred by an instrument which took effect before that commencement.

9   Options relating to land

(1) The rule against perpetuities shall not apply to a disposition consisting of the conferring of an option to acquire for valuable consideration an interest reversionary (whether directly or indirectly) on the term of a lease if –

   (a) the option is exercisable only by the lessee or his successors in title, and

   (b) it ceases to be exercisable at or before the expiration of one year following the determination of the lease.

This subsection shall apply in relation to an agreement for a lease as it applies in relation to a lease, and 'lessee' shall be construed accordingly.

(2) In the case of a disposition consisting of the conferring of an option to acquire for valuable consideration any interest in land, the perpetuity period under the rule against perpetuities shall be twenty-one years, and section 1 of this Act shall not apply: provided that this subsection shall not apply to a right of pre-emption conferred on a public or local authority in respect of land used or to be used for religious purposes where the right becomes exercisable only if the land ceases to be used for such purposes.

10   Avoidance of contractual and other rights in cases of remoteness

Where a disposition inter vivos would fall to be treated as void for remoteness if the rights and duties thereunder were capable of transmission to persons other than the original parties and had been so transmitted, it shall be treated as void as between the person by whom it was made and the person to whom or in whose favour it was made or any successor of his, and no remedy shall lie in contract or otherwise for giving effect to it or making restitution for its lack of effect.

11   Rights for enforcement of rentcharges

(1) The rule against perpetuities shall not apply to any powers or remedies for recovering or compelling the payment of an annual sum to which section 121 or 122 of the Law of Property Act 1925 applies, or otherwise becoming exercisable or enforceable on the breach of any condition or other requirement relating to that sum ...

12   Possibilities of reverter, conditions subsequent, exceptions and reservations

(1) In the case of –

(a) a possibility of reverter on the determination of a determinable fee simple, or

(b) a possibility of a resulting trust on the determination of any other determinable interest in property,

the rule against perpetuities shall apply in relation to the provision causing the interest to be determinable as it would apply if that provision were expressed in the form of a condition subsequent giving rise, on breach thereof, to a right of re-entry or an equivalent right in the case of property other than land, and where the provision falls to be treated as void for remoteness the determinable interest shall become an absolute interest.

(2) Where a disposition is subject to any such provision, or to any such condition subsequent, or to any exception or reservation, the disposition shall be treated for the purposes of this Act as including a separate disposition of any rights arising by virtue of the provision, condition subsequent, exception or reservation.

13   Amendment of s164 of Law of Property Act 1925

(1) The periods for which accumulations of income under a settlement or other disposition are permitted by section 164 of the Law of Property Act 1925 shall include –

(a) a term of twenty-one years from the date of the making of the disposition, and

(b) the duration of the minority or respective minorities of any person or persons in being at that date.

(2) It is hereby declared that the restrictions imposed by the said section 164 apply in relation to a power to accumulate income whether or not there is a duty to exercise that power, and that they apply whether or not the power to accumulate extends to income produced by the investment of income previously accumulated.

14 Right to stop accumulations

Section 2 above shall apply to any question as to the right of beneficiaries to put an end to accumulations of income under any disposition as it applies to questions arising on the rule against perpetuities.

15 Short title, interpretation and extent

(1) This Act may be cited as the Perpetuities and Accumulations Act 1964.

(2) In this Act –

'disposition' includes the conferring of a power of appointment and any other disposition of an interest in or right over property, and references to the interest disposed of shall be construed accordingly;

'in being' means living or en ventre sa mère;

'power of appointment' includes any discretionary power to transfer a beneficial interest in property without the furnishing of valuable consideration;

'will' includes a codicil;

and for the purposes of this Act a disposition contained in a will shall be deemed to be made at the death of the testator.

(3) For the purposes of this Act a person shall be treated as a member of a class if in his case all the conditions identifying a member of the class are satisfied, and shall be treated as a potential member if in his case some only of those conditions are satisfied but there is a possibility that the remainder will in time be satisfied.

(4) Nothing in this Act shall affect the operation of the rule of law rendering void for remoteness certain dispositions under which property is limited to be applied for purposes other than the benefit of any person or class of persons in cases where the property may be so applied after the end of the perpetuity period.

(5) The foregoing sections of this Act shall apply (except as provided in section 8(2) above) only in relation to instruments taking effect after the commencement of this Act, and in the case of an instrument made in the exercise of a special power of appointment shall apply only where the instrument creating the power takes effect after that commencement: provided that section 7 above shall apply in all cases for construing the foregoing reference to a special power of appointment.

(6) This Act shall apply in relation to a disposition made otherwise than by an instrument as if the disposition had been contained in an instrument taking effect when the disposition was made.

(7) This Act binds the Crown ...

As amended by the Children Act 1975, s108(1)(a), Schedule 3, para 43.

LAW OF PROPERTY (JOINT TENANTS) ACT 1964

(1964 c 63)

1   Assumptions on sale of land by survivor of joint tenants

(1) For the purposes of section 36(2) of the Law of Property Act 1925, as amended by section 7 of and the Schedule to the Law of Property (Amendment) Act 1926, the survivor of two or more joint tenants shall in favour of a purchaser of the legal estate, be deemed to be solely and beneficially interested if the conveyance includes a statement that he is so interested.

Provided that the foregoing provisions of this subsection shall not apply if, at any time before the date of the conveyance by the survivor –

(a) a memorandum of severance (that is to say a note or memorandum signed by the joint tenants or one of them and recording that the joint tenancy was severed in equity on a date therein specified) had been endorsed on or annexed to the conveyance by virtue of which the legal estate was vested in the joint tenants; or

(b) a bankruptcy order made against any of the joint tenants, or a petition for such an order, had been registered under the Land Charges Act 1925, being an order or petition of which the purchaser has notice, by virtue of the registration, on the date of the conveyance by the survivor.

(2) The foregoing provisions of this section shall apply with the necessary modifications in relation to a conveyance by the personal representatives of the survivor of joint tenants as they apply in relation to a conveyance by such a survivor.

3   Exclusion of registered land

This Act shall not apply to registered land.

As amended by the Insolvency Act 1985, s235(1), Schedule 8, para 13; Law of Property (Miscellaneous Provisions) Act 1994, s21(1), (2), Schedule 1, para 3, Schedule 2; Land Registration Act 2002, s133, Schedule 11, para 5.

COMMONS REGISTRATION ACT 1965
(1965 c 64)

1 Registration of commons and towns or village greens and ownership of and rights over them

(1) There shall be registered, in accordance with the provisions of this Act and subject to the exceptions mentioned therein –

(a) land in England or Wales which is common land or a town or village green;

(b) rights of common over such land; and

(c) persons claiming to be or found to be owners of such land or becoming the owners thereof by virtue of this Act;

and no rights of common over land which is capable of being registered under this Act shall be registered in the register of title.

(2) After the end of such period, not being less than three years from the commencement of this Act, as the Minister may by order determine –

(a) no land capable of being registered under this Act shall be deemed to be common land or a town or village green unless it is so registered; and

(b) no rights of common shall be exercisable over any such land unless they are registered either under this Act or in the register of title.

(3) Where any land is registered under this Act but no person is registered as the owner thereof under this Act in the register of title, it shall –

(a) if it is a town or village green, be vested in accordance with the following provisions of this Act; and

(b) if it is common land, be vested as Parliament may hereafter determine.

8 Vesting of unclaimed land

(1) Where the registration under section 4 of this Act [provisional registration] of any land as common land or as a town or village green has become final but no person is registered under that section as the owner of the land, then unless the land is registered in the register of title, the registration authority shall refer the question of the ownership of the land to a Commons Commissioner.

(2) After the registration authority has given such notices as may be prescribed, the Commons Commissioner shall inquire into the matter and shall, if satisfied that

any person is the owner of the land, direct the registration authority to register that person accordingly; and the registration authority shall comply with the direction.

(3) If the Commons Commissioner is not so satisfied and the land is a town or village green he shall direct the registration authority to register as the owner of the land the local authority specified in subsection (5) of this section [as substituted]; and the registration authority shall comply with the direction ...

9   Protection of unclaimed common land

Where the registration under section 4 of this Act of any land as common land has become final but no person is registered under this Act or in the register of title as the owner of the land, then, until the land is vested under any provision hereafter made by Parliament, any local authority in whose area the land or part of the land is situated may take such steps for the protection of the land against unlawful interference as could be taken by an owner in possession of the land, and may (without prejudice to any power exercisable apart from this section) institute proceedings for any offence committed in respect of that land.

10   Effect of registration

The registration under this Act of any land as common land or as a town or village green, or of any rights of common over any such land, shall be conclusive evidence of the matters registered, as at the date of registration, except where the registration is provisional only.

12   Subsequent registration under Land Registration Acts 1925 and 1936

The following provisions shall have effect with respect to the registration in the register of title of any land after the ownership of the land has been registered under this Act, that is to say –

(b) if the registration authority is notified by the Chief Land Registrar that the land has been registered in the register of title the authority shall delete the registration of the ownership under this Act and indicate in the register in the prescribed manner that it has been registered under those Acts.

16   Disregard of certain interruptions in prescriptive claims to rights of common

(1) Where during any period a right of common claimed over any land was not exercised, but during the whole or part of that period either –

(a) the land was requisitioned; or

(b) where the right claimed is a right to graze animals, the right could not be or was not exercised for reasons of animal health;

that period or part shall be left out of account, both –

(i) in determining for the purposes of the Prescription Act 1832 whether there was an interruption within the meaning of that Act of the actual enjoyment of the right; and

(ii) in computing the period of thirty or sixty years mentioned in section 1 of that Act.

(2) For the purposes of the said Act any objection under this Act to the registration of a right of common shall be deemed to be such a suit or action as is referred to in section 4 of that Act.

(3) In this section 'requisitioned' means in the possession of a Government department in the exercise or purported exercise of powers conferred by regulations made under the Emergency Powers (Defence) Act 1939 or by Part VI of the Requisitioned Land and War Works Act 1945; and in determining in any proceedings any question arising under this section whether any land was requisitioned during any period a document purporting to be a certificate to that effect issued by a Government department shall be admissible in evidence.

(4) Where it is necessary for the purposes of this section to establish that a right to graze animals on any land could not be or was not exercised for reasons of animal health it shall be sufficient to prove either –

(a) that the movement of the animals to that land was prohibited or restricted by or under the Diseases of Animals Act 1950 or any enactment repealed by that Act; or

(b) that the land was not, but some other land was, approved for grazing under any scheme in force under that Act or any such enactment and the animals were registered, or were undergoing tests with a view to registration, under the scheme.

21   Savings

(1) Section 1(2) of this Act shall not affect the application to any land registered under this Act of section 193 or section 194 of the Law of Property Act 1925 (rights of access to, and restriction on inclosure of, land over which rights of common are exercisable).

(2) Section 10 of this Act shall not apply for the purpose of deciding whether any land forms part of a highway.

22   Interpretation

(1) In this Act, unless the context otherwise requires –

'common land' means –

(a) land subject to rights of common (as defined in this Act) whether those rights are exercisable at all times or only during limited periods;

(b) waste land of a manor not subject to rights of common;

but does not include a town or village green or any land which forms part of a highway;

'land' includes land covered with water;

'local authority' means the council of a county, London borough or county district, the council of a parish;

'the Minister' means the Minister of Housing and Local Government;

'prescribed' means prescribed by regulations under this Act;

'register of title' means the register kept under section 1 of the Land Registration Act 2002;

'registration' includes an entry in the register made in pursuance of section 13 of this Act [amendment of registers];

'rights of common' includes cattlegates or beastgates (by whatever name known) and rights of sole or several vesture or herbage or of sole or several pasture, but does not include rights held for a term of years or from year to year;

'town or village green' means land which has been allotted by or under any Act for the exercise or recreation of the inhabitants of any locality or on which the inhabitants of any locality have a customary right to indulge in lawful sports and pastimes or which falls within subsection (1A) of this section.

(1A) Land falls within this subsection if it is land on which for not less than twenty years a significant number of the inhabitants of any locality, or of any neighbourhood within a locality, have indulged in lawful sports and pastimes as of right, and either –

(a) continue to do so, or

(b) have ceased to do so for not more than such period as may be prescribed, or determined in accordance with prescribed provisions.

(1B) If regulations made for the purposes of paragraph (b) of subsection (1A) of this section provide for the period mentioned in that paragraph to come to an end unless prescribed steps are taken, the regulations may also require registration authorities to make available in accordance with the regulations, on payment of any prescribed fee, information relating to the taking of any such steps.

(2) References in this Act to the ownership and the owner of any land are references to the ownership of a legal estate in fee simple in any land and to the person holding that estate, and references to land registered in the register of title are references to land the fee simple of which is so registered.

As amended by the Local Government Act 1972, s272(1), Schedule 30; Local Government Act 1985, s102(2), Schedule 17; Land Registration Act 1997, s4(2), Schedule 2, Pt I; Countryside and Rights of Way Act 2000, s98; Land Registration Act 2002, s133, Schedule 11, para 7.

MISREPRESENTATION ACT 1967
(1967 c 7)

1   Removal of certain bars to rescission for innocent misrepresentation

Where a person has entered into a contract after a misrepresen-tation has been made to him, and –

(a) the misrepresentation has become a term of the contract; or

(b) the contract has been performed;

or both, then, if otherwise he would be entitled to rescind the contract without alleging fraud, he shall be so entitled, subject to the provisions of this Act, notwithstanding the matters mentioned in paragraphs (a) and (b) of this section.

2   Damages for misrepresentation

(1) Where a person has entered into a contract after a misrepresentation has been made to him by another party thereto and as a result thereof he has suffered loss, then, if the person making the misrepresentation would be liable to damages in respect thereof had the misrepresentation been made fraudulently, that person shall be so liable notwithstanding that the misrepresentation was not made fraudulently, unless he proves that he had reasonable ground to believe and did believe up to the time the contract was made that the facts represented were true.

(2) Where a person has entered into a contract after a misrepresentation has been made to him otherwise than fraudulently, and he would be entitled, by reason of the misrepresentation, to rescind the contract, then, if it is claimed, in any proceedings arising out of the contract, that the contract ought to be or has been rescinded the court or arbitrator may declare the contract subsisting and award damages in lieu of rescission, if of opinion that it would be equitable to do so, having regard to the nature of the misrepresentation and the loss that would be caused by it if the contract were upheld, as well as to the loss that rescission would cause to the other party.

(3) Damages may be awarded against a person under subsection (2) of this section whether or not he is liable to damages under subsection (1) thereof, but where he is so liable any award under the said subsection (2) shall be taken into account in assessing his liability under the said subsection (1).

3   Avoidance of provision excluding liability for misrepresentation

If a contract contains a term which would exclude or restrict –

(a) any liability to which a party to a contract may be subject by reason of any misrepresentation made by him before the contract was made; or

(b) any remedy available to another party to the contract by reason of such misrepresentation,

that term shall be of no effect except in so far as it satisfies the requirement of reasonableness stated in section 11(1) of the Unfair Contract Terms Act 1977; and it is for those claiming that the term satisfies that requirement to show that it does.

As amended by the Unfair Contract Terms Act 1977, s8(1).

LEASEHOLD REFORM ACT 1967
(1967 c 88)

PART I

ENFRANCHISEMENT AND EXTENSION OF LONG LEASEHOLDS

1   Tenants entitled to enfranchisement or extension

(1) This Part of this Act shall have effect to confer on a tenant of a leasehold house a right to acquire on fair terms the freehold or an extended lease of the house and premises where –

(a) his tenancy is a long tenancy at a low rent and –

(i) if the tenancy was entered into before 1st April 1990, or on or after 1st April 1990 in pursuance of a contract made before that date, and the house and premises had a rateable value at the date of commencement of the tenancy or else at any time before 1st April 1990, subject to subsections (5) and (6) below, the rateable value of the house and premises on the appropriate day was not more than £200 or, if it is in Greater London, than £400; and

(ii) if the tenancy does not fall within sub-paragraph (i) above, on the date the contract for the grant of the tenancy was made or, if there was no such contract, on the date the tenancy was entered into R did not exceed £25,000 under the formula –

$$R = \frac{P \times I}{1 - (1 + I)^{-T}}$$

where –

P is the premium payable as a condition of the grant of the tenancy (and includes a payment of money's worth) or, where no premium is so payable, zero,

I is 0.06, and

T is the term, expressed in years, granted by the tenancy (disregarding any right to terminate the tenancy before the end of the term or to extend the tenancy); and

(b) at the relevant time (that is to say, at the time when he gives notice in accordance with this Act of his desire to have the freehold or to have an extended lease, as the case may be) he has been tenant of the house under a long tenancy at a low rent for the last two years;

and to confer the like right in the other cases for which provision is made in this Part of this Act.

(1ZA) Where a house is for the time being let under two or more tenancies, a tenant under any of those tenancies which is superior to that held by any tenant on whom this Part of this Act confers a right does not have any right under this Part of this Act.

(1ZB) Where a flat forming part of a house is let to a person who is a qualifying tenant of the flat for the purposes of Chapter 1 or 2 of Part 1 of the Leasehold Reform, Housing and Urban Development Act 1993 (c 28), a tenant of the house does not have any right under this Part of this Act unless, at the relevant time, he has been occupying the house, or any part of it, as his only or main residence (whether or not he has been using it for other purposes) –

(a) for the last two years; or

(b) for periods amounting to two years in the last ten years.

(1ZC) The references in subsection (1)(a) and (b) to a long tenancy do not include a tenancy to which Part 2 of the Landlord and Tenant Act 1954 (business tenancies) applies unless –

(a) it is granted for a term of years certain exceeding thirty-five years, whether or not it is (or may become) terminable before the end of that term by notice given by or to the tenant or by re-entry, forfeiture or otherwise,

(b) it is for a term fixed by law under a grant with a covenant or obligation for perpetual renewal, unless it is a tenancy by sub-demise from one which is not a tenancy which falls within any of the paragraphs in this subsection,

(c) it is a tenancy taking effect under section 149(6) of the Law of Property Act 1925 (c 20) (leases terminable after a death or marriage or the formation of a civil partnership), or

(d) it is a tenancy which –

(i) is or has been granted for a term of years certain not exceeding thirty-five years, but with a covenant or obligation for renewal without payment of a premium (but not for perpetual renewal), and

(ii) is or has been once or more renewed so as to bring to more than thirty-five years the total of the terms granted (including any interval between the end of a tenancy and the grant of a renewal).

(1ZD) Where this Part of this Act applies as if there were a single tenancy of property comprised in two or more separate tenancies, then, if each of the separate tenancies falls within any of the paragraphs of subsection (1ZC) above, that subsection shall apply as if the single tenancy did so.

(1A) The references in subsection (1)(a) and (b) to a long tenancy at a low rent do not include a tenancy excluded from the operation of this Part by section 33A of and Schedule 4A to this Act.

(1B) This Part of this Act shall not have effect to confer any right on the tenant of a house under a tenancy to which Part 2 of the Landlord and Tenant Act 1954 (c 56) (business tenancies) applies unless, at the relevant time, the tenant has been occupying the house, or any part of it, as his only or main residence (whether or not he has been using it for other purposes) –

(a) for the last two years; or

(b) for periods amounting to two years in the last ten years.

(3) This Part of this Act shall not confer on the tenant of a house any right by reference to his being a tenant of it at any time when –

(a) it is let to him with other land or premises to which it is ancillary; or

(b) it is comprised in –

(i) an agricultural holding within the meaning of the Agricultural Holdings Act 1986 held under a tenancy in relation to which that Act applies, or

(ii) the holding held under a farm business tenancy within the meaning of the Agricultural Tenancies Act 1995;

or, in the case of any right to which subsection (3A) below applies, at any time when the tenant's immediate landlord is a charitable housing trust and the house forms part of the housing accommodation provided by the trust in the pursuit of its charitable purposes.

(3A) For the purposes of subsection (3) above this subsection applies as follows –

(a) where the tenancy was created after the commencement of Chapter III of Part I of the Leasehold Reform, Housing and Urban Development Act 1993, this subsection applies to any right to acquire the freehold of the house and premises; but

(b) where the tenancy was created before that commencement, this subsection applies only to any such right exercisable by virtue of any one or more of the provisions of sections 1A, 1AA and 1B below;

and in that subsection 'charitable housing trust' means a housing trust within the meaning of the Housing Act 1985 which is a charity within the meaning of the Charities Act 1993.

(4) In subsection (1)(a) above, 'the appropriate day', in relation to any house and premises, means the 23rd March 1965 or such later day as by virtue of section 25(3) of the Rent Act 1977 would be the appropriate day for purposes of that Act in relation to a dwelling house consisting of that house.

(4A) Schedule 8 to the Housing Act 1974 shall have effect to enable a tenant to have the rateable value of the house and premises reduced for purposes of this section in consequence of tenant's improvements.

(5) If, in relation to any house and premises, the appropriate day for the purposes of subsection (1)(a) above falls on or after 1st April 1973 that subsection shall have effect in relation to the house and premises –

(a) in a case where the tenancy was created on or before 18th February 1966, as if for the sums of £200 and £400 specified in that subsection there were substituted respectively the sums of £750 and £1,500; and

(b) in a case where the tenancy was created after 18th February 1966, as if for those sums of £200 and £400 there were substituted respectively the sums of £500 and £1,000.

(6) If, in relation to any house and premises –

(a) the appropriate day for the purposes of subsection (1)(a) above falls before 1st April 1973, and

(b) the rateable value of the house and premises on the appropriate day was more than £200 or, if it was then in Greater London, £400, and

(c) the tenancy was created on or before 18th February 1966,

subsection (1)(a) above shall have effect in relation to the house and premises as if for the reference to the appropriate day there were substituted a reference to 1st April 1973 and as if for the sums of £200 and £400 specified in that subsection there were substituted respectively the sums of £750 and £1,500.

(7) The Secretary of State may by order replace any amount referred to in subsection (1)(a)(ii) above and the number in the definition of 'T' in that subsection by such amount or number as is specified in the order …

1A   Right to enfranchisement only in case of houses whose value or rent exceeds applicable limit under section 1 or 4

(1) Where subsection (1) of section 1 above would apply in the case of the tenant of a house but for the fact that the applicable financial limit specified in subsection (1)(a)(i) or (ii) or (as the case may be) subsection (5) or (6) of that section is exceeded, this Part of this Act shall have effect to confer on the tenant the same right to acquire the freehold of the house and premises as would be conferred by subsection (1) of that section if that limit were not exceeded.

(2) Where a tenancy of any property is not a tenancy at a low rent in accordance with section 4(1) below but is a tenancy falling within section 4A(1) below, the tenancy shall nevertheless be treated as a tenancy at a low rent for the purposes of this Part of this Act so far as it has effect for conferring on any person a right to acquire the freehold of a house and premises.

1AA Additional right to enfranchisement only in case of houses whose rent exceeds applicable limit under section 4

(1) Where –

(a) section 1(1) above would apply in the case of the tenant of a house but for the fact that the tenancy is not a tenancy at a low rent, and

(b) the tenancy is not an excluded tenancy,

this Part of this Act shall have effect to confer on the tenant the same right to acquire the freehold of the house and premises as would be conferred by section 1(1) above if it were a tenancy at a low rent.

(3) A tenancy is an excluded tenancy for the purposes of subsection (1) above if –

(a) the house which the tenant occupies under the tenancy is in an area designated for the purposes of this provision as a rural area by order made by the Secretary of State,

(b) the freehold of that house is owned together with adjoining land which is not occupied for residential purposes and has been owned together with such land since 1st April 1997 (the date on which section 106 of the Housing Act 1996 came into force), and

(c) the tenancy either –

(i) was granted on or before that date, or

(ii) was granted after that date, but on or before the coming into force of section 141 of the Commonhold and Leasehold Reform Act 2002, for a term of years certain not exceeding thirty-five years. ...

1B   Right of enfranchisement only in case of certain tenancies terminable after death or marriage

Where a tenancy granted so as to become terminable by notice after a death, a marriage or the formation of a civil partnership –

(a) is (apart from this section) a long tenancy in accordance with section 3(1) below, but

(b) was granted before 18th April 1980 or in pursuance of a contract entered into before that date,

then (notwithstanding section 3(1)) the tenancy shall be a long tenancy for the purposes of this Part of this Act only so far as this Part has effect for conferring on any person a right to acquire the freehold of a house and premises.

2   Meaning of 'house' and 'house and premises', and adjustment of boundary

(1) For purposes of this Part of this Act, 'house' includes any building designed or adapted for living in and reasonably so called, notwithstanding that the building is not structurally detached, or was or is not solely designed or adapted for living in, or is divided horizontally into flats or maisonettes; and –

(a) where a building is divided horizontally, the flats or other units into which it is so divided are not separate 'houses', though the building as a whole may be; and

(b) where a building is divided vertically the building as a whole is not a 'house' though any of the units into which it is divided may be.

(2) References in this Part of this Act to a house do not apply to a house which is not

structurally detached and of which a material part lies above or below a part of the structure not comprised in the house ...

3   Meaning of 'long tenancy'

(1) In this Part of this Act 'long tenancy' means, subject to the provisions of this section, a tenancy granted for a term of years certain exceeding twenty-one years, whether or not the tenancy is (or may become) terminable before the end of that term by notice given by or to the tenant or by re-entry, forfeiture or otherwise, and includes both a tenancy taking effect under section 149(6) of the Law of Property Act 1925 (leases terminable after a death or marriage or the formation of a civil partnership) and a tenancy for a term fixed by law under a grant with a covenant or obligation for perpetual renewal unless it is a tenancy by sub-demise from one which is not a long tenancy: provided that a tenancy granted so as to become terminable by notice after a death or marriage is not to be treated as a long tenancy if –

(a) the notice is capable of being given at any time after the death or marriage of the tenant;

(b) the length of the notice is not more than three months; and

(c) the terms of the tenancy preclude both –

(i) its assignment otherwise than by virtue of section 92 of the Housing Act 1985 (assignments by way of exchange), and

(ii) the sub-letting of the whole of the premises comprised in it ...

4   Meaning of 'low rent'

(1) For purposes of this Part of this Act a tenancy of any property is a tenancy at a low rent at any time when rent is not payable under the tenancy in respect of the property at a yearly rate –

(i) if the tenancy was entered into before 1st April 1990, or on or after 1st April 1990 in pursuance of a contract made before that date, and the property had a rateable value other than nil at the date of the commencement of the tenancy or else at any time before 1st April 1990, equal to or more than two-thirds of the rateable value of the property on the appropriate day or, if later, the first day of the term;

(ii) if the tenancy does not fall within paragraph (i) above, more than £1,000 if the property is in Greater London and £250 if the property is elsewhere ...

4A   Alternative rent limits for purposes of section 1A(2)

(1) For the purposes of section 1A(2) above a tenancy of any property falls within this subsection if either no rent was payable under it in respect of the property during the initial year or the aggregate amount of rent so payable during the year did not exceed the following amount, namely –

(a) where the tenancy was entered into before 1st April 1963, two-thirds of the letting value of the property (on the same terms) on the date of the commencement of the tenancy;

(b) where –

(i) the tenancy was entered into either on or after 1st April 1963 but before 1st April 1990, or on or after 1st April 1990 in pursuance of a contract made before that date, and

(ii) the property had a rateable value other than nil at the date of commencement of the tenancy or else at any time before 1st April 1990,

two-thirds of the rateable value of the property on the relevant date; or

(c) in any other case, £1,000 if the property is in Greater London or £250 if elsewhere.

(2) For the purposes of subsection (1) above –

(a) 'the initial year', in relation to any tenancy, means the period of one year beginning with the date of the commencement of the tenancy;

(b) 'the relevant date' means the date of the commencement of the tenancy or, if the property did not have a rateable value or had a rateable value of nil, on that date, the date on which it first had a rateable value other than nil; and

(c) paragraphs (b) and (c) of section 4(1) above shall apply as they apply for the purposes of section 4(1);

and it is hereby declared that in subsection (1) above the reference to the letting value of any property is to be construed in like manner as the reference in similar terms which appears in the proviso to section 4(1) above.

(3) Section 1(7) above applies to any amount referred to in subsection (1)(c) above as it applies to the amount referred to in subsection (1)(a)(ii) of that section.

As amended by the Housing Act 1974, s118(1); Housing and Planning Act 1968, s18, Schedule 4, paras 3, 11(1); Rent Act 1977, s155, Schedule 23, para 42; Housing Act 1980, s141, Schedule 21, paras 1, 2; Agricultural Holdings Act 1986, s100, Schedule 14, para 13; References to Rating (Housing) Regulations 1990, as amended; Leasehold Reform, Housing and Urban Development Act 1993, ss63, 64(1), (2), 65, 67; Agricultural Tenancies Act 1995, s40, Schedule, para 22; Housing Act 1996, ss105(1), (2), 106, 114, Schedule 9, paras 1, 2(2); Commonhold and Leasehold Reform Act 2002, ss138(1)–(3), 139(1), (2), 140, 141, 180, Schedule 14; Civil Partnership Act 2004, s80, Schedule 8, paras 3–5.

LAW OF PROPERTY ACT 1969
(1969 c 59)

23   Reduction of statutory period of title

Section 44(1) of the Law of Property Act 1925 (under which the period of commencement of title which may be required under a contract expressing no contrary intention is thirty years except in certain cases) shall have effect, in its application to contracts made after the commencement of this Act, as if it specified fifteen years instead of thirty years as the period of commencement of title which may be so required.

24   Contracts for purchase of land affected by land charge, etc

(1) Where under a contract for the sale or other disposition of any estate or interest in land the title to which is not registered under the Land Registration Act 2002 or any enactment replaced by it any question arises whether the purchaser had knowledge, at the time of entering into the contract, of a registered land charge, that question shall be determined by reference to his actual knowledge and without regard to the provisions of section 198 of the Law of Property Act 1925 (under which registration under the Land Charges Act 1925 or any enactment replaced by it is deemed to constitute actual notice).

(2) Where any estate or interest with which such a contract is concerned is affected by a registered land charge and the purchaser, at the time of entering into the contract, had not received notice and did not otherwise actually know that the estate or interest was affected by the charge, any provision of the contract shall be void so far as it purports to exclude the operation of subsection (1) above or to exclude or restrict any right or remedy that might otherwise be exercisable by the purchaser on the ground that the estate or interest is affected by the charge.

(3) In this section –

'purchaser' includes a lessee, mortgagee or other person acquiring or intending to acquire an estate or interest in land; and

'registered land charge' means any instrument or matter registered, otherwise than in a register of local land charges, under the Land Charges Act 1925 or any Act replaced by it.

(4) For the purposes of this section any knowledge acquired in the course of a transaction by a person who is acting therein as counsel, or as solicitor or other agent, for another shall be treated as the knowledge of that other ...

25 Compensation in certain cases for loss due to undisclosed land charges

(1) Where a purchaser of any estate or interest in land under a disposition to which this section applies has suffered loss by reason that the estate or interest is affected by a registered land charge, then if –

(a) the date of completion was after the commencement of this Act; and

(b) on that date the purchaser had no actual knowledge of the charge; and

(c) the charge was registered against the name of an owner of an estate in the land who was not as owner of any such estate a party to any transaction, or concerned in any event, comprised in the relevant title;

the purchaser shall be entitled to compensation for the loss.

(2) For the purposes of subsection (1)(b) above, the question whether any person had actual knowledge of a charge shall be determined without regard to the provisions of section 198 of the Law of Property Act 1925 (under which registration under the Land Charges Act 1925 or any enactment replaced by it is deemed to constitute actual notice).

(3) Where a transaction comprised in the relevant title was effected or evidenced by a document which expressly provided that it should take effect subject to an interest or obligation capable of registration in any of the relevant registers, the transaction which created that interest or obligation shall be treated for the purposes of subsection (1)(c) above as comprised in the relevant title.

(4) Any compensation for loss under this section shall be paid by the Chief Land Registrar, and where the purchaser of the estate or interest in question has incurred expenditure for the purpose –

(a) of securing that the estate or interest is no longer affected by the registered land charge or is so affected to a less extent; or

(b) of obtaining compensation under this section;

the amount of the compensation shall include the amount of the expenditure (so far as it would not otherwise fall to be treated as compensation for loss) reasonably incurred by the purchaser for that purpose.

(5) In the case of an action to recover compensation under this section, the cause of action shall be deemed for the purposes of the Limitation Act 1980 to accrue at the time when the registered land charge affecting the estate or interest in question comes to the notice of the purchaser ...

(8) Where compensation under this section has been paid in a case where the purchaser would have had knowledge of the registered land charge but for the fraud of any person, the Chief Land Registrar, on behalf of the Crown, may recover the amount paid from that person.

(9) This section applies to the following dispositions, that is to say –

(a) any sale or exchange and, subject to the following provisions of this subsection, any mortgage of an estate or interest in land;

(b) any grant of a lease for a term of years derived out of a leasehold interest;

(c) any compulsory purchase, by whatever procedure, of land; and

(d) any conveyance of a fee simple in land under Part I of the Leasehold Reform Act 1967;

but does not apply to the grant of a term of years derived out of the freehold or the mortgage of such a term by the lessee; and references in this section to a purchaser shall be construed accordingly.

(10) In this section –

'date of completion', in relation to land which vests in the Land Commission or another acquiring authority by virtue of a general vesting declaration under the Land Commission Act 1967 or the Town and Country Planning Act 1968, means the date on which it so vests;

'mortgage' includes any charge;

'registered land charge' means any instrument or matter registered, otherwise than in a register of local land charges, under the Land Charges Act 1925 or any Act replaced by it, except that –

(a) in relation to an assignment of a lease or underlease or a mortgage by an assignee under such an assignment, it does not include any instrument or matter affecting the title to the freehold or to any relevant leasehold reversion; and

(b) in relation to the grant of an underlease or the mortgage by the underlessee of the term of years created by an underlease, it does not include any instrument or matter affecting the title to the freehold or to any leasehold reversion superior to the leasehold interest out of which the term of years is derived;

'relevant registers' means the registers kept under section 1 of the Land Charges Act [1972];

'relevant title' means –

(a) in relation to a disposition made under a contract, the title which the purchaser was, apart from any acceptance by him (by agreement or otherwise) of a shorter or an imperfect title, entitled to require; or

(b) in relation to any other disposition, the title which he would have been entitled to require if the disposition had been made under a contract to which section 44(1) of the Law of Property Act 1925 applied and that contract had been made on the date of completion.

(11) For the purposes of this section any knowledge acquired in the course of a transaction by a person who is acting therein as counsel, or as solicitor or other agent, for another shall be treated as the knowledge of that other.

As amended by the Limitation Act 1980, s40(2), Schedule 3, para 9; Land Registration Act 2002, s133, Schedule 11, para 9.

ADMINISTRATION OF JUSTICE ACT 1970
(1970 c 31)

36 Additional powers of court in action by mortgagee for possession of dwelling-house

(1) Where the mortgagee under a mortgage of land which consists of or includes a dwelling-house brings an action in which he claims possession of the mortgaged property, not being an action for foreclosure in which a claim for possession of the mortgaged property is also made, the court may exercise any of the powers conferred on it by subsection (2) below if it appears to the court that in the event of its exercising the power the mortgagor is likely to be able within a reasonable period to pay any sums due under the mortgage or to remedy a default consisting of a breach of any other obligation arising under or by virtue of the mortgage.

(2) The court –

(a) may adjourn the proceedings, or

(b) on giving judgment, or making an order, for delivery of possession of the mortgaged property, or at any time before the execution of such judgment or order, may –

(i) stay or suspend execution of the judgment or order, or

(ii) postpone the date for delivery of possession,

for such period or periods as the court thinks reasonable.

(3) Any such adjournment, stay, suspension or postponement as is referred to in subsection (2) above may be made subject to such conditions with regard to payment by the mortgagor of any sum secured by the mortgage or the remedying of any default as the court thinks fit.

(4) The court may from time to time vary or revoke any condition imposed by virtue of this section. ...

39 Interpretation of Part IV

(1) In this Part of this Act –

'dwelling-house' includes any building or part thereof which is used as a dwelling;

'mortgage' includes a charge and 'mortgagor' and 'mortgagee' shall be construed accordingly;

'mortgagor' and 'mortgagee' includes any person deriving title under the original mortgagor or mortgagee.

(2) The fact that part of the premises comprised in a dwelling-house is used as a shop or office or for business, trade or professional purposes shall not prevent the dwelling-house from being a dwelling-house for the purposes of this Part of this Act.

As amended by the Statute Law (Repeals) Act 2004, s1(1), Schedule 1, Pt 12.

DEFECTIVE PREMISES ACT 1972
(1972 c 35)

4   Landlord's duty of care in virtue of obligation or right to repair premises demised

(1) Where premises are let under a tenancy which puts on the landlord an obligation to the tenant for the maintenance or repair of the premises, the landlord owes to all persons who might reasonably be expected to be affected by defects in the state of the premises a duty to take such care as is reasonable in all the circumstances to see that they are reasonably safe from personal injury or from damage to their property caused by a relevant defect.

(2) The said duty is owed if the landlord knows (whether as the result of being notified by the tenant or otherwise) or if he ought in all the circumstances to have known of the relevant defect.

(3) In this section 'relevant defect' means a defect in the state of the premises existing at or after the material time and arising from, or continuing because of, an act or omission by the landlord which constitutes or would if he had had notice of the defect have constituted a failure by him to carry out his obligation to the tenant for the maintenance or repair of the premises; and for the purposes of the foregoing provision 'the material time' means –

  (a) where the tenancy commenced before this Act, the commencement of this Act; and

  (b) in all other cases, the earliest of the following times, that is to say –

    (i) the time when the tenancy commences;

    (ii) the time when the tenancy agreement is entered into;

    (iii) the time when possession is taken of the premises in contemplation of the letting.

(4) Where premises are let under a tenancy which expressly or impliedly gives the landlord the right to enter the premises to carry out any description of maintenance or repair of the premises, then, as from the time when he first is, or by notice or otherwise can put himself, in a position to exercise the right and so long as he is or can put himself in that position, he shall be treated for the purposes of subsections (1) to (3) above (but for no other purpose) as if he were under an obligation to the tenant for that description of maintenance or repair of the premises; but the landlord shall not owe the tenant any duty by virtue of this subsection in respect

of any defect in the state of the premises arising from, or continuing because of, a failure to carry out an obligation expressly imposed on the tenant by the tenancy.

(5) For the purposes of this section obligations imposed or rights given by any enactment in virtue of a tenancy shall be treated as imposed or given by the tenancy.

(6) This section applies to a right of occupation given by contract or any enactment and not amounting to a tenancy as if the right were a tenancy, and 'tenancy' and cognate expressions shall be construed accordingly.

6   Supplemental

(1) In this Act –

...

'personal injury' includes any disease and any impairment of a person's physical or mental condition;

'tenancy' means –

(a) a tenancy created either immediately or derivatively out of the freehold, whether by a lease or underlease, by an agreement for a lease or underlease or by a tenancy agreement, but not including a mortgage term or any interest arising in favour of a mortgagor by his attorning tenant to his mortgagee; or

(b) a tenancy at will or a tenancy on sufferance; or

(c) a tenancy, whether or not constituting a tenancy at common law, created by or in pursuance of any enactment; and cognate expressions shall be construed accordingly.

(2) Any duty imposed by or enforceable by virtue of any provision of this Act is in addition to any duty a person may owe apart from that provision.

(3) Any term of an agreement which purports to exclude or restrict, or has the effect of excluding or restricting, the operation of any of the provisions of this Act, or any liability arising by virtue of any such provision, shall be void.

LAND CHARGES ACT 1972
(1972 c 61)

1   The registers and the index

(1) The registrar shall continue to keep at the registry in the prescribed manner the following registers, namely –

    (a) a register of land charges;

    (b) a register of pending actions;

    (c) a register of writs and orders affecting land,

    (d) a register of deeds of arrangement affecting land;

    (e) a register of annuities,

and shall also continue to keep there an index whereby all entries made in any of those registers can readily be traced.

(2) Every application to register shall be in the prescribed form and shall contain the prescribed particulars.

(3) Where any charge or other matter is registrable in more than one of the registers kept under this Act, it shall be sufficient if it is registered in one such register, and if it is so registered the person entitled to the benefit of it shall not be prejudicially affected by any provision of this Act as to the effect of non-registration in any other such register.

(3A) Where any charge or other matter is registrable in a register kept under this Act and was also, before the commencement of the Local Land Charges Act 1975, registrable in a local land charges register, then, if before the commencement of the said Act it was registered in the appropriate local land charges register, it shall be treated for the purposes of the provisions of this Act as to the effect of non-registration as if it had been registered in the appropriate register under this Act; and any certificate setting out the result of an official search of the appropriate local land charges register shall, in relation to it, have effect as if it were a certificate setting out the result of an official search under this Act.

(4) Schedule 1 to this Act shall have effect in relation to the register of annuities.

(5) An office copy of an entry in any register kept under this section shall be admissible in evidence in all proceedings and between all parties to the same extent as the original would be admissible.

(6) Subject to the provisions of this Act, registration may be vacated pursuant to an order of the court.

(6A) The county courts have jurisdiction under subsection (6) above –

(a) in the case of a land charge of Class C(i), C(ii) or D(i), if the amount does not exceed £30,000;

(b) in the case of a land charge of Class C(iii), if it is for a specified capital sum of money not exceeding £30,000 or, where it is not for a specified capital sum, if the capital value of the land affected does not exceed £30,000;

(c) in the case of a land charge of Class A, Class B, Class C(iv), Class D(ii), Class D(iii) or Class E if the capital value of the land affected does not exceed £30,000;

(d) in the case of a land charge of Class F, if the land affected by it is the subject of an order made by the court under section 1 of the Matrimonial Homes Act 1983 or section 33 of the Family Law Act 1996 or an application for an order under either of those sections relating to that land has been made to the court;

(e) in a case where an application under section 23 of the Deeds of Arrangement Act 1914 could be entertained by the court.

(7) In this section 'index' includes any device or combination of devices serving the purpose of an index.

2   The register of land charges

(1) If a charge on or obligation affecting land falls into one of the classes described in this section, it may be registered in the register of land charges as a land charge of that class.

(2) A Class A land charge is –

(a) a rent or annuity or principal money payable by instalments or otherwise, with or without interest, which is not a charge created by deed but is a charge upon land (other than a rate) created pursuant to the application of some person under the provisions of any Act of Parliament, for securing to any person either the money spent by him or the costs, charges and expenses incurred by him under such Act, or the money advanced by him for repaying the money spent or the costs, charges and expenses incurred by another person under the authority of an Act of Parliament; or

(b) a rent or annuity or principal money payable as mentioned in paragraph (a) above which is not a charge created by deed but is a charge upon land (other than a rate) created pursuant to the application of some person under any of the enactments mentioned in Schedule 2 to this Act.

(3) A Class B land charge is a charge on land (not being a local land charge) of any of the kinds described in paragraph (a) of subsection (2) above, created otherwise than pursuant to the application of any person.

(4) A Class C land charge is any of the following (not being a local land charge), namely –

(i) a puisne mortgage;

(ii) a limited owner's charge;

(iii) a general equitable charge;

(iv) an estate contract;

and for this purpose –

(i) a puisne mortgage is a legal mortgage which is not protected by a deposit of documents relating to the legal estate affected;

(ii) a limited owner's charge is an equitable charge acquired by a tenant for life or statutory owner under the Capital Transfer Tax Act 1984 or under any other statute by reason of the discharge by him of any capital transfer tax or other liabilities and to which special priority is given by the statute;

(iii) a general equitable charge is any equitable charge which –

(a) is not secured by a deposit of documents relating to the legal estate affected; and

(b) does not arise or affect an interest arising under a trust of land or a settlement; and

(c) is not a charge given by way of indemnity against rents equitably apportioned or charged exclusively on land in exoneration of other land and against the breach or non-observance of covenants or conditions; and

(d) is not included in any other class of land charge;

(iv) an estate contract is a contract by an estate owner or by a person entitled at the date of the contract to have a legal estate conveyed to him to convey or create a legal estate, including a contract conferring either expressly or by statutory implication a valid option to purchase, a right of pre-emption or any other like right.

(5) A Class D land charge is any of the following (not being a local land charge), namely –

(i) an Inland Revenue charge;

(ii) a restrictive covenant;

(iii) an equitable easement;

and for this purpose –

(i) an Inland Revenue charge is a charge on land, being a charge acquired by the Board under the Capital Transfer Tax Act 1984;

(ii) a restrictive covenant is a covenant or agreement (other than a covenant or agreement between a lessor and a lessee) restrictive of the user of land and entered into on or after 1st January 1926;

(iii) an equitable easement is an easement, right or privilege over or affecting land created or arising on or after 1st January 1926, and being merely an equitable interest.

(6) A Class E land charge is an annuity created before 1st January 1926 and not registered in the register of annuities.

(7) A Class F land charge is a charge affecting any land by virtue of Part IV of the Family Law Act 1996.

(8) A charge or obligation created before 1st January 1926 can only be registered as a Class B land charge or a Class C land charge if it is acquired under a conveyance made on or after that date.

3   Registration of land charges

(1) A land charge shall be registered in the name of the estate owner whose estate is intended to be affected.

(1A) Where a person has died and a land charge created before his death would apart from his death have been registered in his name, it shall be so registered notwithstanding his death.

(4) The expenses incurred by the person entitled to the charge in registering a land charge of Class A, Class B or Class C (other than an estate contract) or by the Board in registering an Inland Revenue charge shall be deemed to form part of the land charge, and shall be recoverable accordingly on the day for payment of any part of the land charge next after such expenses are incurred.

(5) Where a land charge is not created by an instrument, short particulars of the effect of the charge shall be furnished with the application to register the charge.

(6) An application to register an Inland Revenue charge shall state the tax in respect of which the charge is claimed and, so far as possible, shall define the land affected, and such particulars shall be entered or referred to in the register.

(7) In the case of a land charge for securing money created by a company before 1st January 1970 or so created at any time as a floating charge, registration under any of the enactments mentioned in subsection (8) below shall be sufficient in place of registration under this Act, and shall have effect as if the land charge had been registered under this Act.

(8) The enactments referred to in subsection (7) above are section 93 of the Companies (Consolidation) Act 1908, section 79 of the Companies Act 1929, section 95 of the Companies Act 1948 and sections 395 to 398 of the Companies Act 1985.

4   Effect of land charges and protection of purchasers

(1) A land charge of Class A (other than a land improvement charge registered after 31st December 1969) or of Class B shall, when registered, take effect as if it had been created by a deed of charge by way of legal mortgage, but without prejudice to the priority of the charge.

(2) A land charge of Class A created after 31st December 1888 shall be void as against a purchaser of the land charged with it or of any interest in such land, unless the land charge is registered in the register of land charges before the completion of the purchase.

(3) After the expiration of one year from the first conveyance occurring on or after

1st January 1889 of a land charge of Class A created before that date the person entitled to the land charge shall not be able to recover the land charge or any part of it as against a purchaser of the land charged with it or of any interest in the land, unless the land charge is registered in the register of land charges before the completion of the purchase.

(4) If a land improvement charge was registered as a land charge of Class A before 1st January 1970, any body corporate which, but for the charge, would have power to advance money on the security of the estate or interest affected by it shall have that power notwithstanding the charge.

(5) A land charge of Class B and a land charge of Class C (other than an estate contract) created or arising on or after 1st January 1926 shall be void as against a purchaser of the land charged with it, or of any interest in such land, unless the land charge is registered in the appropriate register before the completion of the purchase.

(6) An estate contract and a large charge of Class D created or entered into on or after 1st January 1926 shall be void as against a purchaser for money or money's worth (or, in the case of an Inland Revenue charge, a purchaser within the meaning of the Capital Transfer Tax Act 1984) of a legal estate in the land charged with it, unless the land charge is registered in the appropriate register before the completion of the purchase.

(7) After the expiration of one year from the first conveyance occurring on or after 1st January 1926 of a land charge of Class B or Class C created before that date the person entitled to the land charge shall not be able to enforce or recover the land charge or any part of it as against a purchaser of the land charged with it, or of any interest in the land, unless the land charge is registered in the appropriate register before the completion of the purchase.

(8) A land charge of Class F shall be void as against a purchaser of the land charged with it, or of any interest in such land, unless the land charge is registered in the appropriate register before the completion of the purchase.

5   The register of pending actions

(1) There may be registered in the register of pending actions –

    (a) a pending land action;

    (b) a petition in bankruptcy filed on or after 1st January 1926.

(2) Subject to general rules under section 16 of this Act, every application for registration under this section shall contain particulars of the title of the proceedings and the name, address and description of the estate owner or other person whose estate or interest is intended to be affected.

(3) An application for registration shall also state –

    (a) if it relates to a pending land action, the court in which and the day on which the action was commenced; and

(b) if it relates to a petition in bankruptcy, the court in which and the day on which the petition was filed.

(4) The registrar shall forthwith enter the particulars in the register, in the name of the estate owner or other person whose estate or interest is intended to be affected.

(4A) Where a person has died and a pending land action would apart from his death have been registered in his name, it shall be so registered notwithstanding his death.

(7) A pending land action shall not bind a purchaser without express notice of it unless it is for the time being registered under this section.

(8) A petition in bankruptcy shall not bind a purchaser of a legal estate in good faith, for money or money's worth, unless it is for the time being registered under this section.

(10) The court, if it thinks fit, may upon the determination of the proceedings, or during the pendency of the proceedings if satisfied that they are not prosecuted in good faith, make an order vacating a registration under this section, and direct the party on whose behalf it was made to pay all or any of the costs and expenses occasioned by the registration and by its vacation ...

6 The register of writs and orders affecting land

(1) There may be registered in the register of writs and orders affecting land –

(a) any writ or order affecting land issued or made by any court for the purpose of enforcing a judgment or recognisance;

(b) any order appointing a receiver or sequestrator of land;

(c) any bankruptcy order, whether or not the bankrupt's estate is known to include land;

(d) any access order under the Access to Neighbouring Land Act 1992.

(1A) No writ or order affecting an interest under a trust of land may be registered under subsection (1) above.

(2) Every entry made pursuant to this section shall be made in the name of the estate owner or other person whose land, if any, is affected by the writ or order registered.

(2A) Where a person has died and any such writ or order as is mentioned in subsection (1)(a) or (b) above would apart from his death have been registered in his name, it shall be so registered notwithstanding his death ...

(4) Except as provided by subsection (5) below and by section 37(5) of the Supreme Court Act 1981 and section 107(3) of the County Courts Act 1984 (which make special provision as to receiving orders in respect of land of judgment debtors) every such writ and order as is mentioned in subsection (1) above, and every delivery in execution or other proceeding taken pursuant to any such writ or order, or in obedience to any such writ or order, shall be void as against a purchaser of the land unless the writ or order is for the time being registered under this section ...

7   The register of deeds of arrangement affecting land

(1) The deed of arrangement affecting land may be registered in the register of deeds of arrangement affecting land, in the name of the debtor, on the application of a trustee of the deed or a creditor assenting to or taking the benefit of the deed.

(2) Every deed of arrangement shall be void as against a purchaser of land comprised in it or affected by it unless it is for the time being registered under this section.

8   Expiry and renewal of registrations

A registration under section 5, section 6 or section 7 of this Act shall cease to have effect at the end of the period of five years from the date on which it is made, but may be renewed from time to time and, if so renewed, shall have effect for five years from the date of renewal.

9   Searches

(1) Any person may search in any register kept under this Act on paying the prescribed fee.

(2) Without prejudice to subsection (1) above, the registrar may provide facilities for enabling persons entitled to search in any such register to see photographic or other images or copies of any portion of the register which they may wish to examine.

10   Official searches

(1) Where any person requires search to be made at the registry for entries of any matters or documents, entries of which are required or allowed to be made in the registry by this Act, he may make a requisition in that behalf to the registrar, which may be either –

   (a) a written requisition delivered at or sent by post to the registry; or

   (b) a requisition communicated by teleprinter, telephone or other means in such manner as may be prescribed in relation to the means in question, in which case it shall be treated as made to the registrar if, but only if, he accepts it;

and the registrar shall not accept a requisition made in accordance with paragraph (b) above unless it is made by a person maintaining a credit account at the registry, and may at his discretion refuse to accept it notwithstanding that it is made by such a person ...

(3) Where a requisition is made under subsection (1) above and the fee payable in respect of it is paid or debited in accordance with subsection (2) above, the registrar shall thereupon make the search required and –

   (a) shall issue a certificate setting out the result of the search; and

   (b) without prejudice to paragraph (a) above, may take such other steps as he considers appropriate to communicate that result to the person by whom the requisition was made.

(4) In favour of a purchaser or an intending purchaser, as against persons interested under or in respect of matters or documents entries of which are required or allowed as aforesaid, the certificate, according to its tenor, shall be conclusive, affirmatively or negatively, as the case may be ...

11 Date of effective registration and priority notices

(1) Any person intending to make an application for the registration of any contemplated charge, instrument or other matter in pursuance of this Act or any rule made under this Act may give a priority notice in the prescribed form at least the relevant number of days before the registration is to take effect.

(2) Where a notice is given under subsection (1) above, it shall be entered in the register to which the intended application when made will relate.

(3) If the application is presented within the relevant number of days thereafter and refers in the prescribed manner to the notice, the registration shall take effect as if the registration had been made at the time when the charge, instrument or matter was created, entered into, made or arose, and the date at which the registration so takes effect shall be deemed to be the date of registration ...

(5) Where a purchaser has obtained a certificate under section 10 above, any entry which is made in the register after the date of the certificate and before the completion of the purchase, and is not made pursuant to a priority notice entered in the register on or before the date of the certificate, shall not affect the purchaser if the purchase is completed before the expiration of the relevant number of days after the date of the certificate.

(6) The relevant number of days is –

    (a) for the purposes of subsections (1) and (5) above, fifteen;

    (b) for the purposes of subsection (3) above, thirty;

or such other number as may be prescribed; but in reckoning the relevant number of days for any of the purposes of this section any days when the registry is not open to the public shall be excluded.

12 Protection of solicitors, trustees, etc

A solicitor, or a trustee, personal representative, agent or other person in a fiduciary position, shall not be answerable –

    (a) in respect of any loss occasioned by reliance on an office copy of an entry in any register kept under this Act;

    (b) for any loss that may arise from error in a certificate under section 10 above obtained by him.

13 Saving for overreaching powers

(1) The registration of any charge, annuity or other interest under this Act shall not

prevent the charge, annuity or interest being overreached under any other Act, except where otherwise provided by that other Act.

(2) The registration as a land charge of a puisne mortgage or charge shall not operate to prevent that mortgage or charge being overreached in favour of a prior mortgagee or a person deriving title under him where, by reason of a sale or foreclosure, or otherwise, the right of the puisne mortgagee or subsequent chargee to redeem is barred.

14 Exclusion of matters affecting registered land or created by instruments necessitating registration of land

(1) This Act shall not apply to instruments or matters required to be registered or re-registered on or after 1st January 1926, if and so far as they affect registered land, and can be protected under the Land Registration Act 2002.

(2) Nothing in this Act imposes on the registrar any obligation to ascertain whether or not an instrument or matter affects registered land.

(3) Where an instrument executed on or after 27th July 1971 conveys, grants or assigns an estate in land and creates a land charge affecting that estate, this Act shall not apply to the land charge, so far as it affects that estate, if under section 7 of the Land Registration Act 2002 (effect of failure to comply with requirement of registration) the instrument will, unless the necessary application for registration under that Act is made within the time allowed by or under section 6 of that Act, become void so far as respects the conveyance, grant or assignment of that estate.

17 Interpretation

(1) In this Act, unless the context otherwise requires –

'annuity' means a rentcharge or an annuity for a life or lives or for any term of years or greater estate determinable on a life or on lives and created after 25th April 1855 and before 1st January 1926, but does not include an annuity created by a marriage settlement or will;

'the Board' means the Commissioners of Inland Revenue;

'conveyance' includes a mortgage, charge, lease, assent, vesting declaration, vesting instrument, release and every other assurance of property, or of an interest in property, by an instrument except a will, and 'convey' has a corresponding meaning;

'court' means the High Court, or the county court in a case where that court has jurisdiction;

'deed of arrangement' has the same meaning as in the Deeds of Arrangement Act 1914;

'estate owner', 'legal estate', 'equitable interest', 'charge by way of legal mortgage' and 'will' have the same meanings as in the Law of Property Act 1925;

'judgment' includes any order or decree having the effect of a judgment;

'land' includes land of any tenure and mines and minerals, whether or not severed from the surface, buildings or parts of buildings (whether the division is horizontal, vertical or made in any other way) and other corporeal hereditaments, also a manor, an advowson and a rent and other incorporeal hereditaments, and an easement, right, privilege or benefit in, over or derived from land, but not an undivided share in land, and 'hereditament' means real property which, on an intestacy occurring before 1st January 1926, might have devolved on an heir;

'land improvement charge' means any charge under the Improvement of Land Act 1864 or under any special improvement Act within the meaning of the Improvement of Land Act 1899;

'pending land action' means any action or proceedings pending in court relating to land or any interest in or charge on land;

'prescribed' means prescribed by rules made pursuant to this Act;

'purchaser' means any person (including a mortgagee or lessee) who, for valuable consideration, takes any interest in land or in a charge on land, and 'purchase' has a corresponding meaning;

'registrar' means the Chief Land Registrar, 'registry' means Her Majesty's Land Registry, and 'registered land' has the same meaning as in the Land Registration Act 2002;

'tenant for life', 'statutory owner', 'vesting instrument' and 'settlement' have the same meanings as in the Settled Land Act 1925 ...

SCHEDULE 1

ANNUITIES

1. No further entries shall be made in the register of annuities ...

SCHEDULE 2

CLASS A LAND CHARGES

1. Charges created pursuant to applications under the enactments mentioned in this Schedule may be registered as land charges of Class A by virtue of paragraph (b) of section 2(2) of this Act – ...

(i) The Agricultural Holdings Act 1986

Section 85 (charges in respect of sums due to tenant of agricultural holding).

Section 86 (charges in favour of landlord of agricultural holdings in respect of compensation for or cost of certain improvements) ...

As amended by the Local Land Charges Act 1975, ss17(1)(a), (b), 19, Schedule 2; Finance Act 1975, s52(1), Schedule 12, paras 2, 18(1), (2), (4), (5), (6); Supreme Court Act 1981, s152(1), Schedule 5; Matrimonial Homes Act 1983, s12, Schedule 2; Capital Transfer Act 1984, s276, Schedule 8, para 3(1)(a), (b), (2); County Courts Act 1984, s148(1), Schedule 2, Pt IV, para 18; Companies Consolidation (Consequential Provisions) Act 1985, s30, Schedule 2;

Insolvency Act 1985, s235(1), (3), Schedule 8, para 21(2), (3), Schedule 10, Pt III; Agricultural Holdings Act 1986, ss100, 101, Schedule 14, para 51, Schedule 15, Pt I; High Court and County Courts Jurisdiction Order 1991, art 2(8), Schedule; Access to Neighbouring Land Act 1992, s5(1); Law of Property (Miscellaneous Provisions) Act 1994, s15(2)–(4); Trusts of Land and Appointment of Trustees Act 1996, s25(1), Schedule 3, para 12; Family Law Act 1996, s66(1), Schedule 8, Pt III, paras 46, 47; Land Registration Act 1997, s4(1), Schedule 1, Pt I, para 3; Land Registration Act 2002, s133, Schedule 11, para 10(1), (2), (4).

ADMINISTRATION OF JUSTICE ACT 1973
(1973 c 15)

8   Extension of powers of court in action by mortgagee of dwelling-house

(1) Where by a mortgage of land which consists of or includes a dwelling-house, or by any agreement between the mortgagee under such a mortgage and the mortgagor, the mortgagor is entitled or is to be permitted to pay the principal sum secured by instalments or otherwise to defer payment of it in whole or in part, but provision is also made for earlier payment in the event of any default by the mortgagor or of a demand by the mortgagee or otherwise, then for purposes of section 36 of the Administration of Justice Act 1970 (under which a court has power to delay giving a mortgagee possession of the mortgaged property so as to allow the mortgagor a reasonable time to pay any sums due under the mortgage) a court may treat as due under the mortgage on account of the principal sum secured and of interest on it only such amounts as the mortgagor would have expected to be required to pay if there had been no such provision for earlier payment.

(2) A court shall not exercise by virtue of subsection (1) above the powers conferred by section 36 of the Administration of Justice Act 1970 unless it appears to the court not only that the mortgagor is likely to be able within a reasonable period to pay any amounts regarded (in accordance with subsection (1) above) as due on account of the principal sum secured, together with the interest on those amounts, but also that he is likely to be able by the end of that period to pay any further amounts that he would have expected to be required to pay by then on account of that sum and of interest on it if there had been no such provision as is referred to in subsection (1) above for earlier payment.

(3) Where subsection (1) above would apply to an action in which a mortgagee only claimed possession of the mortgaged property, and the mortgagee brings an action for foreclosure (with or without also claiming possession of the property), then section 36 of the Administration of Justice Act 1970 together with subsections (1) and (2) above shall apply as they would apply if it were an action in which the mortgagee only claimed possession of the mortgaged property, except that –

    (a) section 36(2)(b) shall apply only in relation to any claim for possession; and

    (b) section 36(5) shall not apply.

(4) For purposes of this section the expressions 'dwelling-house', 'mortgage', 'mortgagee' and 'mortgagor' shall be construed in the same way as for the purposes of Part IV of the Administration of Justice Act 1970. ...

As amended by the Statute Law (Repeals) Act 2004, s1(1), Schedule 1, Pt 12.

MATRIMONIAL CAUSES ACT 1973
(1973 c 18)

24 Property adjustment orders in connection with divorce proceedings, etc

(1) On granting a decree of divorce, a decree of nullity of marriage or a decree of judicial separation or at any time thereafter (whether, in the case of a decree of divorce, or of nullity of marriage, before or after the decree is made absolute), the court may make any one or more of the following orders, that is to say –

(a) an order that a party to the marriage shall transfer to the other party, to any child of the family or to such person as may be specified in the order for the benefit of such a child such property as may be so specified, being property to which the first-mentioned party is entitled, either in possession or reversion;

(b) an order that a settlement of such property as may be so specified, being property to which a party to the marriage is so entitled, be made to the satisfaction of the court for the benefit of the other party to the marriage and of the children of the family or either or any of them;

(c) an order varying for the benefit of the parties to the marriage and of the children of the family or either or any of them any ante-nuptial or post-nuptial settlement (including such a settlement made by will or codicil) made on the parties to the marriage, other than one in the form of a pension arrangement (within the meaning of section 25D below);

(d) an order extinguishing or reducing the interest of either of the parties to the marriage under any such settlement, other than one in the form of a pension arrangement (within the meaning of section 25D below);

subject, however, in the case of an order under paragraph (a) above, to the restrictions imposed by section 29(1) and (3) below on the making of orders for a transfer of property in favour of children who have attained the age of eighteen.

(2) The court may make an order under subsection (1)(c) above notwithstanding that there are no children of the family.

(3) Without prejudice to the power to give a direction under section 30 below for the settlement of an instrument by conveyancing counsel, where an order is made under this section on or after granting a decree of divorce or nullity of marriage, neither the order nor any settlement made in pursuance of the order shall take effect unless the decree has been made absolute.

24A Orders for sale of property

(1) Where the court makes under section 23 or 24 of this Act a secured periodical payments order, an order for the payment of a lump sum or a property adjustment order, then, on making that order or at any time thereafter, the court may make a further order for the sale of such property as may be specified in the order, being property in which or in the proceeds of sale of which either or both of the parties to the marriage has or have a beneficial interest, either in possession or reversion.

(2) Any order made under subsection (1) above may contain such consequential or supplementary provisions as the court thinks fit and, without prejudice to the generality of the foregoing provision, may include –

(a) provision requiring the making of a payment out of the proceeds of sale of the property to which the order relates, and

(b) provision requiring any such property to be offered for sale to a person, or class of persons, specified in the order.

(3) Where an order is made under subsection (1) above on or after the grant of a decree of divorce or nullity of marriage, the order shall not take effect unless the decree has been made absolute.

(4) Where an order is made under subsection (1) above, the court may direct that the order, or such provision thereof as the court may specify, shall not take effect until the occurrence of an event specified by the court or the expiration of a period so specified.

(5) Where an order under subsection (1) above contains a provision requiring the proceeds of sale of the property to which the order relates to be used to secure periodical payments to a party to the marriage, the order shall cease to have effect on the death or re-marriage, or formation of a civil partnership by, of that person.

(6) Where a party to a marriage has a beneficial interest in any property, or in the proceeds of sale thereof, and some other person who is not a party to the marriage also has a beneficial interest in that property or in the proceeds of sale thereof, then, before deciding whether to make an order under this section in relation to that property, it shall be the duty of the court to give that other person an opportunity to make representations with respect to the order; and any representations made by that other person shall be included among the circumstances to which the court is required to have regard under section 25(1) below.

As amended by the Matrimonial Homes and Property Act 1981, s7; Matrimonial and Family Proceedings Act 1984, s46(1), Schedule 1, para 11; Welfare Reform and Pensions Act 1999, s19, Schedule 3, paras 1, 3; Civil Partnership Act 2004, s261(1), Schedule 27, para 42.

CONSUMER CREDIT ACT 1974
(1974 c 39)

8   Consumer credit agreements

(1) A personal credit agreement is an agreement between an individual ('the debtor') and any other person ('the creditor') by which the creditor provides the debtor with credit of any amount.

(2) A consumer credit agreement is a personal credit agreement by which the creditor provides the debtor with credit not exceeding £25,000.

(3) A consumer credit agreement is a regulated agreement within the meaning of this Act if it is not an agreement (an 'exempt agreement') specified in or under section 16.

9   Meaning of credit

(1) In this Act 'credit' includes a cash loan, and any other form of financial accommodation …

94   Right to complete payments ahead of time

(1) The debtor under a regulated consumer credit agreement is entitled at any time, by notice to the creditor and the payment to the creditor of all amounts payable by the debtor to him under the agreement (less any rebate allowable under section 95), to discharge the debtor's indebtedness under the agreement.

(2) A notice under subsection (1) may embody the exercise by the debtor of any option to purchase goods conferred on him by the agreement, and deal with any other matter arising on, or in relation to, the termination of the agreement.

137   Extortionate credit bargains

(1) If the court finds a credit bargain extortionate it may reopen the credit agreement so as to do justice between the parties.

(2) In this section and sections 138 to 140 –

    (a) 'credit agreement' means any agreement (other than an agreement which is an exempt agreement as a result of section 16(6C)) between an individual (the 'debtor') and any other person (the 'creditor') by which the creditor provides the debtor with credit of any amount, and

(b) 'credit bargain' –

(i) where no transaction other than the credit agreement is to be taken into account in computing the total charge for credit, means the credit agreement, or

(ii) where one or more other transactions are to be so taken into account, means the credit agreement and those other transactions, taken together.

138 When bargains are extortionate

(1) A credit bargain is extortionate if it –

(a) requires the debtor or a relative of his to make payments (whether unconditionally, or on certain contingencies) which are grossly exorbitant, or

(b) otherwise grossly contravenes ordinary principles of fair dealing.

(2) In determining whether a credit bargain is extortionate, regard shall be had to such evidence as is adduced concerning –

(a) interest rates prevailing at the time it was made,

(b) the factors mentioned in subsections (3) to (5), and

(c) any other relevant considerations.

(3) Factors applicable under subsection (2) in relation to the debtor include –

(a) his age, experience, business capacity and state of health; and

(b) the degree to which, at the time of making the credit bargain, he was under financial pressure, and the nature of that pressure.

(4) Factors applicable under subsection (2) in relation to the creditor include –

(a) the degree of risk accepted by him, having regard to the value of any security provided;

(b) his relationship to the debtor; and

(c) whether or not a colourable cash price was quoted for any goods or services included in the credit bargain.

(5) Factors applicable under subsection (2) in relation to a linked transaction include the question how far the transaction was reasonably required for the protection of debtor or creditor, or was in the interest of the debtor.

139 Reopening of extortionate agreements

(1) A credit agreement may, if the court thinks just, be reopened on the ground that the credit bargain is extortionate –

(a) on an application for the purpose made by the debtor or any surety to the High Court, county court ...; or

(b) at the instance of the debtor or a surety in any proceedings to which the debtor and creditor are parties, being proceedings to enforce the agreement, any security relating to it, or any linked transaction; or

(c) at the instance of the debtor or a surety in other proceedings in any court where the amount paid or payable under the credit agreement is relevant.

(2) In reopening the agreement, the court may, for the purpose of relieving the debtor or a surety from payment of any sum in excess of that fairly due and reasonable, by order –

(a) direct accounts to be taken ... between any persons,

(b) set aside the whole or part of any obligation imposed on the debtor or a surety by the credit bargain or any related agreement,

(c) require the creditor to repay the whole or part of any sum paid under the credit bargain or any related agreement by the debtor or a surety, whether paid to the creditor or any other person,

(d) direct the return to the surety of any property provided for the purposes of the security, or

(e) alter the terms of the credit agreement or any security instrument.

(3) An order may be made under subsection (2) notwithstanding that its effect is to place a burden on the creditor in respect of an advantage unfairly enjoyed by another person who is a party to a linked transaction ...

140 Interpretation of sections 137 to 139

Where the credit agreement is not a regulated agreement, expressions used in sections 137 to 139 which, apart from this section, apply only to regulated agreements, shall be construed as nearly as may be as if the credit agreement were a regulated agreement.

NB Section 16 of the 1974 Act exempts consumer credit agreements where the creditor is a local authority or is specified in the Consumer Credit (Exempt Agreements) Order 1989, as amended and modified. Section 16 does not regulate a consumer credit agreement if it is secured by a land mortgage or affect the application of ss137 to 140: s16(6C)(a), (7).

As amended by the Consumer Credit (Increase of Monetary Limits) Order 1983, as amended by SI 1998/996; Financial Services and Markets Act 2000 (Regulated Activities) Order 2001, art 90(1), (6).

LOCAL LAND CHARGES ACT 1975
(1975 c 76)

1   Local land charges

(1) A charge or other matter affecting land is a local land charge if it falls within any of the following descriptions and is not one of the matters set out in section 2 below –

(a) any charge acquired either before or after the commencement of this Act by a local authority or National Park authority, water authority, sewerage undertaker or new town development corporation under the Public Health Acts 1936 and 1937, the Public Health Act 1961 or the Highways Act 1980 (or any Act repealed by that Act) or the Building Act 1984 or any similar charge acquired by a local authority or National Park authority under any other Act, whether passed before or after this Act, being a charge that is binding on successive owners of the land affected;

(b) any prohibition of or restriction on the use of land –

(i) imposed by a local authority or National Park authority on or after 1st January 1926 (including any prohibition or restriction embodied in any condition attached to a consent, approval or licence granted by a local authority or National Park authority on or after that date), or

(ii) enforceable by a local authority or National Park authority under any covenant or agreement made with them on or after that date,

being a prohibition or restriction binding on successive owners of the land affected;

(c) any prohibition of or restriction on the use of land –

(i) imposed by a Minister of the Crown or government department on or after the date of the commencement of this Act (including any prohibition or restriction embodied in any condition attached to a consent, approval or licence granted by such a Minister or department on or after that date), or

(ii) enforceable by such a Minister or department under any covenant or agreement made with him or them on or after that date, being a prohibition or restriction binding on successive owners of the land affected;

(d) any positive obligation affecting land enforceable by a Minister of the Crown, government department or local authority or National Park authority under any covenant or agreement made with him or them on or after the date of the commencement of this Act and binding on successive owners of the land affected;

(e) any charge or other matter which is expressly made a local land charge by any statutory provision not contained in this section.

(2) For the purposes of subsection (1)(a) above, any sum which is recoverable from successive owners or occupiers of the land in respect of which the sum is recoverable shall be treated as a charge, whether the sum is expressed to be a charge on the land or not.

(3) For the purposes of this section and section 2 of this Act, the Broads Authority shall be treated as a local authority or National Park authority.

2   Matters which are not local land charges

The following matters are not local land charges –

(a) a prohibition or restriction enforceable under a covenant or agreement made between a lessor and a lessee;

(b) a positive obligation enforceable under a covenant or agreement made between a lessor and a lessee;

(c) a prohibition or restriction enforceable by a Minister of the Crown, government department or local authority or National Park authority under any covenant or agreement, being a prohibition or restriction binding on successive owners of the land affected by reason of the fact that the covenant or agreement is made for the benefit of land of the Minister, government department or local authority or National Park authority;

(d) a prohibition or restriction embodied in any bye-laws;

(e) a condition or limitation subject to which planning permission was granted at any time before the commencement of this Act or was or is (at any time) deemed to be granted under any statutory provision relating to town and country planning, whether by a Minister of the Crown, government department or local authority or National Park authority;

(f) a prohibition or restriction embodied in a scheme under the Town and Country Planning Act 1932 or any enactment repealed by that Act;

(g) a prohibition or restriction enforceable under a forestry dedication covenant entered into pursuant to section 5 of the Forestry Act 1967;

(h) a prohibition or restriction affecting the whole or any of the following areas –

(i) England, Wales or England and Wales;

(ii) England, or England and Wales, with the exception of, or of any part of, Greater London;

(iii) Greater London.

3   Registering authorities, local land charges registers, and indexes

(1) Each of the following local authorities –

(a) the council of any district;

(aa) a Welsh county council;

(ab) a county borough council;

(b) the council of any London borough; and

(c) the Common Council of the City of London,

shall be a registering authority for the purposes of this Act.

(2) There shall continue to be kept for the area of each registering authority –

(a) a local land charges register, and

(b) an index whereby all entries made in that register can readily be traced,

and as from the commencement of this Act the register and index kept for the area of a registering authority shall be kept by that authority.

(3) Neither a local land charges register nor an index such as is mentioned in subsection (2(b) above need be kept in documentary form.

(4) For the purposes of this Act the area of the Common Council of the City of London includes the Inner Temple and the Middle Temple.

4   The appropriate local land charges register

In this Act, unless the context otherwise requires, 'the appropriate local land charges register', in relation to any land or to a local land charge, means the local land charges register for the area in which the land or, as the case may be, the land affected by the charge is situated or, if the land in question is situated in two or more areas for which local land charges registers are kept, each of the local land charges registers kept for those areas respectively.

6   Local authority's right to register a general charge against land in certain circumstances

(1) Where a local authority have incurred any expenditure in respect of which, when any relevant work is completed and any requisite resolution is passed or order is made, there will arise in their favour a local land charge (in this section referred to as 'the specific charge'), the following provisions of this section shall apply.

(2) At any time before the specific charge comes into existence, a general charge against the land, without any amount being specified, may be registered in the appropriate local land charges register by the registering authority if they are the originating authority and, if they are not, shall be registered therein by them if the originating authority make an application for that purpose.

(3) A general charge registered under this section shall be a local land charge ...

(5) Where a general charge is registered under this section its registration shall be cancelled within such period starting with the day on which the specific charge comes into existence, and not being less than one year, as may be prescribed, and the specific charge shall not be registered before the general charge is cancelled ...

7   Effect of registering certain financial charges

A local land charge falling within section 1(1)(a) above shall, when registered, take effect as if it had been created by a deed of charge by way of legal mortgage within the meaning of the Law of Property Act 1925, but without prejudice to the priority of the charge.

10   Compensation for non-registration or defective official search certificate

(1) Failure to register a local land charge in the appropriate local land charges register shall not affect the enforceability of the charge but where a person has purchased any land affected by a local land charge, then –

(a) in a case where a material personal search of the appropriate local land charges register was made in respect of the land in question before the relevant time, if at the time of the search the charge was in existence but not registered in that register; or

(aa) in a case where the appropriate local land charges register is kept otherwise than in documentary form and a material personal search of that register was made in respect of the land in question before the relevant time, if the entitlement to search in that register conferred by section 8 above was not satisfied as mentioned in subsection (1A) [availability in visible and legible form] of that section; or

(b) in a case where a material official search of the appropriate local land charges register was made in respect of the land in question before the relevant time, if the charge was in existence at the time of the search but (whether registered or not) was not shown by the official search certificate as registered in that register,

the purchaser shall (subject to section 11(1) below) be entitled to compensation for any loss suffered by him in consequence ...

(3) For the purposes of this section –

(a) a person purchases land where, for valuable consideration, he acquires any interest in land or the proceeds of sale of land, and this includes cases where he acquires as lessee or mortgagee and shall be treated as including cases where an interest is conveyed or assigned at his direction to another person;

(b) the relevant time –

(i) where the acquisition of the interest in question was preceded by a contract for its acquisition, other than a qualified liability contract, is the time when that contract was made;

(ii) in any other case, is the time when the purchaser acquired the interest in question or, if he acquired it under a disposition which took effect only when registered in the register of title kept under the Land Registration Act 2002, the time when that disposition was made; and for the purposes of sub-paragraph (i) above, a qualified liability contract is a contract containing a term the effect of which is to make the liability of the purchaser dependent upon, or avoidable by reference to, the outcome of a search for local land charges affecting the land to be purchased.

(c) a personal search is material if, but only if –

(i) it is made after the commencement of this Act, and

(ii) it is made by or on behalf of the purchaser or, before the relevant time, the purchaser or his agent has knowledge of the result of it;

(d) an official search is material if, but only if –

(i) it is made after the commencement of this Act, and

(ii) it is requisitioned by or on behalf of the purchaser or, before the relevant time, the purchaser or his agent has knowledge of the contents of the official search certificate.

(4) Any compensation for loss under this section shall be paid by the registering authority in whose area the land affected is situated; and where the purchaser has incurred expenditure for the purpose of obtaining compensation under this section, the amount of the compensation shall include the amount of the expenditure reasonably incurred by him for that purpose (so far as that expenditure would not otherwise fall to be treated as loss for which he is entitled to compensation under this section).

(5) Where any compensation for loss under this section is paid by a registering authority in respect of a local land charge as respects which they are not the originating authority, then, unless an application for registration of the charge was made to the registering authority in time for it to be practicable for the registering authority to avoid incurring liability to pay that compensation, an amount equal thereto shall be recoverable from the originating authority by the registering authority.

(6) Where any compensation for loss under this section is paid by a registering authority, no part of the amount paid, or of any corresponding amount paid to that authority by the originating authority under subsection (5) above, shall be recoverable by the registering authority or the originating authority from any other person except as provided by subsection (5) above or under a policy of insurance or on grounds of fraud.

(7) In the case of an action to recover compensation under this section the cause of action shall be deemed for the purposes of the Limitation Act [1980] to accrue at the time when the local land charge comes to the notice of the purchaser; and for the purposes of this subsection the question when the charge came to his notice shall be determined without regard to the provisions of section 198 of the Law of Property Act 1925 (under which registration under certain enactments is deemed to constitute actual notice).

(8) Where the amount claimed by way of compensation under this section does not exceed £5,000, proceedings for the recovery of such compensation may be begun in the county court.

(9) If in any proceedings for the recovery of compensation under this section the court dismisses a claim to compensation, it shall not order the purchaser to pay the registering authority's costs unless it considers that it was unreasonable for the purchaser to commence the proceedings.

11 Mortgages, trusts [of land] and settled land

(1) Where there appear to be grounds for a claim under section 10 above in respect of an interest that is subject to a mortgage –

(a) the claim may be made by any mortgagee of the interest as if he were the person entitled to that interest but without prejudice to the making of a claim by that person;

(b) no compensation shall be payable under that section in respect of the interest of the mortgagee (as distinct from the interest which is subject to the mortgage);

(c) any compensation payable under that section in respect of the interest that is subject to the mortgage shall be paid to the mortgagee or, if there is more than one mortgagee, to the first mortgagee and shall in either case be applied by him as if it were proceeds of sale.

(2) Where an interest is subject to a trust of land any compensation payable in respect of it under section 10 above shall be dealt with as if it were proceeds of sale arising under the trust.

(3) Where an interest is settled land for the purposes of the Settled Land Act 1925 any compensation payable in respect of it under section 10 above shall be treated as capital money arising under that Act.

12 Office copies as evidence

An office copy of an entry in any local land charges register shall be admissible in evidence in all proceedings and between all parties to the same extent as the original would be admissible.

13 Protection of solicitors, trustees, etc

A solicitor or a trustee, personal representative, agent or other person in a fiduciary position, shall not be answerable in respect of any loss occasioned by reliance on an erroneous official search certificate or an erroneous office copy of an entry in a local land charges register.

As amended by the Interpretation Act 1978, s25(1), Schedule 3; Highways Act 1980, s343(2), Schedule 24, para 26; Local Government (Miscellaneous Provisions) Act 1982, s34(a), (d)(i), (ii); Building Act 1984, s133(1), Schedule 6, para 16; Norfolk and Suffolk Broads Act 1988, s21, Schedule 6, para 14; Water Act 1989, s190(1), Schedule 25, para 52; High Court and County Courts Jurisdiction Order 1991, art 2(8), Schedule; Local Government (Wales) Act 1994, s66(6), Schedule 16, para 49; Environment Act 1995, s78, Schedule 10, para 14; Trusts of Land and Appointment of Trustees Act 1996, s25(1), Schedule 3, para 14; Land Registration Act 2002, s133, Schedule 11, para 13.

RACE RELATIONS ACT 1976
(1976 c 74)

21 Disposal or management of premises

(1) It is unlawful for a person, in relation to premises in Great Britain of which he has power to dispose, to discriminate against another –

(a) in the terms on which he offers him those premises; or

(b) by refusing his application for those premises; or

(c) in his treatment of him in relation to any list of persons in need of premises of that description.

(2) It is unlawful for a person, in relation to premises managed by him, to discriminate against a person occupying the premises –

(a) in the way he affords him access to any benefits or facilities, or by refusing or deliberately omitting to afford him access to them; or

(b) by evicting him, or subjecting him to any other detriment.

(2A) It is unlawful for a person, in relation to such premises as are referred to in subsection (1) or (2), to subject to harassment a person who applies for or, as the case may be, occupies such premises.

(3) Subsection (1) does not apply to discrimination on grounds other than those of race or ethnic or national origins in either a person who owns an estate or interest in the premises and wholly occupies them unless he uses the services of an estate agent for the purposes of the disposal of the premises, or publishes or causes to be published an advertisement in connection with the disposal.

22 Exception from ss20(1) and 21: small dwellings

(1) Sections 20(1) [discrimination in provision of goods, facilities or services] and 21 do not apply to discrimination on grounds other than those of race or ethnic or national origins in either the provision by a person of accommodation in any premises, or the disposal of premises by him, if –

(a) that person or a near relative of his ('the relevant occupier') resides, and intends to continue to reside, on the premises; and

(b) there is on the premises, in addition to the accommodation occupied by the relevant occupier, accommodation (not being storage accommodation or means of access) shared by the relevant occupier with other persons residing on the premises who are not members of his household; and

(c) the premises are small premises.

(2) Premises shall be treated for the purposes of this section as small premises if –

(a) in the case of premises comprising residential accommodation for one or more households (under separate letting or similar agreements) in addition to the accommodation occupied by the relevant occupier, there is not normally residential accommodation for more than two such households and only the relevant occupier and any member of his household reside in the accommodation occupied by him;

(b) in the case of premises not falling within paragraph (a), there is not normally residential accommodation on the premises for more than six persons in addition to the relevant occupier and any members of his household.

23   Further exceptions from ss20 and 21

...

(2) Section 20(1) does not apply to anything done by a person as a participant in arrangements under which he (for reward or not) takes into his home, and treats as if they were members of his family, children, elderly persons, or persons requiring a special degree of care and attention.

24   Consent for assignment or sub-letting

(1) Where the licence or consent of the landlord or of any other person is required for the disposal to any person of premises in Great Britain comprised in a tenancy, it is unlawful for the landlord or other person –

(a) to discriminate against a person by withholding the licence or consent for disposal of the premises to him, or

(b) in relation to such a licence or consent, to subject to harassment a person who applies for the licence or consent, or from whom the licence or consent is withheld.

(2) Subsection (1) does not apply to discrimination on grounds other than those of race or ethnic or national origins if –

(a) the person withholding a licence or consent, or a near relative of his ('the relevant occupier') resides, and intends to continue to reside, on the premises; and

(b) there is on the premises, in addition to the accommodation occupied by the relevant occupier, accommodation (not being storage accommodation or means of access) shared by the relevant occupier with other persons residing on the premises who are not members of his household; and

(c) the premises are small premises.

(3) Section 22(2) (meaning of 'small premises') shall apply for the purposes of this as well as of that section.

(4) In this section 'tenancy' means a tenancy created by a lease or sub-lease, by an agreement for a lease or sub-lease or by a tenancy agreement or in pursuance of any enactment; and 'disposal', in relation to premises comprised in a tenancy, includes assignment or assignation of the tenancy and sub-letting or parting with possession of the premises or any part of the premises.

(5) This section applies to tenancies created before the passing of this Act, as well as to others.

78   General interpretation provisions

(1) In this Act, unless the context otherwise requires –

'advertisement' includes every form of advertisement or notice, whether to the public or not, and whether in a newspaper or other publication, by television or radio, by display of notices, signs, labels, showcards or goods, by distribution of samples, circulars, catalogues, price lists or other material, by exhibition of pictures, models or films, or in any other way, and references to the publishing of advertisements shall be construed accordingly; ...

'dispose', in relation to premises, includes granting a right to occupy the premises, and any reference to acquiring premises shall be construed accordingly; ...

'estate agent' means a person who, by way of profession or trade, provides services for the purpose of finding premises for persons seeking to acquire them or assisting in the disposal of premises; ...

(2) It is hereby declared that in this Act 'premises', unless the context otherwise requires, includes land of any description ...

(5) For the purposes of this Act a person is a near relative of another if that person is the wife or husband, a parent or child, a grandparent or grandchild, or a brother or sister of the other (whether of full blood or half-blood or by affinity), and 'child' includes an illegitimate child and the wife or husband of an illegitimate child ...

NB For provisions equivalent to ss21, 22 and 24 above against discrimination on grounds of sex, see ss30, 31 and 32 of the Sex Discrimination Act 1975.

As amended by the Race Relations Act 1976 (Amendment) Regulations 2003, regs 23–26.

RENT ACT 1977
(1977 c 42)

PART I

PRELIMINARY

1   Protected tenants and tenancies

Subject to this Part of the Act, a tenancy under which a dwelling-house (which may be a house or part of a house) is let as a separate dwelling is a protected tenancy for the purposes of this Act.

Any reference in this Act to a protected tenant shall be construed accordingly.

2   Statutory tenants and tenancies

(1) Subject to this Part of this Act –

(a) after the termination of a protected tenancy of a dwelling-house the person who, immediately before that termination, was the protected tenant of the dwelling-house shall, if and so long as he occupies the dwelling-house as his residence, be the statutory tenant of it; and

(b) Part I of Schedule 1 to this Act shall have effect for determining what person (if any) is the statutory tenant of a dwelling-house or, as the case may be, is entitled to an assured tenancy of a dwelling-house by succession at any time after the death of a person who, immediately before his death, was either a protected tenant of the dwelling-house or the statutory tenant of it by virtue of paragraph (a) above.

(2) In this Act a dwelling-house is referred to as subject to a statutory tenancy when there is a statutory tenant of it.

(3) In subsection (1)(a) above and in Part I of Schedule 1, the phrase 'if and so long as he occupies the dwelling-house as his residence' shall be construed as it was immediately before the commencement of this Act (that is to say, in accordance with section 3(2) of the Rent Act 1968).

(4) A person who becomes a statutory tenant of a dwelling-house as mentioned in subsection (1)(a) above is, in this Act, referred to as a statutory tenant by virtue of his previous protected tenancy.

(5) A person who becomes a statutory tenant as mentioned in subsection (1)(b) above is, in this Act, referred to as a statutory tenant by succession.

3   Terms and conditions of statutory tenancies

(1) So long as he retains possession, a statutory tenant shall observe and be entitled to the benefit of all the terms and conditions of the original contract of tenancy, so far as they are consistent with the provisions of this Act.

(2) It shall be a condition of a statutory tenancy of a dwelling-house that the statutory tenant shall afford to the landlord access to the dwelling-house and all reasonable facilities for executing therein any repairs which the landlord is entitled to execute.

(3) Subject to section 5 of the Protection from Eviction Act 1977 (under which at least four weeks' notice to quit is required), a statutory tenant of a dwelling-house shall be entitled to give up possession of the dwelling-house if, and only if, he gives such notice as would have been required under the provisions of the original contract of tenancy, or, if no notice would have been so required, on giving not less than three months' notice.

(4) Notwithstanding anything in the contract of tenancy, a landlord who obtains an order for possession of a dwelling-house as against a statutory tenant shall not be required to give to the statutory tenant any notice to quit.

(5) Part II of Schedule 1 of this Act shall have effect in relation to the giving up of possession of statutory tenancies and the changing of statutory tenants by agreement.

4   Dwelling-houses above certain rateable values

(1) A tenancy which is entered into before 1st April 1990 or (where the dwelling-house had a rateable value on 31st March 1990) is entered into on or after 1st April 1990 in pursuance of a contract made before that date is not a protected tenancy if the dwelling-house falls within one of the Classes set out in subsection (2) below.

(2) Where alternative rateable values are mentioned in this subsection, the higher applies if the dwelling-house is in Greater London and the lower applies if it is elsewhere.

Class A

The appropriate day in relation to the dwelling-house falls or fell on or after 1st April 1973 and the dwelling-house on the appropriate day has or had a rateable value exceeding £1,500 or £750.

Class B

The appropriate day in relation to the dwelling-house fell on or after 22nd March 1973, but before 1st April 1973, and the dwelling-house –

   (a) on the appropriate day had a rateable value exceeding £600 or £300, and

(b) on 1st April 1973 had a rateable value exceeding £1,500 or £750.

Class C

The appropriate day in relation to the dwelling-house fell before 22nd March 1973 and the dwelling-house –

(a) on the appropriate day had a rateable value exceeding £400 or £200, and

(b) on 22nd March 1973 had a rateable value exceeding £600 or £300, and

(c) on 1st April 1973 had a rateable value exceeding £1,500 or £750.

(3) If any question arises in any proceedings whether a dwelling-house falls within a Class in subsection (2) above, by virtue of its rateable value at any time, it shall be deemed not to fall within that Class unless the contrary is shown.

(4) A tenancy is not a protected tenancy if –

(a) it is entered into on or after 1st April 1990 (otherwise than, where the dwelling-house had a rateable value on 31st March 1990, in pursuance of a contract made before 1st April 1990), and

(b) under it the rent payable for the time being is payable at a rate exceeding £25,000 a year.

(5) In subsection (4) above 'rent' does not include any sum payable by the tenant as is expressed (in whatever terms) to be payable in respect of rates, council tax, services, repairs, maintenance or insurance, unless it could not have been regarded by the parties as a sum so payable.

(6) If any question arises in any proceedings whether a tenancy is precluded from being a protected tenancy by subsection (4) above, the tenancy shall be deemed to be a protected tenancy unless the contrary is shown.

(7) The Secretary of State may by order replace the amount referred to in subsection (4) above by an amount specified in the order ...

5   Tenancies at low rents

(1) A tenancy which was entered into before 1st April 1990 or (where the dwelling-house had a rateable value on 31st March 1990) is entered into on or after 1st April 1990 in pursuance of a contract made before that date is not a protected tenancy if under the tenancy either no rent is payable or the rent payable is less than two-thirds of the rateable value which is or was the rateable value of the dwelling-house on the appropriate day.

(2) Where –

(a) the appropriate day in relation to a dwelling-house fell before 22nd March 1973, and

(b) the dwelling-house had on the appropriate day a rateable value exceeding, if it is in Greater London, £400 or, if it is elsewhere, £200, subsection (1) above shall apply in relation to the dwelling-house as if the reference to the appropriate day were a reference to 22nd March 1973.

(2A) A tenancy is not a protected tenancy if –

(a) it is entered into on or after 1st April 1990 (otherwise than, where the dwelling-house had a rateable value on 31st March 1990, in pursuance of a contract made before 1st April 1990), and

(b) under the tenancy for the time being either no rent is payable or the rent is payable at a rate of, if the dwelling-house is in Greater London, £1,000 or less a year, and, if the dwelling-house is elsewhere, £250 or less a year.

(2B) Subsection (7) of section 4 above shall apply to any amount referred to in subsection (2A) above as it applies to the amount referred to in subsection (4) of that section.

(3) In this Act a tenancy falling within subsection (1) above, is referred to as a 'tenancy at a low rent'.

(4) In determining whether a long tenancy is a tenancy at a low rent, there shall be disregard such part (if any) of the sums payable by the tenant as is expressed (in whatever terms) to be payable in respect of rates, council tax, services, repairs, maintenance, or insurance, unless it could not have been regarded by the parties as a part so payable.

(5) In subsection (4) above 'long tenancy' means a tenancy granted for a term certain exceeding 21 years, other than a tenancy which is, or may become, terminable before the end of that term by notice given to the tenant.

5A Certain shared ownership leases

(1) A tenancy is not a protected tenancy if it is a qualifying shared ownership lease, that is –

(a) a lease granted [after 11th December 1987] in pursuance of the right to be granted a shared ownership lease under Part V of the Housing Act 1985, or

(b) a lease granted [after 11th December 1987] by a housing association and which complies with the conditions set out in subsection (2) below.

(2) The conditions referred to in subsection (1)(b) above are that the lease –

(a) was granted for a term of 99 years or more and is not (and cannot become) terminable except in pursuance of a provision for re-entry or forfeiture;

(b) was granted at a premium, calculated by reference to the value of the dwelling-house or the cost of providing it, of not less than 25 per cent, or such other percentage as may be prescribed, of the figure by reference to which it was calculated;

(c) provides for the tenant to acquire additional shares in the dwelling-house on terms specified in the lease and complying with such requirements as may be prescribed;

(d) does not restrict the tenant's powers to assign, mortgage or charge his interest in the dwelling-house;

(e) if it enables the landlord to require payment for outstanding shares in the dwelling-house, does so only in such circumstances as may be prescribed;

(f) provides, in the case of a house, for the tenant to acquire the landlord's interest on terms specified in the lease and complying with such requirements as may be prescribed; and

(g) states the landlord's opinion that by virtue of this section the lease is excluded from the operation of this Act ...

(5) In any proceedings the court may, if of opinion that it is just and equitable to do so, treat a lease as a qualifying shared ownership lease notwithstanding that the condition specified in subsection (2)(g) above is not satisfied.

(6) In this section –

'house' has the same meaning as in Part I of the Leasehold Reform Act 1967;

'housing association' has the same meaning as in the Housing Associations Act 1985; and

'lease' includes an agreement for a lease, and references to the grant of a lease shall be construed accordingly.

6   Dwelling-houses let with other land

Subject to section 26 of this Act, a tenancy is not a protected tenancy if the dwelling-house which is subject to the tenancy is let together with land other than the site of the dwelling-house.

7   Payments for board or attendance

(1) A tenancy is not a protected tenancy if under the tenancy the dwelling-house is bona fide let at a rent which includes payments in respect of board or attendance.

(2) For the purposes of subsection (1) above, a dwelling-house shall not be taken to be bona fide let at a rent which includes payments in respect of attendance unless the amount of rent which is fairly attributable to attendance, having regard to the value of the attendance to the tenant, forms a substantial part of the whole rent.

8   Lettings to students

(1) A tenancy is not a protected tenancy if it is granted to a person who is pursuing, or intends to pursue, a curse of study provided by a specified educational institution and is so granted either by that institution or by another specified institution or body of persons.

(2) In subsection (1) above 'specified' means specified, or of a class specified, for the purposes of this section by regulations made by the Secretary of State by statutory instrument ...

9 Holiday lettings

A tenancy is not a protected tenancy if the purpose of the tenancy is to confer on the tenant the right to occupy the dwelling-house for a holiday.

10 Agricultural holdings, etc

(1) A tenancy is not a protected tenancy if –

(a) the dwelling-house is comprised in an agricultural holding and is occupied by the person responsible for the control (whether as tenant or as servant or agent of the tenant) of the farming of the holding, or

(b) the dwelling-house is comprised in the holding held under a farm business tenancy and is occupied by the person responsible for the control (whether as tenant or as servant or agent of the tenant) of the management of the holding.

(2) In subsection (1) above –

'agricultural holding' means any agricultural holding within the meaning of the Agricultural Holdings Act 1986 held under a tenancy in relation to which that Act applies, and

'farm business tenancy', and 'holding' in relation to such a tenancy, have the same meaning as in the Agricultural Tenancies Act 1995.

11 Licensed premises

A tenancy of a dwelling-house which consists of or comprises premises licensed for the sale of intoxicating liquors for consumption on the premises shall not be a protected tenancy, nor shall such a dwelling-house be the subject of a statutory tenancy.

12 Resident landlords

(1) Subject to subsection (2) below, a tenancy of a dwelling-house granted on or after 14th August 1974 shall not be a protected tenancy at any time if –

(a) the dwelling-house forms part only of a building and, except in a case where the dwelling-house also forms part of a flat, the building is not a purpose-built block of flats; and

(b) the tenancy was granted by a person who, at the time when he granted it, occupied as his residence another dwelling-house which –

(i) in the case mentioned in paragraph (a) above, also forms part of the flat; or

(ii) in any other case, also forms part of the building; and

(c) subject to paragraph 1 of Schedule 2 of this Act, at all times since the tenancy was granted the interest of the landlord under the tenancy has belonged to a person who, at the time he owed that interest, occupied as his residence another dwelling-house which –

(i) in the case mentioned in paragraph (a) above, also formed part of the flat; or

(ii) in any other case, also formed part of the building.

(2) This section does not apply to a tenancy of a dwelling-house which forms part of a building if the tenancy is granted to a person who, immediately before it was granted, was a protected or statutory tenant of that dwelling-house or of any other dwelling-house in that building.

(4) Schedule 2 to this Act shall have effect for the purpose of supplementing this section.

14   Landlord's interest belonging to local authority, etc

A tenancy shall not be a protected tenancy at any time when the interest of the landlord under that tenancy belongs to –

(a) the council of a county or county borough;

(b) the council of a district or, in the application of this Act to the Isles of Scilly, the Council of the Isles of Scilly;

(bb) the Broads Authority;

(bc) a National Park authority;

(c) the council of a London borough or the Common Council of the City of London;

(caa) a police authority established under section 3 of the Police Act 1996;

(cb) a joint authority established by Part IV of the Local Government Act 1985;

(cc) the London Fire and Emergency Planning Authority;

(d) the Commission for the New Towns;

(e) a development corporation established by an order made, or having effect as if made, under the New Towns Act 1981;

(g) an urban development corporation within the meaning of Part XVI of the Local Government, Planning and Land Act 1980;

(h) a housing action trust established under Part III of the Housing Act 1988;

(i) the Residuary Body for Wales (Corff Gweddilliol Cymru);

nor shall a person at any time be a statutory tenant of a dwelling-house if the interest of his immediate landlord would belong at that time to any of those bodies.

15   Landlord's interest belonging to housing association, etc

(1) A tenancy shall not be a protected tenancy at any time when the interest of the landlord under that tenancy belongs to a housing association falling within subsection (3) below; nor shall a person at any time be a statutory tenant of a dwelling-house if the interest of his immediate landlord would belong at that time to such a housing association.

(2) A tenancy shall not be a protected tenancy at any time when the interest of the landlord under that tenancy belongs to –

(a) the Housing Corporation; or

(b) a housing trust which is a charity within the meaning of the Charities Act 1993;

nor shall a person at any time be a statutory tenant of a dwelling-house if the interest of his immediate landlord would belong at that time to any of those bodies ...

16 Landlord's interest belonging to housing co-operative

A tenancy shall not be a protected tenancy at any time when the interest of the landlord under that tenancy belongs to a housing co-operative, within the meaning of section 27B of the Housing Act 1985 (agreements with housing co-operatives under certain superseded provisions) and the dwelling-house is comprised in a housing co-operative agreement within the meaning of that section.

18 Regulated tenancies

(1) Subject to sections 24(3) and 143 [release by order from rent regulation of dwelling-houses within particular areas] of this Act, a 'regulated tenancy' is, for the purposes of this Act, a protected or statutory tenancy.

(2) Where a regulated tenancy is followed by a statutory tenancy of the same dwelling-house, the two shall be treated for the purposes of this Act as together constituting one regulated tenancy.

24 Premises with a business use

(3) A tenancy shall not be a regulated tenancy if it is a tenancy to which Part II of the Landlord and Tenant Act 1954 applies (but this provision is without prejudice to the application of any other provisions of this Act to a sub-tenancy of any part of the premises comprised in such a tenancy).

26 Land and premises let with dwelling-house

(1) For the purposes of this Act, any land or premises let together with a dwelling-house shall, unless it consists of agricultural land exceeding two acres in extent, be treated as part of the dwelling-house.

(2) For the purposes of subsection (1) above 'agricultural land' has the meaning set out in section 26(3)(a) of the General Rate Act 1967 (exclusion of agricultural land and premises from liability for rating).

PART VII

SECURITY OF TENURE

98   Grounds for possession of certain dwelling-houses

(1) Subject to this Part of this Act, a court shall not make an order for possession of a dwelling-house which is for the time being let on a protected tenancy or subject to a statutory tenancy unless the court considers it reasonable to make such an order and either –

(a) the court is satisfied that suitable alternative accommodation is available for the tenant or will be available for him when the order in question takes effect, or

(b) the circumstances are as specified in any of the Cases in Part I of Schedule 15 to this Act.

(2) If, apart from subsection (1) above, the landlord would be entitled to recover possession of a dwelling-house which is for the time being let on or subject to a regulated tenancy, the court shall make an order for possession if the circumstances of the case are as specified in any of the Cases in Part II of Schedule 15.

(3) Part III of Schedule 15 shall have effect in relation to Case 9 in that Schedule and for determining the relevant date for the purposes of the Cases in Part II of that Schedule.

(4) Part IV of Schedule 15 shall have effect for determining whether, for the purposes of subsection (1)(a) above, suitable alternative accommodation is or will be available for a tenant.

(5) Part V of Schedule 15 shall have effect for the purpose of setting out conditions which are relevant to Cases 11 and 12 of that Schedule.

PART IX

PREMIUMS, ETC

119   Prohibition of premiums and loans on grant of protected tenancies

(1) Any person who, as a condition of the grant, renewal or continuance of a protected tenancy, requires, in addition to the rent, the payment of any premium or the making of any loan (whether secured or unsecured) shall be guilty of an offence.

(2) Any person who, in connection with the grant, renewal or continuance of a protected tenancy, receives any premium in addition to the rent shall be guilty of an offence ...

(4) The court by which a person is convicted of an offence under this section relating to requiring or receiving any premium may order the amount of the premium to be repaid to the person by whom it was paid.

123 Excessive price for furniture to be treated as premium

Where the purchase of any furniture has been required as a condition of the grant, renewal, continuance or assignment –

(a) of a protected tenancy, or

(b) of rights under a restricted contract which relates to premises falling within section 122(1) of this Act,

then, if the price exceeds the reasonable price of the furniture, the excess shall be treated, for the purposes of this Part of this Act, as if it were a premium required to be paid as a condition of the grant, renewal, continuance or assignment of the protected tenancy or, as the case may be, the rights under the restricted contract.

128 Interpretation of Part IX

(1) In this Part of this Act, unless the context otherwise requires –

'furniture' includes fittings and other articles; and
'premium' includes –

(a) any fine or other like sum;

(b) any other pecuniary consideration in addition to rent; and

(c) any sum paid by way of a deposit, other than one which does not exceed one-sixth of the annual rent and is reasonable in relation to the potential liability in respect of which it is paid.

(2) For the avoidance of doubt it is hereby declared that nothing in this Part of this Act shall render any amounts recoverable more than once.

SCHEDULE 15

GROUNDS FOR POSSESSION OF DWELLING-HOUSES LET ON OR SUBJECT TO PROTECTED OR STATUTORY TENANCIES

PART I

CASES IN WHICH COURT MAY ORDER POSSESSION

Case 1

Where any rent lawfully due from the tenant has not been paid, or any obligation of the protected or statutory tenancy which arises under this Act, or –

(a) in the case of a protected tenancy, or other obligation of the tenancy, in so far as is consistent with the provisions of Part VII of that Act, or

(b) in the case of a statutory tenancy, any other obligation of the previous protected tenancy which is applicable to the statutory tenancy,

has been broken or not performed.

Case 2

Where the tenant or any person residing or lodging with him or any sub-tenant of his has been guilty of conduct which is a nuisance or annoyance to adjoining occupiers, or has been convicted of using the dwelling-house or allowing the dwelling-house to be used for immoral or illegal purposes.

Case 3

Where the condition of the dwelling-house has, in the opinion of the court, deteriorated owing to acts of waste by, or the neglect or default of, the tenant or any person residing or lodging with him or any sub-tenant of his and, in the case of any act of waste by, or the neglect or default of, a person lodging with the tenant or a sub-tenant of his, where the court is satisfied that the tenant has not, before the making of the order in question, taken such steps as he ought reasonably to have taken for the removal of the lodger or sub-tenant, as the case may be.

Case 4

Where the condition of any furniture provided for use under the tenancy has, in the opinion of the court, deteriorated owing to ill-treatment by the tenant or any person residing or lodging with him or any sub-tenant of his and, in the case of any ill-treatment by a person lodging with the tenant or a sub-tenant of his, where the court is satisfied that the tenant has not, before the making of the order in question, taken such steps as he ought reasonably to have taken for the removal of the lodger or sub-tenant, as the case may be.

Case 5

Where the tenant has given notice to quit and, in consequence of that notice, the landlord has contracted to sell or let the dwelling-house or has taken any other steps as the result of which he would, in the opinion of the court, be seriously prejudiced if he could not obtain possession.

Case 6

Where, without the consent of the landlord, the tenant has, at any time after –

    (b) 22nd March 1973, in the case of a tenancy which became a regulated tenancy by virtue of section 14 of the Counter-Inflation Act 1973;

    (bb) the commencement of section 73 of the Housing Act 1980, in the case of a tenancy which became a regulated tenancy by virtue of that section;

    (c) 14th August 1974, in the case of a regulated furnished tenancy; or

    (d) 8th December 1965, in the case of any other tenancy,

assigned or sublet the whole of the dwelling-house or sublet part of the dwelling-house, the remainder being already sublet.

Case 8

Where the dwelling-house is reasonably required by the landlord for occupation as a residence for some person engaged in his whole-time employment, or in the whole-time employment of some tenant from him or with whom, conditional on housing being provided, a contract for such employment has been entered into, and the tenant was in the employment of the landlord or a former landlord, and the dwelling-house was let to him in consequence of that employment and he has ceased to be in that employment.

Case 9

Where the dwelling-house is reasonably required by the landlord for occupation as a residence for –

(a) himself, or

(b) any son or daughter of his over 18 years of age, or

(c) his father or mother, or

(d) if the dwelling-house is let on or subject to a regulated tenancy, the father or mother of his spouse or civil partner,

and the landlord did not become landlord by purchasing the dwelling-house or any interest therein after –

(i) 7th November 1956, in the case of a tenancy which was then a controlled tenancy;

(ii) 8th March 1973, in the case of a tenancy which became a regulated tenancy by virtue of section 14 of the Counter-Inflation Act 1973;

(iii) 24th May 1974, in the case of a regulated furnished tenancy; or

23rd March 1965, in the case of any other tenancy. ...

PART II

CASES IN WHICH COURT MUST ORDER POSSESSION WHERE DWELLING-HOUSE SUBJECT TO REGULATED TENANCY

Case 11

Where a person (in this Case referred to as 'the owner-occupier') who let the dwelling-house on a regulated tenancy had, at any time before the letting, occupied it as his residence and –

(a) not later than the relevant date the landlord gave notice in writing to the tenant that possession might be recovered under this Case, and

(b) the dwelling-house has not, since –

(i) 22nd March 1973, in the case of a tenancy which became a regulated tenancy by virtue of section 14 of the Counter-Inflation Act 1973;

(ii) 14th August 1974, in the case of a regulated furnished tenancy; or

(iii) 8th December 1965, in the case of any other tenancy,

been let by the owner-occupier on a protected tenancy with respect to which the condition mentioned in paragraph (a) above was not satisfied, and

(c) the court is of the opinion that of the conditions set out in Part V of this Schedule one of those in paragraphs (a) and (c) to (f) is satisfied.

If the court is of the opinion that, notwithstanding that the condition in paragraph (a) or (b) above is not complied with, it is just and equitable to make an order for possession of the dwelling-house, the court may dispense with the requirements of either or both of those paragraphs, as the case may require ...

Where the dwelling-house has been let by the owner-occupier on a protected tenancy (in this paragraph referred to as 'the earlier tenancy') granted on or after 16th November 1984 but not later than the end of the period of two months beginning with the commencement of the Rent (Amendment) Act 1985 and either –

(i) the earlier tenancy was granted for a term certain (whether or not to be followed by a further term or to continue thereafter from year to year or some other period) and was during that term a protected shorthold tenancy as defined in section 52 of the Housing Act 1980, or

(ii) the conditions mentioned in paragraphs (a) to (c) of Case 20 were satisfied with respect to the dwelling-house and the earlier tenancy,

then for the purposes of paragraph (b) above the condition in paragraph (a) above is to be treated as having been satisfied with respect to the earlier tenancy.

Case 12

Where the landlord (in this Case referred to as 'the owner') intends to occupy the dwelling-house as his residence at such time as he might retire from regular employment and has let it on a regulated tenancy before he has so retired and –

(a) not later than the relevant date the landlord gave notice in writing to the tenant that possession might be recovered under this Case; and

(b) the dwelling-house has not, since 14th August 1974, been let by the owner on a protected tenancy with respect to which the condition mentioned in paragraph (a) above was not satisfied; and

(c) the court is of the opinion that of the conditions set out in Part V of this Schedule one of those paragraphs (b) to (e) is satisfied.

If the court is of the opinion that, notwithstanding that the condition in paragraph (a) or (b) above is not complied with, it is just and equitable to make an order for possession of the dwelling-house, the court may dispense with the requirements of either or both of those paragraphs, as the case may require.

Case 13

Where the dwelling-house is let under a tenancy for a term of years certain not exceeding 8 months and –

(a) not later than the relevant date the landlord gave notice in writing to the tenant that possession might be recovered under this Case; and

(b) the dwelling-house was, at some time within the period of 12 months ending on the relevant date, occupied under a right to occupy it for a holiday.

For the purposes of this Case a tenancy shall be treated as being for a term of years certain notwithstanding that it is liable to determination by re-entry or on the happening of any event other than the giving of notice by the landlord to determine the term.

Case 14

Where the dwelling-house is let under a tenancy for a term of years certain not exceeding 12 months and –

(a) not later than the relevant date the landlord gave notice in writing to the tenant that possession might be recovered under this Case; and

(b) at some time within the period of 12 months ending on the relevant date, the dwelling-house was subject to such a tenancy as is referred to in section 8(1) of this Act.

For the purposes of this Case a tenancy shall be treated as being for a term of years certain notwithstanding that it is liable to determination by re-entry or on the happening of any event other than the giving of notice by the landlord to determine the term.

Case 15

Where the dwelling-house is held for the purpose of being available for occupation by a minister of religion as a residence from which to perform the duties of his office and –

(a) not later than the relevant date the tenant was given notice in writing that possession might be recovered under this Case, and

(b) the court is satisfied that the dwelling-house is required for occupation by a minister of religion as such a residence.

Case 16

Where the dwelling-house was at any time occupied by a person under the terms of his employment as a person employed in agriculture, and

(a) the tenant neither is nor at any time was so employed by the landlord and is not the widow of a person who was so employed, and

(b) not later than the relevant date, the tenant was given notice in writing that possession might be recovered under this Case, and

(c) the court is satisfied that the dwelling-house is required for occupation by a person employed, or to be employed, by the landlord in agriculture.

For the purposes of this Case 'employed', 'employment' and 'agriculture' have the same meanings as in the Agricultural Wages Act 1948 ...

Case 19

Where the dwelling-house was let under a protected shorthold tenancy (or is treated under section 55 of the Housing Act 1980 as having been so let) and –

(a) there either has been no grant of a further tenancy of the dwelling-house since the end of the protected shorthold tenancy or, if there was such a grant, it was to a person who immediately before the grant was in possession of the dwelling-house as a protected or statutory tenant; and

(b) the proceedings for possession were commenced after appropriate notice by the landlord to the tenant and not later than three months after the expiry of the notice.

A notice is appropriate for this Case if –

(i) it is in writing and states that proceedings for possession under this Case may be brought after its expiry; and

(ii) it expires not earlier than three months after it is served nor, if, when it is served, the tenancy is a periodic tenancy, before that periodic tenancy could be brought to an end by a notice to quit served by the landlord on the same day;

(iii) it is served –

(a) in the period of three months immediately preceding the date on which the protected shorthold tenancy comes to an end; or

(b) if that date has passed, in the period of three months immediately preceding any anniversary of that date; and

(iv) in a case where a previous notice has been served by the landlord on the tenant n respect of the dwelling-house, and that notice was an appropriate notice, it is served not earlier than three months after the expiry of the previous notice. ...

PART III

PROVISIONS APPLICABLE TO CASE 9 AND PART II OF THIS SCHEDULE

Provision for Case 9

1. A court shall not make an order for possession of a dwelling-house by reason only that the circumstances of the case fall within Case 9 in Part I of this Schedule if the court is satisfied that, having regard to all the circumstances of the case,

including the question whether other accommodation is available for the landlord or the tenant, greater hardship would be caused by granting the order than by refusing to grant it.

Provision for Part II

2. Any reference in Part II of this Schedule to the relevant date shall be construed as follows –

(a) except in a case falling within paragraph (b) or (c) below, if the protected tenancy, or, in the case of a statutory tenancy, the previous contractual tenancy, was created before 8th December 1965, the relevant date means 7th June 1966; and

(b) except in a case falling within paragraph (c) below, if the tenancy became a regulated tenancy by virtue of section 14 of the Counter-Inflation Act 1973 and the tenancy or, in the case of a statutory tenancy, the previous contractual tenancy, was created before 22nd March 1973, the relevant date means 22nd September 1973; and

(c) in the case of a regulated furnished tenancy, if the tenancy or, in the case of a statutory furnished tenancy, the previous contractual tenancy was created before 14th August 1974, the relevant date means 13th February 1975; and

(d) in any other case, the relevant date means the date of the commencement of the regulated tenancy in question.

PART IV

SUITABLE ALTERNATIVE ACCOMMODATION

3. For the purposes of section 98(1)(a) of this Act, a certificate of the local housing authority for the district in which the dwelling-house in question is situated, certifying that the authority will provide suitable alternative accommodation for the tenant by a date specified in the certificate, shall be conclusive evidence that suitable alternative accommodation will be available for him by that date.

4.–(1) Where no such certificate as is mentioned in paragraph 3 above is produced to the court, accommodation shall be deemed to be suitable for the purposes of section 98(1)(a) of this Act if it consists of either –

(a) premises which are to be let as a separate dwelling such that they will then be let on a protected tenancy (other than one under which the landlord might recover possession of the dwelling-house under one of the Cases in Part II of this Schedule), or

(b) premises to be let as a separate dwelling on terms which will, in the opinion of the court, afford to the tenant security of tenure reasonably equivalent to the security afforded by Part VII of this Act in the case of a protected tenancy of a kind mentioned in paragraph (a) above, and, in the opinion of the court, the accommodation fulfils the relevant condition as defined in paragraph 5 below.

5.–(1) For the purposes of paragraph 4 above, the relevant conditions are that the accommodation is reasonably suitable to the needs of the tenant and his family as regards proximity to place of work, and either –

(a) similar as regards rental and extent to the accommodation afforded by dwelling-houses provided in the neighbourhood by any local housing authority for persons whose needs as regards extent are, in the opinion of the court, similar to those of the tenant and of his family; or

(b) reasonably suitable to the means of the tenant and to the needs of the tenant and his family as regards extent and character; and

that if any furniture was provided for use under the protected or statutory tenancy in question, furniture is provided for use in the accommodation which is either similar to that so provided or is reasonably suitable to the needs of the tenant and his family.

(2) For the purposes of sub-paragraph (1)(a) above, a certificate of a local housing authority stating –

(a) the extent of the accommodation afforded by dwelling-houses provided by the authority to meet the needs of tenants with families of such number as may be specified in the certificate, and

(b) the amount of the rent charged by the authority for dwelling-houses affording accommodation of that extent,

shall be conclusive evidence of the facts so stated.

6. Accommodation shall not be deemed to be suitable to the needs of the tenant and his family if the result of their occupation of the accommodation would be that it would be an overcrowded dwelling-house for the purposes of Part X of the Housing Act 1985.

7. Any document purporting to be a certificate of a local housing authority named therein issued for the purposes of this Schedule and to be signed by the proper officer of that authority shall be received in evidence and, unless the contrary is shown, shall be deemed to be such a certificate without further proof.

8. In this Part 'local housing authority' and 'district' in relation to such an authority have the same meaning as in the Housing Act 1985.

PART V

PROVISIONS APPLYING TO CASES 11, 12 AND 20

1. In this Part of this Schedule –

'mortgage' includes a charge and 'mortgagee' shall be construed accordingly;

'owner' means, in relation to Case 11, the owner-occupier; and 'successor in title' means any person deriving title from the owner, other than a purchaser for value or a person deriving title from a purchaser for value.

2. The condition referred to in paragraph (c) in each of Cases 11 and 12 and in paragraph (e)(ii) of Case 20 are that –

(a) the dwelling-house is required as a residence for the owner or any member of his family who resided with the owner when he last occupied the dwelling-house as a residence;

(b) the owner has retired from regular employment and requires the dwelling-house as a residence;

(c) the owner has died and the dwelling-house is required as a residence for a member of his family who was residing with him at the time of his death;

(d) the owner has died and the dwelling-house is required by a successor in title as his residence or for the purpose of disposing of it with vacant possession;

(e) the dwelling-house is subject to a mortgage, made by deed and granted before the tenancy, and the mortgagee –

(i) is entitled to exercise a power of sale conferred on him by the mortgage or by section 101 of the Law of Property Act 1925; and

(ii) requires the dwelling-house for the purpose of disposing of it with vacant possession in exercise of that power; and

(f) the dwelling-house is not reasonably suitable to the needs of the owner, having regard to his place of work, and he requires it for the purpose of disposing of it with vacant possession and of using the proceeds of that disposal in acquiring, as his residence, a dwelling-house which is more suitable to those needs.

NB For the phasing out of the Rent Acts, see Housing Act 1988, chapter V, below.

As amended by the Local Government, Planning and Land Act 1980, s155(1); Housing Act 1980, ss55(1), 65(1), 66(1–6), 69(4), 73, 79, 152, Schedule 7, Schedule 8, para 2, Schedule 25, paras 28, 35, 57, 75, Schedule 26; New Towns Act 1981, s81, Schedule 12, para 24; Local Government Act 1985, ss84, 102(2), Schedule 14, para 56, Schedule 17; Rent (Amendment) Act 1985, s1(1), (2), (4); Housing (Consequential Provisions) Act 1985, s4, Schedule 2, para 35(1), (12); Agricultural Holdings Act 1986, s100, Schedule 14, para 59; Housing and Planning Act 1986, s24(2), Schedule 5, Pt II, para 15; Housing Act 1988, ss39(1), 62(7), 140(1), Schedule 17, Pt II, para 99; Norfolk and Suffolk Broads Act 1988, s21, Schedule 6, para 18; References to Rating (Housing) Regulations 1990, reg 2, Schedule, paras 15, 16, 17, 18; Local Government Finance (Housing) (Consequential Amendments) Order 1993, art 2(1), Schedule 1, paras 3, 4; Charities Act 1993, s98(1), Schedule 6, para 30; Local Government (Wales) Act 1994, ss22(2), 39(2), Schedule 8, para 3(1), Schedule 13, para 28; Police and Magistrates' Courts Act 1994, s43, Schedule 4, Pt II, para 53; Agricultural Tenancies Act 1995, s40, Schedule, para 27; Environment Act 1995, s78, Schedule 10, para 18; Police Act 1996, s103(1), Schedule 7, Pt I, para 1(1), (2)(n); Police Act 1997, s134(1), Schedule 9, para 39; Government of Wales Act 1998, ss131, 141, 152, Schedule 18, Pts IV, VI; Greater London Authority Act 1999, s328(8), Schedule 9, Pt I, para 26; Criminal Justice and Police Act 2001, s128(1), Schedule 6, Pt 3, para 63, Schedule 7, Pt 5(1); Civil Partnership Act 2004, s81, Schedule 8, para 14.

PROTECTION FROM EVICTION ACT 1977
(1977 c 43)

1   Unlawful eviction and harassment of occupier

(1) In this section 'residential occupier', in relation to any premises, means a person occupying the premises as a residence, whether under a contract or by virtue of any enactment or rule of law giving him the right to remain in occupation or restricting the right of any other person to recover possession of the premises.

(2) If any person unlawfully deprives the residential occupier of any premises of his occupation of the premises or any part thereof, or attempts to do so, he shall be guilty of an offence unless he proves that he believed, and had reasonable cause to believe, that the residential occupier had ceased to reside in the premises.

(3) If any person with intent to cause the residential occupier of any premises –

(a) to give up the occupation of the premises or any part thereof; or

(b) to refrain from exercising any right or pursuing any remedy in respect of the premises or part thereof;

does acts likely to interfere with the peace or comfort of the residential occupier or members of his household, or persistently withdraws or withholds services reasonably required for the occupation of the premises as a residence, he shall be guilty of an offence.

(3A) Subject to subsection (3B) below, the landlord of a residential occupier or an agent of the landlord shall be guilty of an offence if –

(a) he does acts likely to interfere with the peace or comfort of the residential occupier or members of his household, or

(b) he persistently withdraws or withholds services reasonably required for the occupation of the premises in question as a residence,

and (in either case) he knows, or has reasonable cause to believe, that that conduct is likely to cause the residential occupier to give up the occupation of the whole or part of the premises or to refrain from exercising any right or pursuing any remedy in respect of the whole or part of the premises.

(3B) A person shall not be guilty of an offence under subsection (3A) above if he proves that he had reasonable grounds for doing the acts or withdrawing or withholding the services in question.

(3C) In subsection (3A) above 'landlord', in relation to a residential occupier of any premises, means the person who, but for –

(a) the residential occupier's right to remain in occupation of the premises, or

(b) a restriction on the person's rights to recover possession of the premises,

would be entitled to occupation of the premises and any superior landlord under whom that person derives title ...

(5) Nothing in this section shall be taken to prejudice any liability or remedy to which a person guilty of an offence thereunder may be subject in civil proceedings ...

2 Restriction on re-entry without due process of law

Where any premises are let as a dwelling on a lease which is subject to a right of re-entry or forfeiture it shall not be lawful to enforce that right otherwise than by proceedings in the court while any person is lawfully residing in the premises or part of them.

3 Prohibition of eviction without due process of law

(1) Where any premises have been let as a dwelling under a tenancy which is neither a statutorily protected tenancy nor an excluded tenancy and –

(a) the tenancy (in this section referred to as the former tenancy) has come to an end, but

(b) the occupier continues to reside in the premises or part of them,

it shall not be lawful for the owner to enforce against the occupier, otherwise than by proceedings in the court, his right to recover possession of the premises.

(2) In this section 'the occupier', in relation to any premises, means any person lawfully residing in the premises or part of them at the termination of the former tenancy.

(2A) Subsections (1) and (2) above apply in relation to any restricted contract (within the meaning of the Rent Act 1977) which –

(a) creates a licence; and

(b) is entered into after the commencement of section 69 of the Housing Act 1980;

as they apply in relation to a restricted contract which creates a tenancy.

(2B) Subsections (1) and (2) above apply in relation to any premises occupied as a dwelling under a licence, other than an excluded licence, as they apply in relation to premises let as a dwelling under a tenancy, and in those subsections the expression 'let' and 'tenancy' shall be construed accordingly.

(2C) References in the preceding provisions of this section and section 4(2A) below to an excluded tenancy do not apply to –

(a) a tenancy entered into before the date on which the Housing Act 1988 came into force, or

(b) a tenancy entered into on or after that date but pursuant to a contract made before that date, but, subject to that, 'excluded tenancy' and 'excluded licence' shall be construed in accordance with section 3A below.

(3) This section shall, with the necessary modifications, apply where the owner's right to recover possession arises on the death of the tenant under a statutory tenancy within the meaning of the Rent Act 1977 or the Rent (Agriculture) Act 1976.

3A   Excluded tenancies and licences

(1) Any reference in this Act to an excluded tenancy or an excluded licence is a reference to a tenancy or licence which is excluded by virtue of any of the following provisions of this section.

(2) A tenancy or licence is excluded if –

(a) under its terms the occupier shares any accommodation with the landlord or licensor; and

(b) immediately before the tenancy or licence was granted and also at the time it comes to an end, the landlord or licensor occupied as his only or principal home premises of which the whole or part of the shared accommodation formed part.

(3) A tenancy or licence is also excluded if –

(a) under its terms the occupier shares any accommodation with a member of the family of the landlord or licensor;

(b) immediately before the tenancy or licence was granted and also at the time it comes to a end, the member of the family of the landlord or licensor occupied as his only or principal home premises of which the whole or part of the shared accommodation formed part; and

(c) immediately before the tenancy or licence was granted and also at the time it comes to an end, the landlord or licensor occupied as his only or principal home premises in the same building as the shared accommodation and that building is not a purpose-built block of flats.

(4) For the purposes of subsections (2) and (3) above, an occupier shares accommodation with another person if he has the use of it in common with that person (whether or not also in common with others) and any reference in those subsections to shared accommodation shall be construed accordingly, and if, in relation to any tenancy or licence, there is at any time more than one person who is the landlord or licensor, any reference in those subsections to the landlord or licensor shall be construed as a reference to any one of those persons.

(5) In subsections (2) to (4) above –

(a) 'accommodation' includes neither an area used for storage nor a staircase, passage, corridor or other means of access;

(b) 'occupier' means, in relation to a tenancy, the tenant and, in relation to a licence, the licensee; and

(c) 'purpose-built block of flats' has the same meaning as in Part III of Schedule 1 to the Housing Act 1988;

and section 113 of the Housing Act 1985 shall apply to determine whether a person is for the purposes of subsection (3) above a member of another's family as it applies for the purposes of Part IV of that Act.

(6) A tenancy or licence is excluded if it was granted as a temporary expedient to a person who entered the premises in question or any other premises as a trespasser (whether or not, before the beginning of that tenancy or licence, another tenancy or licence to occupy the premises or any other premises had been granted to him).

(7) A tenancy or licence is excluded if –

(a) it confers on the tenant or licensee the right to occupy the premises for a holiday only, or

(b) it is granted otherwise than for money or money's worth.

(7A) A tenancy or licence is excluded if it is granted in order to provide accommodation under Part VI of the Immigration and Asylum Act 1999

(8) A licence is excluded if it confers rights of occupation in a hostel, within the meaning of the Housing Act 1985, which is provided by –

(a) the council of a county, county borough, district or London Borough, the Common Council of the City of London, the Council of the Isles of Scilly, the London Fire and Emergency Planning Authority, a joint authority within the meaning of the Local Government Act 1985 or a residuary body within the meaning of that Act;

(b) a development corporation within the meaning of the New Towns Act 1981;

(c) the Commission for the New Towns;

(d) an urban development corporation established by an order under section 135 of the Local Government, Planning and Land Act 1980;

(e) a housing action trust established under Part III of the Housing Act 1988;

(g) the Housing Corporation;

(ga) the Secretary of State under section 89 of the Housing Associations Act 1985;

(h) a housing trust (within the meaning of the Housing Associations Act 1985) which is a charity or a registered social landlord (within the meaning of the Housing Act 1985); or

(i) any other person who is, or who belongs to a class of person which is, specified in an order made by the Secretary of State ...

5 Validity of notices to quit

(1) Subject to subsection (1B) below no notice by a landlord or a tenant to quit any premises let (whether before or after the commencement of this Act) as a dwelling shall be valid unless –

(a) it is in writing and contains such information as may be prescribed, and

(b) it is given not less than four weeks before the date on which it is to take effect.

(1A) Subject to subsection (1B) below, no notice by a licensor or a licensee to determine a periodic licence to occupy premises as a dwelling (whether the licence was granted before or after the passing of this Act) shall be valid unless –

(a) it is in writing and contains such information as may be prescribed, and

(b) it is given not less than four weeks before the date on which it is to take effect.

(1B) Nothing in subsection (1) or subsection (1A) above applies to –

(a) premises let on an excluded tenancy which is entered into on or after the date on which the Housing Act 1988 came into force unless it is entered into pursuant to a contract made before that date; or

(b) premises occupied under an excluded licence.

(2) In this section 'prescribed' means prescribed by regulations made by the Secretary of State by statutory instrument ...

8   Interpretation

(1) In this Act 'statutorily protected tenancy' means –

(a) a protected tenancy within the meaning of the Rent Act 1977 or a tenancy to which Part I of the Landlord and Tenant Act 1954 applies:

(b) a protected occupancy or statutory tenancy as defined in the Rent (Agriculture) Act 1976;

(c) a tenancy to which Part II of the Landlord and Tenant Act 1954 applies;

(d) a tenancy of an agricultural holding within the meaning of the Agricultural Holdings Act 1986 which is a tenancy in relation to which that Act applies;

(e) an assured tenancy or assured agricultural occupancy under Part I of the Housing Act 1988;

(f) a tenancy to which Schedule 10 to the Local Government and Housing Act 1989 applies;

(g) a farm business tenancy within the meaning of the Agricultural Tenancies Act 1995.

(2) For the purposes of Part I of this Act [sections 1–4] a person who, under the terms of his employment, had exclusive possession of any premises other than as a tenant shall be deemed to have been a tenant and the expression 'let' and 'tenancy' shall be construed accordingly.

(3) In Part I of this Act 'the owner', in relation to any premises, means the person who, as against the occupier, is entitled to possession thereof.

(4) In this Act 'excluded tenancy' and 'excluded licence' have the meaning assigned by section 3A of this Act.

(5) If, on or after the date on which the Housing Act 1988 came into force, the terms of an excluded tenancy or excluded licence entered into before that date are varied, then –

    (a) if the variation affects the amount of the rent which is payable under the tenancy or licence, the tenancy or licence shall be treated for the purposes of sections 3(2C) and 5(1B) above as a new tenancy or licence entered into at the time of the variation; and

    (b) if the variation does not affect the amount of the rent which is so payable nothing in this Act shall affect the determination of the question whether the variation is such as to give rise to a new tenancy or licence.

(6) Any reference in subsection (5) above to a variation affecting the amount of the rent which is payable under a tenancy or licence does not include a reference to –

    (a) a reduction or increase effected under Part III or Part VI of the Rent Act 1977 (rents under regulated tenancies and housing association tenancies), section 78 of that Act (power of rent tribunal in relation to restricted contracts) or sections 11 to 14 of the Rent (Agriculture) Act 1976; or

    (b) a variation which is made by the parties and has the effect of making the rent expressed to be payable under the tenancy or licence the same as a rent for the dwelling which is entered in the register under Part IV or section 79 of the Rent Act 1977.

As amended by the Agricultural Holdings Act 1986, s100, Schedule 14, para 61; Housing Act 1988, ss29, 30(1), (2), 31, 32, 33; Local Government and Housing Act 1989, s194(1), Schedule 11, para 54; Local Government (Wales) Act 1994, s22(2), Schedule 8, para 4(1); Agricultural Tenancies Act 1995, s40, Schedule, para 29; Housing Act 1996 (Consequential Provisions) Order 1996, art 5, Schedule 2, para 7; Government of Wales Act 1998, ss131, 140, 141, 152, Schedule 16, para 2, Schedule 18, Pts IV, VI; Greater London Authority Act 1999, s328(8), Schedule 29, Pt I, para 27; Immigration and Asylum Act 1999, s169(1), Schedule 14, para 73.

CRIMINAL LAW ACT 1977
(1977 c 45)

6   Violence for securing entry

(1) Subject to the following provisions of this section, any person who, without lawful authority, uses or threatens violence for the purpose of securing entry into any premises for himself or for any other person is guilty of an offence, provided that –

(a) there is someone present on those premises at the time who is opposed to the entry which the violence is intended to secure; and

(b) the person using or threatening the violence knows that this is the case.

(1A) Subsection (1) above does not apply to a person who is a displaced residential occupier or a protected intending occupier of the premises in question or who is acting on behalf of such an occupier; and if the accused adduces sufficient evidence that he was, or was acting on behalf of, such an occupier he shall be presumed to be, or to be acting on behalf of, such an occupier unless the contrary is proved by the prosecution.

(2) Subject to subsection (1A) above, the fact that a person has any interest in or right to possession or occupation of any premises shall not for the purposes of subsection (1) above constitute lawful authority for the use or threat of violence by him or anyone else for the purpose of securing his entry into those premises.

(4) It is immaterial for the purposes of this section –

(a) whether the violence in question is directed against the person or against property; and

(b) whether the entry which the violence is intended to secure is for the purpose of acquiring possession of the premises in question or for any other purpose.

(5) A person guilty of an offence under this section shall be liable on summary conviction to imprisonment for a term not exceeding six months or to a fine not exceeding level 5 on the standard scale or to both.

(6) A constable in uniform may arrest without warrant anyone who is, or whom he, with reasonable cause, suspects to be, guilty of an offence under this section.

(7) Section 12 below contains provisions which apply for determining when any person is to be regarded for the purposes of this Part of this Act as a displaced residential occupier of any premises or of any access to any premises and section 12A below contains provisions which apply for determining when any person is to

be regarded for the purposes of this Part of this Act as a protected intending occupier of any premises or of any access to any premises.

7   Adverse occupation of residential premises

(1) Subject to the following provisions of this section and to section 12A(9) below, any person who is on any premises as a trespasser after having entered as such is guilty of an offence if he fails to leave those premises on being required to do so by or on behalf of –

(a) a displaced residential occupier of the premises; or

(b) an individual who is a protected intending occupier of the premises.

(2) In any proceedings for an offence under this section it shall be a defence for the accused to prove that he believed that the person requiring him to leave the premises was not a displaced residential occupier or protected intending occupier of the premises or a person acting on behalf of a displaced residential occupier or protected intending occupier.

(3) In any proceedings for an offence under this section it shall be a defence for the accused to prove –

(a) that the premises in question are or form part of premises used mainly for non-residential purposes; and

(b) that he was not on any part of the premises used wholly or mainly for residential purposes.

(4) Any reference in the preceding provisions of this section to any premises includes a reference to any access to them, whether or not any such access itself constitutes premises, within the meaning of this Part of this Act.

(5) A person guilty of an offence under this section shall be liable on summary conviction to imprisonment for a term not exceeding six months or to a fine not exceeding level 5 on the standard scale or to both.

(6) A constable in uniform may arrest without warrant anyone who is, or whom he, with reasonable cause, suspects to be, guilty of an offence under this section.

(7) Section 12 below contains provisions which apply for determining when any person is to be regarded for the purposes of this Part of this Act as a displaced residential occupier of any premises or of any access to any premises and section 12A below contains provisions which apply for determining when any person is to be regarded for the purposes of this Part of this Act as a protected intending occupier of any premises or of any access to any premises.

12   Supplementary provisions

(3) Subject to subsection (4) below, any person who was occupying any premises as a residence immediately before being excluded from occupation by anyone who entered those premises, or any access to those premises, as a trespasser is a displaced residential occupier of the premises for the purposes of this Part of this

Act so long as he continues to be excluded from occupation of the premises by the original trespasser or by any subsequent trespasser.

(4) A person who was himself occupying the premises in question as a trespasser immediately before being excluded from occupation shall not by virtue of subsection (3) above be a displaced residential occupier of the premises for the purposes of this Part of this Act.

(5) A person who by virtue of subsection (3) above is a displaced residential occupier of any premises shall be regarded for the purposes of this Part of this Act as a displaced residential occupier also of any access to those premises.

(6) Anyone who entered or is on or in occupation of any premises by virtue of –

> (a) any title derived from a trespasser; or
>
> (b) any licence or consent given by a trespasser or by a person deriving title from a trespasser,

shall himself be treated as a trespasser for the purposes of this Part of this Act (without prejudice to whether or not he would be a trespasser apart from this provision); and references in this Part of this Act to a person's entering or being on or occupying any premises as a trespasser shall be construed accordingly.

(7) Anyone who is on any premises as a trespasser shall not cease to be a trespasser for the purposes of this Part of this Act by virtue of being allowed time to leave the premises, nor shall anyone cease to be a displaced residential occupier of any premises by virtue of any such allowance of time to a trespasser. ...

12A Protected intending occupiers: supplementary provisions

(1) For the purposes of this Part of this Act an individual is a protected intending occupier of any premises at any time if at that time he falls within subsection (2), (4) or (6) below.

(2) An individual is a protected intending occupier of any premises if –

> (a) he has in those premises a freehold interest or a leasehold interest with not less than two years still to run;
>
> (b) he requires the premises for his own occupation as a resident;
>
> (c) he is excluded from occupation of the premises by a person who entered them, or any access to them, as a trespasser; and
>
> (d) he or a person acting on his behalf holds a written statement
>
>> (i) which specifies his interest in the premises;
>>
>> (ii) which states that he requires the premises for occupation as a residence for himself; and
>>
>> (iii) with respect to which the requirements in subsection (3) below are fulfilled.

(3) The requirements referred to in subsection (2)(d)(iii) above are –

(a) that the statement is signed by the person whose interest is specified in it in the presence of a justice of the peace or commissioner for oaths; and

(b) that the justice of the peace or commissioner for oaths has subscribed his name as a witness to the signature.

(4) An individual is also a protected intending occupier of any premises if –

(a) he has a tenancy of those premises (other than a tenancy falling within subsection (2)(a) above or (6)(a) below) or a licence to occupy those premises granted by a person with a freehold interest or a leasehold interest with not less than two years still to run in the premises;

(b) he requires the premises for his own occupation as a residence;

(c) he is excluded from occupation of the premises by a person who entered them, or any access to them, as a trespasser; and

(d) he or a person acting on his behalf holds a written statement –

(i) which states that he has been granted a tenancy of those premises or a licence to occupy those premises;

(ii) which specifies the interest in the premises of the person who granted that tenancy or licence to occupy ('the landlord');

(iii) which states that he requires the premises for occupation as a residence for himself; and

(iv) with respect to which the requirements in subsection (5) below are fulfilled.

(5) The requirements referred to in subsection (4)(d)(iv) above are –

(a) that the statement is signed by the landlord and by the tenant or licensee in the presence of a justice of the peace or commissioner for oaths;

(b) that the justice of the peace or commissioner for oaths has subscribed his name as a witness to the signatures.

(6) An individual is also a protected intending occupier of any premises if –

(a) he has a tenancy of those premises (other than a tenancy falling within subsection (2)(a) or (4)(a) above) or a licence to occupy those premises granted by an authority to which this subsection applies;

(b) he requires the premises for his own occupation as a residence;

(c) he is excluded from occupation of the premises by a person who entered the premises, or any access to them, as a trespasser; and

(d) there has been issued to him by or on behalf of the authority referred to in paragraph (a) above a certificate stating that –

(i) he has been granted a tenancy of those premises or a licence to occupy those premises as a residence by the authority; and

(ii) the authority which granted that tenancy or licence to occupy is one to which this subsection applies, being of a description specified in the certificate.

(7) Subsection (6) above applies to the following authorities –

(a) any body mentioned in section 14 of the Rent Act 1977 (landlord's interest belonging to local authority etc.);

(b) the Housing Corporation; and

(d) a registered social landlord within the meaning of the Housing Act 1985 (see section 5(4) and (5) of that Act).

(7A) Subsection (6) also applies to the Secretary of State if the tenancy or licence is granted by him under Part III of the Housing Associations Act 1985.

(8) A person is guilty of an offence if he makes a statement for the purposes of subsection (2)(d) or (4)(d) above which he knows to be false in a material particular or if he recklessly makes such a statement which is false in a material particular.

(9) In any proceedings for an offence under section 7 of this Act where the accused was requested to leave the premises by a person claiming to be or to act on behalf of a protected intending occupier of the premises –

(a) it shall be a defence for the accused to prove that, although asked to do so by the accused at the time the accused was requested to leave, that person failed at that time to produce to the accused such a statement as is referred to in subsection (2)(d) or (4)(d) above or such a certificate as is referred to in subsection (6)(d) above; and

(b) any document purporting to be a certificate under subsection (6)(d) above shall be received in evidence and, unless the contrary is proved, shall be deemed to have been issued by or on behalf of the authority stated in the certificate.

(10) A person guilty of an offence under subsection (8) above shall be liable on summary conviction to imprisonment for a term not exceeding six months or to a fine not exceeding level 5 on the standard scale or to both.

(11) A person who is a protected intending occupier of any premises shall be regarded for the purposes of this Part of this Act as a protected intending occupier also of any access to those premises.

As amended by the Criminal Justice and Public Order Act 1994, ss72, 73, 74, 168(3), Schedule 11; Housing Act 1996 (Consequential Provisions) Order 1996, art 5, Schedule 2, para 8; Government of Wales Act 1998, ss140, 141, 152, Schedule 16, para 3, Schedule 18, Pt VI.

CHARGING ORDERS ACT 1979
(1979 c 53)

1   Charging orders

(1) Where, under a judgment or order of the High Court or a county court, a person (the 'debtor') is required to pay a sum of money to another person (the 'creditor') then, for the purpose of enforcing that judgment or order, the appropriate court may make an order in accordance with the provisions of this Act imposing on any such property of the debtor as may be specified in the order a charge for securing the payment of any money due or to become due under the judgment or order ...

(3) An order under subsection (1) above is referred to in this Act as a 'charging order' ...

(5) In deciding whether to make a charging order the court shall consider all the circumstances of the case and, in particular, any evidence before it as to –

(a) the personal circumstances of the debtor, and

(b) whether any other creditor of the debtor would be likely to be unduly prejudiced by the making of the order.

2   Property which may be charged

(1) Subject to subsection (3) below, a charge may be imposed by a charging order only on –

(a) any interest held by the debtor beneficially –

(i) in any asset of a kind mentioned in subsection (2) below, or

(ii) under any trust; or

(b) any interest held by a person as trustee of a trust ('the trust'), if the interest is in such an asset or is an interest under another trust and –

(i) the judgment or order in respect of which a charge is to be imposed was made against that person as trustee of the trust, or

(ii) the whole beneficial interest under the trust is held by the debtor unencumbered and for his own benefit, or

(iii) in a case where there are two or more debtors all of whom are liable to the creditor for the same debt, they together hold the whole beneficial interest under the trust unencumbered and for their own benefit.

(2) The assets referred to in subsection (1) above are –

(a) land ...

3   Provisions supplementing sections 1 and 2

(1) A charging order may be made either absolutely or subject to conditions as to notifying the debtor or as to the time when the charge is to become enforceable, or as to other matters.

(2) The Land Charges Act 1972 and the Land Registration Act 2002 shall apply in relation to charging orders as they apply in relation to other orders or writs issued or made for the purposes of enforcing judgments.

(4) Subject to the provisions of this Act, a charge imposed by a charging order shall have the like effect and shall be enforceable in the same courts and in the same manner as an equitable charge created by the debtor by writing under his hand.

(5) The court by which a charging order was made may at any time, on the application of the debtor or of any person interested in any property to which the order relates, make an order discharging or varying the charging order.

(6) Where a charging order has been protected by an entry registered under the Land Charges Act 1972 or the Land Registration Act 2002, an order under subsection (5) above discharging the charging order may direct that the entry be cancelled ...

6   Interpretation ...

(2) For the purposes of section 1 of this Act references to a judgment or order of the High Court or a county court shall be taken to include references to a judgment, order, decree or award (however called) of any court or arbitrator (including any foreign court or arbitrator) which is or has become enforceable (whether wholly or to a limited extent) as if it were a judgment or order of the High Court or a county court ...

As amended by the Land Registration Act 2002, ss 133, 135, Schedule 11, para 15, Schedule 13.

LIMITATION ACT 1980
(1980 c 58)

PART I

ORDINARY TIME LIMITS FOR DIFFERENT CLASSES OF ACTION

1   Time limits under Part I subject to extension or exclusion under Part II

(1) This Part of this Act gives the ordinary time limits for bringing actions of the various classes mentioned in the following provisions of this Part.

(2) The ordinary time limits given in this Part of this Act are subject to extension or exclusion in accordance with the provisions of Part II of this Act.

5   Time limit for actions founded on simple contract

An action founded on simple contract shall not be brought after the expiration of six years from the date on which the cause of action accrued.

15   Time limit for actions to recover land

(1) No action shall be brought by any person to recover any land after the expiration of twelve years form the date on which the right of action accrued to him or, if it first accrued to some person through whom he claims, to that person.

(2) Subject to the following provisions of this section, where –

(a) the estate or interest claimed was an estate or interest in reversion or remainder or any other future estate or interest and the right of action to recover the land accrued on the date on which the estate or interest fell into possession by the determination of the preceding estate or interest; and

(b) the person entitled to the preceding estate or interest (not being a term of years absolute) was not in possession of the land on that date;

no action shall be brought by the person entitled to the succeeding estate or interest after the expiration of twelve years from the date on which the right of action accrued to the person entitled to the preceding estate or interest or six years from the date on which the right of action accrued to the person entitled to the succeeding estate or interest, which ever period last expires.

(3) Subsection (2) above shall not apply to any estate or interest which falls into

possession on the determination of an entailed interest and which might have been barred by the person entitled to the entailed interest.

(4) No person shall bring an action to recover any estate or interest in land under an assurance taking effect after the right of action to recover the land had accrued to the person by whom the assurance was made or some person through whom he claimed or some person entitled to a preceding estate or interest, unless the action is brought within the period during which the person by whom the assurance was made could have brought such an action.

(5) Where any person is entitled to any estate or interest in land in possession and, while so entitled, is also entitled to any future estate or interest in that land, and his right to recover the estate or interest in possession is barred under this Act, no action shall be brought by that person, or by any person claiming through him, in respect of the future estate or interest, unless in the meantime possession of the land has been recovered by a person entitled to an intermediate estate or interest.

(6) Part I of Schedule 1 to this Act contains provisions for determining the date of accrual of rights of action to recover land in the cases there mentioned.

(7) Part II of that Schedule contains provisions modifying the provisions of this section in their application to actions brought by, or by a person claiming through, the Crown or any spiritual or eleemosynary corporation sole.

16 Time limit for redemption actions

When a mortgagee of land has been in possession of any of the mortgaged land for a period of twelve years, no action to redeem the land of which the mortgagee has been so in possession shall be brought after the end of that period by the mortgagor or any person claiming through him.

17 Extinction of title to land after expiration of time limit

Subject to –

(a) section 18 of this Act;

at the expiration of the period prescribed by this Act for any person to bring an action to recover land (including a redemption action) the title of that person to the land shall be extinguished.

18 Settled land and land held on trust

(1) Subject to section 21(1) and (2) of this Act, the provisions of this Act shall apply to equitable interests in land as they apply to legal estates. Accordingly a right to action to recover the land shall, for the purposes of this Act but not otherwise, be treated as accruing to a person entitled in possession to such an equitable interest in the like manner and circumstances, and on the same date, as it would accrue if his interest were a legal estate in the land (and any relevant provision of Part I of Schedule 1 to this Act shall apply in any such case accordingly).

(2) Where the period prescribed by this Act has expired for the bringing of an action to recover land by a tenant for life or a statutory owner of settled land –

(a) his legal estate shall not be extinguished if and so long as the right of action to recover the land of any person entitled to a beneficial interest in the land either has not accrued or has not been barred by this Act; and

(b) the legal estate shall accordingly remain vested in the tenant for life or statutory owner and shall devolve in accordance with the Settled Land Act 1925;

but if and when every such right of action has been barred by this Act, his legal estate shall be extinguished.

(3) Where any land is held upon trust and the period prescribed by this Act has expired for the bringing of an action to recover the land by the trustees, the estate of the trustees shall not be extinguished if and so long as the right of action to recover the land of any person entitled to a beneficial interest in the land either has not accrued or has not been barred by this Act; but if and when every such right of action has been so barred the estate of the trustees shall be extinguished.

(4) Where –

(a) any settled land is vested in a statutory owner; or

(b) any land is held upon trust;

an action to recover the land may be brought by the statutory owner or trustees on behalf of any person entitled to a beneficial interest in possession in the land whose right of action has not been barred by this Act, notwithstanding that the right of action of the statutory owner or trustees would apart from this provision have been barred by this Act.

19   Time limit for actions to recover rent

No action shall be brought, or distress made, to recover arrears of rent, or damages in respect of arrears of rent, after the expiration of six years from the date on which the arrears became due.

19A Actions for breach of commonhold duty

An action in respect of a right or duty of a kind referred to in section 37(1) of the Commonhold and Leasehold Reform Act 2002 (enforcement) shall not be brought after the expiration of six years from the date on which the cause of action accrued.

20   Time limit for actions to recover money secured by a mortgage or charge or to recover proceeds of the sale of land

(1) No action shall be brought to recover –

(a) any principal sum of money secured by a mortgage or other charge on property (whether real or personal); or

(b) proceeds of the sale of land;

after the expiration of twelve years from the date on which the right to receive the money accrued.

(2) No foreclosure action in respect of mortgaged personal property shall be brought after the expiration of twelve years from the date on which the right to foreclose accrued.

But if the mortgagee was in possession of the mortgaged property after that date, the right to foreclose on the property which was in his possession shall not be treated as having accrued for the purposes of this subsection until the date on which his possession discontinued.

(3) The right to receive any principal sum of money secured by a mortgage or other charge and the right to foreclose on the property subject to the mortgage or charge shall not be treated as accruing so long as that property comprises any future interest or any life insurance policy which has not matured or been determined.

(4) Nothing in this section shall apply to a foreclosure action in respect of mortgaged land, but the provisions of this Act relating to actions to recover land shall apply to such an action.

(5) Subject to subsections (6) and (7) below, no action to recover arrears of interest payable in respect of any sum of money secured by a mortgage or other charge or payable in respect of proceeds of the sale of land, or to recover damages in respect of such arrears [,] shall be brought after the expiration of six years from the date on which the interest became due.

(6) Where –

(a) a prior mortgagee or other incumbrancer has been in possession of the property charged; and

(b) an action is brought within one year of the discontinuance of that possession by the subsequent incumbrancer;

the subsequent incumbrancer may recover by that action all the arrears of interest which fell due during the period of possession by the prior incumbrancer or damages in respect of those arrears, notwithstanding that the period exceeded six years.

(7) Where –

(a) the property subject to the mortgage or charge comprises any future interest or life insurance policy; and

(b) it is a term of the mortgage or charge that arrears of interest shall be treated as part of the principal sum of money secured by the mortgage or charge;

interest shall not be treated as becoming due before the right to recover the principal sum of money has accrued or is treated as having accrued.

28   Extension of limitation period in case of disability

(1) Subject to the following provisions of this section, if on the date when any right of action accrued for which a period of limitation is prescribed by this Act, the person to whom it accrued was under a disability, the action may be brought at any time before the expiration of six years from the date when he ceased to be under a disability or died (whichever first occurred) notwithstanding that the period of limitation has expired.

(2) This section shall not affect any case where the right of action first accrued to some person (not under a disability) through whom the person under a disability claims.

(3) When a right of action which has accrued to a person under a disability accrues, on the death of that person while still under a disability, to another person under a disability, no further extension of time shall be allowed by reason of the disability of the second person.

(4) No action to recover land or money charged on land shall be brought by virtue of this section by any person after the expiration of thirty years from the date on which the right of action accrued to that person or some person through whom he claims. ...

29   Fresh accrual of action on acknowledgment or part payment

(1) Subsections (2) and (3) below apply where any right of action (including a foreclosure action) to recover land or an advowson or any right of a mortgagee of personal property to bring a foreclosure action in respect of the property has accrued.

(2) If the person in possession of the land, benefice or personal property in question acknowledges the title of the person to whom the right of action has accrued –

   (a) the right shall be treated as having accrued on and not before the date of the acknowledgment; and

   (b) in the case of a right of action to recover land which has accrued to a person entitled to an estate or interest taking effect on the determination of an entailed interest against whom time is running under section 27 [cure of defective disentailing assurance] of this Act, section 27 shall thereupon cease to apply to the land.

(3) In the case of a foreclosure or other action by a mortgagee, if the person in possession of the land, benefice or personal property in question or the person liable for the mortgage debt makes any payment in respect of the debt (whether of principal or interest) the right shall be treated as having accrued on and not before the date of the payment.

(4) Where a mortgagee is by virtue of the mortgage in possession of any mortgaged land and either –

(a) receives any sum in respect of the principal or interest of the mortgage debt; or

(b) acknowledges the title of the mortgagor, or his equity of redemption;

an action to redeem the land in his possession may be brought at any time before the expiration of twelve years from the date of the payment or acknowledgment.

(5) Subject to subsection (6) below, where any right of action has accrued to recover –

(a) any debt or other liquidated pecuniary claim; or

(b) any claim to the personal estate of a deceased person or to any share or interest in any such estate;

and the person liable or accountable for the claim acknowledges the claim or makes any payment in respect of it the right shall be treated as having accrued on and not before the date of the acknowledgment or payment.

(6) A payment of a part of the rent or interest due at any time shall not extend the period for claiming the remainder then due, but any payment of interest shall be treated as a payment in respect of the principal debt.

(7) Subject to subsection (6) above, a current period of limitation may be repeatedly extended under this section by further acknowledgments or payments, but a right of action, once barred by this Act, shall not be revived by any subsequent acknowledgment or payment.

30   Formal provisions as to acknowledgments and part payments

(1) To be effective for the purposes of section 29 of this Act, an acknowledgment must be in writing and signed by the person making it.

(2) For the purposes of section 29, any acknowledgment or payment –

(a) may be made by the agent of the person by whom it is required to be made under that section; and

(b) shall be made to the person, or to an agent of the person, whose title or claim is being acknowledged or, as the case may be, in respect of whose claim the payment is being made.

31   Effect of acknowledgment or part payment on persons other than the maker or recipient

(1) An acknowledgement of the title to any land, benefice, or mortgaged personalty by any person in possession of it shall bind all other persons in possession during the ensuing period of limitation.

(2) A payment in respect of a mortgage debt by the mortgagor or any other person liable for the debt, or by any person in possession of the mortgaged property, shall, so far as any right of the mortgagee to foreclose or otherwise to recover the property is concerned, bind all other persons in possession of the mortgaged property during the ensuing period of limitation.

(3) Where two or more mortgagees are by virtue of the mortgage in possession of the mortgaged land, an acknowledgement of the mortgagor's title or of his equity of redemption by one of the mortgagees shall only bind him and his successors and shall not bind any other mortgagee or his successors.

(4) Where in a case within subsection (3) above the mortgagee by whom the acknowledgement is given is entitled to a part of the mortgaged land and not to any ascertained part of the mortgage debt the mortgagor shall be entitled to redeem that part of the land on payment, with interest, of the part of the mortgage debt which bears the same proportion to the whole of the debt as the value of the part of the land bears to the whole of the mortgaged land.

(5) Where there are two or more mortgagors, and the title or equity of redemption of one of the mortgagors is acknowledged as mentioned above in this section, the acknowledgement shall be treated as having been made to all the mortgagors.

(6) An acknowledgment of any debt or other liquidated pecuniary claim shall bind the acknowledgor and his successors but not any other person.

(7) A payment made in respect of any debt or other liquidated pecuniary claim shall bind all persons liable in respect of the debt or claim.

(8) An acknowledgment by one of several personal representatives of any claim to the personal estate of a deceased person or to any share or interest in any such estate, or a payment by one of several personal representatives in respect of any such claim, shall bind the estate of the deceased person.

(9) In this section 'successor', in relation to any mortgagee or person liable in respect of any debt or claim, means his personal representatives and any other person on whom the rights under the mortgage or, as the case may be, the liability in respect of the debt or claim devolve (whether on death or bankruptcy or the disposition of property or the determination of a limited estate or interest in settled property or otherwise).

32 Postponement of limitation period in case of fraud, concealment or mistake

(1) Subject to subsections (3) and (4A) below, where in the case of any action for which a period of limitation is prescribed by this Act, either –

(a) the action is based upon the fraud of the defendant; or

(b) any fact relevant to the plaintiff's right of action has been deliberately concealed from him by the defendant; or

(c) the action is for relief from the consequences of a mistake;

the period of limitation shall not begin to run until the plaintiff has discovered the fraud, concealment or mistake (as the case may be) or could with reasonable diligence have discovered it.

References in this subsection to the defendant include references to the defendant's agent and to any person through whom the defendant claims and his agent.

(2) For the purposes of subsection (1) above, deliberate commission of a breach of duty in circumstances in which it is unlikely to be discovered for some time amounts to deliberate concealment of the facts involved in that breach of duty.

(3) Nothing in this section shall enable any action –

(a) to recover, or recover the value of, any property; or

(b) to enforce any charge against, or set aside any transaction affecting, any property;

to be brought against the purchaser of the property or any person claiming through him in any case where the property has been purchased for valuable consideration by an innocent third party since the fraud or concealment or (as the case may be) the transaction in which the mistake was made took place.

(4) A purchase is an innocent third party for the purposes of this section –

(a) in the case of fraud or concealment of any fact relevant to the plaintiff's right of action, if he was not a party to the fraud or (as the case may be) to the concealment of that fact and did not at the time of the purchase know or have reason to believe that the fraud or concealment had taken place; and

(b) in the case of mistake, if he did not at the time of the purchase know or have reason to believe that the mistake had been made.

(4A) Subsection (1) above shall not apply in relation to the time limit prescribed by section 11A(3) of this Act or in relation to that time limit as applied by virtue of section 12(1) of this Act. ...

PART III

MISCELLANEOUS AND GENERAL

36   Equitable jurisdiction and remedies

(1) The following time limits under this Act, that is to say – ...

(b) the time limit under section 5 for actions founded on simple contract;

(c) the time limit under section 7 for actions to enforce awards where the submission is not by an instrument under seal;

(d) the time limit under section 8 for actions on a specialty; ...

shall not apply to any claim for specific performance of a contract or for an injunction or for other equitable relief, except in so far as any such time limit may be applied by the court by analogy in like manner as the corresponding time limit under any enactment repealed by the Limitation Act 1939 was applied before 1st July 1940.

(2) Nothing in this Act shall affect any equitable jurisdiction to refuse relief on the ground of acquiescence or otherwise.

38   Interpretation

(1) In this Act, unless the context otherwise requires –

'action' includes any proceeding in a court of law, including an ecclesiastical court;

'land' includes corporeal hereditaments, tithes and rent charges and any legal or equitable estate or interest therein, but except as provided above in this definition does not include any incorporeal hereditament;

'personal estate' and 'personal property' do not include chattels real;

'personal injuries' includes any disease and any impairment of a person's physical or mental condition, and 'injury' and cognate expressions shall be construed accordingly;

'rent' includes a rentcharge and a rent service;

'rentcharge' means any annuity or periodical sum of money charged upon or payable out of land, except a rent service or interest on a mortgage on land;

'settled land', 'statutory owner' and 'tenant for life' have the same meanings respectively as in the Settled Land Act 1925;

'trust' and 'trustee' have the same meanings respectively as in the Trustee Act 1925.

(2) For the purposes of this Act a person shall be treated as under a disability while he is an infant, or of unsound mind.

(3) For the purposes of subsection (2) above a person is of unsound mind if he is a person who, by reason of mental disorder is incapable of managing and administering his property and affairs; and in this section 'mental disorder' has the same meaning as in the Mental Health Act 1983.

(4) Without prejudice to the generality of subsection (3) above, a person shall be conclusively presumed for the purposes of subsection (2) above to be of unsound mind:

(a) while he is liable to be detained or subject to guardianship under the Mental Health Act 1983 (otherwise than by virtue of section 35 or 89); and

(b) while he is receiving treatment for mental disorder as an in-patient in any hospital within the meaning of the Mental Health Act 1983 or independent hospital or care home within the meaning of the Care Standards Act 2000 without being liable to be detained under the said Act of 1983 (otherwise than by virtue of section 35 or 89), being treatment which follows without any interval a period during which he was liable to be detained or subject to guardianship under the Mental Health Act 1959, or the said Act of 1983 (otherwise than by virtue of section 35 or 89) or by virtue of any enactment repealed or excluded by the Mental Health Act 1959.

(5) Subject to subsection (6) below, a person shall be treated as claiming through another person if he became entitled by, through, under, or by the act of that other person to the right claimed, and any person whose estate or interest might have been barred by a person entitled to an entailed interest in possession shall be treated as claiming through the person so entitled.

(6) A person becoming entitled to any estate or interest by virtue of a special power of appointment shall not be treated as claiming through the appointor.

(7) References in this Act to a right of action to recover land shall include references to a right to enter into possession of the land or, in the case of rentcharges and tithes, to distrain for arrears of rent or tithe, and references to the bringing of such an action shall include references to the making of such an entry or distress.

(8) References in this Act to the possession of land shall, in the case of tithes and rentcharges, be construed as references to the receipt of the tithe or rent, and references to the date of dispossession or discontinuance of possession of land shall, in the case of rentcharges, be construed as references to the date of the last receipt of rent.

(9) References in Part II of this Act to a right of action shall include references to –

(a) a cause of action;

(b) a right to receive money secured by a mortgage or charge on any property;

(c) a right to recover proceeds of the sale of land; and

(d) a right to receive a share or interest in the personal estate of a deceased person.

(10) References in Part II to the date of the accrual of a right of action shall be construed –

(a) in the case of an action upon a judgment, as references to the date on which the judgment became enforceable; and

(b) in the case of an action to recover arrears of rent or interest, or damages in respect of arrears of rent or interest, as references to the date on which the rent or interest became due.

SCHEDULE 1

PROVISIONS WITH RESPECT TO ACTIONS TO RECOVER LAND

PART I

ACCRUAL OF RIGHTS OF ACTION TO RECOVER LAND

1. Where the person bringing an action to recover land, or some person through whom he claims, has been in possession of the land, and has while entitled to the land been dispossessed or discontinued his possession, the right of action shall be treated as having accrued on the date of the dispossession or discontinuance.

2. Where any person brings an action to recover any land of a deceased person (whether under a will or on intestacy) and the deceased person –

(a) was on the date of his death in possession of the land or, in the case of a rentcharge created by will or taking effect upon his death, in possession of the land charged; and

(b) was the last person entitled to the land to be in possession of it;

the right of action shall be treated as having accrued on the date of his death.

3. Where any person brings an action to recover land, being an estate or interest in possession assured otherwise than by will to him, or to some person through whom he claims, and –

(a) the person making the assurance was on the date when the assurance took effect in possession of the land or, in the case of a rentcharge created by the assurance, in possession of the land charged; and

(b) no person has been in possession of the land by virtue of the assurance;

the right of action shall be treated as having accrued on the date when the assurance took effect.

4. The right of action to recover any land shall, in a case where –

(a) the estate or interest claimed was an estate or interest in reversion or remainder or any other future estate or interest; and

(b) no person has taken possession of the land by virtue of the estate or interest claimed;

be treated as having accrued on the date on which the estate or interest fell into possession by the determination of the preceding estate or interest.

5.–(1) Subject to sub-paragraph (2) below, a tenancy from year to year or other period, without a lease in writing, shall for the purposes of this Act be treated as being determined at the expiration of the first year or other period; and accordingly the right of action of the person entitled to the land subject to the tenancy shall be treated as having accrued at the date on which in accordance with this sub-paragraph the tenancy is determined.

(2) Where any rent has subsequently been received in respect of the tenancy, the right of action shall be treated as having accrued on the date of the last receipt of rent.

6.–(1) Where –

(a) any person is in possession of land by virtue of a lease in writing by which a rent of not less than ten pounds a year is reserved; and

(b) the rent is received by some person wrongfully claiming to be entitled to the land in reversion immediately expectant on the determination of the lease; and

(c) no rent is subsequently received by the person rightfully so entitled;

the right of action to recover the land of the person rightfully so entitled shall be treated as having accrued on the date when the rent was first received by the person wrongfully claiming to be so entitled and not on the date of the determination of the lease ...

7.–(1) Subject to sub-paragraph (2) below, a right of action to recover land by virtue of a forfeiture or breach of condition shall be treated as having accrued on the date on which the forfeiture was incurred or the condition broken.

(2) If any such right has accrued to a person entitled to an estate or interest in reversion or remainder and the land was not recovered by virtue of that right, the right of action to recover the land shall not be treated as having accrued to that person until his estate or interest fell into possession, as if no such forfeiture or breach of condition had occurred.

8.–(1) No right of action to recover land shall be treated as accruing unless the land is in the possession of some person in whose favour the period of limitation can run (referred to below in this paragraph as 'adverse possession'); and where under the preceding provisions of this Schedule any such right of action is treated as accruing on a certain date and no person is in adverse possession on that date, the right of action shall not be treated as accruing unless and until adverse possession is taken on the land.

(2) Where a right of action to recover land has accrued and after its accrual, before the right is barred, the land ceases to be in adverse possession, the right of action shall no longer be treated as having accrued and no fresh right of action shall be treated as accruing unless and until the land is again taken into adverse possession.

(3) For the purposes of this paragraph –

(a) possession of any land subject to a rentcharge by a person (other than the person entitled to the rentcharge) who does not pay the rent shall be treated as adverse possession of the rentcharge; and

(b) receipt of rent under a lease by a person wrongfully claiming to be entitled to the land in reversion immediately expectant on the determination of the lease shall be treated as adverse possession of the land.

(4) For the purpose of determining whether a person occupying any land is in adverse possession of the land it shall not be assumed by implication of law that his occupation is by permission of the person entitled to the land merely by virtue of the fact that his occupation is not inconsistent with the latter's present or future enjoyment of the land. This provision shall not be taken as prejudicing a finding to the effect that a person's occupation of any land is by implied permission of the person entitled to the land in any case where such a finding is justified on the actual facts of the case.

9. Where any settled land or any land subject to a trust of land is in the possession of a person entitled to a beneficial interest in the land (not being a person solely or absolutely entitled to the land), no right of action to recover the land shall be treated for the purposes of this Act as accruing during that possession to any person in whom the land is vested as tenant for life, statutory owner or trustee, or to any other person entitled to a beneficial interest in the land.

As amended by the Mental Health Act 1983, s148, Schedule 4, para 55; Consumer Protection Act 1987, s6(6), Schedule 1, paras 4, 6; Trusts of Land and Appointment of Trustees Act 1996, s25(1), (2), Schedule 3, para 18, Schedule 4; Land Registration Act 2002,, s135, Schedule 13; Commonhold and Leasehold Reform Act 2002, s68, Schedule 5, para 4; Care Standards Act 2000, s116, Schedule 4, para 8.

SUPREME COURT ACT 1981
(1981 c 54)

37   Powers of High Court with respect to injunctions and receivers

(1) The High Court may by order (whether interlocutory or final) grant an injunction or appoint a receiver in all cases in which it appears to the court to be just and convenient to do so.

(2) Any such order may be made either unconditionally or on such terms and conditions as the court thinks just.

(3) The power of the High Court under subsection (1) to grant an interlocutory injunction restraining a party to any proceedings from removing from the jurisdiction of the High Court, or otherwise dealing with, assets located within that jurisdiction shall be exercisable in cases where that party is, as well as in cases where he is not, domiciled, resident or present within that jurisdiction.

(4) The power of the High Court to appoint a receiver by way of equitable execution shall operate in relation to all legal estates and interests in land; and that power –

   (a) may be exercised in relation to an estate or interest in land whether or not a charge has been imposed on that land under section 1 of the Charging Orders Act 1979 for the purpose of enforcing the judgment, order or award in question; and

   (b) shall be in addition to, and not in derogation of, any power of any court to appoint a receiver in proceedings for enforcing such a charge.

(5) Where an order under the said section 1 imposing a charge for the purpose of enforcing a judgment, order or award has been, or has effect as if, registered under section 6 of the Land Charges Act 1972, subsection (4) of the said section 6 (effect of non-registration of writs and orders registrable under that section) shall not apply to an order appointing a receiver made either –

   (a) in proceedings for enforcing the charge; or

   (b) by way of equitable execution of the judgment, order or award or, as the case may be, of so much of it as requires payment of moneys secured by the charge.

38   Relief against forfeiture for non-payment of rent

(1) In any action in the High Court for the forfeiture of a lease for non-payment of rent, the court shall have power to grant relief against forfeiture in a summary manner, and may do so subject to the same terms and conditions as to the payment

of rent, costs or otherwise as could have been imposed by it in such an action immediately before the commencement of this Act.

(2) Where the lessee or a person deriving title under him is granted relief under this section, he shall hold the demised premises in accordance with the terms of the lease without the necessity for a new lease.

39 Execution of instrument by person nominated by High Court

(1) Where the High Court has given or made a judgment or order directing a person to execute any conveyance, contract or other document, or to indorse any negotiable instrument, then, if that person –

(a) neglects or refuses to comply with the judgment or order; or

(b) cannot after reasonable inquiry be found, the High Court may, on such terms and conditions, if any, as may be just, order that the conveyance, contract or other document shall be executed, or that the negotiable instrument shall be indorsed, by such person as the court may nominate for that purpose.

(2) A conveyance, contract, document or instrument executed or indorsed in pursuance of an order under this section shall operate, and be for all purposes available, as if it had been executed or indorsed by the person originally directed to execute or indorse it.

CIVIL AVIATION ACT 1982
(1982 c 16)

76 Liability of aircraft in respect of trespass, nuisance and surface damage

(1) No action shall lie in respect of trespass or in respect of nuisance, by reason only of the flight of an aircraft over any property at a height above the ground which, having regard to wind, weather and all the circumstances of the case is reasonable, or the ordinary incidents of such flight, so long as the provisions of any Air Navigation Order and of any orders under section 62 [orders in time of war or great national emergency] above have been duly complied with and there has been no breach of section 81 [dangerous flying] below.

(2) Subject to subsection (3) below, where material loss or damage is caused to any person or property on land or water by, or by a person in, or an article, animal or person falling from, an aircraft while in flight, taking off or landing, then unless the loss or damage was caused or contributed to by the negligence of the person by whom it was suffered, damages in respect of the loss or damage shall be recoverable without proof of negligence or intention or other cause of action, as if the loss or damage had been caused by the wilful act, neglect, or default of the owner of the aircraft.

(3) Where material loss or damage is caused as aforesaid in circumstances in which –

(a) damages are recoverable in respect of the said loss or damage by virtue only of subsection (2) above, and

(b) a legal liability is created in some person other than the owner to pay damages in respect of the said loss or damage,

the owner shall be entitled to be indemnified by that other person against any claim in respect of the said loss or damage.

(4) Where the aircraft concerned has been bona fide demised, let or hired out for any period exceeding fourteen days to any other person by the owner thereof, and no pilot, commander, navigator or operative member of the crew of the aircraft is in the employment of the owner, this section shall have effect as if for references to the owner there were substituted references to the person to whom the aircraft has been so demised, let or hired out.

105 General interpretation

(1) In this Act, except where the context otherwise requires –

'Air Navigation Order' means an Order in Council under section 60 above; ...

'flight' means a journey by air beginning when the aircraft in question takes off and ending when it next lands; ...

'loss or damage' includes, in relation to persons, loss of life and personal injury; ...

COUNTY COURTS ACT 1984
(1984 c 28)

138 Provisions as to forfeiture for non-payment of rent

(1) This section has effect where a lessor is proceeding by action in a county court (being an action in which the county court has jurisdiction) to enforce against a lessee a right of re-entry or forfeiture in respect of any land for non-payment of rent.

(2) If the lessee pays into court or to the lessor not less than five clear days before the return day all the rent in arrear and the costs of the action, the action shall cease, and the lessee shall hold the land according to the lease without any new lease.

(3) If –

(a) the action does not cease under subsection (2); and

(b) the court at the trial is satisfied that the lessor is entitled to enforce the right of re-entry or forfeiture,

the court shall order possession of the land to be given to the lessor at the expiration of such period, not being less than four weeks from the date of the order, as the court thinks fit, unless within that period the lessee pays into court or to the lessor all the rent in arrear and the costs of the action.

(4) The court may extend the period specified under subsection (3) at any time before possession of the land is recovered in pursuance of the order under that subsection.

(5) If –

(a) within the period specified in the order; or

(b) within that period as extended under subsection (4),

the lessee pays into court or to the lessor –

(i) all the rent in arrear; and

(ii) the costs of the action,

he shall hold the land according to the lease without any new lease.

(6) Subsection (2) shall not apply where the lessor is proceeding in the same action to enforce a right of re-entry or forfeiture on any other ground as well as for non-payment of rent, or to enforce any other claim as well as the right of re-entry or forfeiture and the claim for arrears of rent.

(7) If the lessee does not –

(a) within the period specified in the order; or

(b) within that period as extended under subsection (4), pay into court or to the lessor –

(i) all the rent in arrear; and

(ii) the costs of the action,

the order shall be enforceable in the prescribed manner and so long as the order remains unreversed the lessee shall, subject to subsections (8) and (9A), be barred from all relief.

(8) The extension under subsection (4) of a period fixed by a court shall not be treated as relief from which the lessee is barred by subsection (7) if he fails to pay into court or to the lessor all the rent in arrear and the costs of the action within that period.

(9) Where the court extends a period under subsection (4) at a time when –

(a) that period has expired; and

(b) a warrant has been issued for the possession of the land, the court shall suspend the warrant for the extended period; and, if, before the expiration period, the lessee pays into court or to the lessor all the rent in arrear and all the costs of the action, the court shall cancel the warrant.

(9A) Where the lessor recovers possession of the land at any time after the making of the order under subsection (3) (whether as a result of the enforcement of the order or otherwise) the lessee may, at any time within six months from the date on which the lessor recovers possession, apply to the courts for relief; and on any such application the court may, if it thinks fit, grant to the lessee such relief, subject to such terms and conditions, as it thinks fit.

(9B) Where the lessee is granted relief on an application under subsection (9A) he shall hold the land according to the lease without any new lease.

(9C) An application under subsection (9A) may be made by a person with an interest under a lease of the land derived (whether immediately or otherwise) from the lessee's interest therein in like manner as if he were the lessee; and on any such application the court may make an order which (subject to such terms and conditions as the court thinks fit) vests the land in such a person, as lessee of the lessor, for the remainder of the term of the lease under which he has any such interest as aforesaid, or for any lesser term.

In this subsection any reference to the land includes a reference to a part of the land.

(10) Nothing in this section or section 139 shall be taken to affect –

(a) the power of the court to make any order which it would otherwise have power to make as respects a right of re-entry or forfeiture on any ground other than non-payment of rent; or

(b) section 146(4) of the Law of Property Act 1925 (relief against forfeiture).

139 Service of summons and re-entry

(1) In a case where section 138 has effect if –

(a) one-half year's rent is in arrear at the time of the commencement of the action; and

(b) the lessor has a right to re-enter for non-payment of that rent; and

(c) no sufficient distress is to be found on the premises countervailing the arrears then due,

the service of the summons in the action in the prescribed manner shall stand in lieu of a demand and re-entry.

(2) Where a lessor has enforced against a lessee, by re-entry without action, a right of re-entry or forfeiture as respects any land for non-payment of rent, the lessee may at any time within six months from the date on which the lessor re-entered apply to the county court for relief, and on any such application the court may, if it thinks fit, grant to the lessee such relief as the High Court could have granted.

(3) Subsections (9B) and (9C) of section 138 shall have effect in relation to an application under subsection (2) of this section as they have effect in relation to an application under subsection (9A) of that section.

140 Interpretation of sections 138 and 139

For the purposes of sections 138 and 139 –

'lease' includes –

(a) an original or derivative under-lease;

(b) an agreement for a lease where the lessee has become entitled to have his lease granted; and

(c) a grant at a fee farm rent, or under a grant securing a rent by condition;

'lessee' includes –

(a) an original or derivative under-lessee;

(b) the persons deriving title under a lessee;

(c) a grantee under a grant at a fee farm rent, or under a grant securing a rent by condition; and

(d) the persons deriving title under such a grantee;

'lessor' includes –

(a) an original or derivative under-lessor;

(b) the persons deriving title under a lessor;

(c) a person making a grant at a fee farm rent, or a grant securing a rent by condition; and

(d) the persons deriving title under such a grantor;

'under-lease' includes an agreement for an under-lease where the under-lessee has become entitled to have his underlease granted; and

'under-lessee' includes any person deriving title under an under-lessee.

As amended by the Administration of Justice Act 1985, ss55(1)–(5), 67(2), Schedule 8, Pt III; Courts and Legal Services Act 1990, s125(2), Schedule 17, para 17; High Court and County Courts Jurisdiction Order 1991, art 2(8), Schedule.

MATRIMONIAL AND FAMILY PROCEEDINGS ACT 1984

(1984 c 42)

22   Powers of court in relation to certain tenancies of dwelling-houses

(1) This section applies if –

(a) an application is made by a party to a marriage for an order for financial relief, and

(b) one of the parties is entitled, either in his own right or jointly with the other party, to occupy a dwelling-house situated in England or Wales by virtue of a tenancy which is a relevant tenancy within the meaning of Schedule 7 to the Family Law Act 1996 (certain statutory tenancies).

(2) The court may make in relation to that dwelling-house any order which it could make under Part II of that Schedule if a decree of divorce, a decree of nullity of marriage or a decree of judicial separation has been granted in England and Wales in respect of the marriage.

(3) The provisions of paragraphs 10, 11 and 14(1) in Part III of that Schedule apply in relation to any order under this section as they apply to any order under Part II of that Schedule.

As substituted by the Family Law Act 1996, s66(1), Schedule 8, Pt III, para 52 and modified by the Family Law Act 1996 (Commencement No 2) Order 1997, art 3(2) until such time as Part II of the 1996 Act is brought into force.

HOUSING ACT 1985
(1985 c 68)

PART IV

SECURE TENANCIES AND RIGHTS OF SECURE TENANTS

79 Secure tenancies

(1) A tenancy under which a dwelling-house is let as a separate dwelling is a secure tenancy at any time when the conditions described in sections 80 and 81 as the landlord condition and the tenant condition are satisfied.

(2) Subsection (1) has effect subject to –

(a) the exceptions in Schedule 1 (tenancies which are not secure tenancies),

(b) sections 89(3) and (4) and 90(3) and (4) (tenancies ceasing to be secure after death of tenant), and

(c) sections 91(2) and 93(2) (tenancies ceasing to be secure in consequence of assignment or subletting).

(3) The provisions of this Part apply in relation to a licence to occupy a dwelling-house (whether or not granted for a consideration) as they apply in relation to a tenancy.

(4) Subsection (3) does not apply to a licence granted as a temporary expedient to a person who entered the dwelling-house or any other land as a trespasser (whether or not, before the grant of that licence, another licence to occupy that or another dwelling-house had been granted to him).

80 The landlord condition

(1) The landlord condition is that the interest of the landlord belongs to one of the following authorities or bodies –

a local authority,

a new town corporation,

a housing action trust,

an urban development corporation.

(3) If a co-operative housing association ceases to be a registered social landlord, it shall, within the period of 21 days beginning with the date on which it ceases to be a registered social landlord, notify each of its tenants who thereby becomes a secure tenant, in writing, that he has become a secure tenant. ...

81   The tenant condition

The tenant condition is that the tenant is an individual and occupies the dwelling-house as his only or principal home; or, where the tenancy is a joint tenancy, that each of the joint tenants is an individual and at least one of them occupies the dwelling-house as his only or principal home.

82   Security of tenure

(1) A secure tenancy which is either –

(a) a weekly or other periodic tenancy, or

(b) a tenancy for a term certain but subject to termination by the landlord,

cannot be brought to an end by the landlord except by obtaining an order mentioned in subsection (1A).

(1A) These are the orders –

(a) an order of the court for the possession of the dwelling-house;

(b) an order under subsection (3);

(c) a demotion order under section 82A.

(2) Where the landlord obtains an order for the possession of the dwelling-house, the tenancy ends on the date on which the tenant is to give up possession in pursuance of the order.

(3) Where a secure tenancy is a tenancy for a term certain but with a provision for re-entry or forfeiture, the court shall not order possession of the dwelling-house in pursuance of that provision, but in a case where the court would have made such an order it shall instead make an order terminating the tenancy on a date specified in the order and section 86 (periodic tenancy arising on termination of fixed term) shall apply.

(4) Section 146 of the Law of Property Act 1925 (restriction on and relief against forfeiture), except subsection (4) (vesting in under-lessee), and any other enactment or rule of law relating to forfeiture, shall apply in relation to proceedings for an order under subsection (3) of this section as if they were proceedings to enforce a right of re-entry or forfeiture.

82A Demotion because of anti-social behaviour

(1) This section applies to a secure tenancy if the landlord is –

(a) a local housing authority;

(b) a housing action trust;

(c) a registered social landlord.

(2) The landlord may apply to a county court for a demotion order.

(3) A demotion order has the following effect –

(a) the secure tenancy is terminated with effect from the date specified in the order;

(b) if the tenant remains in occupation of the dwelling-house after that date a demoted tenancy is created with effect from that date;

(c) it is a term of the demoted tenancy that any arrears of rent payable at the termination of the secure tenancy become payable under the demoted tenancy;

(d) it is also a term of the demoted tenancy that any rent paid in advance or overpaid at the termination of the secure tenancy is credited to the tenant's liability to pay rent under the demoted tenancy.

(4) The court must not make a demotion order unless it is satisfied –

(a) that the tenant or a person residing in or visiting the dwelling-house has engaged or has threatened to engage in conduct to which section 153A or 153B of the Housing Act 1996 (anti-social behaviour or use of premises for unlawful purposes) applies, and

(b) that it is reasonable to make the order. ...

PART V

THE RIGHT TO BUY

118 The right to buy

(1) A secure tenant has the right to buy, that is to say, the right, in the circumstances and subject to the conditions and exceptions stated in the following provisions of this Part –

(a) if the dwelling-house is a house and the landlord owns the freehold, to acquire the freehold of the dwelling-house;

(b) if the landlord does not own the freehold or if the dwelling-house is a flat (whether or not the landlord owns the freehold), to be granted a lease of the dwelling-house.

(2) Where a secure tenancy is a joint tenancy then, whether or not each of the joint tenants occupies the dwelling-house as his only or principal home, the right to buy belongs jointly to all of them or to such one or more of them as may be agreed between them; but such an agreement is not valid unless the person or at least one of the persons to whom the right to buy is to belong occupies the dwelling-house as his only or principal home.

(3) For the purposes of this Part, a dwelling-house which is a commonhold unit (within the meaning of the Commonhold and Leasehold Reform Act 2002) shall be treated as a house and not as a flat.

119 Qualifying period for right to buy

(1) The right to buy does not arise unless the period which, in accordance with Schedule 4, is to be taken into account for the purposes of this section is at least five years.

(2) Where the secure tenancy is a joint tenancy the condition in subsection (1) need be satisfied with respect to one only of the joint tenants.

120 Exceptions to the right to buy

The right to buy does not arise in the cases specified in Schedule 5 (exceptions to the right to buy).

121 Circumstances in which the right to buy cannot be exercised

(1) The right to buy cannot be exercised if the tenant is obliged to give up possession of the dwelling-house in pursuance of an order of the court or will be so obliged at a date specified in the order.

(2) The right to buy cannot be exercised if the person, or one of the persons, to whom the right to buy belongs –

  (a) has a bankruptcy petition pending against him,

  (c) is an undischarged bankrupt, or

  (d) has made a composition or arrangement with his creditors the terms of which remain to be fulfilled.

(3) The right to buy cannot be exercised at any time during the suspension period under an order made under section 121A in respect of the secure tenancy.

121A Order suspending right to buy because of anti-social behaviour

(1) The court may, on the application of the landlord under a secure tenancy, make a suspension order in respect of the tenancy.

(2) A suspension order is an order providing that the right to buy may not be exercised in relation to the dwelling-house during such period as is specified in the order ('the suspension period').

(3) The court must not make a suspension order unless it is satisfied –

  (a) that the tenant, or a person residing in or visiting the dwelling-house, has engaged or threatened to engage in conduct to which section 153A or 153B of the Housing Act 1996 applies (anti-social behaviour or use of premises for unlawful purposes), and

  (b) that it is reasonable to make the order. ...

183 Meaning of 'house', 'flat' and 'dwelling-house'

(1) The following provisions apply to the interpretation of 'house', 'flat' and 'dwelling-house' when used in this Part.

(2) A dwelling-house is a house if, and only if, it (or so much of it as does not consist of land included by virtue of section 184) is a structure reasonably so called; so that –

(a) where a building is divided horizontally, the flats or other units into which it is divided are not houses;

(b) where a building is divided vertically, the units into which it is divided may be houses;

(c) where a building is not structurally detached, it is not a house if a material part of it lies above or below the remainder of the structure.

(3) A dwelling-house which is not a house is a flat.

PART XVIII

MISCELLANEOUS AND GENERAL PROVISIONS

610 Power of court to authorise conversion of premises into flats

(1) The local housing authority or a person interested in any premises may apply to the county court where –

(a) owing to changes in the character of the neighbourhood in which the premises are situated, they cannot readily be let as a single dwelling-house but could readily be let for occupation if converted into two or more dwelling-houses, or

(b) planning permission has been granted under Part III of the Town and Country Planning Act 1990 (general planning control) for the use of the premises as converted into two or more separate dwelling-houses instead of as a single dwelling-house,

and the conversion is prohibited or restricted by the provisions of the lease of the premises, or by a restrictive covenant affecting the premises, or otherwise.

(2) The court may, after giving any person interested an opportunity of being heard, vary the terms of the lease or other instrument imposing the prohibition or restriction, subject to such conditions and upon such terms as the court may think just.

SCHEDULE 5

EXCEPTIONS TO THE RIGHT TO BUY

1. The right to buy does not arise if the landlord is a housing trust or a housing association and is a charity.

2. The right to buy does not arise if the landlord is a co-operative housing association ...

10.–(1) The right to buy does not arise if the dwelling-house is one of a group of dwelling-houses –

(a) which are particularly suitable, having regard to their location, size, design, heating systems and other features, for occupation by elderly persons, and

(b) which it is the practice of the landlord to let for occupation by persons aged 60 or more, or for occupation by such persons and physically disabled persons,

and special facilities such as are mentioned in sub-paragraph (2) are provided wholly or mainly for the purposes of assisting those persons.

(2) The facilities referred to above are facilities which consist of or include –

(a) the services of a resident warden, or

(b) the services of a non-resident warden, a system for calling him and the use of a common room in close proximity to the group of dwelling-houses ...

NB On 1 May 2005 the amendments made by the Anti-social Behaviour Act 2003 (see below) were not in force in Wales. The insertion of sections 121(3) and 121A was not in force on 1 May 2005.

As amended by the Insolvency Act 1985, s235(3), Schedule 10, Pt III; Housing Act 1988, ss83(1), (2), 140(2), Schedule 18, para 4; Local Government and Housing Act 1989, s165(1), Schedule 9, Pt V, para 89; Planning (Consequential Provisions) Act 1990, s4, Schedule 2, para 71(5); Leasehold Reform, Housing and Urban Development Act 1993, s106(1); Housing Act 1996 (Consequential Provisions) Order 1996, art 5, Schedule 2, para 14(1), 8(a), (b); Government of Wales Act 1998, ss131, 152, Schedule 18, Pt IV; Commonhold and Leasehold Reform Act 2002, s68, Schedule 5, para 5; Anti-social Behaviour Act 2003, s14(1), (2); Housing Act 2004, ss180(1), 192(1), (2).

LANDLORD AND TENANT ACT 1985
(1985 c 70)

8   Implied terms as to fitness for human habitation

(1) In a contract to which this section applies for the letting of a house for human habitation there is implied, notwithstanding any stipulation to the contrary –

(a) a condition that the house is fit for human habitation at the commencement of the tenancy, and

(b) an undertaking that the house will be kept by the landlord fit for human habitation during the tenancy.

(2) The landlord, or a person authorised by him in writing, may at reasonable times of the day, on giving 24 hours' notice in writing to the tenant or occupier, enter premises to which this section applies for the purpose of viewing their state and condition.

(3) This section applies to a contract if –

(a) the rent does not exceed the figure applicable in accordance with subsection (4), and

(b) the letting is not on such terms as to the tenant's responsibility as are mentioned in subsection (5).

(4) The rent limit for the application of this section is shown by the following Table, by reference to the date of making of the contract and the situation of the premises:

TABLE

Date of making of contract	Rent limit
Before 31st July 1923.	In London: £40. Elsewhere: £26 or £16 …
On or after 31st July 1923 and before 6th July 1957.	In London: £40. Elsewhere: £26.
On or after 6th July 1957.	In London: £80. Elsewhere: £52 …

(5) This section does not apply where a house is let for a term of three years or more (the lease not being determinable at the option of either party before the expiration of three years) upon terms that the tenant puts the premises into a condition reasonably fit for human habitation.

(6) In this section 'house' includes –

(a) a part of a house, and

(b) any yard, garden, outhouses and appurtenances belonging to the house or usually enjoyed with it.

9 Application of s8 to certain houses occupied by agricultural workers

(1) Where under the contract of employment of a worker employed in agriculture the provision of a house for his occupation forms part of his remuneration and the provisions of section 8 (implied terms as to fitness for human habitation) are inapplicable by reason only of the house not being let to him –

(a) there are implied as part of the contract of employment, notwithstanding any stipulation to the contrary, the like condition and undertaking as would be implied under that section if the house were so let, and

(b) the provisions of that section apply accordingly, with the substitution of 'employer' for 'landlord' and such other modifications as may be necessary.

(2) This section does not affect any obligation of a person other than the employer to repair a house to which this section applies, or any remedy for enforcing such an obligation.

(3) In this section 'house' includes –

(a) a part of a house, and

(b) any yard, garden, outhouses and appurtenances belonging to the house or usually enjoyed with it.

10 Fitness for human habitation

In determining for the purposes of this Act whether a house is unfit for human habitation, regard shall be had to its condition in respect of the following matters –

repair,
stability,
freedom from damp,
internal arrangement,
natural lighting,
ventilation,
water supply,
drainage and sanitary conveniences,
facilities for preparation and cooking of food and for the disposal of waste water;

and the house shall be regarded as unfit for human habitation if, and only if, it is so far defective in one or more of those matters that it is not reasonably suitable for occupation in that condition.

11 Repairing obligations in short leases

(1) In a lease to which this section applies (as to which, see sections 13 and 14) there is implied a covenant by the lessor –

(a) to keep in repair the structure and exterior of the dwelling-house (including drains, gutters and external pipes),

(b) to keep in repair and proper working order the installations in the dwelling-house for the supply of water, gas and electricity and for sanitation (including basins, sinks, baths and sanitary conveniences, but not other fixtures, fittings and appliances for making use of the supply of water, gas or electricity), and

(c) to keep in repair and proper working order the installations in the dwelling-house for space heating and heating water.

(1A) If a lease to which this section applies is a lease of a dwelling-house which forms part only of a building, then, subject to subsection (1B), the covenant implied by subsection (1) shall have effect as if –

(a) the reference in paragraph (a) of that subsection to the dwelling-house included a reference to any part of the building in which the lessor has an estate or interest; and

(b) any reference in paragraphs (b) and (c) of that subsection to an installation in the dwelling-house included a reference to an installation which, directly or indirectly, serves the dwelling-house and which either –

(i) forms part of any part of a building in which the lessor has an estate or interest; or

(ii) is owned by the lessor or under his control.

(1B) Nothing in subsection (1A) shall be construed as requiring the lessor to carry out any works or repairs unless the disrepair (or failure to maintain in working order) is such as to affect the lessee's enjoyment of the dwelling-house or of any common parts, as defined in section 60(1) of the Landlord and Tenant Act 1987, which the lessee, as such, is entitled to use.

(2) The covenant implied by subsection (1) ('the lessor's repairing covenant') shall not be construed as requiring the lessor –

(a) to carry out works or repairs for which the lessee is liable by virtue of his duty to use the premises in a tenant-like manner, or would be so liable but for an express covenant on his part,

(b) to rebuild or reinstate the premises in the case of destruction or damage by fire, or by tempest, flood or other inevitable accident, or

(c) to keep in repair or maintain anything which the lessee is entitled to remove from the dwelling-house.

(3) In determining the standard of repair required by the lessor's repairing covenant, regard shall be had to the age, character and prospective life of the dwelling-house and the locality in which it is situated.

(3A) In any case where –

(a) the lessor's repairing covenant has effect as mentioned in subsection (1A), and

(b) in order to comply with the covenant the lessor needs to carry out works or repairs otherwise than in, or to an installation in, the dwelling-house, and

(c) the lessor does not have a sufficient right in the part of the building or the installation concerned to enable him to carry out the required works or repairs,

then, in any proceedings relating to a failure to comply with the lessor's repairing covenant, so far as it requires the lessor to carry out the works or repairs in question, it shall be a defence for the lessor to prove that he used all reasonable endeavours to obtain, but was unable to obtain, such rights as would be adequate to enable him to carry out the works or repairs.

(4) A covenant by the lessee for the repair of the premises is of no effect so far as it relates to the matters mentioned in subsection (1)(a) to (c), except so far as it imposes on the lessee any of the requirements mentioned in subsection (2)(a) or (c).

(5) The reference in subsection (4) to a covenant by the lessee for the repair of the premises includes a covenant –

(a) to put in repair or deliver up in repair,

(b) to paint, point or render,

(c) to pay money in lieu of repairs by the lessee, or

(d) to pay money on account of repairs by the lessor.

(6) In a lease in which the lessor's repairing covenant is implied there is also implied a covenant by the lessee that the lessor, or any person authorised by him in writing, may at reasonable times of the day and on giving 24 hours' notice in writing to the occupier, enter the premises comprised in the lease for the purpose of viewing their condition and state of repair.

12 Restriction on contracting out of s11

(1) A covenant or agreement, whether contained in a lease to which section 11 applies or in an agreement collateral to such a a lease, is void in so far as it purports –

(a) to exclude or limit the obligations of the lessor or the immunities of the lessee under that section, or

(b) to authorise any forfeiture or impose on the lessee any penalty, disability or obligation in the event of his enforcing or relying upon those obligations or immunities,

unless the inclusion of the provision was authorised by the county court.

(2) The county court may, by order made with the consent of the parties, authorise the inclusion in a lease, or in an agreement collateral to a lease, of provisions excluding or modifying in relation to the lease, the provisions of section 11 with respect to the repairing obligations of the parties if it appears to the court that it is reasonable to do so, having regard to all the circumstances of the case, including the other terms and conditions of the lease.

13 Leases to which s11 applies: general rule

(1) Section 11 (repairing obligations) applies to a lease of a dwelling-house granted on or after 24th October 1961 for a term of less than seven years.

(2) In determining whether a lease is one to which section 11 applies –

(a) any part of the term which falls before the grant shall be left out of account and the lease shall be treated as a lease for a term commencing with the grant,

(b) a lease which is determinable at the option of the lessor before the expiration of seven years from the commencement of the term shall be treated as a lease for a term of less than seven years, and

(c) a lease (other than a lease to which paragraph (b) applies) shall not be treated as a lease for a term of less than seven years if it confers on the lessee an option for renewal for a term which, together with the original term, amounts to seven years or more.

(3) This section has effect subject to –

section 14 (leases to which section 11 applies: exceptions), and

section 32(2) (provisions not applying to tenancies with Part II of the Landlord and Tenant Act 1954).

14 Leases to which s11 applies: exceptions

(1) Section 11 (repairing obligations) does not apply to a new lease granted to an existing tenant, or to a former tenant still in possession, if the previous lease was not a lease to which section 11 applied (and, in the case of a lease granted before 24th October 1961, would not have been if it had been granted on or after that date).

(2) In subsection (1) –

'existing tenant' means a person who is when, or immediately before, the new lease is granted, the lessee under another lease of the dwelling-house;
'former tenant still in possession' means a person who –

(a) was the lessee under another lease of the dwelling-house which terminated at some time before the new lease was granted, and

(b) between the termination of that other lease and the grant of the new lease was continuously in possession of the dwelling-house or of the rents and profits of the dwelling-house; and 'the previous lease' means the other lease referred to in the above definitions.

(3) Section 11 does not apply to a lease of a dwelling-house which is a tenancy of an agricultural holding within the meaning of the Agricultural Holdings Act 1986 and in relation to which that Act applies or to a farm business tenancy within the meaning of the Agricultural Tenancies Act 1995.

(4) Section 11 does not apply to a lease granted on or after 3rd October 1980 to –

a local authority,

a National Park authority,

a new town corporation,

an urban development corporation,

the Development Board for Rural Wales,

a registered social landlord,

a co-operative housing association,

an educational institution or other body specified, or of a class specified, by regulations under section 8 of the Rent Act 1977 or paragraph 8 of Schedule 1 to the Housing Act 1988 (bodies making student lettings), or

a housing action trust established under Part III of the Housing Act 1988.

(5) Section 11 does not apply to a lease granted on or after 3rd October 1980 to –

(a) Her Majesty in right of the Crown (unless the lease is under the management of the Crown Estate Commissioners), or

(b) a government department or a person holding in trust for Her Majesty for the purposes of a government department.

15   Jurisdiction of county court

The county court has jurisdiction to make a declaration that section 11 (repairing obligations) applies, or does not apply, to a lease –

(a) whatever the net annual value of the property in question, and

(b) notwithstanding that no other relief is sought than a declaration.

16   Meaning of 'lease' and related expressions

In sections 11 to 15 (repairing obligations in short leases) –

(a) 'lease' does not include a mortgage term;

(b) 'lease of a dwelling-house' means a lease by which a building or part of a building is let wholly or mainly as a private residence, and 'dwelling-house' means that building or part of a building;

(c) 'lessee' and 'lessor' mean, respectively, the person for the time being entitled to the term of a lease and to the reversion expectant on it.

17 Specific performance of landlord's repairing obligations

(1) In proceedings in which a tenant of a dwelling alleges a breach on the part of his landlord of a repairing covenant relating to any part of the premises in which the dwelling is comprised, the court may order specific performance of the covenant whether or not the breach relates to a part of the premises let to the tenant and notwithstanding any equitable rule restricting the scope of the remedy, whether on the basis of a lack of mutuality or otherwise.

(2) In this section –

(a) 'tenant' includes a statutory tenant,

(b) in relation to a statutory tenant the reference to the premises let to him is to the premises of which he is a statutory tenant,

(c) 'landlord', in relation to a tenant, includes any person against whom the tenant has a right to enforce a repairing covenant, and

(d) 'repairing covenant' means a covenant to repair, maintain, renew, construct or replace any property.

18 Meaning of 'service charge' and 'relevant costs'

(1) In the following provisions of this Act 'service charge' means an amount payable by a tenant of a dwelling as part of or in addition to the rent –

(a) which is payable, directly or indirectly, for services, repairs, maintenance, improvements or insurance or the landlord's costs of management, and

(b) the whole or part of which varies or may vary according to the relevant costs.

(2) The relevant costs are the costs or estimated costs incurred or to be incurred by or on behalf of the landlord, or a superior landlord, in connection with the matters for which the service charge is payable.

(3) For this purpose –

(a) 'costs' includes overheads, and

(b) costs are relevant costs in relation to a service charge whether they are incurred, or to be incurred, in the period for which the service charge is payable or in an earlier or later period.

19 Limitation of service charges: reasonableness

(1) Relevant costs shall be taken into account in determining the amount of a service charge payable for a period –

(a) only to the extent that they are reasonably incurred, and

(b) where they are incurred on the provision of services or the carrying out of works, only if the services or works are of a reasonable standard;

and the amount payable shall be limited accordingly.

(2) Where a service charge is payable before the relevant costs are incurred, no greater amount than is reasonable is so payable, and after the relevant costs have been incurred any necessary adjustment shall be made by repayment, reduction or subsequent charges or otherwise.

(5) If a person takes any proceedings in the High Court in pursuance of any of the provisions of this Act relating to service charges and he could have taken those proceedings in the county court, he shall not be entitled to recover any costs.

32 Provisions not applying to tenancies within Part II of the Landlord and Tenant Act 1954

(1) The following provisions do not apply to a tenancy to which Part II of the Landlord and Tenant Act 1954 (business tenancies) applies –

sections 1 to 3A (information to be given to tenant),
section 17 (specific performance of landlord's repairing obligations).

(2) Section 11 (repairing obligations) does not apply to a new lease granted to an existing tenant, or to a former tenant still in possession, if the new lease is a tenancy to which Part II of the Landlord and Tenant Act 1954 applies and the previous lease either is such a tenancy or would be but for section 28 of that Act (tenancy not within Part II if renewal agreed between the parties).

In this subsection 'existing tenant', 'former tenant still in possession' and 'previous lease' have the same meaning as in section 14(2).

(3) Section 31 (reserve power to limit rents) does not apply to a dwelling forming part of a property subject to a tenancy to which Part II of the Landlord and Tenant Act 1954 applies; but without prejudice to the application of that section in relation to a sub-tenancy of a part of the premises comprised in such a tenancy.

36 Meaning of 'lease' and 'tenancy' and related expressions

(1) In this Act 'lease' and 'tenancy' have the same meaning.

(2) Both expressions include –

(a) a sub-lease or sub-tenancy, and
(b) an agreement for a lease or tenancy (or sub-lease or sub-tenancy).

(3) The expressions 'lessor' and 'lessee' and 'landlord' and 'tenant', and references to letting, to the grant of a lease or to covenants or terms, shall be construed accordingly.

37 Meaning of 'statutory tenant' and related expressions

In this Act –

(a) 'statutory tenancy' and 'statutory tenant' mean a statutory tenancy or statutory tenant within the meaning of the Rent Act 1977 or the Rent (Agriculture) Act 1976; and

(b) 'landlord', in relation to a statutory tenant, means the person who, apart from the statutory tenancy, would be entitled to possession of the premises.

38   Minor definitions

In this Act –

...

'co-operative housing association' has the same meaning as in the Housing Associations Act 1985;

'dwelling' means a building or part of a building occupied or intended to be occupied as a separate dwelling, together with any yard, garden, outhouses and appurtenances belonging to it or usually enjoyed with it;

'housing association' has the same meaning as in the Housing Associations Act 1985;

'local authority' means a district, county, county borough or London borough council, the Common Council of the City of London or the Council of the Isles of Scilly and in sections 14(4), 26(1) and 28(6) includes the Broads Authority, a police authority established under section 3 of the Police Act 1996, the Metropolitan Police Authority, a joint authority established by Part IV of the Local Government Act 1985 and the London Fire and Emergency Planning Authority; ...

'new town corporation' means –

(a) a development corporation established by an order made, or treated as made, under the New Towns Act 1981, or

(b) the Commission for the New Towns; ...

'registered social landlord' has the same meaning as in the Housing Act 1985 (see section 5(4) and (5) of that Act); ...

'urban development corporation' has the same meaning as in Part XVI of the Local Government, Planning and Land Act 1980.

NB Section 11(1A), (1B) and (3A) above do not apply to leases (or contracts for leases) made before 15 January 1989.

As amended by the Agricultural Holdings Act 1986, s100, Schedule 14, para 64; Landlord and Tenant Act 1987, s41(1), Schedule 2, paras 1, 2; Housing Act 1988, s116(1)–(3), (4); Norfolk and Suffolk Broads Act 1988, s21, Schedule 6, para 26; Education Reform Act 1988, s237(2), Schedule 13, Pt I; Local Government and Housing Act 1989, s194(1), Schedule 11, para 89; Local Government (Wales) Act 1994, s22(2), Schedule 8, para 7; Police and Magistrates' Courts Act 1994, s43, Schedule 4, Pt II, para 60; Agricultural Tenancies Act 1995, s40, Schedule, para 31; Environment Act 1995, s78, Schedule 10, para 25(1); Housing Act 1996, ss 83(1), 93(2), 227, Schedule 19, Pt III; Police Act 1996, s103(1), Schedule 7, Pt I, para 1(1), (2)(X); Housing Act 1996 (Consequential Provisions) Order 1996, art 5, Schedule 2, para 16(1), (2), (4); Greater London Authority Act 1999, ss325, 328(8), 423, Schedule 27, para 53, Schedule 29, Pt I, para 44, Schedule 34, Pt VIII; Commonhold and Leasehold Reform Act 2002, ss150, 180, Schedule 9, para 7, Schedule 14.

AGRICULTURAL HOLDINGS ACT 1986
(1986 c 5)

1 Principal definitions

(1) In this Act 'agricultural holding' means the aggregate of the land (whether agricultural land or not) comprised in a contract of tenancy which is a contract for an agricultural tenancy, not being a contract under which the land is let to the tenant during his continuance in any office, appointment or employment held under the landlord.

(2) For the purposes of this section, a contract of tenancy relating to any land is a contract for an agricultural tenancy if, having regard to –

(a) the terms of the tenancy,

(b) the actual or contemplated use of the land at the time for the conclusion of the contract and subsequently, and

(c) any other relevant circumstances,

the whole of the land comprised in the contract, subject to such exceptions only as do not substantially affect the character of the tenancy, is let for use as agricultural land.

(3) A change in user of the land concerned subsequent to the conclusion of a contract of tenancy which involves any breach of the terms of the tenancy shall be disregarded for the purpose of determining whether a contract which was not originally a contract for an agricultural tenancy has subsequently become one unless it is effected with the landlord's permission, consent or acquiescence.

(4) In this Act 'agricultural land' means –

(a) land used for agriculture which is so used for the purposes of a trade or business, and

(b) any other land which, by virtue of a designation under section 109(1) of the Agriculture Act 1947, is agricultural land within the meaning of that Act.

(5) In this Act 'contract of tenancy' means a letting of land, or agreement for letting land, for a term of years or from year to year; and for the purposes of this definition a letting of land, or an agreement for letting land, which, by virtue of subsection (6) of section 149 of the Law of Property Act 1925, takes effect as such a letting of land or agreement for letting land as is mentioned in that subsection shall be deemed to be a letting of land or, as the case may be, an agreement for letting land, for a term of years.

2 Restriction on letting agricultural land for less than from year to year

(1) An agreement to which this section applies shall take effect, with the necessary modifications, as if it were an agreement for the letting of land for a tenancy from year to year unless the agreement was approved by the Minister before it was entered into.

(2) Subject to subsection (3) below, this section applies to an agreement under which –

(a) any land is let to a person for use as agricultural land for an interest less than a tenancy from year to year, or

(b) a person is granted a licence to occupy land for use as agricultural land,

if the circumstances are such that if his interest were a tenancy from year to year he would in respect of that land be the tenant of an agricultural holding.

(3) This section does not apply to an agreement for the letting of land, or the granting of a licence to occupy land –

(a) made (whether or not it expressly so provides) in contemplation of the use of the land only for grazing or mowing (or both) during some specified period of the year, or

(b) by a person whose interest in the land is less than a tenancy from year to year and has not taken effect as such a tenancy by virtue of this section.

(4) Any dispute arising as to the operation of this section in relation to any agreement shall be determined by arbitration under this Act.

3 Tenancies for two years or more to continue from year to year unless terminated by notice

(1) Subject to section 5 below, a tenancy of an agricultural holding for a term of two years or more shall, instead of terminating on the term date, continue (as from that date) as a tenancy from year to year, but otherwise on the terms of the original tenancy so far as applicable, unless –

(a) not less than one year nor more than two years before the term date a written notice has been given by either party to the other of his intention to terminate the tenancy, or

(b) section 4 below applies.

(2) A notice given under subsection (1) above shall be deemed, for the purposes of this Act, to be a notice to quit.

(3) This section does not apply to a tenancy which, by virtue of subsection (6) of section 149 of the Law of Property Act 1925, takes effect as such a term of years as is mentioned in that subsection.

(4) In this section 'term date', in relation to a tenancy granted for a term of years, means the date fixed for the expiry of that term.

4 Death of tenant before term date

(1) This section applies where –

(a) a tenancy such as is mentioned in subsection (1) of section 3 above is granted on or after 12th September 1984 to any person or persons,

(b) the person, or the survivor of the persons, dies before the term date, and

(c) no notice effective to terminate the tenancy on the term date has been given under that subsection.

(2) Where this section applies, the tenancy, instead of continuing as mentioned in section 3(1) above –

(a) shall, if the death is one year or more before the term date, terminate on that date, or

(b) shall, if the death is at any other time, continue (as from the term date) for a further period of twelve months, but otherwise on the terms of the tenancy so far as applicable, and shall accordingly terminate on the first anniversary of the term date.

(3) For the purposes of the provisions of this Act with respect to compensation any tenancy terminating in accordance with this section shall be deemed to terminate by reason of a notice to quit given by the landlord of the holding.

(4) In this section 'term date' has the same meaning as in section 3 above.

5 Restriction on agreements excluding effect of section 3

(1) Except as provided in this section, section 3 above shall have effect notwithstanding any agreement to the contrary.

(2) Where before the grant of a tenancy of an agricultural holding for a term of not less than two, and not more than five, years –

(a) the persons who will be the landlord and the tenant in relation to the tenancy agree that section 3 above shall not apply to the tenancy, and

(b) those persons make a joint application in writing to the Minister for his approval of that agreement, and

(c) the Minister notifies them of his approval,

section 3 shall not apply to the tenancy if it satisfies the requirements of subsection (3) below.

(3) A tenancy satisfies the requirements of this subsection if the contract of tenancy is in writing and it, or a statement endorsed upon it, indicates (in whatever terms) that section 3 does not apply to the tenancy.

10 Tenant's right to remove fixtures and buildings

(1) Subject to the provisions of this section –

(a) any engine, machinery, fencing or other fixture (of whatever description) affixed, whether for the purposes of agriculture or not, to an agricultural holding by the tenant, and

(b) any building erected by him on holding,

shall be removable by the tenant at any time during the continuance of the tenancy or before the expiry of two months from its termination, and shall remain his property so long as he may remove it by virtue of this subsection.

(2) Subsection (1) above shall not apply –

(a) to a fixture affixed or a building erected in pursuance of some obligation,

(b) to a fixture affixed or a building erected instead of some fixture or building belonging to the landlord,

(c) to a building in respect of which the tenant is entitled to compensation under this Act or otherwise, or

(d) to a fixture affixed or a building erected before 1st January 1884.

(3) The right conferred by subsection (1) above shall not be exercisable in relation to a fixture or building unless the tenant –

(a) has paid all rent owing by him and has performed or satisfied all his other obligations to the landlord in respect of the holding, and

(b) has, at least one month before both the exercise of the right and the termination of the tenancy, given to the landlord notice in writing of his intention to remove the fixture or building.

(4) If, before the expiry of the notice mentioned in subsection (3) above, the landlord gives to the tenant a counter-notice in writing electing to purchase a fixture or building comprised in the notice, subsection (1) above shall cease to apply to that fixture or building, but the landlord shall be liable to pay to the tenant the fair value of the fixture or building to an incoming tenant of the holding.

(5) In the removal of a fixture or building by virtue of subsection (1) above, the tenant shall not do any avoidable damage to any other building or other part of the holding, and immediately after the removal shall make good all damage so done that is occasioned by the removal.

(6) Any dispute between the landlord and the tenant with respect to the amount payable by the landlord under subsection (4) above in respect of any fixture or building shall be determined by arbitration under this Act.

(7) This section shall apply to a fixture or building acquired by a tenant as it applies to a fixture or building affixed or erected by him.

(8) This section shall not be taken as prejudicing any right to remove a fixture that subsists otherwise than by virtue of this section.

16 No distress for rent due more than a year previously

(1) Subject to subsection (2) below, the landlord of an agricultural holding shall not be entitled to distrain for rent which became due in respect of that holding more than one year before the making of the distress.

(2) Where it appears that, according to the ordinary course of dealing between the landlord and the tenant of the holding, the payment of rent has been deferred until the expiry of a quarter or half-year after the date at which the rent legally became due, the rent shall, for the purposes of subsection (1) above, be deemed to have become due at the expiry of that quarter or half-year and not at the date at which it became legally due.

17 Compensation to be set off against rent for purposes of distress

Where the amount of any compensation due to the tenant of an agricultural holding, whether under this Act or under custom or agreement, has been ascertained before the landlord distrains for rent, that amount may be set off against the rent and the landlord shall not be entitled to distrain for more than the balance.

18 Restrictions on distraining on property of third party

(1) Property belonging to a person other than the tenant of an agricultural holding shall not be distrained for rent if –

   (a) the property is agricultural or other machinery and is on the holding under an agreement with the tenant for its hire or use in the conduct of his business, or

   (b) the property is livestock and is on the holding solely for breeding purposes.

(2) Agisted livestock shall not be distrained by the landlord of an agricultural holding for rent where there is other sufficient distress to be found; and if such livestock is distrained by him by reason of other sufficient distress not being found, there shall not be recovered by that distress a sum exceeding the amount of the price agreed to be paid for the feeding, or any part of the price which remains unpaid.

(3) The owner of the agisted livestock may, at any time before it is sold, redeem it by paying to the distrainer a sum equal to the amount mentioned in subsection (2) above, and payment of that sum to the distrainer shall be in full discharge as against the tenant of any sum of that amount which would otherwise be due from the owner of the livestock to the tenant in respect of the price of feeding.

(4) Any portion of the agisted livestock shall, so long as it remains on the holding, continue liable to be distrained for the amount for which the whole of the livestock is distrainable.

(5) In this section 'livestock' includes any animal capable of being distrained; and 'agisted livestock' means livestock belonging to another person which has been taken by the tenant of an agricultural holding to be fed at a fair price.

23 Landlord's power of entry

The landlord of an agricultural holding or any person authorised by him may at all reasonable times enter on the holding for any of the following purposes, namely –

(a) viewing the state of the holding,

(b) fulfilling the landlord's responsibilities to manage the holding in accordance with the rules of good estate management,

(c) providing or improving fixed equipment on the holding otherwise than in fulfilment of those responsibilities.

24   Restriction of landlord's remedies for breach of contract of tenancy

Notwithstanding any provision in a contract of tenancy of an agricultural holding making the tenant liable to pay a higher rent or other liquidated damages in the event of a breach or non-fulfilment of a term or condition of the contract, the landlord shall not be entitled to recover in consequence of any such breach or non-fulfilment, by distress or otherwise, any sum in excess of the damage actually suffered by him in consequence of the breach or non-fulfilment.

96   Interpretation

(1) In this Act, unless the context otherwise requires –

'agreement' includes an agreement arrived at by means of valuation or otherwise, and 'agreed' has a corresponding meaning;

'agricultural holding' has the meaning given by section 1 above;

'agricultural land' has the meaning given by section 1 above; ...

'agriculture' includes horticulture, fruit growing, seed growing, dairy farming and livestock breeding and keeping, the use of land as grazing land, meadow land, osier land, market gardens and nursery grounds, and the use of land for woodlands where that use is ancillary to the farming of land for other agricultural purposes and 'agricultural' shall be construed accordingly;

'building' includes any part of a building; ...

'contract of tenancy' has the meaning given by section 1 above; ...

'landlord' means any person for the time being entitled to receive the rents and profits of any land;

'livestock' includes any creature kept for the production of food, wool, skins, or fur or for the purpose of its use in the farming of land or the carrying on in relation to land of any agricultural activity; ...

'the Minister' means –

(a) in relation to England, the Secretary of State, and

(b) in relation to Wales, the Secretary of State, ...

'tenant' means the holder of land under a contract of tenancy, and includes the executors, administrators, assigns, or trustee in bankruptcy of a tenant, or other person deriving title from a tenant;

'termination', in relation to a tenancy, means the cesser of the contract of tenancy by reason of effluxion of time or from any other cause; ...

(3) Sections 10 and 11 of the Agriculture Act 1947 (which specify the circumstances

in which an owner of agricultural land is deemed for the purposes of that Act to fulfil his responsibilities to manage the land in accordance with the rules of good estate management and an occupier of such land is deemed for those purposes to fulfil his responsibilities to farm it in accordance with the rules of good husbandry) shall apply for the purposes of this Act.

(4) References in this Act to the farming of land include references to the carrying on in relation to the land of any agricultural activity.

(5) References in this Act to the use of land for agriculture include, in relation to land forming part of an agricultural unit, references to any use of the land in connection with the farming of the unit.

(6) The designations of landlord and tenant shall continue to apply to the parties until the conclusion of any proceedings taken under or in pursuance of this Act in respect of compensation.

As amended by the Ministry of Agriculture, Fisheries and Food (Dissolution) Order 2002, art 5(1), Schedule 1, para 27.

REVERTER OF SITES ACT 1987
(1987 c 15)

1 Right of reverter replaced by trust

(1) Where any relevant enactment provides for land to revert to the ownership of any person at any time, being a time when the land ceases, or has ceased for a specified period, to be used for particular purposes, that enactment shall have effect, and (subject to subsection (4) below) shall be deemed always to have had effect, as if it provided (instead of for the reverter) for the land to be vested after that time, on the trust arising under this section, in the persons in whom it was vested immediately before that time.

(2) Subject to the following provisions of this Act, the trust arising under this section in relation to any land is a trust for the persons who (but for this Act) would from time to time be entitled to the ownership of the land by virtue of its reverter with a power, without consulting them, to sell the land and to stand possessed of the net proceeds of sale (after payment of costs and expenses) and of the net rents and profits until sale (after payment of rates, taxes, costs of insurance, repairs and other outgoings) in trust for those persons; but they shall not be entitled by reason of their interest to occupy the land.

(3) Where –

(a) a trust in relation to any land has arisen or is treated as having arisen under this section at such a time as is mentioned in subsection (1) above; and

(b) immediately before that time the land was vested in any persons in their capacity as the minister and churchwardens of any parish,

those persons shall be treated as having become trustees under this section in that capacity and, accordingly, their interest in the land shall pass and, if the case so requires, be treated as having passed to their successors from time to time.

(4) This section shall not confer any right on any person as a beneficiary –

(a) in relation to any property in respect of which that person's claim was statute-barred before the commencement of this Act, or in relation to any property derived from any such property; or

(b) in relation to any rents or profits received, or breach of trust committed, before the commencement of this Act;

and anything validly done before the commencement of this Act in relation to any land which by virtue of this section is deemed to have been held at the time in trust shall, if done by the beneficiaries, be deemed, so far as necessary for preserving its validity, to have been done by the trustees.

(5) Where any property is held by any persons as trustees of a trust which has arisen under this section and, in consequence of subsection (4) above, there are no beneficiaries of that trust, the trustees shall have no power to act in relation to that property except –

(a) for the purpose for which they could have acted in relation to that property if this Act had not been passed; or

(b) for the purpose of securing the establishment of a scheme under section 2 below or the making of an order under section 554 of the Education Act 1996 (special powers as to trusts for religious education).

(6) In this section –

'churchwardens' includes chapel wardens;

'minister' includes a rector, vicar or perpetual curate; and

'parish' includes a parish of the Church in Wales;

and the reference to a person's claim being statute-barred is a reference to the Limitation Act 1980 providing that no proceedings shall be brought by that person to recover the property in respect of which the claim subsists.

2   Charity Commissioners' schemes

(1) Subject to the following provisions of this section and to sections 3 and 4 [provisions supplemental to sections 2 and 3] below, where any persons hold any property as trustees of a trust which has arisen under section 1 above, the Charity Commissioners may, on the application of the trustees, by order establish a scheme which –

(a) extinguishes the rights of beneficiaries under the trust; and

(b) requires the trustees to hold the property on trust for such charitable purposes as may be specified in the order.

(2) Subject to subsections (3) and (4) below, an order made under this section –

(a) may contain any such provision as may be contained in an order made by the High Court for establishing a scheme for the administration of a charity; and

(b) shall have the same effect as an order so made.

(3) The charitable purposes specified in an order made under this section on an application with respect to any trust shall be as similar in character as the Charity Commissioners think is practicable in all the circumstances to the purposes (whether charitable or not) for which the trustees held the relevant land before the cesser of use in consequence of which the trust arose; but in determining the character of the last-mentioned purposes the Commissioners, if they think it appropriate to do so, may give greater weight to the persons or locality benefited by the purposes than to the nature of the benefit.

(4) An order made under this section on an application with respect to any trust shall be so framed as to secure that if a person who –

(a) but for the making of the order would have been a beneficiary under the trust; and

(b) has not consented to the establishment of a scheme under this section,

notifies a claim to the trustees within the period of five years after the date of the making of the order, that person shall be paid an amount equal to the value of his rights at the time of their extinguishment.

(5) The Charity Commissioners shall not make any order under this section establishing a scheme unless –

(a) the requirements of section 3 below with respect to the making of the application for the order are satisfied or, by virtue of subsection (4) of that section, do not apply;

(b) one of the conditions specified in subsection (6) below is fulfilled;

(c) public notice of the Commissioners' proposals has been given inviting representations to be made to them within a period specified in the notice, being a period ending not less than one month after the date of the giving of the notice; and

(d) that period has ended and the Commissioners have taken into consideration any representations which have been made within that period and not withdrawn.

(6) The conditions mentioned in subsection (5)(b) above are –

(a) that there is no claim by any person to be a beneficiary in respect of rights proposed to be extinguished –

(i) which is outstanding; or

(ii) which has at any time been accepted as valid by the trustees or by persons whose acceptance binds the trustees; or

(iii) which has been upheld in proceedings that have been concluded;

(b) that consent to the establishment of a scheme under this section has been given by every person whose claim to be a beneficiary in respect of those rights is outstanding or has been so accepted or upheld.

(7) The Charity Commissioners shall refuse to consider an application under this section unless it is accompanied by a statutory declaration by the applicants –

(a) that the requirements of section 3 below are satisfied with respect to the making of the application or, if the declaration so declares, do not apply; and

(b) that a condition specified in subsection (6) above and identified in the declaration is fulfilled;

and the declaration shall be conclusive for the purposes of this section of the matters declared therein.

(8) A notice given for the purposes of subsection (5)(c) above shall contain such

particulars of the Commissioners' proposals, or such directions for obtaining information about them, and shall be given in such manner, as they think sufficient and appropriate; and a further such notice shall not be required where the Commissioners decide, before proceeding with any proposals of which notice has been given, to modify them.

3   Applications for schemes

(1) Where an application is made under section 2 above by the trustees of any trust that has arisen under section 1 above, the requirements of this section are satisfied with respect to the making of that application if, before the application is made –

(a) notices under subsection (2) below have been published in two national newspapers and in a local newspaper circulating in the locality where the relevant land is situated;

(b) each of those notices specified a period for the notification to the trustees of claims by beneficiaries, being a period ending not less than three months after the date of publication of the last of those notices to be published;

(c) that period has ended;

(d) for a period of not less than twenty-one days during the first month of that period, a copy of one of those notices was affixed to some object on the relevant land in such a position and manner as, so far as practicable, to make the notice easy for members of the public to see and read without going to the land; and

(e) the trustees have considered what other steps could be taken to trace the persons who are or may be beneficiaries and to inform those persons of the application to be made under section 2 above and have taken such of the steps considered by them as it was reasonably practicable for them to take.

(2) A notice under this subsection shall –

(a) set out the circumstances that have resulted in a trust having arisen under section 1 above;

(b) state that an application is to be made for the establishment of a scheme with respect to the property subject to the trust; and

(c) contain a warning to every beneficiary that, if he wishes to oppose the extinguishment of his rights, he should notify his claim to the trustees in the manner, and within the period, specified in the notice.

(3) Where at the time when the trustees publish a notice for the purposes of subsection (2) above –

(a) the relevant land is not under their control; and

(b) it is not reasonably practicable for them to arrange for a copy of the notice to be affixed as required by paragraph (d) of subsection (1) above to some object on the land,

that paragraph shall be disregarded for the purposes of this section.

(4) The requirements of this section shall not apply in the case of an application made in respect of any trust if –

(a) the time when that trust is treated as having arisen was before the commencement of this Act; and

(b) more than twelve years have elapsed since that time.

6   Clarification of status, etc of land before reverter

(1) Nothing in this Act shall require any land which is or has been the subject of any grant, conveyance or other assurance under any relevant enactment to be treated as or as having been settled land.

(2) It is hereby declared –

(a) that the power conferred by section 14 of the School Sites Act 1841 (power of sale etc) is exercisable at any time in relation to land in relation to which (but for the exercise of the power) a trust might subsequently arise under section 1 above; and

(b) that the exercise of that power in respect of any land prevents any trust from arising under section 1 above in relation to that land or any land representing the proceeds of sale of that land.

7   Construction

(1) In this Act –

'relevant enactment' means any enactment contained in –

(a) the School Sites Acts;

(b) the Literary and Scientific Institutions Act 1854; or

(c) the Places of Worship Sites Act 1873;

'relevant land', in relation to a trust which has arisen under section 1 above, means the land which but for this Act would have reverted to the persons who are the first beneficiaries under the trust.

(2) In this Act references to land include references to –

(a) any part of any land which has been the subject of a grant, conveyance or other assurance under any relevant enactment;

(b) any land an interest in which (including any future or contingent interest arising under any such enactment) belongs to the Crown, the Duchy of Lancaster or the Duchy of Cornwall.

(3) For the purposes of this Act a claim by any person to be a beneficiary under trust is outstanding if –

(a) it has been notified to the trustees;

(b) it has not been withdrawn; and

(c) proceedings for determining whether it should be upheld have not been commenced or (if commenced) have not been concluded.

(4) For the purposes of this Act proceedings shall not, in relation to any person's

claim, be treated as concluded where the time for appealing is unexpired or an appeal is pending unless that person has indicated his intention not to appeal or, as the case may be, not to continue with the appeal.

As amended by the Trusts of Land and Appointment of Trustees Act 1996, s5, Schedule 2, para 6; Edication Act 1996, s582(1), Schedule 37, Pt I, para 67.

LANDLORD AND TENANT ACT 1988
(1988 c 26)

1   Qualified duty to consent to assigning, underletting, etc of premises

(1) This section applies in any case where –

(a) a tenancy includes a covenant on the part of the tenant not to enter into one or more of the following transactions, that is –

(i) assigning,

(ii) underletting,

(iii) charging, or

(iv) parting with the possession of,

the premises comprised in the tenancy or any part of the premises without the consent of the landlord or some other person, but

(b) the covenant is subject to the qualification that the consent is not to be unreasonably withheld (whether or not it is also subject to any other qualification).

(2) In this section and section 2 [duty to pass on applications] of this Act –

(a) references to a proposed transaction are to any assignment, underletting, charging or parting with possession to which the covenant relates, and

(b) references to the person who may consent to such a transaction are to the person who under the covenant may consent to the tenant entering into the proposed transaction.

(3) Where there is served on the person who may consent to a proposed transaction a written application by the tenant for consent to the transaction, he owes a duty to the tenant within a reasonable time –

(a) to give consent, except in a case where it is reasonable not to give consent,

(b) to serve on the tenant written notice of his decision whether or not to give consent specifying in addition –

(i) if the consent is given subject to conditions, the conditions,

(ii) if the consent is withheld, the reasons for withholding it.

(4) Giving consent subject to any condition that is not a reasonable condition does not satisfy the duty under subsection (3)(a) above.

(5) For the purposes of this Act it is reasonable for a person not to give consent to a

proposed transaction only in a case where, if he withheld consent and the tenant completed the transaction, the tenant would be in breach of a covenant.

(6) It is for the person who owed any duty under subsection (3) above –

(a) if he gave consent and the question arises whether he gave it within a reasonable time, to show that he did,

(b) if he gave consent subject to any condition and the question arises whether the condition was a reasonable condition, to show that it was,

(c) if he did not give consent and the question arises whether it was reasonable for him not to do so, to show that it was reasonable,

and, if the question arises whether he served notice under that subsection within a reasonable time, to show that he did.

3   Qualified duty to approve consent by another

(1) This section applies in any case where –

(a) a tenancy includes a covenant on the part of the tenant not without the approval of the landlord to consent to the sub-tenant –

(i) assigning,

(ii) underletting,

(iii) charging, or

(iv) parting with the possession of,

the premises comprised in the sub-tenancy or any part of the premises, but

(b) the covenant is subject to the qualification that the approval is not to be unreasonably withheld (whether or not it is also subject to any other qualification).

(2) Where there is served on the landlord a written application by the tenant for approval or a copy of a written application to the tenant by the sub-tenant for consent to a transaction to which the covenant relates the landlord owes a duty to the sub-tenant within a reasonable time –

(a) to give approval, except in a case where it is reasonable not to give approval,

(b) to serve on the tenant and the sub-tenant written notice of his decision whether or not to give approval specifying in addition –

(i) if approval is given subject to conditions, the conditions,

(ii) if approval is withheld, the reasons for withholding.

(3) Giving approval subject to any condition that is not a reasonable condition does not satisfy the duty under subsection (2)(a) above.

(4) For the purposes of this section it is reasonable for the landlord not to give approval only in a case where, if he withheld approval and the tenant gave his consent, the tenant would be in breach of covenant.

(5) It is for a landlord who owed any duty under subsection (2) above –

(a) if he gave approval and the question arises whether he gave it within a reasonable time, to show that he did,

(b) if he gave approval subject to any condition and the question arises whether the condition was a reasonable condition, to show that it was,

(c) if he did not give approval and the question arises whether it was reasonable for him not to do so, to show that it was reasonable,

and, if the question arises whether he served notice under that subsection within a reasonable time, to show that he did.

4   Breach of duty

A claim that a person has broken any duty under this Act may be made the subject of civil proceedings in like manner as any other claim in tort for breach of statutory duty.

5   Interpretation

(1) In this Act –

'covenant' includes condition and agreement,

'consent' includes licence,

'landlord' includes any superior landlord from whom the tenant's immediate landlord directly or indirectly holds,

'tenancy', subject to subsection (3) below, means any lease or other tenancy (whether made before or after the coming into force of this Act) and includes –

(a) a sub-tenancy, and

(b) an agreement for a tenancy

and references in this Act to the landlord and to the tenant are to be interpreted accordingly, and

'tenant', where the tenancy is affected by a mortgage (within the meaning of the Law of Property Act 1925) and the mortgagee proposes to exercise his statutory or express power of sale, includes the mortgagee.

(2) An application or notice is to be treated as served for the purposes of this Act if –

(a) served in any manner provided in the tenancy, and

(b) in respect of any matter for which the tenancy makes no provision, served in any manner provided by section 23 of the Landlord and Tenant Act 1927.

(3) This Act does not apply to a secure tenancy (defined in section 79 of the Housing Act 1985) or to an introductory tenancy (within the meaning of Chapter I of Part V of the Housing Act 1996). ...

As amended by the Housing Act 1996 (Consequential Amendments) Order 1997, art 2, Schedule, para 5.

HOUSING ACT 1988
(1988 c 50)

PART I

RENTED ACCOMMODATION

CHAPTER I

ASSURED TENANCIES

1   Assured tenancies

(1) A tenancy under which a dwelling-house is let as a separate dwelling is for the purposes of this Act an assured tenancy if and so long as –

(a) the tenant or, as the case may be, each of the joint tenants is an individual; and

(b) the tenant or, as the case may be, at least one of the joint tenants occupies the dwelling-house as his only or principal home; and

(c) the tenancy is not one which, by virtue of subsection (2) or subsection (6) below, cannot be an assured tenancy.

(2) Subject to subsection (3) below, if and so long as a tenancy falls within any paragraph in Part I of Schedule 1 to this Act, it cannot be an assured tenancy; and in that Schedule –

(a) 'tenancy' means a tenancy under which a dwelling-house is let as a separate dwelling;

(b) Part II has effect for determining the rateable value of a dwelling-house for the purposes of Part I; and

(c) Part III has effect for supplementing paragraph 10 in Part I.

(2A) The Secretary of State may by order replace any amount referred to in paragraphs 2 and 3A of Schedule 1 to this Act by such amount as is specified in the order ...

(3) Except as provided in Chapter V below, at the commencement of this Act, a tenancy –

(a) under which a dwelling-house was then let as a separate dwelling, and

(b) which immediately before that commencement was an assured tenancy for the purposes of sections 56 to 58 of the Housing Act 1980 (tenancies granted by approved bodies),

shall become an assured tenancy for the purposes of this Act.

(4) In relation to an assured tenancy falling within subsection (3) above –

(a) Part I of Schedule 1 to this Act shall have effect, subject to subsection (5) below, as if it consisted only of paragraphs 11 and 12; and

(b) sections 56 to 58 of the Housing Act 1980 (and Schedule 5 to that Act) shall not apply after the commencement of this Act.

(5) In any case where –

(a) immediately before the commencement of this Act the landlord under a tenancy is a fully mutual housing association, and

(b) at the commencement of this Act the tenancy becomes an assured tenancy by virtue of subsection (3) above,

then, so long as that association remains the landlord under that tenancy (and under any statutory periodic tenancy which arises on the coming to an end of that tenancy), paragraph 12 of Schedule 1 to this Act shall have effect in relation to that tenancy with the omission of sub-paragraph (1)(h).

2   Letting of a dwelling-house together with other land

(1) If, under a tenancy, a dwelling-house is let together with other land, then, for the purpose of this Part of this Act, –

(a) if and so long as the main purpose of the letting is the provision of a home for the tenant or, where there are joint tenants, at least one of them, the other land shall be treated as part of the dwelling-house; and

(b) if and so long as the main purpose of the letting is not as mentioned in paragraph (a) above, the tenancy shall be treated as not being one under which a dwelling-house is let as a separate dwelling.

(2) Nothing in subsection (1) above affects any question whether a tenancy is precluded from being an assured tenancy by virtue of any provision of Schedule 1 to this Act.

3   Tenant sharing accommodation with persons other than landlord

(1) Where a tenant has the exclusive occupation of any accommodation (in this section referred to as 'the separate accommodation') and –

(a) the terms as between the tenant and his landlord on which he holds the separate accommodation include the use of other accommodation (in this section referred to as 'the shared accommodation') in common with another person or other persons, not being or including the landlord, and

(b) by reason only of the circumstances mentioned in paragraph (a) above, the separate accommodation would not, apart form this section, be a dwelling house let on an assured tenancy, the separate accommodation shall be deemed to be a dwelling-house let on an assured tenancy and the following provisions of this section shall have effect.

(2) For the avoidance of doubt it is hereby declared that where, for the purpose of determining the rateable value of the separate accommodation, it is necessary to make an apportionment under Part II of Schedule 1 to this Act, regard is to be had to the circumstances mentioned in subsection (1)(a) above.

(3) While the tenant is in possession of the separate accommodation, any term of the tenancy terminating or modifying, or providing for the termination or modification of, his right to the use of any of the shared accommodation which is living accommodation shall be of no effect.

(4) Where the terms of the tenancy are such that, at any time during the tenancy, the persons in common with whom the tenant is entitled to the use of the shared accommodation could be varied or their number could be increased, nothing in subsection (3) above shall prevent those terms from having effect so far as they relate to any such variation or increase.

(5) In this section 'living accommodation' means accommodation of such a nature that the fact that it constitutes or is included in the shared accommodation is sufficient, apart from this section, to prevent the tenancy from constituting an assured tenancy of a dwelling-house.

4 Certain sublettings not to exclude any part of sub-lessor's premises from assured tenancy

(1) Where the tenant of a dwelling-house has sub-let a part but not the whole of the dwelling-house, then, as against his landlord or any superior landlord, no part of the dwelling-house shall be treated as excluded from being a dwelling-house let on an assured tenancy by reason only that the terms on which any person claiming under the tenant holds any part of the dwelling-house include the use of accommodation in common with other persons.

(2) Nothing in this section affects the rights against, and liabilities to, each other of the tenant and any person claiming under him, or of any two such persons.

5 Security of tenure

(1) An assured tenancy cannot be brought to an end by the landlord except by obtaining an order of the court in accordance with the following provisions of this Chapter or Chapter II below or, in the case of a fixed term tenancy which contains power for the landlord to determine the tenancy in certain circumstances, by the exercise of that power and, accordingly, the service by the landlord of a notice to quit shall be of no effect in relation to a periodic assured tenancy.

(2) If an assured tenancy which is a fixed term tenancy comes to an end otherwise than by virtue of –

(a) an order of the court, or

(b) a surrender or other action on the part of the tenant,

then, subject to section 7 and Chapter II below, the tenant shall be entitled to remain in possession of the dwelling-house let under that tenancy and, subject to subsection (4) below, his right to possession shall depend upon a periodic tenancy arising by virtue of this section.

(3) The periodic tenancy referred to in subsection (2) above is one –

(a) taking effect in possession immediately on the coming to an end of the fixed term tenancy;

(b) deemed to have been granted by the person who was the landlord under the fixed term tenancy immediately before it came to an end to the person who was then the tenant under that tenancy;

(c) under which the premises which are let are the same dwelling-house as was let under the fixed term tenancy;

(d) under which the periods of the tenancy are the same as those for which rent was last payable under the fixed term tenancy; and

(e) under which, subject to the following provisions of this Part of this Act, the other terms are the same as those of the fixed term tenancy immediately before it came to an end, except that any term which makes provision for determination by the landlord or the tenant shall not have effect while the tenancy remains an assured tenancy.

(4) The periodic tenancy referred to in subsection (2) above shall not arise if, on the coming to an end of the fixed term tenancy, the tenant is entitled, by virtue of the grant of another tenancy, to possession of the same or substantially the same dwelling-house as was let to him under the fixed term tenancy.

(5) If, on or before the date on which a tenancy is entered into or is deemed to have been granted as mentioned in subsection (3)(b) above, the person who is to be the tenant under that tenancy –

(a) enters into an obligation to do any act which (apart from this subsection) will cause the tenancy to come to an end at a time when it is an assured tenancy, or

(b) executes, signs or gives any surrender, notice to quit or other document which (apart from this subsection) has the effect of bringing the tenancy to an end at a time when it is an assured tenancy,

the obligation referred to in paragraph (a) above shall not be enforceable or, as the case may be, the surrender, notice to quit or other document referred to in paragraph (b) above shall be of no effect.

(6) If, by virtue of any provision of this Part of this Act, Part I of Schedule 1 to this Act has effect in relation to a fixed term tenancy as if it consisted only of paragraphs 11 and 12, that Part shall have the like effect in relation to any periodic tenancy which arises by virtue of this section on the coming to an end of the fixed term tenancy.

(7) Any reference in this Part of this Act to a statutory periodic tenancy is a reference to a periodic tenancy arising by virtue of this section.

6   Fixing of terms of statutory periodic tenancy

(1) In this section, in relation to a statutory periodic tenancy, –

(a) 'the former tenancy' means the fixed term tenancy on the coming to an end of which the statutory periodic tenancy arises; and

(b) 'the implied terms' means the terms of the tenancy which have effect by virtue of section 5(3)(e) above, other than terms as to the amount of the rent;

but nothing in the following provisions of this section applies to a statutory periodic tenancy at a time when, by virtue of paragraph 11 or paragraph 12 in Part 1 of Schedule 1 to this Act, it cannot be an assured tenancy.

(2) Not later than the first anniversary of the day on which the former tenancy came to an end, the landlord may serve on the tenant, or the tenant may serve on the landlord, a notice in the prescribed form proposing terms of the statutory periodic tenancy different from the implied terms and, if the landlord or the tenant considers it appropriate, proposing an adjustment of the amount of the rent to take account of the proposed terms.

(3) Where a notice has been served under subsection (2) above, –

(a) within the period of three months beginning on the date on which the notice was served on him, the landlord or the tenant, as the case may be, may, by an application in the prescribed form, refer the notice to a rent assessment committee under subsection (4) below; and

(b) if the notice is not so referred, then, with effect from such date, not falling within the period referred to in paragraph (a) above, as may be specified in the notice, the terms proposed in the notice shall become terms of the tenancy in substitution for any of the implied terms dealing with the same subject matter and the amount of the rent shall be varied in accordance with any adjustment so proposed.

(4) Where a notice under subsection (2) above is referred to a rent assessment committee, the committee shall consider the terms proposed in the notice and shall determine whether those terms, or some other terms (dealing with the same subject matter as the proposed terms), are such as, in the committee's opinion, might reasonably be expected to be found in an assured periodic tenancy of the dwelling-house concerned, being a tenancy –

(a) which begins on the coming to an end of the former tenancy; and

(b) which is granted by a willing landlord on terms which, except in so far as they relate to the subject matter of the proposed terms, are those of the statutory periodic tenancy at the time of the committee's consideration.

(5) Whether or not a notice under subsection (2) above proposes an adjustment of the amount of the rent under the statutory periodic tenancy, where a rent assessment committee determine any terms under subsection (4) above, they shall, if they consider it appropriate, specify such an adjustment to take account of the terms so determined.

(6) In making a determination under subsection (4) above, or specifying an adjustment of an amount of rent under subsection (5) above, there shall be disregarded any effect on the terms or the amount of the rent attributable to the granting of a tenancy to a sitting tenant.

(7) Where a notice under subsection (2) above is referred to a rent assessment committee, then, unless the landlord and the tenant otherwise agree, with effect from such date as the committee may direct –

(a) the terms determined by the committee shall become terms of the statutory periodic tenancy in substitution for any of the implied terms dealing with the same subject matter; and

(b) the amount of the rent under the statutory periodic tenancy shall be altered to accord with any adjustment specified by the committee;

but for the purposes of paragraph (b) above the committee shall not direct a date earlier than the date specified, in accordance with subsection (3)(b) above, in the notice referred to them.

(8) Nothing in this section requires a rent assessment committee to continue with a determination under subsection (4) above if the landlord and tenant give notice writing that they no longer require such a determination or if the tenancy has come to an end.

6A   Demotion because of anti-social behaviour

(1) This section applies to an assured tenancy if the landlord is a registered social landlord.

(2) The landlord may apply to a county court for a demotion order.

(3) A demotion order has the following effect –

(a) the assured tenancy is terminated with effect from the date specified in the order;

(b) if the tenant remains in occupation of the dwelling-house after that date a demoted tenancy is created with effect from that date;

(c) it is a term of the demoted tenancy that any arrears of rent payable at the termination of the assured tenancy become payable under the demoted tenancy;

(d) it is also a term of the demoted tenancy that any rent paid in advance or overpaid at the termination of the assured tenancy is credited to the tenant's liability to pay rent under the demoted tenancy.

(4) The court must not make a demotion order unless it is satisfied –

(a) that the tenant or a person residing in or visiting the dwelling-house has engaged or has threatened to engage in conduct to which section 153A or 153B of the Housing Act 1996 (anti-social behaviour or use of premises for unlawful purposes) applies, and

(b) that it is reasonable to make the order.

(5) The court must not entertain proceedings for a demotion order unless –

(a) the landlord has served on the tenant a notice under subsection (6), or

(b) the court thinks it is just and equitable to dispense with the requirement of the notice.

(6) The notice must –

(a) give particulars of the conduct in respect of which the order is sought;

(b) state that the proceedings will not begin before the date specified in the notice;

(c) state that the proceedings will not begin after the end of the period of twelve months beginning with the date of service of the notice.

(7) The date specified for the purposes of subsection (6)(b) must not be before the end of the period of two weeks beginning with the date of service of the notice.

(8) Each of the following has effect in respect of a demoted tenancy at the time it is created by virtue of an order under this section as it has effect in relation to the assured tenancy at the time it is terminated by virtue of the order –

(a) the parties to the tenancy;

(b) the period of the tenancy;

(c) the amount of the rent;

(d) the dates on which the rent is payable.

(9) Subsection (8)(b) does not apply if the assured tenancy was for a fixed term and in such a case the demoted tenancy is a weekly periodic tenancy.

(10) If the landlord of the demoted tenancy serves on the tenant a statement of any other express terms of the assured tenancy which are to apply to the demoted tenancy such terms are also terms of the demoted tenancy.

(11) For the purposes of this section a demoted tenancy is a tenancy to which section 20B of the Housing Act 1988 applies.

7   Orders for possession

(1) The court shall not make an order for possession of a dwelling-house let on an assured tenancy except on one or more of the grounds set out in Schedule 2 to this Act; but nothing in this Part of this Act relates to proceedings for possession of such a dwelling-house which are brought by a mortgagee, within the meaning of the Law of Property Act 1925, who has lent money on the security of the assured tenancy.

(2) The following provisions of this section have effect, subject to section 8 [notice of proceedings for possession] below, in relation to proceedings for the recovery of possession of a dwelling-house let on an assured tenancy.

(3) If the court is satisfied that any of the grounds in Part 1 of Schedule 2 to this Act is established then, subject to subsections (5A) and (6) below, the court shall make an order for possession.

(4) If the court is satisfied that any of the grounds in Part II of Schedule 2 to this Act is established, then, subject to subsections (5A) and (6) below, the court may make an order for possession if it considers it reasonable to do so.

(5) Part III of Schedule 2 to this Act shall have effect for supplementing Ground 9 in that Schedule and Part IV of that Schedule shall have effect in relation to notices given as mentioned in Grounds 1 to 5 of that Schedule.

(5A) The court shall not make an order for possession of a dwelling-house let on an assured periodic tenancy arising under Schedule 10 to the Local Government and Housing Act 1989 on any of the following grounds, that is to say, –

(a) Grounds 1, 2 and 5 in Part I of Schedule 2 to this Act;

(b) Ground 16 in Part II of that Schedule; and

(c) if the assured periodic tenancy arose on the termination of a former 1954 Act tenancy, within the meaning of the said Schedule 10, Ground 6 in Part I of Schedule 2 to this Act.

(6) The court shall not make an order for possession of a dwelling-house to take effect at a time when it is let on an assured fixed term tenancy unless –

(a) the ground for possession is Ground 2 or Ground 8 in Part I of Schedule 2 to this Act or any of the grounds in Part II of that Schedule, other than Ground 9 or Ground 16; and

(b) the terms of the tenancy make provision for it to be brought to an end on the ground in question (whether that provision takes the form of a provision for re-entry, for forfeiture, for determination by notice or otherwise).

(7) Subject to the proceeding provisions of this section, the court may make an order for possession of a dwelling-house on grounds relating to a fixed term tenancy which has come to an end; and where an order is made in such circumstances, any statutory periodic tenancy which has arisen on the ending of the fixed term tenancy shall end (without any notice and regardless of the period) on the day on which the order takes effect.

15　Limited prohibition on assignment, etc without consent

(1) Subject to subsection (3) below, it shall be an implied term of every assured tenancy which is a periodic tenancy that, except with the consent of the landlord, the tenant shall not –

(a) assign the tenancy (in whole or in part); or

(b) sub-let or part with possession of the whole or any part of the dwelling-house let on the tenancy.

(2) Section 19 of the Landlord and Tenant Act 1927 (consents to assign not to be unreasonably withheld etc) shall not apply to a term which is implied into an assured tenancy by subsection (1) above.

(3) In the case of a periodic tenancy which is not a statutory periodic tenancy or an

assured periodic tenancy arising under Schedule 10 to the Local Government and Housing Act 1989 subsection (1) above does not apply if –

(a) there is a provision (whether contained in the tenancy or not) under which the tenant is prohibited (whether absolutely or conditionally) from assigning or sub-letting or parting with possession or is permitted (whether absolutely or conditionally) to assign, sub-let or part with possession; or

(b) a premium is required to be paid on the grant or renewal of the tenancy.

(4) In subsection (3)(b) above 'premium' includes –

(a) any fine or other like sum;

(b) any other pecuniary consideration in addition to rent; and

(c) any sum paid by way of deposit, other than one which does not exceed one-sixth of the annual rent payable under the tenancy immediately after the grant or renewal in question.

16   Access for repairs

It shall be an implied term of every assured tenancy that the tenant shall afford to the landlord access to the dwelling-house let on the tenancy and all reasonable facilities for executing therein any repairs which the landlord is entitled to execute.

CHAPTER II

ASSURED SHORTHOLD TENANCIES

19A   Assured shorthold tenancies: post-Housing Act 1996 tenancies

An assured tenancy which –

(a) is entered into on or after the day on which section 96 of the Housing Act 1996 comes into force (otherwise than pursuant to a contract made before that day), or

(b) comes into being by virtue of section 5 above on the coming to an end of an assured tenancy within paragraph (a) above,

is an assured shorthold tenancy unless it falls within any paragraph in Schedule 2A to this Act.

20   Assured shorthold tenancies: pre-Housing Act 1996 tenancies

(1) Subject to subsection (3) below, an assured tenancy which is not one to which section 19A above applies is an assured shorthold tenancy if –

(a) it is a fixed term tenancy granted for a term certain of not less than six months,

(b) there is no power for the landlord to determine the tenancy at any time earlier than six months from the beginning of the tenancy, and

(c) a notice in respect of it is served as mentioned in subsection (2) below.

(2) The notice referred to in subsection (1)(c) above is one which –

(a) is in such form as may be prescribed;

(b) is served before the assured tenancy is entered into;

(c) is served by the person who is to be the landlord under the assured tenancy on the person who is to be the tenant under that tenancy; and

(d) states that the assured tenancy to which it relates is to be a shorthold tenancy.

(3) Notwithstanding anything in subsection (1) above, where –

(a) immediately before a tenancy (in this subsection referred to as 'the new tenancy') is granted, the person to whom it is granted or, as the case may be, at least one of the persons to whom it is granted was a tenant under an assured tenancy which was not a shorthold tenancy, and

(b) the new tenancy is granted by the person who, immediately before the beginning of the tenancy, was the landlord under the assured tenancy referred to in paragraph (a) above,

the new tenancy cannot be an assured shorthold tenancy.

(4) Subject to subsection (5) below, if, on the coming to an end of an assured shorthold tenancy (including a tenancy which was an assured shorthold but ceased to be assured before it came to an end), a new tenancy of the same or substantially the same premises comes into being under which the landlord and the tenant are the same as at the coming to an end of the earlier tenancy, then, if and so long as the new tenancy is an assured tenancy, it shall be an assured shorthold tenancy, whether or not it fulfils the conditions in paragraphs (a) to (c) of subsection (1) above.

(5) Subsection (4) above does not apply if, before the new tenancy is entered into (or, in the case of a statutory periodic tenancy, take effect in possession), the landlord serves notice on the tenant that the new tenancy is not to be a shorthold tenancy.

(5A) Subsections (3) and (4) above do not apply where the new tenancy is one to which section 19A above applies.

(6) In the case of joint landlords –

(a) the reference in subsection (2)(c) above to the person who is to be the landlord is a reference to at least one of the persons who are to be joint landlords; and

(b) the reference in subsection (5) above to the landlord is a reference to at least one of the joint landlords.

20A Post-Housing Act 1996 tenancies: duty of landlord to provide statement as to terms of tenancy

(1) Subject to subsection (3) below, a tenant under an assured shorthold tenancy to which section 19A above applies may, by notice in writing, require the landlord

under that tenancy to provide him with a written statement of any term of the tenancy which –

(a) falls within subsection (2) below, and

(b) is not evidenced in writing.

(2) The following terms of a tenancy fall within this subsection, namely –

(a) the date on which the tenancy began or, if it is a statutory periodic tenancy or a tenancy to which section 39(7) below applies, the date on which the tenancy came into being,

(b) the rent payable under the tenancy and the dates on which that rent is payable,

(c) any-term providing for a review of the rent payable under the tenancy, and

(d) in the case of a fixed term tenancy, the length of the fixed term.

(3) No notice may be given under subsection (1) above in relation to a term of the tenancy if –

(a) the landlord under the tenancy has provided a statement of that term in response to an earlier notice under that subsection given by the tenant under the tenancy, and

(b) the term has not been varied since the provision of the statement referred to in paragraph (a) above.

(4) A landlord who fails, without reasonable excuse, to comply with a notice under subsection (1) above within the period of 28 days beginning with the date on which he received the notice is liable on summary conviction to a fine not exceeding level 4 on the standard scale.

(5) A statement provided for the purposes of subsection (1) above shall not be regarded as conclusive evidence of what was agreed by the parties to the tenancy in question.

(6) Where

(a) a term of a statutory periodic tenancy is one which has effect by virtue of section 5(3)(e) above, or

(b) a term of a tenancy to which subsection (7) of section 39 below applies is one which has effect by virtue of subsection (6)(e) of that section,

subsection (1) above shall have effect in relation to it as if paragraph (b) related to the term of the tenancy from which it derives.

(7) In subsections (1) and (3) above –

(a) references to the tenant under the tenancy shall, in the case of joint tenants, be taken to be references to any of the tenants, and

(b) references to the landlord under the tenancy shall, in the case of joint landlords, be taken to be references to any of the landlords.

20B Demoted assured shorthold tenancies

(1) An assured tenancy is an assured shorthold tenancy to which this section applies (a demoted assured shorthold tenancy) if –

(a) the tenancy is created by virtue of an order of the court under section 82A of the Housing Act 1985 or section 6A of this Act (a demotion order), and

(b) the landlord is a registered social landlord.

(2) At the end of the period of one year starting with the day when the demotion order takes effect a demoted assured shorthold tenancy ceases to be an assured shorthold tenancy unless subsection (3) applies.

(3) This subsection applies if before the end of the period mentioned in subsection (2) the landlord gives notice of proceedings for possession of the dwelling house.

(4) If subsection (3) applies the tenancy continues to be a demoted assured shorthold tenancy until the end of the period mentioned in subsection (2) or (if later) until one of the following occurs –

(a) the notice of proceedings for possession is withdrawn;

(b) the proceedings are determined in favour of the tenant;

(c) the period of six months beginning with the date on which the notice is given ends and no proceedings for possession have been brought.

(5) Registered social landlord has the same meaning as in Part 1 of the Housing Act 1996.

21 Recovery of possession on expiry or termination of assured shorthold tenancy

(1) Without prejudice to any right of the landlord under an assured shorthold tenancy to recover possession of the dwelling-house let on the tenancy in accordance with Chapter I above, on or after the coming to an end of an assured shorthold tenancy which was a fixed term tenancy, a court shall make an order for possession of the dwelling-house if it is satisfied –

(a) that the assured shorthold tenancy has come to an end and no further assured tenancy (whether shorthold or not) is for the time being in existence, other than an assured shorthold periodic tenancy (whether statutory or not); and

(b) the landlord or, in the case of joint landlords, at least one of them has given to the tenant not less than two months' notice in writing stating that he requires possession of the dwelling-house.

(2) A notice under paragraph (b) of subsection (1) above may be given before or on the day on which the tenancy comes to an end; and that subsection shall have effect notwithstanding that on the coming to an end of the fixed term tenancy a statutory periodic tenancy arises.

(3) Where a court makes an order for possession of a dwelling-house by virtue of subsection (1) above, any statutory periodic tenancy which has arisen on the coming to an end of the assured shorthold tenancy shall end (without further notice and regardless of the period) on the day on which the order takes effect.

(4) Without prejudice to any such right as is referred to in subsection (1) above, a court shall make an order for possession of a dwelling-house let on an assured shorthold tenancy which is a periodic tenancy if the court is satisfied –

(a) that the landlord or, in the case of joint landlords, at least one of them has given to the tenant a notice in writing stating that, after a date specified in the notice, being the last day of a period of the tenancy and not earlier than two months after the date the notice was given, possession of the dwelling-house is required by virtue of this section; and

(b) that the date specified in the notice under paragraph (a) above is not earlier than the earliest day on which, apart from section 5(1) above, the tenancy could be brought to an end by a notice to quit given by the landlord on the same date as the notice under paragraph (a) above

(5) Where an order for possession under subsection (1) or (4) above is made in relation to a dwelling-house let on a tenancy to which section 19A above applies, the order may not be made so as to take effect earlier than –

(a) in the case of a tenancy which is not a replacement tenancy, six months after the beginning of the tenancy, and

(b) in the case of a replacement tenancy, six months after the beginning of the original tenancy.

(5A) Subsection (5) above does not apply to an assured shorthold tenancy to which section 20B (demoted assured shorthold tenancies) applies.

(6) In subsection (5)(b) above, the reference to the original tenancy is –

(a) where the replacement tenancy came into being on the coming to an end of a tenancy which was not a replacement tenancy, to the immediately preceding tenancy, and

(b) where there have been successive replacement tenancies, to the tenancy immediately preceding the first in the succession of replacement tenancies.

(7) For the purposes of this section, a replacement tenancy is a tenancy –

(a) which comes into being on the coming to an end of an assured shorthold tenancy, and

(b) under which, on its coming into being –

(i) the landlord and tenant are the same as under the earlier tenancy as at its coming to an end, and

(ii) the premises let are the same or substantially the same as those let under the earlier tenancy as at that time.

CHAPTER IV

PROTECTION FROM EVICTION

27   Damages for unlawful eviction

(1) This section applies if, at any time after 9th June 1988, a landlord (in this section referred to as 'the landlord in default') or any person acting on behalf of the landlord in default unlawfully deprives the residential occupier of any premises of his occupation of the whole or part of the premises.

(2) This section also applies if, at any time after 9th June 1988, a landlord (in this section referred to as 'the landlord in default') or any person acting on behalf of the landlord in default –

(a) attempts unlawfully to deprive the residential occupier of any premises of his occupation of the whole or part of the premises, or

(b) knowing or having reasonable cause to believe that the conduct is likely to cause the residential occupier of any premises –

(i) to give up his occupation of the premises or any part thereof, or

(ii) to refrain from exercising any right or pursuing any remedy in respect of the premises or any part thereof,

does acts likely to interfere with the peace or comfort of the residential occupier or members of his household, or persistently withdraws or withholds services reasonably required for the occupation of the premises as a residence,

and, as a result, the residential occupier gives up his occupation of the premises as a residence.

(3) Subject to the following provisions of this section, where this section applies, the landlord in default shall, by virtue of this section, be liable to pay to the former residential occupier, in respect of his loss of the right to occupy the premises in question as his residence, damages assessed on the basis set out in section 28 below.

(4) Any liability arising by virtue of subsection (3) above –

(a) shall be in the nature of a liability in tort; and

(b) subject to subsection (5) below, shall be in addition to any liability arising apart from this section (whether in tort, contract or otherwise).

(5) Nothing in this section affects the right of a residential occupier to enforce any liability which arises apart from this section in respect of his loss of the right to occupy premises as his residence; but damages shall not be awarded both in respect of such a liability and in respect of a liability arising by virtue of this section on account of the same loss.

(6) No liability shall arise by virtue of subsection (3) above if –

(a) before the date on which proceedings to enforce the liability are finally disposed of, the former residential occupier is reinstated in the premises in question in such circumstances that he becomes again the residential occupier of them; or

(b) at the request of the former residential occupier, a court makes an order (whether in the nature of an injunction or otherwise) as a result of which he is reinstated as mentioned in paragraph (a) above;

and, for the purposes of paragraph (a) above, proceedings to enforce a liability are finally disposed of on the earliest date by which the proceedings (including any proceedings on or in consequence of an appeal) have been determined and any time for appealing or further appealing has expired, except that if any appeal is abandoned, the proceedings shall be taken to be disposed of on the date of the abandonment.

(7) If, in proceedings to enforce a liability arising by virtue of subsection (3) above, it appears to the court –

(a) that, prior to the event which gave rise to the liability, the conduct of the former residential occupier or any person living with him in the premises concerned was such that it is reasonable to mitigate the damages for which the landlord in default would otherwise be liable, or

(b) that, before the proceedings were begun, the landlord in default offered to reinstate the former residential occupier in the premises in question and either it was unreasonable of the former residential occupier to refuse that offer or, if he had obtained alternative accommodation before the offer was made, it would have been unreasonable of him to refuse that offer if he had not obtained that accommodation,

the court may reduce the amount of damages which would otherwise be payable to such amount as it thinks appropriate.

(8) In proceedings to enforce a liability arising by virtue of subsection (3) above, it shall be a defence for the defendant to prove that he believed, and had reasonable cause to believe –

(a) that the residential occupier had ceased to reside in the premises in question at the time when he was deprived of occupation as mentioned in subsection (1) above or, as the case may be, when the attempt was made or the acts were done as a result of which he gave up his occupation of those premises; or

(b) that, where the liability would otherwise arise by virtue only of the doing of acts or the withdrawal or withholding of services, he had reasonable grounds for doing the acts or withdrawing or withholding the services in question.

(9) In this section –

(a) 'residential occupier', in relation to any premises, has the same meaning as in section 1 of the [Protection from Eviction Act 1977];

(b) 'the right to occupy', in relation to a residential occupier, includes any restriction on the right of another person to recover possession of the premises in question;

(c) 'landlord', in relation to a residential occupier, means the person who, but for the occupier's right to occupy, would be entitled to occupation of the premises and any superior landlord under whom that person derives title;

(d) 'former residential occupier', in relation to any premises, means the person who was the residential occupier until he was deprived of or gave up his occupation as mentioned in subsection (1) or subsection (2) above (and, in relation to a former residential occupier, 'the right to occupy' and 'landlord' shall be construed accordingly).

CHAPTER V

PHASING OUT OF RENT ACTS AND OTHER TRANSITIONAL PROVISIONS

34 New protected tenancies and agricultural occupancies restricted to special cases

(1) A tenancy which is entered into on or after the commencement of this Act cannot be a protected tenancy, unless –

(a) it is entered into in pursuance of a contract made before the commencement of this Act; or

(b) it is granted to a person (alone or jointly with others) who, immediately before the tenancy was granted, was a protected or statutory tenant and is so granted by the person who at that time was the landlord (or one of the joint landlords) under the protected or statutory tenancy; or

(c) it is granted to a person (alone or jointly with others) in the following circumstances –

(i) prior to the grant of the tenancy, an order for possession of a dwelling-house was made against him (alone or jointly with others) on the court being satisfied as mentioned in section 98(1)(a) of, or Case 1 in Schedule 16 to, the Rent Act 1977 or Case 1 of Schedule 4 to the Rent (Agriculture) Act 1976 (suitable alternative accommodation available); and

(ii) the tenancy is of the premises which constitute the suitable alternative accommodation as to which the court was so satisfied; and

(iii) in the proceedings for possession the court considered that, in the circumstances, the grant of an assured tenancy would not afford the required security and, accordingly, directed that the tenancy would be a protected tenancy; or

(d) it is a tenancy under which the interest of the landlord was at the time the tenancy was granted held by a new town corporation, within the meaning of section 80 of the Housing Act 1985, and, before the date which has effect by virtue of paragraph (a) or paragraph (b) of subsection (4) of section 38 below, ceased to be so held by virtue of a disposal by the Commission for the New Towns made pursuant to a direction under section 37 of the New Towns Act 1981.

(2) In subsection (1)(b) above 'protected tenant' and 'statutory tenant' do not include –

(a) a tenant under a protected shorthold tenancy;

(b) a protected or statutory tenant of a dwelling-house which was let under a protected shorthold tenancy which ended before the commencement of this Act and in respect of which at that commencement either there has been no grant of a further tenancy or any grant of a further tenancy has been to the person who, immediately before the grant, was in possession of the dwelling-house as a protected or statutory tenant;

and in this subsection 'protected shorthold tenancy' includes a tenancy which, in proceedings for possession under Case 19 in Schedule 15 to the Rent Act 1977, is treated as a protected shorthold tenancy.

(3) In any case where –

(a) by virtue of subsections (1) and (2) above, a tenancy entered into on or after the commencement of this Act is an assured tenancy, but

(b) apart from subsection (2) above, the effect of subsection (1)(b) above would be that the tenancy would be a protected tenancy, and

(c) the landlord and the tenant under the tenancy are the same as at the coming to an end of the protected or statutory tenancy which, apart from subsection (2) above, would fall within subsection (1)(b) above,

the tenancy shall be an assured shorthold tenancy (whether or not, in the case of a tenancy to which the provision applies, it fulfils the conditions in section 20(1) above) unless, before the tenancy is entered into, the landlord serves notice on the tenant that it is not to be a shorthold tenancy.

(4) A licence or tenancy which is entered into on or after the commencement of this Act cannot be a relevant licence or relevant tenancy for the purposes of the Rent (Agriculture) Act 1976 (in this subsection referred to as 'the 1976 Act') unless –

(a) it is entered into in pursuance of a contract made before the commencement of this Act; or

(b) it is granted to a person (alone or jointly with others) who, immediately before the licence or tenancy was granted, was a protected occupier or statutory tenant, within the meaning of the 1976 Act, and is so granted by the person who at that time was the landlord or licensor (or one of the joint landlords or licensors) under the protected occupancy or statutory tenancy in question.

(5) Except as provided in subsection (4) above, expressions used in this section have the same meaning as in the Rent Act 1977.

35 Removal of special regimes for tenancies of housing associations, etc

(1) In this section 'housing association tenancy' has the same meaning as in Part VI of the Rent Act 1977.

(2) A tenancy which is entered into on or after the commencement of this Act cannot be a housing association tenancy unless –

(a) it is entered into in pursuance of a contract made before the commencement of this Act; or

(b) it is granted to a person (alone or jointly with others) who, immediately before the tenancy was granted, was a tenant under a housing association tenancy and is so granted by the person who at that time was the landlord under that housing association tenancy; or

(c) it is granted to a person (alone or jointly with others) in the following circumstances –

(i) prior to the grant of the tenancy, an order for possession of a dwelling-house was made against him (alone or jointly with others) on the court being satisfied as mentioned in paragraph (b) or paragraph (c) of subsection (2) of section 94 of the Housing Act 1985; and

(ii) the tenancy is of the premises which constitute the suitable accommodation as to which the court was so satisfied; and

(iii) in the proceedings for possession the court directed that the tenancy would be a housing association tenancy; or

(d) it is a tenancy under which the interest of the landlord was at the time the tenancy was granted held by a new town corporation, within the meaning of section 80 of the Housing Act 1985, and, before the date which has effect by virtue of paragraph (a) or paragraph (b) of subsection (4) of section 38 below, ceased to be so held by virtue of a disposal by the Commission for the New Towns made pursuant to a direction under section 37 of the New Towns Act 1981.

(3) Where, on or after the commencement of this Act, a registered social landlord, within the meaning of the Housing Act 1985 (see section 5(4) and (5) of that Act), grants a secure tenancy pursuant to an obligation under section 554(2A) of the Housing Act 1985 (as set out in Schedule 17 to this Act) then, in determining whether that tenancy is a housing association tenancy, it shall be assumed for the purposes only of section 86(2)(b) of the Rent Act 1977 (tenancy would be a protected tenancy but for section 15 or 16 of that Act) that the tenancy was granted before the commencement of this Act.

(4) Subject to section 38(4A) below, a tenancy or licence which is entered into on or after the commencement of this Act cannot be a secure tenancy unless –

(a) the interest of the landlord belongs to a local authority, a new town corporation or an urban development corporation, all within the meaning of section 80 of the Housing Act 1985 or a housing action trust established under Part III of this Act; or

(b) the interest of the landlord belongs to a housing co-operative within the meaning of section 27B of the Housing Act 1985 (agreements between local housing authorities and housing co-operatives) and the tenancy or licence is of a dwelling-house comprised in a housing co-operative agreement falling within that section; or

(c) it is entered into in pursuance of a contract made before the commencement of this Act; or

(d) it is granted to a person (alone or jointly with others) who, immediately before it was entered into, was a secure tenant and is so granted by the body which at that time was the landlord or licensor under the secure tenancy; or

(e) it is granted to a person (alone or jointly with others) in the following circumstances –

(i) prior to the grant of the tenancy or licence, an order for possession of a dwelling-house was made against him (alone or jointly with others) on the court being satisfied as mentioned in paragraph (b) or paragraph (c) of subsection (2) of section 84 of the Housing Act 1985; and

(ii) the tenancy or licence is of the premises which constitute the suitable accommodation as to which the court was so satisfied; and

(iii) in the proceedings for possession the court considered that, in the circumstances, the grant of an assured tenancy would not afford the required security and, accordingly, directed that the tenancy or licence would be a secure tenancy; or

(f) it is granted pursuant to an obligation under section 554(2A) of the Housing Act 1985 (as set out in Schedule 17 to this Act).

(5) If, on or after the commencement of this Act, the interest of the landlord under a protected or statutory tenancy becomes held by a housing association, a housing trust or the Housing Corporation or, where that interest becomes held by him as the result of the exercise by him of functions under Part III of the Housing Associations Act 1985, the Secretary of State, nothing in the preceding provisions of this section shall prevent the tenancy from being a housing association tenancy or a secure tenancy and, accordingly, in such a case section 80 of the Housing Act 1985 (and any enactment which refers to that section) shall have effect without regard to the repeal of provisions of that section effected by this Act.

(6) In subsection (5) above 'housing association' and 'housing trust' have the same meaning as in the Housing Act 1985.

36 New restricted contracts limited to transitional cases

(1) A tenancy or other contract entered into after the commencement of this Act cannot be a restricted contract for the purposes of the Rent Act 1977 unless it is entered into in pursuance of a contract made before the commencement of this Act.

(2) If the terms of a restricted contract are varied after this Act comes into force then, subject to subsection (3) below, –

(a) if the variation affects the amount of the rent which, under the contract, is payable for the dwelling in question, the contract shall be treated as a new contract entered into at the time of the variation (and subsection (1) above shall have effect accordingly); and

(b) if the variation does not affect the amount of the rent which, under the contract, is so payable, nothing in this section shall affect the determination of the question whether the variation is such as to give rise to a new contract.

(3) Any reference in subsection (2) above to a variation affecting the amount of the rent which, under a contract, is payable for a dwelling does not include a reference to –

(a) a reduction or increase effected under section 78 of the Rent Act 1977 (power of rent tribunal); or

(b) a variation which is made by the parties and has the effect of making the rent expressed to be payable under the contract the same as the rent for the dwelling which is entered in the register under section 79 of the Rent Act 1977. ...

(5) In this section 'rent' has the same meaning as in Part V of the Rent Act 1977.

37   No further assured tenancies under Housing Act 1980

(1) A tenancy which is entered into on or after the commencement of this Act cannot be an assured tenancy for the purposes of section 56 to 58 of the Housing Act 1980 (in this section referred to as a '1980 Act tenancy').

(2) In any case where –

(a) before the commencement of this Act, a tenant under a 1980 Act tenancy made an application to the court under section 24 of the Landlord and Tenant Act 1954 (for the grant of a new tenancy), and

(b) at the commencement of this Act the 1980 Act tenancy is continuing by virtue of that section or of any provision of Part IV of the said Act of 1954,

section 1(3) of this Act shall not apply to the 1980 Act tenancy.

(3) If, in a case falling within subsection (2) above, the court makes an order for the grant of a new tenancy under section 29 of the Landlord and Tenant Act 1954, that tenancy shall be an assured tenancy for the purposes of this Act.

(4) In any case where –

(a) before the commencement of this Act a contract was entered into for the grant of a 1980 Act tenancy, but

(b) at the commencement of this Act the tenancy had not been granted,

the contract shall have effect as a contract for the grant of an assured tenancy (within the meaning of this Act).

(5) In relation to an assured tenancy falling within subsection (3) above or granted pursuant to a contract falling within subsection (4) above, Part I of Schedule 1 to this Act shall have effect as if it consisted only of paragraphs 11 and 12; and, if the landlord granting the tenancy is a fully mutual housing association, then, so long as that association remains the landlord under that tenancy (and under any statutory periodic tenancy which arises on the coming to an end of that tenancy), the said

paragraph 12 shall have effect in relation to that tenancy with the omission of sub-paragraph (1)(h).

(6) Any reference in this section to a provision of the Landlord and Tenant Act 1954 is a reference only to that provision as applied by section 58 of the Housing Act 1980.

38   Transfer of existing tenancies from public to private sector

(1) The provisions of subsection (3) below apply in relation to a tenancy which was entered into before, or pursuant to a contract made before, the commencement of this Act if, –

(a) at that commencement or, if it is later, at the time it is entered into, the interest of the landlord is held by a public body (within the meaning of subsection (5) below); and

(b) at some time after that commencement, the interest of the landlord ceases to be so held.

(2) The provisions of subsection (3) below also apply in relation to a tenancy which was entered into before, or pursuant to a contract made before, the commencement of this Act if, –

(a) at the commencement of this Act or, if it is later, at the time it is entered into, it is a housing association tenancy; and

(b) at some time after that commencement, it ceases to be such a tenancy.

(3) Subject to subsections (4), (4A) and (4B) below, on and after the time referred to in subsection (1)(b) or, as the case may be, subsection (2)(b) above –

(a) the tenancy shall not be capable of being a protected tenancy, a protected occupancy or a housing association tenancy;

(b) the tenancy shall not be capable of being a secure tenancy unless (and only at a time when) the interest of the landlord under the tenancy is (or is again) held by a public body; and

(c) paragraph 1 of Schedule 1 to this Act shall not apply in relation to it, and the question whether at any time thereafter it becomes (or remains) an assured tenancy shall be determined accordingly.

(4) In relation to a tenancy under which, at the commencement of this Act or, if it is later, at the time the tenancy is entered into, the interest of the landlord is held by a new town corporation, within the meaning of section 80 of the Housing Act 1985 and which subsequently ceases to be so held by virtue of a disposal by the Commission for the New Towns made pursuant to a direction under section 37 of the New Towns Act 1981, subsections (1) and (3) above shall have effect as if any reference in subsection (1) above to the commencement of this Act were a reference to –

(a) the date on which expires the period of two years beginning on the day this Act is passed; or

(b) if the Secretary of State by order made by statutory instrument within that period so provides, such other date (whether earlier or later) as may be specified by the order for the purposes of this subsection.

(4A) Where, by virtue of a disposal falling within subsection (4) above and made before the date which has effect by virtue of paragraph (a) or paragraph (b) of that subsection, the interest of the landlord under a tenancy passes to a registered social landlord (within the meaning of the Housing Act 1985 (see section 5(4) and (5) of that Act)), then, notwithstanding anything in subsection (3) above, so long as the tenancy continues to be held by a body which would have been specified in subsection (1) of section 80 of the Housing Act 1985 if the repeal of provisions of that section effected by this Act had not been made, the tenancy shall continue to be a secure tenancy and to be capable of being a housing association tenancy.

(4B) Where, by virtue of a disposal by the Secretary of State made in the exercise by him of functions under Part III of the Housing Associations Act 1985, the interest of the landlord under a secure tenancy passes to a registered social landlord (within the meaning of the Housing Act 1985) then, notwithstanding anything in subsection (3) above, so long as the tenancy continues to be held by a body which would have been specified in subsection (1) of section 80 of the Housing Act 1985 if the repeal of provisions of that section effected by this Act had not been made, the tenancy shall continue to be a secure tenancy and to be capable of being a housing association tenancy.

(5) For the purposes of this section, the interest of a landlord under a tenancy is held by a public body at a time when –

(a) it belongs to a local authority, a new town corporation or an urban development corporation, all within the meaning of section 80 of the Housing Act 1985; or

(b) it belongs to a housing action trust established under Part III of this Act; or

(d) it belongs to Her Majesty in right of the Crown or to a government department or is held in trust for Her Majesty for the purposes of a government department.

(6) In this section –

(a) 'housing association tenancy' means a tenancy to which Part VI of the Rent Act 1977 applies;

(b) 'protected tenancy' has the same meaning as in that Act; and

(c) 'protected occupancy' has the same meaning as in the Rent (Agriculture) Act 1976.

SCHEDULE 1

TENANCIES WHICH CANNOT BE ASSURED TENANCIES

PART I

THE TENANCIES

Tenancies entered into before commencement

1. A tenancy which is entered into before, or pursuant to a contract made before, the commencement of this Act.

Tenancies of dwelling-houses with high rateable values

2.– (1) A tenancy –

(a) which is entered into on or after 1st April 1990 (otherwise than, where the dwelling-house had a rateable value on 31st March 1990, in pursuance of a contract made before 1st April 1990), and

(b) under which the rent payable for the time being is payable at a rate exceeding £25,000 a year.

(2) In sub-paragraph (1) 'rent' does not include any sum payable by the tenant as is expressed (in whatever terms) to be payable in respect of rates, council tax, services, management, repairs, maintenance or insurance, unless it could not have been regarded by the parties to the tenancy as a sum so payable.

2A. A tenancy –

(a) which was entered into before 1st April 1990 or on or after that date in pursuance of a contract made before that date, and

(b) under which the dwelling-house had a rateable value on the 31st March 1990 which, if it is in Greater London, exceeded £1,500 and, if it is elsewhere, exceeded £750.

Tenancies at a low rent

3. A tenancy under which for the time being no rent is payable.

3A. A tenancy –

(a) which is entered into on or after 1st April 1990 (otherwise than, where the dwelling-house had a rateable value on 31st March 1990, in pursuance of a contract made before 1st April 1990), and

(b) under which the rent payable for the time being is payable at a rate of, if the dwelling-house is in Greater London, £1,000 or less a year and, if it is elsewhere, £250 or less a year.

3B. A tenancy –

(a) which was entered into before 1st April 1990 or, where the dwelling-house had a rateable value on 31st March 1990, on or after 1st April 1990 in pursuance of a contract made before that date, and

(b) under which the rent for the time being payable is less than two-thirds of the rateable value of the dwelling-house on 31st March 1990.

3C. Paragraph 2(2) above applies for the purposes of paragraphs 3, 3A and 3B as it applies for the purposes of paragraph 2(1).

Business tenancies

4. A tenancy to which Part II of the Landlord and Tenant Act 1954 applies (business tenancies).

Licensed premises

5. A tenancy under which the dwelling-house consists of or comprises premises licensed for the sale of intoxicating liquors for consumption on the premises.

Tenancies of agricultural land

6.– (1) A tenancy under which agricultural land, exceeding two acres, is let together with the dwelling-house.

(2) In this paragraph 'agricultural land' has the meaning set out in section 26(3)(a) of the General Rate Act 1967 (exclusion of agricultural land and premises from liability for rating).

Tenancies of agricultural holdings, etc

7. A tenancy under which the dwelling-house –

(a) is comprised in an agricultural holding, and

(b) is occupied by the person responsible for the control (whether as tenant or as servant or agent of the tenant) of the farming of the holding.

(2) A tenancy under which the dwelling-house –

(a) is comprised in the holding held under a farm business tenancy, and

(b) is occupied by the person responsible for the control (whether as tenant or as servant or agent of the tenant) of the management of the holding.

(3) In this paragraph –

'agricultural holding' means any agricultural holding within the meaning of the Agricultural Holdings Act 1986 held under a tenancy in relation to which that Act applies, and

'farm business tenancy' and 'holding', in relation to such a tenancy, have the same meaning as in the Agricultural Tenancies Act 1995.

Lettings to students

8.– (1) A tenancy which is granted to a person who is pursuing, or intends to pursue, a course of study provided by a specified educational institution and is so granted either by that institution or by another specified institution or body of persons.

(2) In sub-paragraph (1) above 'specified' means specified, or of a class specified, for the purposes of this paragraph by regulations made by the Secretary of State by statutory instrument.

(3) A statutory instrument made in the exercise of the power conferred by sub-paragraph (2) above shall be subject to annulment in pursuance of a resolution of either House of Parliament.

Holiday lettings

9. A tenancy the purpose of which is to confer on the tenant the right to occupy the dwelling-house for a holiday.

Resident landlords

10.– (1) A tenancy in respect of which the following conditions are fulfilled –

(a) that the dwelling-house forms part only of a building and, except in a case where the dwelling-house also forms part of a flat, the building is not a purpose-built block of flats; and

(b) that, subject to Part III of this Schedule, the tenancy was granted by an individual who, at the time when the tenancy was granted, occupied as his only or principal home another dwelling-house which, –

(i) in the case mentioned in paragraph (a) above, also forms part of the flat; or

(ii) in any other case, also forms part of the building; and

(c) that, subject to Part III of this Schedule, at all times since the tenancy was granted the interest of the landlord under the tenancy has belonged to an individual who, at the time he owned that interest, occupied as his only or principal home another dwelling-house which, –

(i) in the case mentioned in paragraph (a) above, also forms part of the flat; or

(ii) in any other case, also formed part of the building; and

(d) that the tenancy is not one which is excluded from this sub-paragraph by sub-paragraph (3) below.

(2) If a tenancy was granted by two or more persons jointly, the reference in sub-paragraph (1)(b) above to an individual is a reference to any one of those persons and if the interest of the landlord is for the time being held by two or more persons jointly, the reference in sub-paragraph (1)(c) above to an individual is a reference to any one of those persons.

(3) A tenancy (in this sub-paragraph referred to as 'the new tenancy') is excluded from sub-paragraph (1) above if –

(a) it is granted to a person (alone, or jointly with others) who, immediately before it was granted, was a tenant under an assured tenancy (in this sub-paragraph referred to as 'the former tenancy') of the same dwelling-house or of another dwelling-house which forms part of the building in question; and

(b) the landlord under the new tenancy and under the former tenancy is the same person or, if either of those tenancies is or was granted by two or more persons jointly, the same person is the landlord or one of the landlords under each tenancy.

Crown tenancies

11.– (1) A tenancy under which the interest of the landlord belongs to Her Majesty in right of the Crown or to a government department or is held in trust for Her Majesty for the purposes of a government department.

(2) The reference in sub-paragraph (1) above to the case where the interest of the landlord belongs to Her Majesty in right of the Crown does not include the case where that interest is under the management of the Crown Estate Commissioners or it is held by the Secretary of State as the result of the exercise by him of functions under Part III of the Housing Associations Act 1985.

Local authority tenancies, etc

12.– (1) A tenancy under which the interest of the landlord belongs to –

(a) a local authority, as defined in sub-paragraph (2) below;

(b) the Commission for the New Towns;

(d) an urban development corporation established by an order under section 135 of the Local Government, Planning and Land Act 1980;

(e) a development corporation, within the meaning of the New Towns Act 1981;

(f) an authority established under section 10 of the Local Government Act 1985 (waste disposal authorities);

(g) a residuary body, within the meaning of the Local Government Act 1985;

(gg) the Residuary Body for Wales (Corff Gweddilliol Cymru);

(h) a fully mutual housing association; or

(i) a housing action trust established under Part III of this Act.

(2) The following are local authorities for the purposes of sub-paragraph (1)(a) above –

(a) the council of a county, county borough, district or London borough;

(b) the Common Council of the City of London;

(c) the Council of the Isles of Scilly;

(d) the Broads Authority;

(da) a National Park authority;

(ee) the London Fire and Emergency Planning Authority;

(f) a joint authority, within the meaning of the Local Government Act 1985; and

(g) a police authority established under section 3 of the Police Act 1996.

Accommodation for asylum-seekers

12A.– (1) Tenancy granted by a private landlord under arrangements for the provision of support for asylum-seekers or dependants of asylum-seekers made under Part VI of the Immigration and Asylum Act 1999.

(2) 'Private landlord' means a landlord who is not within section 80(1) of the Housing Act 1985.

Transitional cases

13.– (1) A protected tenancy, within the meaning of the Rent Act 1977.

(2) A housing association tenancy, within the meaning of Part VI of that Act.

(3) A secure tenancy.

(4) Where a person is a protected occupier of a dwelling-house, within the meaning of the Rent (Agriculture) Act 1976, the relevant tenancy, within the meaning of that Act, by virtue of which he occupies the dwelling-house.

SCHEDULE 2

GROUNDS FOR POSSESSION OF DWELLING-HOUSES LET ON ASSURED TENANCIES

PART I

GROUNDS ON WHICH COURT MUST ORDER POSSESSION

Ground 1

Not later than the beginning of the tenancy the landlord gave notice in writing to the tenant that possession might be recovered on this ground or the court is of the opinion that it is just and equitable to dispense with the requirement of notice and (in either case) –

(a) at some time before the beginning of the tenancy, the landlord who is seeking possession or, in the case of joint landlords seeking possession, at least one of them occupied the dwelling-house as his only or principal home; or

(b) the landlord who is seeking possession or, in the case of joint landlords seeking possession, at least one of them requires the dwelling-house as his or his spouse's only or principal home and neither the landlord (or, in the case of joint landlords, any one of them) nor any other person who, as landlord, derived title under the landlord who gave notice mentioned above acquired the reversion on the tenancy for money or money's worth.

Ground 2

The dwelling-house is subject to a mortgage granted before the beginning of the tenancy and –

(a) the mortgagee is entitled to exercise a power of sale conferred on him by the mortgage or by section 101 of the Law of Property Act 1925; and

(b) the mortgagee requires possession of the dwelling-house for the purpose of disposing of it with vacant possession in exercise of that power; and

(c) either notice was given as mentioned in Ground 1 above or the court is satisfied that it is just and equitable to dispense with the requirement of notice;

and for the purposes of this ground 'mortgage' includes a charge and 'mortgagee' shall be construed accordingly.

Ground 3

The tenancy is a fixed term tenancy for a term not exceeding eight months and –

(a) not later than the beginning of the tenancy the landlord gave notice in writing to the tenant that possession might be recovered on this ground; and

(b) at some time within the period of twelve months ending with the beginning of the tenancy, the dwelling-house was occupied under a right to occupy it for a holiday.

Ground 4

The tenancy is a fixed term tenancy for a term not exceeding twelve months and –

(a) not later than the beginning of the tenancy the landlord gave notice in writing to the tenant that possession might be recovered on this ground; and

(b) at some time within the period of twelve months ending with the beginning of the tenancy, the dwelling-house was let on a tenancy falling within paragraph 8 of Schedule 1 to this Act.

Ground 5

The dwelling-house is held for the purpose of being available for occupation by a minister of religion as a residence from which to perform the duties of his office and –

(a) not later than the beginning of the tenancy the landlord gave notice in writing to the tenant that possession might be recovered on this ground; and

(b) the court is satisfied that the dwelling-house is required for occupation by a minister of religion as such a residence.

Ground 6

[Landlord intends to demolish or reconstruct.]

Ground 7

The tenancy is a periodic tenancy (including a statutory periodic tenancy) which has devolved under the will or intestacy of the former tenant and the proceedings for the recovery of possession are begun not later than twelve months after the death of the former tenant or, if the court so directs, after the date on which, in the opinion of the court, the landlord or, in the case of joint landlords, any one of them became aware of the former tenant's death.

For the purposes of this ground, the acceptance by the landlord of rent from a new tenant after the death of the former tenant shall not be regarded as creating a new periodic tenancy, unless the landlord agrees in writing to a change (as compared with the tenancy before the death) in the amount of the rent, the period of the tenancy, the premises which are let or any other term of the tenancy.

Ground 8

Both at the date of the service of the notice under section 8 of this Act relating to the proceedings for possession and at the date of the hearing –

(a) if rent is payable weekly or fortnightly, at least eight weeks' rent is unpaid;

(b) if rent is payable monthly, at least two months' rent is unpaid;

(c) if rent is payable quarterly, at least one quarter's rent is more than three months in arrears; and

(d) if rent is payable yearly, at least three months' rent is more than three months in arrears;

and for the purpose of this ground 'rent' means rent lawfully due from the tenant.

Part II

GROUNDS ON WHICH COURT MAY ORDER POSSESSION

Ground 9

Suitable alternative accommodation is available for the tenant or will be available for him when the order for possession takes effect.

Ground 10

Some rent lawfully due from the tenant –

(a) is unpaid on the date on which the proceedings for possession are begun; and

(b) except where subsection (1)(b) of section 8 of this Act applies, was in arrears at the date of the service of the notice under that section relating to those proceedings.

Ground 11

Whether or not any rent is in arrears on the date on which proceedings for possession are begun, the tenant has persistently delayed paying rent which has become lawfully due.

Ground 12

Any obligation of the tenancy (other than one related to the payment of rent) has been broken or not performed.

Ground 13

The condition of the dwelling-house or any of the common parts has deteriorated owing to acts of waste by, or the neglect or default of, the tenant or any other person residing in the dwelling-house and, in the case of an act of waste by, or the neglect or default of, a person lodging with the tenant or a sub-tenant of his, the tenant has not taken such steps as he ought reasonably to have taken for the removal of the lodger or sub-tenant.

For the purposes of this ground, 'common parts' means any part of a building comprising the dwelling-house and any other premises which the tenant is entitled under the terms of the tenancy to use in common with the occupiers of other dwelling-houses in which the landlord has an estate or interest.

Ground 14

The tenant or a person residing in or visiting the dwelling-house –

(a) has been guilty of conduct causing or likely to cause a nuisance or annoyance to a person residing, visiting or otherwise engaging in a lawful activity in the locality, or

(b) has been convicted of –

(i) using the dwelling-house or allowing it to be used for immoral or illegal purposes, or

(ii) an arrestable offence committed in, or in the locality of, the dwelling-house.

Ground 14A

The dwelling-house was occupied (whether alone or with others) by a married couple or a couple living together as husband and wife and –

(a) one or both of the partners is a tenant of the dwelling-house,

(b) the landlord who is seeking possession is a registered social landlord or a charitable housing trust,

(c) one partner has left the dwelling-house because of violence or threats of violence by the other towards –

(i) that partner, or

(ii) a member of the family of that partner who was residing with that partner immediately before the partner left, and

(d) the court is satisfied that the partner who has left is unlikely to return.

For the purposes of this ground 'registered social landlord' and 'member of the family' have the same meaning as in Part I of the Housing Act 1996 and 'charitable housing trust' means a housing trust, within the meaning of the Housing Associations Act 1985, which is a charity within the meaning of the Charities Act 1993.

Ground 15

The condition of any furniture provided for use under the tenancy has, in the opinion of the court, deteriorated owing to ill-treatment by the tenant or any other person residing in the dwelling-house and, in the case of ill-treatment by a person lodging with the tenant or by a sub-tenant of his, the tenant has not taken such steps as he ought reasonably to have taken for the removal of the lodger or sub-tenant.

Ground 16

The dwelling-house was let to the tenant in consequence of his employment by the landlord seeking possession or a previous landlord under the tenancy and the tenant has ceased to be in that employment.

For the purposes of this ground, at a time when the landlord is or was the Secretary of State, employment by a health service body, as defined in section 60(7) of the National Health Service and Community Care Act 1990, or by a Local Health Board, shall be regarded as employment by the Secretary of State.

Ground 17

The tenant is the person, or one of the persons, to whom the tenancy was granted and the landlord was induced to grant the tenancy by a false statement made knowingly or recklessly by –

(a) the tenant, or

(b) a person acting at the tenant's instigation.

PART III

SUITABLE ALTERNATIVE ACCOMMODATION

1. For the purposes of Ground 9 above, a certificate of the local housing authority for the district in which the dwelling-house in question is situated, certifying that the authority will provide suitable alternative accommodation for the tenant by a date specified in the certificate, shall be conclusive evidence that suitable alternative accommodation will be available for him by that date.

2. Where no such certificate as is mentioned in paragraph 1 above is produced to the court, accommodation shall be deemed to be suitable for the purposes of Ground 9 above if it consists of either –

(a) premises which are to be let as a separate dwelling such that they will then be let on an assured tenancy, other than –

(i) a tenancy in respect of which notice is given not later than the beginning of the tenancy that possession might be recovered on any of Grounds 1 to 5 above, or

(ii) an assured shorthold tenancy, within the meaning of Chapter II of Part I of this Act, or

(b) premises to be let as a separate dwelling on terms which will, in the opinion of the court, afford to the tenant security of tenure reasonably equivalent to the security afforded by Chapter I of Part I of this Act in the case of an assured tenancy of a kind mentioned in sub-paragraph (a) above,

and, in the opinion of the court, the accommodation fulfils the relevant conditions as defined in paragraph 3 below.

3.– (1) For the purposes of paragraph 2 above, the relevant conditions are that the accommodation is reasonably suitable to the needs of the tenant and his family as regards proximity to place of work, and either –

(a) similar as regards rental and extent to the accommodation afforded by dwelling-houses provided in the neighbourhood by any local housing authority for persons whose needs as regards extent are, in the opinion of the court, similar to those of the tenant and of family; or

(b) reasonably suitable to the means of the tenant and to the needs of the tenant and his family as regards extent and character; and

that if any furniture was provided for use under the assured tenancy in question, furniture is provided for use in the accommodation which is either similar to that so provided or is reasonable to the needs of the tenant and his family ...

SCHEDULE 2A

ASSURED TENANCIES: NON-SHORTHOLDS

Tenancies excluded by notice

1. – (1) An assured tenancy in respect of which a notice is served as mentioned in sub-paragraph (2) below.

(2) The notice referred to in sub-paragraph (1) above is one which –

(a) is served before the assured tenancy is entered into,

(b) is served by the person who is to be the landlord under the assured tenancy on the person who is to be the tenant under that tenancy, and

(c) states that the assured tenancy to which it relates is not to be an assured shorthold tenancy.

2. – (1) An assured tenancy in respect of which a notice is served as mentioned in sub-paragraph (2) below.

(2) The notice referred to in sub-paragraph (1) above is one which –

(a) is served after the assured tenancy has been entered into,

(b) is served by the landlord under the assured tenancy on the tenant under that tenancy, and

(c) states that the assured tenancy to which it relates is no longer an assured shorthold tenancy.

Tenancies containing exclusionary provision

3. An assured tenancy which contains a provision to the effect that the tenancy is not an assured shorthold tenancy.

Tenancies under section 39

4. An assured tenancy arising by virtue of section 39 [statutory tenants: succession] above, other than one to which subsection (7) of that section applies.

Former secure tenancies

5. An assured tenancy which became an assured tenancy on ceasing to be a secure tenancy.

Former demoted tenancies

5A. An assured tenancy which ceases to be an assured shorthold tenancy by virtue of section 20B(2) or (4).

Tenancies under Schedule 10 to the Local Government and Housing Act 1989

6. An assured tenancy arising by virtue of Schedule 10 to the Local Government and Housing Act 1989 (security of tenure on ending of long residential tenancies).

Tenancies replacing non-shortholds

7. – (1) An assured tenancy which –

(a) is granted to a person (alone or jointly with others) who, immediately before the tenancy was granted, was the tenant (or, in the case of joint tenants, one of the tenants) under an assured tenancy other than a shorthold tenancy ('the old tenancy'),

(b) is granted (alone or jointly with others) by a person who was at that time the landlord (or one of the joint landlords) under the old tenancy, and

(c) is not one in respect of which a notice is served as mentioned in sub-paragraph (2) below.

(2) The notice referred to in sub-paragraph (1)(c) above is one which –

(a) is in such form as may be prescribed,

(b) is served before the assured tenancy is entered into,

(c) is served by the person who is to be the tenant under the assured tenancy on the person who is to be the landlord under that tenancy (or, in the case of joint landlords, on at least one of the persons who are to be joint landlords), and

(d) states that the assured tenancy to which it relates is to be a shorthold tenancy.

8. An assured tenancy which comes into being by virtue of section 5 above on the coming to an end of an assured tenancy which is not a shorthold tenancy.

Assured agricultural occupancies

9. – (1) An assured tenancy –

(a) in the case of which the agricultural worker condition is, by virtue of any provision of Schedule 3 to this Act, for the time being fulfilled with respect to the dwelling-house subject to the tenancy, and

(b) which does not fall within sub-paragraph (2) or (4) below.

(2) An assured tenancy falls within this sub-paragraph if –

(a) before it is entered into, a notice –

(i) in such form as may be prescribed, and

(ii) stating that the tenancy is to be a shorthold tenancy,

is served by the person who is to be the landlord under the tenancy on the person who is to be the tenant under it, and

(b) it is not an excepted tenancy.

(3) For the purposes of sub-paragraph (2)(b) above, an assured tenancy is an excepted tenancy if –

(a) the person to whom it is granted or, as the case may be, at least one of the persons to whom it is granted was, immediately before it is granted, a tenant or licensee under an assured agricultural occupancy, and

(b) the person by whom it is granted or, as the case may be, at least one of the persons by whom it is granted was, immediately before it is granted, a landlord or licensor under the assured agricultural occupancy referred to in paragraph (a) above.

(4) An assured tenancy falls within this sub-paragraph if it comes into being by virtue of section 5 above on the coming to an end of a tenancy falling within sub-paragraph (2) above.

NB On 1 May 2005 the amendments made by the Anti-social Behaviour Act 2003 (see below were not in force in Wales, save for the power to make regulations.

As amended by the Local Government and Housing Act 1989, s194(1), Schedule 11, paras 101–106; National Health Service and Community Care Act 1990, s60, Schedule 8, Pt II, para 10; References to Rating (Housing) Regulations 1990, reg 2, Schedule, paras 27, 29, 30; Local Government Finance (Housing) (Consequential Amendments) Order 1993, art 2(1), Schedule 1, para 19; Local Government (Wales) Act 1994 ss22(2), 39(2), Schedule 8, para 9(2), Schedule 13, para 31; Police and Magistrates' Courts Act 1994, s43, Schedule 4, Pt II, para 62; Agricultural Tenancies Act 1995, s40, Schedule, para 34; Environment Act 1995, s78, Schedule 10, para 28; Police Act 1996, s103(1), Schedule 7, Pt I, para 1(1), (2)(ZC); Housing Act 1996, ss96, 99–102, 104, 148, 149, 227, Schedule 8, para 2(1), (3), (4), (7), Schedule 19, Pts IV, VIII; Housing Act 1996 (Consequential Provisions) Order 1996, art 5, Schedule 2, para 18(1)–(3); Government of Wales Act 1998, ss129(2), 131, 140(1), 152, Schedule 15, para 15, Schedule 16, paras 59, 60, Schedule 18, Pt IV; Government of Wales Act 1998 (Housing) (Amendments) Order 1999, art 2, Schedule, para 3(1)–(4); Greater London Authority Act 1999, ss325, 328(8), Schedule 27, para 59, Schedule 29, Pt I, para 53; Immigration and Asylum Act 1999, s169(1), Schedule 14, para 88; Police Reform Act 2002, ss100(2), 107, Schedule 8; National Health Service Reform and Health Care Professions Act 2002, s6(2), Schedule 5, para 28; Anti-social Behaviour Act 2003, ss14(4), 15(1)–(3).

LAW OF PROPERTY (MISCELLANEOUS PROVISIONS) ACT 1989

(1989 c 34)

1 Deeds and their execution

(1) Any rule of law which –

(a) restricts the substances on which a deed may be written;

(b) requires a seal for the valid execution of an instrument as a deed by an individual; or

(c) requires authority by one person to another to deliver an instrument as a deed on his behalf to be given by deed,

is abolished.

(2) An instrument shall not be a deed unless –

(a) it makes it clear on its face that it is intended to be a deed by the person making it or, as the case may be, by the parties to it (whether by describing itself as a deed or expressing itself to be executed or signed as a deed or otherwise); and

(b) it is validly executed as a deed by that person or, as the case may be, one or more of those parties.

(3) An instrument is validly executed as a deed by an individual if, and only if –

(a) it is signed –

(i) by him in the presence of a witness who attests the signature; or

(ii) at his direction and in his presence and the presence of two witnesses who each attest the signature; and

(b) it is delivered as a deed by him or a person authorised to do so on his behalf.

(4) In subsections (2) and (3) above 'sign', in relation to an instrument, includes making one's mark on the instrument and 'signature' is to be construed accordingly.

(5) Where a solicitor, duly certificated notary public or licensed conveyancer, or an agent or employee of a solicitor, duly certificated notary public or licensed conveyancer, in the course of or in connection with a transaction involving the disposition or creation of an interest in land, purports to deliver an instrument as a deed on behalf of a party to the instrument, it shall be conclusively presumed in favour of a purchaser that he is authorised so to deliver the instrument.

(6) In subsection (5) above –

'disposition' and 'purchaser' have the same meanings as in the Law of Property Act 1925;

'duly certificated notary public' has the same meaning as it has in the Solicitors Act 1974 by virtue of section 87 of that Act; and

'interest in land' means any estate, interest or charge in or over land.

(7) Where an instrument under seal that constitutes a deed is required for the purposes of an Act passed before this section comes into force, this section shall have effect as to signing, sealing or delivery of an instrument by an individual in place of any provision of that Act as to signing, sealing or delivery.

(9) Nothing in subsection (1)(b), (2), (3), (7) or (8) above applies in relation to deeds required or authorised to be made under –

(a) the seal of the County Palatine of Lancaster;

(b) the seal of the Duchy of Lancaster; or

(c) the seal of the Duchy of Cornwall.

(10) The references in this section to the execution of a deed by an individual do not include execution by a corporation sole and the reference in subsection (7) above to signing, sealing or delivery by an individual does not include signing, sealing or delivery by such a corporation.

(11) Nothing in this section applies in relation to instruments delivered as deeds before this section comes into force.

2   Contracts for sale, etc of land to be made by signed writing

(1) A contract for the sale or other disposition of an interest in land can only be made in writing and only by incorporating all the terms which the parties have expressly agreed in one document or, where contracts are exchanged, in each.

(2) The terms may be incorporated in a document either by being set out in it or by reference to some other document.

(3) The document incorporating the terms or, where contracts are exchanged, one of the documents incorporating them (but not necessarily the same one) must be signed by or on behalf of each party to the contract.

(4) Where a contract for the sale or other disposition of an interest in land satisfies the conditions of this section by reason only of the rectification of one or more documents in pursuance of an order of a court, the contract shall come into being, or be deemed to have come into being, at such time as may be specified in the order.

(5) This section does not apply in relation to –

(a) a contract to grant such a lease as is mentioned in section 54(2) of the Law of Property Act 1925 (short leases);

(b) a contract made in the course of a public auction; or

(c) a contract regulated under the Financial Services and Markets Act 2002, other than a regulated mortgage contract;

and nothing in this section affects the creation or operation of resulting, implied or constructive trusts.

(6) In this section –

'disposition' has the same meaning as in the Law of Property Act 1925;

'interest in land' means any estate, interest or charge in or over land;

'regulated mortgage contract' must be read with –

(a) section 22 of the Financial Services and Markets Act 2000,

(b) any relevant order under that section, and

(c) Schedule 22 to that Act.

(7) Nothing in this section shall apply in relation to contracts made before this section comes into force.

(8) Section 40 of the Law of Property Act 1925 (which is superseded by this section) shall cease to have effect.

NB The repeal of s40 of the Law of Property Act 1925 took effect on 27 September 1989.

As amended by the Courts and Legal Services Act 1990, s125(2), Schedule 17, para 20(1), (2); Trusts of Land and Appointment of Trustees Act 1996, s25(2), Schedule 4; Financial Services and Markets Act 2000 (Consequential Amendments and Repeals) Order 2001, art 317.

LOCAL GOVERNMENT AND HOUSING ACT 1989

(1989 c 42)

186 Security of tenure on ending of long residential tenancies

(1) Schedule 10 to this Act shall have effect (in place of Part I of the Landlord and Tenant Act 1954) to confer security of tenure on certain tenants under long tenancies and, in particular, to establish assured periodic tenancies when such long tenancies come to an end.

(2) Schedule 10 to this Act applies, and section 1 of the Landlord and Tenant Act 1954 does not apply, to a tenancy of a dwelling-house –

(a) which is a long tenancy at a low rent, as defined in Schedule 10 to this Act; and

(b) which is entered into on or after the day appointed for the coming into force of this section, otherwise than in pursuance of a contract made before that day.

(3) If a tenancy –

(a) is in existence on 15th January 1999, and

(b) does not fall within subsection (2) above, and

(c) immediately before that date was, or was deemed to be, a long tenancy at a low rent for the purposes of Part I of the Landlord and Tenant Act 1954,

then, on and after that date (and so far as concerns any notice specifying a date of termination on or after that date and any steps taken in consequence thereof), section 1 of that Act shall cease to apply to it and Schedule 10 to this Act shall apply to it unless, before that date, the landlord has served a notice under section 4 of that Act specifying a date of termination which is earlier than that date.

(4) The provisions of Schedule 10 to this Act have effect notwithstanding any agreement to the contrary, but nothing in this subsection or that Schedule shall be construed as preventing the surrender of a tenancy ...

(6) Where, by virtue of subsection (3) above, Schedule 10 to this Act applies to a tenancy which is not a long tenancy at a low rent as defined in that Schedule, it shall be deemed to be such a tenancy for the purposes of that Schedule.

SCHEDULE 10

SECURITY OF TENURE ON ENDING OF
LONG RESIDENTIAL TENANCIES

1– (1) This Schedule applies to a long tenancy of a dwelling-house at a low rent as respects which for the time being the following condition (in this Schedule referred to as 'the qualifying condition') is fulfilled, that is to say, that the circumstances (as respects the property let under the tenancy, the use of that property and all other relevant matters) are such that, if the tenancy were not at a low rent, it would at that time be an assured tenancy within the meaning of Part I of the Housing Act 1988.

(2) For the purpose only of determining whether the qualifying condition is fulfilled with respect to a tenancy, Schedule 1 to the Housing Act 1988 (tenancies which cannot be assured tenancies) shall have effect with the omission of paragraph 1 (which excludes tenancies entered into before, or pursuant to contracts made before, the coming into force of Part I of that Act) …

NB Section 186 above came into force on 1st April 1990.

TOWN AND COUNTRY PLANNING ACT 1990

(1990 c 8)

55 Meaning of 'development' and 'new development'

(1) Subject to the following provisions of this section, in this Act, except where the context otherwise requires, 'development' means the carrying out of building, engineering, mining or other operations in, on, over or under land, or the making of any material change in the use of any buildings or other land.

(1A) For the purposes of this Act 'building operations' includes –

(a) demolition of buildings;

(b) rebuilding;

(c) structural alterations of or additions to buildings; and

(d) other operations normally undertaken by a person carrying on business as a builder.

(2) The following operations or uses of land shall not be taken for the purposes of this Act to involve development of the land –

(a) the carrying out for the maintenance, improvement or other alteration of any building of works which –

(i) affect only the interior of the building, or

(ii) do not materially affect the external appearance of the building,

and are not works for making good war damage or works begun after 5th December 1968 for the alteration of a building by providing additional space in it underground;

(b) the carrying out on land within the boundaries of a road by a local highway authority of any works required for the maintenance or improvement of the road but, in the case of any such works which are not exclusively for the maintenance of the road, not including any works which may have significant adverse effects on the environment;

(c) the carrying out by a local authority or statutory undertakers of any works for the purpose of inspecting, repairing or renewing any sewers, mains, pipes, cables or other apparatus, including the breaking open of any street or other land for that purpose;

(d) the use of any building or other land within the curtilage of a dwelling-house for any purpose incidental to the enjoyment of the dwelling-house as such;

(e) the use of any land for the purposes of agriculture or forestry (including afforestation) and the use for any of those purposes of any building occupied together with land so used;

(f) in the case of buildings or other land which are used for a purpose of any class specified in an order made by the Secretary of State under this section, the use of the buildings or other land or, subject to the provisions of the order, of any part of the buildings or the other land, for any other purpose of the same class.

(g) the demolition of any description of building specified in a direction given by the Secretary of State to local planning authorities generally or to a particular local planning authority.

(3) For the avoidance of doubt it is hereby declared that for the purposes of this section –

(a) the use as two or more separate dwelling-houses of any building previously used as a single dwelling-house involves a material change in the use of the building and of each part of it which is so used;

(b) the deposit of refuse or waste materials on land involves a material change in its use, notwithstanding that the land is comprised in a site already used for that purpose, if –

(i) the superficial area of the deposit is extended, or

(ii) the height of the deposit is extended and exceeds the level of the land adjoining the site.

(4) For the purposes of this Act mining operations include –

(a) the removal of material of any description –

(i) from a mineral-working deposit;

(ii) from a deposit of pulverised fuel ash or other furnace ash or clinker; or

(iii) from a deposit of iron, steel or other metallic slags; and

(b) the extraction of minerals from a disused railway embankment.

(4A) Where the placing or assembly of any tank in any part of any inland waters for the purpose of fish farming there would not, apart from this subsection, involve development of the land below, this Act shall have effect as if the tank resulted from carrying out engineering operations over that land; and in this subsection –

'fish farming' means the breeding, rearing or keeping of fish or shellfish (which includes any kind of crustacean and mollusc));

'inland waters' means waters which do not form part of the sea or of any creek, bay or estuary or of any river as far as the tide flows; and

'tank' includes any cage and any other structure for use in fish farming.

(5) Without prejudice to any regulations made under the provisions of this Act relating to the control of advertisements, the use for the display of advertisements

of any external part of a building which is not normally used for that purpose shall be treated for the purposes of this section as involving a material change in the use of that part of the building.

57   Planning permission required for development

(1) Subject to the following provisions of this section, planning permission is required for the carrying out of any development of land.

(2) Where planning permission to develop land has been granted for a limited period, planning permission is not required for the resumption, at the end of that period, of its use for the purpose for which it was normally used before the permission was granted.

(3) Where by a development order planning permission to develop land has been granted subject to limitations, planning permission is not required for the use of that land which (apart from its use in accordance with that permission) is its normal use.

(4) Where an enforcement notice has been issued in respect of any development of land, planning permission is not required for its use for the purpose for which (in accordance with the provisions of this Part of this Act) it could lawfully have been used if that development had not been carried out.

(5) In determining for the purposes of subsections (2) and (3) what is or was the normal use of land, no account shall be taken of any use begun in contravention of this Part or of previous planning control.

(6) For the purposes of this section a use of land shall be taken to have begun in contravention of previous planning control if it was begun in contravention of Part III of the [Town and Country Planning Act 1947], Part III of the [Town and Country Planning Act 1962] or Part III of the [Town and Country Planning Act 1971].

(7) Subsection (1) has effect subject to Schedule 4 (which makes special provision about use of land on 1st July 1948).

58   Granting of planning permission: general

(1) Planning permission may be granted –

   (a) by a development order;

   (b) by the local planning authority (or, in the cases provided in this Part, by the Secretary of State) on application to the authority in accordance with a development order;

   (c) on the adoption or approval of a simplified planning zone scheme or alterations to such a scheme in accordance with section 82 or, as the case may be, section 86; or

   (d) on the designation of an enterprise zone or the approval of a modified scheme under Schedule 32 to the Local Government, Planning and Land Act 1980 in accordance with section 88 of this Act.

(2) Planning permission may also be deemed to be granted under section 90 (development with government authorisation).

(3) This section is without prejudice to any other provisions of this Act providing for the granting of permission.

59 Development orders: general

(1) The Secretary of State shall by order (in this Act referred to as a 'development order') provide for the granting of planning permission.

(2) A development order may either –

(a) itself grant planning permission for development specified in the order or for development of any class specified; or

(b) in respect of development for which planning permission is not granted by the order itself, provide for the granting of planning permission by the local planning authority (or, in the cases provided in the following provisions, by the Secretary of State) on application to the authority in accordance with the provisions of the order.

(3) A development order may be made either –

(a) as a general order applicable, except so far as the order otherwise provides, to all land, or

(b) as a special order applicable only to such land or descriptions of land as may be specified in the order.

62 Form and content of applications for planning permission

Any application to a local planning authority for planning permission –

(a) shall be made in such manner as may be prescribed by regulations under this Act; and

(b) shall include such particulars and be verified by such evidence as may be required by the regulations or by directions given by the local planning authority under them.

70 Determination of applications: general considerations

(1) Where an application is made to a local planning authority for planning permission –

(a) subject to sections 91 and 92, they may grant planning permission, either unconditionally or subject to such conditions as they think fit; or

(b) they may refuse planning permission.

(2) In dealing with such an application the authority shall have regard to the provisions of the development plan, so far as material to the application, and to any other material considerations.

(3) Subsection (1) has effect subject to section 65 and to the following provisions of this Act, to sections 66, 67, 72 and 73 of the Planning (Listed Buildings and Conservation Areas) Act 1990 and to section 15 of the Health Services Act 1976.

70A Power of local planning authority to decline to determine applications

(1) A local planning authority may decline to determine an application for planning permission for the development of any land if –

(a) within the period of two years ending with the date on which the application is received, the Secretary of State has refused a similar application referred to him under section 77 or has dismissed an appeal against the refusal of a similar application; and

(b) in the opinion of the authority there has been no significant change since the refusal or, as the case may be, dismissal mentioned in paragraph (a) in the development plan, so far as material to the application, or in any other material considerations.

(2) For the purposes of this section an application for planning permission for the development of any land shall only be taken to be similar to a later application if the development and the land to which the applications relate are in the opinion of the local planning authority the same or substantially the same.

(3) The reference in subsection (1)(a) to an appeal against the refusal of an application includes an appeal under section 78(2) in respect of an application.

106 Planning obligations

(1) Any person interested in land in the area of a local planning authority may, by agreement or otherwise, enter into an obligation (referred to in this section and sections 106A and 106B as 'a planning obligation'), enforceable to the extent mentioned in subsection (3) –

(a) restricting the development or use of the land in any specified way;

(b) requiring specified operations or activities to be carried out in, on, under or over the land;

(c) requiring the land to be used in any specified way; or

(d) requiring a sum or sums to be paid to the authority on a specified date or dates or periodically.

(2) A planning obligation may –

(a) be unconditional or subject to conditions;

(b) impose any restriction or requirement mentioned in subsection (1)(a) to (c) either indefinitely or for such period or periods as may be specified; and

(c) if it requires a sum or sums to be paid, require the payment of a specified amount or an amount determined in accordance with the instrument by which the obligation is entered into and, if it requires the payment of periodical sums, require them to be paid indefinitely or for a specified period.

(3) Subject to subsection (4) a planning obligation is enforceable by the authority identified in accordance with subsection (9)(d) –

(a) against the person entering into the obligation; and

(b) against any person deriving title from that person.

(4) The instrument by which a planning obligation is entered into may provide that a person shall not be bound by the obligation in respect of any period during which he no longer has an interest in the land ...

(11) A planning obligation shall be a local land charge and for the purposes of the Local Land Charges Act 1975 the authority by whom the obligation is enforceable shall be treated as the originating authority as respects such a charge ...

(13) In this section 'specified' means specified in the instrument by which the planning obligation is entered into and in this section and section 106A [modification and discharge of planning obligations] 'land' has the same meaning as in the Local Land Charges Act 1975.

242 Overriding of rights of possession

If the Secretary of State certifies that possession of a house which –

(a) has been acquired or appropriated by a local authority for planning purposes, and

(b) is for the time being held by the authority for the purposes for which it was acquired or appropriated,

is immediately required for those purposes, nothing in the Rent Act 1977 or Part I of the Housing Act 1988 shall prevent the acquiring or appropriating authority from obtaining possession of the house.

328 Settled land ...

(1) The purposes authorised for the application of capital money –

(a) by section 73 of the Settled Land Act 1925 ...

shall include the payment of any sum recoverable under section 111 or 112 [compensation on subsequent development].

(2) The purposes authorised as purposes for which money may be raised by mortgage –

(a) by section 71 of the Settled Land Act 1925 ...

shall include the payment of any sum so recoverable.

As amended by the Planning and Compensation Act 1991, ss12(1), 13(1), (2), 14(1), 17(1), 31(4), 84(6), Schedule 6, paras 8, 9, 37, Schedule 19, Pts I, II; Trusts of Land and Appointment of Trustees Act 1996, s25(2), Schedule 4; Town and Country Planning (Environmental Impact Assessment) (England and Wales) Regulations 1999, reg 35(1).

PLANNING (LISTED BUILDINGS AND CONSERVATION AREAS) ACT 1990
(1990 c 9)

1 Listing of buildings of special architectural or historic interest

(1) For the purposes of this Act and with a view to the guidance of local planning authorities in the performance of their functions under this Act and the [Town and Country Planning Act 1990] in relation to buildings of special architectural or historic interest, the Secretary of State shall compile lists of such buildings, or approve, with or without modifications, such lists compiled by the Historic Buildings and Monuments Commission for England (in this Act referred to as 'the Commission') or by other persons or bodies of persons, and may amend any list so compiled or approved ...

(5) In this Act 'listed building' means a building which is for the time being included in a list compiled or approved by the Secretary of State under this section; and for the purposes of this Act –

(a) any object or structure fixed to the building;

(b) any object or structure within the curtilage of the building which, although not fixed to the building, forms part of the land and has done so since before 1st July 1948,

shall be treated as part of the building ...

72 General duty as respects conservation areas in exercise of planning functions

(1) In the exercise, with respect to any buildings or other land in a conservation area, of any functions under or by virtue of any of the provisions mentioned in subsection (2), special attention shall be paid to the desirability of preserving or enhancing the character or appearance of that area.

(2) The provisions referred to in subsection (1) are the planning Acts and Part I of the Historic Buildings and Ancient Monuments Act 1953 and sections 70 and 73 of the Leasehold Reform, Housing and Urban Development Act 1993.

(3) In subsection (2), references to provisions of the Leasehold Reform, Housing and Urban Development Act 1993 include reference to those provisions as they have effect by virtue of section 118(1) of the Housing Act 1996.

87   Settled land

The classes of works specified in Part II of Schedule 3 to the Settled Land Act 1925 (which specifies improvements which may be paid for out of capital money, subject to provisions under which repayment out of income may be required to be made) shall include works specified by the Secretary of State as being required for properly maintaining a listed building which is settled land within the meaning of that Act.

As amended by the Leasehold Reform, Housing and Urban Development Act 1993, s187(1), Schedule 21, para 30; Housing Act 1996, s118(7).

WATER RESOURCES ACT 1991
(1991 c 57)

24   Restrictions on abstraction

(1) Subject to the following provisions of this Chapter [Chapter II] and to any drought order or drought permit under Chapter III of this Part, no person shall –

  (a) abstract water from any source of supply; or

  (b) cause or permit any other person so to abstract any water,

except in pursuance of a licence under this Chapter granted by the Agency and in accordance with the provision of that licence.

(2) Where by virtue of subsection (1) above the abstraction of water contained in any underground strata is prohibited except in pursuance of a licence under this Chapter, no person shall begin, or cause or permit any other person to begin –

  (a) to construct any well, borehole or other work by which water may be abstracted from those strata;

  (b) to extend any such well, borehole or other work; or

  (c) to install or modify any machinery or apparatus by which additional quantities of water may be abstracted from those strata by means of a well, borehole or other work,

unless the conditions specified in subsection (3) below are satisfied.

(3) The conditions mentioned in subsection (2) above are –

  (a) that the abstraction of the water or, as the case may be, of the additional quantities of water is authorised by a licence under this Chapter; and

  (b) that –

    (i) the well, borehole or work, as constructed or extended; or

    (ii) the machinery or apparatus, as installed or modified,

  fulfils the requirements of that licence as to the means by which water is authorised to be abstracted ...

(6) The restrictions imposed by this section shall have effect notwithstanding anything in any enactment contained in any Act passed before the passing of the Water Resources Act 1963 on 31st July 1963 or in any statutory provision made or issued, whether before or after the passing of that Act, by virtue of such an enactment.

27 Rights to abstract small quantities

(1) The restriction on abstraction shall not apply to any abstraction of a quantity of water not exceeding twenty cubic metres in any period of twenty-four hours, if the abstraction does not form part of a continuous operation, or of a series of operations, by which a quantity of water which, in aggregate, is more than twenty cubic metres is abstracted during the period.

(2) In the case of any abstraction of water from underground strata which falls within subsection (1) above, the restriction imposed by section 24(2) above shall not apply –

  (a) to the construction or extension of any well, borehole or other work; or

  (b) to the installation or modification of machinery or other apparatus,

if the well, borehole or other work is constructed or extended, or the machinery or apparatus is installed or modified, for the purpose of abstracting the water.

(3) Where a person is authorised by a licence under this Chapter to carry on a particular abstraction operation (or series of operations), this section does not permit him to carry it on beyond the authorisation conferred by the licence.

27A Variation of small quantity threshold

(1) The Secretary of State may by order made by statutory instrument provide that section 27(1) above is to have effect in relation to –

  (a) a geographical area; or

  (b) a class of inland waters; or

  (c) a class of underground strata; or

  (d) a class of inland waters or of underground strata within a geographical area,

(in each case as specified in the order) as if for 'twenty cubic metres' there were substituted another quantity specified in the order. ...

72 Interpretation of Chapter II

(1) In this Chapter –

  ...

  'the restriction on abstraction' means the restriction imposed by section 24(1) above; ...

  'spray irrigation' means (subject to subsection (5) below) the irrigation of land or plants (including seeds) by means of water or other liquid emerging (in whatever form) from apparatus designed or adapted to eject liquid into the air in the form of jets or spray; and

  'statutory provision' means a provision (whether of a general or special nature) which is contained in, or in any document made or issued under, any Act (whether of a general or special nature) ...

(4) For the purposes of this Chapter land shall be taken to be contiguous to any inland waters notwithstanding that it is separated from those waters by a towpath or by any other land used, or acquired for use, in connection with the navigation of the inland waters, unless that other land comprises any building or works other than a lock, pier, wharf, landing-stage or similar works.

(5) The Ministers may by order direct that references to spray irrigation in this Chapter, and in any other enactments in which 'spray irrigation' is given the same meaning as in this Chapter, or such of those references as may be specified in the order –

(a) shall be construed as not including spray irrigation if carried out by such methods or in such circumstances or for such purposes as may be specified in the order; and

(b) without prejudice to the exercise of the power conferred by virtue of paragraph (a) above, shall be construed as including references to the carrying out, by such methods or in such circumstances or for such purposes as may be specified in the order, of irrigation of any such description, other than spray irrigation, as may be so specified.

221 General interpretation

(1) In this Act, except in so far as the context otherwise requires – ...

'abstraction', in relation to water contained in any source of supply, means the doing of anything whereby any of that water is removed from that source of supply, whether temporarily or permanently, including anything whereby the water is so removed for the purpose of being transferred to another source of supply; and 'abstract' shall be construed accordingly; ...

'the Agency' means the Environment Agency;

'agriculture' has the same meaning as in the Agriculture Act 1947 and 'agricultural' shall be construed accordingly; ...

'inland waters' means the whole or any part of –

(a) any river, stream or other watercourse (within the meaning of Chapter II of Part II of this Act), whether natural or artificial and whether tidal or not;

(b) any lake or pond, whether natural or artificial, or any reservoir or dock, in so far as the lake, pond, reservoir or dock does not fall within paragraph (a) of this definition; and

(c) so much of any channel, creek, bay, estuary or arm of the sea as does not fall within paragraph (a) or (b) of this definition; ...

'source of supply' means –

(a) any inland waters except, without prejudice to subsection (3) below in its application to paragraph (b) of this definition, any which are discrete waters; or

(b) any underground strata in which water is or at any time may be contained; ...

'underground strata' means strata subjacent to the surface of any land; ...

As amended by the Environment Act 1995, s120, Schedule 22, paras 128, 177, Schedule 24; Environment Act 1995 (Consequential Amendments) Regulations 1996, reg 3, Schedule 2, para 8; Water Act 2003, s6(1).

ACCESS TO NEIGHBOURING LAND ACT 1992

(1992 c 23)

1 Access orders

(1) A person –

    (a) who, for the purpose of carrying out works to any land (the 'dominant land'), desires to enter upon any adjoining or adjacent land (the 'servient land'), and

    (b) who needs, but does not have, the consent of some other person to that entry,

may make an application to the court for an order under this section ('an access order') against that person.

(2) On an application under this section, the court shall make an access order if, and only if, it is satisfied –

    (a) that the works are reasonably necessary for the preservation of the whole or any part of the dominant land; and

    (b) that they cannot be carried out, or would be substantially more difficult to carry out, without entry upon the servient land;

but this subsection is subject to subsection (3) below.

(3) The court shall not make an access order in any case where it is satisfied that, were it to make such an order –

    (a) the respondent or any other person would suffer interference with, or disturbance of, his use or enjoyment of the servient land, or

    (b) the respondent, or any other person (whether of full age or capacity or not) in occupation of the whole or any part of the servient land, would suffer hardship,

to such a degree by reason of the entry (notwithstanding any requirement of this Act or any term or condition that may be imposed under it) that it would be unreasonable to make the order.

(4) Where the court is satisfied on an application under this section that it is reasonably necessary to carry out any basic preservation works to the dominant land, those works shall be taken for the purposes of this Act to be reasonably necessary for the preservation of the land; and in this subsection 'basic preservation works' means any of the following, that is to say –

(a) the maintenance, repair or renewal of any part of a building or other structure comprised in, or situate on, the dominant land;

(b) the clearance, repair or renewal of any drain, sewer, pipe or cable so comprised or situate;

(c) the treatment, cutting back, felling, removal or replacement of any hedge, tree, shrub or other growing thing which is so comprised and which is, or is in danger of becoming, damaged, diseased, dangerous, insecurely rooted or dead;

(d) the filling in, or clearance, of any ditch so comprised;

but this subsection is without prejudice to the generality of the works which may, apart from it, be regarded by the court as reasonably necessary for the preservation of any land.

(5) If the court considers it fair and reasonable in all the circumstances of the case, works may be regarded for the purposes of this Act as being reasonably necessary for the preservation of any land (or, for the purposes of subsection (4) above, as being basic preservation works which it is reasonably necessary to carry out to any land) notwithstanding that the works incidentally involve –

(a) the making of some alteration, adjustment or improvement to the land, or

(b) the demolition of the whole or any part of a building or structure comprised in or situate upon the land.

(6) Where any works are reasonably necessary for the preservation of the whole or any part of the dominant land, the doing to the dominant land of anything which is requisite for, incidental to, or consequential on, the carrying out of those works shall be treated for the purposes of this Act as the carrying out of works which are reasonably necessary for the preservation of that land; and references in this Act to works, or to the carrying out of works, shall be construed accordingly.

(7) Without prejudice to the generality of subsection (6) above, if it is reasonably necessary for a person to inspect the dominant land –

(a) for the purpose of ascertaining whether any works may be reasonably necessary for the preservation of the whole or any part of that land,

(b) for the purpose of making any map or plan, or ascertaining the course of any drain, sewer, pipe or cable, in preparation for, or otherwise in connection with, the carrying out of works which are so reasonably necessary, or

(c) otherwise in connection with the carrying out of any such works,

the making of such an inspection shall be taken for the purposes of this Act to be the carrying out to the dominant land of works which are reasonably necessary for the preservation of that land; and references in this Act to works, or to the carrying out of works, shall be construed accordingly.

3   Effect of access orders

(1) An access order requires the respondent, so far as he has power to do so, to permit the applicant or any of his associates to do anything which the applicant or

associate is authorised or required to do under or by virtue of the order or this section.

(2) Except as otherwise provided by or under this Act, an access order authorises the applicant or any of his associates, without the consent of the respondent, –

(a) to enter upon the servient land for the purpose of carrying out the specified works;

(b) to bring on to that land, leave there during the period permitted by the order and, before the end of that period, remove, such materials, plant and equipment as are reasonably necessary for the carrying out of those works; and

(c) to bring on to that land any waste arising from the carrying out of those works, if it is reasonably necessary to do so in the course of removing it from the dominant land;

but nothing in this Act or in any access order shall authorise the applicant or any of his associates to leave anything in, on or over the servient land (otherwise than in discharge of their duty to make good that land) after their entry for the purpose of carrying out works to the dominant land ceases to be authorised under or by virtue of the order.

(3) An access order requires the applicant –

(a) to secure that any waste arising from the carrying out of the specified works is removed from the servient land forthwith;

(b) to secure that, before the entry ceases to be authorised under or by virtue of the order, the servient land is, so far as reasonably practicable, made good; and

(c) to indemnify the respondent against any damage which may be caused to the servient land or any goods by the applicant or any of his associates which would not have been so caused had the order not been made;

but this subsection is subject to subsections (4) and (5) below.

(4) In making an access order, the court may vary or exclude, in whole or in part, –

(a) any authorisation that would otherwise be conferred by subsection (2)(b) or (c) above; or

(b) any requirement that would otherwise be imposed by subsection (3) above.

(5) Without prejudice to the generality of subsection (4) above, if the court is satisfied that it is reasonably necessary for any such waste as may arise from the carrying out of the specified works to be left on the servient land for some period before removal, the access order may, in place of subsection (3)(a) above, include provision –

(a) authorising the waste to be left on that land for such period as may be permitted by the order; and

(b) requiring the applicant to secure that the waste is removed before the end of that period.

(6) Where the applicant or any of his associates is authorised or required under or by virtue of an access order or this section to enter, or do any other thing, upon the servient land, he shall not (as respects that access order) be taken to be a trespasser from the beginning on account of his, or any other person's, subsequent conduct.

(7) For the purposes of this section, the applicant's 'associates' are such number of persons (whether or not servants or agents of his) whom he may reasonably authorise under this subsection to exercise the power of entry conferred by the access order as may be reasonably necessary for the carrying out the specified works.

4 Persons bound by access order, unidentified persons and bar on contracting out

(1) In addition to the respondent, an access order shall, subject to the provisions of the Land Charges Act 1972 and the Land Registration Act 2002, be binding on –

    (a) any of his successors in title to the servient land; and

    (b) any person who has an estate or interest in, or right over, the whole or any part of the servient land which was created after the making of the order and who derives his title to that estate, interest or right under the respondent;

and references to the respondent shall be construed accordingly.

(2) If and to the extent that the court considers it just and equitable to allow him to do so, a person on whom an access order becomes binding by virtue of subsection (1)(a) or (b) above shall be entitled, as respects anything falling to be done after the order becomes binding on him, to enforce the order or any of its terms or conditions as if he were the respondent, and references to the respondent shall be construed accordingly ...

(4) Any agreement, whenever made, shall be void if and to the extent that it would, apart from this subsection, prevent a person from applying for an access order or restrict his right to do so.

5 Registration of access orders and of applications for such orders ...

(4) In any case where –

    (a) an access order is discharged [by the court] under s6(1)(a) below, and

    (b) the order has been protected by an entry registered under the Land Charges Act 1972 or by a notice under the Land Registration Act 2002,

the court may by order direct that the entry or notice shall be cancelled.

(5) The rights conferred on a person by or under an access order shall not be capable of falling within paragraph 2 of Schedule 1 or 3 to the Land Registration Act 2002 (overriding status of interest of person in actual occupation).

(6) An application for an access order shall be regarded as a pending land action for the purposes of the Land Charges Act 1972 and the Land Registration Act 2002.

8   Interpretation and application

(1) Any reference in this Act to an 'entry' upon any servient land includes a reference to the doing on that land of anything necessary for carrying out the works to the dominant land which are reasonably necessary for its preservation; and 'enter' shall be construed accordingly.

(2) This Act applies in relation to any obstruction of, or other interference with, a right over, or interest in, any land as it applies in relation to an entry upon that land; and 'enter' and 'entry' shall be construed accordingly.

(3) In this Act –

'access order' has the meaning given by section 1(1) above;

'applicant' means a person making an application for an access order and, subject to section 4 above, 'the respondent' means the respondent, or any of the respondents, to such an application;

'the court' means the High Court or a county court;

'the dominant land' and 'the servient land' respectively have the meanings given by section 1(1) above, but subject, in the case of servient land, to section 2(1) above;

'land' does not include a highway;

'the specified works' means the works specified in the access order in pursuance of section 2(1)(a) above.

As amended by the Land Registration Act 2002, ss 133, 135, Schedule 11, para 26, Schedule 13.

CHARITIES ACT 1993
(1993 c 10)

35 Application of provisions to trust corporations appointed under s16 or 18

(1) In the definition of 'trust corporation' contained in the following provisions –

 (a) section 117(xxx) of the Settled Land Act 1925,

 (b) section 68(18) of the Trustee Act 1925,

 (c) section 205(xxviii) of the Law of Property Act 1925,

 (d) section 55(xxvi) of the Administration of Estates Act 1925 ...

the reference to a corporation appointed by the court in any particular case to be a trustee includes a reference to a corporation appointed by the Commissioners under this Act to be a trustee ...

36 Restrictions on dispositions

(1) Subject to the following provisions of this section and section 40 below, no land held by or in trust for a charity shall be sold, leased or otherwise disposed of without an order of the court or of the Commissioners.

(2) Subsection (1) above shall not apply to a disposition of such land if –

 (a) the disposition is made to a person who is not –

 (i) a connected person (as defined in Schedule 5 to this Act), or

 (ii) a trustee for, or nominee of, a connected person; and

 (b) the requirements of subsection (3) or (5) below have been complied with in relation to it.

(3) Except where the proposed disposition is the granting of such a lease as is mentioned in subsection (5) below, the charity trustees must, before entering into an agreement for the sale, or (as the case may be) for a lease or other disposition, of the land –

 (a) obtain and consider a written report on the proposed disposition from a qualified surveyor instructed by the trustees and acting exclusively for the charity;

 (b) advertise the proposed disposition for such period and in such manner as the surveyor has advised in his report (unless he has there advised that it would not be in the best interests of the charity to advertise the proposed disposition); and

(c) decide that they are satisfied, having considered the surveyor's report, that the terms on which the disposition is proposed to be made are the best that can reasonably be obtained for the charity ...

(5) Where the proposed disposition is the granting of a lease for a term ending not more than seven years after it is granted (other than one granted wholly or partly in consideration of a fine), the charity trustees must, before entering into an agreement for the lease –

(a) obtain and consider the advice on the proposed disposition of a person who is reasonably believed by the trustees to have the requisite ability and practical experience to provide them with competent advice on the proposed disposition; and

(b) decide that they are satisfied, having considered that person's advice, that the terms on which the disposition is proposed to be made are the best that can reasonably be obtained for the charity ...

LEASEHOLD REFORM, HOUSING AND URBAN DEVELOPMENT ACT 1993

(1993 c 28)

PART I

LANDLORD AND TENANT

CHAPTER I

COLLECTIVE ENFRANCHISEMENT IN CASE OF TENANTS OF FLATS

1 The right to collective enfranchisement

(1) This Chapter has effect for the purpose of conferring the right to acquire the freehold of premises to which this Chapter applies on the relevant date, at a price determined in accordance with this Chapter, exercisable subject to and in accordance with this Chapter by a company (referred to in this Chapter as a RTE company) of which qualifying tenants of flats contained in the premises are members;

and that right is referred to in this Chapter as 'the right to collective enfranchisement'.

(2) Where the right to collective enfranchisement is exercised in relation to any such premises ('the relevant premises') –

(a) the RTE company by which the right to collective enfranchisement is exercised is entitled, subject to and in accordance with this Chapter, to acquire, in like manner, the freehold of any property which is not comprised in the relevant premises but to which this paragraph applies by virtue of subsection (3); and

(b) section 2 has effect with respect to the acquisition of leasehold interests to which paragraph (a) or (b) of subsection (1) of that section applies.

(3) Subsection (2)(a) applies to any property if at the relevant date either –

(a) it is appurtenant property which is demised by the lease held by a qualifying tenant of a flat contained in the relevant premises; or

(b) it is property which any such tenant is entitled under the terms of the lease of his flat to use in common with the occupiers of other premises (whether those premises are contained in the relevant premises or not).

(4) The right of acquisition in respect of the freehold of any such property as is mentioned in subsection (3)(b) shall, however, be taken to be satisfied with respect to that property if, on the acquisition of the relevant premises in pursuance of this Chapter, either –

(a) there are granted by the person who owns the freehold of that property –

(i) over that property, or

(ii) over any other property,

such permanent rights as will ensure that thereafter the occupier of the flat referred to in that provision has as nearly as may be the same rights as those enjoyed in relation to that property on the relevant date by the qualifying tenant under the terms of his lease; or

(b) there is acquired from the person who owns the freehold of that property the freehold of any other property over which any such permanent rights may be granted.

(5) A claim by a RTE company to exercise the right to collective enfranchisement may be made in relation to any premises to which this Chapter applies despite the fact that those premises are less extensive than the entirety of the premises in relation to which the RTE company is entitled to exercise that right.

(6) Any right or obligation under this Chapter to acquire any interest in property shall not extend to underlying minerals in which that interest subsists if –

(a) the owner of the interest requires the minerals to be excepted, and

(b) proper provision is made for the support of the property as it is enjoyed on the relevant date.

(7) In this section –

'appurtenant property', in relation to a flat, means any garage, outhouse, garden, yard or appurtenances belonging to, or usually enjoyed with, the flat;

'the relevant premises' means any such premises as are referred to in subsection (2).

(8) In this Chapter 'the relevant date', in relation to any claim to exercise the right to collective enfranchisement, means the date on which notice of the claim is given under section 13.

2   Acquisition of leasehold interests

(1) Where the right to collective enfranchisement is exercised by a RTE company in relation to any premises to which this Chapter applies ('the relevant premises'), then, subject to and in accordance with this Chapter –

(a) there shall be acquired by the RTE company every interest to which this paragraph applies by virtue of subsection (2); and

(b) the RTE company shall be entitled to acquire any interest to which this paragraph applies by virtue of subsection (3);

and any interest which the RTE company so acquires shall be acquired in the manner mentioned in section 1(1).

(2) Paragraph (a) of subsection (1) above applies to the interest of the tenant under any lease which is superior to the lease held by a qualifying tenant of a flat contained in the relevant premises.

(3) Paragraph (b) of subsection (1) above applies to the interest of the tenant under any lease (not falling within subsection (2) above) under which the demised premises consist of or include –

(a) any common parts of the relevant premises, or

(b) any property falling within section 1(2)(a) which is to be acquired by virtue of that provision,

where the acquisition of that interest is reasonably necessary for the proper management or maintenance of those common parts, or (as the case may be) that property ...

(7) In this section 'the relevant premises' means any such premises as are referred to in subsection (1).

3   Premises to which this Chapter applies

(1) Subject to section 4, this Chapter applies to any premises if –

(a) they consist of a self-contained building or part of a building;

(b) they contain two or more flats held by qualifying tenants; and

(c) the total number of flats held by such tenants is not less than two thirds of the total number of flats contained in the premises. ...

4   Premises excluded from right

(1) This Chapter does not apply to premises falling within section 3(1) if –

(a) any part or parts of the premises is or are neither –

(i) occupied, or intended to be occupied, for residential purposes, nor

(ii) comprised in any common parts of the premises; and

(b) the internal floor area of that part or of those parts (taken together) exceeds 25 per cent of the internal floor area of the premises (taken as a whole).

(2) Where in the case of any such premises any part of the premises (such as, for example, a garage, parking space or storage area) is used, or intended for use, in conjunction with a particular dwelling contained in the premises (and accordingly is not comprised in any common parts of the premises), it shall be taken to be occupied, or intended to be occupied, for residential purposes.

(3) For the purpose of determining the internal floor area of a building or of any part of a building, the floor or floors of the building or part shall be taken to extend (without interruption) throughout the whole of the interior of the building or part,

except that the area of any common parts of the building or part shall be disregarded.

(3A) Where different persons own the freehold of different parts of premises within subsection (1) of section 3, this Chapter does not apply to the premises if any of those parts is a self-contained part of a building for the purposes of that section.

(4) This Chapter does not apply to premises falling within section 3(1) if the premises are premises with a resident landlord and do not contain more than four units. ...

4A   RTE companies

(1) A company is a RTE company in relation to premises if –

(a) it is a private company limited by guarantee, and

(b) its memorandum of association states that its object, or one of its objects, is the exercise of the right to collective enfranchisement with respect to the premises.

(2) But a company is not a RTE company if it is a commonhold association (within the meaning of Part 1 of the Commonhold and Leasehold Reform Act 2002).

(3) And a company is not a RTE company in relation to premises if another company which is a RTE company in relation to –

(a) the premises, or

(b) any premises containing or contained in the premises,

has given a notice under section 13 with respect to the premises, or any premises containing or contained in the premises, and the notice continues in force in accordance with subsection (11) of that section.

4B   RTE companies: membership

(1) Before the execution of a relevant conveyance to a company which is a RTE company in relation to any premises the following persons are entitled to be members of the company –

(a) qualifying tenants of flats contained in the premises, and

(b) if the company is also a RTM company which has acquired the right to manage the premises, landlords under leases of the whole or any part of the premises.

(2) In this section –

'relevant conveyance' means a conveyance of the freehold of the premises or of any premises containing or contained in the premises; and

'RTM company' has the same meaning as in Chapter 1 of Part 2 of the Commonhold and Leasehold Reform Act 2002.

(3) On the execution of a relevant conveyance to the RTE company, any member of the company who is not a participating member ceases to be a member.

(4) In this Chapter 'participating member', in relation to a RTE company, means a person who is a member by virtue of subsection (1)(a) of this section and who-

(a) has given a participation notice to the company before the date when the company gives a notice under section 13 or during the participation period, or

(b) is a participating member by virtue of either of the following two subsections.

(5) A member who is the assignee of a lease by virtue of which a participating member was a qualifying tenant of his flat is a participating member if he has given a participation notice to the company within the period beginning with the date of the assignment and ending 28 days later (or, if earlier, on the execution of a relevant conveyance to the company).

(6) And if the personal representatives of a participating member are a member, they are a participating member if they have given a participation notice to the company at any time (before the execution of a relevant conveyance to the company). ...

5   Qualifying tenants

(1) Subject to the following provisions of this section, a person is a qualifying tenant of a flat for the purpose of this Chapter if he is tenant of the flat under a long lease.

(2) Subsection (1) does not apply where –

(a) the lease is a business lease; or

(b) the immediate landlord under the lease is a charitable housing trust and the flat forms part of the housing accommodation provided by it in the pursuit of its charitable purposes;

and in paragraph (b) 'charitable housing trust' means a housing trust within the meaning of the Housing Act 1985 which is a charity within the meaning of the Charities Act 1993.

(3) No flat shall have more than one qualifying tenant at any one time ...

7   Meaning of 'long lease'

(1) In this Chapter 'long lease' means (subject to the following provisions of this section) –

(a) a lease granted for a term of years certain exceeding 21 years, whether or not it is (or may become) terminable before the end of that term by notice given by or to the tenant or by re-entry, forfeiture or otherwise;

(b) a lease for a term fixed by law under a grant with a covenant or obligation for perpetual renewal (other than a lease by sub-demise from one which is not a long lease) or a lease taking effect under section 149(6) of the Law of Property Act 1925 (leases terminable after death or marriage or the formation of a civil partnership);

(c) a lease granted in pursuance of the right to buy conferred by Part V of the

Housing Act 1985 or in pursuance of the right to acquire on rent to mortgage terms conferred by that Part of that Act;

(d) a shared ownership lease, whether granted in pursuance of that Part of that Act or otherwise, where the tenant's total share is 100 per cent; or

(e) a lease granted in pursuance of that Part of that Act as it has effect by virtue of section 17 of the Housing Act 1996 (the right to acquire). ...

CHAPTER II

INDIVIDUAL RIGHT OF TENANT OF FLAT TO ACQUIRE NEW LEASE

39 Right of qualifying tenant of flat to acquire new lease

(1) This Chapter has effect for the purpose of conferring on a tenant of a flat, in the circumstances mentioned in subsection (2), the right, exercisable subject to and in accordance with this Chapter, to acquire a new lease of the flat on payment of a premium determined in accordance with this Chapter.

(2) Those circumstances are that on the relevant date for the purposes of this Chapter –

(a) the tenant has for the last two years been a qualifying tenant of the flat.

(3) The following provisions, namely –

(a) section 5 (with the omission of subsections (5) and (6)), and

(b) section 7,

shall apply for the purposes of this Chapter as they apply for the purposes of Chapter I; and references in this Chapter to a qualifying tenant of a flat shall accordingly be construed by reference to those provisions.

(3A) On the death of a person who has for the two years before his death been a qualifying tenant of a flat, the right conferrred by this Chapter is exercisable, subject to and in accordance with this Chapter, by his personal representatives; and, accordingly, in such a case references in this Chapter to the tenant shall, in so far as the context permits, be to the personal representatives.

(4) For the purposes of this Chapter a person can be (or be among those constituting) the qualifying tenant of each of two or more flats at the same time, whether he is tenant of those flats under one lease or under two or more separate leases.

(7) The right conferred by this Chapter on a tenant to acquire a new lease shall not extend to underlying minerals comprised in his existing lease if –

(a) the landlord requires the minerals to be excepted, and

(b) proper provision is made for the support of the premises demised by that existing lease as they are enjoyed on the relevant date.

(8) In this Chapter 'the relevant date', in relation to a claim by a tenant under this

Chapter, means the date on which notice of the claim is given to the landlord under section 42.

As amended by the Housing Act 1996, ss105(3)(a), 106, 107, 111(1), 112, 227, Schedule 9, para 3(1)–(3), 4(1), (2), Schedule 10, paras 1, 2, Schedule 19, Pt V; Housing Act 1996 (Consequential Amendments) (No 2) Order 1997, art 2, Schedule, para 7; Commonhold and Leasehold Reform Act 2002, ss115, 117(1), 122, 124, 130(1)–(3), 131, 132(1), 180, Schedule 8, paras 2, 3, Schedule 14; Civil Partnership Act 2004, s81, Schedule 8, para 47(1).

LAW OF PROPERTY (MISCELLANEOUS PROVISIONS) ACT 1994
(1994 c 36)

1   Covenants to be implied on a disposition of property

(1) In an instrument effecting or purporting to effect a disposition of property there shall be implied on the part of the person making the disposition, whether or not the disposition is for valuable consideration, such of the covenants specified in sections 2 to 5 as are applicable to the disposition.

(2) Of those sections –

(a) sections 2, 3(1) and (2), 4 and 5 apply where dispositions are expressed to be made with full title guarantee; and

(b) sections 2, 3(3), 4 and 5 apply where dispositions are expressed to be made with limited title guarantee.

(3) Sections 2 to 4 have effect subject to section 6 (no liability under covenants in certain cases); and sections 2 to 5 have effect subject to section 8(1) (limitation or extension of covenants by instrument effecting the disposition).

(4) In this Part –

'disposition' includes the creation of a term of years;

'instrument' includes an instrument which is not a deed; and

'property' includes a thing in action, and any interest in real or personal property.

2   Right to dispose and further assurance

(1) If the disposition is expressed to be made with full title guarantee or with limited title guarantee there shall be implied the following covenants –

(a) that the person making the disposition has the right (with the concurrence of any other person conveying the property) to dispose of the property as he purports to, and

(b) that that person will at his own cost do all that he reasonably can to give the person to whom he disposes of the property the title he purports to give.

(2) The latter obligation includes –

(a) in relation to a disposition of an interest in land the title to which is registered, doing all that he reasonably can to ensure that the person to whom the disposition is made is entitled to be registered as proprietor with at least the class of title registered immediately before the disposition; and

(b) in relation to a disposition of an interest in land the title to which is required to be registered by virtue of the disposition, giving all reasonable assistance fully to establish to the satisfaction of the Chief Land Registrar the right of the person to whom the disposition is made to registration as proprietor.

(3) In the case of a disposition of an existing legal interest in land, the following presumptions apply, subject to the terms of the instrument, in ascertaining for the purposes of the covenants implied by this section what the person making the disposition purports to dispose of –

(a) where the title to the interest is registered, it shall be presumed that the disposition is of the whole of that interest;

(b) where the title to the interest is not registered, then –

(i) if it appears from the instrument that the interest is a leasehold interest, it shall be presumed that the disposition is of the property for the unexpired portion of the term of years created by the lease; and

(ii) in any other case, it shall be presumed that what is disposed of is the fee simple.

3   Charges, incumbrances and third party rights

(1) If the disposition is expressed to be made with full title guarantee there shall be implied a covenant that the person making the disposition is disposing of the property free –

(a) from all charges and incumbrances (whether monetary or not), and

(b) from all other rights exercisable by third parties,

other than any charges, incumbrances or rights which that person does not and could not reasonably be expected to know about.

(2) In its application to charges, incumbrances and other third party rights subsection (1) extends to liabilities imposed and rights conferred by or under any enactment, except to the extent that such liabilities and rights are, by reason of –

(a) being, at the time of the disposition, only potential liabilities and rights in relation to the property, or

(b) being liabilities and rights imposed or conferred in relation to property generally,

not such as to constitute defects in title.

(3) If the disposition is expressed to be made with limited title guarantee there shall be implied a covenant that the person making the disposition has not since the last disposition for value –

(a) charged or incumbered the property by means of any charge or incumbrance which subsists at the time when the disposition is made, or granted third party rights in relation to the property which so subsists, or

(b) suffered the property to be so charged or incumbered or subjected to any such rights,

and that he is not aware that anyone else has done so since the last disposition for value.

4   Validity of lease

(1) Where the disposition is of leasehold land and is expressed to be made with full title guarantee or with limited title guarantee, the following covenants shall also be implied –

(a) that the lease is subsisting at the time of the disposition, and

(b) that there is no subsisting breach of a condition or tenant's obligation, and nothing which at that time would render the lease liable to forfeiture.

(2) If the disposition is the grant of an underlease, the references to 'the lease' in subsection (1) are references to the lease out of which the underlease is created.

5   Discharge of obligations where property subject to rentcharge or leasehold land

(1) Where the disposition is a mortgage of property subject to a rentcharge, of leasehold land or of a commonhold unit, and is expressed to be made with full title guarantee or with limited title guarantee, the following covenants shall also be implied.

(2) If the property is subject to a rentcharge, there shall be implied a covenant that the mortgagor will fully and promptly observe and perform all the obligations under the instrument creating the rentcharge that are for the time being enforceable with respect to the property by the owner of the rentcharge in his capacity as such.

(3) If the property is leasehold land, there shall be implied a covenant that the mortgagor will fully and promptly observe and perform all the obligations under the lease subject to the mortgage that are for the time being imposed on him in his capacity as tenant under the lease.

(3A) If the property is a commonhold unit, there shall be implied a covenant that the mortgagor will fully and promptly observe and perform all the obligations under the commonhold community statement that are for the time being imposed on him in his capacity as a unit-holder or as a joint unit-holder.

(4) In this section –

(a) 'commonhold community statement', 'commonhold unit', 'joint unit-holder' and 'unit-holder' have the same meanings as in the Commonhold and Leasehold Reform Act 2002, and

(b) 'mortgage' includes charge, and 'mortgagor' shall be construed accordingly.

6   No liability under covenants in certain cases

(1) The person making the disposition is not liable under the covenants implied by virtue of –

(a) section 2(1)(a) (right to dispose),

(b) section 3 (charges, incumbrances and third party rights), or

(c) section 4 (validity of lease),

in respect of any particular matter to which the disposition is expressly made subject.

(2) Furthermore that person is not liable under any of those covenants for anything (not falling within subsection (1)) –

(a) which at the time of the disposition is within the actual knowledge, or

(b) which is a necessary consequence of facts that are then within the actual knowledge,

of the person to whom the disposition is made.

(3) For this purpose section 198 of the Law of Property Act 1925 (deemed notice by virtue of registration) shall be disregarded.

(4) Moreover, where the disposition is of an interest the title to which is registered under the Land Registration Act 2002, that person is not liable under any of those covenants for anything (not falling within subsection (1) or (2)) which at the time of the disposition was entered in relation to that interest in the register of title under that Act.

7   Annexation of benefit of covenants

The benefit of a covenant implied by virtue of this Part shall be annexed and incident to, and shall go with, the estate or interest of the person to whom the disposition is made, and shall be capable of being enforced by every person in whom that estate or interest is (in whole or in part) for the time being vested.

8   Supplementary provisions

(1) The operation of any covenant implied in an instrument by virtue of this Part may be limited or extended by a term of that instrument.

(2) Sections 81 and 83 of the Law of Property Act 1925 (effect of covenant with two or more jointly; construction of implied covenants) apply to a covenant implied by virtue of this Part as they apply to a covenant implied by virtue of that Act.

(3) Where in an instrument effecting or purporting to effect a disposition of property a person is expressed to direct the disposition, this Part applies to him as if he were the person making the disposition.

(4) This Part has effect –

(a) where 'gyda gwarant teitl llawn' is used instead of 'with full title guarantee', and

(b) where 'gyda gwarant teitl cyfyngedig' is used instead of 'with limited title guarantee',

as it has effect where the English words are used.

9   Modifications of statutory forms

(1) Where a form set out in an enactment, or in an instrument made under an enactment, includes words which (in an appropriate case) would have resulted in the implication of a covenant by virtue of section 76 of the Law of Property Act 1925, the form shall be taken to authorise instead the use of the words 'with full title guarantee' or 'with limited title guarantee' or their Welsh equivalent given in section 8(4).

(2) This applies in particular to the forms set out in Schedule 4 to the Law of Property Act 1925.

10   General saving for covenants in old form

(1) Except as provided by section 11 below (cases in which covenants in old form implied on disposition after commencement), the following provisions, namely –

(a) section 76 of the Law of Property Act 1925, and

(b) section 24(1)(a) of the Land Registration Act 1925,

are repealed as regards dispositions of property made after the commencement of this Part.

(2) The repeal of those provisions by this Act accordingly does not affect the enforcement of a covenant implied by virtue of either of them on a disposition before the commencement of this Part

11   Covenants in old form implied in certain cases

(1) Section 76 of the Law of Property Act 1925 applies in relation to a disposition of property made after the commencement of this Part in pursuance of a contract entered into before commencement where –

(a) the contract contains a term providing for a disposition to which that section would have applied if the disposition had been made before commencement, and

(b) the existence of the contract and of that term is apparent on the face of the instrument effecting the disposition, unless there has been an intervening disposition of the property expressed, in accordance with this Part, to be made with full title guarantee.

(2) Section 24(1)(a) of the Land Registration Act 1925 applies in relation to a disposition of a leasehold interest in land made after the commencement of this Part in pursuance of a contract entered into before commencement where –

(a) the covenant specified in that provision would have been implied on the disposition if it had been made before commencement, and

(b) the existence of the contract is apparent on the face of the instrument effecting the disposition,

unless there has been an intervening disposition of the leasehold interest expressed, in accordance with this Part, to be made with full title guarantee.

(3) In subsections (1) and (2) an 'intervening disposition' means a disposition after the commencement of this Part to, or to a predecessor in title of, the person by whom the disposition in question is made.

(4) Where in order for subsection (1) or (2) to apply it is necessary for certain matters to be apparent on the face of the instrument effecting the disposition, the contract shall be deemed to contain an implied term that they should so appear.

12   Covenants in new form to be implied in other cases

(1) This section applies to a contract for the disposition of property entered into before the commencement of this Part where the disposition is made after commencement and section 11 (cases in which covenants in old form to be implied) does not apply because there has been an intervening disposition expressed, in accordance with this Part, to be with full title guarantee.

(2) A contract which contains a term that the person making the disposition shall do so as beneficial owner shall be construed as requiring that person to do so by an instrument expressed to be made with full title guarantee.

(3) A contract which contains a term that the person making the disposition shall do so –

(a) as settlor, or

(b) as trustee or mortgagee or personal representative,

shall be construed as requiring that person to do so by an instrument expressed to be made with limited title guarantee.

(4) A contract for the disposition of a leasehold interest in land entered into at a date when the title to the leasehold interest was registered shall be construed as requiring the person making the disposition for which it provides to do so by an instrument expressed to be made with full title guarantee.

(5) Where this section applies and the contract provides that any of the covenants to be implied by virtue of section 76 of the Law of Property Act 1925 or section 24(1)(a) of the Land Registration Act 1925 shall be implied in a modified form, the contract

shall be construed as requiring a corresponding modification of the covenants implied by virtue of this Part.

13   Application of transitional provisions in relation to options

For the purposes of sections 11 and 12 (transitional provisions implication of covenants in old form in certain cases and new form in others) as they apply in relation to a disposition of property in accordance with an option granted before the commencement of this Part and exercised after commencement, the contract for the disposition shall be deemed to have been entered into on the grant of the option.

PART II

MATTERS ARISING IN CONNECTION WITH DEATH

14   Vesting of estate in case of intestacy or lack of executors ...

(2) Any real or personal estate of a person dying before the commencement of this section shall, if it is property to which this subsection applies, vest in the Public Trustee on the commencement of this section.

(3) Subsection (2) above applies to any property –

(a) if it was vested in the Probate Judge under section 9 of the Administration of Estates Act 1925 immediately before the commencement of this section, or

(b) if it was not so vested but as at commencement there has been no grant of representation in respect of it and there is no executor with power to obtain such a grant.

(4) Any property vesting in the Public Trustee by virtue of subsection (2) above shall –

(a) if the deceased died intestate, be treated as vesting in the Public Trustee under section 9(1) of the Administration of Estates Act 1925 (as substituted by subsection (1) above); and

(b) otherwise be treated as vesting in the Public Trustee under section 9(2) of that Act (as so substituted).

(5) Anything done by or in relation to the Probate Judge with respect to property vested in him as mentioned in subsection (3)(a) above shall be treated as having been done by or in relation to the Public Trustee.

(6) So far as may be necessary in consequence of the transfer to the Public Trustee of the functions of the Probate Judge under section 9 of the Administration of Estates Act 1925, any reference in an enactment or instrument to the Probate Judge shall be construed as a reference to the Public Trustee.

15   Registration of land charges after death ...

(5) The amendments made by this section [to sections 3, 5 and 6 of the Land Charges Act 1972] do not apply where the application for registration was made

before the commencement of this section, but without prejudice to a person's right to make a new application after commencement.

16   Concurrence of personal representatives in dealings with interests in land ...

(3) The amendments made by subsection (1) apply to contracts made after the commencement of this section.

17   Notices affecting land: absence of knowledge of intended recipient's death

(1) Service of a notice affecting land which would be effective but for the death of the intended recipient is effective despite his death if the person service the notice has no reason to believe that he has died.

(2) Where the person serving a notice affecting land has no reason to believe that the intended recipient has died, the proper address for the purposes of section 7 of the Interpretation Act 1978 (service of documents by post) shall be what would be the proper address apart from his death.

(3) The above provisions do not apply to a notice authorised or required to be served for the purposes of proceedings before –

(a) any court,

(b) any tribunal specified in Schedule 1 to the Tribunals and Inquiries Act 1992 (tribunals within general supervision of Council on Tribunals), or

(c) the Chief Land Registrar or the Adjudicator to Her Majesty's Land Registry;

but this is without prejudice to the power to make provision in relation to such proceedings by rules of court, procedural rules within the meaning of section 8 of the Tribunals and Inquiries Act 1992 or rules under the Land Registration Act 2002.

18   Notices affecting land: service on personal representatives before filing of grant

(1) A notice affecting land which would have been authorised or required to be served on a person but for his death shall be sufficiently served before a grant of representation has been filed if –

(a) it is addressed to 'The Personal Representatives of' the deceased (naming him) and left at or sent by post to his last known place of residence or business in the United Kingdom, and

(b) a copy of it, similarly addressed, is served on the Public Trustee.

(2) The reference in subsection (1) to the filing of a grant of representation is to the filing at the Principal Registry of the Family Division of the High Court of a copy of a grant of representation in respect of the deceased's estate or, as the case may be, the part of his estate which includes the land in question.

(3) The method of service provided for by this section is not available where provision is made –

(a) by or under any enactment, or

(b) by an agreement in writing,

requiring a different method of service, or expressly prohibiting the method of service provided for by this section, in the circumstances.

PART III

GENERAL PROVISIONS

20   Crown application

This Act binds the Crown.

21   Consequential amendments and repeals ...

(3) In the case of section 76 of the Law of Property Act 1925 and section 24(1)(a) of the Land Registration Act 1925, those provisions are repealed in accordance with section 10(1) above (general saving for covenants in old form).

(4) The amendments consequential on Part I of this Act (namely those in paragraphs 1, 2, 3, 5, 7, 9 and 12 of Schedule 1) shall not have effect in relation to any disposition of property to which, by virtue of section 10(1) or 11 above (transitional provisions), section 76 of the Law of Property Act 1925 or section 24(1)(a) of the Land Registration Act 1925 continues to apply.

23   Commencement

(1) The provisions of this Act come into force on such day as the Lord Chancellor may appoint by order made by statutory instrument.

(2) Different days may be appointed for different provisions and for different purposes.

NB All of the above provisions came into force on 1 July1995 and the Act was fully in force on that date.

As amended by the Trusts of Land and Appointment of Trustees Act 1996, s25(2), Schedule 4; Land Registration Act 2002, s133, Schedule 11, para 31(1)–(3); Commonhold and Leasehold Reform Act 2002, s68, Schedule 5, para 7; Statute Law (Repeals) Act 2004, s1(1), Schedule 1, Pt 12.

AGRICULTURAL TENANCIES ACT 1995

(1995 c 8)

PART I

GENERAL PROVISIONS

1   Meaning of 'farm business tenancy'

(1) A tenancy is a 'farm business tenancy' for the purposes of this Act if –

(a) it meets the business conditions together with either the agriculture condition or the notice conditions, and

(b) it is not a tenancy which, by virtue of section 2 of this Act, cannot be a farm business tenancy.

(2) The business conditions are –

(a) that all or part of the land comprised in the tenancy is farmed for the purposes of a trade or business, and

(b) that, since the beginning of the tenancy, all or part of the land so comprised has been so farmed.

(3) The agriculture condition is that, having regard to –

(a) the terms of the tenancy,

(b) the use of the land comprised in the tenancy,

(c) the nature of any commercial activities carried on on that land, and

(d) any other relevant circumstances,

the character of the tenancy is primarily or wholly agricultural.

(4) The notice conditions are –

(a) that, on or before the relevant day, the landlord and the tenant each gave the other a written notice –

(i) identifying (by name or otherwise) the land to be comprised in the tenancy or proposed tenancy, and

(ii) containing a statement to the effect that the person giving the notice intends that the tenancy or proposed tenancy is to be, and remain, a farm business tenancy, and

(b) that, at the beginning of the tenancy, having regard to the terms of the tenancy and any other relevant circumstances, the character of the tenancy was primarily or wholly agricultural.

(5) In subsection (4) above 'the relevant day' means whichever is the earlier of the following –

(a) the day on which the parties enter into any instrument creating the tenancy, other than an agreement to enter into a tenancy on a future date, or

(b) the beginning of the tenancy.

(6) The written notice referred to in subsection (4) above must not be included in any instrument creating the tenancy.

(7) If in any proceedings –

(a) any question arises as to whether a tenancy was a farm business tenancy at any time, and

(b) it is proved that all or part of the land comprised in the tenancy was farmed for the purposes of a trade or business at that time,

it shall be presumed, unless the contrary is proved, that all or part of the land so comprised has been so farmed since the beginning of the tenancy.

(8) Any use of land in breach of the terms of the tenancy, any commercial activities carried on in breach of those terms, and any cessation of such activities in breach of those terms, shall be disregarded in determining whether at any time the tenancy meets the business conditions or the agriculture condition, unless the landlord or his predecessor in title has consented to the breach or the landlord has acquiesced in the breach.

2 Tenancies which cannot be farm business tenancies

(1) A tenancy cannot be a farm business tenancy for the purposes of this Act if –

(a) the tenancy begins before 1st September 1995, or

(b) it is a tenancy of an agricultural holding beginning on or after that date with respect to which, by virtue of section 4 of this Act, the Agricultural Holdings Act 1986 applies.

(2) In this section 'agricultural holding' has the same meaning as in the Agricultural Holdings Act 1986.

4 Agricultural Holdings Act 1986 not to apply in relation to new tenancies except in special cases

(1) The Agricultural Holdings Act 1986 (in this section referred to as 'the 1986 Act') shall not apply in relation to any tenancy beginning on or after 1st September 1995 (including any agreement to which section 2 of that Act would otherwise apply beginning on or after that date), except any tenancy of agricultural holding which –

(a) is granted by a written contract of tenancy entered into before 1st September

1995 and indicating (in whatever terms) that the 1986 Act is to apply in relation to the tenancy,

(b) is obtained by virtue of a direction of an Agricultural Land Tribunal under section 39 or 53 of the 1986 Act,

(c) is granted (following a direction under section 39 of that Act) in circumstances falling within section 45(6) of that Act,

(d) is granted on an agreed succession by a written contract of tenancy indicating (in whatever terms) that Part IV of the 1986 Act is to apply in relation to the tenancy,

(e) is created by the acceptance of a tenant, in accordance with the provisions as to compensation known as the 'Evesham custom' and set out in subsections (3) to (5) of section 80 of the 1986 Act, on the terms and conditions of the previous tenancy, or

(f) is granted to a person who, immediately before the grant of the tenancy, was the tenant of the holding, or of any agricultural holding which comprised the whole or a substantial part of the land comprised in the holding, under a tenancy in relation to which the 1986 Act applied ('the previous tenancy') and is so granted merely because a purported variation of the previous tenancy (not being an agreement expressed to take effect as a new tenancy between the parties) has effect as an implied surrender followed by the grant of the tenancy.

(2) For the purposes of subsection (1)(d) above, a tenancy ('the current tenancy') is granted on an agreed succession if, and only if, –

(a) the previous tenancy of the holding or a related holding was a tenancy in relation to which Part IV of the 1986 Act applied, and

(b) the current tenancy is granted otherwise than as mentioned in paragraph (b) or (c) of subsection (1) above but in such circumstances that if –

(i) Part IV of the 1986 Act applied in relation to the current tenancy, and

(ii) a sole (or surviving) tenant under the current tenancy were to die and be survived by a close relative of his,

the occasion on which the current tenancy is granted would for the purposes of subsection (1) of section 37 of the 1986 Act be taken to be an occasion falling within paragraph (a) or (b) of that subsection.

(3) In this section –

(a) 'agricultural holding' and 'contract of tenancy' have the same meaning as in the 1986 Act, and

(b) 'close relative' and 'related holding' have the meaning given by section 35(2) of that Act.

5 Tenancies for more than two years to continue from year to year unless terminated by notice

(1) A farm business tenancy for a term of more than two years shall, instead of terminating on the term date, continue (as from that date) as a tenancy from year

to year, but otherwise on the terms of the original tenancy so far as applicable, unless at least twelve months but less than twenty-four months before the term date a written notice has been given by either party to the other of his intention to terminate the tenancy.

(2) In subsection (1) above 'the term date', in relation to a fixed term tenancy, means the date fixed for the expiry of the term.

(3) For the purposes of section 140 of the Law of Property Act 1925 (apportionment of conditions on severance of reversion), a notice under subsection 1) above shall be taken to be a notice to quit.

(4) This section has effect notwithstanding any agreement to the contrary.

8   Tenant's right to remove fixtures and buildings

(1) Subject to the provision of this section –

> (a) any fixture (of whatever description) affixed, whether for the purposes of agriculture or not, to the holding by the tenant under a farm business tenancy, and
>
> (b) any building erected by him on the holding,

may be removed by the tenant at any time during the continuance of the tenancy or at any time after the termination of the tenancy when he remains in possession as tenant (whether or not under a new tenancy), and shall remain his property so long as he may remove it by virtue of this subsection.

(2) Subsection (1) above shall not apply –

> (a) to a fixture affixed or a building erected in pursuance of some obligation,
>
> (b) to a fixture affixed or a building erected instead of some fixture or building belonging to the landlord,
>
> (c) to a fixture or building in respect of which the tenant has obtained compensation under section 16 of this Act or otherwise, or
>
> (d) to a fixture or building in respect of which the landlord has given his consent under section 17 of this Act on condition that the tenant agrees not to remove it and which the tenant has agreed not to remove.

(3) In the removal of a fixture or building by virtue of subsection (1) above, the tenant shall not do any avoidable damage to the holding,

(4) Immediately after removing a fixture or building by virtue of subsection (1) above, the tenant shall make good all damage to the holding that is occasioned by the removal.

(5) This section applies to a fixture or building acquired by a tenant as it applies to a fixture or building affixed or erected by him.

(6) Except as provided by subsection (2)(d) above, this section has effect notwithstanding any agreement or custom to the contrary.

(7) No right to remove fixtures that subsists otherwise than by virtue of this section shall be exercisable by the tenant under a farm business tenancy.

PART II

RENT REVIEW UNDER FARM BUSINESS TENANCY

9 Application of Part II

This part of this Act applies in relation to a farm business tenancy (notwithstanding any agreement to the contrary) unless the tenancy is created by an instrument which –

(a) expressly states that the rent is not to be reviewed during the tenancy, or

(b) provides that the rent is to be varied, at a specified time or times during the tenancy –

(i) by or to a specified amount, or

(ii) in accordance with a specified formula which does not preclude a reduction and which does not require or permit the exercise by any person of any judgment or discretion in relation to the determination of the rent of the holding,

but otherwise is to remain fixed.

10 Notice requiring statutory rent review

(1) The landlord or tenant under a farm business tenancy in relation to which this Part of this Act applies may by notice in writing given to the other (in this Part of this Act referred to as a 'statutory review notice') require that the rent to be payable in respect of the holding as from the review date shall be referred to arbitration in accordance with this Act.

(2) In this Part of this Act 'the review date', in relation to a statutory review notice, means a date which –

(a) is specified in the notice, and

(b) complies with subsections (3) to (6) below.

(3) The review date must be at least twelve months but less than twenty-four months after the day on which the statutory review notice is given …

12 Appointment of arbitrator

Where a statutory review notice has been given in relation to a farm business tenancy, but –

(a) no arbitrator has been appointed under an agreement made since the notice was given, and

(b) no person has been appointed under such an agreement to determine the question of the rent (otherwise than as arbitrator) on a basis agreed by the parties,

either party may, at any time during the period of six months ending with the review date, apply to the President of the Royal Institution of Chartered Surveyors (in this Act referred to as 'the RICS') for the appointment of an arbitrator by him.

13   Amount of rent

(1) On any reference made in pursuance of a statutory review notice, the arbitrator shall determine the rent properly payable in respect of the holding at the review date and accordingly shall, with effect from that date, increase or reduce the rent previously payable or direct that it shall continue unchanged. ...

14   Interpretation of Part II

In this Part of this Act, unless the context otherwise requires –

'the review date', in relation to a statutory review notice, has the meaning given by section 10(2) of this Act;

'statutory review notice' has the meaning given by section 10(1) of this Act.

PART III

COMPENSATION ON TERMINATION OF FARM BUSINESS TENANCY

15   Meaning of 'tenant's improvement'

For the purposes of this Part of this Act a 'tenant's improvement', in relation to any farm business tenancy, means –

(a) any physical improvement which is made on the holding by the tenant by his own effort or wholly or partly at his own expense, or

(b) any intangible advantage which –

(i) is obtained for the holding by the tenant by his own effort or wholly or partly at his own expense, and

(ii) becomes attached to the holding,

and references to the provision of a tenant's improvement are references to the making by the tenant of any physical improvement falling within paragraph (a) above or the obtaining by the tenant of any intangible advantage falling within paragraph (b) above.

16   Tenant's right to compensation for tenant's improvement

(1) The tenant under a farm business tenancy shall, subject to the provisions of this Part of this Act, be entitled on the termination of the tenancy, on quitting the holding, to obtain from his landlord compensation in respect of any tenant's improvement.

(2) A tenant shall not be entitled to compensation under this section in respect of –

(a) any physical improvement which is removed from the holding, or

(b) any intangible advantage which does not remain attached to the holding.
...

17 Consent of landlord as condition of compensation for tenant's improvement

(1) A tenant shall not be entitled to compensation under section 16 of this Act in respect of any tenant's improvement unless the landlord has given his consent in writing to the provision of the tenant's improvement.

(2) Any such consent may be given in the instrument creating the tenancy or elsewhere. ...

18 Conditions in relation to compensation for planning permission

(1) A tenant shall not be entitled to compensation under section 16 of this Act in respect of a tenant's improvement which consists of planning permission unless –

(a) the landlord has given his consent in writing to the making of the application for planning permission,

(b) that consent is expressed to be given for the purpose –

(i) of enabling a specified physical improvement falling within paragraph (a) of section 15 of this Act lawfully to be provided by the tenant, or

(ii) of enabling the tenant lawfully to effect a specified change of use, and

(c) on the termination of the tenancy, the specified physical improvement has not been completed or the specified change of use has not been effected. ...

19 Reference to arbitration of refusal or failure to give consent or of condition attached to consent

(1) Where, in relation to any tenant's improvement, the tenant under a farm business tenancy is aggrieved by –

(a) the refusal of his landlord to give his consent under section 17(1) of this Act,

(b) the failure of his landlord to give such consent within two months of a written request by the tenant for such consent, or

(c) any variation in the terms of the tenancy required by the landlord as a condition of giving such consent,

the tenant may by notice in writing given to the landlord demand that the question shall be referred to arbitration under this section; ...

(7) If the arbitrator gives his approval, that approval shall have effect for the purposes of this Part of this Act and for the purposes of the terms of the farm business tenancy as if it were the consent of the landlord. ...

20 Amount of compensation for tenant's improvement not consisting of planning permission

(1) The amount of compensation payable to the tenant under section 16 of this Act in respect of any tenant's improvement shall be an amount equal to the increase attributable to the improvement in the value of the holding at the termination of the tenancy as land comprised in a tenancy.

(2) Where a landlord and the tenant have entered into an agreement in writing whereby any benefit is given or allowed to the tenant in consideration of the provision of a tenant's improvement, the amount of compensation otherwise payable in respect of that improvement shall be reduced by the proportion which the value of the benefit bears to the amount of the total cost of providing the improvement. ...

(5) This section does not apply where the tenant's improvement consists of planning permission.

21 Amount of compensation for planning permission

(1) The amount of compensation payable to the tenant under section 16 of this Act in respect of a tenant's improvement which consists of planning permission shall be an amount equal to the increase attributable to the fact that the relevant development is authorised by the planning permission in the value of the holding at the termination of the tenancy as land comprised in a tenancy.

(2) In subsection (1) above, 'the relevant development' means the physical improvement or change of use specified in the landlord's consent under section 18 of this Act in accordance with subsection (1)(b) of that section.

(3) Where the landlord and the tenant have entered into an agreement in writing whereby any benefit is given or allowed to the tenant in consideration of the obtaining of planning permission by the tenant, the amount of compensation otherwise payable in respect of that permission shall be reduced by the proportion which the value of the benefit bears to the amount of the total cost of obtaining the permission.

22 Settlement of claims for compensation

(1) Any claim by the tenant under a farm business tenancy for compensation under section 16 of this Act shall, subject to the provisions of this section, be determined by arbitration under this section.

(2) No such claim for compensation shall be enforceable unless before the end of the period of two months beginning with the date of the termination of the tenancy the tenant has given notice in writing to his landlord of his intention to make the claim and of the nature of the claim. ...

27 Interpretation of Part III

In this Part of this Act, unless the context otherwise requires –

'planning permission' has the meaning given by section 336(1) of the Town and Country Planning Act 1990;

'tenant's improvement', and references to the provision of such an improvement, have the meaning given by section 15 of this Act.

30 General provisions applying to arbitrations under Act

(1) Any matter which is required to be determined by arbitration under this Act shall be determined by the arbitration of a sole arbitrator. ...

32 Power of limited owners to give consents, etc

The landlord under a farm business tenancy, whatever his estate or interest in the holding, may, for the purposes of this Act, give any consent, make any agreement or do or have done to him any other act which he might give, make, do or have done to him if he were owner in fee simple or, if his interest is an interest in a leasehold, were absolutely entitled to that leasehold.

33 Power to apply and raise capital money

(1) The purposes authorised by section 73 of the Settled Land Act 1925 or section 26 of the Universities and College Estates Act 1925 for the application of capital money shall include –

(a) the payment of expenses incurred by a landlord under a farm business tenancy in, or in connection with, the making of any physical improvement on the holding,

(b) the payment of compensation under section 16 of this Act, and

(c) the payment of the costs, charges and expenses incurred by him on a reference to arbitration under section 19 or 22 of this Act.

(2) The purposes authorised by section 71 of the Settled Land Act 1925 as purposes for which money may be raised by mortgage shall include the payment of compensation under section 16 of this Act.

(3) Where the landlord under a farm business tenancy –

(a) is a tenant for life or in a fiduciary position, and

(b) is liable to pay compensation under section 16 of this Act,

he may require the sum payable as compensation and any costs, charges and expenses incurred by him in connection with the tenant's claim under that section to be paid out of any capital money held on the same trusts as the settled land.

(4) In subsection (3) above –

'capital money' includes any personal estate held on the same trusts as the land.

34   Estimation of best rent for purposes of Acts and other instruments

(1) In estimating the best rent or reservation in the nature of rent of land comprised in a farm business tenancy for the purposes of a relevant instrument, it shall not be necessary to take into account against the tenant any increase in the value of that land arising from any tenant's improvements.

(2) In subsection (1) above –

'a relevant instrument' means any Act of Parliament, deed or other instrument which authorises a lease to be made on the condition that the best rent or reservation in the nature of rent is reserved;

'tenant's improvement' has the meaning given by section 15 of this Act.

37   Crown land

(1) This Act shall apply in relation to land in which there subsists, or has at any material time subsisted, a Crown interest as it applies in relation to land in which no such interest subsists or has ever subsisted. ...

(3) If any question arises as to who is to be treated as the owner of a Crown interest, that question shall be referred to the Treasury, whose decision shall be final.

(4) In subsections (1) and (3) above 'Crown interest' means an interest which belongs to Her Majesty in right of the Crown or of the Duchy of Lancaster or to the Duchy of Cornwall, or to a government department, or which is held in trust for Her Majesty for the purposes of a government department. ...

38   Interpretation

(1) In this Act, unless the context otherwise requires –

'agriculture' includes horticulture, fruit growing, seed growing, dairy farming and livestock breeding and keeping, the use of land as grazing land, meadow land, osier land, market gardens and nursery grounds, and the use of land for woodlands where that use is ancillary to the farming of land for other agricultural purposes, and 'agricultural' shall be construed accordingly;

'building' includes any part of a building;

'fixed term tenancy' means any tenancy other than a periodic tenancy;

'holding', in relation to a farm business tenancy, means the aggregate of the land comprised in the tenancy;

'landlord' includes any person from time to time deriving title from the original landlord;

'livestock' includes any creature kept for the production of food, wool, skins or fur or for the purpose of its use in the farming of land; ...

'tenancy' means any tenancy other than a tenancy at will, and includes a sub-tenancy and an agreement for a tenancy or sub-tenancy;

'tenant' includes a sub-tenant and any person deriving title from the original tenant or sub-tenant;

'termination', in relation to a tenancy, means the cesser of the tenancy by reason of effluxion of time or from any other cause.

(2) References in this Act to the farming of land include references to the carrying on in relation to land of any agricultural activity.

(3) A tenancy granted pursuant to a contract shall be taken for the purposes of this Act to have been granted when the contract was entered into.

(4) For the purposes of this Act a tenancy begins on the day on which, under the terms of the tenancy, the tenant is entitled to possession under that tenancy; and references in this Act to the beginning of the tenancy are references to that day.

(5) The designations of landlord and tenant shall continue to apply until the conclusion of any proceedings taken under this Act in respect of compensation.

41   Short title, commencement and extent ...

(2) This Act shall come into force on 1st September 1995. ...

As amended by the Trusts of Land and Appointment of Trustees Act 1996, s25(2), Schedule 4.

LANDLORD AND TENANT (COVENANTS) ACT 1995

(1995 c 30)

1 Tenancies to which the Act applies

(1) Sections 3 to 16 and 21 apply only to new tenancies.

(2) Sections 17 to 20 apply to both new and other tenancies.

(3) For the purposes of this section a tenancy is a new tenancy if it is granted on or after the date on which this Act comes into force otherwise than in pursuance of—

    (a) an agreement entered into before that date, or

    (b) an order of a court made before that date.

(4) Subsection (3) has effect subject to section 20(1) in the case of overriding leases granted under section 19.

(5) Without prejudice to the generality of subsection (3), that subsection applies to the grant of a tenancy where by virtue of any variation of a tenancy there is a deemed surrender and regrant as it applies to any other grant of a tenancy.

(6) Where a tenancy granted on or after the date on which this Act comes into force is so granted in pursuance of an option granted before that date, the tenancy shall be regarded for the purposes of subsection (3) as granted in pursuance of an agreement entered into before that date (and accordingly is not a new tenancy), whether or not the option was exercised before that date.

(7) In subsection (6) 'option' includes right of first refusal.

2 Covenants to which the Act applies

(1) This Act applies to a landlord covenant or a tenant covenant of a tenancy –

    (a) whether or not the covenant has reference to the subject matter of the tenancy, and

    (b) whether the covenant is express, implied or imposed by law,

but does not apply to a covenant falling within subsection (2).

(2) Nothing in this Act affects any covenant imposed in pursuance of –

    (a) section 35 or 155 of the Housing Act 1985 (covenants for repayment of discount on early disposals);

(b) paragraph 1 of Schedule 6A to that Act (covenants requiring redemption of landlord's share); or

(c) section 11 or 13 of the Housing Act 1996 or paragraph 1 or 3 of Schedule 2 to the Housing Associations Act 1985 (covenants for repayment of discount on early disposals or for restricting disposals).

3   Transmission of benefit and burden of covenants

(1) The benefit and burden of all landlord and tenant covenants of a tenancy –

(a) shall be annexed and incident to the whole, and to each and every part, of the premises demised by the tenancy and of the reversion in them, and

(b) shall in accordance with this section pass on an assignment of the whole or any part of those premises or of the reversion in them.

(2) Where the assignment is by the tenant under the tenancy, then as from the assignment the assignee –

(a) becomes bound by the tenant covenants of the tenancy except to the extent that –

(i) immediately before the assignment they did not bind the assignor, or

(ii) they fall to be complied with in relation to any demised premises not comprised in the assignment; and

(b) becomes entitled to the benefit of the landlord covenants of the tenancy except to the extent that they fall to be complied with in relation to any such premises.

(3) Where the assignment is by the landlord under the tenancy, then as from the assignment the assignee –

(a) becomes bound by the landlord covenants of the tenancy except to the extent that –

(i) immediately before the assignment they did not bind the assignor, or

(ii) they fall to be complied with in relation to any demised premises not comprised in the assignment; and

(b) becomes entitled to the benefit of the tenant covenants of the tenancy except to the extent that they fall to be complied with in relation to any such premises.

(4) In determining for the purposes of subsection (2) or (3) whether any covenant bound the assignor immediately before the assignment, any waiver or release of the covenant which (in whatever terms) is expressed to be personal to the assignor shall be disregarded.

(5) Any landlord or tenant covenant of a tenancy which is restrictive of the user of land shall, as well as being capable of enforcement against an assignee, be capable of being enforced against any other person who is the owner or occupier of any demised premises to which the covenant relates, even though there is no express provision in the tenancy to that effect.

(6) Nothing in this section shall operate –

(a) in the case of a covenant which (in whatever terms) is expressed to be personal to any person, to make the covenant enforceable by or (as the case may be) against any other person; or

(b) to make a covenant enforceable against any person if, apart from this section, it would not be enforceable against him by reason of its not having been registered under the Land Registration Act 2002 or the Land Charges Act 1972.

(7) To the extent that there remains in force any rule of law by virtue of which the burden of a covenant whose subject matter is not in existence at the time when it is made does not run with the land affected unless the covenantor covenants on behalf of himself and his assigns, that rule of law is hereby abolished in relation to tenancies.

4   Transmission of rights of re-entry

The benefit of a landlord's right of re-entry under a tenancy –

(a) shall be annexed and incident to the whole, and to each and every part, of the reversion in the premises demised by the tenancy,

and

(b) shall pass on an assignment of the whole or any part of the reversion in those premises.

5   Tenant released from covenants on assignment of tenancy

(1) This section applies where a tenant assigns premises demised to him under a tenancy.

(2) If the tenant assigns the whole of the premises demised to him, he –

(a) is released from the tenant covenants of the tenancy, and

(b) ceases to be entitled to the benefit of the landlord covenants of the tenancy,

as from the assignment.

(3) If the tenant assigns part only of the premises demised to him, then as from the assignment he –

(a) is released from the tenant covenants of the tenancy, and

(b) ceases to be entitled to the benefit of the landlord covenants of the tenancy,

only to the extent that those covenants fall to be complied with in relation to that part of the demised premises.

(4) This section applies as mentioned in subsection (1) whether or not the tenant is tenant of the whole of the premises comprised in the tenancy.

6 Landlord may be released from covenants on assignment of reversion

(1) This section applies where a landlord assigns the reversion in premises of which he is the landlord under a tenancy.

(2) If the landlord assigns the reversion in the whole of the premises of which he is the landlord –

(a) he may apply to be released from the landlord covenants of the tenancy in accordance with section 8; and

(b) if he is so released from all of those covenants, he ceases to be entitled to the benefit of the tenant covenants of the tenancy as from the assignment.

(3) If the landlord assigns the reversion in part only of the premises of which he is the landlord –

(a) he may apply to be so released from the landlord covenants of the tenancy to the extent that they fall to be complied with in relation to that part of those premises; and

(b) if he is, to that extent, so released from all of those covenants, then as from the assignment he ceases to be entitled to the benefit of the tenant covenants only to the extent that they fall to be complied with in relation to that part of those premises.

(4) This section applies as mentioned in subsection (1) whether or not the landlord is landlord of the whole of the premises comprised in the tenancy.

7 Former landlord may be released from covenants on assignment of reversion

(1) This section applies where –

(a) a landlord assigns the reversion in premises of which he is the landlord under a tenancy, and

(b) immediately before the assignment a former landlord of the premises remains bound by a landlord covenant of the tenancy ('the relevant covenant').

(2) If immediately before the assignment the former landlord does not remain the landlord of any other premises demised by the tenancy, he may apply to be released from the relevant covenant in accordance with section 8.

(3) In any other case the former landlord may apply to be so released from the relevant covenant to the extent that it falls to be complied with in relation to any premises comprised in the assignment.

(4) If the former landlord is so released from every landlord covenant by which he remained bound immediately before the assignment, he ceases to be entitled to the benefit of the tenant covenants of the tenancy.

(5) If the former landlord is so released from every such landlord covenant to the extent that it falls to be complied with in relation to any premises comprised in

the assignment, he ceases to be entitled to the benefit of the tenant covenants of the tenancy to the extent that they fall to be so complied with.

(6) This section applies as mentioned in subsection (1) –

(a) whether or not the landlord making the assignment is landlord of the whole of the premises comprised in the tenancy; and

(b) whether or not the former landlord has previously applied (whether under section 6 or this section) to be released from the relevant covenant.

8 Procedure for seeking release from a covenant under section 6 or 7

(1) For the purposes of section 6 or 7 an application for the release of a covenant to any extent is made by serving on the tenant, either before or within the period of four weeks beginning with the date of the assignment in question, a notice informing him of –

(a) the proposed assignment or (as the case may be) the fact that the assignment has taken place, and

(b) the request for the covenant to be released to that extent.

(2) Where an application for the release of a covenant is made in accordance with subsection (1), the covenant is released to the extent mentioned in the notice if –

(a) the tenant does not, within the period of four weeks beginning with the day on which the notice is served, serve on the landlord or former landlord a notice in writing objecting to the release, or

(b) the tenant does so serve such a notice but the court, on the application of the landlord or former landlord, makes a declaration that it is reasonable for the covenant to be so released, or

(c) the tenant serves on the landlord or former landlord a notice in writing consenting to the release and, if he has previously served a notice objecting to it, stating that that notice is withdrawn.

(3) Any release from a covenant in accordance with this section shall be regarded as occurring at the time when the assignment in question takes place.

(4) In this section –

(a) 'the tenant' means the tenant of the premises comprised in the assignment in question (or, if different parts of those premises are held under the tenancy by different tenants, each of those tenants);

(b) any reference to the landlord or the former landlord is a reference to the landlord referred to in section 6 or the former landlord referred to in section 7, as the case may be; and

(c) 'the court' means a county court.

9 Apportionment of liability under covenants binding both assignor and assignee of tenancy or reversion

(1) This section applies where –

(a) a tenant assigns part only of the premises demised to him by a tenancy;

(b) after the assignment both the tenant and his assignee are to be bound by a non-attributable tenant covenant of the tenancy; and

(c) the tenant and his assignee agree that as from the assignment liability under the covenant is to be apportioned between them in such manner as is specified in the agreement.

(2) This section also applies where –

(a) a landlord assigns the reversion in part only of the premises of which he is the landlord under a tenancy;

(b) after the assignment both the landlord and his assignee are to be bound by a non-attributable landlord covenant of the tenancy; and

(c) the landlord and his assignee agree that as from the assignment liability under the covenant is to be apportioned between them in such manner as is specified in the agreement.

(3) Any such agreement as is mentioned in subsection (1) or (2) may apportion liability in such a way that a party to the agreement is exonerated from all liability under a covenant.

(4) In any case falling within subsection (1) or (2) the parties to the agreement may apply for the apportionment to become binding on the appropriate person in accordance with section 10.

(5) In any such case the parties to the agreement may also apply for the apportionment to become binding on any person (other than the appropriate person) who is for the time being entitled to enforce the covenant in question; and section 10 shall apply in relation to such an application as it applies in relation to an application made with respect to the appropriate person.

(6) For the purposes of this section a covenant is, in relation to an assignment, a 'non-attributable' covenant if it does not fall to be complied with in relation to any premises comprised in the assignment.

(7) In this section 'the appropriate person' means either –

(a) the landlord of the entire premises referred to in subsection (1)(a) (or, if different parts of those premises are held under the tenancy by different landlords, each of those landlords), or

(b) the tenant of the entire premises referred to in subsection (2)(a) (or, if different parts of those premises are held under the tenancy by different tenants, each of those tenants),

depending on whether the agreement in question falls within subsection (1) or subsection (2).

10   Procedure for making apportionment bind other party to lease

(1) For the purposes of section 9 the parties to an agreement falling within subsection (1) or (2) of that section apply for an apportionment to become binding on

the appropriate person if, either before or within the period of four weeks beginning with the date of the assignment in question, they serve on that person a notice informing him of –

(a) the proposed assignment or (as the case may be) the fact that the assignment has taken place;

(b) the prescribed particulars of the agreement; and

(c) their request that the apportionment should become binding on him.

(2) Where an application for an apportionment to become binding has been made in accordance with subsection (1), the apportionment becomes binding on the appropriate person if –

(a) he does not, within the period of four weeks beginning with the day on which the notice is served under subsection (1), serve on the parties to the agreement a notice in writing objecting to the apportionment becoming binding on him, or

(b) he does so serve such a notice but the court, on the application of the parties to the agreement, makes a declaration that it is reasonable for the apportionment to become binding on him, or

(c) he serves on the parties to the agreement a notice in writing consenting to the apportionment becoming binding on him and, if he has previously served a notice objecting thereto, stating that that notice is withdrawn.

(3) Where any apportionment becomes binding in accordance with this section, this shall be regarded as occurring at the time when the assignment in question takes place.

(4) In this section –

'the appropriate person' has the same meaning as in section 9;

'the court' means a county court;

'prescribed' means prescribed by virtue of section 27.

11 Assignments in breach of covenant or by operation of law

(1) This section provides for the operation of sections 5 to 10 in relation to assignments in breach of a covenant of a tenancy or assignments by operation of law ('excluded assignments').

(2) In the case of an excluded assignment subsection (2) or (3) of section 5 –

(a) shall not have the effect mentioned in that subsection in relation to the tenant as from that assignment, but

(b) shall have that effect as from the next assignment (if any) of the premises assigned by him which is not an excluded assignment.

(3) In the case of an excluded assignment subsection (2) or (3) of section 6 or 7 –

(a) shall not enable the landlord or former landlord to apply for such a release as is mentioned in that subsection as from that assignment, but

(b) shall apply on the next assignment (if any) of the reversion assigned by the landlord which is not an excluded assignment so as to enable the landlord or former landlord to apply for any such release as from that subsequent assignment.

(4) Where subsection (2) or (3) of section 6 or 7 does so apply –

(a) any reference in that section to the assignment (except where it relates to the time as from which the release takes effect) is a reference to the excluded assignment; but

(b) in that excepted case and in section 8 as it applies in relation to any application under that section made by virtue of subsection (3) above, any reference to the assignment or proposed assignment is a reference to any such subsequent assignment as is mentioned in that subsection.

(5) In the case of an excluded assignment section 9 –

(a) shall not enable the tenant or landlord and his assignee to apply for an agreed apportionment to become binding in accordance with section 10 as from that assignment, but

(b) shall apply on the next assignment (if any) of the premises or reversion assigned by the tenant or landlord which is not an excluded assignment so as to enable him and his assignee to apply for such an apportionment to become binding in accordance with section 10 as from that subsequent assignment.

(6) Where section 9 does so apply –

(a) any reference in that section to the assignment or the assignee under it is a reference to the excluded assignment and the assignee under that assignment; but

(b) in section 10 as it applies in relation to any application under section 9 made by virtue of subsection (5) above, any reference to the assignment or proposed assignment is a reference to any such subsequent assignment as is mentioned in that subsection.

(7) If any such subsequent assignment as is mentioned in subsection (2), (3) or (5) above comprises only part of the premises assigned by the tenant or (as the case may be) only part of the premises the reversion in which was assigned by the landlord on the excluded assignment –

(a) the relevant provision or provisions of section 5, 6, 7 or 9 shall only have the effect mentioned in that subsection to the extent that the covenants or covenant in question fall or falls to be complied with in relation to that part of those premises; and

(b) that subsection may accordingly apply on different occasions in relation to different parts of those premises.

12   Covenants with management companies, etc

(1) This section applies where –

(a) a person other than the landlord or tenant ('the third party') is under a covenant of a tenancy liable (as principal) to discharge any function with respect to all or any of the demised premises ('the relevant function'); and

(b) that liability is not the liability of a guarantor or any other financial liability referable to the performance or otherwise of a covenant of the tenancy by another party to it.

(2) To the extent that any covenant of the tenancy confers any rights against the third party with respect to the relevant function, then for the purposes of the transmission of the benefit of the covenant in accordance with this Act it shall be treated as if it were –

(a) a tenant covenant of the tenancy to the extent that those rights are exercisable by the landlord; and

(b) a landlord covenant of the tenancy to the extent that those rights are exercisable by the tenant.

(3) To the extent that any covenant of the tenancy confers any rights exercisable by the third party with respect to the relevant function, then for the purposes mentioned in subsection (4), it shall be treated as if it were –

(a) a tenant covenant of the tenancy to the extent that those rights are exercisable against the tenant; and

(b) a landlord covenant of the tenancy to the extent that those rights are exercisable against the landlord.

(4) The purposes mentioned in subsection (3) are –

(a) the transmission of the burden of the covenant in accordance with this Act; and

(b) any release from, or apportionment of liability in respect of, the covenant in accordance with this Act.

(5) In relation to the release of the landlord from any covenant which is to be treated as a landlord covenant by virtue of subsection (3), section 8 shall apply as if any reference to the tenant were a reference to the third party.

13   Covenants binding two or more persons

(1) Where in consequence of this Act two or more persons are bound by the same covenant, they are so bound both jointly and severally.

(2) Subject to section 24(2), where by virtue of this Act –

(a) two or more persons are bound jointly and severally by the same covenant, and

(b) any of the persons so bound is released from the covenant,

the release does not extend to any other of those persons.

(3) For the purpose of providing for contribution between persons who, by virtue of

this Act, are bound jointly and severally by a covenant, the Civil Liability (Contribution) Act 1978 shall have effect as if –

(a) liability to a person under a covenant were liability in respect of damage suffered by that person;

(b) references to damage accordingly included a breach of a covenant of a tenancy; and

(c) section 7(2) of that Act were omitted.

15 Enforcement of covenants

(1) Where any tenant covenant of a tenancy, or any right of re-entry contained in a tenancy, is enforceable by the reversioner in respect of any premises demised by the tenancy, it shall also be so enforceable by –

(a) any person (other than the reversioner) who, as the holder of the immediate reversion in those premises, is for the time being entitled to the rents and profits under the tenancy in respect of those premises, or

(b) any mortgagee in possession of the reversion in those premises who is so entitled.

(2) Where any landlord covenant of a tenancy is enforceable against the reversioner in respect of any premises demised by the tenancy, it shall also be so enforceable against any person falling within subsection (1)(a) or (b).

(3) Where any landlord covenant of a tenancy is enforceable by the tenant in respect of any premises demised by the tenancy, it shall also be so enforceable by any mortgagee in possession of those premises under a mortgage granted by the tenant.

(4) Where any tenant covenant of a tenancy, or any right of re-entry contained in a tenancy, is enforceable against the tenant in respect of any premises demised by the tenancy, it shall also be so enforceable against any such mortgagee.

(5) Nothing in this section shall operate –

(a) in the case of a covenant which (in whatever terms) is expressed to be personal to any person, to make the covenant enforceable by or (as the case may be) against any other person; or

(b) to make a covenant enforceable against any person if, apart from this section, it would not be enforceable against him by reason of its not having been registered under the Land Registration Act 2002 or the Land Charges Act 1972.

(6) In this section –

'mortgagee' and 'mortgage' include 'chargee' and 'charge' respectively;

'the reversioner', in relation to a tenancy, means the holder for the time being of the interest of the landlord under the tenancy.

16 Tenant guaranteeing performance of covenant by assignee

(1) Where on an assignment a tenant is to any extent released from a tenant

covenant of a tenancy by virtue of this Act ('the relevant covenant'), nothing in this Act (and in particular section 25) shall preclude him from entering into an authorised guarantee agreement with respect to the performance of that covenant by the assignee.

(2) For the purposes of this section an agreement is an authorised guarantee agreement if –

(a) under it the tenant guarantees the performance of the relevant covenant to any extent by the assignee; and

(b) it is entered into in the circumstances set out in subsection (3); and

(c) its provisions conform with subsections (4) and (5).

(3) Those circumstances are as follows –

(a) by virtue of a covenant against assignment (whether absolute or qualified) the assignment cannot be effected without the consent of the landlord under the tenancy or some other person;

(b) any such consent is given subject to a condition (lawfully imposed) that the tenant is to enter into an agreement guaranteeing the performance of the covenant by the assignee; and

(c) the agreement is entered into by the tenant in pursuance of that condition.

(4) An agreement is not an authorised guarantee agreement to the extent that it purports –

(a) to impose on the tenant any requirement to guarantee in any way the performance of the relevant covenant by any person other than the assignee; or

(b) to impose on the tenant any liability, restriction or other requirement (of whatever nature) in relation to any time after the assignee is released from that covenant by virtue of this Act.

(5) Subject to subsection (4), an authorised guarantee agreement may –

(a) impose on the tenant any liability as sole or principal debtor in respect of any obligation owed by the assignee under the relevant covenant;

(b) impose on the tenant liabilities as guarantor in respect of the assignee's performance of that covenant which are no more onerous than those to which he would be subject in the event of his being liable as sole or principal debtor in respect of any obligation owed by the assignee under that covenant;

(c) require the tenant, in the event of the tenancy assigned by him being disclaimed, to enter into a new tenancy of the premises comprised in the assignment –

(i) whose term expires not later than the term of the tenancy assigned by the tenant, and

(ii) whose tenant covenants are no more onerous than those of that tenancy;

(d) make provision incidental or supplementary to any provision made by virtue of any of paragraphs (a) to (c).

(6) Where a person ('the former tenant') is to any extent released from a covenant of a tenancy by virtue of section 11(2) as from an assignment and the assignor under the assignment enters into an authorised guarantee agreement with the landlord with respect to the performance of that covenant by the assignee under the assignment –

(a) the landlord may require the former tenant to enter into an agreement under which he guarantees, on terms corresponding to those of that authorised guarantee agreement, the performance of that covenant by the assignee under the assignment; and

(b) if its provisions conform with subsections (4) and (5), any such agreement shall be an authorised guarantee agreement for the purposes of this section; and

(c) in the application of this section in relation to any such agreement –

(i) subsections (2)(b) and (c) and (3) shall be omitted, and

(ii) any reference to the tenant or to the assignee shall be read as a reference to the former tenant or to the assignee under the assignment.

(7) For the purposes of subsection (1) it is immaterial that –

(a) the tenant has already made an authorised guarantee agreement in respect of a previous assignment by him of the tenancy referred to in that subsection, it having been subsequently revested in him following a disclaimer on behalf of the previous assignee, or

(b) the tenancy referred to in that subsection is a new tenancy entered into by the tenant in pursuance of an authorised guarantee agreement;

and in any such case subsections (2) to (5) shall apply accordingly.

(8) It is hereby declared that the rules of law relating to guarantees (and in particular those relating to the release of sureties) are, subject to its terms, applicable in relation to any authorised guarantee agreement as in relation to any other guarantee agreement.

17 Restriction on liability of former tenant or his guarantor for rent or service charge, etc

(1) This section applies where a person ('the former tenant') is as a result of an assignment no longer a tenant under a tenancy but –

(a) (in the case of a tenancy which is a new tenancy) he has under an authorised guarantee agreement guaranteed the performance by his assignee of a tenant covenant of the tenancy under which any fixed charge is payable; or

(b) (in the case of any tenancy) he remains bound by such a covenant.

(2) The former tenant shall not be liable under that agreement or (as the case may be) the covenant to pay any amount in respect of any fixed charge payable under the covenant unless, within the period of six months beginning with the date when the charge becomes due, the landlord serves on the former tenant a notice informing him –

(a) that the charge is now due; and

(b) that in respect of the charge the landlord intends to recover from the former tenant such amount as is specified in the notice and (where payable) interest calculated on such basis as is so specified.

(3) Where a person ('the guarantor') has agreed to guarantee the performance by the former tenant of such a covenant as is mentioned in subsection (1), the guarantor shall not be liable under the agreement to pay any amount in respect of any fixed charge payable under the covenant unless, within the period of six months beginning with the date when the charge becomes due, the landlord serves on the guarantor a notice informing him –

(a) that the charge is now due; and

(b) that in respect of the charge the landlord intends to recover from the guarantor such amount as is specified in the notice and (where payable) interest calculated on such basis as is so specified.

(4) Where the landlord has duly served a notice under subsection (2) or (3), the amount (exclusive of interest) which the former tenant or (as the case may be) the guarantor is liable to pay in respect of the fixed charge in question shall not exceed the amount specified in the notice unless –

(a) his liability in respect of the charge is subsequently determined to be for a greater amount,

(b) the notice informed him of the possibility that that liability would be so determined, and

(c) within the period of three months beginning with the date of the determination, the landlord serves on him a further notice informing him that the landlord intends to recover that greater amount from him (plus interest, where payable).

(5) For the purposes of subsection (2) or (3) any fixed charge which has become due before the date on which this Act comes into force shall be treated as becoming due on that date; but neither of those subsections applies to any such charge if before that date proceedings have been instituted by the landlord for the recovery from the former tenant of any amount in respect of it.

(6) In this section –

'fixed charge', in relation to a tenancy, means –

(a) rent,

(b) any service charge as defined by section 18 of the Landlord and Tenant Act 1985 (the words 'of a dwelling' being disregarded for this purpose), and

(c) any amount payable under a tenant covenant of the tenancy providing for the payment of a liquidated sum in the event of a failure to comply with any such covenant;

'landlord', in relation to a fixed charge, includes any person who has a right to enforce payment of the charge.

18 Restriction of a liability of former tenant or his guarantor where tenancy subsequently varied

(1) This section applies where a person ('the former tenant') is as a result of an assignment no longer a tenant under a tenancy but –

(a) (in the case of a new tenancy) he has under an authorised guarantee agreement guaranteed the performance by his assignee of any tenant covenant of the tenancy; or

(b) (in the case of any tenancy) he remains bound by such a covenant.

(2) The former tenant shall not be liable under the agreement or (as the case may be) the covenant to pay any amount in respect of the covenant to the extent that the amount is referable to any relevant variation of the tenant covenants of the tenancy effected after the assignment.

(3) Where a person ('the guarantor') has agreed to guarantee the performance by the former tenant of a tenant covenant of the tenancy, the guarantor (where his liability to do so is not wholly discharged by any such variation of the tenant covenants of the tenancy) shall not be liable under the agreement to pay any amount in respect of the covenant to the extent that the amount is referable to any such variation.

(4) For the purposes of this section a variation of the tenant covenants of a tenancy is a 'relevant variation' if either –

(a) the landlord has, at the time of the variation, an absolute right to refuse to allow it; or

(b) the landlord would have had such a right if the variation had been sought by the former tenant immediately before the assignment by him but, between the time of that assignment and the time of the variation, the tenant covenants of the tenancy have been so varied as to deprive the landlord of such a right.

(5) In determining whether the landlord has or would have had such a right at any particular time regard shall be had to all the circumstances (including the effect of any provision made by or under any enactment).

(6) Nothing in this section applies to any variation of the tenant covenants of a tenancy effected before the date on which this Act comes into force.

(7) In this section 'variation' means a variation whether effected by deed or otherwise.

19 Right of former tenant or his guarantor to overriding lease

(1) Where in respect of any tenancy ('the relevant tenancy') any person ('the claimant') makes full payment of an amount which he has been duly required to pay in accordance with section 17, together with any interest payable, he shall be entitled (subject to and in accordance with this section) to have the landlord under that tenancy grant him an overriding lease of the premises demised by the tenancy.

(2) For the purposes of this section 'overriding lease' means a tenancy of the reversion expectant on the relevant tenancy which –

(a) is granted for a term equal to the remainder of the term of the relevant tenancy plus three days or the longest period (less than three days) that will not wholly displace the landlord's reversionary interest expectant on the relevant tenancy, as the case may require; and

(b) (subject to subsections (3) and (4) and to any modifications agreed to by the claimant and the landlord) otherwise contains the same covenants as the relevant tenancy, as they have effect immediately before the grant of the lease.

(3) An overriding lease shall not be required to reproduce any covenant of the relevant tenancy to the extent that the covenant is (in whatever terms) expressed to be a personal covenant between the landlord and the tenant under that tenancy.

(4) If any right, liability or other matter arising under a covenant of the relevant tenancy falls to be determined or otherwise operates (whether expressly or otherwise) by reference to the commencement of that tenancy –

(a) the corresponding covenant of the overriding lease shall be so framed that that right, liability or matter falls to be determined or otherwise operates by reference to the commencement of that tenancy; but

(b) the overriding lease shall not be required to reproduce any covenant of that tenancy to the extent that it has become spent by the time that that lease is granted.

(5) A claim to exercise the right to an overriding lease under this section is made by the claimant making a request for such a lease to the landlord; and any such request –

(a) must be made to the landlord in writing and specify the payment by virtue of which the claimant claims to be entitled to the lease ('the qualifying payment'); and

(b) must be so made at the time of making the qualifying payment or within the period of 12 months beginning with the date of that payment.

(6) Where the claimant duly makes such a request –

(a) the landlord shall (subject to subsection (7)) grant and deliver to the claimant an overriding lease of the demised premises within a reasonable time of the request being received by the landlord; and

(b) the claimant –

(i) shall thereupon deliver to the landlord a counterpart of the lease duly executed by the claimant, and

(ii) shall be liable for the landlord's reasonable costs of and incidental to the grant of the lease.

(7) The landlord shall not be under any obligation to grant an overriding lease of the demised premises under this section at a time when the relevant tenancy has been determined; and a claimant shall not be entitled to the grant of such a lease if at the time when he makes his request –

(a) the landlord has already granted such a lease and that lease remains in force; or

(b) another person has already duly made a request for such a lease to the landlord and that request has been neither withdrawn nor abandoned by that person.

(8) Where two or more requests are duly made on the same day, then for the purposes of subsection (7) –

(a) a request made by a person who was liable for the qualifying payment as a former tenant shall be treated as made before a request made by a person who was so liable as a guarantor; and

(b) a request made by a person whose liability in respect of the covenant in question commenced earlier than any such liability of another person shall be treated as made before a request made by that other person.

(9) Where a claimant who has duly made a request for an overriding lease under this section subsequently withdraws or abandons the request before he is granted such a lease by the landlord, the claimant shall be liable for the landlord's reasonable costs incurred in pursuance of the request down to the time of its withdrawal or abandonment; and for the purposes of this section –

(a) a claimant's request is withdrawn by the claimant notifying the landlord in writing that he is withdrawing his request; and

(b) a claimant is to be regarded as having abandoned his request if –

(i) the landlord has requested the claimant in writing to take, within such reasonable period as is specified in the landlord's request, all or any of the remaining steps required to be taken by the claimant before the lease can be granted, and

(ii) the claimant fails to comply with the landlord's request,

and is accordingly to be regarded as having abandoned it at the time when that period expires.

(10) Any request or notification under this section may be sent by post.

(11) The preceding provisions of this section shall apply where the landlord is the tenant under an overriding lease granted under this section as they apply where no such lease has been granted; and accordingly there may be two or more such leases interposed between the first such lease and the relevant tenancy.

20 Overriding leases: supplementary provisions

(1) For the purposes of section 1 an overriding lease shall be a new tenancy only if the relevant tenancy is a new tenancy.

(2) Every overriding lease shall state –

(a) that it is a lease granted under section 19, and

(b) whether it is or is not a new tenancy for the purposes of section 1;

and any such statement shall comply with such requirements as may be prescribed by land registration rules under the Land Registration Act 2002.

(3) A claim that the landlord has failed to comply with subsection (6)(a) of section 19 may be made the subject of civil proceedings in like manner as any other claim in tort for breach of statutory duty; and if the claimant under that section fails to comply with subsection (6)(b)(i) of that section he shall not be entitled to exercise any of the rights otherwise exercisable by him under the overriding lease.

(4) An overriding lease –

(a) shall be deemed to be authorised as against the persons interested in any mortgage of the landlord's interest (however created or arising); and

(b) shall be binding on any such persons;

and if any such person is by virtue of such a mortgage entitled to possession of the documents of title relating to the landlord's interest –

(i) the landlord shall within one month of the execution of the lease deliver to that person the counterpart executed in pursuance of section 19(6)(b)(i); and

(ii) if he fails to do so, the instrument creating or evidencing the mortgage shall apply as if the obligation to deliver a counterpart were included in the terms of the mortgage as set out in that instrument.

(5) It is hereby declared –

(a) that the fact that an overriding lease takes effect subject to the relevant tenancy shall not constitute a breach of any covenant of the lease against subletting or parting with possession of the premises demised by the lease or any part of them; and

(b) that each of sections 16, 17 and 18 applies where the tenancy referred to in subsection (1) of that section is an overriding lease as it applies in other cases falling within that subsection.

(6) No tenancy shall be registrable under the Land Charges Act 1972 or be taken to be an estate contract within the meaning of that Act by reason of any right or obligation that may arise under section 19, and any right arising from a request made under that section shall not be capable of falling within paragraph 2 of Schedule 1 or 3 to the Land Registration Act 2002; but any such request shall be registrable under the Land Charges Act 1972, or may be the subject of a notice under the Land Registration Act 2002, as if it were an estate contract.

(7) In this section –

(a) 'mortgage' includes 'charge'; and

(b) any expression which is also used in section 19 has the same meaning as in that section.

21 Forfeiture or disclaimer limited to part only of demised premises

(1) Where –

(a) as a result of one or more assignments a person is the tenant of part only of the premises demised by a tenancy, and

(b) under a proviso or stipulation in the tenancy there is a right of re-entry or forfeiture for a breach of a tenant covenant of the tenancy, and

(c) the right is (apart from this subsection) exercisable in relation to that part and other land demised by the tenancy,

the right shall nevertheless, in connection with a breach of any such covenant by that person, be taken to be a right exercisable only in relation to that part.

(2) Where –

(a) a company which is being wound up, or a trustee in bankruptcy, is as a result of one or more assignments the tenant of part only of the premises demised by a tenancy, and

(b) the liquidator of the company exercises his power under section 178 of the Insolvency Act 1986, or the trustee in bankruptcy exercises his power under section 315 of that Act, to disclaim property demised by the tenancy,

the power is exercisable only in relation to the part of the premises referred to in paragraph (a).

23   Effects of becoming subject to liability under, or entitled to benefit of, covenant, etc

(1) Where as a result of an assignment a person becomes, by virtue of this Act, bound by or entitled to the benefit of a covenant, he shall not by virtue of this Act have any liability or rights under the covenant in relation to any time falling before the assignment.

(2) Subsection (1) does not preclude any such rights being expressly assigned to the person in question.

(3) Where as a result of an assignment a person becomes, by virtue of this Act, entitled to a right of re-entry contained in a tenancy, that right shall be exercisable in relation to any breach of a covenant of the tenancy occurring before the assignment as in relation to one occurring thereafter, unless by reason of any waiver or release it was not so exercisable immediately before the assignment.

24   Effects of release from liability under, or loss of benefit of, covenant

(1) Any release of a person from a covenant by virtue of this Act does not affect any liability of his arising from a breach of the covenant occurring before the release.

(2) Where –

(a) by virtue of this Act a tenant is released from a tenant covenant of a tenancy, and

(b) immediately before the release another person is bound by a covenant of the tenancy imposing any liability or penalty in the event of a failure to comply with that tenant covenant,

then, as from the release of the tenant, that other person is released from the covenant mentioned in paragraph (b) to the same extent as the tenant is released from that tenant covenant.

(3) Where a person bound by a landlord or tenant covenant of a tenancy –

(a) assigns the whole or part of his interest in the premises demised by the tenancy, but

(b) is not released by virtue of this Act from the covenant (with the result that subsection (1) does not apply),

the assignment does not affect any liability of his arising from a breach of the covenant occurring before the assignment.

(4) Where by virtue of this Act a person ceases to be entitled to the benefit of a covenant, this does not affect any rights of his arising from a breach of the covenant occurring before he ceases to be so entitled.

25 Agreement void if it restricts operation of the Act

(1) Any agreement relating to a tenancy is void to the extent that –

(a) it would apart from this section have effect to exclude, modify or otherwise frustrate the operation of any provision of this Act, or

(b) it provides for –

(i) the termination or surrender of the tenancy, or

(ii) the imposition on the tenant of any penalty, disability or liability,

in the event of the operation of any provision of this Act, or

(c) it provides for any of the matters referred to in paragraph (b)(i) or (ii) and does so (whether expressly or otherwise) in connection with, or in consequence of, the operation of any provision of this Act.

(2) To the extent that an agreement relating to a tenancy constitutes a covenant (whether absolute or qualified) against the assignment, or parting with the possession, of the premises demised by the tenancy or any part of them –

(a) the agreement is not void by virtue of subsection (1) by reason only of the fact that as such the covenant prohibits or restricts any such assignment or parting with possession; but

(b) paragraph (a) above does not otherwise affect the operation of that subsection in relation to the agreement (and in particular does not preclude its application to the agreement to the extent that it purports to regulate the giving of, or the making of any application for, consent to any such assignment or parting with possession).

(3) In accordance with section 16(1) nothing in this section applies to any agreement to the extent that it is an authorised guarantee agreement; but (without prejudice to the generality of subsection (1) above) an agreement is void to the extent that it is one falling within section 16(4)(a) or (b).

(4) This section applies to an agreement relating to a tenancy whether or not the agreement is –

(a) contained in the instrument creating the tenancy; or

(b) made before the creation of the tenancy.

26 Miscellaneous savings, etc

(1) Nothing in this Act is to be read as preventing –

(a) a party to a tenancy from releasing a person from a landlord covenant or a tenant covenant of the tenancy; or

(b) the parties to a tenancy from agreeing to an apportionment of liability under such a covenant.

(2) Nothing in this Act affects the operation of section 3(3A) of the Landlord and Tenant Act 1985 (preservation of former landlord's liability until tenant notified of new landlord).

(3) No apportionment which has become binding in accordance with section 10 shall be affected by any order or decision made under or by virtue of any enactment not contained in this Act which relates to apportionment.

28 Interpretation

(1) In this Act (unless the context otherwise requires) –

'assignment' includes equitable assignment and in addition (subject to section 11) assignment in breach of a covenant of a tenancy or by operation of law;

'authorised guarantee agreement' means an agreement which is an authorised guarantee agreement for the purposes of section 16;

'collateral agreement', in relation to a tenancy, means any agreement collateral to the tenancy, whether made before or after its creation;

'consent' includes licence;

'covenant' includes term, condition and obligation, and references to a covenant (or any description of covenant) of a tenancy include a covenant (or a covenant of that description) contained in a collateral agreement;

'landlord' and 'tenant', in relation to a tenancy, mean the person for the time being entitled to the reversion expectant on the term of the tenancy and the person so entitled to that term respectively;

'landlord covenant', in relation to a tenancy, means a covenant falling to be complied with by the landlord of premises demised by the tenancy;

'new tenancy' means a tenancy which is a new tenancy for the purposes of section 1;

'reversion' means the interest expectant on the termination of a tenancy;

'tenancy' means any lease or other tenancy and includes –

(a) a sub-tenancy, and

(b) an agreement for a tenancy,

but does not include a mortgage term;

'tenant covenant', in relation to a tenancy, means a covenant falling to be complied with by the tenant of premises demised by the tenancy.

(2) For the purposes of any reference in this Act to a covenant falling to be complied with in relation to a particular part of the premises demised by a tenancy, a covenant falls to be so complied with if –

(a) it in terms applies to that part of the premises, or

(b) in its practical application it can be attributed to that part of the premises (whether or not it can also be so attributed to other individual parts of those premises).

(3) Subsection (2) does not apply in relation to covenants to pay money; and, for the purposes of any reference in this Act to a covenant falling to be complied with in relation to a particular part of the premises demised by a tenancy, a covenant of a tenancy which is a covenant to pay money falls to be so complied with if –

(a) the covenant in terms applies to that part; or

(b) the amount of the payment is determinable specifically by reference –

(i) to that part, or

(ii) to anything falling to be done by or for a person as tenant or occupier of that part (if it is a tenant covenant), or

(iii) to anything falling to be done by or for a person as landlord of that part (if it is a landlord covenant).

(4) Where two or more persons jointly constitute either the landlord or the tenant in relation to a tenancy, any reference in this Act to the landlord or the tenant is a reference to both or all of the persons who jointly constitute the landlord or the tenant, as the case may be (and accordingly nothing in section 13 applies in relation to the rights and liabilities of such persons between themselves).

(5) References in this Act to the assignment by a landlord of the reversion in the whole or part of the premises demised by a tenancy are to the assignment by him of the whole of his interest (as owner of the reversion) in the whole or part of those premises.

(6) For the purposes of this Act –

(a) any assignment (however effected) consisting in the transfer of the whole of the landlord's interest (as owner of the reversion) in any premises demised by a tenancy shall be treated as an assignment by the landlord of the reversion in those premises even if it is not effected by him; and

(b) any assignment (however effected) consisting in the transfer of the whole of the tenant's interest in any premises demised by a tenancy shall be treated as an assignment by the tenant of those premises even if it is not effected by him.

29   Crown application

This Act binds the Crown.

30   Consequential amendments and repeals

(1) The enactments specified in Schedule 1 are amended in accordance with that Schedule, the amendments being consequential on the provisions of this Act.

(2) The enactments specified in Schedule 2 are repealed to the extent specified.

(3) Subsections (1) and (2) do not affect the operation of –

(a) section 77 of, or Part IX or X of Schedule 2 to, the Law of Property Act 1925, or

(b) section 24(1)(b) or (2) of the Land Registration Act 1925,

in relation to tenancies which are not new tenancies.

(4) In consequence of this Act nothing in the following provisions, namely –

(a) sections 78 and 79 of the Law of Property Act 1925 (benefit and burden of covenants relating to land), and

(b) sections 141 and 142 of that Act (running of benefit and burden of covenants with reversion),

shall apply in relation to new tenancies ...

31   Commencement

(1) The provisions of this Act come into force on such a day as the Lord Chancellor may appoint by order made by statutory instrument. ...

NB This Act came into force on 1 January 1996.

As amended by the Housing Act 1996 (Consequential Provisions) Order 1996, art 5, Schedule 2, para 22; Land Registration Act 2002, s133, Schedule 11, para 33.

DISABILITY DISCRIMINATION ACT 1995
(1995 c 50)

PART II

THE EMPLOYMENT FIELD

18A Alterations to premises occupied under leases

(1) This section applies where –

(a) a person to whom a duty to make reasonable adjustments applies ('the occupier') occupies premises under a lease;

(b) but for this section, the occupier would not be entitled to make a particular alteration to the premises; and

(c) the alteration is one which the occupier proposes to make in order to comply with that duty.

(2) Except to the extent to which it expressly so provides, the lease shall have effect by virtue of this subsection as if it provided –

(a) for the occupier to be entitled to make the alteration with the written consent of the lessor;

(b) for the occupier to have to make a written application to the lessor for consent if he wishes to make the alteration;

(c) if such an application is made, for the lessor not to withhold his consent unreasonably; and

(d) for the lessor to be entitled to make his consent subject to reasonable conditions.

(3) In this section –

'lease' includes a tenancy, sub-lease or sub-tenancy and an agreement for a lease, tenancy, sub-lease or sub-tenancy; and

'sub-lease' and 'sub-tenancy' have such meaning as may be prescribed.

(4) If the terms and conditions of a lease –

(a) impose conditions which are to apply if the occupier alters the premises, or

(b) entitle the lessor to impose conditions when consenting to the occupier's altering the premises,

the occupier is to be treated for the purposes of subsection (1) as not being entitled to make the alteration …

18B Reasonable adjustments: supplementary

(1) In determining whether it is reasonable for a person to have to take a particular step in order to comply with a duty to make reasonable adjustments, regard shall be had, in particular, to –

(a) the extent to which taking the step would prevent the effect in relation to which the duty is imposed;

(b) the extent to which it is practicable for him to take the step;

(c) the financial and other costs which would be incurred by him in taking the step and the extent to which taking it would disrupt any of his activities;

(d) the extent of his financial and other resources;

(e) the availability to him of financial or other assistance with respect to taking the step;

(f) the nature of his activities and the size of his undertaking;

(g) where the step would be taken in relation to a private household, the extent to which taking it would –

(i) disrupt that household, or

(ii) disturb any person residing there. ...

PART III

DISCRIMINATION IN OTHER AREAS

22 Discrimination in relation to premises

(1) It is unlawful for a person with power to dispose of any premises to discriminate against a disabled person –

(a) in the terms on which he offers to dispose of those premises to the disabled person;

(b) by refusing to dispose of those premises to the disabled person; or

(c) in his treatment of the disabled person in relation to any list of persons in need of premises of that description.

(2) Subsection (1) does not apply to a person who owns an estate or interest in the premises and wholly occupies them unless, for the purpose of disposing of the premises, he –

(a) uses the services of an estate agent, or

(b) publishes an advertisement or causes an advertisement to be published.

(3) It is unlawful for a person managing any premises to discriminate against a disabled person occupying those premises –

(a) in the way he permits the disabled person to make use of any benefits or facilities;

(b) by refusing or deliberately omitting to permit the disabled person to make use of any benefits or facilities; or

(c) by evicting the disabled person, or subjecting him to any other detriment.

(4) It is unlawful for any person whose licence or consent is required for the disposal of any premises comprised in ... a tenancy to discriminate against a disabled person by withholding his licence or consent for the disposal of the premises to the disabled person.

(5) Subsection (4) applies to tenancies created before as well as after the passing of this Act.

(6) In this section –

'advertisement' includes every form of advertisement or notice, whether to the public or not;

'dispose', in relation to premises, includes granting a right to occupy the premises, and, in relation to premises comprised in, or (in Scotland) the subject of, a tenancy, includes –

(a) assigning the tenancy, and

(b) sub-letting or parting with possession of the premises or any part of the premises;

and 'disposal' shall be construed accordingly;

'estate agent' means a person who, by way of profession or trade, provides services for the purpose of finding premises for persons seeking to acquire them or assisting in the disposal of premises; and

'tenancy' means a tenancy created –

(a) by a lease or sub-lease,

(b) by an agreement for a lease or sub-lease,

(c) by a tenancy agreement, or

(d) in pursuance of any enactment ...

23   Exemption for small dwellings

(1) Where the conditions mentioned in subsection (2) are satisfied, subsection (1), (3) or (as the case may be) (4) of section 22 does not apply.

(2) The conditions are that –

(a) the relevant occupier resides, and intends to continue to reside, on the premises;

(b) the relevant occupier shares accommodation on the premises with persons who reside on the premises and are not members of his household;

(c) the shared accommodation is not storage accommodation or a means of access; and

(d) the premises are small premises.

(3) For the purposes of this section, premises are 'small premises' if they fall within subsection (4) or (5).

(4) Premises fall within this subsection if –

(a) only the relevant occupier and members of his household reside in the accommodation occupied by him;

(b) the premises comprise, in addition to the accommodation occupied by the relevant occupier, residential accommodation for at least one other household;

(c) the residential accommodation for each other household is let, or available for letting, on a separate tenancy or similar agreement; and

(d) there are not normally more than two such other households.

(5) Premises fall within this subsection if there is not normally residential accommodation on the premises for more than six persons in addition to the relevant occupier and any members of his household.

(6) For the purposes of this section 'the relevant occupier' means –

(a) in a case falling within section 22(1), the person with power to dispose of the premises, or a near relative of his;

(b) in a case falling within section 22(4), the person whose licence or consent is required for the disposal of the premises, or a near relative of his.

(7) For the purposes of this section –

'near relative' means a person's spouse or civil partner, partner, parent, child, grandparent, grandchild, or brother or sister (whether of full or half blood or by marriage or civil partnership); and

'partner' means the other member of a couple consisting of –

(a) a man and a woman who are not married to each other but are living together as husband and wife, or

(b) two people of the same sex who are not civil partners of each other but are living together as if they were civil partners.

24 Meaning of 'discrimination'

(1) For the purposes of section 22, a person ('A') discriminates against a disabled person if –

(a) for a reason which relates to the disabled person's disability, he treats him less favourably than he treats or would treat others to whom that reason does not or would not apply; and

(b) he cannot show that the treatment in question is justified.

(2) For the purposes of this section, treatment is justified only if –

(a) in A's opinion, one or more of the conditions mentioned in subsection (3) are satisfied; and

(b) it is reasonable, in all the circumstances of the case, for him to hold that opinion.

(3) The conditions are that –

(a) in any case, the treatment is necessary in order not to endanger the health or safety of any person (which may include that of the disabled person);

(b) in any case, the disabled person is incapable of entering into an enforceable agreement, or of giving an informed consent, and for that reason the treatment is reasonable in that case;

(c) in a case falling within section 22(3)(a), the treatment is necessary in order for the disabled person or the occupiers of other premises forming part of the building to make use of the benefit or facility;

(d) in a case falling within section 22(3)(b), the treatment is necessary in order for the occupiers of other premises forming part of the building to make use of the benefit or facility. ...

25   Enforcement, remedies and procedure

(1) A claim by any person that another person –

(a) has discriminated against him in a way which is unlawful under this Part;
...

may be made the subject of civil proceedings in the same way as another claim in tort ... for breach of statutory duty.

(2) For the avoidance of doubt it is hereby declared that damages in respect of discrimination in a way which is unlawful under this Part may include compensation for injury to feelings whether or not they include compensation under any other head.

(3) Proceedings in England and Wales shall be brought only in a county court ...

As amended by the Disability Discrimination Act 1995 (Amendment) Regulations 2003, regs 3(1), 4(1), 14(2), (3), 17(2); Civil Partnership Act 2004, s261(1), Schedule 27, para 150.

TREASURE ACT 1996
(1996 c 24)

1   Meaning of 'treasure'

(1) Treasure is –

(a) any object at least 300 years old when found which –

(i) is not a coin but has metallic content of which at least 10 per cent by weight is precious metal;

(ii) when found, is one of at least two coins in the same find which are at least 300 years old at that time and have that percentage of precious metal; or

(iii) when found, is one of at least ten coins in the same find which are at least 300 years old at that time;

(b) any object at least 200 years old when found which belongs to a class designated under section 2(1);

(c) any object which would have been treasure trove if found before the commencement of section 4;

(d) any object which, when found, is part of the same find as –

(i) an object within paragraph (a), (b) or (c) found at the same time or earlier; or

(ii) an object found earlier which would be within paragraph (a) or (b) if it had been found at the same time.

(2) Treasure does not include objects which are –

(a) unworked natural objects, or

(b) minerals as extracted from a natural deposit,

or which belong to a class designated under section 2(2).

2   Power to alter meaning

(1) The Secretary of State may by order, for the purposes of section 1(1)(b), designate any class of object which he considers to be of outstanding historical, archaeological or cultural importance.

(2) The Secretary of State may by order, for the purposes of section 1(2), designate any class of object which (apart from the order) would be treasure. ...

3   Supplementary

(1) This section supplements section 1.

(2) 'Coin' includes any metal token which was, or can reasonably be assumed to have been, used or intended for use as or instead of money.

(3) 'Precious metal' means gold or silver.

(4) When an object is found, it is part of the same find as another object if –

(a) they are found together,

(b) the other object was found earlier in the same place where they had been left together,

(c) the other object was found earlier in a different place, but they had been left together and had become separated before being found.

(5) If the circumstances in which objects are found can reasonably be taken to indicate that they were together at some time before being found, the objects are to be presumed to have been left together, unless shown not to have been.

(6) An object which can reasonably be taken to be at least a particular age is to be presumed to be at least that age, unless shown not to be.

(7) An object is not treasure if it is wreck within the meaning of Part IX of the Merchant Shipping Act 1995.

4   Ownership of treasure which is found

(1) When treasure is found, it vests, subject to prior interests and rights –

(a) in the franchisee, if there is one;

(b) otherwise, in the Crown.

(2) Prior interests and rights are any which, or which derive from any which –

(a) were held when the treasure was left where it was found, or

(b) if the treasure had been moved before being found, were held when it was left where it was before being moved.

(3) If the treasure would have been treasure trove if found before the commencement of this section, neither the Crown nor any franchisee has any interest in it or right over it except in accordance with this Act.

(4) This section applies –

(a) whatever the nature of the place where the treasure was found, and

(b) whatever the circumstances in which it was left (including being lost or being left with no intention of recovery).

5   Meaning of 'franchisee'

(1) The franchisee for any treasure is the person who –

(a) was, immediately before the commencement of section 4, or

(b) apart from this Act, as successor in title, would have been,

the franchisee of the Crown in right of treasure trove for the place where the treasure was found.

(2) It is as franchisees in right of treasure trove that Her Majesty and the Duke of Cornwall are to be treated as having enjoyed the rights to treasure trove which belonged respectively to the Duchy of Lancaster and the Duchy of Cornwall immediately before the commencement of section 4.

6 Treasure vesting in the Crown

(1) Treasure vesting in the Crown under this Act is to be treated as part of the hereditary revenues of the Crown to which section 1 of the Civil List Act 1952 applies (surrender of hereditary revenues to the Exchequer).

(2) Any such treasure may be transferred, or otherwise disposed of, in accordance with directions given by the Secretary of State.

(3) The Crown's title to any such treasure may be disclaimed at any time by the Secretary of State.

(4) If the Crown's title is disclaimed, the treasure –

(a) is deemed not to have vested in the Crown under this Act, and

(b) without prejudice to the interests or rights of others, may be delivered to any person in accordance with the code published under section 11.

7 Jurisdiction of coroners

(1) The jurisdiction of coroners which is referred to in section 30 of the Coroners Act 1988 (treasure) is exercisable in relation to anything which is treasure for the purposes of this Act.

(2) That jurisdiction is not exercisable for the purposes of the law relating to treasure trove in relation to anything found after the commencement of section 4.

(3) The Act of 1988 and anything saved by virtue of section 36(5) of that Act (saving for existing law and practice etc) has effect subject to this section.

(4) An inquest held by virtue of this section is to be held without a jury, unless the coroner orders otherwise.

8 Duty of finder to notify coroner.

(1) A person who finds an object which he believes or has reasonable grounds for believing is treasure must notify the coroner for the district in which the object was found before the end of the notice period.

(2) The notice period is fourteen days beginning with –

(a) the day after the find; or

(b) if later, the day on which the finder first believes or has reason to believe the object is treasure.

(3) Any person who fails to comply with subsection (1) is guilty of an offence ...

(4) In proceedings for an offence under this section, it is a defence for the defendant to show that he had, and has continued to have, a reasonable excuse for failing to notify the coroner.

(5) If the office of coroner for a district is vacant, the person acting as coroner for that district is the coroner for the purposes of subsection (1).

9   Procedure for inquests

(1) In this section, 'inquest' means an inquest held under section 7.

(2) A coroner proposing to conduct an inquest must notify –

(a) the British Museum, if his district is in England; or
(b) the National Museum of Wales, if it is in Wales.

(3) Before conducting the inquest, the coroner must take reasonable steps to notify –

(a) any person who it appears to him may have found the treasure; and
(b) any person who, at the time the treasure was found, occupied land which it appears to him may be where it was found. ...

10   Rewards

(1) This section applies if treasure –

(a) has vested in the Crown under section 4; and
(b) is to be transferred to a museum.

(2) The Secretary of State must determine whether a reward is to be paid by the museum before the transfer.

(3) If the Secretary of State determines that a reward is to be paid, he must also determine, in whatever way he thinks fit –

(a) the treasure's market value;
(b) the amount of the reward;
(c) to whom the reward is to be payable; and
(d) if it is to be payable to more than one person, how much each is to receive.

(4) The total reward must not exceed the treasure's market value.

(5) The reward may be payable to –

(a) the finder or any other person involved in the find;
(b) the occupier of the land at the time of the find;
(c) any person who had an interest in the land at that time, or has had such an interest at any time since then.

(6) Payment of the reward is not enforceable against a museum or the Secretary of State.

(7) In a determination under this section, the Secretary of State must take into account anything relevant in the code of practice issued under section 11.

(8) This section also applies in relation to treasure which has vested in a franchisee under section 4, if the franchisee makes a request to the Secretary of State that it should.

11   Codes of practice

(1) The Secretary of State must –

  (a) prepare a code of practice relating to treasure;

  (b) keep the code under review; and

  (c) revise it when appropriate.

(2) The code must, in particular, set out the principles and practice to be followed by the Secretary of State –

  (a) when considering to whom treasure should be offered;

  (b) when making a determination under section 10; and

  (c) where the Crown's title to treasure is disclaimed.

(3) The code may include guidance for –

  (a) those who search for or find treasure; and

  (b) museums and others who exercise functions in relation to treasure.

(4) Before preparing the code or revising it, the Secretary of State must consult such persons appearing to him to be interested as he thinks appropriate. ...

(7) The Secretary of State must publish the code in whatever way he considers appropriate for bringing it to the attention of those interested. ...

12   Report on operation of Act

As soon as reasonably practicable after each anniversary of the coming into force of this section, the Secretary of State shall lay before Parliament a report on the operation of this Act in the preceding year.

15   Short title, commencement and extent ...

(2) This Act comes into force on such day as the Secretary of State may by order made by statutory instrument appoint; and different days may be appointed for different purposes. ...

PARTY WALL ETC ACT 1996
(1996 c 40)

1   New building on line of junction

(1) This section shall have effect where lands of different owners adjoin and –

(a) are not built on at the line of junction; or

(b) are built on at the line of junction only to the extent of a boundary wall (not being a party fence wall or the external wall of a building),

and either owner is about to build on any part of the line of junction.

(2) If a building owner desires to build a party wall or party fence wall on the line of junction he shall, at least one month before he intends the building work to start, serve on any adjoining owner a notice which indicates his desire to build and describes the intended wall.

(3) If, having been served with notice described in subsection (2), an adjoining owner serves on the building owner a notice indicating his consent to the building of a party wall or party fence wall –

(a) the wall shall be built half on the land of each of the two owners or in such other position as may be agreed between the two owners; and

(b) the expense of building the wall shall be from time to time defrayed by the two owners in such proportion as has regard to the use made or to be made of the wall by each of them and to the cost of labour and materials prevailing at the time when that use is made by each owner respectively.

(4) If, having been served with notice described in subsection (2), an adjoining owner does not consent under this subsection to the building of a party wall or party fence wall, the building owner may only build the wall –

(a) at his own expense; and

(b) as an external wall or a fence wall, as the case may be, placed wholly on his own land,

and consent under this subsection is consent by a notice served within the period of fourteen days beginning with the day on which the notice described in subsection (2) is served.

(5) If the building owner desires to build on the line of junction a wall placed wholly on his own land he shall, at least one month before he intends the building work to start, serve on any adjoining owner a notice which indicates his desire to build and describes the intended wall.

(6) Where the building owner builds a wall wholly on his own land in accordance with subsection (4) or (5) he shall have the right, at any time in the period which –

(a) begins one month after the day on which the notice mentioned in the subsection concerned was served, and

(b) ends twelve months after that day,

to place below the level of the land of the adjoining owner such projecting footings and foundations as are necessary for the construction of the wall.

(7) Where the building owner builds a wall wholly on his own land in accordance with subsection (4) or (5) he shall do so at his own expense and shall compensate any adjoining owner and any adjoining occupier for any damage to his property occasioned by –

(a) the building of the wall;

(b) the placing of any footings or foundations placed in accordance with subsection (6).

(8) Where any dispute arises under this section between the building owner and any adjoining owner or occupier it is to be determined in accordance with section 10.

2   Repair, etc of party wall: rights of owner

(1) This section applies where lands of different owners adjoin and at the line of junction the said lands are built on or a boundary wall, being a party fence wall or the external wall of a building, has been erected.

(2) A building owner shall have the following rights –

(a) to underpin, thicken or raise a party structure, a party fence wall, or an external wall which belongs to the building owner and is built against a party structure or party fence wall;

(b) to make good, repair, or demolish and rebuild, a party structure or party fence wall in a case where such work is necessary on account of defect or want of repair of the structure or wall;

(c) to demolish a partition which separates buildings belonging to different owners but does not conform with statutory requirements and to build instead a party wall which does so conform;

(d) in the case of buildings connected by arches or structures over public ways or over passages belonging to other persons, to demolish the whole or part of such buildings, arches or structures which do not conform with statutory requirements and to rebuild them so that they do so conform;

(e) to demolish a party structure which is of insufficient strength or height for the purposes of any intended building of the building owner and to rebuild it of sufficient strength or height for the said purposes (including rebuilding to a lesser height or thickness where the rebuilt structure is of sufficient strength and height for the purposes of any adjoining owner);

(f) to cut into a party structure for any purpose (which may be or include the purpose of inserting a damp proof course);

(g) to cut away from a party wall, party fence wall, external wall or boundary wall any footing or any projecting chimney breast, jamb or flue, or other projection on or over the land of the building owner in order to erect, raise or underpin any such wall or for any other purpose;

(h) to cut away or demolish parts of any wall or building of an adjoining owner overhanging the land of the building owner or overhanging a party wall, to the extent that it is necessary to cut away or demolish the parts to enable a vertical wall to be erected or raised against the wall or building of the adjoining owner;

(j) to cut into the wall of an adjoining owner's building in order to insert a flashing or other weather-proofing of a wall erected against that wall;

(k) to execute any other necessary works incidental to the connection of a party structure with the premises adjoining it;

(l) to raise a party fence wall, or to raise such a wall for use as a party wall, and to demolish a party fence wall and rebuild it as a party fence wall or as a party wall;

(m) subject to the provisions of section 11(7), to reduce, or to demolish and rebuild, a party wall or party fence wall to –

(i) a height of not less than two metres where the wall is not used by an adjoining owner to any greater extent than a boundary wall; or

(ii) a height currently enclosed upon by the building of an adjoining owner;

(n) to expose a party wall or party structure hitherto enclosed subject to providing adequate weathering.

(3) Where work mentioned in paragraph (a) of subsection (2) is not necessary on account of defect or want of repair of the structure or wall concerned, the right falling within that paragraph is exercisable –

(a) subject to making good all damage occasioned by the work to the adjoining premises or to their internal furnishings and decorations; and

(b) where the work is to a party structure or external wall, subject to carrying any relevant flues and chimney stacks up to such a height and in such materials as may be agreed between the building owner and the adjoining owner concerned or, in the event of dispute, determined in accordance with section 10;

and relevant flues and chimney stacks are those which belong to an adjoining owner and either form part of or rest on or against the party structure or external wall.

(4) The right falling within subsection (2)(e) is exercisable subject to –

(a) making good all damage occasioned by the work to the adjoining premises or to their internal furnishings and decorations; and

(b) carrying any relevant flues and chimney stacks up to such a height and in such materials as may be agreed between the building owner and the adjoining owner concerned or, in the event of dispute, determined in accordance with section 10;

and relevant flues and chimney stacks are those which belong to an adjoining owner and either form part of or rest on or against the party structure.

(5) Any right falling within subsection (2)(f), (g) or (h) is exercisable subject to making good all damage occasioned by the work to the adjoining premises or to their internal furnishings and decorations.

(6) The right falling within subsection (2)(j) is exercisable subject to making good all damage occasioned by the work to the wall of the adjoining owner's building.

(7) The right falling within subsection (2)(m) is exercisable subject to –

(a) reconstructing any parapet or replacing an existing parapet with another one; or

(b) constructing a parapet where one is needed but did not exist before.

(8) For the purposes of this section a building or structure which was erected before the day on which this Act was passed shall be deemed to conform with statutory requirements if it conforms with the statutes regulating buildings or structures on the date on which it was erected.

3   Party structure notices

(1) Before exercising any right conferred on him by section 2 a building owner shall serve on any adjoining owner a notice (in this Act referred to as a 'party structure notice') stating –

(a) the name and address of the building owner;

(b) the nature and particulars of the proposed work including, in cases where the building owner proposes to construct special foundations, plans, sections and details of construction of the special foundations together with reasonable particulars of the loads to be carried thereby; and

(c) the date on which the proposed work will begin.

(2) A party structure notice shall –

(a) be served at least two months before the date on which the proposed work will begin;

(b) cease to have effect if the work to which it relates –

(i) has not begun within the period of twelve months beginning with the day on which the notice is served; and

(ii) is not prosecuted with due diligence.

(3) Nothing in this section shall –

(a) prevent a building owner from exercising with the consent in writing of the adjoining owners and of the adjoining occupiers any right conferred on him by section 2; or

(b) require a building owner to serve any party structure notice before complying with any notice served under any statutory provisions relating to dangerous or neglected structures.

4   Counter notices

(1) An adjoining owner may, having been served with a party structure notice serve on the building owner a notice (in this Act referred to as a 'counter notice') setting out –

(a) in respect of a party fence wall or party structure, a requirement that the building owner build in or on the wall or structure to which the notice relates such chimney copings, breasts, jambs or flues, or such piers or recesses or other like works, as may reasonably be required for the convenience of the adjoining owner;

(b) in respect of special foundations to which the adjoining owner consents under section 7(4) below, a requirement that the special foundations –

(i) be placed at a specified greater depth than that proposed by the building owner; or

(ii) be constructed of sufficient strength to bear the load to be carried by columns of any intended building of the adjoining owner,

or both.

(2) A counter notice shall –

(a) specify the works required by the notice to be executed and shall be accompanied by plans, sections and particulars of such works; and

(b) be served within the period of one month beginning with the day on which the party structure notice is served.

(3) A building owner on whom a counter notice has been served shall comply with the requirements of the counter notice unless the execution of the works required by the counter notice would –

(a) be injurious to him;

(b) cause unnecessary inconvenience to him; or

(c) cause unnecessary delay in the execution of the works pursuant to the party structure notice.

5   Disputes arising under sections 3 and 4

If an owner on whom a party structure notice or a counter notice has been served does not serve a notice indicating his consent to it within the period of fourteen days beginning with the day on which the party structure notice or counter notice was served, he shall be deemed to have dissented from the notice and a dispute shall be deemed to have arisen between the parties.

6   Adjacent excavation and construction

(1) This section applies where –

(a) a building owner proposes to excavate, or excavate for and erect a building or structure, within a distance of three metres measured horizontally from any part of a building or structure of an adjoining owner; and

(b) any part of the proposed excavation, building or structure will within those three metres extend to a lower level than the level of the bottom of the foundations of the building or structure of the adjoining owner.

(2) This section also applies where –

(a) a building owner proposes to excavate, or excavate for and erect a building or structure, within a distance of six metres measured horizontally from any part of a building or structure of an adjoining owner; and

(b) any part of the proposed excavation, building or structure will within those six metres meet a plane drawn downwards in the direction of the excavation, building or structure of the building owner at an angle of forty-five degrees to the horizontal from the line formed by the intersection of the plane of the level of the bottom of the foundations of the building or structure of the adjoining owner with the plane of the external face of the external wall of the building or structure of the adjoining owner.

(3) The building owner may, and if required by the adjoining owner shall, at his own expense underpin or otherwise strengthen or safeguard the foundations of the building or structure of the adjoining owner so far as may be necessary.

(4) Where the buildings or structures of different owners are within the respective distances mentioned in subsections (1) and (2) the owners of those buildings or structures shall be deemed to be adjoining owners for the purposes of this section.

(5) In any case where this section applies the building owner shall, at least one month before beginning to excavate, or excavate for and erect a building or structure, serve on the adjoining owner a notice indicating his proposals and stating whether he proposes to underpin or otherwise strengthen or safeguard the foundations of the building or structure of the adjoining owner.

(6) The notice referred to in subsection (5) shall be accompanied by plans and sections showing –

(a) the site and depth of any excavation the building owner proposes to make;

(b) if he proposes to erect a building or structure, its site.

(7) If an owner on whom a notice referred to in subsection (5) has been served does not serve a notice indicating his consent to it within the period of fourteen days beginning with the day on which the notice referred to in subsection (5) was served, he shall be deemed to have dissented from the notice and a dispute shall be deemed to have arisen between the parties.

(8) The notice referred to in subsection (5) shall cease to have effect if the work to which the notice relates –

(a) has not begun within the period of twelve months beginning with the day on which the notice was served; and

(b) is not prosecuted with due diligence.

(9) On completion of any work executed in pursuance of this section the building owner shall if so requested by the adjoining owner supply him with particulars including plans and sections of the work.

(10) Nothing in this section shall relieve the building owner from any liability to which he would otherwise be subject for injury to any adjoining owner or any adjoining occupier by reason of work executed by him.

7   Compensation, etc

(1) A building owner shall not exercise any right conferred on him by this Act in such a manner or at such time as to cause unnecessary inconvenience to any adjoining owner or to any adjoining occupier.

(2) The building owner shall compensate any adjoining owner and any adjoining occupier for any loss or damage which may result to any of them by reason of any work executed in pursuance of this Act.

(3) Where a building owner in exercising any right conferred on him by this Act lays open any part of the adjoining land or building he shall at his own expense make and maintain so long as may be necessary a proper hoarding, shoring or fans or temporary construction for the protection of the adjoining land or building and the security of any adjoining occupier.

(4) Nothing in this Act shall authorise the building owner to place special foundations on land of an adjoining owner without his previous consent in writing.

(5) Any works executed in pursuance of this Act shall –

    (a) comply with the provisions of statutory requirements; and

    (b) be executed in accordance with such plans, sections and particulars as may be agreed between the owners or in the event of dispute determined in accordance with section 10;

and no deviation shall be made from those plans, sections and particulars except such as may be agreed between the owners (or surveyors acting on their behalf) or in the event of dispute determined in accordance with section 10.

8   Rights of entry

(1) A building owner, his servants, agents and workmen may during usual working hours enter and remain on any land or premises for the purpose of executing any work in pursuance of this Act and may remove any furniture or fittings or take any other action necessary for that purpose.

(2) If the premises are closed, the building owner, his agents and workmen may, if accompanied by a constable or other police officer, break open any fences or doors in order to enter the premises.

(3) No land or premises may be entered by any person under subsection (1) unless the building owner serves on the owner and the occupier of the land or premises –

    (a) in case of emergency, such notice of the intention to enter as may be reasonably practicable;

    (b) in any other case, such notice of the intention to enter as complies with subsection (4).

(4) Notice complies with this subsection if it is served in a period of not less than fourteen days ending with the day of the proposed entry.

(5) A surveyor appointed or selected under section 10 may during usual working hours enter and remain on any land or premises for the purpose of carrying out the object for which he is appointed or selected.

(6) No land or premises may be entered by a surveyor under subsection (5) unless the building owner who is a party to the dispute concerned serves on the owner and the occupier of the land or premises –

(a) in case of emergency, such notice of the intention to enter as may be reasonably practicable;

(b) in any other case, such notice of the intention to enter as complies with subsection (4).

9   Easements

Nothing in this Act shall –

(a) authorise any interference with an easement of light or other easements in or relating to a party wall; or

(b) prejudicially affect any right of any person to preserve or restore any right or other thing in or connected with a party wall in case of the party wall being pulled down or rebuilt.

10   Resolution of disputes

(1) Where a dispute arises or is deemed to have arisen between a building owner and an adjoining owner in respect of any matter connected with any work to which this Act relates either –

(a) both parties shall concur in the appointment of one surveyor (in this section referred to as an 'agreed surveyor'); or

(b) each party shall appoint a surveyor and the two surveyors so appointed shall forthwith select a third surveyor (all of whom are in this section referred to as 'the three surveyors').

(2) All appointments and selections made under this section shall be in writing and shall not be rescinded by either party. ...

(10) The agreed surveyor or as the case may be the three surveyors or any two of them shall settle by award any matter –

(a) which is connected with any work to which this Act relates, and

(b) which is in dispute between the building owner and the adjoining owner.

(11) Either of the parties or either of the surveyors appointed by the parties may call upon the third surveyor selected in pursuance of this section to determine the disputed matters and he shall make the necessary award.

(12) An award may determine –

(a) the right to execute any work;

(b) the time and manner of executing any work; and

(c) any other matter arising out of or incidental to the dispute including the costs of making the award;

but any period appointed by the award for executing any work shall not unless otherwise agreed between the building owner and the adjoining owner begin to run until after the expiration of the period prescribed by this Act for service of the notice in respect of which the dispute arises or is deemed to have arisen.

(13) The reasonable costs incurred in –

(a) making or obtaining an award under this section;

(b) reasonable inspections of work to which the award relates; and

(c) any other matter arising out of the dispute,

shall be paid by such of the parties as the surveyor or surveyors making the award determine.

(14) Where the surveyors appointed by the parties make an award the surveyors shall serve it forthwith on the parties.

(15) Where an award is made by the third surveyor –

(a) he shall, after payment of the costs of the award, serve it forthwith on the parties or their appointed surveyors; and

(b) if it is served on their appointed surveyors, they shall serve it forthwith on the parties.

(16) The award shall be conclusive and shall not except as provided by this section be questioned in any court.

(17) Either of the parties to the dispute may, within the period of fourteen days beginning with the day on which an award made under this section is served on him, appeal to the county court against the award and the county court may –

(a) rescind the award or modify it in such manner as the court thinks fit; and

(b) make such order as to costs as the court thinks fit.

11   Expenses

(1) Except as provided under this section expenses of work under this Act shall be defrayed by the building owner.

(2) Any dispute as to responsibility for expenses shall be settled as provided in section 10.

(3) An expense mentioned in section 1(3)(b) shall be defrayed as there mentioned.

(4) Where work is carried out in exercise of the right mentioned in section 2(2)(a), and the work is necessary on account of defect or want of repair of the structure or wall concerned, the expenses shall be defrayed by the building owner and the adjoining owner in such proportion as has regard to –

(a) the use which the owners respectively make or may make of the structure or wall concerned; and

(b) responsibility for the defect or want of repair concerned, if more than one owner makes use of the structure or wall concerned.

(5) Where work is carried out in exercise of the right mentioned in section 2(2)(b) the expenses shall be defrayed by the building owner and the adjoining owner in such proportion as has regard to –

(a) the use which the owners respectively make or may make of the structure or wall concerned; and

(b) responsibility for the defect or want of repair concerned, if more than one owner makes use of the structure or wall concerned.

(6) Where the adjoining premises are laid open in exercise of the right mentioned in section 2(2)(e) a fair allowance in respect of disturbance and inconvenience shall be paid by the building owner to the adjoining owner or occupier.

(7) Where a building owner proposes to reduce the height of a party wall or party fence wall under section 2(2)(m) the adjoining owner may serve a counter notice under section 4 requiring the building owner to maintain the existing height of the wall, and in such case the adjoining owner shall pay to the building owner a due proportion of the cost of the wall so far as it exceeds –

(a) two metres in height; or

(b) the height currently enclosed upon by the building of the adjoining owner.

(8) Where the building owner is required to make good damage under this Act the adjoining owner has a right to require that the expenses of such making good be determined in accordance with section 10 and paid to him in lieu of the carrying out of work to make the damage good.

(9) Where –

(a) works are carried out, and

(b) some of the works are carried out at the request of the adjoining owner or in pursuance of a requirement made by him,

he shall defray the expenses of carrying out the works requested or required by him.

(10) Where –

(a) consent in writing has been given to the construction of special foundations on land of an adjoining owner; and

(b) the adjoining owner erects any building or structure and its cost is found to be increased by reason of the existence of the said foundations,

the owner of the building to which the said foundations belong shall, on receiving an account with any necessary invoices and other supporting documents within the period of two months beginning with the day of the completion of the work by the adjoining owner, repay to the adjoining owner so much of the cost as is due to the existence of the said foundations.

(11) Where use is subsequently made by the adjoining owner of work carried out solely at the expense of the building owner the adjoining owner shall pay a due proportion of the expenses incurred by the building owner in carrying out that work; and for this purpose he shall be taken to have incurred expenses calculated by reference to what the cost of the work would be if it were carried out at the time when that subsequent use is made.

12   Security for expenses

(1) An adjoining owner may serve a notice requiring the building owner before he begins any work in the exercise of the rights conferred by this Act to give such security as may be agreed between the owners or in the event of dispute determined in accordance with section 10.

(2) Where –

(a) in the exercise of the rights conferred by this Act an adjoining owner requires the building owner to carry out any work the expenses of which are to be defrayed in whole or in part by the adjoining owner; or

(b) an adjoining owner serves a notice on the building owner under subsection (1),

the building owner may before beginning the work to which the requirement or notice relates serve a notice on the adjoining owner requiring him to give such security as may be agreed between the owners or in the event of dispute determined in accordance with section 10.

(3) If within the period of one month beginning with –

(a) the day on which a notice is served under subsection (2); or

(b) in the event of dispute, the date of the determination by the surveyor or surveyors,

the adjoining owner does not comply with the notice or the determination, the requirement or notice by him to which the building owner's notice under that subsection relates shall cease to have effect.

13   Account for work carried out

(1) Within the period of two months beginning with the day of the completion of any work executed by a building owner of which the expenses are to be wholly or partially defrayed by an adjoining owner in accordance with section 11 the building owner shall serve on the adjoining owner an account in writing showing –

(a) particulars and expenses of the work; and

(b) any deductions to which the adjoining owner or any other person is entitled in respect of old materials or otherwise;

and in preparing the account the work shall be estimated and valued at fair average rates and prices according to the nature of the work, the locality and the cost of labour and materials prevailing at the time when the work is executed.

(2) Within the period of one month beginning with the day of service of the said account the adjoining owner may serve on the building owner a notice stating any objection he may have thereto and thereupon a dispute shall be deemed to have arisen between the parties.

(3) If within that period of one month the adjoining owner does not serve notice under subsection (2) he shall be deemed to have no objection to the account.

14 Settlement of account

(1) All expenses to be defrayed by an adjoining owner in accordance with an account served under section 13 shall be paid by the adjoining owner.

(2) Until an adjoining owner pays to the building owner such expenses as aforesaid the property in any works executed under this Act to which the expenses relate shall be vested solely in the building owner.

16 Offences

(1) If –

(a) an occupier of land or premises refuses to permit a person to do anything which he is entitled to do with regard to the land or premises under section 8(1) or (5); and

(b) the occupier knows or has reasonable cause to believe that the person is so entitled,

the occupier is guilty of an offence.

(2) If –

(a) a person hinders or obstructs a person in attempting to do anything which he is entitled to do with regard to land or premises under section 8(1) or (5); and

(b) the first-mentioned person knows or has reasonable cause to believe that the other person is so entitled,

the first-mentioned person is guilty of an offence. ...

17 Recovery of sums

Any sum payable in pursuance of this Act (otherwise than by way of fine) shall be recoverable summarily as a civil debt. ...

19 The Crown

(1) This Act shall apply to land in which there is –

(a) an interest belonging to Her Majesty in right of the Crown,

(b) an interest belonging to a government department, or

(c) an interest held in trust for Her Majesty for the purposes of any such department.

(2) This Act shall apply to –

(a) land which is vested in, but not occupied by, Her Majesty in right of the Duchy of Lancaster;

(b) land which is vested in, but not occupied by, the possessor for the time being of the Duchy of Cornwall.

20   Interpretation

In this Act, unless the context otherwise requires, the following expressions have the meanings hereby respectively assigned to them –

'adjoining owner' and 'adjoining occupier' respectively mean any owner and any occupier of land, buildings, storeys or rooms adjoining those of the building owner and for the purposes only of section 6 within the distances specified in that section;

'appointing officer' means the person appointed under this Act by the local authority to make such appointments as are required under section 10(8);

'building owner' means an owner of land who is desirous of exercising rights under this Act;

'foundation', in relation to a wall, means the solid ground or artificially formed support resting on solid ground on which the wall rests;

'owner' includes –

(a) a person in receipt of, or entitled to receive, the whole or part of the rents or profits of land;

(b) a person in possession of land, otherwise than as a mortgagee or as a tenant from year to year or for a lesser term or as a tenant at will;

(c) a purchaser of an interest in land under a contract for purchase or under an agreement for a lease, otherwise than under an agreement for a tenancy from year to year or for a lesser term;

'party fence wall' means a wall (not being part of a building) which stands on lands of different owners and is used or constructed to be used for separating such adjoining lands, but does not include a wall constructed on the land of one owner the artificially formed support of which projects into the land of another owner;

'party structure' means a party wall and also a floor partition or other structure separating buildings or parts of buildings approached solely by separate staircases or separate entrances;

'party wall' means –

(a) a wall which forms part of a building and stands on lands of different owners to a greater extent than the projection of any artificially formed support on which the wall rests; and

(b) so much of a wall not being a wall referred to in paragraph (a) above as separates buildings belonging to different owners;

'special foundations' means foundations in which an assemblage of beams or rods is employed for the purpose of distributing any load; and

'surveyor' means any person not being a party to the matter appointed or selected under section 10 to determine disputes in accordance with the procedures set out in this Act.

21 Other statutory provisions

(1) The Secretary of State may by order amend or repeal any provision of a private or local Act passed before or in the same session as this Act, if it appears to him necessary or expedient to do so in consequence of this Act. ...

TRUSTS OF LAND AND APPOINTMENT OF TRUSTEES ACT 1996

(1996 c 47)

PART I

TRUSTS OF LAND

1 Meaning of 'trust of land'

(1) In this Act –

(a) 'trust of land' means (subject to subsection (3)) any trust of property which consists of or includes land, and

(b) 'trustees of land' means trustees of a trust of land.

(2) The reference in subsection (1)(a) to a trust –

(a) is to any description of a trust (whether express, implied, resulting or constructive), including a trust for sale and a bare trust, and

(b) includes a trust created, or arising, before the commencement of this Act,

(3) The reference to land in subsection (1)(a) does not include land which (despite section 2) is settled land or which is land to which the Universities and College Estates Act 1925 applies.

2 Trusts in place of settlements

(1) No settlement created after the commencement of this Act is a settlement for the purposes of the Settled Land Act 1925; and no settlement shall be deemed to be made under that Act after that commencement.

(2) Subsection (1) does not apply to a settlement created on the occasion of an alteration in any interest in, or of a person becoming entitled under, a settlement which –

(a) is in existence at the commencement of this Act, or

(b) derives from a settlement within paragraph (a) or this paragraph.

(3) But a settlement created as mentioned in subsection (2) is not a settlement for the purposes of the Settled land Act 1925 if provision to the effect that it is not is made in the instrument, or any of the instruments, by which it is created.

(4) Where at any time after the commencement of this Act there is in the case of any settlement which is a settlement for the purposes of the Settled land Act 1925 no relevant property which is, or is deemed to be, subject to the settlement, the settlement permanently ceases at that time to be a settlement for the purposes of that Act. In this subsection 'relevant property' means land and personal chattels to which section 67(1) of the Settled Land Act 1925 (heirlooms) applies.

(5) No land held on charitable, ecclesiastical or public trusts shall be or be deemed to be settled land after the commencement of this Act, even if it was or was deemed to be settled land before that commencement.

(6) Schedule 1 has effect to make provision consequential on this section (including provision to impose a trust in circumstances in which, apart from this section, there would be a settlement for the purposes of the Settled Land Act 1925 (and there would not otherwise be a trust)).

3   Abolition of doctrine of conversion

(1) Where land is held by trustees subject to a trust for sale, the land is not to be regarded as personal property; and where personal property is subject to a trust for sale in order that the trustees may acquire land, the personal property is not to be regarded as land.

(2) Subsection (1) does not apply to a trust created by a will if the testator died before the commencement of this Act.

(3) Subject to that, subsection (1) applies to a trust whether it is created, or arises, before or after that commencement.

4   Express trusts for sale as trusts of land

(1) In the case of every trust for sale of land created by a disposition there is to be implied, despite any provision to the contrary made by the disposition, a power for the trustees to postpone sale of the land; and the trustees are not liable in any way for postponing sale of the land, in the exercise of their discretion, for an indefinite period.

(2) Subsection (1) applies to a trust whether it is created, or arises, before or after the commencement of this Act

(3) Subsection (1) does not affect any liability incurred by trustees before that commencement.

5   Implied trusts for sale as trusts of land

(1) Schedule 2 has effect in relation to statutory provisions which impose a trust for sale of land in certain circumstances so that in those circumstances there is instead a trust of the land (without a duty to sell).

(2) Section 1 of the Settled Land Act 1925 does not apply to land held on any trust arising by virtue of that Schedule (so that any such land is subject to a trust of land).

6   General powers of trustees

(1) For the purpose of exercising their functions as trustees, the trustees of land have in relation to the land subject to the trust all the powers of an absolute owner.

(2) Where in the case of any land subject to a trust of land each of the beneficiaries interested in the land is a person of full age and capacity who is absolutely entitled to the land, the powers conferred on the trustees by subsection (1) include the power to convey the land to the beneficiaries even though they have not required the trustees to do so; and where land is conveyed by virtue of this subsection –

  (a) the beneficiaries shall do whatever is necessary to secure that it vests in them, and

  (b) if they fail to do so, the court may make an order requiring them to do so.

(3) The trustees of land have power to acquire land under the power conferred by section 8 of the Trustee Act 2000.

(5) In exercising the powers conferred by this section trustees shall have regard to the rights of the beneficiaries.

(6) The powers conferred by this section shall not be exercised in contravention of, or of any order made in pursuance of, any other enactment or any rule of law or equity.

(7) The reference in subsection (6) to an order includes an order of any court or of the Charity Commissioners.

(8) Where any enactment other than this section confers on trustees authority to act subject to any restriction, limitation or condition, trustees of land may not exercise the powers conferred by this section to do any act which they are prevented from doing under the other enactment by reason of the restriction, limitation or condition.

(9) The duty of care under section 1 of the Trustee Act 2000 applies to trustees of land when exercising the powers conferred by this section.

7   Partition by trustees

(1) The trustees of land may, where beneficiaries of full age are absolutely entitled in undivided shares to land subject to the trust, partition the land, or any part of it, and provide (by way of mortgage or otherwise) for the payment of any equality money.

(2) The trustees shall give effect to any such partition by conveying the partitioned land in severalty (whether or not subject to any legal mortgage created for raising equality money), either absolutely or in trust, in accordance with the rights of those beneficiaries.

(3) Before exercising their powers under subsection (2) the trustees shall obtain the consent of each of those beneficiaries.

(4) Where a share in the land is affected by an incumbrance, the trustees may

either give effect to it or provide for its discharge from the property allotted to that share as they think fit.

(5) If a share in the land is absolutely vested in a minor, subsections (1) to (4) apply as if he were of full age, except that the trustees may act on his behalf and retain land or other property representing his share in trust for him.

(6) Subsection (1) is subject to sections 21 (part-unit: interests) and 22 (part-unit: charging) of the Commonhold and Leasehold Reform Act 2002.

8 Exclusion and restriction of powers

(1) Sections 6 and 7 do not apply in the case of a trust of land created by a disposition in so far as provision to the effect that they do not apply is made by the disposition.

(2) If the disposition creating such a trust makes provision requiring any consent to be obtained to the exercise of any power conferred by section 6 or 7, the power may not be exercised without that consent.

(3) Subsection (1) does not apply in the case of charitable, ecclesiastical or public trusts.

(4) Subsections (1) and (2) have effect subject to any enactment which prohibits or restricts the effect of provision of the description mentioned in them.

9 Delegation by trustees

(1) The trustees of land may, by power of attorney, delegate to any beneficiary or beneficiaries of full age and beneficially entitled to an interest in possession in land subject to the trust any of their functions as trustees which relate to the land.

(2) Where trustees purport to delegate to a person by a power of attorney under subsection (1) functions relating to any land and another person in good faith deals with him in relation to the land, he shall be presumed in favour of that other person to have been a person to whom the functions could be delegated unless that other person has knowledge at the time of the transaction that he was not such a person. And it shall be conclusively presumed in favour of any purchaser whose interest depends on the validity of that transaction that that other person dealt in good faith and did not have such knowledge if that other person makes a statutory declaration to that effect before or within three months after the completion of the purchase.

(3) A power of attorney under subsection (1) shall be given by all the trustees jointly and (unless expressed to be irrevocable and to be given by way of security) may be revoked by any one or more of them; and such a power is revoked by the appointment as a trustee of a person other than those by whom it is given (though not by any of those persons dying or otherwise ceasing to be a trustee).

(4) Where a beneficiary to whom functions are delegated by a power of attorney under subsection (1) ceases to be a person beneficially entitled to an interest in possession in land subject to the trust –

(a) if the functions are delegated to him alone, the power is revoked,

(b) if the functions are delegated to him and to other beneficiaries to be exercised by them jointly (but not separately), the power is revoked if each of the other beneficiaries ceases to be so entitled (but otherwise functions exercisable in accordance with the power are so exercisable by the remaining beneficiary or beneficiaries), and

(c) if the functions are delegated to him and to other beneficiaries to be exercised by them separately (or either separately or jointly), the power is revoked in so far as it relates to him.

(5) A delegation under subsection (1) may be for any period or indefinite.

(6) A power of attorney under subsection (1) cannot be an enduring power within the meaning of the Enduring Powers of Attorney Act 1985.

(7) Beneficiaries to whom functions have been delegated under subsection (1) are, in relation to the exercise of the functions, in the same position as trustees (with the same duties and liabilities); but such beneficiaries shall not be regarded as trustees for any other purposes (including, in particular, the purposes of any enactment permitting the delegation of functions by trustees or imposing requirements relating to the payment of capital money).

(9) Neither this section nor the repeal by this Act of section 29 of the Law of Property Act 1925 (which is superseded by this section) affects the operation after the commencement of this Act of any delegation effected before that commencement.

9A   Duties of trustees in connection with delegation, etc

(1) The duty of care under section 1 of the Trustee Act 2000 applies to trustees of land in deciding whether to delegate any of their functions under section 9.

(2) Subsection (3) applies if the trustees of land –

(a) delegate any of their functions under section 9, and

(b) the delegation is not irrevocable.

(3) While the derogation continues, the trustees –

(a) must keep the delegation under review,

(b) if circumstances make it appropriate to do so, must consider whether there is a need to exercise any power of intervention that they have, and

(c) if they consider that there is a need to exercise such a power, must do so.

(4) 'Power of intervention' includes –

(a) a power to give directions to the beneficiary;

(b) a power to revoke the delegation.

(5) The duty of care under section 1 of the 2000 Act applies to trustees in carrying out any duty under subsection (3).

(6) A trustee of land is not liable for any act or default of the beneficiary, or beneficiaries, unless the trustee fails to comply with the duty of care in deciding to delegate any of the trustees' functions under section 9 or in carrying out any duty under subsection (3).

(7) Neither this section nor the repeal of section 9(8) by the Trustee Act 2000 affects the operation after the commencement of this section of any delegation effected before that commencement.

10 Consents

(1) If a disposition creating a trust of land requires the consent of more than two persons to the exercise by the trustees of any function relating to the land, the consent of any two of them to the exercise of the function is sufficient in favour of a purchaser.

(2) Subsection (1) does not apply to the exercise of a function by trustees of land held on charitable, ecclesiastical or public trusts.

(3) Where at any time a person whose consent is expressed by a disposition creating a trust of land to be required to the exercise by the trustees of any function relating to the land is not of full age –

(a) his consent is not, in favour of a purchaser, required to the exercise of the function, but

(b) the trustees shall obtain the consent of a parent who has parental responsibility for him (within the meaning of the Children Act 1989) or of a guardian of his.

11 Consultation with beneficiaries

(1) The trustees of land shall in the exercise of any function relating to land subject to the trust –

(a) so far as is practicable, consult the beneficiaries of full age and beneficially entitled to an interest in possession in the land, and

(b) so far as consistent with the general interest of the trust, give effect to the wishes of those beneficiaries, or (in case of dispute) of the majority (according to the value of their combined interests).

(2) Subsection (1) does not apply –

(a) in relation to a trust created by a disposition in so far as provision that it does not apply is made by the disposition,

(b) in relation to a trust created or arising under a will made before the commencement of this Act, or

(c) in relation to the exercise of the power mentioned in section 6(2).

(3) Subsection (1) does not apply to a trust created before the commencement of this Act by a disposition, or a trust created after that commencement by reference to

such a trust, unless provision to the effect that it is to apply is made by a deed executed –

(a) in a case in which the trust was created by one person and he is of full capacity, by that person, or

(b) in a case in which the trust was created by more than one person, by such of the persons who created the trust as are alive and of full capacity.

(4) A deed executed for the purposes of subsection (3) is irrevocable.

12   The right to occupy

(1) A beneficiary who is beneficially entitled to an interest in possession in land subject to a trust of land is entitled by reason of his interest to occupy the land at any time if at that time –

(a) the purposes of the trust include making the land available for his occupation (or for the occupation of beneficiaries of a class of which he is a member or of beneficiaries in general), or

(b) the land is held by the trustees so as to be so available.

(2) Subsection (1) does not confer on a beneficiary a right to occupy land if it is either unavailable or unsuitable for occupation by him.

(3) This section is subject to section 13.

13   Exclusion and restriction of right to occupy

(1) Where two or more beneficiaries are (or apart from this subsection would be) entitled under section 12 to occupy land, the trustees of land may exclude or restrict the entitlement of any one or more (but not all) of them.

(2) Trustees may not under subsection (1) –

(a) unreasonably exclude any beneficiary's entitlement to occupy land, or

(b) restrict any such entitlement to an unreasonable extent.

(3) The trustees of land may from time to time impose reasonable conditions on any beneficiary in relation to his occupation of land by reason of his entitlement under section 12.

(4) The matters to which trustees are to have regard in exercising the powers conferred by this section include –

(a) the intentions of the person or persons (if any) who created the trust,

(b) the purposes for which the land is held, and

(c) the circumstances and wishes of each of the beneficiaries who is (or apart from any previous exercise by the trustees of those powers would be) entitled to occupy the land under section 12.

(5) The conditions which may be imposed on a beneficiary under subsection (3) include, in particular, conditions requiring him –

(a) to pay any outgoings or expenses in respect of the land, or

(b) to assume any other obligation in relation to the land or to any activity which is or is proposed to be conducted there.

(6) Where the entitlement of any beneficiary to occupy land under section 12 has been excluded or restricted, the conditions which may be imposed on any other beneficiary under subsection (3) include, in particular, conditions requiring him to –

(a) make payments by way of compensation to the beneficiary whose entitlement has been excluded or restricted, or

(b) forgo any payment or other benefit to which he would otherwise be entitled under the trust so as to benefit that beneficiary.

(7) The powers conferred on trustees by this section may not be exercised –

(a) so as to prevent any person who is in occupation of land (whether or not by reason of an entitlement under section 12) from continuing to occupy the land, or

(b) in a manner likely to result in any such person ceasing to occupy the land,

unless he consents or the court has given approval.

(8) The matters to which the court is to have regard in determining whether to give approval under subsection (7) include the matters mentioned in subsection (4)(a) to (c).

14   Applications for order

(1) Any person who is a trustee of land or has an interest in property subject to a trust of land may make an application to the court for an order under this section.

(2) On application for an order under this section the court may make any such order –

(a) relating to the exercise by the trustees of any of their functions (including an order relieving them of any obligation to obtain the consent of, or to consult, any person in connection with the exercise of any of their functions), or

(b) declaring the nature or extent of a person's interest in property subject to the trust,

as the court thinks fit.

(3) The court may not under this section make any order as to the appointment or removal of trustees.

(4) The powers conferred on the court by this section are exercisable on an application whether it is made before or after the commencement of this Act.

15   Matters relevant in determining applications

(1) The matters to which the court is to have regard in determining an application for an order under section 14 include –

(a) the intentions of the person or persons (if any) who created the trust,

(b) the purposes for which the property subject to the trust is held,

(c) the welfare of any minor who occupies or might reasonably be expected to occupy any land subject to the trust as his home, and

(d) the interests of any secured creditor of any beneficiary.

(2) In the case of an application relating to the exercise in relation to any land of the powers conferred on the trustees by section 13, the matters to which the court is to have regard also include the circumstances and wishes of each of the beneficiaries who is (or apart from any previous exercise by the trustees of those powers would be) entitled to occupy the land under section 12.

(3) In the case of any other application, other than one relating to the exercise of the power mentioned in section 6(2), the matters to which the court is to have regard also include the circumstances and wishes of any beneficiaries of full age and entitled to an interest in possession in property subject to the trust or (in case of dispute) of the majority (according to the value of their combined interests).

(4) This section does not apply to an application if section 335A of the Insolvency Act 1986 (which is inserted by Schedule 3 and relates to applications by a trustee of a bankrupt) applies to it.

16 Protection of purchasers

(1) A purchaser of land which is or has been subject to a trust need not be concerned to see that any requirement imposed on the trustees by section 6(5), 7(3) or 11(1) has been complied with.

(2) Where –

(a) trustees of land who convey land which (immediately before it is conveyed) is subject to the trust contravene section 6(6) or (8), but

(b) the purchaser of the land from the trustees has no actual notice of the contravention,

the contravention does not invalidate the conveyance.

(3) Where the powers of trustees of land are limited by virtue of section 8 –

(a) the trustees shall take all reasonable steps to bring the limitation to the notice of any purchaser of the land from them, but

(b) the limitation does not invalidate any conveyance by the trustees to a purchaser who has no actual notice of the limitation.

(4) Where trustees of land convey land which (immediately before it is conveyed) is subject to the trust to persons believed by them to be beneficiaries absolutely entitled to the land under the trust and of full age and capacity –

(a) the trustees shall execute a deed declaring that they are discharged from the trust in relation to that land, and

(b) if they fail to do so, the court may make an order requiring them to do so.

(5) A purchaser of land to which a deed under subsection (4) relates is entitled to assume that, as from the date of the deed, the land is not subject to the trust unless he has actual notice that the trustees were mistaken in their belief that the land was conveyed to beneficiaries absolutely entitled to the land under the trust and of full age and capacity.

(6) Subsections (2) and (3) do not apply to land held on charitable, ecclesiastical or public trusts.

(7) This section does not apply to registered land.

17   Application of provisions to trusts of proceeds of sale

(2) Section 14 applies in relation to a trust of proceeds of sale of land and trustees of such a trust as in relation to a trust of land and trustees of land.

(3) In this section 'trust of proceeds of sale of land' means (subject to subsection (5)) any trust of property (other than a trust of land) which consists of or includes –

(a) any proceeds of a disposition of land held in trust (including settled land), or

(b) any property representing any such proceeds.

(4) The references in subsection (3) to a trust –

(a) are to any description of trust (whether express, implied, resulting or constructive), including a trust for sale and a bare trust, and

(b) include a trust created, or arising, before the commencement of this Act.

(5) A trust which (despite section 2) is a settlement for the purposes of the Settled Land Act 1925 cannot be a trust of proceeds of sale of land.

(6) In subsection (3) –

(a) 'disposition' includes any disposition made, or coming into operation, before the commencement of this Act, and

(b) the reference to settled land includes personal chattels to which section 67(1) of the Settled Land Act 1925 (heirlooms) applies.

18   Application of Part to personal representatives

(1) The provisions of this Part relating to trustees, other than sections 10, 11 and 14, apply to personal representatives, but with appropriate modifications and without prejudice to the functions of personal representatives for the purposes of administration.

(2) The appropriate modifications include –

(a) the substitution of references to persons interested in the due administration of the estate for references to beneficiaries, and

(b) the substitution of references to the will for references to the disposition creating the trust.

(3) Section 3(1) does not apply to personal representatives if the death occurs before the commencement of this Act.

PART II

APPOINTMENT AND RETIREMENT OF TRUSTEES

19   Appointment and retirement of trustee at instance of beneficiaries

(1) This section applies in the case of a trust where –

(a) there is no person nominated for the purpose of appointing new trustees by the instrument, if any, creating the trust, and

(b) the beneficiaries under the trust are of full age and capacity and (taken together) are absolutely entitled to the property subject to the trust.

(2) The beneficiaries may give a direction or directions of either or both of the following descriptions –

(a) a written direction to a trustee or trustees to retire from the trust, and

(b) a written direction to the trustees or trustee for the time being (or, if there are none, to the personal representative of the last person who was a trustee) to appoint by writing to be a trustee or trustees the person or persons specified in the direction.

(3) Where –

(a) a trustee has been given a direction under subsection (2)(a),

(b) reasonable arrangements have been made for the protection of any rights of his in connection with the trust,

(c) after he has retired there will be either a trust corporation or at least two persons to act as trustees to perform the trust, and

(d) either another person is to be appointed to be a new trustee on his retirement (whether in compliance with a direction under subsection (2)(b) or otherwise) or the continuing trustees by deed consent to his retirement,

he shall make a deed declaring his retirement and shall be deemed to have retired and be discharged from the trust.

(4) Where a trustee retires under subsection (3) he and the continuing trustees (together with any new trustee) shall (subject to any arrangements for the protection of his rights) do anything necessary to vest the trust property in the continuing trustees (or the continuing and new trustees).

(5) This section has effect subject to the restrictions imposed by the Trustee Act 1925 on the number of trustees.

20   Appointment of substitute for incapable trustee

(1) This section applies where –

(a) a trustee is incapable by reason of mental disorder of exercising his functions as trustee,

(b) there is no person who is both entitled and willing and able to appoint a trustee in place of him under section 36(1) of the Trustee Act 1925, and

(c) the beneficiaries under the trust are of full age and capacity and (taken together) are absolutely entitled to the property subject to the trust.

(2) The beneficiaries may give to –

(a) a receiver of the trustee,

(b) an attorney acting for him under the authority of a power of attorney created by an instrument which is registered under section 6 of the Enduring Powers of Attorney Act 1985, or

(c) a person authorised for the purpose by the authority having jurisdiction under Part VII of the Mental Health Act 1983,

a written direction to appoint by writing the person or persons specified in the direction to be a trustee or trustees in place of the incapable trustee.

21   Supplementary

(1) For the purposes of section 19 or 20 a direction is given by beneficiaries if –

(a) a single direction is jointly given by all of them, or

(b) (subject to subsection (2)) a direction is given by each of them (whether solely or jointly with one or more, but not all, of the others),

and none of them by writing withdraws the direction given by him before it has been complied with.

(2) Where more than one direction is given each must specify for appointment or retirement the same person or persons.

(3) Subsection (7) of section 36 of the Trustee Act 1925 (powers of trustees appointed under that section) applies to a trustee appointed under section 19 or 20 as if he were appointed under that section.

(4) A direction under section 19 or 20 must not specify a person or persons for appointment if the appointment of that person or those persons would be in contravention of section 35(1) of the Trustee Act 1925 or section 24(1) of the Law of Property Act 1925 (requirements as to identity of trustees).

(5) Sections 19 and 20 do not apply in relation to a trust created by a disposition in so far as provision that they do not apply is made by the disposition.

(6) Sections 19 and 20 do not apply in relation to a trust created before the commencement of this Act by a disposition in so far as provision to the effect that they do not apply is made by a deed executed –

(a) in a case in which the trust was created by one person and he is of full capacity, by that person, or

(b) in a case in which the trust was created by more than one person, by such of the persons who created the trust as are alive and of full capacity.

(7) A deed executed for the purposes of subsection (6) is irrevocable.

(8) Where a deed is executed for the purposes of subsection (6) –

(a) it does not affect anything done before its execution to comply with a direction under section 19 or 20, but

(b) a direction under section 19 or 20 which has been given but not complied with before its execution shall cease to have effect.

PART III

SUPPLEMENTARY

22 Meaning of 'beneficiary'

(1) In this Act 'beneficiary', in relation to a trust, means any person who under the trust has an interest in property subject to the trust (including a person who has such an interest as a trustee or a personal representative).

(2) In this Act references to a beneficiary who is beneficially entitled do not include a beneficiary who has an interest in property subject to the trust only by reason of being a trustee or personal representative.

(3) For the purposes of this Act a person who is a beneficiary only by reason of being an annuitant is not to be regarded as entitled to an interest in possession in land subject to the trust.

23 Other interpretation provisions

(1) In this Act 'purchaser' has the same meaning as in Part I of the Law of Property Act 1925.

(2) Subject to that, where an expression used in this Act is given a meaning by the Law of Property Act 1925 it has the same meaning as in that Act unless the context otherwise requires.

(3) In this Act 'the court' means –

(a) the High Court, or

(b) a county court.

24 Application to Crown

(1) Subject to subsection (2), this Act binds the Crown.

(2) This Act (except so far as it relates to undivided shares and joint ownership) does not affect or alter the descent, devolution or nature of the estates and interests of or in –

(a) land for the time being vested in Her Majesty in right of the Crown or of the Duchy of Lancaster, or

(b) land for the time being belonging to the Duchy of Cornwall and held in right or respect of the Duchy.

25 Amendments, repeals, etc ...

(4) The amendments and repeals made by this Act do not affect any entailed interest created before the commencement of this Act.

(5) The amendments and repeals made by this Act in consequence of section 3 –

(a) do not affect a trust created by a will if the testator died before the commencement of this Act, and

(b) do not affect personal representatives of a person who died before that commencement;

and the repeal of section 22 of the Partnership Act 1890 does not apply in any circumstances involving the personal representatives of a partner who died before that commencement.

26 Power to make consequential provision

(1) The Lord Chancellor may by order made by statutory instrument make any such supplementary, transitional or incidental provision as appears to him to be appropriate for any of the purposes of this Act or in consequence of any of the provisions of this Act. ...

SCHEDULE 1

PROVISIONS CONSEQUENTIAL ON SECTION 2

Minors

1. (1) Where after commencement of this Act a person purports to convey a legal estate in land to a minor, or two or more minors, alone, the conveyance –

(a) is not effective to pass the legal estate, but

(b) operates as a declaration that the land is held in trust for the minor or minors (or if he purports to convey it to the minor or minors in trust for any persons, for those persons).

(2) Where after the commencement of this Act a person purports to convey a legal estate in land to –

(a) a minor or two or more minors, and

(b) another person who is, or other persons who are, of full age,

the conveyance operates to vest the land in the other person or persons in trust for the minor or minors and the other person or persons (or if he purports to convey it to them in trust for any persons, for those persons).

(3) Where immediately before the commencement of this Act a conveyance is operating (by virtue of section 27 of the Settled Land Act 1925) as an agreement to execute a settlement in favour of a minor or minors –

(a) the agreement ceases to have effect on the commencement of this Act, and

(b) the conveyance subsequently operates instead as a declaration that the land is held in trust for the minor or minors.

2. Where after the commencement of this Act a legal estate in land would, by reason of intestacy or in any other circumstances not dealt with in paragraph 1, vest in a person who is a minor if he were a person of full age, the land is held in trust for the minor.

Family charges

3. Where by virtue of an instrument coming into operation after the commencement of this Act, land becomes charged voluntarily (or in consideration of marriage or the formation of a civil partnership) or by way of family arrangement, whether immediately or after an interval, with the payment of –

(a) a rent charge for the life of a person or a shorter period, or

(b) capital, annual or periodical sums for the benefit of a person,

the instrument operates as a declaration that the land is held in trust for giving effect to the charge.

Charitable, ecclesiastical and public trusts

4. (1) This paragraphs applies in the case of land held on charitable, ecclesiastical or public trusts (other than land to which the Universities and College Estates Act 1925 applies).

(2) Where there is a conveyance of such land –

(a) if neither section 37(1) nor section 39(1) of the Charities Act 1993 applies to the conveyance, it shall state that the land is held on such trusts, and

(b) if neither section 37(2) nor section 39(2) of that Act has been complied with in relation to the conveyance and a purchaser has notice that the land is held on such trusts, he must see that any consents or orders necessary to authorise the transaction have been obtained.

(3) Where any trustees or the majority of any set of trustees have power to transfer or create any legal estate in the land, the estate shall be transferred or created by them in the names and on behalf of the persons in whom it is vested.

Entailed interests

5. (1) Where a person purports by an instrument coming into operation after the commencement of this Act to grant to another person an entailed interest in real or personal property, the instrument –

(a) is not effective to grant an entailed interest, but

(b) operates instead as a declaration that the property is held in trust absolutely for the person to whom an entailed interest in the property was purportedly granted.

(2) Where a person purports by an instrument coming into operation after the commencement of this Act to declare himself a tenant in tail of real or personal property, the instrument is not effective to create an entailed interest.

Property held on settlement ceasing to exist

6. Where a settlement ceases to be a settlement for the purposes of the Settled land Act 1925 because no relevant property (within the meaning of section 2(4)) is, or is deemed to be, subject to the settlement, any property which is or later becomes subject to the settlement is held in trust for the persons interested under the settlement.

SCHEDULE 2

AMENDMENTS OF STATUTORY PROVISIONS IMPOSING TRUST FOR SALE

1. (1)–(6) [Amends s31 of the Law of Property Act 1925]

(7) The amendments made by this paragraph –

(a) apply whether the right of redemption is discharged before or after the commencement of this Act, but

(b) are without prejudice to any dealings or arrangements made before the commencement of this Act.

2. (1) [Repeals s32 of the Law of Property Act 1925]

(2) The repeal made by this paragraph applies in relation to land purchased after the commencement of this Act whether the trust or will in pursuance of which it is purchased comes into operation before or after the commencement of this Act.

3. (1)–(5) [Amends s34 of the Law of Property Act 1925]

(6) The amendments made by this paragraph apply whether the disposition is made, or comes into operation, before or after the commencement of this Act.

4. (1)–(3) [Amends s36 of the Law of Property Act 1925]

(4) The amendments made by this paragraph apply whether the legal estate is limited, or becomes held in trust, before or after the commencement of this Act.

5. (1)–(4) [Amends s33 of the Administration of Estates Act 1925]

(5) The amendments made by this paragraph apply whether the death occurs before or after the commencement of this Act.

6. (1)–(5) [Amends s1 of the Reverter of Sites Act 1987]

(6) The amendments made by this paragraph apply whether the trust arises before or after the commencement of this Act.

Trusts deemed to arise in 1926

(7) Where at the commencement of this Act any land is held on trust for sale, or on the statutory trusts, by virtue of Schedule 1 to the Law of Property Act 1925 (transitional provisions), it shall after that commencement be held in trust for the persons interested in the land; and references in that Schedule to trusts for sale or trustees for sale or to the statutory trusts shall be construed accordingly.

NB This Act came into force on 1 January 1997.

As amended by the Trustee Act 2000, s40(1), Schedule 2, Pt II, paras 45–48; Commonhold and Leasehold Reform Act 2002, s68, Schedule 5, para 8; Civil Partnership Act 2004, s261(1), Schedule 27, para 153.

FAMILY LAW ACT 1996
(1996 c 27)

PART IV

FAMILY HOMES AND DOMESTIC VIOLENCE

30 Rights concerning home where one spouse or civil partner has no estate, etc

(1) This section applies if –

(a) one spouse or civil partner ('A') is entitled to occupy a dwelling-house by virtue of –

(i) a beneficial estate or interest or contract; or

(ii) any enactment giving A the right to remain in occupation; and

(b) the other spouse or civil partner ('B') is not so entitled.

(2) Subject to the provisions of this Part, B has the following rights ('home rights') –

(a) if in occupation, a right not to be evicted or excluded from the dwelling-house or any part of it by A except with the leave of the court given by an order under section 33;

(b) if not in occupation, a right with the leave of the court so given to enter into and occupy the dwelling-house.

(3) If B is entitled under this section to occupy a dwelling-house or any part of a dwelling-house, any payment or tender made or other thing done by B in or towards satisfaction of any liability of A in respect of rent, mortgage payments or other outgoings affecting the dwelling-house is, whether or not it is made or done in pursuance of an order under section 40, as good as if made or done by A.

(4) B's occupation by virtue of this section –

(a) is to be treated, for the purposes of the Rent (Agriculture) Act 1976 and the Rent Act 1977 (other than Part V and sections 103 to 106 of that Act), as occupation by A at A's residence, and

(b) if B occupies the dwelling-house as B's only or principal home, is to be treated, for the purposes of the Housing Act 1985, Part I of the Housing Act 1988 and Chapter I of Part V of the Housing Act 1996, as occupation by A as A's only or principal home.

(5) If B –

(a) is entitled under this section to occupy a dwelling-house or any part of a dwelling-house, and

(b) makes any payment in or towards satisfaction of any liability of A in respect of mortgage payments affecting the dwelling-house,

the person to whom the payment is made may treat it as having been made by A, but the fact that the person has treated any such payment as having been so made does not affect any claim of B against A to an interest in the dwelling-house by virtue of the payment.

(6) If B is entitled under this section to occupy a dwelling-house or part of a dwelling-house by reason of an interest of A under a trust, all the provisions of subsections (3) to (5) apply in relation to the trustees as they apply in relation to A.

(7) This section does not apply to a dwelling-house which –

(a) in the case of spouses, has at no time been, and was at no time intended by them to be, a matrimonial home of theirs; and

(b) in the case of civil partners, has at no time been, and was at no time intended by them to be, a civil partnership home of theirs.

(8) B's home rights continue –

(a) only so long as the marriage or civil partnership subsists, except to the extent that an order under section 33(5) otherwise provides; and

(b) only so long as A is entitled as mentioned in subsection (1) to occupy the dwelling-house, except where provision is made by section 31 for those rights to be a charge on an estate or interest in the dwelling-house.

(9) It is hereby declared that a person –

(a) who has an equitable interest in a dwelling-house or in its proceeds of sale, but

(b) is not a person in whom there is vested (whether solely or as joint tenant) a legal estate in fee simple or a legal term of years absolute in the dwelling-house,

is to be treated, only for the purpose of determining whether he has home rights, as not being entitled to occupy the dwelling-house by virtue of that interest.

31   Effect of home rights as charge on dwelling-house

(1) Subsections (2) and (3) apply if, at any time during a marriage or civil partnership, A is entitled to occupy a dwelling-house by virtue of a beneficial estate or interest.

(2) B's home rights are a charge on the estate or interest.

(3) The charge created by subsection (2) has the same priority as if it were an equitable interest created at whichever is the latest of the following dates –

(a) the date on which A acquires the estate or interest;

(b) the date of the marriage or of the formation of the civil partnership; and

(c) 1st January 1968 (the commencement date of the Matrimonial Homes Act 1967).

(4) Subsections (5) and (6) apply if, at any time when B's home rights are a charge on an interest of A under a trust, there are, apart from A or B, no persons, living or unborn, who are or could become beneficiaries under the trust.

(5) The rights are a charge also on the estate or interest of the trustees for A.

(6) The charge created by subsection (5) has the same priority as if it were an equitable interest created (under powers overriding the trusts) on the date when it arises.

(7) In determining for the purposes of subsection (4) whether there are any persons who are not, but could become, beneficiaries under the trust, there is to be disregarded any potential exercise of a general power of appointment exercisable by either or both of A and B alone (whether or not the exercise of it requires the consent of another person).

(8) Even though B's home rights are a charge on an estate or interest in the dwelling-house, those rights are brought to an end by –

(a) the death of A, or

(b) the termination (otherwise than by death) of the marriage or civil partnership,

unless the court directs otherwise by an order made under section 33(5).

(9) If –

(a) B's home rights are a charge on an estate or interest in the dwelling-house, and

(b) that estate or interest is surrendered to merge in some other estate or interest expectant on it in such circumstances that, but for the merger, the person taking the estate or interest would be bound by the charge,

the surrender has effect subject to the charge and the persons thereafter entitled to the other estate or interest are, for so long as the estate or interest surrendered would have endured if not so surrendered, to be treated for all purposes of this Part as deriving title to the other estate or interest under A or, as the case may be, under the trustees for A, by virtue of the surrender.

(10) If the title to the legal estate by virtue of which A is entitled to occupy a dwelling-house (including any legal estate held by trustees for A) is registered under the Land Registration Act 2002 or any enactment replaced by that Act –

(a) registration of a land charge affecting the dwelling-house by virtue of this Part is to be effected by registering a notice under that Act; and

(b) B's home rights are not to be capable of falling within paragraph 2 of Schedule 1 or 3 to that Act.

(12) If –

(a) B's home rights are a charge on the estate of A or of trustees of A, and

(b) that estate is the subject of a mortgage,

then if, after the date of the creation of the mortgage ('the first mortgage'), the charge is registered under section 2 of the Land Charges Act 1972, the charge is, for the purposes of section 94 of the Law of Property Act 1925 (which regulates the rights of mortgagees to make further advances ranking in priority to subsequent mortgages), to be deemed to be a mortgage subsequent in date to the first mortgage.

(13) It is hereby declared that a charge under subsection (2) or (5) is not registrable under subsection (10) or under section 2 of the Land Charges Act 1972 unless it is a charge on a legal estate.

32 Further provisions relating to home rights

Schedule 4 (provisions supplementary to sections 30 and 31) has effect.

33 Occupation orders where applicant has estate or interest, etc or has home rights

(1) If –

(a) a person ('the person entitled') –

(i) is entitled to occupy a dwelling-house by virtue of a beneficial estate or interest or contract or by virtue of any enactment giving him the right to remain in occupation, or

(ii) has home rights in relation to a dwelling-house, and

(b) the dwelling-house –

(i) is or at any time has been the home of the person entitled and of another person with whom he is associated, or

(ii) was at any time intended by the person entitled and any such other person to be their home,

the person entitled may apply to the court for an order containing any of the provisions specified in subsections (3), (4) and (5).

(2) If an agreement to marry is terminated, no application under this section may be made by virtue of section 62(3)(e) by reference to that agreement after the end of the period of three years beginning with the day on which it is terminated.

(2A) If a civil partnership agreement (as defined by section 73 of the Civil Partnership Act 2004) is terminated, no application under this section may be made by virtue of section 62(3)(eza) by reference to that agreement after the end of the period of three years beginning with the day on which it is terminated.

(3) An order under this section may –

(a) enforce the applicant's entitlement to remain in occupation as against the other person ('the respondent');

(b) require the respondent to permit the applicant to enter and remain in the dwelling-house or part of the dwelling-house;

(c) regulate the occupation of the dwelling-house by either or both parties;

(d) if the respondent is entitled as mentioned in subsection (1)(a)(i), prohibit, suspend or restrict the exercise by him of his right to occupy the dwelling-house;

(e) if the respondent has home rights in relation to the dwelling-house and the applicant is the other spouse or civil partner, restrict or terminate those rights;

(f) require the respondent to leave the dwelling-house or part of the dwelling-house; or

(g) exclude the respondent from a defined area in which the dwelling-house is included.

(4) An order under this section may declare that the applicant is entitled as mentioned in subsection (1)(a)(i) or has home rights.

(5) If the applicant has home rights and the respondent is the other spouse or civil partner, an order under this section made during the marriage or civil partnership may provide that those rights are not brought to an end by –

(a) the death of the other spouse or civil partner; or

(b) the termination (otherwise than by death) of the marriage or civil partnership.

(6) In deciding whether to exercise its powers under subsection (3) and (if so) in what manner, the court shall have regard to all the circumstances including –

(a) the housing needs and housing resources of each of the parties and of any relevant child;

(b) the financial resources of each of the parties;

(c) the likely effect of any order, or of any decision by the court not to exercise its powers under subsection (3), on the health, safety or well-being of the parties and of any relevant child; and

(d) the conduct of the parties in relation to each other and otherwise.

(7) If it appears to the court that the applicant or any relevant child is likely to suffer significant harm attributable to conduct of the respondent if an order under this section containing one or more of the provisions mentioned in subsection (3) is not made, the court shall make the order unless it appears to it that –

(a) the respondent or any relevant child is likely to suffer significant harm if the order is made; and

(b) the harm likely to be suffered by the respondent or child in that event is as great as, or greater than, the harm attributable to conduct of the respondent which is likely to be suffered by the applicant or child if the order is not made.

(8) The court may exercise its powers under subsection (5) in any case where it considers that in all the circumstances it is just and reasonable to do so.

(9) An order under this section –

(a) may not be made after the death of either of the parties mentioned in subsection (1); and

(b) except in the case of an order made by virtue of subsection (5)(a), ceases to have effect on the death of either party.

(10) An order under this section may, in so far as it has continuing effect, be made for a specified period, until the occurrence of a specified event or until further order.

34 Effect of order under section 33 where rights are charge on dwelling-house

(1) If B's home rights are a charge on the estate or interest of A or of trustees for A –

(a) an order under section 33 against A has, except so far as a contrary intention appears, the same effect against persons deriving title under A or under the trustees and affected by the charge, and

(b) sections 33(1), (3), (4) and (10) and 30(3) to (6) apply in relation to any person deriving title under A or under the trustees and affected by the charge as they apply in relation to A.

(2) The court may make an order under section 33 by virtue of subsection (1)(b) if it considers that in all the circumstances it is just and reasonable to do so.

35 One former spouse or former civil partner with no existing right to occupy

(1) This section applies if –

(a) one former spouse or former civil partner is entitled to occupy a dwelling-house by virtue of a beneficial estate or interest or contract, or by virtue of any enactment giving him the right to remain in occupation;

(b) the other former spouse or former civil partner is not so entitled; and

(c) the dwelling-house –

(i) in the case of former spouses, was at any time their matrimonial home or was at any time intended by them to be their matrimonial home, or

(ii) in the case of former civil partners, was at any time their civil partnership home or was at any time intended by them to be their civil partnership home.

(2) The former spouse or former civil partner not so entitled may apply to the court for an order under this section against the other former spouse or former civil partner ('the respondent').

(3) If the applicant is in occupation, an order under this section must contain provision –

(a) giving the applicant the right not to be evicted or excluded from the dwelling-house or any part of it by the respondent for the period specified in the order; and

(b) prohibiting the respondent from evicting or excluding the applicant during that period.

(4) If the applicant is not in occupation, an order under this section must contain provision –

(a) giving the applicant the right to enter into and occupy the dwelling-house for the period specified in the order; and

(b) requiring the respondent to permit the exercise of that right.

(5) An order under this section may also –

(a) regulate the occupation of the dwelling-house by either or both of the parties;

(b) prohibit, suspend or restrict the exercise by the respondent of his right to occupy the dwelling-house;

(c) require the respondent to leave the dwelling-house or part of the dwelling-house; or

(d) exclude the respondent from a defined area in which the dwelling-house is included.

(6) In deciding whether to make an order under this section containing provision of the kind mentioned in subsection (3) or (4) and (if so) in what manner, the court shall have regard to all the circumstances including –

(a) the housing needs and housing resources of each of the parties and of any relevant child;

(b) the financial resources of each of the parties;

(c) the likely effect of any order, or of any decision by the court not to exercise its powers under subsection (3) or (4), on the health, safety or well-being of the parties and of any relevant child;

(d) the conduct of the parties in relation to each other and otherwise;

(e) the length of time that has elapsed since the parties ceased to live together;

(f) the length of time that has elapsed since the marriage or civil partnership was dissolved or annulled; and

(g) the existence of any pending proceedings between the parties –

(i) for an order under section 23A or 24 of the Matrimonial Causes Act 1973 (property adjustment orders in connection with divorce proceedings etc);

(ia) for a property adjustment order under Part 2 of Schedule 5 to the Civil Partnership Act 2004;

(ii) for an order under paragraph 1(2)(d) or (e) of Schedule 1 to the Children Act 1989 (orders for financial relief against parents); or

(iii) relating to the legal or beneficial ownership of the dwelling-house.

(7) In deciding whether to exercise its power to include one or more of the provisions referred to in subsection (5) ('a subsection (5) provision') and (if so) in what manner, the court shall have regard to all the circumstances including the matters mentioned in subsection (6)(a) to (e).

(8) If the court decides to make an order under this section and it appears to it that, if the order does not include a subsection (5) provision, the applicant or any relevant child is likely to suffer significant harm attributable to conduct of the respondent, the court shall include the subsection (5) provision in the order unless it appears to the court that –

(a) the respondent or any relevant child is likely to suffer significant harm if the provision is included in the order; and

(b) the harm likely to be suffered by the respondent or child in that event is as great as or greater than the harm attributable to conduct of the respondent which is likely to be suffered by the applicant or child if the provision is not included.

(9) An order under this section –

(a) may not be made after the death of either of the former spouses or former civil partners; and

(b) ceases to have effect on the death of either of them.

(10) An order under this section must be limited so as to have effect for a specified period not exceeding six months, but may be extended on one or more occasions for a further specified period not exceeding six months.

(11) A former spouse or former civil partner who has an equitable interest in the dwelling-house or in the proceeds of sale of the dwelling-house but in whom there is not vested (whether solely or as joint tenant) a legal estate in fee simple or a legal term of years absolute in the dwelling-house is to be treated (but only for the purpose of determining whether he is eligible to apply under this section) as not being entitled to occupy the dwelling-house by virtue of that interest.

(12) Subsection (11) does not prejudice any right of such a former spouse or former civil partner to apply for an order under section 33.

(13) So long as an order under this section remains in force, subsections (3) to (6) of section 30 apply in relation to the applicant –

(a) as if he were B (the person entitled to occupy the dwelling-house by virtue of that section; and

(b) as if the respondent were A (the person entitled as mentioned in subsection (1)(a) of that section).

36 One cohabitant or former cohabitant with no existing right to occupy

(1) This section applies if –

(a) one cohabitant or former cohabitant is entitled to occupy a dwelling-house by virtue of a beneficial estate or interest or contract or by virtue of any enactment giving him the right to remain in occupation;

(b) the other cohabitant or former cohabitant is not so entitled; and

(c) that dwelling-house is the home in which they live together as husband and wife or a home in which they at any time so lived together or intended so to live together.

(2) The cohabitant or former cohabitant not so entitled may apply to the court for an order under this section against the other cohabitant or former cohabitant ('the respondent').

(3) If the applicant is in occupation, an order under this section must contain provision –

(a) giving the applicant the right not to be evicted or excluded from the dwelling-house or any part of it by the respondent for the period specified in the order; and

(b) prohibiting the respondent from evicting or excluding the applicant during that period.

(4) If the applicant is not in occupation, an order under this section must contain provision –

(a) giving the applicant the right to enter into and occupy the dwelling-house for the period specified in the order; and

(b) requiring the respondent to permit the exercise of that right.

(5) An order under this section may also –

(a) regulate the occupation of the dwelling-house by either or both of the parties;

(b) prohibit, suspend or restrict the exercise by the respondent of his right to occupy the dwelling-house;

(c) require the respondent to leave the dwelling-house or part of the dwelling-house; or

(d) exclude the respondent from a defined area in which the dwelling-house is included.

(6) In deciding whether to make an order under this section containing provision of the kind mentioned in subsection (3) or (4) and (if so) in what manner, the court shall have regard to all the circumstances including –

(a) the housing needs and housing resources of each of the parties and of any relevant child;

(b) the financial resources of each of the parties;

(c) the likely effect of any order, or of any decision by the court not to exercise its powers under subsection (3) or (4), on the health, safety or well-being of the parties and of any relevant child;

(d) the conduct of the parties in relation to each other and otherwise;

(e) the nature of the parties' relationship;

(f) the length of time during which they have lived together as husband and wife;

(g) whether there are or have been any children who are children of both parties or for whom both parties have or have had parental responsibility;

(h) the length of time that has elapsed since the parties ceased to live together; and

(i) the existence of any pending proceedings between the parties –

(i) for an order under paragraph 1(2)(d) or (e) of Schedule 1 to the Children Act 1989 (orders for financial relief against parents); or

(ii) relating to the legal or beneficial ownership of the dwelling-house.

(7) In deciding whether to exercise its powers to include one or more of the provisions referred to in subsection (5) ('a subsection (5) provision') and (if so) in what manner, the court shall have regard to all the circumstances including –

(a) the matters mentioned in subsection (6)(a) to (d); and

(b) the questions mentioned in subsection (8).

(8) The questions are –

(a) whether the applicant or any relevant child is likely to suffer significant harm attributable to conduct of the respondent if the subsection (5) provision is not included in the order; and

(b) whether the harm likely to be suffered by the respondent or child if the provision is included is as great as or greater than the harm attributable to conduct of the respondent which is likely to be suffered by the applicant or child if the provision is not included.

(9) An order under this section –

(a) may not be made after the death of either of the parties; and

(b) ceases to have effect on the death of either of them.

(10) An order under this section must be limited so as to have effect for a specified period not exceeding six months, but may be extended on one occasion for a further specified period not exceeding six months.

(11) A person who has an equitable interest in the dwelling-house or in the proceeds of sale of the dwelling-house but in whom there is not vested (whether solely or as joint tenant) a legal estate in fee simple or a legal term of years absolute in the dwelling-house is to be treated (but only for the purpose of determining whether he is eligible to apply under this section) as not being entitled to occupy the dwelling-house by virtue of that interest.

(12) Subsection (11) does not prejudice any right of such a person to apply for an order under section 33.

(13) So long as the order remains in force, subsections (3) to (6) of section 30 apply in relation to the applicant –

(a) as if he were B (the person entitled to occupy the dwelling-house by virtue of that section); and

(b) as if the respondent were A (the person entitled as mentioned in subsection (1)(a) of that section).

37 Neither spouse or civil partner entitled to occupy

(1) This section applies if –

(a) one spouse or former spouse and the other spouse or former spouse occupy a dwelling-house which is or was the matrimonial home; but

(b) neither of them is entitled to remain in occupation –

(i) by virtue of a beneficial estate or interest or contract; or

(ii) by virtue of any enactment giving him the right to remain in occupation.

(1A) This section also applies if –

(a) one civil partner or former civil partner and the other civil partner or former civil partner occupy a dwelling-house which is or was the civil partnership home; but

(b) neither of them is entitled to remain in occupation –

(i) by virtue of a beneficial estate or interest or contract; or

(ii) by virtue of any enactment giving him the right to remain in occupation.

(2) Either of the parties may apply to the court for an order against the other under this section.

(3) An order under this section may –

(a) require the respondent to permit the applicant to enter and remain in the dwelling-house or part of the dwelling-house;

(b) regulate the occupation of the dwelling-house by either or both of the parties;

(c) require the respondent to leave the dwelling-house or part of the dwelling-house; or

(d) exclude the respondent from a defined area in which the dwelling-house is included.

(4) Subsections (6) and (7) of section 33 apply to the exercise by the court of its powers under this section as they apply to the exercise by the court of its powers under subsection (3) of that section.

(5) An order under this section must be limited so as to have effect for a specified period not exceeding six months, but may be extended on one or more occasions for a further specified period not exceeding six months.

38 Neither cohabitant or former cohabitant entitled to occupy

(1) This section applies if –

(a) one cohabitant or former cohabitant and the other cohabitant or former cohabitant occupy a dwelling-house which is the home in which they live or lived together as husband and wife; but

(b) neither of them is entitled to remain in occupation –

(i) by virtue of a beneficial estate or interest or contract; or

(ii) by virtue of any enactment giving him the right to remain in occupation.

(2) Either of the parties may apply to the court for an order against the other under this section.

(3) An order under this section may –

(a) require the respondent to permit the applicant to enter and remain in the dwelling-house or part of the dwelling-house;

(b) regulate the occupation of the dwelling-house by either or both of the parties;

(c) require the respondent to leave the dwelling-house or part o the dwelling-house; or

(d) exclude the respondent from a defined area in which the dwelling-house is included.

(4) In deciding whether to exercise its powers to include one or more of the provisions referred to in subsection (3) ('a subsection (3) provision') and (if so) in what manner, the court shall have regard to all the circumstances including –

(a) the housing needs and housing resources of each of the parties and of any relevant child;

(b) the financial resources of each of the parties;

(c) the likely effect of any order, or of any decision by the court not to exercise its powers under subsection (3), on the health, safety or well-being of the parties and of any relevant child;

(d) the conduct of the parties in relation to each other and otherwise; and

(e) the questions mentioned in subsection (5).

(5) The questions are –

(a) whether the applicant or any relevant child is likely to suffer significant harm attributable to conduct of the respondent if the subsection (3) provision is not included in the order; and

(b) whether the harm likely to be suffered by the respondent or child if the provision is included is as great as or greater than the harm attributable to conduct of the respondent which is likely to be suffered by the applicant or child if the provision is not included.

(6) An order under this section shall be limited so as to have effect for a specified period not exceeding six months, but may be extended on one occasion for a further specified period not exceeding six months.

39 Supplementary provisions

(1) In this Part an 'occupation order' means an order under section 33, 35, 36, 37 or 38.

(2) An application for an occupation order may be made in other family proceedings or without any other family proceedings being instituted.

(3) If –

(a) an application for an occupation order is made under section 33, 35, 36, 37 or 38, and

(b) the court considers that it has no power to make the order under the section concerned, but that it has power to make an order under one of the other sections,

the court may make an order under that other section.

(4) The fact that a person has applied for an occupation order under sections 35 to 38, or that an occupation order has been made, does not affect the right of any person to claim a legal or equitable interest in any property in any subsequent proceedings (including subsequent proceedings under this Part).

40 Additional provisions that may be included in certain occupation orders

(1) The court may on, or at any time after, making an occupation order under section 33, 35 or 36 –

(a) impose on either party obligations as to –

(i) the repair and maintenance of the dwelling-house; or

(ii) the discharge of rent, mortgage payments or other outgoings affecting the dwelling-house;

(b) order a party occupying the dwelling-house or any part of it (including a party who is entitled to do so by virtue of a beneficial estate or interest or contract or by virtue of any enactment giving him the right to remain in occupation) to make periodical payments to the other party in respect of the accommodation, if the other party would (but for the order) be entitled to occupy the dwelling-house by virtue of a beneficial estate or interest or contract or by virtue of any such enactment;

(c) grant either party possession or use of furniture or other contents of the dwelling-house;

(d) order either party to take reasonable care of any furniture or other contents of the dwelling-house;

(e) order either party to take reasonable steps to keep the dwelling-house and any furniture or other contents secure.

(2) In deciding whether and, if so, how to exercise its powers under this section, the court shall have regard to all the circumstances of the case including –

(a) the financial needs and financial resources of the parties; and

(b) the financial obligations which they have, or are likely to have in the foreseeable future, including financial obligations to each other and to any relevant child.

(3) An order under this section ceases to have effect when the occupation order to which it relates ceases to have effect.

41 Additional considerations if parties are cohabitants or former cohabitants

(1) This section applies if the parties are cohabitants or former cohabitants.

(2) Where the court is required to consider the nature of the parties' relationship, it is to have regard to the fact that they have not given each other the commitment involved in marriage.

42 Non-molestation orders

(1) In this Part a 'non-molestation order' means an order containing either or both of the following provisions –

(a) provision prohibiting a person ('the respondent') from molesting another person who is associated with the respondent;

(b) provision prohibiting the respondent from molesting a relevant child. ...

43 Leave of court required for applications by children under sixteen

(1) A child under the age of sixteen may not apply for an occupation order or a non-molestation order except with the leave of the court.

(2) The court may grant leave for the purpose of subsection (1) only if it is satisfied that the child has sufficient understanding to make the proposed application for the occupation order or non-molestation order.

44 Evidence of agreement to marry or form a civil partnership

(1) Subject to subsection (2), the court shall not make an order under section 33 or 42 by virtue of section 62(3)(e) unless there is produced to it evidence in writing of the existence of the agreement to marry.

(2) Subsection (1) does not apply if the court is satisfied that the agreement to marry was evidenced by –

(a) the gift of an engagement ring by one party to the agreement to the other in contemplation of their marriage, or

(b) a ceremony entered into by the parties in the presence of one or more other persons assembled for the purpose of witnessing the ceremony.

(3) Subject to subsection (4), the court shall not make an order under section 33 or 42 by virtue of section 62(3)(eza) unless there is produced to it evidence in writing of the existence of the civil partnership agreement (as defined by section 73 of the Civil Partnership Act 2004).

(4) Subsection (3) does not apply if the court is satisfied that the civil partnership agreement was evidence by –

(a) a gift by one party to the agreement to the other as a token of the agreement, or

(b) a ceremony entered into by the parties in the presence of one or more other persons assembled for the purpose of witnessing the ceremony.

45 Ex parte orders

(1) The court may, in any case where it considers that it is just and convenient to do so, make an occupation order or a non-molestation order even though the respondent has not been given such notice of the proceedings as would otherwise be required by rules of court.

(2) In determining whether to exercise its powers under subsection (1), the court shall have regard to all the circumstances including –

(a) any risk of significant harm to the applicant or a relevant child, attributable to conduct of the respondent, if the order is not made immediately;

(b) whether it is likely that the applicant will be deterred or prevented from pursuing the application if an order is not made immediately; and

(c) whether there is reason to believe that the respondent is aware of the proceedings but is deliberately evading service and that the applicant or a relevant child will be seriously prejudiced by the delay involved –

(i) where the court is a magistrates' court, in effecting service of proceedings; or

(ii) in any other case, in effecting substituted service.

(3) If the court makes an order by virtue of subsection (1) it must afford the respondent an opportunity to make representations relating to the order as soon as just and convenient at a full hearing.

(4) If, at a full hearing, the court makes an occupation order ('the full order'), then –

(a) for the purposes of calculating the maximum period for which the full order may be made to have effect, the relevant section is to apply as if the period for which the full order will have effect began on the date on which the initial order first had effect; and

(b) the provisions of section 36(10) or 38(6) as to the extension of orders are to apply as if the full order and the initial order were a single order.

(5) In this section –

'full hearing' means a hearing of which notice has been given to all the parties in accordance with rules of court;

'initial order' means an occupation order made by virtue of subsection (1); and

'relevant section' means section 33(10), 35(10), 36(10), 37(5) or 38(6).

46 Undertakings

(1) In any case where the court has power to make an occupation order or non-molestation order, the court may accept an undertaking from any party to the proceedings.

(2) No power of arrest may be attached to any undertaking given under subsection (1).

(3) The court shall not accept an undertaking under subsection (1) in any case where apart from this section a power of arrest would be attached to the order.

(4) An undertaking given to a court under subsection (1) is enforceable as if it were an order of the court.

(5) This section has effect without prejudice to the powers of the High Court and the county court apart from this section.

47 Arrest for breach of order

(1) In this section 'a relevant order' means an occupation order or a non-molestation order.

(2) If –

(a) the court makes a relevant order; and

(b) it appears to the court that the respondent has used or threatened violence against the applicant or a relevant child,

it shall attach a power of arrest to one or more provisions of the order unless satisfied that in all the circumstances of the case the applicant or child will be adequately protected without such a power of arrest. ...

49 Variation and discharge of orders

(1) An occupation order or non-molestation order may be varied or discharged by the court on an application by –

(a) the respondent, or

(b) the person on whose application the order was made.

(2) In the case of a non-molestation order made by virtue of section 42(2)(b), the order may be varied or discharged by the court even though no such application has been made.

(3) If B's home rights are, under section 31, a charge on the estate or interest of A or of trustees for A, an order under section 33 against A may also be varied or discharged by the court on an application by any person deriving title under A or under the trustees and affected by the charge. ...

53 Transfer of certain tenancies

Schedule 7 makes provision in relation to the transfer of certain tenancies on divorce etc or on separation of cohabitants.

54 Dwelling-house subject to mortgage

(1) In determining for the purposes of this Part whether a person is entitled to

occupy a dwelling-house by virtue of an estate or interest, any right to possession of the dwelling-house conferred on a mortgagee of the dwelling-house under or by virtue of his mortgage is to be disregarded.

(2) Subsection (1) applies whether or not the mortgagee is in possession.

(3) Where a person ('A') is entitled to occupy a dwelling-house by virtue of an estate or interest, a connected person does not by virtue of –

(a) any home rights conferred by section 30, or

(b) any rights conferred by an order under section 35 or 36,

have any larger right against the mortgagee to occupy the dwelling-house than A has by virtue of his estate or interest and of any contract with the mortgagee.

(4) Subsection (3) does not apply, in the case of home rights, if under section 31 those rights are a charge, affecting the mortgagee, on the estate or interest mortgaged.

(5) In this section 'connected person', in relation to any person, means that person's spouse, former spouse, civil partner, former civil partner, cohabitant or former cohabitant.

55 Actions by mortgagees: joining connected persons as parties

(1) This section applies if a mortgagee of land which consists of or includes a dwelling-house brings an action in any court for the enforcement of his security.

(2) A connected person who is not already a party to the action is entitled to be made a party in the circumstances mentioned in subsection (3).

(3) The circumstances are that –

(a) the connected person is enabled by section 30(3) or (6) (or by section 30(3) or (6) as applied by section 35(13) or 36(13)), to meet the mortgagor's liabilities under the mortgage;

(b) he has applied to the court before the action is finally disposed of in that court; and

(c) the court sees no special reason against his being made a party to the action and is satisfied –

(i) that he may be expected to make such payments or do such other things in or towards satisfaction of the mortgagor's liabilities or obligations as might affect the outcome of the proceedings; or

(ii) that the expectation of it should be considered under section 36 of the Administration of Justice Act 1970.

(4) In this section 'connected person' has the same meaning as in section 54.

56 Actions by mortgagees: service of notice on certain persons

(1) This section applies if a mortgagee of and which consists, or substantially

consists, of a dwelling-house brings an action for the enforcement of his security, and at the relevant time there is –

(a) in the case of unregistered land, a land charge of Class F registered against the person who is the estate owner at the relevant time or any person who, where the estate owner is a trustee, preceded him as trustee during the subsistence of the mortgagee; or

(b) in the case of registered land, a subsisting registration of –

(i) a notice under section 31(10);

(ii) a notice under section 2(8) of the Matrimonial Homes Act 1983; or

(iii) a notice or caution under section 2(7) of the Matrimonial Homes Act 1967.

(2) If the person on whose behalf –

(a) the land charge is registered, or

(b) the notice or caution is entered,

is not a party to the action, the mortgagee must serve notice of the action on him.

(3) If –

(a) an official search has been made on behalf of the mortgagee which would disclose any land charge of Class F, notice or caution within subsection (1)(a) or (b),

(b) a certificate of the result of the search has been issued, and

(c) the action is commenced within the priority period,

the relevant time is the date of the certificate.

(4) In any other case the relevant time is the time when the action is commenced.

(5) The priority period is, for both registered and unregistered land, the period for which, in accordance with section 11(5) and (6) of the Land Charges Act 1972, a certificate on an official search operates in favour of a purchaser.

62   Meaning of 'cohabitants', 'relevant child' and 'associated persons'

(1) For the purposes of this Part –

(a) 'cohabitants' are two persons who are neither married to each other nor civil partners of each other but are living together as husband and wife or as if they were civil partners; and

(b) 'former cohabitants' is to be read accordingly, but does not include cohabitants who have subsequently married each other or become civil partners of each other.

(2) In this Part, 'relevant child', in relation to any proceedings under this Part, means –

(a) any child who is living with or might reasonably be expected to live with either party to the proceedings;

(b) any child in relation to whom an order under the Adoption Act 1976, the Adoption and Children Act 2002 or the Children Act 1989 is in question in the proceedings; and

(c) any other child whose interests the court considers relevant.

(3) For the purposes of this Part, a person is associated with another person if –

(a) they are or have been married to each other;

(aa) they are or have been civil partners of each other;

(b) they are cohabitants or former cohabitants;

(c) they live or have lived in the same household, otherwise than merely by reason of one of them being the other's employee, tenant, lodger or boarder;

(d) they are relatives;

(e) they have agreed to marry one another (whether or not that agreement has been terminated);

(eza) they have entered into a civil partnership agreement (as defined by section 73 of the Civil Partnership Act 2004) (whether or not that agreement has been terminated);

(f) in relation to any child, they are both persons falling within subsection (4); or

(g) they are parties to the same family proceedings (other than proceedings under this Part).

(4) A person falls within this subsection in relation to a child if –

(a) he is a parent of the child; or

(b) he has or has had parental responsibility for the child.

(5) If a child has been adopted or has been freed for adoption by virtue of any of the enactments mentioned in section 16(1) of the Adoption Act 1976, two persons are also associated with each other for the purposes of this Part if –

(a) one is a natural parent of the child or a parent of such a natural parent; and

(b) the other is the child or any person –

(i) who has become a parent of the child by virtue of an adoption order or has applied for an adoption order, or

(ii) with whom the child has at any time been placed for adoption.

(6) A body corporate and another person are not, by virtue of subsection (3)(f) or (g), to be regarded for the purposes of this Part as associated with each other.

63   Interpretation of Part IV

(1) In this Part –

'adoption order' has the meaning given by section 72(1) of the Adoption Act 1976;

'associated', in relation to a person, is to be read with section 62(3) to (6);

'child' means a person under the age of eighteen years;

'cohabitant' and 'former cohabitant' have the meaning given by section 62(1);

'the court' is to be read with section 57;

'development' means physical, intellectual, emotional, social or behavioural development;

'dwelling-house' includes (subject to subsection (4)) –

(a) any building or part of a building which is occupied as a dwelling,

(b) any caravan, house-boat or structure which is occupied as a dwelling,

and any yard, garden, garage or outhouse belonging to it and occupied with it;

'family proceedings' means any proceedings –

(a) under the inherent jurisdiction of the High Court in relation to children; or

(b) under the enactments mentioned in subsection (2);

'harm' –

(a) in relation to a person who has reached the age of eighteen years, means ill-treatment or the impairment of health; and

(b) in relation to a child, means ill-treatment or impairment of health or development;

'health' includes physical or mental health;

'home rights' has the meaning given by section 30;

'ill-treatment' includes forms of ill-treatment which are not physical and, in relation to a child, includes sexual abuse;

'mortgage', 'mortgagor' and 'mortgagee' have the same meaning as in the Law of Property Act 1925;

'mortgage payments' includes any payments which, under the terms of the mortgage, the mortgagor is required to make to any person;

'non-molestation order' has the meaning given by section 42(1);

'occupation order' has the meaning given by section 39;

'parental responsibility' has the same meaning as in the Children Act 1989;

'relative', in relation to a person, means –

(a) the father, mother, stepfather, stepmother, son, daughter, stepson, stepdaughter, grandmother, grandfather, grandson or granddaughter of that person or of that person's spouse, former spouse, civil partner or former civil partner, or

(b) the brother, sister, uncle, aunt, niece or nephew (whether of the full blood or of the half blood or by marriage or civil partnership) of that person or of that person's spouse, former spouse, civil partner or former civil partner,

and includes, in relation to a person who is living or has lived with another person as husband and wife, any person who would fall within paragraph (a) or (b) if the parties were married to each other or were civil partners of each other;

'relevant child', in relation to any proceedings under this Part, has the meaning given by section 62(2);

'the relevant judicial authority', in relation to any order under this Part, means –

(a) where the order was made by the High Court, a judge of that court;

(b) where the order was made by a county court, a judge or district judge of that or any other county court; or

(c) where the order was made by a magistrates' court, any magistrates' court.

(2) The enactments referred to in the definition of 'family proceedings' are –

(a) Part II;

(b) this Part;

(c) the Matrimonial Causes Act 1973;

(d) the Adoption Act 1976;

(e) the Domestic Proceedings and Magistrates' Courts Act 1978;

(f) Part III of the Matrimonial and Family Proceedings Act 1984;

(g) Parts I, II and IV of the Children Act 1989;

(h) section 30 of the Human Fertilisation and Embryology Act 1990;

(i) the Adoption and Children Act 2002;

(j) Schedules 5 to 7 to the Civil Partnership Act 2004.

(3) Where the question of whether harm suffered by a child is significant turns on the child's health or development, his health or development shall be compared with that which could reasonably be expected of a similar child.

(4) For the purposes of sections 31, 32, 53 and 54 and such other provisions of this Part (if any) as may be prescribed, this Part is to have effect as if paragraph (b) of the definition of 'dwelling-house' were omitted.

(5) It is hereby declared that this Part applies as between the parties to a marriage even though either of them is, or has at any time during the marriage been, married to more than one person.

SCHEDULE 7

TRANSFER OF CERTAIN TENANCIES ON DIVORCE ETC
OR ON SEPARATION OF COHABITANTS

PART I

GENERAL

1. In this Schedule –

'civil partner', except in paragraph 2, includes (where the context requires) former civil partner;

'cohabitant', except in paragraph 3, includes (where the context requires) former cohabitant;

'the court' does not include a magistrates' court,

'landlord' includes –

(a) any person from time to time deriving title under the original landlord; and

(b) in relation to any dwelling-house, any person other than the tenant who is, or (but for Part VII of the Rent Act 1977 or Part II of the Rent (Agriculture) Act 1976) would be, entitled to possession of the dwelling-house;

'Part II order' means an order under Part II of this Schedule;

'a relevant tenancy' means –

(a) a protected tenancy or statutory tenancy within the meaning of the Rent Act 1977;

(b) a statutory tenancy within the meaning of the Rent (Agriculture) Act 1976;

(c) a secure tenancy within the meaning of section 79 of the Housing Act 1985;

(d) an assured tenancy or assured agricultural occupancy within the meaning of Part I of the Housing Act 1988; or

(e) an introductory tenancy within the meaning of Chapter I of Part V of the Housing Act 1996;

'spouse', except in paragraph 2, includes (where the context requires) former spouse; and

'tenancy' includes sub-tenancy.

2. – (1) This paragraph applies if one spouse or civil partner is entitled, either in his own right or jointly with the other spouse or civil partner, to occupy a dwelling-house by virtue of a relevant tenancy.

(2) The court may make a Part II order –

(a) on granting a decree of divorce, a decree of nullity of marriage or a decree of judicial separation or at any time thereafter (whether, in the case of a decree of divorce or nullity of marriage, before or after the decree is made absolute), or

(b) at any time when it has power to make a property adjustment order under Part 2 of Schedule 5 to the Civil Partnership Act 2004 with respect to the civil partnership.

3. – (1) This paragraph applies if one cohabitant is entitled, either in his own right or jointly with the other cohabitant, to occupy a dwelling-house by virtue of a relevant tenancy.

(2) If the cohabitants cease to live together as husband and wife, the court may make a Part II order.

4. The court shall not make a Part II order unless the dwelling-house is or was –

(a) in the case of spouses, a matrimonial home;

(aa) in the case of civil partners, a civil partnership home; or

(b) in the case of cohabitants, a home in which they lived together as husband and wife.

5. In determining whether to exercise its powers under Part II of this Schedule and, if so, in what manner, the court shall have regard to all the circumstances of the case including –

(a) the circumstances in which the tenancy was granted to either or both of the spouses, civil partners or cohabitants or, as the case requires, the circumstances in which either or both of them became tenant under the tenancy;

(b) the matters mentioned in section 33(6)(a), (b) and

(c) and, where the parties are cohabitants and only one of them is entitled to occupy the dwelling-house by virtue of the relevant tenancy, the further matters mentioned in section 36(6)(e), (f), (g) and (h); and (c) the suitability of the parties as tenants.

PART II

ORDERS THAT MAY BE MADE

6. References in this Part of this Schedule to a spouse, a civil partner or a cohabitant being entitled to occupy a dwelling-house by virtue of a relevant tenancy apply whether that entitlement is in his own right or jointly with the other spouse, civil partner or cohabitant.

Protected, secure or assured tenancy or assured
agricultural occupancy

7. – (1) If a spouse, civil partner or cohabitant is entitled to occupy the dwelling-house by virtue of a protected tenancy within the meaning of the Rent Act 1977, a secure tenancy within the meaning of the Housing Act 1985, an assured tenancy or assured agricultural occupancy within the meaning of Part I of the Housing Act 1988 or an introductory tenancy within the meaning of Chapter I of Part V of the Housing Act 1996, the court may by order direct that, as from such date as may be specified in the order, there shall, by virtue of the order and without further assurance, be transferred to, and vested in, the other spouse, civil partner or cohabitant –

(a) the estate or interest which the spouse, civil partner or cohabitant so entitled had in the dwelling-house immediately before that date by virtue of the lease or agreement creating the tenancy and any assignment of that lease or agreement, with all rights, privileges and appurtenances attaching to that estate or interest but subject to all covenants, obligations, liabilities and incumbrances to which it is subject; and

(b) where the spouse, civil partner or cohabitant so entitled is an assignee of such lease or agreement, the liability of that spouse, civil partner or cohabitant under any covenant of indemnity by the assignee express or implied in the assignment of the lease or agreement to that spouse, civil partner or cohabitant.

(2) If an order is made under this paragraph, any liability or obligation to which the spouse, civil partner or cohabitant so entitled is subject under any covenant having reference to the dwelling-house in the lease or agreement, being a liability or obligation falling due to be discharged or performed on or after the date so specified, shall not be enforceable against that spouse, civil partner or cohabitant.

(3) If the spouse, civil partner or cohabitant so entitled is a successor within the meaning of Part 4 of the Housing Act 1985 –

(a) his former spouse (or, in the case of judicial separation, his spouse),

(b) his former civil partner (or, if a separation order is in force, his civil partner), or

(c) his former cohabitant,

is to be deemed also to be a successor within the meaning of that Part.

(3A) If the spouse, civil partner or cohabitant so entitled is a successor within the meaning of section 132 of the Housing Act 1996 –

(a) his former spouse (or, in the case of judicial separation, his spouse),

(b) his former civil partner (or, if a separation order is in force, his civil partner), or

(c) his former cohabitant,

is to be deemed also to be a successor within the meaning of that section.

(4) If the spouse, civil partner or cohabitant so entitled is for the purposes of section 17 of the Housing Act 1998 a successor in relation to the tenancy or occupancy –

(a) his former spouse (or, in the case of judicial separation, his spouse),

(b) his former civil partner (or, if a separation order is in force, his civil partner), or

(c) his former cohabitant,

is to be deemed to be a successor in relation to the tenancy or occupancy for the purposes of that section.

(5) If the transfer under sub-paragraph (1) is of an assured agricultural occupancy, then, for the purposes of Chapter III of Part I of the Housing Act 1988 –

(a) the agricultural worker condition is fulfilled with respect to the dwelling-house while the spouse, civil partner or cohabitant to whom the assured agricultural occupancy is transferred continues to be the occupier under that occupancy, and

(b) that condition is to be treated as so fulfilled by virtue of the same paragraph of Schedule 3 to the Housing Act 1988 as was applicable before the transfer.

Statutory tenancy within the meaning of the Rent Act 1977

8. – (1) This paragraph applies if the spouse, civil partner or cohabitant is entitled to occupy the dwelling-house by virtue of a statutory tenancy within the meaning of the Rent Act 1977.

(2) The court may by order direct that, as from the date specified in the order –

(a) that spouse, civil partner or cohabitant is to cease to be entitled to occupy the dwelling-house; and

(b) the other spouse, civil partner or cohabitant is to be deemed to be the tenant or, as the case may be, the sole tenant under that statutory tenancy.

(3) The question whether the provisions of paragraphs 1 to 3, or (as the case may be) paragraphs 5 to 7 of Schedule 1 to the Rent Act 1977, as to the succession by the surviving spouse, or surviving civil partner of a deceased tenant, or by a member of the deceased tenant's family, to the right to retain possession are capable of having effect in the event of the death of the person deemed by an order under this paragraph to be the tenant or sole tenant under the statutory tenancy is to be determined according as those provisions have or have not already had effect in relation to the statutory tenancy.

Statutory tenancy within the meaning of the Rent (Agriculture) Act 1976

9. – (1) This paragraph applies if the spouse, civil partner or cohabitant is entitled to occupy the dwelling-house by virtue of a statutory tenancy within the meaning of the Rent (Agriculture) Act 1976.

(2) The court may by order direct that, as from such date as may be specified in the order –

(a) that spouse, civil partner or cohabitant is to cease to be entitled to occupy the dwelling-house; and

(b) the other spouse, civil partner or cohabitant is to be deemed to be the tenant or, as the case may be, the sole tenant under that statutory tenancy.

(3) A spouse, civil partner or cohabitant who is deemed under this paragraph to be the tenant under a statutory tenancy is (within the meaning of that Act) a statutory tenant in his own right, or a statutory tenant by succession, according as the other spouse, civil partner or cohabitant was a statutory tenant in his own right or a statutory tenant by succession.

Part III

SUPPLEMENTARY PROVISIONS

10. – (1) If the court makes a Part II order, it may by the order direct the making of a payment by the spouse, civil partner or cohabitant to whom the tenancy is transferred ('the transferee') to the other spouse, civil partner or cohabitant ('the transferor').

(2) Without prejudice to that, the court may, on making an order by virtue of sub-paragraph (1) for the payment of a sum –

(a) direct that payment of that sum or any part of it is to be deferred until a specified date or until the occurrence of a specified event, or

(b) direct that that sum or any part of it is to be paid by instalments.

(3) Where an order has been made by virtue of sub-paragraph (1), the court may, on the application of the transferee or the transferor –

(a) exercise its powers under sub-paragraph (2), or

(b) vary any direction previously given under that sub-paragraph,

at any time before the sum whose payment is required by the order is paid in full.

(4) In deciding whether to exercise its powers under this paragraph and, if so, in what manner, the court shall have regard to all the circumstances including –

(a) the financial loss that would otherwise be suffered by the transferor as a result of the order;

(b) the financial needs and financial resources of the parties; and

(c) the financial obligations which the parties have, or are likely to have in the foreseeable future, including financial obligations to each other and to any relevant child.

(5) The court shall not give any direction under sub-paragraph (2) unless it appears to it that immediate payment of the sum required by the order would cause the transferee financial hardship which is greater than any financial hardship that would be caused to the transferor if the direction were given.

11. – (1) If the court makes a Part II order, it may by the order direct that both spouses, civil partners or cohabitants are to be jointly and severally liable to discharge or perform any or all of the liabilities and obligations in respect of the dwelling-house (whether arising under the tenancy or otherwise) which –

(a) have at the date of the order fallen due to be discharged or performed by one only of them; or

(b) but for the direction, would before the date specified as the date on which the order is to take effect fall due to be discharged or performed by one only of them.

(2) If the court gives such a direction, it may further direct that either spouse, civil partner or cohabitant is to be liable to indemnify the other in whole or in part against any payment made or expenses incurred by the other in discharging or performing any such liability or obligation.

12. The date specified in a Part II order as the date on which the order is to take effect must not be earlier than –

(a) in the case of a marriage in respect of which a decree of divorce or nullity has been granted, the date on which the decree is made absolute;

(b) in the case of a civil partnership in respect of which a dissolution or nullity order has been made, the date on which the order is made final.

13. – (1) If after the grant of a decree dissolving or annulling a marriage either spouse remarries or forms a civil partnership, that spouse is not entitled to apply, by reference to the grant of that decree, for a Part II order.

(2) If after the making of a dissolution or nullity order either civil partner forms a subsequent civil partnership or marries, that civil partner is not entitled to apply, by reference to the making of that order, for a Part II order.

(3) In sub-paragraohs (1) and (2) –

(a) the references to remarrying and marrying include references to cases where the marriage is by law void or voidable, and

(b) the references to forming a civil partnership include references to cases where the civil partnership is by law void or voidable.

14. – (1) Rules of court shall be made requiring the court, before it makes an order under this Schedule, to give the landlord of the dwelling-house to which the order will relate an opportunity of being heard.

(2) Rules of court may provide that an application for a Part II order by reference to an order or decree may not, without the leave of the court by which that order was made or decree was granted, be made after the expiration of such period from the order or grant as may be prescribed by the rules.

15. – (1) If a spouse or civil partner is entitled to occupy a dwelling-house by virtue of a tenancy, this Schedule does not affect the operation of sections 30 and 31 in relation to the other spouse's or civil partner's home rights.

(2) If a spouse, civil partner or cohabitant is entitled to occupy a dwelling-house by virtue of a tenancy, the court's powers to make orders under this Schedule are additional to those conferred by sections 33, 35 and 36.

SCHEDULE 9

MODIFICATIONS, SAVING AND TRANSITIONAL ...

7. In paragraphs 8 to 15 'the 1983 Act' means the Matrimonial Homes Act 1983. ...

NB The insertion in section 62(2)(b) and of section 63(2)(i), above, was not in force on 1 May 2005.

As amended by the Housing Act 1996 (Consequential Amendments) Order 1997, art 2, Schedule, para 10(a), (b); Land Registration Act 2002, ss133, 135, Schedule 11, para 34(1), (2), Schedule 13; Adoption and Children Act 2002, s139(1), Schedule 3, paras 85, 88; Civil Partnership Act 2004, s82, Schedule 9, Pt 1, paras 1–8, 10–14, 16.

HOUSING ACT 1996
(1996 c 52)

1   The register of social landlords

(1) The Relevant Authority shall maintain a register of social landlords which shall be open to inspection at all reasonable times.

(1A) In this Part 'the Relevant Authority' means the Housing Corporation or the Secretary of State, as provided by section 56.

(1B) The register maintained by the Housing Corporation shall be maintained at its head office.

2   Eligibility for registration

(1) A body is eligible for registration as a social landlord if it is –

(a) a registered charity which is a housing association,

(b) a society registered under the Industrial and Provident Societies Act 1965 which satisfies the conditions in subsection (2), or

(c) a company registered under the Companies Act 1985 which satisfies those conditions.

(2) The conditions are that the body is non-profit-making and is established for the purpose of, or has among its objects or powers, the provision, construction, improvement or management of –

(a) houses to be kept available for letting,

(b) houses for occupation by members of the body, where the rules of the body restrict membership to persons entitled or prospectively entitled (as tenants or otherwise) to occupy a house provided or managed by the body, or

(c) hostels,

and that any additional purposes or objects are among those specified in subsection (4).

(3) For the purposes of this section a body is non-profit-making if –

(a) it does not trade for profit, or

(b) its constitution or rules prohibit the issue of capital with interest or dividend exceeding the rate prescribed by the Treasury for the purposes of section 1(1)(b) of the Housing Associations Act 1985.

(4) The permissible additional purposes or objects are –

(a) providing land, amenities or services, or providing, constructing, repairing or improving buildings, for its residents, either exclusively or together with other persons;

(b) acquiring, or repairing and improving, or creating by the conversion of houses or other property, houses to be disposed of on sale, on lease or on shared ownership terms;

(c) constructing houses to be disposed of on shared ownership terms;

(d) managing houses held on leases or other lettings (not being houses within subsection (2)(a) or (b)) or blocks of flats;

(e) providing services of any description for owners or occupiers of houses in arranging or carrying out works of maintenance, repair or improvement, or encouraging or facilitating the carrying out of such works;

(f) encouraging and giving advice on the forming of housing associations or providing services for, and giving advice on the running of, such associations and other voluntary organisations concerned with housing, or matters connected with housing.

(5) A body is not ineligible for registration as a social landlord by reason only that its powers include power –

(a) to acquire commercial premises or businesses as an incidental part of a project or series of projects undertaken for purposes or objects falling within subsection (2) or (4);

(b) to repair, improve or convert commercial premises acquired as mentioned in paragraph (a) or to carry on for a limited period any business so acquired;

(c) to repair or improve houses, or buildings in which houses are situated, after a disposal of the houses by the body by way of sale or lease or on shared ownership terms.

(6) In this section –

'block of flats' means a building containing two or more flats which are held on leases or other lettings and which are occupied or intended to be occupied wholly or mainly for residential purposes;

'disposed of on shared ownership terms' means disposed of on a lease –

(a) granted on a payment of a premium calculated by reference to a percentage of the value of the house or of the cost of providing it, or

(b) under which the tenant (or his personal representatives) will or may be entitled to a sum calculated by reference directly or indirectly to the value of the house;

'letting' includes the grant of a licence to occupy;

'residents', in relation to a body, means persons occupying a house or hostel provided or managed by the body; and

'voluntary organisation' means an organisation whose activities are not carried on for profit.

(7) The Secretary of State may by order specify permissible purposes, objects or powers additional to those specified in subsections (4) and (5).

CHAPTER II

DISPOSAL OF LAND AND RELATED MATTERS

8   Power of registered social landlord to dispose of land

(1) A registered social landlord has power by virtue of this section and not otherwise to dispose, in such manner as it thinks fit, of land held by it.

(2) Section 39 of the Settled Land Act 1925 (disposal of land by trustees) does not apply to the disposal of land by a registered social landlord; and accordingly the disposal need not be for the best consideration in money that can reasonably be obtained. Nothing in this subsection shall be taken to authorise any action on the part of a charity which would conflict with the trusts of the charity.

(3) This section has effect subject to section 9 (control by Relevant Authority of land transactions).

9   Consent required for disposal of land by registered social landlord

(1) The consent of the Relevant Authority is required for any disposal of land by a registered social landlord under section 8.

(1A) The consent –

(a) if given by the Housing Corporation, shall be given by order under its seal, and

(b) if given by the Secretary of State, shall be given by order in writing.

(2) The consent of the Relevant Authority may be so given –

(a) generally to all registered social landlords or to a particular landlord or description of landlords;

(b) in relation to particular land or in relation to a particular description of land,

and may be given subject to conditions.

(3) Before giving any consent other than a consent in relation to a particular

landlord or particular land, the Relevant Authority shall consult such bodies representative of registered social landlords as it thinks fit.

(4) A disposal of a house by a registered social landlord made without the consent required by this section is void unless –

    (a) the disposal is to an individual (or to two or more individuals),

    (b) the disposal does not extend to any other house, and

    (c) the landlord reasonably believes that the individual or individuals intend to use the house as their principal dwelling.

(5) Any other disposal by a registered social landlord which requires consent under this section is valid in favour of a person claiming under the landlord notwithstanding that that consent has not been given; and a person dealing with a registered social landlord, or with a person claiming under such a landlord, shall not be concerned to see or inquire whether any such consent has been given.

(6) Where at the time of its removal from the register of social landlords a body owns land, this section continues to apply to that land after the removal as if the body concerned continued to be a registered social landlord.

(7) For the purposes of this section 'disposal' means sale, lease, mortgage, charge or any other disposition.

(8) This section has effect subject to section 10 (lettings and other disposals not requiring consent of Relevant Authority).

10   Lettings and other disposals not requiring consent of Relevant Authority

(1) A letting by a registered social landlord does not require consent under section 9 if it is –

    (a) a letting of land under an assured tenancy or an assured agricultural occupancy, or what would be an assured tenancy or an assured agricultural occupancy but for any of paragraphs 4 to 8, or paragraph 12(1)(h), of Schedule 1 to the Housing Act 1988, or

    (b) a letting of land under a secure tenancy or what would be a secure tenancy but for any of paragraphs 2 to 12 of Schedule 1 to the Housing Act 1985.

(2) Consent under section 9 is not required in the case of a disposal to which section 81 or 133 of the Housing Act 1988 applies (certain disposals for which the consent of the Secretary of State is required).

(3) Consent under section 9 is not required for a disposal under Part V [ss118 to 188] of the Housing Act 1985 (the right to buy) or under the right conferred by section 16 below (the right to acquire).

16   Right of tenant to acquire dwelling

(1) A tenant of a registered social landlord has the right to acquire the dwelling of which he is a tenant if –

(a) he is a tenant under an assured tenancy, other than an assured shorthold tenancy or a long tenancy, or under a secure tenancy,

(b) the dwelling was provided with public money and has remained in the social rented sector, and

(c) he satisfies any further qualifying conditions applicable under Part V of the Housing Act 1985 (the right to buy) as it applies in relation to the right conferred by this section.

(2) For this purpose a dwelling shall be regarded as provided with public money if –

(a) it was provided or acquired wholly or in part by means of a grant under section 18 (social housing grant),

(b) it was provided or acquired wholly or in part by applying or appropriating sums standing in the disposal proceeds fund of a registered social landlord (see section 25), or

(c) it was acquired by a registered social landlord after the commencement of this paragraph on a disposal by a public sector landlord at a time when it was capable of being let as a separate dwelling.

(3) A dwelling shall be regarded for the purposes of this section as having remained within the social rented sector if, since it was so provided or acquired –

(a) the person holding the freehold interest in the dwelling has been either a registered social landlord or a public sector landlord; and

(b) any person holding an interest as lessee (otherwise than as mortgagee) in the dwelling has been –

(i) an individual holding otherwise than under a long tenancy; or

(ii) a registered social landlord or a public sector landlord.

(3A) In subsection (3)(a) the reference to the freehold interest in the dwelling includes a reference to such an interest in the dwelling as is held by the landlord under a lease granted in pursuance of paragraph 3 of Schedule 9 to the Leasehold Reform, Housing and Urban Development Act 1993 (mandatory leaseback to former freeholder on collective enfrachisement).

(4) A dwelling shall be regarded for the purposes of this section as provided by means of a grant under section 18 (social housing grant) if, and only if, the Relevant Authority when making the grant notified the recipient that the dwelling was to be so regarded. The Relevant Authority shall before making the grant inform the applicant that it proposes to give such a notice and allow him an opportunity to withdraw his application within a specified time.

(5) But notice must be taken to be given to a registered social landlord under subsection (4) by the Housing Corporation if it is sent using electronic communications to such number or address as the registered social landlord has for the time being notified to the Housing Corporation for that purpose.

(6) The means by which notice is sent by virtue of subsection (5) must be such as to enable the registered social landlord to reproduce the notice by electronic means in a form which is visible and legible.

(7) An electronic communication is a communication transmitted (whether from one person to another, from one device to another, or from a person to a device or vice versa) –

(a) by means of an electronic communications network; or

(b) by other means but while in electronic form.

17 Right of tenant to acquire dwelling: supplementary provisions

(1) The Secretary of State may by order –

(a) specify the amount or rate of discount to be given on the exercise of the right conferred by section 16; and

(b) designate rural areas in relation to dwellings in which the right conferred by that section does not arise.

(2) The provisions of Part V of the Housing Act 1985 apply in relation to the right to acquire under section 16 –

(a) subject to any order under subsection (1) above, and

(b) subject to such other exceptions, adaptations and other modifications as may be specified by regulations made by the Secretary of State. ...

CHAPTER IV

GENERAL POWERS OF THE RELEVANT AUTHORITY

37 Powers of entry

(1) This section applies where it appears to the Relevant Authority that a registered social landlord may be failing to maintain or repair any premises in accordance with guidance issued under section 36.

(2) A person authorised by the Relevant Authority may at any reasonable time, on giving not less than 28 days' notice of his intention to the landlord concerned, enter any such premises for the purpose of survey and examination.

(3) Where such notice is given to the landlord, the landlord shall give the occupier or occupiers of the premises not less than seven days' notice of the proposed survey and examination. ...

(6) The Relevant Authority shall give a copy of any survey carried out in exercise of the powers conferred by this section to the landlord concerned. ...

38 Penalty for obstruction of person exercising power of entry

(1) It is an offence for a registered social landlord or any of its officers or employees to obstruct a person authorised under section 37 (powers of entry) to enter premises in the performance of anything which he is authorised by that section to do. ...

CHAPTER V

MISCELLANEOUS AND GENERAL PROVISIONS

63   Minor definitions: Part I

(1) In this Part –

'dwelling' means a building or part of a building occupied or intended to be occupied as a separate dwelling, together with any yard, garden, outhouses and appurtenances belonging to it or usually enjoyed with it; ...

'hostel' means a building in which is provided for persons generally or for a class or classes of persons –

(a) residential accommodation otherwise than in separate and self-contained premises, and

(b) either board or facilities for the preparation of food adequate to the needs of those persons, or both;

'house' includes –

(a) any part of a building occupied or intended to be occupied as a separate dwelling, and

(b) any yard, garden, outhouses and appurtenances belonging to it or usually enjoyed with it; ...

'long tenancy' has the same meaning as in Part V of the Housing Act 1985;

'modifications' includes additions, alterations and omissions and cognate expressions shall be construed accordingly;

'notice' means notice in writing;

'public sector landlord' means any of the authorities or bodies within section 80(1) of the Housing Act 1985 (the landlord condition for secure tenancies); ...

(2) References in this Part to the provision of a dwelling or house include the provision of a dwelling or house –

(a) by erecting the dwelling or house, or converting a building into dwellings or a house, or

(b) by altering, enlarging, repairing or improving an existing dwelling or house;

and references to a dwelling or house provided by means of a grant or other financial assistance are to its being so provided directly or indirectly.

PART III

LANDLORD AND TENANT

CHAPTER I

TENANTS' RIGHTS

81   Restriction on termination of tenancy for failure to pay service charge

(1) A landlord may not, in relation to premises let as a dwelling, exercise a right of re-entry or forfeiture for failure by a tenant to pay a service charge or administration charge unless –

(a) it is finally determined by (or on appeal from) a leasehold valuation tribunal or by a court, or by an arbitral tribunal in proceedings pursuant to a post-dispute arbitration agreement, that the amount of the service charge or administration charge is payable by him, or

(b) the tenant has admitted that it is so payable.

(2) The landlord may not exercise a right of re-entry or forfeiture by virtue of subsection (1)(a) until after the end of the period of 14 days beginning with the day after that on which the final determination is made.

(3) For the purposes of this section it is finally determined that the amount of a service charge or administration charge is payable –

(a) if a decision that it is payable is not appealed against or otherwise challenged, at the end of the time for bringing an appeal or other challenge, or

(b) if such a decision is appealed against or otherwise challenged and not set aside in consequence of the appeal or other challenge, at the time specified in subsection (3A).

(3A) The time referred to in subsection (3)(b) is the time when the appeal or other challenge is disposed of –

(a) by the determination of the appeal or other challenge and the expiry of the time for bringing a subsequent appeal (if any), or

(b) by its being abandoned or otherwise ceasing to have effect.

(4) The reference in subsection (1) to premises let as a dwelling does not include premises let on –

(a) a tenancy to which Part II of the Landlord and Tenant Act 1954 applies (business tenancies),

(b) a tenancy of an agricultural holding within the meaning of the Agricultural Holdings Act 1986 in relation to which that Act applies, or

(c) a farm business tenancy within the meaning of the Agricultural Tenancies Act 1995.

(4A) References in this section to the exercise of a right of re-entry or forfeiture include the service of a notice under section 146(1) of the Law of Property Act 1925 (restriction on re-entry or forfeiture).

(5) In this section –

(a) 'administration charge' has the meaning given by Part 1 of Schedule 11 to the Commonhold and Leasehold Reform Act 2002,

(b) 'arbitration agreement' and 'arbitral tribunal' have the same meaning as in Part 1 of the Arbitration Act 1996 (c 23) and 'post-dispute arbitration agreement', in relation to any matter, means an arbitration agreement made after a dispute about the matter has arisen,

(c) 'dwelling' has the same meaning as in the Landlord and Tenant Act 1985 (c 70), and

(d) 'service charge' means a service charge within the meaning of section 18(1) of the Landlord and Tenant Act 1985, other than one excluded from that section by section 27 of that Act (rent of dwelling registered and not entered as variable).

(5A) Any order of a court to give effect to a determination of a leasehold valuation tribunal shall be treated as a determination by the court for the purposes of this section.

(6) Nothing in this section affects the exercise of a right of re-entry or forfeiture on other grounds.

PART V

CONDUCT OF TENANTS

CHAPTER I

INTRODUCTORY TENANCIES

124 Introductory tenancies

(1) A local housing authority or a housing action trust may elect to operate an introductory tenancy regime.

(2) When such an election is in force, every periodic tenancy of a dwelling-house entered into or adopted by the authority or trust shall, if it would otherwise be a secure tenancy, be an introductory tenancy, unless immediately before the tenancy was entered into or adopted the tenant or, in the case of joint tenants, one or more of them was –

(a) a secure tenant of the same or another dwelling-house, or

(b) an assured tenant of a registered social landlord (otherwise than under an assured shorthold tenancy) in respect of the same or another dwelling-house.

(3) Subsection (2) does not apply to a tenancy entered into or adopted in pursuance of a contract made before the election was made.

(4) For the purposes of this Chapter a periodic tenancy is adopted by a person if that person becomes the landlord under the tenancy, whether on a disposal or surrender of the interest of the former landlord.

(5) An election under this section may be revoked at any time, without prejudice to the making of a further election.

125 Duration of introductory tenancy

(1) A tenancy remains an introductory tenancy until the end of the trial period, unless one of the events mentioned in subsection (5) occurs before the end of that period.

(2) The 'trial period' is the period of one year beginning with –

(a) in the case of a tenancy which was entered into by a local housing authority or housing action trust –

(i) the date on which the tenancy was entered into, or

(ii) if later, the date on which a tenant was first entitled to possession under the tenancy; or

(b) in the case of a tenancy which was adopted by a local housing authority or housing action trust, the date of adoption;

but this is subject to subsections (3) and (4) and to section 125A (extension of trial period by six months).

(3) Where the tenant under an introductory tenancy was formerly a tenant under another introductory tenancy, or held an assured shorthold tenancy from a registered social landlord, any period or periods during which he was such a tenant shall count towards the trial period, provided –

(a) if there was one such period, it ended immediately before the date specified in subsection (2), and

(b) if there was more than one such period, the most recent period ended immediately before that date and each period succeeded the other without interruption.

(4) Where there are joint tenants under an introductory tenancy, the reference in subsection (3) to the tenant shall be construed as referring to the joint tenant in whose case the application of that subsection produces the earliest starting date for the trial period.

(5) A tenancy ceases to be an introductory tenancy if, before the end of the trial period –

(a) the circumstances are such that the tenancy would not otherwise be a secure tenancy,

(b) a person or body other than a local housing authority or housing action trust becomes the landlord under the tenancy,

(c) the election in force when the tenancy was entered into or adopted is revoked, or

(d) the tenancy ceases to be an introductory tenancy by virtue of section 133(3) (succession).

(6) A tenancy does not come to an end merely because it ceases to be an introductory tenancy, but a tenancy which has once ceased to be an introductory tenancy cannot subsequently become an introductory tenancy.

(7) This section has effect subject to section 130 (effect of beginning proceedings for possession).

125A Extension of trial period by 6 months

(1) If both of the following conditions are met in relation to an introductory tenancy, the trial period is extended by 6 months.

(2) The first condition is that the landlord has served a notice of extension on the tenant at least 8 weeks before the original expiry date.

(3) The second condition is that either –

(a) the tenant has not requested a review under section 125B in accordance with subsection (1) of that section, or

(b) if he has, the decision on the review was to confirm the landlord's decision to extend the trial period.

(4) A notice of extension is a notice –

(a) stating that the landlord has decided that the period for which the tenancy is to be an introductory tenancy should be extended by 6 months, and

(b) complying with subsection (5).

(5) A notice of extension must –

(a) set out the reasons for the landlord's decision, and

(b) inform the tenant of his right to request a review of the landlord's decision and of the time within which such a request must be made.

(6) In this section and section 125B 'the original expiry date' means the last day of the period of one year that would apply as the trial period apart from this section.

125B Review of decision to extend trial period

(1) A request for review of the landlord's decision that the trial period for an introductory tenancy should be extended under section 125A must be made before the end of the period of 14 days beginning with the day on which the notice of extension is served.

(2) On a request being duly made to it, the landlord shall review its decision.

(3) The Secretary of State may make provision by regulations as to the procedure to be followed in connection with a review under this section.

Nothing in the following provisions affects the generality of this power.

(4) Provision may be made by regulations –

(a) requiring the decision on review to be made by a person of appropriate seniority who was not involved in the original decision, and

(b) as to the circumstances in which the person concerned is entitled to an oral hearing, and whether and by whom he may be represented at such a hearing.

(5) The landlord shall notify the tenant of the decision on the review.

If the decision is to confirm the original decision, the landlord shall also notify him of the reasons for the decision.

(6) The review shall be carried out and the tenant notified before the original expiry date.

126 Licences

(1) The provisions of this Chapter apply in relation to a licence to occupy a dwelling-house (whether or not granted for a consideration) as they apply in relation to a tenancy.

(2) Subsection (1) does not apply to a licence granted as a temporary expedient to a person who entered the dwelling-house or any other land as a trespasser (whether or not, before the grant of that licence, another licence to occupy that or another dwelling-house had been granted to him).

127 Proceedings for possession

(1) The landlord may only bring an introductory tenancy to an end by obtaining an order of the court for the possession of the dwelling-house.

(2) The court shall make such an order unless the provisions of section 128 apply.

(3) Where the court makes such an order, the tenancy comes to an end on the date on which the tenant is to give up possession in pursuance of the order.

128 Notice of proceedings for possession

(1) The court shall not entertain proceedings for the possession of a dwelling-house let under an introductory tenancy unless the landlord has served on the tenant a notice of proceedings complying with this section.

(2) The notice shall state that the court will be asked to make an order for the possession of the dwelling-house.

(3) The notice shall set out the reasons for the landlord's decision to apply for such an order.

(4) The notice shall specify a date after which proceedings for the possession of the dwelling-house may be begun. The date so specified must not be earlier than the date on which the tenancy could, apart from this Chapter, be brought to an end by notice to quit given by the landlord on the same date as the notice of proceedings. ...

131 Persons qualified to succeed tenant

A person is qualified to succeed the tenant under an introductory tenancy if he occupies the dwelling-house as his only or principal home at the time of the tenant's death and either –

(a) he is the tenant's spouse, or

(b) he is another member of the tenant's family and has resided with the tenant throughout the period of twelve months ending with the tenant's death;

unless, in either case, the tenant was himself a successor, as defined in section 132.

132 Cases where the tenant is a successor

(1) The tenant is himself a successor if –

(a) the tenancy vested in him by virtue of section 133 (succession to introductory tenancy),

(b) he was a joint tenant and has become the sole tenant,

(c) he became the tenant on the tenancy being assigned to him (but subject to subsections (2) and (3)), or

(d) he became the tenant on the tenancy being vested in him on the death of the previous tenant.

(2) A tenant to whom the tenancy was assigned in pursuance of an order under section 24 of the Matrimonial Causes Act 1973 (property adjustment orders in connection with matrimonial proceedings) or section 17(1) of the Matrimonial and Family Proceedings Act 1984 (property adjustment orders after overseas divorce, &c) is a successor only if the other party to the marriage was a successor.

(2A) A tenant to whom the tenancy was assigned in pursuance of an order under Part 2 of Schedule 5, or paragraph 9(2) or (3) of Schedule 7, to the Civil Partnership Act 2004 (property adjustment orders in connection with civil partnership proceedings or after overseas dissolution of civil partnership, etc) is a successor only if the other civil partner was a successor.

(3) Where within six months of the coming to an end of an introductory tenancy ('the former tenancy') the tenant becomes a tenant under another introductory tenancy, and –

(a) the tenant was a successor in relation to the former tenancy, and

(b) under the other tenancy either the dwelling-house or the landlord, or both, are the same as under the former tenancy,

the tenant is also a successor in relation to the other tenancy unless the agreement creating that tenancy otherwise provides.

133 Succession to introductory tenancy

(1) This section applies where a tenant under an introductory tenancy dies.

(2) Where there is a person qualified to succeed the tenant, the tenancy vests by virtue of this section in that person, or if there is more than one such person in the one to be preferred in accordance with the following rules –

(a) the tenant's spouse or civil partner is to be preferred to another member of the tenant's family;

(b) of two or more other members of the tenant's family such of them is to be preferred as may be agreed between them or as may, where there is no such agreement, be selected by the landlord.

(3) Where there is no person qualified to succeed the tenant, the tenancy ceases to be an introductory tenancy –

(a) when it is vested or otherwise disposed of in the course of the administration of the tenant's estate, unless the vesting or other disposal is in pursuance of an order made under –

(i) section 24 of the Matrimonial Causes Act 1973 (property adjustment orders made in connection with matrimonial proceedings),

(ii) section 17(1) of the Matrimonial and Family Proceedings Act 1984 (property adjustment orders after overseas divorce, &c),

(iii) paragraph 1 of Schedule 1 to the Children Act 1989 (orders for financial relief against parents), or

(iv) Part 2 of Schedule 5, or paragraph 9(2) or (3) of Schedule 7, to the Civil Partnership Act 2004 (property adjustment orders in connection with civil partnership proceedings or after overseas dissolution of civil partnership, etc); or

(b) when it is known that when the tenancy is so vested or disposed of it will not be in pursuance of such an order.

134 Assignment in general prohibited

(1) An introductory tenancy is not capable of being assigned except in the cases mentioned in subsection (2).

(2) The exceptions are –

(a) an assignment in pursuance of an order made under –

(i) section 24 of the Matrimonial Causes Act 1973 (property adjustment orders in connection with matrimonial proceedings),

(ii) section 17(1) of the Matrimonial and Family Proceedings Act 1984 (property adjustment orders after overseas divorce, &c),

(iii) paragraph 1 of Schedule 1 to the Children Act 1989 (orders for financial relief against parents), or

(iv) Part 2 of Schedule 5, or paragraph 9(2) or (3) of Schedule 7, to the Civil Partnership Act 2004 (property adjustment orders in connection with civil partnership proceedings or after overseas dissolution of civil partnership, etc);

(b) an assignment to a person who would be qualified to succeed the tenant if the tenant died immediately before the assignment.

(3) Subsection (1) also applies to a tenancy which is not an introductory tenancy but would be if the tenant, or where the tenancy is a joint tenancy, at least one of the tenants, were occupying or continuing to occupy the dwelling-house as his only or principal home.

138 Jurisdiction of county court

(1) A county court has jurisdiction to determine questions arising under this Chapter and to entertain proceedings brought under this Chapter and claims, for whatever amount, in connection with an introductory tenancy. ...

139 Meaning of 'dwelling-house'

(1) For the purposes of this Chapter a dwelling-house may be a house or a part of a house.

(2) Land let together with a dwelling-house shall be treated for the purposes of this Chapter as part of the dwelling-house unless the land is agricultural land which would not be treated as part of a dwelling-house for the purposes of Part IV of the Housing Act 1985 (see section 112(2) of that Act).

140 Members of a person's family: Chapter I

(1) A person is a member of another's family within the meaning of this Chapter if –

(a) he is the spouse or civil partner of that person, or he and that person live together as husband and wife or as if they were civil partners, or

(b) he is that person's parent, grandparent, child, grandchild, brother, sister, uncle, aunt, nephew or niece.

(2) For the purpose of subsection (1)(b) –

(a) a relationship by marriage or civil partnership shall be treated as a relationship by blood,

(b) a relationship of the half-blood shall be treated as a relationship of the whole blood, and

(c) the stepchild of a person shall be treated as his child.

CHAPTER IA

DEMOTED TENANCIES

143A Demoted tenancies

(1) This section applies to a periodic tenancy of a dwelling-house if each of the following conditions is satisfied.

(2) The first condition is that the landlord is either a local housing authority or a housing action trust.

(3) The second condition is that the tenant condition in section 81 of the Housing Act 1985 is satisfied.

(4) The third condition is that the tenancy is created by virtue of a demotion order under section 82A of that Act.

(5) In this Chapter –

(a) a tenancy to which this section applies is referred to as a demoted tenancy;

(b) references to demoted tenants must be construed accordingly.

143B   Duration of demoted tenancy

(1) A demoted tenancy becomes a secure tenancy at the end of the period of one year (the demotion period) starting with the day the demotion order takes effect; but this is subject to subsections (2) to (5).

(2) A tenancy ceases to be a demoted tenancy if any of the following paragraphs applies –

(a) either of the first or second conditions in section 143A ceases to be satisfied;

(b) the demotion order is quashed;

(c) the tenant dies and no one is entitled to succeed to the tenancy.

(3) If at any time before the end of the demotion period the landlord serves a notice of proceedings for possession of the dwelling-house subsection (4) applies.

(4) The tenancy continues as a demoted tenancy until the end of the demotion period or (if later) until any of the following occurs –

(a) the notice of proceedings is withdrawn by the landlord;

(b) the proceedings are determined in favour of the tenant;

(c) the period of 6 months beginning with the date on which the notice is served ends and no proceedings for possession have been brought.

(5) A tenancy does not come to an end merely because it ceases to be a demoted tenancy.

143D   Proceedings for possession

(1) The landlord may only bring a demoted tenancy to an end by obtaining an order of the court for possession of the dwelling-house.

(2) The court must make an order for possession unless it thinks that the procedure under sections 143E {Notice of proceedings for possession] and 143F [Review of decision to seek possession] has not been followed.

(3) If the court makes such an order the tenancy comes to an end on the date on which the tenant is to give up possession in pursuance of the order.

143H   Succession to demoted tenancy

(1) This section applies if the tenant under a demoted tenancy dies.

(2) If the tenant was a successor, the tenancy –

(a) ceases to be a demoted tenancy, but

(b) does not become a secure tenancy.

(3) In any other case a person is qualified to succeed the tenant if –

(a) he occupies the dwelling-house as his only or principal home at the time of the tenant's death,

(b) he is a member of the tenant's family, and

(c) he has resided with the tenant throughout the period of 12 months ending with the tenant's death.

(4) If only one person is qualified to succeed under subsection (3) the tenancy vests in him by virtue of this section.

(5) If there is more than one such person the tenancy vests by virtue of this section in the person preferred in accordance with the following rules –

(a) the tenant's spouse or civil partner or (if the tenant has neither spouse nor civil partner) the person mentioned in section 143P(1)(b) is to be preferred to another member of the tenant's family;

(b) if there are two or more other members of the tenant's family the person preferred may be agreed between them or (if there is no such agreement) selected by the landlord.

143K   Restriction on assignment

(1) A demoted tenancy is not capable of being assigned except as mentioned in subsection (2).

(2) The exceptions are assignment in pursuance of an order made under –

(a) section 24 of the Matrimonial Causes Act 1973 (property adjustment orders in connection with matrimonial proceedings);

(b) section 17(1) of the Matrimonial and Family Proceedings Act 1984 (property adjustment orders after overseas divorce, etc.);

(c) paragraph 1 of Schedule 1 to the Children Act 1989 (orders for financial relief against parents);

(d) Part 2 of Schedule 5, or paragraph 9(2) or (3) of Schedule 7, to the Civil Partnership Act 2004 (property adjustment orders in connection with civil partnership proceedings or after overseas dissolution of civil partnership, etc).

143O   Meaning of dwelling house

(1) For the purposes of this Chapter a dwelling-house may be a house or a part of a house.

(2) Land let together with a dwelling-house must be treated for the purposes of this Chapter as part of the dwelling-house unless the land is agricultural land which would not be treated as part of a dwelling-house for the purposes of Part 4 of the Housing Act 1985.

143P Members of a person's family

(1) For the purposes of this Chapter a person is a member of another's family if –

(a) he is the spouse or civil partner of that person;

(b) he and that person live together as a couple in an enduring family relationship, but he does not fall within paragraph (c);

(c) he is that person's parent, grandparent, child, grandchild, brother, sister, uncle, aunt, nephew or niece.

(2) For the purposes of subsection (1)(b) it is immaterial that two persons living together in an enduring family relationship are of the same sex.

(3) For the purposes of subsection (1)(c) –

(a) a relationship by marriage or civil partnership must be treated as a relationship by blood;

(b) a relationship of the half-blood must be treated as a relationship of the whole blood;

(c) a stepchild of a person must be treated as his child.

CHAPTER III

INJUNCTIONS AGAINST ANTI-SOCIAL BEHAVIOUR

153A Anti-social behaviour injunction

(1) This section applies to conduct –

(a) which is capable of causing nuisance or annoyance to any person, and

(b) which directly or indirectly relates to or affects the housing management functions of a relevant landlord.

(2) The court on the application of a relevant landlord may grant an injunction (an anti-social behaviour injunction) if each of the following two conditions is satisfied.

(3) The first condition is that the person against whom the injunction is sought is engaging, has engaged or threatens to engage in conduct to which this section applies.

(4) The second condition is that the conduct is capable of causing nuisance or annoyance to any of the following –

(a) a person with a right (of whatever description) to reside in or occupy housing accommodation owned or managed by the relevant landlord;

(b) a person with a right (of whatever description) to reside in or occupy other housing accommodation in the neighbourhood of housing accommodation mentioned in paragraph (a);

(c) a person engaged in lawful activity in or in the neighbourhood of housing accommodation mentioned in paragraph (a);

(d) a person employed (whether or not by the relevant landlord) in connection with the exercise of the relevant landlord's housing management functions.

(5) It is immaterial where conduct to which this section applies occurs.

(6) An anti-social behaviour injunction prohibits the person in respect of whom it is granted from engaging in conduct to which this section applies.

153B   Injunction against unlawful use of premises

(1) This section applies to conduct which consists of or involves using or threatening to use housing accommodation owned or managed by a relevant landlord for an unlawful purpose.

(2) The court on the application of the relevant landlord may grant an injunction prohibiting the person in respect of whom the injunction is granted from engaging in conduct to which this section applies.

153E   Injunctions: supplementary

(1) This section applies for the purposes of sections 153A to 153D.

(2) An injunction may –

(a) be made for a specified period or until varied or discharged;

(b) have the effect of excluding a person from his normal place of residence.

(3) An injunction may be varied or discharged by the court on an application by –

(a) the person in respect of whom it is made;

(b) the relevant landlord.

(4) If the court thinks it just and convenient it may grant or vary an injunction without the respondent having been given such notice as is otherwise required by rules of court.

(5) If the court acts under subsection (4) it must give the person against whom the injunction is made an opportunity to make representations in relation to the injunction as soon as it is practicable for him to do so.

(6) The court is the High Court or a county court.

(7) Each of the following is a relevant landlord –

(a) a housing action trust;

(b) a local authority (within the meaning of the Housing Act 1985);

(c) a registered social landlord.

(8) A charitable housing trust which is not a registered social landlord is also a relevant landlord for the purposes of section 153D.

(9) Housing accommodation includes –

(a) flats, lodging-houses and hostels;

(b) any yard, garden, outhouses and appurtenances belonging to the accommodation or usually enjoyed with it;

(c) in relation to a neighbourhood, the whole of the housing accommodation owned or managed by a relevant landlord in the neighbourhood and any common areas used in connection with the accommodation.

(10) A landlord owns housing accommodation if either of the following paragraphs applies to him –

(a) he is a person (other than a mortgagee not in possession) who is for the time being entitled to dispose of the fee simple in the premises, whether in possession or in reversion;

(b) he is a person who holds or is entitled to the rents and profits of the premises under a lease which (when granted) was for a term of not less than three years.

(11) The housing management functions of a relevant landlord include –

(a) functions conferred by or under any enactment;

(b) the powers and duties of the landlord as the holder of an estate or interest in housing accommodation.

(12) Harm includes serious ill-treatment or abuse (whether physical or not).

PART VIII

MISCELLANEOUS AND GENERAL PROVISIONS

229 Meaning of 'lease' and 'tenancy' and related expressions

(1) In this Act 'lease' and 'tenancy' have the same meaning.

(2) Both expressions include –

(a) a sub-lease or a sub-tenancy, and

(b) an agreement for a lease or tenancy (or sub-lease or sub-tenancy).

(3) The expressions 'lessor' and 'lessee' and 'landlord' and 'tenant', and references to letting, to the grant of a lease or to covenants or terms, shall be construed accordingly.

230 Minor definitions: general

In this Act –

'assured tenancy', 'assured shorthold tenancy' and 'assured agricultural occupancy' have the same meaning as in Part I of the Housing Act 1988;

'enactment' includes an enactment comprised in subordinate legislation (within the meaning of the Interpretation Act 1978);

'housing action trust' has the same meaning as in the Housing Act 1988;

'housing association' has the same meaning as in the Housing Associations Act 1985;

'introductory tenancy' and 'introductory tenant' have the same meaning as in Chapter I of Part V of this Act;

'local housing authority' has the same meaning as in the Housing Act 1985;

'registered social landlord' has the same meaning as in Part I of this Act;

'secure tenancy' and 'secure tenant' have the same meaning as in Part IV of the Housing Act 1985.

NB The insertion in section 16 of subsections (5)–(7) applies to England only. The insertion of sections 16(3A), 125A and 125B was not in force on 1 May 2005.

As amended by the Government of Wales Act 1998, ss140, 141, 152, Schedule 16, paras 81–84, Schedule 18, Pt VI; Housing (Right to Acquire) (Electronic Communications) (England) Order 2001; Commonhold and Leasehold Reform Act 2002, ss170, 176, Schedule 13, para 16; Communications Act 2003, s406(1), Schedule 17, para 136; Anti-social Behaviour Act 2003, ss13(1)–(3), 14, Schedule 1, para 1; Housing Act 2004, ss179, 202, Civil Partnership Act 2004, ss81, 261(4), Schedule 8, paras 51–55, 58, 59, Schedule 30.

TRUSTEE ACT 2000
(2000 c 29)

PART I

THE DUTY OF CARE

1   The duty of care

(1) Whenever the duty under this subsection applies to a trustee, he must exercise such care and skill as is reasonable in the circumstances, having regard in particular –

(a) to any special knowledge or experience that he has or holds himself out as having, and

(b) if he acts as trustee in the course of a business or profession, to any special knowledge or experience that it is reasonable to expect of a person acting in the course of that kind of business or profession.

(2) In this Act the duty under subsection (1) is called 'the duty of care'.

2   Application of duty of care

Schedule 1 makes provision about when the duty of care applies to a trustee.

PART III

ACQUISITION OF LAND

8   Power to acquire freehold and leasehold land

(1) A trustee may acquire freehold or leasehold land in the United Kingdom –

(a) as an investment,

(b) for occupation by a beneficiary, or

(c) for any other reason.

(2) 'Freehold or leasehold land' means –

(a) in relation to England and Wales, a legal estate in land, ...

(3) For the purposes of exercising his functions as a trustee, a trustee who acquires land under this section has all the powers of an absolute owner in relation to the land.

9   Restriction or exclusion of this Part, etc

The powers conferred by this Part are –

(a) in addition to powers conferred on trustees otherwise than by this Part, but

(b) subject to any restriction or exclusion imposed by the trust instrument or by any enactment or any provision of subordinate legislation.

10   Existing trusts

(1) This Part does not apply in relation to –

(a) a trust of property which consists of or includes land which (despite section 2 of the Trusts of Land and Appointment of Trustees Act 1996) is settled land, or

(b) a trust to which the Universities and College Estates Act 1925 applies.

(2) Subject to subsection (1), this Part applies in relation to trusts whether created before or after its commencement.

PART VI

MISCELLANEOUS AND SUPPLEMENTARY ...

35   Personal representatives

(1) Subject to the following provisions of this section, this Act applies in relation to a personal representative administering an estate according to the law as it applies to a trustee carrying out a trust for beneficiaries.

(2) For this purpose this Act is to be read with the appropriate modifications and in particular –

(a) references to the trust instrument are to be read as references to the will,

(b) references to a beneficiary or to beneficiaries, apart from the reference to a beneficiary in section 8(1)(b), are to be read as references to a person or the persons interested in the due administration of the estate, and

(c) the reference to a beneficiary in section 8(1)(b) is to be read as a reference to a person who under the will of the deceased or under the law relating to intestacy is beneficially interested in the estate. ...

SCHEDULE 1

APPLICATION OF DUTY OF CARE ...

ACQUISITION OF LAND

2. The duty of care applies to a trustee –

(a) when exercising the power under section 8 to acquire land;

(b) when exercising any other power to acquire land, however conferred;

(c) when exercising any power in relation to land acquired under a power mentioned in sub-paragraph (a) or (b). ...

LAND REGISTRATION ACT 2002
(2002 c 9)

PART 1

PRELIMINARY

1 Register of title

(1) There is to continue to be a register of title kept by the registrar.

(2) Rules may make provision about how the register is to be kept and may, in particular, make provision about –

(a) the information to be included in the register,

(b) the form in which information included in the register is to be kept, and

(c) the arrangement of that information.

2 Scope of title registration

This Act makes provision about the registration of title to –

(a) unregistered legal estates which are interests of any of the following kinds –

(i) an estate in land,

(ii) a rentcharge,

(iii) a franchise,

(iv) a profit a prendre in gross, and

(v) any other interest or charge which subsists for the benefit of, or is a charge on, an interest the title to which is registered; and

(b) interests capable of subsisting at law which are created by a disposition of an interest the title to which is registered.

PART 2

FIRST REGISTRATION OF TITLE

CHAPTER 1

FIRST REGISTRATION

3 When title may be registered

(1) This section applies to any unregistered legal estate which is an interest of any of the following kinds –

  (a) an estate in land,

  (b) a rentcharge,

  (c) a franchise, and

  (d) a profit a prendre in gross.

(2) Subject to the following provisions, a person may apply to the registrar to be registered as the proprietor of an unregistered legal estate to which this section applies if –

  (a) the estate is vested in him, or

  (b) he is entitled to require the estate to be vested in him.

(3) Subject to subsection (4), an application under subsection (2) in respect of a leasehold estate may only be made if the estate was granted for a term of which more than seven years are unexpired.

(4) In the case of an estate in land, subsection (3) does not apply if the right to possession under the lease is discontinuous.

(5) A person may not make an application under subsection (2)(a) in respect of a leasehold estate vested in him as a mortgagee where there is a subsisting right of redemption.

(6) A person may not make an application under subsection (2)(b) if his entitlement is as a person who has contracted to buy under a contract.

(7) If a person holds in the same right both –

  (a) a lease in possession, and

  (b) a lease to take effect in possession on, or within a month of, the end of the lease in possession,

then, to the extent that they relate to the same land, they are to be treated for the purposes of this section as creating one continuous term.

4 When title must be registered

(1) The requirement of registration applies on the occurrence of any of the following events –

(a) the transfer of a qualifying estate –

(i) for valuable or other consideration, by way of gift or in pursuance of an order of any court, or

(ii) by means of an assent (including a vesting assent);

(b) the transfer of an unregistered legal estate in land in circumstances where section 171A of the Housing Act 1985 (c 68) applies (disposal by landlord which leads to a person no longer being a secure tenant);

(c) the grant out of a qualifying estate of an estate in land –

(i) for a term of years absolute of more than seven years from the date of the grant, and

(ii) for valuable or other consideration, by way of gift or in pursuance of an order of any court;

(d) the grant out of a qualifying estate of an estate in land for a term of years absolute to take effect in possession after the end of the period of three months beginning with the date of the grant;

(e) the grant of a lease in pursuance of Part 5 of the Housing Act 1985 (the right to buy) out of an unregistered legal estate in land;

(f) the grant of a lease out of an unregistered legal estate in land in such circumstances as are mentioned in paragraph (b);

(g) the creation of a protected first legal mortgage of a qualifying estate.

(2) For the purposes of subsection (1), a qualifying estate is an unregistered legal estate which is –

(a) a freehold estate in land, or

(b) a leasehold estate in land for a term which, at the time of the transfer, grant or creation, has more than seven years to run.

(3) In subsection (1)(a), the reference to transfer does not include transfer by operation of law.

(4) Subsection (1)(a) does not apply to –

(a) the assignment of a mortgage term, or

(b) the assignment or surrender of a lease to the owner of the immediate reversion where the term is to merge in that reversion.

(5) Subsection (1)(c) does not apply to the grant of an estate to a person as a mortgagee.

(6) For the purposes of subsection (1)(a) and (c), if the estate transferred or granted has a negative value, it is to be regarded as transferred or granted for valuable or other consideration.

(7) In subsection (1)(a) and (c), references to transfer or grant by way of gift include transfer or grant for the purpose of –

(a) constituting a trust under which the settlor does not retain the whole of the beneficial interest, or

(b) uniting the bare legal title and the beneficial interest in property held under a trust under which the settlor did not, on constitution, retain the whole of the beneficial interest.

(8) For the purposes of subsection (1)(g) –

(a) a legal mortgage is protected if it takes effect on its creation as a mortgage to be protected by the deposit of documents relating to the mortgaged estate, and

(b) a first legal mortgage is one which, on its creation, ranks in priority ahead of any other mortgages then affecting the mortgaged estate.

(9) In this section –

'land' does not include mines and minerals held apart from the surface;

'vesting assent' has the same meaning as in the Settled Land Act 1925 (c 18).

6   Duty to apply for registration of title

(1) If the requirement of registration applies, the responsible estate owner, or his successor in title, must, before the end of the period for registration, apply to the registrar to be registered as the proprietor of the registrable estate.

(2) If the requirement of registration applies because of section 4(1)(g) –

(a) the registrable estate is the estate charged by the mortgage, and

(b) the responsible estate owner is the owner of that estate.

(3) If the requirement of registration applies otherwise than because of section 4(1)(g) –

(a) the registrable estate is the estate which is transferred or granted, and

(b) the responsible estate owner is the transferee or grantee of that estate.

(4) The period for registration is 2 months beginning with the date on which the relevant event occurs, or such longer period as the registrar may provide under subsection (5).

(5) If on the application of any interested person the registrar is satisfied that there is good reason for doing so, he may by order provide that the period for registration ends on such later date as he may specify in the order.

(6) Rules may make provision enabling the mortgagee under any mortgage falling within section 4(1)(g) to require the estate charged by the mortgage to be registered whether or not the mortgagor consents.

7   Effect of non-compliance with section 6

(1) If the requirement of registration is not complied with, the transfer, grant or creation becomes void as regards the transfer, grant or creation of a legal estate.

(2) On the application of subsection (1) –

(a) in a case falling within section 4(1)(a) or (b), the title to the legal estate reverts to the transferor who holds it on a bare trust for the transferee, and

(b) in a case falling within section 4(1)(c) to (g), the grant or creation has effect as a contract made for valuable consideration to grant or create the legal estate concerned.

(3) If an order under section 6(5) is made in a case where subsection (1) has already applied, that application of the subsection is to be treated as not having occurred.

(4) The possibility of reverter under subsection (1) is to be disregarded for the purposes of determining whether a fee simple is a fee simple absolute.

8   Liability for making good void transfers, etc

If a legal estate is retransferred, regranted or recreated because of a failure to comply with the requirement of registration, the transferee, grantee or, as the case may be, the mortgagor –

(a) is liable to the other party for all the proper costs of and incidental to the retransfer, regrant or recreation of the legal estate, and

(b) is liable to indemnify the other party in respect of any other liability reasonably incurred by him because of the failure to comply with the requirement of registration.

9   Titles to freehold estates

(1) In the case of an application for registration under this Chapter of a freehold estate, the classes of title with which the applicant may be registered as proprietor are –

(a) absolute title,

(b) qualified title, and

(c) possessory title;

and the following provisions deal with when each of the classes of title is available.

(2) A person may be registered with absolute title if the registrar is of the opinion that the person's title to the estate is such as a willing buyer could properly be advised by a competent professional adviser to accept.

(3) In applying subsection (2), the registrar may disregard the fact that a person's title appears to him to be open to objection if he is of the opinion that the defect will not cause the holding under the title to be disturbed.

(4) A person may be registered with qualified title if the registrar is of the opinion that the person's title to the estate has been established only for a limited period or subject to certain reservations which cannot be disregarded under subsection (3).

(5) A person may be registered with possessory title if the registrar is of the opinion –

Land: The Law of Real Property

(a) that the person is in actual possession of the land, or in receipt of the rents and profits of the land, by virtue of the estate, and

(b) that there is no other class of title with which he may be registered.

10   Titles to leasehold estates

(1) In the case of an application for registration under this Chapter of a leasehold estate, the classes of title with which the applicant may be registered as proprietor are –

(a) absolute title,

(b) good leasehold title,

(c) qualified title, and

(d) possessory title;

and the following provisions deal with when each of the classes of title is available.

(2) A person may be registered with absolute title if –

(a) the registrar is of the opinion that the person's title to the estate is such as a willing buyer could properly be advised by a competent professional adviser to accept, and

(b) the registrar approves the lessor's title to grant the lease.

(3) A person may be registered with good leasehold title if the registrar is of the opinion that the person's title to the estate is such as a willing buyer could properly be advised by a competent professional adviser to accept.

(4) In applying subsection (2) or (3), the registrar may disregard the fact that a person's title appears to him to be open to objection if he is of the opinion that the defect will not cause the holding under the title to be disturbed.

(5) A person may be registered with qualified title if the registrar is of the opinion that the person's title to the estate, or the lessor's title to the reversion, has been established only for a limited period or subject to certain reservations which cannot be disregarded under subsection (4).

(6) A person may be registered with possessory title if the registrar is of the opinion –

(a) that the person is in actual possession of the land, or in receipt of the rents and profits of the land, by virtue of the estate, and

(h) that there is no other class of title with which he may be registered.

11   Freehold estates

(1) This section is concerned with the registration of a person under this Chapter as the proprietor of a freehold estate.

(2) Registration with absolute title has the effect described in subsections (3) to (5).

—— 532 ——

(3) The estate is vested in the proprietor together with all interests subsisting for the benefit of the estate.

(4) The estate is vested in the proprietor subject only to the following interests affecting the estate at the time of registration –

(a) interests which are the subject of an entry in the register in relation to the estate,

(b) unregistered interests which fall within any of the paragraphs of Schedule 1, and

(c) interests acquired under the Limitation Act 1980 (c 58) of which the proprietor has notice.

(5) If the proprietor is not entitled to the estate for his own benefit, or not entitled solely for his own benefit, then, as between himself and the persons beneficially entitled to the estate, the estate is vested in him subject to such of their interests as he has notice of.

(6) Registration with qualified title has the same effect as registration with absolute title, except that it does not affect the enforcement of any estate, right or interest which appears from the register to be excepted from the effect of registration.

(7) Registration with possessory title has the same effect as registration with absolute title, except that it does not affect the enforcement of any estate, right or interest adverse to, or in derogation of, the proprietor's title subsisting at the time of registration or then capable of arising.

12   Leasehold estates

(1) This section is concerned with the registration of a person under this Chapter as the proprietor of a leasehold estate.

(2) Registration with absolute title has the effect described in subsections (3) to (5).

(3) The estate is vested in the proprietor together with all interests subsisting for the benefit of the estate.

(4) The estate is vested subject only to the following interests affecting the estate at the time of registration –

(a) implied and express covenants, obligations and liabilities incident to the estate,

(b) interests which are the subject of an entry in the register in relation to the estate,

(c) unregistered interests which fall within any of the paragraphs of Schedule 1, and

(d) interests acquired under the Limitation Act 1980 (c 58) of which the proprietor has notice.

(5) If the proprietor is not entitled to the estate for his own benefit, or not entitled

solely for his own benefit, then, as between himself and the persons beneficially entitled to the estate, the estate is vested in him subject to such of their interests as he has notice of.

(6) Registration with good leasehold title has the same effect as registration with absolute title, except that it does not affect the enforcement of any estate, right or interest affecting, or in derogation of, the title of the lessor to grant the lease.

(7) Registration with qualified title has the same effect as registration with absolute title except that it does not affect the enforcement of any estate, right or interest which appears from the register to be excepted from the effect of registration.

(8) Registration with possessory title has the same effect as registration with absolute title, except that it does not affect the enforcement of any estate, right or interest adverse to, or in derogation of, the proprietor's title subsisting at the time of registration or then capable of arising.

14   Rules about first registration

Rules may –

> (a) make provision about the making of applications for registration under this Chapter;
>
> (b) make provision about the functions of the registrar following the making of such an application, including provision about –

>> (i) the examination of title, and
>>
>> (ii) the entries to be made in the register where such an application is approved;

> (c) make provision about the effect of any entry made in the register in pursuance of such an application.

CHAPTER 2

CAUTIONS AGAINST FIRST REGISTRATION

15   Right to lodge

(1) Subject to subsection (3), a person may lodge a caution against the registration of title to an unregistered legal estate if he claims to be –

> (a) the owner of a qualifying estate, or
>
> (b) entitled to an interest affecting a qualifying estate.

(2) For the purposes of subsection (1), a qualifying estate is a legal estate which –

> (a) relates to land to which the caution relates, and
>
> (b) is an interest of any of the following kinds –

>> (i) an estate in land,
>>
>> (ii) a rentcharge,

(iii) a franchise, and

(iv) a profit a prendre in gross.

(3) No caution may be lodged under subsection (1) –

(a) in the case of paragraph (a), by virtue of ownership of –

(i) a freehold estate in land, or

(ii) a leasehold estate in land granted for a term of which more than seven years are unexpired;

(b) in the case of paragraph (b), by virtue of entitlement to such a leasehold estate as is mentioned in paragraph (a)(ii) of this subsection.

(4) The right under subsection (1) is exercisable by application to the registrar.

16   Effect

(1) Where an application for registration under this Part relates to a legal estate which is the subject of a caution against first registration, the registrar must give the cautioner notice of the application and of his right to object to it.

(2) The registrar may not determine an application to which subsection (1) applies before the end of such period as rules may provide, unless the cautioner has exercised his right to object to the application or given the registrar notice that he does not intend to do so.

(3) Except as provided by this section, a caution against first registration has no effect and, in particular, has no effect on the validity or priority of any interest of the cautioner in the legal estate to which the caution relates.

(4) For the purposes of subsection (1), notice given by a person acting on behalf of an applicant for registration under this Part is to be treated as given by the registrar if –

(a) the person is of a description provided by rules, and

(b) notice is given in such circumstances as rules may provide.

17   Withdrawal

The cautioner may withdraw a caution against first registration by application to the registrar.

18   Cancellation

(1) A person may apply to the registrar for cancellation of a caution against first registration if he is –

(a) the owner of the legal estate to which the caution relates, or

(b) a person of such other description as rules may provide.

(2) Subject to rules, no application under subsection (1)(a) may be made by a person who –

(a) consented in such manner as rules may provide to the lodging of the caution, or

(b) derives title to the legal estate by operation of law from a person who did so.

(3) Where an application is made under subsection (1), the registrar must give the cautioner notice of the application and of the effect of subsection (4).

(4) If the cautioner does not exercise his right to object to the application before the end of such period as rules may provide, the registrar must cancel the caution.

19   Cautions register

(1) The registrar must keep a register of cautions against first registration.

(2) Rules may make provision about how the cautions register is to be kept and may, in particular, make provision about –

(a) the information to be included in the register,

(b) the form in which information included in the register is to be kept, and

(c) the arrangement of that information.

22   Supplementary

In this Chapter, 'the cautioner', in relation to a caution against first registration, means the person who lodged the caution, or such other person as rules may provide.

PART 3

DISPOSITIONS OF REGISTERED LAND

23   Owner's powers

(1) Owner's powers in relation to a registered estate consist of –

(a) power to make a disposition of any kind permitted by the general law in relation to an interest of that description, other than a mortgage by demise or sub-demise, and

(b) power to charge the estate at law with the payment of money.

(2) Owner's powers in relation to a registered charge consist of –

(a) power to make a disposition of any kind permitted by the general law in relation to an interest of that description, other than a legal sub-mortgage, and

(b) power to charge at law with the payment of money indebtedness secured by the registered charge.

(3) In subsection (2)(a), 'legal sub-mortgage' means –

(a) a transfer by way of mortgage,

(b) a sub-mortgage by sub-demise, and

(c) a charge by way of legal mortgage.

24 Right to exercise owner's powers

A person is entitled to exercise owner's powers in relation to a registered estate or charge if he is –

(a) the registered proprietor, or

(b) entitled to be registered as the proprietor.

25 Mode of exercise

(1) A registrable disposition of a registered estate or charge only has effect if it complies with such requirements as to form and content as rules may provide.

(2) Rules may apply subsection (1) to any other kind of disposition which depends for its effect on registration.

26 Protection of disponees

(1) Subject to subsection (2), a person's right to exercise owner's powers in relation to a registered estate or charge is to be taken to be free from any limitation affecting the validity of a disposition.

(2) Subsection (1) does not apply to a limitation –

(a) reflected by an entry in the register, or

(b) imposed by, or under, this Act.

(3) This section has effect only for the purpose of preventing the title of a disponee being questioned (and so does not affect the lawfulness of a disposition).

27 Dispositions required to be registered

(1) If a disposition of a registered estate or registered charge is required to be completed by registration, it does not operate at law until the relevant registration requirements are met.

(2) In the case of a registered estate, the following are the dispositions which are required to be completed by registration –

(a) a transfer,

(b) where the registered estate is an estate in land, the grant of a term of years absolute –

(i) for a term of more than seven years from the date of the grant,

(ii) to take effect in possession after the end of the period of three months beginning with the date of the grant,

(iii) under which the right to possession is discontinuous,

(iv) in pursuance of Part 5 of the Housing Act 1985 (c 68) (the right to buy), or

(v) in circumstances where section 171A of that Act applies (disposal by landlord which leads to a person no longer being a secure tenant),

(c) where the registered estate is a franchise or manor, the grant of a lease,

(d) the express grant or reservation of an interest of a kind falling within section 1(2)(a) of the Law of Property Act 1925 (c 20), other than one which is capable of being registered under the Commons Registration Act 1965 (c 64),

(e) the express grant or reservation of an interest of a kind falling within section 1(2)(b) or (e) of the Law of Property Act 1925, and

(f) the grant of a legal charge.

(3) In the case of a registered charge, the following are the dispositions which are required to be completed by registration –

(a) a transfer, and

(b) the grant of a sub-charge.

(4) Schedule 2 to this Act (which deals with the relevant registration requirements) has effect.

(5) This section applies to dispositions by operation of law as it applies to other dispositions, but with the exception of the following –

(a) a transfer on the death or bankruptcy of an individual proprietor,

(b) a transfer on the dissolution of a corporate proprietor, and

(c) the creation of a legal charge which is a local land charge.

(6) Rules may make provision about applications to the registrar for the purpose of meeting registration requirements under this section.

(7) In subsection (2)(d), the reference to express grant does not include grant as a result of the operation of section 62 of the Law of Property Act 1925 (c 20).

28   Basic rule

(1) Except as provided by sections 29 and 30, the priority of an interest affecting a registered estate or charge is not affected by a disposition of the estate or charge.

(2) It makes no difference for the purposes of this section whether the interest or disposition is registered.

29   Effect of registered dispositions: estates

(1) If a registrable disposition of a registered estate is made for valuable consideration, completion of the disposition by registration has the effect of postponing to the interest under the disposition any interest affecting the estate immediately before the disposition whose priority is not protected at the time of registration.

(2) For the purposes of subsection (1), the priority of an interest is protected –

(a) in any case, if the interest –

(i) is a registered charge or the subject of a notice in the register,

(ii) falls within any of the paragraphs of Schedule 3, or

(iii) appears from the register to be excepted from the effect of registration, and

(b) in the case of a disposition of a leasehold estate, if the burden of the interest is incident to the estate.

(3) Subsection (2)(a)(ii) does not apply to an interest which has been the subject of a notice in the register at any time since the coming into force of this section.

(4) Where the grant of a leasehold estate in land out of a registered estate does not involve a registrable disposition, this section has effect as if –

(a) the grant involved such a disposition, and

(b) the disposition were registered at the time of the grant.

30 Effect of registered dispositions: charges

(1) If a registrable disposition of a registered charge is made for valuable consideration, completion of the disposition by registration has the effect of postponing to the interest under the disposition any interest affecting the charge immediately before the disposition whose priority is not protected at the time of registration.

(2) For the purposes of subsection (1), the priority of an interest is protected –

(a) in any case, if the interest –

(i) is a registered charge or the subject of a notice in the register,

(ii) falls within any of the paragraphs of Schedule 3, or

(iii) appears from the register to be excepted from the effect of registration, and

(b) in the case of a disposition of a charge which relates to a leasehold estate, if the burden of the interest is incident to the estate.

(3) Subsection (2)(a)(ii) does not apply to an interest which has been the subject of a notice in the register at any time since the coming into force of this section.

PART 4

NOTICES AND RESTRICTIONS

32 Nature and effect

(1) A notice is an entry in the register in respect of the burden of an interest affecting a registered estate or charge.

(2) The entry of a notice is to be made in relation to the registered estate or charge affected by the interest concerned.

(3) The fact that an interest is the subject of a notice does not necessarily mean that the interest is valid, but does mean that the priority of the interest, if valid, is protected for the purposes of sections 29 and 30.

33 Excluded interests

No notice may be entered in the register in respect of any of the following –

(a) an interest under –

(i) a trust of land, or

(ii) a settlement under the Settled Land Act 1925 (c 18),

(b) a leasehold estate in land which –

(i) is granted for a term of years of three years or less from the date of the grant, and

(ii) is not required to be registered,

(c) a restrictive covenant made between a lessor and lessee, so far as relating to the demised premises,

(d) an interest which is capable of being registered under the Commons Registration Act 1965 (c 64), and

(e) an interest in any coal or coal mine, the rights attached to any such interest and the rights of any person under section 38, 49 or 51 of the Coal Industry Act 1994 (c 21).

34 Entry on application

(1) A person who claims to be entitled to the benefit of an interest affecting a registered estate or charge may, if the interest is not excluded by section 33, apply to the registrar for the entry in the register of a notice in respect of the interest.

(2) Subject to rules, an application under this section may be for –

(a) an agreed notice, or

(b) a unilateral notice.

(3) The registrar may only approve an application for an agreed notice if –

(a) the applicant is the relevant registered proprietor, or a person entitled to be registered as such proprietor,

(b) the relevant registered proprietor, or a person entitled to be registered as such proprietor, consents to the entry of the notice, or

(c) the registrar is satisfied as to the validity of the applicant's claim.

(4) In subsection (3), references to the relevant registered proprietor are to the proprietor of the registered estate or charge affected by the interest to which the application relates.

35   Unilateral notices

(1) If the registrar enters a notice in the register in pursuance of an application under section 34(2)(b) ('a unilateral notice'), he must give notice of the entry to –

   (a) the proprietor of the registered estate or charge to which it relates, and

   (b) such other persons as rules may provide.

(2) A unilateral notice must –

   (a) indicate that it is such a notice, and

   (b) identify who is the beneficiary of the notice.

(3) The person shown in the register as the beneficiary of a unilateral notice, or such other person as rules may provide, may apply to the registrar for the removal of the notice from the register.

36   Cancellation of unilateral notices

(1) A person may apply to the registrar for the cancellation of a unilateral notice if he is –

   (a) the registered proprietor of the estate or charge to which the notice relates, or

   (b) a person entitled to be registered as the proprietor of that estate or charge.

(2) Where an application is made under subsection (1), the registrar must give the beneficiary of the notice notice of the application and of the effect of subsection (3).

(3) If the beneficiary of the notice does not exercise his right to object to the application before the end of such period as rules may provide, the registrar must cancel the notice.

(4) In this section –

   'beneficiary', in relation to a unilateral notice, means the person shown in the register as the beneficiary of the notice, or such other person as rules may provide;

   'unilateral notice' means a notice entered in the register in pursuance of an application under section 34(2)(b).

37   Unregistered interests

(1) If it appears to the registrar that a registered estate is subject to an unregistered interest which –

   (a) falls within any of the paragraphs of Schedule 1, and

   (b) is not excluded by section 33,

he may enter a notice in the register in respect of the interest.

(2) The registrar must give notice of an entry under this section to such persons as rules may provide.

38   Registrable dispositions

Where a person is entered in the register as the proprietor of an interest under a disposition falling within section 27(2)(b) to (e), the registrar must also enter a notice in the register in respect of that interest.

40   Nature

(1) A restriction is an entry in the register regulating the circumstances in which a disposition of a registered estate or charge may be the subject of an entry in the register.

(2) A restriction may, in particular –

(a) prohibit the making of an entry in respect of any disposition, or a disposition of a kind specified in the restriction;

(b) prohibit the making of an entry –

(i) indefinitely,

(ii) for a period specified in the restriction, or

(iii) until the occurrence of an event so specified.

(3) Without prejudice to the generality of subsection (2)(b)(iii), the events which may be specified include –

(a) the giving of notice,

(b) the obtaining of consent, and

(c) the making of an order by the court or registrar.

(4) The entry of a restriction is to be made in relation to the registered estate or charge to which it relates.

41   Effect

(1) Where a restriction is entered in the register, no entry in respect of a disposition to which the restriction applies may be made in the register otherwise than in accordance with the terms of the restriction, subject to any order under subsection (2).

(2) The registrar may by order –

(a) disapply a restriction in relation to a disposition specified in the order or dispositions of a kind so specified, or

(b) provide that a restriction has effect, in relation to a disposition specified in the order or dispositions of a kind so specified, with modifications so specified.

(3) The power under subsection (2) is exercisable only on the application of a person who appears to the registrar to have a sufficient interest in the restriction.

42 Power of registrar to enter

(1) The registrar may enter a restriction in the register if it appears to him that it is necessary or desirable to do so for the purpose of –

(a) preventing invalidity or unlawfulness in relation to dispositions of a registered estate or charge,

(b) securing that interests which are capable of being overreached on a disposition of a registered estate or charge are overreached, or

(c) protecting a right or claim in relation to a registered estate or charge.

(2) No restriction may be entered under subsection (1)(c) for the purpose of protecting the priority of an interest which is, or could be, the subject of a notice.

(3) The registrar must give notice of any entry made under this section to the proprietor of the registered estate or charge concerned, except where the entry is made in pursuance of an application under section 43.

(4) For the purposes of subsection (1)(c), a person entitled to the benefit of a charging order relating to an interest under a trust shall be treated as having a right or claim in relation to the trust property.

43 Applications

(1) A person may apply to the registrar for the entry of a restriction under section 42(1) if –

(a) he is the relevant registered proprietor, or a person entitled to be registered as such proprietor,

(b) the relevant registered proprietor, or a person entitled to be registered as such proprietor, consents to the application, or

(c) he otherwise has a sufficient interest in the making of the entry.

(2) Rules may –

(a) require the making of an application under subsection (1) in such circumstances, and by such person, as the rules may provide;

(b) make provision about the form of consent for the purposes of subsection (1)(b);

(c) provide for classes of person to be regarded as included in subsection (1)(c);

(d) specify standard forms of restriction.

(3) If an application under subsection (1) is made for the entry of a restriction which is not in a form specified under subsection (2)(d), the registrar may only approve the application if it appears to him –

(a) that the terms of the proposed restriction are reasonable, and

(b) that applying the proposed restriction would –

(i) be straightforward, and

(ii) not place an unreasonable burden on him.

(4) In subsection (1), references to the relevant registered proprietor are to the proprietor of the registered estate or charge to which the application relates.

44   Obligatory restrictions

(1) If the registrar enters two or more persons in the register as the proprietor of a registered estate in land, he must also enter in the register such restrictions as rules may provide for the purpose of securing that interests which are capable of being overreached on a disposition of the estate are overreached.

(2) Where under any enactment the registrar is required to enter a restriction without application, the form of the restriction shall be such as rules may provide.

45   Notifiable applications

(1) Where an application under section 43(1) is notifiable, the registrar must give notice of the application, and of the right to object to it, to –

  (a) the proprietor of the registered estate or charge to which it relates, and
  (b) such other persons as rules may provide.

(2) The registrar may not determine an application to which subsection (1) applies before the end of such period as rules may provide, unless the person, or each of the persons, notified under that subsection has exercised his right to object to the application or given the registrar notice that he does not intend to do so.

(3) For the purposes of this section, an application under section 43(1) is notifiable unless it is –

  (a) made by or with the consent of the proprietor of the registered estate or charge to which the application relates, or a person entitled to be registered as such proprietor,
  (b) made in pursuance of rules under section 43(2)(a), or
  (c) an application for the entry of a restriction reflecting a limitation under an order of the court or registrar, or an undertaking given in place of such an order.

46   Power of court to order entry

(1) If it appears to the court that it is necessary or desirable to do so for the purpose of protecting a right or claim in relation to a registered estate or charge, it may make an order requiring the registrar to enter a restriction in the register.

(2) No order under this section may be made for the purpose of protecting the priority of an interest which is, or could be, the subject of a notice.

(3) The court may include in an order under this section a direction that an entry made in pursuance of the order is to have overriding priority.

(4) If an order under this section includes a direction under subsection (3), the registrar must make such entry in the register as rules may provide.

(5) The court may make the exercise of its power under subsection (3) subject to such terms and conditions as it thinks fit.

47   Withdrawal

A person may apply to the registrar for the withdrawal of a restriction if –

(a) the restriction was entered in such circumstances as rules may provide, and

(b) he is of such a description as rules may provide.

PART 5

CHARGES

48   Registered charges

(1) Registered charges on the same registered estate, or on the same registered charge, are to be taken to rank as between themselves in the order shown in the register.

(2) Rules may make provision about –

(a) how the priority of registered charges as between themselves is to be shown in the register, and

(b) applications for registration of the priority of registered charges as between themselves.

49   Tacking and further advances

(1) The proprietor of a registered charge may make a further advance on the security of the charge ranking in priority to a subsequent charge if he has not received from the subsequent chargee notice of the creation of the subsequent charge.

(2) Notice given for the purposes of subsection (1) shall be treated as received at the time when, in accordance with rules, it ought to have been received.

(3) The proprietor of a registered charge may also make a further advance on the security of the charge ranking in priority to a subsequent charge if –

(a) the advance is made in pursuance of an obligation, and

(b) at the time of the creation of the subsequent charge the obligation was entered in the register in accordance with rules.

(4) The proprietor of a registered charge may also make a further advance on the security of the charge ranking in priority to a subsequent charge if –

(a) the parties to the prior charge have agreed a maximum amount for which the charge is security, and

(b) at the time of the creation of the subsequent charge the agreement was entered in the register in accordance with rules.

(5) Rules may –

(a) disapply subsection (4) in relation to charges of a description specified in the rules, or

(b) provide for the application of that subsection to be subject, in the case of charges of a description so specified, to compliance with such conditions as may be so specified.

(6) Except as provided by this section, tacking in relation to a charge over registered land is only possible with the agreement of the subsequent chargee.

50 Overriding statutory charges: duty of notification

If the registrar enters a person in the register as the proprietor of a charge which –

(a) is created by or under an enactment, and

(b) has effect to postpone a charge which at the time of registration of the statutory charge is –

(i) entered in the register, or

(ii) the basis for an entry in the register,

he must in accordance with rules give notice of the creation of the statutory charge to such person as rules may provide.

51 Effect of completion by registration

On completion of the relevant registration requirements, a charge created by means of a registrable disposition of a registered estate has effect, if it would not otherwise do so, as a charge by deed by way of legal mortgage.

52 Protection of disponees

(1) Subject to any entry in the register to the contrary, the proprietor of a registered charge is to be taken to have, in relation to the property subject to the charge, the powers of disposition conferred by law on the owner of a legal mortgage.

(2) Subsection (1) has effect only for the purpose of preventing the title of a disponee being questioned (and so does not affect the lawfulness of a disposition).

53 Powers as sub-chargee

The registered proprietor of a sub-charge has, in relation to the property subject to the principal charge or any intermediate charge, the same powers as the sub-chargor.

54 Proceeds of sale: chargee's duty

For the purposes of section 105 of the Law of Property Act 1925 (c 20) (mortgagee's duties in relation to application of proceeds of sale), in its application to the proceeds of sale of registered land, a person shall be taken to have notice of anything in the register immediately before the disposition on sale.

55 Local land charges

A charge over registered land which is a local land charge may only be realised if the title to the charge is registered.

56 Receipt in case of joint proprietors

Where a charge is registered in the name of two or more proprietors, a valid receipt for the money secured by the charge may be given by –

  (a) the registered proprietors,

  (b) the survivors or survivor of the registered proprietors, or

  (c) the personal representative of the last survivor of the registered proprietors.

57 Entry of right of consolidation

Rules may make provision about entry in the register of a right of consolidation in relation to a registered charge.

PART 6

REGISTRATION: GENERAL

58 Conclusiveness

(1) If, on the entry of a person in the register as the proprietor of a legal estate, the legal estate would not otherwise be vested in him, it shall be deemed to be vested in him as a result of the registration.

(2) Subsection (1) does not apply where the entry is made in pursuance of a registrable disposition in relation to which some other registration requirement remains to be met.

59 Dependent estates

(1) The entry of a person in the register as the proprietor of a legal estate which subsists for the benefit of a registered estate must be made in relation to the registered estate.

(2) The entry of a person in the register as the proprietor of a charge on a registered estate must be made in relation to that estate.

(3) The entry of a person in the register as the proprietor of a sub-charge on a registered charge must be made in relation to that charge.

60 Boundaries

(1) The boundary of a registered estate as shown for the purposes of the register is a general boundary, unless shown as determined under this section.

(2) A general boundary does not determine the exact line of the boundary.

(3) Rules may make provision enabling or requiring the exact line of the boundary of a registered estate to be determined and may, in particular, make provision about –

(a) the circumstances in which the exact line of a boundary may or must be determined,

(b) how the exact line of a boundary may be determined,

(c) procedure in relation to applications for determination, and

(d) the recording of the fact of determination in the register or the index maintained under section 68.

(4) Rules under this section must provide for applications for determination to be made to the registrar.

61 Accretion and diluvion

(1) The fact that a registered estate in land is shown in the register as having a particular boundary does not affect the operation of accretion or diluvion.

(2) An agreement about the operation of accretion or diluvion in relation to a registered estate in land has effect only if registered in accordance with rules.

62 Power to upgrade title

(1) Where the title to a freehold estate is entered in the register as possessory or qualified, the registrar may enter it as absolute if he is satisfied as to the title to the estate.

(2) Where the title to a leasehold estate is entered in the register as good leasehold, the registrar may enter it as absolute if he is satisfied as to the superior title.

(3) Where the title to a leasehold estate is entered in the register as possessory or qualified the registrar may –

(a) enter it as good leasehold if he is satisfied as to the title to the estate, and

(b) enter it as absolute if he is satisfied both as to the title to the estate and as to the superior title.

(4) Where the title to a freehold estate in land has been entered in the register as possessory for at least twelve years, the registrar may enter it as absolute if he is satisfied that the proprietor is in possession of the land.

(5) Where the title to a leasehold estate in land has been entered in the register as possessory for at least twelve years, the registrar may enter it as good leasehold if he is satisfied that the proprietor is in possession of the land.

(6) None of the powers under subsections (1) to (5) is exercisable if there is outstanding any claim adverse to the title of the registered proprietor which is made by virtue of an estate, right or interest whose enforceability is preserved by virtue of the existing entry about the class of title.

(7) The only persons who may apply to the registrar for the exercise of any of the powers under subsections (1) to (5) are –

(a) the proprietor of the estate to which the application relates,

(b) a person entitled to be registered as the proprietor of that estate,

(c) the proprietor of a registered charge affecting that estate, and

(d) a person interested in a registered estate which derives from that estate.

(8) In determining for the purposes of this section whether he is satisfied as to any title, the registrar is to apply the same standards as those which apply under section 9 or 10 to first registration of title.

(9) The Lord Chancellor may by order amend subsection (4) or (5) by substituting for the number of years for the time being specified in that subsection such number of years as the order may provide.

63   Effect of upgrading title

(1) On the title to a registered freehold or leasehold estate being entered under section 62 as absolute, the proprietor ceases to hold the estate subject to any estate, right or interest whose enforceability was preserved by virtue of the previous entry about the class of title.

(2) Subsection (1) also applies on the title to a registered leasehold estate being entered under section 62 as good leasehold, except that the entry does not affect or prejudice the enforcement of any estate, right or interest affecting, or in derogation of, the title of the lessor to grant the lease.

64   Use of register to record defects in title

(1) If it appears to the registrar that a right to determine a registered estate in land is exercisable, he may enter the fact in the register.

(2) Rules may make provision about entries under subsection (1) and may, in particular, make provision about –

(a) the circumstances in which there is a duty to exercise the power conferred by that subsection,

(b) how entries under that subsection are to be made, and

(c) the removal of such entries.

65   Alteration of register

Schedule 4 (which makes provision about alteration of the register) has effect.

66   Inspection of the registers, etc

(1) Any person may inspect and make copies of, or of any part of –

(a) the register of title,

(b) any document kept by the registrar which is referred to in the register of title,

(c) any other document kept by the registrar which relates to an application to him, or

(d) the register of cautions against first registration.

(2) The right under subsection (1) is subject to rules which may, in particular –

(a) provide for exceptions to the right, and

(b) impose conditions on its exercise, including conditions requiring the payment of fees.

67   Official copies of the registers, etc

(1) An official copy of, or of a part of –

(a) the register of title,

(b) any document which is referred to in the register of title and kept by the registrar,

(c) any other document kept by the registrar which relates to an application to him, or

(d) the register of cautions against first registration,

is admissible in evidence to the same extent as the original.

(2) A person who relies on an official copy in which there is a mistake is not liable for loss suffered by another by reason of the mistake.

(3) Rules may make provision for the issue of official copies and may, in particular, make provision about –

(a) the form of official copies,

(b) who may issue official copies,

(c) applications for official copies, and

(d) the conditions to be met by applicants for official copies, including conditions requiring the payment of fees.

70   Official searches

Rules may make provision for official searches of the register, including searches of pending applications for first registration, and may, in particular, make provision about –

(a) the form of applications for searches,

(b) the manner in which such applications may be made,

(c) the form of official search certificates, and

(d) the manner in which such certificates may be issued.

71 Duty to disclose unregistered interests

Where rules so provide –

(a) a person applying for registration under Chapter 1 of Part 2 must provide to the registrar such information as the rules may provide about any interest affecting the estate to which the application relates which –

(i) falls within any of the paragraphs of Schedule 1, and

(ii) is of a description specified by the rules;

(b) a person applying to register a registrable disposition of a registered estate must provide to the registrar such information as the rules may provide about any unregistered interest affecting the estate which –

(i) falls within any of the paragraphs of Schedule 3, and

(ii) is of description specified by the rules.

72 Priority protection

(1) For the purposes of this section, an application for an entry in the register is protected if –

(a) it is one to which a priority period relates, and

(b) it is made before the end of that period.

(2) Where an application for an entry in the register is protected, any entry made in the register during the priority period relating to the application is postponed to any entry made in pursuance of it.

(3) Subsection (2) does not apply if –

(a) the earlier entry was made in pursuance of a protected application, and

(b) the priority period relating to that application ranks ahead of the one relating to the application for the other entry.

(4) Subsection (2) does not apply if the earlier entry is one to which a direction under section 46(3) applies.

(5) The registrar may defer dealing with an application for an entry in the register if it appears to him that subsection (2) might apply to the entry were he to make it.

(6) Rules may –

(a) make provision for priority periods in connection with –

(i) official searches of the register, including searches of pending applications for first registration, or

(ii) the noting in the register of a contract for the making of a registrable disposition of a registered estate or charge;

(b) make provision for the keeping of records in relation to priority periods and the inspection of such records.

(7) Rules under subsection (6)(a) may, in particular, make provision about –

(a) the commencement and length of a priority period,

(b) the applications for registration to which such a period relates,

(c) the order in which competing priority periods rank, and

(d) the application of subsections (2) and (3) in cases where more than one priority period relates to the same application.

73 Objections

(1) Subject to subsections (2) and (3), anyone may object to an application to the registrar.

(2) In the case of an application under section 18, only the person who lodged the caution to which the application relates, or such other person as rules may provide, may object.

(3) In the case of an application under section 36, only the person shown in the register as the beneficiary of the notice to which the application relates, or such other person as rules may provide, may object.

(4) The right to object under this section is subject to rules.

(5) Where an objection is made under this section, the registrar –

(a) must give notice of the objection to the applicant, and

(b) may not determine the application until the objection has been disposed of.

(6) Subsection (5) does not apply if the objection is one which the registrar is satisfied is groundless.

(7) If it is not possible to dispose by agreement of an objection to which subsection (5) applies, the registrar must refer the matter to the adjudicator.

(8) Rules may make provision about references under subsection (7).

74 Effective date of registration

An entry made in the register in pursuance of –

(a) an application for registration of an unregistered legal estate, or

(b) an application for registration in relation to a disposition required to be completed by registration,

has effect from the time of the making of the application.

77 Duty to act reasonably

(1) A person must not exercise any of the following rights without reasonable cause –

(a) the right to lodge a caution under section 15,

(b) the right to apply for the entry of a notice or restriction, and

(c) the right to object to an application to the registrar.

(2) The duty under this section is owed to any person who suffers damage in consequence of its breach.

78 Notice of trust not to affect registrar

The registrar shall not be affected with notice of a trust.

PART 7

SPECIAL CASES

85 Bona vacantia

Rules may make provision about how the passing of a registered estate or charge as bona vacantia is to be dealt with for the purposes of this Act.

86 Bankruptcy

(1) In this Act, references to an interest affecting an estate or charge do not include a petition in bankruptcy or bankruptcy order.

(2) As soon as practicable after registration of a petition in bankruptcy as a pending action under the Land Charges Act 1972 (c 61), the registrar must enter in the register in relation to any registered estate or charge which appears to him to be affected a notice in respect of the pending action.

(3) Unless cancelled by the registrar in such manner as rules may provide, a notice entered under subsection (2) continues in force until –

(a) a restriction is entered in the register under subsection (4), or

(b) the trustee in bankruptcy is registered as proprietor.

(4) As soon as practicable after registration of a bankruptcy order under the Land Charges Act 1972, the registrar must, in relation to any registered estate or charge which appears to him to be affected by the order, enter in the register a restriction reflecting the effect of the Insolvency Act 1986 (c 45).

(5) Where the proprietor of a registered estate or charge is adjudged bankrupt, the title of his trustee in bankruptcy is void as against a person to whom a registrable disposition of the estate or charge is made if –

(a) the disposition is made for valuable consideration,

(b) the person to whom the disposition is made acts in good faith, and

(c) at the time of the disposition –

(i) no notice or restriction is entered under this section in relation to the registered estate or charge, and

(ii) the person to whom the disposition is made has no notice of the bankruptcy petition or the adjudication.

(6) Subsection (5) only applies if the relevant registration requirements are met in relation to the disposition, but, when they are met, has effect as from the date of the disposition.

(7) Nothing in this section requires a person to whom a registrable disposition is made to make any search under the Land Charges Act 1972.

87 Pending land actions, writs, orders and deeds of arrangement

(1) Subject to the following provisions, references in this Act to an interest affecting an estate or charge include –

(a) a pending land action within the meaning of the Land Charges Act 1972,

(b) a writ or order of the kind mentioned in section 6(1)(a) of that Act (writ or order affecting land issued or made by any court for the purposes of enforcing a judgment or recognisance),

(c) an order appointing a receiver or sequestrator, and

(d) a deed of arrangement.

(2) No notice may be entered in the register in respect of –

(a) an order appointing a receiver or sequestrator, or

(b) a deed of arrangement.

(3) None of the matters mentioned in subsection (1) shall be capable of falling within paragraph 2 of Schedule 1 or 3.

(4) In its application to any of the matters mentioned in subsection (1), this Act shall have effect subject to such modifications as rules may provide.

(5) In this section, 'deed of arrangement' has the same meaning as in the Deeds of Arrangement Act 1914 (c 47).

88 Incorporeal hereditaments

In its application to –

(a) rentcharges,

(b) franchises,

(c) profits a prendre in gross, or

(d) manors,

this Act shall have effect subject to such modification as rules may provide.

89 Settlements

(1) Rules may make provision for the purposes of this Act in relation to the application to registered land of the enactments relating to settlements under the Settled Land Act 1925 (c 18).

(2) Rules under this section may include provision modifying any of those enactments in its application to registered land.

(3) In this section, 'registered land' means an interest the title to which is, or is required to be, registered.

PART 9

ADVERSE POSSESSION

96   Disapplication of periods of limitation

(1) No period of limitation under section 15 of the Limitation Act 1980 (c 58) (time limits in relation to recovery of land) shall run against any person, other than a chargee, in relation to an estate in land or rentcharge the title to which is registered.

(2) No period of limitation under section 16 of that Act (time limits in relation to redemption of land) shall run against any person in relation to such an estate in land or rentcharge.

(3) Accordingly, section 17 of that Act (extinction of title on expiry of time limit) does not operate to extinguish the title of any person where, by virtue of this section, a period of limitation does not run against him.

97   Registration of adverse possessor

Schedule 6 (which makes provision about the registration of an adverse possessor of an estate in land or rentcharge) has effect.

98   Defences

(1) A person has a defence to an action for possession of land if –

(a) on the day immediately preceding that on which the action was brought he was entitled to make an application under paragraph 1 of Schedule 6 to be registered as the proprietor of an estate in the land, and

(b) had he made such an application on that day, the condition in paragraph 5(4) of that Schedule would have been satisfied.

(2) A judgment for possession of land ceases to be enforceable at the end of the period of two years beginning with the date of the judgment if the proceedings in which the judgment is given were commenced against a person who was at that time entitled to make an application under paragraph 1 of Schedule 6.

(3) A person has a defence to an action for possession of land if on the day immediately preceding that on which the action was brought he was entitled to make an application under paragraph 6 of Schedule 6 to be registered as the proprietor of an estate in the land.

(4) A judgment for possession of land ceases to be enforceable at the end of the

period of two years beginning with the date of the judgment if, at the end of that period, the person against whom the judgment was given is entitled to make an application under paragraph 6 of Schedule 6 to be registered as the proprietor of an estate in the land.

(5) Where in any proceedings a court determines that –

(a) a person is entitled to a defence under this section, or

(b) a judgment for possession has ceased to be enforceable against a person by virtue of subsection (4),

the court must order the registrar to register him as the proprietor of the estate in relation to which he is entitled to make an application under Schedule 6.

(6) The defences under this section are additional to any other defences a person may have.

(7) Rules may make provision to prohibit the recovery of rent due under a rentcharge from a person who has been in adverse possession of the rentcharge.

PART 10

LAND REGISTRY

99 The land registry

(1) There is to continue to be an office called Her Majesty's Land Registry which is to deal with the business of registration under this Act.

(2) The land registry is to consist of –

(a) the Chief Land Registrar, who is its head, and

(b) the staff appointed by him;

and references in this Act to a member of the land registry are to be read accordingly.

(3) The Lord Chancellor shall appoint a person to be the Chief Land Registrar.

(4) Schedule 7 (which makes further provision about the land registry) has effect.

100 Conduct of business

(1) Any function of the registrar may be carried out by any member of the land registry who is authorised for the purpose by the registrar.

(2) The Lord Chancellor may by regulations make provision about the carrying out of functions during any vacancy in the office of registrar.

(3) The Lord Chancellor may by order designate a particular office of the land registry as the proper office for the receipt of applications or a specified description of application.

(4) The registrar may prepare and publish such forms and directions as he considers

necessary or desirable for facilitating the conduct of the business of registration under this Act.

PART 11

ADJUDICATION

107 The adjudicator

(1) The Lord Chancellor shall appoint a person to be the Adjudicator to Her Majesty's Land Registry.

(2) To be qualified for appointment under subsection (1), a person must have a 10 year general qualification (within the meaning of section 71 of the Courts and Legal Services Act 1990 (c 41)).

(3) Schedule 9 (which makes further provision about the adjudicator) has effect.

108 Jurisdiction

(1) The adjudicator has the following functions –

(a) determining matters referred to him under section 73(7), and

(b) determining appeals under paragraph 4 of Schedule 5 [network access agreements].

(2) Also, the adjudicator may, on application, make any order which the High Court could make for the rectification or setting aside of a document which –

(a) effects a qualifying disposition of a registered estate or charge,

(b) is a contract to make such a disposition, or

(c) effects a transfer of an interest which is the subject of a notice in the register.

(3) For the purposes of subsection (2)(a), a qualifying disposition is –

(a) a registrable disposition, or

(b) a disposition which creates an interest which may be the subject of a notice in the register.

(4) The general law about the effect of an order of the High Court for the rectification or setting aside of a document shall apply to an order under this section.

111 Appeals

(1) Subject to subsection (2), a person aggrieved by a decision of the adjudicator may appeal to the High Court.

(2) In the case of a decision on an appeal under paragraph 4 of Schedule 5 [network access agreements], only appeal on a point of law is possible.

(3) If on an appeal under this section relating to an application under paragraph 1

of Schedule 6 [adverse possession for 10 years] the court determines that it would be unconscionable because of an equity by estoppel for the registered proprietor to seek to dispossess the applicant, but that the circumstances are not such that the applicant ought to be registered as proprietor, the court must determine how the equity due to the applicant is to be satisfied.

112   Enforcement of orders, etc

A requirement of the adjudicator shall be enforceable as an order of the court.

PART 12

MISCELLANEOUS AND GENERAL

115   Rights of pre-emption

(1) A right of pre-emption in relation to registered land has effect from the time of creation as an interest capable of binding successors in title (subject to the rules about the effect of dispositions on priority).

(2) This section has effect in relation to rights of pre-emption created on or after the day on which this section comes into force.

116   Proprietary estoppel and mere equities

It is hereby declared for the avoidance of doubt that, in relation to registered land, each of the following –

(a) an equity by estoppel, and

(b) a mere equity,

has effect from the time the equity arises as an interest capable of binding successors in title (subject to the rules about the effect of dispositions on priority).

117   Reduction in unregistered interests with automatic protection

(1) Paragraphs 10 to 14 of Schedules 1 and 3 shall cease to have effect at the end of the period of ten years beginning with the day on which those Schedules come into force.

(2) If made before the end of the period mentioned in subsection (1), no fee may be charged for –

(a) an application to lodge a caution against first registration by virtue of an interest falling within any of paragraphs 10 to 14 of Schedule 1, or

(b) an application for the entry in the register of a notice in respect of an interest falling within any of paragraphs 10 to 14 of Schedule 3.

120 Conclusiveness of filed copies, etc

(1) This section applies where –

(a) a disposition relates to land to which a registered estate relates, and

(b) an entry in the register relating to the registered estate refers to a document kept by the registrar which is not an original.

(2) As between the parties to the disposition, the document kept by the registrar is to be taken –

(a) to be correct, and

(b) to contain all the material parts of the original document.

(3) No party to the disposition may require production of the original document.

(4) No party to the disposition is to be affected by any provision of the original document which is not contained in the document kept by the registrar.

127 Exercise of powers

(1) Power to make land registration rules is exercisable by the Lord Chancellor with the advice and assistance of the Rule Committee.

(2) The Rule Committee is a body consisting of –

(a) a judge of the Chancery Division of the High Court nominated by the Lord Chancellor,

(b) the registrar,

(c) a person nominated by the General Council of the Bar,

(d) a person nominated by the Council of the Law Society,

(e) a person nominated by the Council of Mortgage Lenders,

(f) a person nominated by the Council of Licensed Conveyancers,

(g) a person nominated by the Royal Institution of Chartered Surveyors,

(h) a person with experience in, and knowledge of, consumer affairs, and

(i) any person nominated under subsection (3).

(3) The Lord Chancellor may nominate to be a member of the Rule Committee any person who appears to him to have qualifications or experience which would be of value to the committee in considering any matter with which it is concerned.

129 Crown application

This Act binds the Crown.

130 Application to internal waters

This Act applies to land covered by internal waters of the United Kingdom which are –

(a) within England or Wales, or

(b) adjacent to England or Wales and specified for the purposes of this section by order made by the Lord Chancellor.

131 'Proprietor in possession'

(1) For the purposes of this Act, land is in the possession of the proprietor of a registered estate in land if it is physically in his possession, or in that of a person who is entitled to be registered as the proprietor of the registered estate.

(2) In the case of the following relationships, land which is (or is treated as being) in the possession of the second-mentioned person is to be treated for the purposes of subsection (1) as in the possession of the first-mentioned person –

(a) landlord and tenant;

(b) mortgagor and mortgagee;

(c) licensor and licensee;

(d) trustee and beneficiary.

(3) In subsection (1), the reference to entitlement does not include entitlement under Schedule 6.

132 General interpretation

(1) In this Act –

'adjudicator' means the Adjudicator to Her Majesty's Land Registry;

'caution against first registration' means a caution lodged under section 15;

'cautions register' means the register kept under section 19(1);

'charge' means any mortgage, charge or lien for securing money or money's worth; ...

'land' includes –

(a) buildings and other structures,

(b) land covered with water, and

(c) mines and minerals, whether or not held with the surface;

'land registration rules' means any rules under this Act, other than rules under section 93, Part 11, section 121 or paragraph 1, 2 or 3 of Schedule 5;

'legal estate' has the same meaning as in the Law of Property Act 1925 (c 20);

'legal mortgage' has the same meaning as in the Law of Property Act 1925;

'mines and minerals' includes any strata or seam of minerals or substances in or under any land, and powers of working and getting any such minerals or substances;

'registrar' means the Chief Land Registrar;

'register' means the register of title, except in the context of cautions against first registration;

'registered' means entered in the register;

'registered charge' means a charge the title to which is entered in the register;

'registered estate' means a legal estate the title to which is entered in the register, other than a registered charge;

'registered land' means a registered estate or registered charge;

'registrable disposition' means a disposition which is required to be completed by registration under section 27;

'requirement of registration' means the requirement of registration under section 4;

'sub-charge' means a charge under section 23(2)(b);

'term of years absolute' has the same meaning as in the Law of Property Act 1925 (c 20);

'valuable consideration' does not include marriage consideration or a nominal consideration in money. ...

(3) In this Act –

(a) references to the court are to the High Court or a county court,

(b) references to an interest affecting an estate or charge are to an adverse right affecting the title to the estate or charge, and

(c) references to the right to object to an application to the registrar are to the right under section 73.

SCHEDULE 1

UNREGISTERED INTERESTS WHICH OVERRIDE FIRST REGISTRATION

1. A leasehold estate in land granted for a term not exceeding seven years from the date of the grant, except for a lease the grant of which falls within section 4(1) (d), (e) or (f).

2. An interest belonging to a person in actual occupation, so far as relating to land of which he is in actual occupation, except for an interest under a settlement under the Settled Land Act 1925 (c 18).

3. A legal easement or profit a prendre.

4. A customary right.

5. A public right.

6. A local land charge.

7. An interest in any coal or coal mine, the rights attached to any such interest and the rights of any person under section 38, 49 or 51 of the Coal Industry Act 1994 (c 21).

8. In the case of land to which title was registered before 1898, rights to mines and minerals (and incidental rights) created before 1898.

9. In the case of land to which title was registered between 1898 and 1925 inclusive,

rights to mines and minerals (and incidental rights) created before the date of registration of the title.

10. A franchise.

11. A manorial right.

12. A right to rent which was reserved to the Crown on the granting of any freehold estate (whether or not the right is still vested in the Crown).

13. A non-statutory right in respect of an embankment or sea or river wall.

14. A right to payment in lieu of tithe.

15. A right acquired under the Limitation Act 1980 before the coming into force of this Schedule [ceases to have effect 13 October 2006].

16. A right in respect of the repair of a church chancel [ceases to have effect 13 October 2013].

SCHEDULE 2

REGISTRABLE DISPOSITIONS: REGISTRATION REQUIREMENTS

PART 1

REGISTERED ESTATES

1. This Part deals with the registration requirements relating to those dispositions of registered estates which are required to be completed by registration.

2. – (1) In the case of a transfer of whole or part, the transferee, or his successor in title, must be entered in the register as the proprietor.

(2) In the case of a transfer of part, such details of the transfer as rules may provide must be entered in the register in relation to the registered estate out of which the transfer is made.

3. – (1) This paragraph applies to a disposition consisting of the grant out of an estate in land of a term of years absolute.

(2) In the case of a disposition to which this paragraph applies –

(a) the grantee, or his successor in title, must be entered in the register as the proprietor of the lease, and

(b) a notice in respect of the lease must be entered in the register.

4. – (1) This paragraph applies to a disposition consisting of the grant out of a franchise or manor of a lease for a term of more than seven years from the date of the grant.

(2) In the case of a disposition to which this paragraph applies –

(a) the grantee, or his successor in title, must be entered in the register as the proprietor of the lease, and

(b) a notice in respect of the lease must be entered in the register.

5. – (1) This paragraph applies to a disposition consisting of the grant out of a franchise or manor of a lease for a term not exceeding seven years from the date of the grant.

(2) In the case of a disposition to which this paragraph applies, a notice in respect of the lease must be entered in the register.

6. – (1) This paragraph applies to a disposition consisting of the creation of a legal rentcharge or profit a prendre in gross, other than one created for, or for an interest equivalent to, a term of years absolute not exceeding seven years from the date of creation.

(2) In the case of a disposition to which this paragraph applies –

(a) the grantee, or his successor in title, must be entered in the register as the proprietor of the interest created, and

(b) a notice in respect of the interest created must be entered in the register.

(3) In sub-paragraph (1), the reference to a legal rentcharge or profit a prendre in gross is to one falling within section 1(2) of the Law of Property Act 1925 (c 20).

7. – (1) This paragraph applies to a disposition which –

(a) consists of the creation of an interest of a kind falling within section 1(2)(a),

(b) or (e) of the Law of Property Act 1925, and

(b) is not a disposition to which paragraph 4, 5 or 6 applies.

(2) In the case of a disposition to which this paragraph applies –

(a) a notice in respect of the interest created must be entered in the register, and

(b) if the interest is created for the benefit of a registered estate, the proprietor of the registered estate must be entered in the register as its proprietor.

(3) Rules may provide for sub-paragraph (2) to have effect with modifications in relation to a right of entry over or in respect of a term of years absolute.

8. In the case of the creation of a charge, the chargee, or his successor in title, must be entered in the register as the proprietor of the charge.

PART 2

REGISTERED CHARGES

9. This Part deals with the registration requirements relating to those dispositions of registered charges which are required to be completed by registration.

10. In the case of a transfer, the transferee, or his successor in title, must be entered in the register as the proprietor.

11. In the case of the creation of a sub-charge, the sub-chargee, or his successor in title, must be entered in the register as the proprietor of the sub-charge.

SCHEDULE 3

UNREGISTERED INTERESTS WHICH OVERRIDE
REGISTERED DISPOSITIONS

1. A leasehold estate in land granted for a term not exceeding seven years from the date of the grant, except for –

(a) a lease the grant of which falls within section 4(1)(d), (e) or (f);

(b) a lease the grant of which constitutes a registrable disposition.

2. An interest belonging at the time of the disposition to a person in actual occupation, so far as relating to land of which he is in actual occupation, except for –

(a) an interest under a settlement under the Settled Land Act 1925 (c 18);

(b) an interest of a person of whom inquiry was made before the disposition and who failed to disclose the right when he could reasonably have been expected to do so;

(c) an interest –

(i) which belongs to a person whose occupation would not have been obvious on a reasonably careful inspection of the land at the time of the disposition, and

(ii) of which the person to whom the disposition is made does not have actual knowledge at that time;

(d) a leasehold estate in land granted to take effect in possession after the end of the period of three months beginning with the date of the grant and which has not taken effect in possession at the time of the disposition.

3. – (1) A legal easement or profit a prendre, except for an easement, or a profit a prendre which is not registered under the Commons Registration Act 1965 (c 64), which at the time of the disposition –

(a) is not within the actual knowledge of the person to whom the disposition is made, and

(b) would not have been obvious on a reasonably careful inspection of the land over which the easement or profit is exercisable.

(2) The exception in sub-paragraph (1) does not apply if the person entitled to the easement or profit proves that it has been exercised in the period of one year ending with the day of the disposition

4. A customary right.

5. A public right.

6. A local land charge.

7. An interest in any coal or coal mine, the rights attached to any such interest and the rights of any person under section 38, 49 or 51 of the Coal Industry Act 1994 (c 21).

8. In the case of land to which title was registered before 1898, rights to mines and minerals (and incidental rights) created before 1898.

9. In the case of land to which title was registered between 1898 and 1925 inclusive, rights to mines and minerals (and incidental rights) created before the date of registration of the title.

10. A franchise.

11. A manorial right.

12. A right to rent which was reserved to the Crown on the granting of any freehold estate (whether or not the right is still vested in the Crown).

13. A non-statutory right in respect of an embankment or sea or river wall.

14. A right to payment in lieu of tithe.

15. A right acquired under the Limitation Act 1980 before the coming into force of this Schedule [ceases to have effect 13 October 2006].

16. A right in respect of the repair of a church chancel [ceases to have effect 13 October 2013].

SCHEDULE 6

REGISTRATION OF ADVERSE POSSESSOR

1. – (1) A person may apply to the registrar to be registered as the proprietor of a registered estate in land if he has been in adverse possession of the estate for the period of ten years ending on the date of the application.

(2) A person may also apply to the registrar to be registered as the proprietor of a registered estate in land if –

(a) he has in the period of six months ending on the date of the application ceased to be in adverse possession of the estate because of eviction by the registered proprietor, or a person claiming under the registered proprietor,

(b) on the day before his eviction he was entitled to make an application under sub-paragraph (1), and

(c) the eviction was not pursuant to a judgment for possession.

(3) However, a person may not make an application under this paragraph if –

(a) he is a defendant in proceedings which involve asserting a right to possession of the land, or

(b) judgment for possession of the land has been given against him in the last two years.

(4) For the purposes of sub-paragraph (1), the estate need not have been registered throughout the period of adverse possession.

2. – (1) The registrar must give notice of an application under paragraph 1 to –

(a) the proprietor of the estate to which the application relates,

(b) the proprietor of any registered charge on the estate,

(c) where the estate is leasehold, the proprietor of any superior registered estate,

(d) any person who is registered in accordance with rules as a person to be notified under this paragraph, and

(e) such other persons as rules may provide.

(2) Notice under this paragraph shall include notice of the effect of paragraph 4.

3. – (1) A person given notice under paragraph 2 may require that the application to which the notice relates be dealt with under paragraph 5.

(2) The right under this paragraph is exercisable by notice to the registrar given before the end of such period as rules may provide.

4. If an application under paragraph 1 is not required to be dealt with under paragraph 5, the applicant is entitled to be entered in the register as the new proprietor of the estate.

5. – (1) If an application under paragraph 1 is required to be dealt with under this paragraph, the applicant is only entitled to be registered as the new proprietor of the estate if any of the following conditions is met.

(2) The first condition is that –

(a) it would be unconscionable because of an equity by estoppel for the registered proprietor to seek to dispossess the applicant, and

(b) the circumstances are such that the applicant ought to be registered as the proprietor.

(3) The second condition is that the applicant is for some other reason entitled to be registered as the proprietor of the estate.

(4) The third condition is that –

(a) the land to which the application relates is adjacent to land belonging to the applicant,

(b) the exact line of the boundary between the two has not been determined under rules under section 60,

(c) for at least ten years of the period of adverse possession ending on the date of the application, the applicant (or any predecessor in title) reasonably believed that the land to which the application relates belonged to him, and

(d) the estate to which the application relates was registered more than one year prior to the date of the application.

(5) In relation to an application under paragraph 1(2), this paragraph has effect as if the reference in sub-paragraph (4)(c) to the date of the application were to the day before the date of the applicant's eviction.

6. – (1) Where a person's application under paragraph 1 is rejected, he may make a further application to be registered as the proprietor of the estate if he is in

adverse possession of the estate from the date of the application until the last day of the period of two years beginning with the date of its rejection.

(2) However, a person may not make an application under this paragraph if –

(a) he is a defendant in proceedings which involve asserting a right to possession of the land,

(b) judgment for possession of the land has been given against him in the last two years, or

(c) he has been evicted from the land pursuant to a judgment for possession.

7. If a person makes an application under paragraph 6, he is entitled to be entered in the register as the new proprietor of the estate.

8. – (1) No one may apply under this Schedule to be registered as the proprietor of an estate in land during, or before the end of twelve months after the end of, any period in which the existing registered proprietor is for the purposes of the Limitation (Enemies and War Prisoners) Act 1945 (8 & 9 Geo 6 c 16) –

(a) an enemy, or

(b) detained in enemy territory.

(2) No-one may apply under this Schedule to be registered as the proprietor of an estate in land during any period in which the existing registered proprietor is –

(a) unable because of mental disability to make decisions about issues of the kind to which such an application would give rise, or

(b) unable to communicate such decisions because of mental disability or physical impairment.

(3) For the purposes of sub-paragraph (2), 'mental disability' means a disability or disorder of the mind or brain, whether permanent or temporary, which results in an impairment or disturbance of mental functioning.

(4) Where it appears to the registrar that sub-paragraph (1) or (2) applies in relation to an estate in land, he may include a note to that effect in the register.

9. – (1) Where a person is registered as the proprietor of an estate in land in pursuance of an application under this Schedule, the title by virtue of adverse possession which he had at the time of the application is extinguished.

(2) Subject to sub-paragraph (3), the registration of a person under this Schedule as the proprietor of an estate in land does not affect the priority of any interest affecting the estate.

(3) Subject to sub-paragraph (4), where a person is registered under this Schedule as the proprietor of an estate, the estate is vested in him free of any registered charge affecting the estate immediately before his registration.

(4) Sub-paragraph (3) does not apply where registration as proprietor is in pursuance of an application determined by reference to whether any of the conditions in paragraph 5 applies.

10. – (1) Where –

(a) a registered estate continues to be subject to a charge notwithstanding the registration of a person under this Schedule as the proprietor, and

(b) the charge affects property other than the estate,

the proprietor of the estate may require the chargee to apportion the amount secured by the charge at that time between the estate and the other property on the basis of their respective values.

(2) The person requiring the apportionment is entitled to a discharge of his estate from the charge on payment of –

(a) the amount apportioned to the estate, and

(b) the costs incurred by the chargee as a result of the apportionment.

(3) On a discharge under this paragraph, the liability of the chargor to the chargee is reduced by the amount apportioned to the estate.

(4) Rules may make provision about apportionment under this paragraph, in particular, provision about –

(a) procedure,

(b) valuation,

(c) calculation of costs payable under sub-paragraph (2)(b), and

(d) payment of the costs of the chargor.

11. – (1) A person is in adverse possession of an estate in land for the purposes of this Schedule if, but for section 96, a period of limitation under section 15 of the Limitation Act 1980 (c 58) would run in his favour in relation to the estate.

(2) A person is also to be regarded for those purposes as having been in adverse possession of an estate in land –

(a) where he is the successor in title to an estate in the land, during any period of adverse possession by a predecessor in title to that estate, or

(b) during any period of adverse possession by another person which comes between, and is continuous with, periods of adverse possession of his own.

(3) In determining whether for the purposes of this paragraph a period of limitation would run under section 15 of the Limitation Act 1980, there are to be disregarded –

(a) the commencement of any legal proceedings, and

(b) paragraph 6 of Schedule 1 to that Act.

12. A person is not to be regarded as being in adverse possession of an estate for the purposes of this Schedule at any time when the estate is subject to a trust, unless the interest of each of the beneficiaries in the estate is an interest in possession.

13. – (1) Where –

(a) a person is in adverse possession of an estate in land,

(b) the estate belongs to Her Majesty in right of the Crown or the Duchy of Lancaster or to the Duchy of Cornwall, and

(c) the land consists of foreshore,

paragraph 1(1) is to have effect as if the reference to ten years were to sixty years.

(2) For the purposes of sub-paragraph (1), land is to be treated as foreshore if it has been foreshore at any time in the previous ten years.

(3) In this paragraph, 'foreshore' means the shore and bed of the sea and of any tidal water, below the line of the medium high tide between the spring and neap tides.

14. Rules must make provision to apply the preceding provisions of this Schedule to registered rentcharges, subject to such modifications and exceptions as the rules may provide.

15. Rules may make provision about the procedure to be followed pursuant to an application under this Schedule.

As amended by the Land Registration Act 2002 (Transitional Provisions) (No 2) Order 2003, art 2.

COMMONHOLD AND LEASEHOLD REFORM ACT 2002

(2002 c 15)

PART 1

COMMONHOLD

1   Commonhold land

(1) Land is commonhold land if –

(a) the freehold estate in the land is registered as a freehold estate in commonhold land,

(b) the land is specified in the memorandum of association of a commonhold association as the land in relation to which the association is to exercise functions, and

(c) a commonhold community statement makes provision for rights and duties of the commonhold association and unit-holders (whether or not the statement has come into force).

(2) In this Part a reference to a commonhold is a reference to land in relation to which a commonhold association exercises functions.

(3) In this Part –

'commonhold association' has the meaning given by section 34,

'commonhold community statement' has the meaning given by section 31,

'commonhold unit' has the meaning given by section 11,

'common parts' has the meaning given by section 25, and

'unit-holder' has the meaning given by sections 12 and 13.

(4) Sections 7 and 9 make provision for the vesting in the commonhold association of the fee simple in possession in the common parts of a commonhold.

2   Application

(1) The Registrar shall register a freehold estate in land as a freehold estate in commonhold land if –

(a) the registered freeholder of the land makes an application under this section, and

(b) no part of the land is already commonhold land.

(2) An application under this section must be accompanied by the documents listed in Schedule 1.

(3) A person is the registered freeholder of land for the purposes of this Part if –

(a) he is registered as the proprietor of a freehold estate in the land with absolute title, or

(b) he has applied, and the Registrar is satisfied that he is entitled, to be registered as mentioned in paragraph (a).

3   Consent

(1) An application under section 2 may not be made in respect of a freehold estate in land without the consent of anyone who –

(a) is the registered proprietor of the freehold estate in the whole or part of the land,

(b) is the registered proprietor of a leasehold estate in the whole or part of the land granted for a term of more than than 21 years,

(c) is the registered proprietor of a charge over the whole or part of the land, or

(d) falls within any other class of person which may be prescribed.

(2) Regulations shall make provision about consent for the purposes of this section …

(3) An order under subsection (2)(f) dispensing with a requirement for consent –

(a) may be absolute or conditional, and

(b) may make such other provision as the court thinks appropriate.

4   Land which may not be commonhold

Schedule 2 (which provides that an application under section 2 may not relate wholly or partly to land of certain kinds) shall have effect.

7   Registration without unit-holders

(1) This section applies where –

(a) a freehold estate in land is registered as a freehold estate in commonhold land in pursuance of an application under section 2, and

(b) the application is not accompanied by a statement under section 9(1)(b).

(2) On registration –

(a) the applicant shall continue to be registered as the proprietor of the freehold estate in the commonhold land, and

(b) the rights and duties conferred and imposed by the commonhold community statement shall not come into force (subject to section 8(2)(b)).

(3) Where after registration a person other than the applicant becomes entitled to be registered as the proprietor of the freehold estate in one or more, but not all, of the commonhold units –

(a) the commonhold association shall be entitled to be registered as the proprietor of the freehold estate in the common parts,

(b) the Registrar shall register the commonhold association in accordance with paragraph (a) (without an application being made),

(c) the rights and duties conferred and imposed by the commonhold community statement shall come into force, and

(d) any lease of the whole or part of the commonhold land shall be extinguished by virtue of this section.

(4) For the purpose of subsection (3)(d) 'lease' means a lease which –

(a) is granted for any term, and

(b) is granted before the commonhold association becomes entitled to be registered as the proprietor of the freehold estate in the common parts.

9   Registration with unit-holders

(1) This section applies in relation to a freehold estate in commonhold land if –

(a) it is registered as a freehold estate in commonhold land in pursuance of an application under section 2, and

(b) the application is accompanied by a statement by the applicant requesting that this section should apply.

(2) A statement under subsection (1)(b) must include a list of the commonhold units giving in relation to each one the prescribed details of the proposed initial unit-holder or joint unit-holders.

(3) On registration –

(a) the commonhold association shall be entitled to be registered as the proprietor of the freehold estate in the common parts,

(b) a person specified by virtue of subsection (2) as the initial unit-holder of a commonhold unit shall be entitled to be registered as the proprietor of the freehold estate in the unit,

(c) a person specified by virtue of subsection (2) as an initial joint unit-holder of a commonhold unit shall be entitled to be registered as one of the proprietors of the freehold estate in the unit,

(d) the Registrar shall make entries in the register to reflect paragraphs (a) to (c) (without applications being made),

(e) the rights and duties conferred and imposed by the commonhold community statement shall come into force, and

(f) any lease of the whole or part of the commonhold land shall be extinguished by virtue of this section.

(4) For the purpose of subsection (3)(f) 'lease' means a lease which –

(a) is granted for any term, and

(b) is granted before the commonhold association becomes entitled to be registered as the proprietor of the freehold estate in the common parts.

10   Extinguished lease: liability

(1) This section applies where –

(a) a lease is extinguished by virtue of section 7(3)(d) or 9(3)(f), and

(b) the consent of the holder of that lease was not among the consents required by section 3 in respect of the application under section 2 for the land to become commonhold land.

(2) If the holder of a lease superior to the extinguished lease gave consent under section 3, he shall be liable for loss suffered by the holder of the extinguished lease.

(3) If the holders of a number of leases would be liable under subsection (2), liability shall attach only to the person whose lease was most proximate to the extinguished lease.

(4) If no person is liable under subsection (2), the person who gave consent under section 3 as the holder of the freehold estate out of which the extinguished lease was granted shall be liable for loss suffered by the holder of the extinguished lease.

11   Definition

(1) In this Part 'commonhold unit' means a commonhold unit specified in a commonhold community statement in accordance with this section.

(2) A commonhold community statement must –

(a) specify at least two parcels of land as commonhold units, and

(b) define the extent of each commonhold unit.

(3) In defining the extent of a commonhold unit a commonhold community statement –

(a) must refer to a plan which is included in the statement and which complies with prescribed requirements,

(b) may refer to an area subject to the exclusion of specified structures, fittings, apparatus or appurtenances within the area,

(c) may exclude the structures which delineate an area referred to, and

(d) may refer to two or more areas (whether or not contiguous).

(4) A commonhold unit need not contain all or any part of a building.

12   Unit-holder

A person is the unit-holder of a commonhold unit if he is entitled to be registered as the proprietor of the freehold estate in the unit (whether or not he is registered).

13   Joint unit-holders

(1) Two or more persons are joint unit-holders of a commonhold unit if they are entitled to be registered as proprietors of the freehold estate in the unit (whether or not they are registered).

(2) In the application of the following provisions to a unit with joint unit-holders a reference to a unit-holder is a reference to the joint unit-holders together –

> (a) section 14(3),
> (b) section 15(1) and (3),
> (c) section 19(2) and (3),
> (d) section 20(1),
> (e) section 23(1),
> (f) section 35(1)(b),
> (g) section 38(1),
> (h) section 39(2), and
> (i) section 47(2).

(3) In the application of the following provisions to a unit with joint unit-holders a reference to a unit-holder includes a reference to each joint unit-holder and to the joint unit-holders together –

> (a) section 1(1)(c),
> (b) section 16,
> (c) section 31(1)(b), (3)(b), (5)(j) and (7),
> (d) section 32(4)(a) and (c),
> (e) section 35(1)(a), (2) and (3),
> (f) section 37(2),
> (g) section 40(1), and
> (h) section 58(3)(a). ...

14   Use and maintenance

(1) A commonhold community statement must make provision regulating the use of commonhold units.

(2) A commonhold community statement must make provision imposing duties in respect of the insurance, repair and maintenance of each commonhold unit.

(3) A duty under subsection (2) may be imposed on the commonhold association or the unit-holder.

15   Transfer

(1) In this Part a reference to the transfer of a commonhold unit is a reference to the transfer of a unit-holder's freehold estate in a unit to another person –

> (a) whether or not for consideration,

(b) whether or not subject to any reservation or other terms, and

(c) whether or not by operation of law.

(2) A commonhold community statement may not prevent or restrict the transfer of a commonhold unit.

(3) On the transfer of a commonhold unit the new unit-holder shall notify the commonhold association of the transfer. ...

16 Transfer: effect

(1) A right or duty conferred or imposed –

(a) by a commonhold community statement, or

(b) in accordance with section 20,

shall affect a new unit-holder in the same way as it affected the former unit-holder.

(2) A former unit-holder shall not incur a liability or acquire a right –

(a) under or by virtue of the commonhold community statement, or

(b) by virtue of anything done in accordance with section 20.

(3) Subsection (2) –

(a) shall not be capable of being disapplied or varied by agreement, and

(b) is without prejudice to any liability or right incurred or acquired before a transfer takes effect.

(4) In this section –

'former unit-holder' means a person from whom a commonhold unit has been transferred (whether or not he has ceased to be the registered proprietor), and

'new unit-holder' means a person to whom a commonhold unit is transferred (whether or not he has yet become the registered proprietor).

17 Leasing: residential

(1) It shall not be possible to create a term of years absolute in a residential commonhold unit unless the term satisfies prescribed conditions.

(2) The conditions may relate to –

(a) length;

(b) the circumstances in which the term is granted;

(c) any other matter.

(3) Subject to subsection (4), an instrument or agreement shall be of no effect to the extent that it purports to create a term of years in contravention of subsection (1).

(4) Where an instrument or agreement purports to create a term of years in contravention of subsection (1) a party to the instrument or agreement may apply to the court for an order –

(a) providing for the instrument or agreement to have effect as if it provided for the creation of a term of years of a specified kind;

(b) providing for the return or payment of money;

(c) making such other provision as the court thinks appropriate.

(5) A commonhold unit is residential if provision made in the commonhold community statement by virtue of section 14(1) requires it to be used only –

(a) for residential purposes, or

(b) for residential and other incidental purposes.

18   Leasing: non-residential

An instrument or agreement which creates a term of years absolute in a commonhold unit which is not residential (within the meaning of section 17) shall have effect subject to any provision of the commonhold community statement.

19   Leasing: supplementary

(1) Regulations may –

(a) impose obligations on a tenant of a commonhold unit;

(b) enable a commonhold community statement to impose obligations on a tenant of a commonhold unit.

(2) Regulations under subsection (1) may, in particular, require a tenant of a commonhold unit to make payments to the commonhold association or a unit-holder in discharge of payments which –

(a) are due in accordance with the commonhold community statement to be made by the unit-holder, or

(b) are due in accordance with the commonhold community statement to be made by another tenant of the unit.

(3) Regulations under subsection (1) may, in particular, provide –

(a) for the amount of payments under subsection (2) to be set against sums owed by the tenant (whether to the person by whom the payments were due to be made or to some other person);

(b) for the amount of payments under subsection (2) to be recovered from the unit-holder or another tenant of the unit.

(4) Regulations may modify a rule of law about leasehold estates (whether deriving from the common law or from an enactment) in its application to a term of years in a commonhold unit. ...

20   Other transactions

(1) A commonhold community statement may not prevent or restrict the creation, grant or transfer by a unit-holder of –

(a) an interest in the whole or part of his unit, or

(b) a charge over his unit.

(2) Subsection (1) is subject to sections 17 to 19 (which impose restrictions about leases).

(3) It shall not be possible to create an interest of a prescribed kind in a commonhold unit unless the commonhold association –

(a) is a party to the creation of the interest, or

(b) consents in writing to the creation of the interest.

(4) A commonhold association may act as described in subsection (3)(a) or (b) only if –

(a) the association passes a resolution to take the action, and

(b) at least 75 per cent. of those who vote on the resolution vote in favour.

(5) An instrument or agreement shall be of no effect to the extent that it purports to create an interest in contravention of subsection (3).

(6) In this section 'interest' does not include –

(a) a charge, or

(b) an interest which arises by virtue of a charge.

21   Part-unit: interests

(1) It shall not be possible to create an interest in part only of a commonhold unit.

(2) But subsection (1) shall not prevent –

(a) the creation of a term of years absolute in part only of a residential commonhold unit where the term satisfies prescribed conditions,

(b) the creation of a term of years absolute in part only of a non-residential commonhold unit, or

(c) the transfer of the freehold estate in part only of a commonhold unit where the commonhold association consents in writing to the transfer.

(3) An instrument or agreement shall be of no effect to the extent that it purports to create an interest in contravention of subsection (1).

(4) Subsection (5) applies where –

(a) land becomes commonhold land or is added to a commonhold unit, and

(b) immediately before that event there is an interest in the land which could not be created after that event by reason of subsection (1).

(5) The interest shall be extinguished by virtue of this subsection to the extent that it could not be created by reason of subsection (1).

(6) Section 17(2) and (4) shall apply (with any necessary modifications) in relation to subsection (2)(a) and (b) above.

(7) Where part only of a unit is held under a lease, regulations may modify the application of a provision which –

(a) is made by or by virtue of this Part, and

(b) applies to a unit-holder or a tenant or both.

(8) Section 20(4) shall apply in relation to subsection (2)(c) above.

(9) Where the freehold interest in part only of a commonhold unit is transferred, the part transferred –

(a) becomes a new commonhold unit by virtue of this subsection, or

(b) in a case where the request for consent under subsection (2)(c) states that this paragraph is to apply, becomes part of a commonhold unit specified in the request.

(10) Regulations may make provision, or may require a commonhold community statement to make provision, about –

(a) registration of units created by virtue of subsection (9);

(b) the adaptation of provision made by or by virtue of this Part or by or by virtue of a commonhold community statement to a case where units are created or modified by virtue of subsection (9).

22 Part-unit: charging

(1) It shall not be possible to create a charge over part only of an interest in a commonhold unit.

(2) An instrument or agreement shall be of no effect to the extent that it purports to create a charge in contravention of subsection (1).

(3) Subsection (4) applies where –

(a) land becomes commonhold land or is added to a commonhold unit, and

(b) immediately before that event there is a charge over the land which could not be created after that event by reason of subsection (1).

(4) The charge shall be extinguished by virtue of this subsection to the extent that it could not be created by reason of subsection (1).

25 Definition

(1) In this Part 'common parts' in relation to a commonhold means every part of the commonhold which is not for the time being a commonhold unit in accordance with the commonhold community statement.

(2) A commonhold community statement may make provision in respect of a specified part of the common parts (a 'limited use area') restricting –

(a) the classes of person who may use it;

(b) the kind of use to which it may be put.

(3) A commonhold community statement –

(a) may make provision which has effect only in relation to a limited use area, and

(b) may make different provision for different limited use areas.

26   Use and maintenance

A commonhold community statement must make provision –

(a) regulating the use of the common parts;

(b) requiring the commonhold association to insure the common parts;

(c) requiring the commonhold association to repair and maintain the common parts.

27   Transactions

(1) Nothing in a commonhold community statement shall prevent or restrict –

(a) the transfer by the commonhold association of its freehold estate in any part of the common parts, or

(b) the creation by the commonhold association of an interest in any part of the common parts.

(2) In this section 'interest' does not include –

(a) a charge, or

(b) an interest which arises by virtue of a charge.

28   Charges: general prohibition

(1) It shall not be possible to create a charge over common parts.

(2) An instrument or agreement shall be of no effect to the extent that it purports to create a charge over common parts.

(3) Where by virtue of section 7 or 9 a commonhold association is registered as the proprietor of common parts, a charge which relates wholly or partly to the common parts shall be extinguished by virtue of this subsection to the extent that it relates to the common parts.

(4) Where by virtue of section 30 land vests in a commonhold association following an amendment to a commonhold community statement which has the effect of adding land to the common parts, a charge which relates wholly or partly to the land added shall be extinguished by virtue of this subsection to the extent that it relates to that land.

(5) This section is subject to section 29 (which permits certain mortgages).

29   New legal mortgages

(1) Section 28 shall not apply in relation to a legal mortgage if the creation of the mortgage is approved by a resolution of the commonhold association.

(2) A resolution for the purposes of subsection (1) must be passed –

(a) before the mortgage is created, and

(b) unanimously.

(3) In this section 'legal mortgage' has the meaning given by section 205(1)(xvi) of the Law of Property Act 1925 (c 20) (interpretation).

31   Form and content: general

(1) A commonhold community statement is a document which makes provision in relation to specified land for –

(a) the rights and duties of the commonhold association, and

(b) the rights and duties of the unit-holders.

(2) A commonhold community statement must be in the prescribed form.

(3) A commonhold community statement may –

(a) impose a duty on the commonhold association;

(b) impose a duty on a unit-holder;

(c) make provision about the taking of decisions in connection with the management of the commonhold or any other matter concerning it.

(4) Subsection (3) is subject to –

(a) any provision made by or by virtue of this Part, and

(b) any provision of the memorandum or articles of the commonhold association.

(5) In subsection (3)(a) and (b) 'duty' includes, in particular, a duty –

(a) to pay money;

(b) to undertake works;

(c) to grant access;

(d) to give notice;

(e) to refrain from entering into transactions of a specified kind in relation to a commonhold unit;

(f) to refrain from using the whole or part of a commonhold unit for a specified purpose or for anything other than a specified purpose;

(g) to refrain from undertaking works (including alterations) of a specified kind;

(h) to refrain from causing nuisance or annoyance;

(i) to refrain from specified behaviour;

(j) to indemnify the commonhold association or a unit-holder in respect of costs arising from the breach of a statutory requirement.

(6) Provision in a commonhold community statement imposing a duty to pay money (whether in pursuance of subsection (5)(a) or any other provision made by or by virtue of this Part) may include provision for the payment of interest in the case of late payment.

(7) A duty conferred by a commonhold community statement on a commonhold association or a unit-holder shall not require any other formality.

(8) A commonhold community statement may not provide for the transfer or loss of an interest in land on the occurrence or non-occurrence of a specified event.

(9) Provision made by a commonhold community statement shall be of no effect to the extent that –

(a) it is prohibited by virtue of section 32,

(b) it is inconsistent with any provision made by or by virtue of this Part,

(c) it is inconsistent with anything which is treated as included in the statement by virtue of section 32, or

(d) it is inconsistent with the memorandum or articles of association of the commonhold association.

32   Regulations

(1) Regulations shall make provision about the content of a commonhold community statement. ...

33   Amendment

(1) Regulations under section 32 shall require a commonhold community statement to make provision about how it can be amended. ...

34   Constitution

(1) A commonhold association is a private company limited by guarantee the memorandum of which –

(a) states that an object of the company is to exercise the functions of a commonhold association in relation to specified commonhold land, and

(b) specifies £1 as the amount required to be specified in pursuance of section 2(4) of the Companies Act 1985 (c. 6) (members' guarantee).

(2) Schedule 3 (which makes provision about the constitution of a commonhold association) shall have effect.

35   Duty to manage

(1) The directors of a commonhold association shall exercise their powers so as to permit or facilitate so far as possible –

(a) the exercise by each unit-holder of his rights, and

(b) the enjoyment by each unit-holder of the freehold estate in his unit.

(2) The directors of a commonhold association shall, in particular, use any right, power or procedure conferred or created by virtue of section 37 for the purpose of preventing, remedying or curtailing a failure on the part of a unit-holder to comply with a requirement or duty imposed on him by virtue of the commonhold community statement or a provision of this Part.

(3) But in respect of a particular failure on the part of a unit-holder (the 'defaulter') the directors of a commonhold association –

(a) need not take action if they reasonably think that inaction is in the best interests of establishing or maintaining harmonious relationships between all the unit-holders, and that it will not cause any unit-holder (other than the defaulter) significant loss or significant disadvantage, and

(b) shall have regard to the desirability of using arbitration, mediation or conciliation procedures (including referral under a scheme approved under section 42) instead of legal proceedings wherever possible.

(4) A reference in this section to a unit-holder includes a reference to a tenant of a unit.

37   Enforcement and compensation

(1) Regulations may make provision (including provision conferring jurisdiction on a court) about the exercise or enforcement of a right or duty imposed or conferred by or by virtue of –

(a) a commonhold community statement;

(b) the memorandum or articles of a commonhold association;

(c) a provision made by or by virtue of this Part. …

57   Multiple site commonholds

(1) A commonhold may include two or more parcels of land, whether or not contiguous.

(2) But section 1(1) of this Act is not satisfied in relation to land specified in the memorandum of association of a commonhold association unless a single commonhold community statement makes provision for all the land.

(3) Regulations may make provision about an application under section 2 made jointly by two or more persons, each of whom is the registered freeholder of part of the land to which the application relates. …

61   Home rights

In the following provisions of this Part a reference to a tenant includes a reference to a person who has home rights (within the meaning of section 30(2) of the Family Law Act 1996 (c 27) (matrimonial or civil partnership home)) in respect of a commonhold unit –

(a) section 19,

(b) section 35, and

(c) section 37.

63   The Crown

This Part binds the Crown.

66   Jurisdiction

(1) In this Part 'the court' means the High Court or a county court.

(2) Provision made by or under this Part conferring jurisdiction on a court shall be subject to provision made under section 1 of the Courts and Legal Services Act 1990 (c 41) (allocation of business between High Court and county courts).

(3) A power under this Part to confer jurisdiction on a court includes power to confer jurisdiction on a tribunal established under an enactment.

(4) Rules of court or rules of procedure for a tribunal may make provision about proceedings brought –

(a) under or by virtue of any provision of this Part, or

(b) in relation to commonhold land.

67   The register

(1) In this Part –

'the register' means the register of title to freehold and leasehold land kept under section 1 of the Land Registration Act 2002,

'registered' means registered in the register, and

'the Registrar' means the Chief Land Registrar.

(2) Regulations under any provision of this Part may confer functions on the Registrar (including discretionary functions).

(3) The Registrar shall comply with any direction or requirement given to him or imposed on him under or by virtue of this Part.

(4) Where the Registrar thinks it appropriate in consequence of or for the purpose of anything done or proposed to be done in connection with this Part, he may –

(a) make or cancel an entry on the register;

(b) take any other action.

(5) Subsection (4) is subject to section 6(2).

69   Interpretation

(1) In this Part –

'instrument' includes any document, and

'object' in relation to a commonhold association means an object stated in the association's memorandum of association in accordance with section 2(1)(c) of the Companies Act 1985 (c 6).

(2) In this Part –

(a) a reference to a duty to insure includes a reference to a duty to use the proceeds of insurance for the purpose of rebuilding or reinstating, and

(b) a reference to maintaining property includes a reference to decorating it and to putting it into sound condition.

(3) A provision of the Law of Property Act 1925 (c 20), the Companies Act 1985 (c 6) or the Land Registration Act 2002 (c 9) defining an expression shall apply to the use of the expression in this Part unless the contrary intention appears.

PART 2

LEASEHOLD REFORM

CHAPTER 1

RIGHT TO MANAGE

71   The right to manage

(1) This Chapter makes provision for the acquisition and exercise of rights in relation to the management of premises to which this Chapter applies by a company which, in accordance with this Chapter, may acquire and exercise those rights (referred to in this Chapter as a RTM company).

(2) The rights are to be acquired and exercised subject to and in accordance with this Chapter and are referred to in this Chapter as the right to manage.

72   Premises to which Chapter applies

(1) This Chapter applies to premises if –

(a) they consist of a self-contained building or part of a building, with or without appurtenant property,

(b) they contain two or more flats held by qualifying tenants, and

(c) the total number of flats held by such tenants is not less than two-thirds of the total number of flats contained in the premises.

(2) A building is a self-contained building if it is structurally detached.

(3) A part of a building is a self-contained part of the building if –

(a) it constitutes a vertical division of the building,

(b) the structure of the building is such that it could be redeveloped independently of the rest of the building, and

(c) subsection (4) applies in relation to it.

(4) This subsection applies in relation to a part of a building if the relevant services provided for occupiers of it –

(a) are provided independently of the relevant services provided for occupiers of the rest of the building, or

(b) could be so provided without involving the carrying out of works likely to result in a significant interruption in the provision of any relevant services for occupiers of the rest of the building.

(5) Relevant services are services provided by means of pipes, cables or other fixed installations.

(6) Schedule 6 (premises excepted from this Chapter) has effect.

73   RTM companies

(1) This section specifies what is a RTM company.

(2) A company is a RTM company in relation to premises if –

(a) it is a private company limited by guarantee, and

(b) its memorandum of association states that its object, or one of its objects, is the acquisition and exercise of the right to manage the premises.

(3) But a company is not a RTM company if it is a commonhold association (within the meaning of Part 1).

(4) And a company is not a RTM company in relation to premises if another company is already a RTM company in relation to the premises or to any premises containing or contained in the premises.

(5) If the freehold of any premises is conveyed or transferred to a company which is a RTM company in relation to the premises, or any premises containing or contained in the premises, it ceases to be a RTM company when the conveyance or transfer is executed.

74   RTM companies: membership and regulations

(1) The persons who are entitled to be members of a company which is a RTM company in relation to premises are –

(a) qualifying tenants of flats contained in the premises, and

(b) from the date on which it acquires the right to manage (referred to in this Chapter as the 'acquisition date'), landlords under leases of the whole or any part of the premises.

(2) The appropriate national authority shall make regulations about the content and form of the memorandum of association and articles of association of RTM companies.

(3) A RTM company may adopt provisions of the regulations for its memorandum or articles.

(4) The regulations may include provision which is to have effect for a RTM company whether or not it is adopted by the company.

(5) A provision of the memorandum or articles of a RTM company has no effect to the extent that it is inconsistent with the regulations.

(6) The regulations have effect in relation to a memorandum or articles –

(a) irrespective of the date of the memorandum or articles, but

(b) subject to any transitional provisions of the regulations.

(7) The following provisions of the Companies Act 1985 (c. 6) do not apply to a RTM company –

(a) sections 2(7) and 3 (memorandum), and

(b) section 8 (articles).

75   Qualifying tenants

(1) This section specifies whether there is a qualifying tenant of a flat for the purposes of this Chapter and, if so, who it is.

(2) Subject as follows, a person is the qualifying tenant of a flat if he is tenant of the flat under a long lease.

(3) Subsection (2) does not apply where the lease is a tenancy to which Part 2 of the Landlord and Tenant Act 1954 (c. 56) (business tenancies) applies.

(4) Subsection (2) does not apply where –

(a) the lease was granted by sub-demise out of a superior lease other than a long lease,

(b) the grant was made in breach of the terms of the superior lease, and

(c) there has been no waiver of the breach by the superior landlord.

(5) No flat has more than one qualifying tenant at any one time; and subsections (6) and (7) apply accordingly.

(6) Where a flat is being let under two or more long leases, a tenant under any of those leases which is superior to that held by another is not the qualifying tenant of the flat.

(7) Where a flat is being let to joint tenants under a long lease, the joint tenants shall (subject to subsection (6)) be regarded as jointly being the qualifying tenant of the flat.

76   Long leases

(1) This section and section 77 specify what is a long lease for the purposes of this Chapter.

(2) Subject to section 77, a lease is a long lease if –

(a) it is granted for a term of years certain exceeding 21 years, whether or not it is (or may become) terminable before the end of that term by notice given by or to the tenant, by re-entry or forfeiture or otherwise,

(b) it is for a term fixed by law under a grant with a covenant or obligation for perpetual renewal (but is not a lease by sub-demise from one which is not a long lease),

(c) it takes effect under section 149(6) of the Law of Property Act 1925 (c 20) (leases terminable after a death or marriage),

(d) it was granted in pursuance of the right to buy conferred by Part 5 of the Housing Act 1985 (c 68) or in pursuance of the right to acquire on rent to mortgage terms conferred by that Part of that Act,

(e) it is a shared ownership lease, whether granted in pursuance of that Part of that Act or otherwise, where the tenant's total share is 100 per cent., or

(f) it was granted in pursuance of that Part of that Act as it has effect by virtue of section 17 of the Housing Act 1996 (c 52) (the right to acquire).

(3) 'Shared ownership lease' means a lease –

(a) granted on payment of a premium calculated by reference to a percentage of the value of the demised premises or the cost of providing them, or

(b) under which the tenant (or his personal representatives) will or may be entitled to a sum calculated by reference, directly or indirectly, to the value of those premises.

(4) 'Total share', in relation to the interest of a tenant under a shared ownership lease, means his initial share plus any additional share or shares in the demised premises which he has acquired.

77   Long leases: further provisions

(1) A lease terminable by notice after a death, a marriage or the formation of a civil partnership is not a long lease if –

(a) the notice is capable of being given at any time after the death or marriage of, or the formation of a civil partnership by, the tenant,

(b) the length of the notice is not more than three months, and

(c) the terms of the lease preclude both its assignment otherwise than by virtue of section 92 of the Housing Act 1985 (assignments by way of exchange) and the sub-letting of the whole of the demised premises.

(2) Where the tenant of any property under a long lease, on the coming to an end of the lease, becomes or has become tenant of the property or part of it under any subsequent tenancy (whether by express grant or by implication of law), that tenancy is a long lease irrespective of its terms.

(3) A lease –

(a) granted for a term of years certain not exceeding 21 years, but with a covenant or obligation for renewal without payment of a premium (but not for perpetual renewal), and

(b) renewed on one or more occasions so as to bring to more than 21 years the total of the terms granted (including any interval between the end of a lease and the grant of a renewal),

is to be treated as if the term originally granted had been one exceeding 21 years.

(4) Where a long lease –

(a) is or was continued for any period under Part 1 of the Landlord and Tenant Act 1954 (c 56) or under Schedule 10 to the Local Government and Housing Act 1989 (c 42), or

(b) was continued for any period under the Leasehold Property (Temporary Provisions) Act 1951 (c 38),

it remains a long lease during that period.

(5) Where in the case of a flat there are at any time two or more separate leases, with the same landlord and the same tenant, and –

(a) the property comprised in one of those leases consists of either the flat or a part of it (in either case with or without appurtenant property), and

(b) the property comprised in every other lease consists of either a part of the flat (with or without appurtenant property) or appurtenant property only,

there shall be taken to be a single long lease of the property comprised in such of those leases as are long leases.

78 Notice inviting participation

(1) Before making a claim to acquire the right to manage any premises, a RTM company must give notice to each person who at the time when the notice is given –

(a) is the qualifying tenant of a flat contained in the premises, but

(b) neither is nor has agreed to become a member of the RTM company.

(2) A notice given under this section (referred to in this Chapter as a 'notice of invitation to participate') must –

(a) state that the RTM company intends to acquire the right to manage the premises,

(b) state the names of the members of the RTM company,

(c) invite the recipients of the notice to become members of the company, and

(d) contain such other particulars (if any) as may be required to be contained in notices of invitation to participate by regulations made by the appropriate national authority.

(3) A notice of invitation to participate must also comply with such requirements (if any) about the form of notices of invitation to participate as may be prescribed by regulations so made.

(4) A notice of invitation to participate must either –

(a) be accompanied by a copy of the memorandum of association and articles of association of the RTM company, or

(b) include a statement about inspection and copying of the memorandum of association and articles of association of the RTM company.

(5) A statement under subsection (4)(b) must –

(a) specify a place (in England or Wales) at which the memorandum of association and articles of association may be inspected,

(b) specify as the times at which they may be inspected periods of at least two hours on each of at least three days (including a Saturday or Sunday or both) within the seven days beginning with the day following that on which the notice is given,

(c) specify a place (in England or Wales) at which, at any time within those seven days, a copy of the memorandum of association and articles of association may be ordered, and

(d) specify a fee for the provision of an ordered copy, not exceeding the reasonable cost of providing it.

(6) Where a notice given to a person includes a statement under subsection (4)(b), the notice is to be treated as not having been given to him if he is not allowed to undertake an inspection, or is not provided with a copy, in accordance with the statement.

(7) A notice of invitation to participate is not invalidated by any inaccuracy in any of the particulars required by or by virtue of this section.

79   Notice of claim to acquire right

(1) A claim to acquire the right to manage any premises is made by giving notice of the claim (referred to in this Chapter as a 'claim notice'); and in this Chapter the 'relevant date', in relation to any claim to acquire the right to manage, means the date on which notice of the claim is given.

(2) The claim notice may not be given unless each person required to be given a notice of invitation to participate has been given such a notice at least 14 days before.

(3) The claim notice must be given by a RTM company which complies with subsection (4) or (5).

(4) If on the relevant date there are only two qualifying tenants of flats contained in the premises, both must be members of the RTM company.

(5) In any other case, the membership of the RTM company must on the relevant date include a number of qualifying tenants of flats contained in the premises which is not less than one-half of the total number of flats so contained.

(6) The claim notice must be given to each person who on the relevant date is –

(a) landlord under a lease of the whole or any part of the premises,

(b) party to such a lease otherwise than as landlord or tenant, or

(c) a manager appointed under Part 2 of the Landlord and Tenant Act 1987 (c

31) (referred to in this Part as 'the 1987 Act') to act in relation to the premises, or any premises containing or contained in the premises.

(7) Subsection (6) does not require the claim notice to be given to a person who cannot be found or whose identity cannot be ascertained; but if this subsection means that the claim notice is not required to be given to anyone at all, section 85 applies.

(8) A copy of the claim notice must be given to each person who on the relevant date is the qualifying tenant of a flat contained in the premises.

(9) Where a manager has been appointed under Part 2 of the 1987 Act to act in relation to the premises, or any premises containing or contained in the premises, a copy of the claim notice must also be given to the leasehold valuation tribunal or court by which he was appointed.

84   Counter-notices

(1) A person who is given a claim notice by a RTM company under section 79(6) may give a notice (referred to in this Chapter as a 'counter-notice') to the company no later than the date specified in the claim notice under section 80(6).

(2) A counter-notice is a notice containing a statement either –

(a) admitting that the RTM company was on the relevant date entitled to acquire the right to manage the premises specified in the claim notice, or

(b) alleging that, by reason of a specified provision of this Chapter, the RTM company was on that date not so entitled,

and containing such other particulars (if any) as may be required to be contained in counter-notices, and complying with such requirements (if any) about the form of counter-notices, as may be prescribed by regulations made by the appropriate national authority.

(3) Where the RTM company has been given one or more counter-notices containing a statement such as is mentioned in subsection (2)(b), the company may apply to a leasehold valuation tribunal for a determination that it was on the relevant date entitled to acquire the right to manage the premises.

(4) An application under subsection (3) must be made not later than the end of the period of two months beginning with the day on which the counter-notice (or, where more than one, the last of the counter-notices) was given.

(5) Where the RTM company has been given one or more counter-notices containing a statement such as is mentioned in subsection (2)(b), the RTM company does not acquire the right to manage the premises unless –

(a) on an application under subsection (3) it is finally determined that the company was on the relevant date entitled to acquire the right to manage the premises, or

(b) the person by whom the counter-notice was given agrees, or the persons by whom the counter-notices were given agree, in writing that the company was so entitled.

(6) If on an application under subsection (3) it is finally determined that the company was not on the relevant date entitled to acquire the right to manage the premises, the claim notice ceases to have effect.

(7) A determination on an application under subsection (3) becomes final –

(a) if not appealed against, at the end of the period for bringing an appeal, or

(b) if appealed against, at the time when the appeal (or any further appeal) is disposed of.

(8) An appeal is disposed of –

(a) if it is determined and the period for bringing any further appeal has ended, or

(b) if it is abandoned or otherwise ceases to have effect.

95 Introductory

Sections 96 to 103 apply where the right to manage premises has been acquired by a RTM company (and has not ceased to be exercisable by it).

96 Management functions under leases

(1) This section and section 97 apply in relation to management functions relating to the whole or any part of the premises.

(2) Management functions which a person who is landlord under a lease of the whole or any part of the premises has under the lease are instead functions of the RTM company.

(3) And where a person is party to a lease of the whole or any part of the premises otherwise than as landlord or tenant, management functions of his under the lease are also instead functions of the RTM company.

(4) Accordingly, any provisions of the lease making provision about the relationship of –

(a) a person who is landlord under the lease, and

(b) a person who is party to the lease otherwise than as landlord or tenant,

in relation to such functions do not have effect.

(5) 'Management functions' are functions with respect to services, repairs, maintenance, improvements, insurance and management.

(6) But this section does not apply in relation to –

(a) functions with respect to a matter concerning only a part of the premises consisting of a flat or other unit not held under a lease by a qualifying tenant, or

(b) functions relating to re-entry or forfeiture.

(7) An order amending subsection (5) or (6) may be made by the appropriate national authority.

97 Management functions: supplementary

(1) Any obligation owed by the RTM company by virtue of section 96 to a tenant under a lease of the whole or any part of the premises is also owed to each person who is landlord under the lease.

(2) A person who is –

(a) landlord under a lease of the whole or any part of the premises,

(b) party to such a lease otherwise than as landlord or tenant, or

(c) a manager appointed under Part 2 of the 1987 Act to act in relation to the premises, or any premises containing or contained in the premises,

is not entitled to do anything which the RTM company is required or empowered to do under the lease by virtue of section 96, except in accordance with an agreement made by him and the RTM company.

(3) But subsection (2) does not prevent any person from insuring the whole or any part of the premises at his own expense.

(4) So far as any function of a tenant under a lease of the whole or any part of the premises –

(a) relates to the exercise of any function under the lease which is a function of the RTM company by virtue of section 96, and

(b) is exercisable in relation to a person who is landlord under the lease or party to the lease otherwise than as landlord or tenant,

it is instead exercisable in relation to the RTM company.

(5) But subsection (4) does not require or permit the payment to the RTM company of so much of any service charges payable by a tenant under a lease of the whole or any part of the premises as is required to meet costs incurred before the right to manage was acquired by the RTM company in connection with matters for which the service charges are payable.

100 Enforcement of tenant covenants

(1) This section applies in relation to the enforcement of untransferred tenant covenants of a lease of the whole or any part of the premises.

(2) Untransferred tenant covenants are enforceable by the RTM company, as well as by any other person by whom they are enforceable apart from this section, in the same manner as they are enforceable by any other such person.

(3) But the RTM company may not exercise any function of re-entry or forfeiture.

(4) In this Chapter 'tenant covenant', in relation to a lease, means a covenant falling

to be complied with by a tenant under the lease; and a tenant covenant is untransferred if, apart from this section, it would not be enforceable by the RTM company.

(5) Any power under a lease of a person who is –

(a) landlord under the lease, or

(b) party to the lease otherwise than as landlord or tenant,

to enter any part of the premises to determine whether a tenant is complying with any untransferred tenant covenant is exercisable by the RTM company (as well as by the landlord or party).

101 Tenant covenants: monitoring and reporting

(1) This section applies in relation to failures to comply with tenant covenants of leases of the whole or any part of the premises.

(2) The RTM company must –

(a) keep under review whether tenant covenants of leases of the whole or any part of the premises are being complied with, and

(b) report to any person who is landlord under such a lease any failure to comply with any tenant covenant of the lease.

(3) The report must be made before the end of the period of three months beginning with the day on which the failure to comply comes to the attention of the RTM company.

(4) But the RTM company need not report to a landlord a failure to comply with a tenant covenant if –

(a) the failure has been remedied,

(b) reasonable compensation has been paid in respect of the failure, or

(c) the landlord has notified the RTM company that it need not report to him failures of the description of the failure concerned.

102 Statutory functions

(1) Schedule 7 (provision for the operation of certain enactments with modifications) has effect.

(2) Other enactments relating to leases (including enactments contained in this Act or any Act passed after this Act) have effect with any such modifications as are prescribed by regulations made by the appropriate national authority.

109 Powers of trustees in relation to right

(1) Where trustees are the qualifying tenant of a flat contained in any premises, their powers under the instrument regulating the trusts include power to be a member of a RTM company for the purpose of the acquisition and exercise of the right to manage the premises.

(2) But subsection (1) does not apply where the instrument regulating the trusts contains an explicit direction to the contrary.

(3) The power conferred by subsection (1) is exercisable with the same consent or on the same direction (if any) as may be required for the exercise of the trustees' powers (or ordinary powers) of investment.

(4) The purposes –

(a) authorised for the application of capital money by section 73 of the Settled Land Act 1925 (c. 18), and

(b) authorised by section 71 of that Act as purposes for which moneys may be raised by mortgage,

include the payment of any expenses incurred by a tenant for life or statutory owner as a member of a RTM company.

112 Definitions

(1) In this Chapter –

'appurtenant property', in relation to a building or part of a building or a flat, means any garage, outhouse, garden, yard or appurtenances belonging to, or usually enjoyed with, the building or part or flat,

'copy', in relation to a document in which information is recorded, means anything onto which the information has been copied by whatever means and whether directly or indirectly,

'document' means anything in which information is recorded,

'dwelling' means a building or part of a building occupied or intended to be occupied as a separate dwelling,

'flat' means a separate set of premises (whether or not on the same floor) –

(a) which forms part of a building,

(b) which is constructed or adapted for use for the purposes of a dwelling, and

(c) either the whole or a material part of which lies above or below some other part of the building,

'relevant costs' has the meaning given by section 18 of the 1985 Act,

'service charge' has the meaning given by that section, and

'unit' means –

(a) a flat,

(b) any other separate set of premises which is constructed or adapted for use for the purposes of a dwelling, or

(c) a separate set of premises let, or intended for letting, on a tenancy to which Part 2 of the Landlord and Tenant Act 1954 (c. 56) (business tenancies) applies.

(2) In this Chapter 'lease' and 'tenancy' have the same meaning and both expressions include (where the context permits) –

(a) a sub-lease or sub-tenancy, and

(b) an agreement for a lease or tenancy (or for a sub-lease or sub-tenancy),

but do not include a tenancy at will or at sufferance.

(3) The expressions 'landlord' and 'tenant', and references to letting, to the grant of a lease or to covenants or the terms of a lease, shall be construed accordingly.

(4) In this Chapter any reference (however expressed) to the lease held by the qualifying tenant of a flat is a reference to a lease held by him under which the demised premises consist of or include the flat (whether with or without one or more other flats).

(5) Where two or more persons jointly constitute either the landlord or the tenant or qualifying tenant in relation to a lease of a flat, any reference in this Chapter to the landlord or to the tenant or qualifying tenant is (unless the context otherwise requires) a reference to both or all of the persons who jointly constitute the landlord or the tenant or qualifying tenant, as the case may require.

(6) In the case of a lease which derives (in accordance with section 77(5)) from two or more separate leases, any reference in this Chapter to the date of the commencement of the term for which the lease was granted shall, if the terms of the separate leases commenced at different dates, have effect as references to the date of the commencement of the term of the lease with the earliest date of commencement.

CHAPTER 5

OTHER PROVISIONS ABOUT LEASES

164 Insurance otherwise than with landlord's insurer

(1) This section applies where a long lease of a house requires the tenant to insure the house with an insurer nominated or approved by the landlord ('the landlord's insurer').

(2) The tenant is not required to effect the insurance with the landlord's insurer if –

(a) the house is insured under a policy of insurance issued by an authorised insurer,

(b) the policy covers the interests of both the landlord and the tenant,

(c) the policy covers all the risks which the lease requires be covered by insurance provided by the landlord's insurer,

(d) the amount of the cover is not less than that which the lease requires to be provided by such insurance, and

(e) the tenant satisfies subsection (3).

(3) To satisfy this subsection the tenant –

(a) must have given a notice of cover to the landlord before the end of the period of fourteen days beginning with the relevant date, and

(b) if (after that date) he has been requested to do so by a new landlord, must have given a notice of cover to him within the period of fourteen days beginning with the day on which the request was given.

(4) For the purposes of subsection (3) –

(a) if the policy has not been renewed the relevant date is the day on which it took effect and if it has been renewed it is the day from which it was last renewed, and

(b) a person is a new landlord on any day if he acquired the interest of the previous landlord under the lease on a disposal made by him during the period of one month ending with that day.

(5) A notice of cover is a notice specifying –

(a) the name of the insurer,

(b) the risks covered by the policy,

(c) the amount and period of the cover, and

(d) such further information as may be prescribed.

(6) A notice of cover –

(a) must be in the prescribed form, and

(b) may be sent by post. ...

(10) In this section –

'authorised insurer', in relation to a policy of insurance, means a person who may carry on in the United Kingdom the business of effecting or carrying out contracts of insurance of the sort provided under the policy without contravening the prohibition imposed by section 19 of the Financial Services and Markets Act 2000 (c 8),

'house' has the same meaning as for the purposes of Part 1 of the 1967 Act,

'landlord' and 'tenant' have the same meanings as in Chapter 1 of this Part,

'long lease' has the meaning given by sections 76 and 77 of this Act, and

'prescribed' means prescribed by regulations made by the appropriate national authority.

100 Requirement to notify long leaseholders that rent is due

(1) A tenant under a long lease of a dwelling is not liable to make a payment of rent under the lease unless the landlord has given him a notice relating to the payment; and the date on which he is liable to make the payment is that specified in the notice.

(2) The notice must specify –

(a) the amount of the payment,

(b) the date on which the tenant is liable to make it, and

(c) if different from that date, the date on which he would have been liable to make it in accordance with the lease,

and shall contain any such further information as may be prescribed.

(3) The date on which the tenant is liable to make the payment must not be –

(a) either less than 30 days or more than 60 days after the day on which the notice is given, or

(b) before that on which he would have been liable to make it in accordance with the lease.

(4) If the date on which the tenant is liable to make the payment is after that on which he would have been liable to make it in accordance with the lease, any provisions of the lease relating to non-payment or late payment of rent have effect accordingly.

(5) The notice –

(a) must be in the prescribed form, and

(b) may be sent by post. ...

(7) In this section 'rent' does not include –

(a) a service charge (within the meaning of section 18(1) of the 1985 Act), or

(b) an administration charge (within the meaning of Part 1 of Schedule 11 to this Act).

(8) In this section 'long lease of a dwelling' does not include –

(a) a tenancy to which Part 2 of the Landlord and Tenant Act 1954 (c 56) (business tenancies) applies,

(b) a tenancy of an agricultural holding within the meaning of the Agricultural Holdings Act 1986 (c 5) in relation to which that Act applies, or

(c) a farm business tenancy within the meaning of the Agricultural Tenancies Act 1995 (c 8).

(9) In this section –

'dwelling' has the same meaning as in the 1985 Act,

'landlord' and 'tenant' have the same meanings as in Chapter 1 of this Part,

'long lease' has the meaning given by sections 76 and 77 of this Act, and

'prescribed' means prescribed by regulations made by the appropriate national authority.

167 Failure to pay small amount for short period

(1) A landlord under a long lease of a dwelling may not exercise a right of re-entry or forfeiture for failure by a tenant to pay an amount consisting of rent, service

charges or administration charges (or a combination of them) ('the unpaid amount') unless the unpaid amount –

(a) exceeds the prescribed sum, or

(b) consists of or includes an amount which has been payable for more than a prescribed period.

(2) The sum prescribed under subsection (1)(a) must not exceed £500.

(3) If the unpaid amount includes a default charge, it is to be treated for the purposes of subsection (1)(a) as reduced by the amount of the charge; and for this purpose 'default charge' means an administration charge payable in respect of the tenant's failure to pay any part of the unpaid amount.

(4) In this section 'long lease of a dwelling' does not include –

(a) a tenancy to which Part 2 of the Landlord and Tenant Act 1954 (c 56) (business tenancies) applies,

(b) a tenancy of an agricultural holding within the meaning of the Agricultural Holdings Act 1986 (c 5) in relation to which that Act applies, or

(c) a farm business tenancy within the meaning of the Agricultural Tenancies Act 1995 (c 8).

(5) In this section –

'administration charge' has the same meaning as in Part 1 of Schedule 11,

'dwelling' has the same meaning as in the 1985 Act,

'landlord' and 'tenant' have the same meaning as in Chapter 1 of this Part,

'long lease' has the meaning given by sections 76 and 77 of this Act, except that a shared ownership lease is a long lease whatever the tenant's total share,

'prescribed' means prescribed by regulations made by the appropriate national authority, and

'service charge' has the meaning given by section 18(1) of the 1985 Act.

168 No forfeiture notice before determination of breach

(1) A landlord under a long lease of a dwelling may not serve a notice under section 146(1) of the Law of Property Act 1925 (c 20) (restriction on forfeiture) in respect of a breach by a tenant of a covenant or condition in the lease unless subsection (2) is satisfied.

(2) This subsection is satisfied if –

(a) it has been finally determined on an application under subsection (4) that the breach has occurred,

(b) the tenant has admitted the breach, or

(c) a court in any proceedings, or an arbitral tribunal in proceedings pursuant to a post-dispute arbitration agreement, has finally determined that the breach has occurred.

(3) But a notice may not be served by virtue of subsection (2)(a) or (c) until after the end of the period of 14 days beginning with the day after that on which the final determination is made.

(4) A landlord under a long lease of a dwelling may make an application to a leasehold valuation tribunal for a determination that a breach of a covenant or condition in the lease has occurred.

(5) But a landlord may not make an application under subsection (4) in respect of a matter which –

(a) has been, or is to be, referred to arbitration pursuant to a post-dispute arbitration agreement to which the tenant is a party,

(b) has been the subject of determination by a court, or

(c) has been the subject of determination by an arbitral tribunal pursuant to a post-dispute arbitration agreement.

169   Section 168: supplementary

(1) An agreement by a tenant under a long lease of a dwelling (other than a post-dispute arbitration agreement) is void in so far as it purports to provide for a determination –

(a) in a particular manner, or

(b) on particular evidence,

of any question which may be the subject of an application under section 168(4).

(2) For the purposes of section 168 it is finally determined that a breach of a covenant or condition in a lease has occurred –

(a) if a decision that it has occurred is not appealed against or otherwise challenged, at the end of the period for bringing an appeal or other challenge, or

(b) if such a decision is appealed against or otherwise challenged and not set aside in consequence of the appeal or other challenge, at the time specified in subsection (3).

(3) The time referred to in subsection (2)(b) is the time when the appeal or other challenge is disposed of –

(a) by the determination of the appeal or other challenge and the expiry of the time for bringing a subsequent appeal (if any), or

(b) by its being abandoned or otherwise ceasing to have effect.

(4) In section 168 and this section 'long lease of a dwelling' does not include –

(a) a tenancy to which Part 2 of the Landlord and Tenant Act 1954 (c 56) (business tenancies) applies,

(b) a tenancy of an agricultural holding within the meaning of the Agricultural Holdings Act 1986 (c 5) in relation to which that Act applies, or

(c) a farm business tenancy within the meaning of the Agricultural Tenancies Act 1995 (c 8).

(5) In section 168 and this section –

'arbitration agreement' and 'arbitral tribunal' have the same meaning as in Part 1 of the Arbitration Act 1996 (c 23) and 'post-dispute arbitration agreement', in relation to any breach (or alleged breach), means an arbitration agreement made after the breach has occurred (or is alleged to have occurred),

'dwelling' has the same meaning as in the 1985 Act,

'landlord' and 'tenant' have the same meaning as in Chapter 1 of this Part, and

'long lease' has the meaning given by sections 76 and 77 of this Act, except that a shared ownership lease is a long lease whatever the tenant's total share.

(6) Section 146(7) of the Law of Property Act 1925 (c 20) applies for the purposes of section 168 and this section.

(7) Nothing in section 168 affects the service of a notice under section 146(1) of the Law of Property Act 1925 in respect of a failure to pay –

(a) a service charge (within the meaning of section 18(1) of the 1985 Act), or

(b) an administration charge (within the meaning of Part 1 of Schedule 11 to this Act).

CHAPTER 6

LEASEHOLD VALUATION TRIBUNALS

173 Leasehold valuation tribunals

(1) Any jurisdiction conferred on a leasehold valuation tribunal by or under any enactment is exercisable by a rent assessment committee constituted in accordance with Schedule 10 to the Rent Act 1977 (c 42).

(2) When so constituted for exercising any such jurisdiction a rent assessment committee is known as a leasehold valuation tribunal.

175 Appeals

(1) A party to proceedings before a leasehold valuation tribunal may appeal to the Lands Tribunal from a decision of the leasehold valuation tribunal.

(2) But the appeal may be made only with the permission of –

(a) the leasehold valuation tribunal, or

(b) the Lands Tribunal.

(3) And it must be made within the time specified by rules under section 3(6) of the Lands Tribunal Act 1949 (c 42).

(4) On the appeal the Lands Tribunal may exercise any power which was available to the leasehold valuation tribunal.

(5) And a decision of the Lands Tribunal on the appeal may be enforced in the same way as a decision of the leasehold valuation tribunal.

(6) The Lands Tribunal may not order a party to the appeal to pay costs incurred by another party in connection with the appeal unless he has, in the opinion of the Lands Tribunal, acted frivolously, vexatiously, abusively, disruptively or otherwise unreasonably in connection with the appeal.

(7) In such a case the amount he may be ordered to pay shall not exceed the maximum amount which a party to proceedings before a leasehold valuation tribunal may be ordered to pay in the proceedings under or by virtue of paragraph 10(3) of Schedule 12.

(8) No appeal lies from a decision of a leasehold valuation tribunal to the High Court by virtue of section 11(1) of the Tribunals and Inquiries Act 1992 (c 53).

(9) And no case may be stated for the opinion of the High Court in respect of such a decision by virtue of that provision.

(10) For the purposes of section 3(4) of the Lands Tribunal Act 1949 (which enables a person aggrieved by a decision of the Lands Tribunal to appeal to the Court of Appeal) a leasehold valuation tribunal is not a person aggrieved.

CHAPTER 7

GENERAL

179 Interpretation

(1) In this Part 'the appropriate national authority' means –

(a) the Secretary of State (as respects England), and

(b) the National Assembly for Wales (as respects Wales).

(2) In this Part –

'the 1967 Act' means the Leasehold Reform Act 1967 (c 88),

'the 1985 Act' means the Landlord and Tenant Act 1985 (c 70),

'the 1987 Act' means the Landlord and Tenant Act 1987 (c 31), and

'the 1993 Act' means the Leasehold Reform, Housing and Urban Development Act 1993 (c 28).

SCHEDULE 1

APPLICATION FOR REGISTRATION: DOCUMENTS

1. This Schedule lists the documents which are required by section 2 to accompany an application for the registration of a freehold estate as a freehold estate in commonhold land.

2. The commonhold association's certificate of incorporation under section 13 of the Companies Act 1985 (c. 6).

3. Any altered certificate of incorporation issued under section 28 of that Act.

4. The memorandum and articles of association of the commonhold association.

5. The commonhold community statement.

6. – (1) Where consent is required under or by virtue of section 3 –

(a) the consent,

(b) an order of a court by virtue of section 3(2)(f) dispensing with the requirement for consent, or

(c) evidence of deemed consent by virtue of section 3(2)(e).

(2) In the case of a conditional order under section 3(2)(f), the order must be accompanied by evidence that the condition has been complied with.

7. A certificate given by the directors of the commonhold association that –

(a) the memorandum and articles of association submitted with the application comply with regulations under paragraph 2(1) of Schedule 3,

(b) the commonhold community statement submitted with the application satisfies the requirements of this Part,

(c) the application satisfies Schedule 2,

(d) the commonhold association has not traded, and

(e) the commonhold association has not incurred any liability which has not been discharged.

SCHEDULE 2

LAND WHICH MAY NOT BE COMMONHOLD LAND

1. – (1) Subject to sub-paragraph (2), an application may not be made under section 2 wholly or partly in relation to land above ground level ('raised land') unless all the land between the ground and the raised land is the subject of the same application.

(2) An application for the addition of land to a commonhold in accordance with section 41 may be made wholly or partly in relation to raised land if all the land between the ground and the raised land forms part of the commonhold to which the raised land is to be added.

2. An application may not be made under section 2 wholly or partly in relation to land if –

(a) it is agricultural land within the meaning of the Agriculture Act 1947 (c 48),

(b) it is comprised in a tenancy of an agricultural holding within the meaning of the Agricultural Holdings Act 1986 (c 5), or

(c) it is comprised in a farm business tenancy for the purposes of the Agricultural Tenancies Act 1995 (c 8).

3. – (1) An application may not be made under section 2 if an estate in the whole or part of the land to which the application relates is a contingent estate.

(2) An estate is contingent for the purposes of this paragraph if (and only if) –

(a) it is liable to revert to or vest in a person other than the present registered proprietor on the occurrence or non-occurrence of a particular event, and

(b) the reverter or vesting would occur by operation of law as a result of an enactment listed in sub-paragraph (3).

(3) The enactments are –

(a) the School Sites Act 1841 (c 38) (conveyance for use as school),

(b) the Lands Clauses Acts (compulsory purchase),

(c) the Literary and Scientific Institutions Act 1854 (c 112) (sites for institutions), and

(d) the Places of Worship Sites Act 1873 (c 50) (sites for places of worship).

(4) Regulations may amend sub-paragraph (3) so as to –

(a) add an enactment to the list, or

(b) remove an enactment from the list.

SCHEDULE 6

PREMISES EXCLUDED FROM RIGHT TO MANAGE

1. – (1) This Chapter does not apply to premises falling within section 72(1) if the internal floor area –

(a) of any non-residential part, or

(b) (where there is more than one such part) of those parts (taken together),

exceeds 25 per cent of the internal floor area of the premises (taken as a whole).

(2) A part of premises is a non-residential part if it is neither –

(a) occupied, or intended to be occupied, for residential purposes, nor

(b) comprised in any common parts of the premises.

(3) Where in the case of any such premises any part of the premises (such as, for example, a garage, parking space or storage area) is used, or intended for use, in conjunction with a particular dwelling contained in the premises (and accordingly is not comprised in any common parts of the premises), it shall be taken to be occupied, or intended to be occupied, for residential purposes.

(4) For the purpose of determining the internal floor area of a building or of any part of a building, the floor or floors of the building or part shall be taken to extend (without interruption) throughout the whole of the interior of the building or part,

except that the area of any common parts of the building or part shall be disregarded.

2. Where different persons own the freehold of different parts of premises falling within section 72(1), this Chapter does not apply to the premises if any of those parts is a self-contained part of a building.

3. – (1) This Chapter does not apply to premises falling within section 72(1) if the premises –

(a) have a resident landlord, and

(b) do not contain more than four units.

(2) Premises have a resident landlord if –

(a) the premises are not, and do not form part of, a purpose-built block of flats (that is, a building which, as constructed, contained two or more flats),

(b) a relevant freeholder, or an adult member of a relevant freeholder's family, occupies a qualifying flat as his only or principal home, and

(c) sub-paragraph (4) or (5) is satisfied.

(3) A person is a relevant freeholder, in relation to any premises, if he owns the freehold of the whole or any part of the premises.

(4) This sub-paragraph is satisfied if –

(a) the relevant freeholder, or

(b) the adult member of his family,

has throughout the last twelve months occupied the flat as his only or principal home.

(5) This sub-paragraph is satisfied if –

(a) immediately before the date when the relevant freeholder acquired his interest in the premises, the premises were premises with a resident landlord, and

(b) he, or an adult member of his family, entered into occupation of the flat during the period of 28 days beginning with that date and has occupied the flat as his only or principal home ever since.

(6) 'Qualifying flat', in relation to any premises and a relevant freeholder or an adult member of his family, means a flat or other unit used as a dwelling –

(a) which is contained in the premises, and

(b) the freehold of the whole of which is owned by the relevant freeholder.

(7) Where the interest of a relevant freeholder in any premises is held on trust, the references in sub-paragraphs (2), (4) and (5)(b) to a relevant freeholder are to a person having an interest under the trust (whether or not also a trustee).

(8) A person is an adult member of another's family if he is –

(a) the other's spouse or civil partner,

(b) a son, daughter, son-in-law or daughter-in-law of the other, or of the other's spouse or civil partner, who has attained the age of 18, or

(c) the father or mother of the other or of the other's spouse or civil partner;

and 'son' and 'daughter' include stepson and stepdaughter ('son-in-law' and 'daughter-in-law' being construed accordingly).

4. – (1) This Chapter does not apply to premises falling within section 72(1) if a local housing authority is the immediate landlord of any of the qualifying tenants of flats contained in the premises.

(2) 'Local housing authority' has the meaning given by section 1 of the Housing Act 1985 (c 68).

5. – (1) This Chapter does not apply to premises falling within section 72(1) at any time if –

(a) the right to manage the premises is at that time exercisable by a RTM company, or

(b) that right has been so exercisable but has ceased to be so exercisable less than four years before that time.

(2) Sub-paragraph (1)(b) does not apply where the right to manage the premises ceased to be exercisable by virtue of section 73(5).

(3) A leasehold valuation tribunal may, on an application made by a RTM company, determine that sub-paragraph (1)(b) is not to apply in any case if it considers that it would be unreasonable for it to apply in the circumstances of the case.

SCHEDULE 7

RIGHT TO MANAGE: STATUTORY PROVISIONS

1. – (1) Section 19 of the Landlord and Tenant Act 1927 (c 36) (covenants not to assign without approval etc.) has effect with the modifications provided by this paragraph.

(2) Subsection (1) applies as if –

(a) the reference to the landlord, and

(b) the final reference to the lessor,

were to the RTM company.

(3) Subsection (2) applies as if the reference to the payment of a reasonable sum in respect of any damage to or diminution in the value of the premises or neighbouring premises belonging to the landlord were omitted.

(4) Subsection (3) applies as if –

(a) the first and final references to the landlord were to the RTM company, and

(b) the reference to the right of the landlord to require payment of a reasonable sum in respect of any damage to or diminution in the value of the premises or neighbouring premises belonging to him were omitted.

2. – (1) Section 4 of the Defective Premises Act 1972 (c 35) (landlord's duty of care by virtue of obligation or right to repair demised premises) has effect with the modifications provided by this paragraph.

(2) References to the landlord (apart from the first reference in subsections (1) and (4)) are to the RTM company.

(3) The reference to the material time is to the acquisition date.

3. – (1) The obligations imposed on a lessor by virtue of section 11 (repairing obligations in short leases) of the Landlord and Tenant Act 1985 (c 70) (referred to in this Part as 'the 1985 Act') are, so far as relating to any lease of any flat or other unit contained in the premises, instead obligations of the RTM company.

(2) The RTM company owes to any person who is in occupation of a flat or other unit contained in the premises otherwise than under a lease the same obligations as would be imposed on it by virtue of section 11 if that person were a lessee under a lease of the flat or other unit.

(3) But sub-paragraphs (1) and (2) do not apply to an obligation to the extent that it relates to a matter concerning only the flat or other unit concerned.

(4) The obligations imposed on the RTM company by virtue of sub-paragraph (1) in relation to any lease are owed to the lessor (as well as to the lessee).

(5) Subsections (3A) to (5) of section 11 have effect with the modifications that are appropriate in consequence of sub-paragraphs (1) to (3).

(6) The references in subsection (6) of section 11 to the lessor include the RTM company; and a person who is in occupation of a flat or other unit contained in the premises otherwise than under a lease has, in relation to the flat or other unit, the same obligation as that imposed on a lessee by virtue of that subsection.

(7) The reference to the lessor in section 12(1)(a) of the 1985 Act (restriction on contracting out of section 11) includes the RTM company.

4. – (1) Sections 18 to 30 of the 1985 Act (service charges) have effect with the modifications provided by this paragraph.

(2) References to the landlord are to the RTM company.

(3) References to a tenant of a dwelling include a person who is landlord under a lease of the whole or any part of the premises (so that sums paid by him in pursuance of section 103 of this Act are service charges).

(4) Section 22(5) applies as if paragraph (a) were omitted and the person referred to in paragraph (b) were a person who receives service charges on behalf of the RTM company.

(5) Section 26 does not apply. ...

As amended by the Civil Partnership Act 2004, ss81, 82, Schedule 8, paras 64–66, Schedule 9, Pt 2, para 24.

GENDER RECOGNITION ACT 2004
(2004 c 7)

1   Applications

(1) A person of either gender who is aged at least 18 may make an application for a gender recognition certificate on the basis of –

(a) living in the other gender, or

(b) having changed gender under the law of a country or territory outside the United Kingdom.

(2) In this Act 'the acquired gender', in relation to a person by whom an application under subsection (1) is or has been made, means –

(a) in the case of an application under paragraph (a) of that subsection, the gender in which the person is living, or

(b) in the case of an application under paragraph (b) of that subsection, the gender to which the person has changed under the law of the country or territory concerned.

(3) An application under subsection (1) is to be determined by a Gender Recognition Panel. …

15   Succession, etc

The fact that a person's gender has become the acquired gender under this Act does not affect the disposal or devolution of property under a will or other instrument made before the appointed day.

16   Peerages, etc

The fact that a person's gender has become the acquired gender under this Act –

(a) does not affect the descent of any peerage or dignity or title of honour, and

(b) does not affect the devolution of any property limited (expressly or not) by a will or other instrument to devolve (as nearly as the law permits) along with any peerage or dignity or title of honour unless an intention that it should do so is expressed in the will or other instrument.

17   Trustees and personal representatives

(1) A trustee or personal representative is not under a duty, by virtue of the law

relating to trusts or the administration of estates, to enquire, before conveying or distributing any property, whether a full gender recognition certificate has been issued to any person or revoked (if that fact could affect entitlement to the property).

(2) A trustee or personal representative is not liable to any person by reason of a conveyance or distribution of the property made without regard to whether a full gender recognition certificate has been issued to any person or revoked if the trustee or personal representative has not received notice of the fact before the conveyance or distribution.

(3) This section does not prejudice the right of a person to follow the property, or any property representing it, into the hands of another person who has received it unless that person has purchased it for value in good faith and without notice.

18   Orders where expectations defeated

(1) This section applies where the disposition or devolution of any property under a will or other instrument (made on or after the appointed day) is different from what it would be but for the fact that a person's gender has become the acquired gender under this Act.

(2) A person may apply to the High Court ... for an order on the ground of being adversely affected by the different disposition or devolution of the property.

(3) The court may, if it is satisfied that it is just to do so, make in relation to any person benefiting from the different disposition or devolution of the property such order as it considers appropriate.

(4) An order may, in particular, make provision for –

   (a) the payment of a lump sum to the applicant,

   (b) the transfer of property to the applicant,

   (c) the settlement of property for the benefit of the applicant,

   (d) the acquisition of property and either its transfer to the applicant or its settlement for the benefit of the applicant.

(5) An order may contain consequential or supplementary provisions for giving effect to the order or for ensuring that it operates fairly as between the applicant and the other person or persons affected by it; and an order may, in particular, confer powers on trustees.

NB The above provisions came into force on 5 April 2005.

CIVIL PARTNERSHIP ACT 2004
(2004 c 33)

PART 1

INTRODUCTION

1   Civil partnership

(1) A civil partnership is a relationship between two people of the same sex ('civil partners') –

   (a) which is formed when they register as civil partners of each other –

      (i) in England or Wales (under Part 2) ...

(2) Subsection (1) is subject to the provisions of this Act under or by virtue of which a civil partnership is void.

(3) A civil partnership ends only on death, dissolution or annulment.

(4) The references in subsection (3) to dissolution and annulment are to dissolution and annulment having effect under or recognised in accordance with this Act. ...

PART 2

CIVIL PARTNERSHIP: ENGLAND AND WALES ...

CHAPTER 3

PROPERTY AND FINANCIAL ARRANGEMENTS

65   Contribution by civil partner to property improvement

(1) This section applies if –

   (a) a civil partner contributes in money or money's worth to the improvement of real or personal property in which or in the proceeds of sale of which either or both of the civil partners has or have a beneficial interest, and
   (b) the contribution is of a substantial nature.

(2) The contributing partner is to be treated as having acquired by virtue of the contribution a share or an enlarged share (as the case may be) in the beneficial interest of such an extent –

(a) as may have been then agreed, or

(b) in default of such agreement, as may seem in all the circumstances just to any court before which the question of the existence or extent of the beneficial interest of either of the civil partners arises (whether in proceedings between them or in any other proceedings).

(3) Subsection (2) is subject to any agreement (express or implied) between the civil partners to the contrary.

66   Disputes between civil partners about property

(1) In any question between the civil partners in a civil partnership as to title to or possession of property, either civil partner may apply to –

(a) the High Court, or

(b) such county court as may be prescribed by rules of court.

(2) On such an application, the court may make such order with respect to the property as it thinks fit (including an order for the sale of the property).

(3) Rules of court made for the purposes of this section may confer jurisdiction on county courts whatever the situation or value of the property in dispute.

67   Applications under section 66 where property not in possession etc

(1) The right of a civil partner ('A') to make an application under section 66 includes the right to make such an application where A claims that the other civil partner ('B') has had in his possession or under his control –

(a) money to which, or to a share of which, A was beneficially entitled, or

(b) property (other than money) to which, or to an interest in which, A was beneficially entitled,

and that either the money or other property has ceased to be in B's possession or under B's control or that A does not know whether it is still in B's possession or under B's control.

(2) For the purposes of subsection (1)(a) it does not matter whether A is beneficially entitled to the money or share –

(a) because it represents the proceeds of property to which, or to an interest in which, A was beneficially entitled, or

(b) for any other reason.

(3) Subsections (4) and (5) apply if, on such an application being made, the court is satisfied that B –

(a) has had in his possession or under his control money or other property as mentioned in subsection (1)(a) or (b), and

(b) has not made to A, in respect of that money or other property, such payment or disposition as would have been appropriate in the circumstances.

(4) The power of the court to make orders under section 66 includes power to order B to pay to A –

(a) in a case falling within subsection (1)(a), such sum in respect of the money to which the application relates, or A's s share of it, as the court considers appropriate, or

(b) in a case falling within subsection (1)(b), such sum in respect of the value of the property to which the application relates, or A's interest in it, as the court considers appropriate.

(5) If it appears to the court that there is any property which –

(a) represents the whole or part of the money or property, and

(b) is property in respect of which an order could (apart from this section) have been made under section 66,

the court may (either instead of or as well as making an order in accordance with subsection (4)) make any order which it could (apart from this section) have made under section 66.

(6) Any power of the court which is exercisable on an application under section 66 is exercisable in relation to an application made under that section as extended by this section.

68   Applications under section 66 by former civil partners

(1) This section applies where a civil partnership has been dissolved or annulled.

(2) Subject to subsection (3), an application may be made under section 66 (including that section as extended by section 67) by either former civil partner despite the dissolution or annulment (and references in those sections to a civil partner are to be read accordingly).

(3) The application must be made within the period of 3 years beginning with the date of the dissolution or annulment.

INDEX

Access orders,   379 et seq
  effect of,   380
  registration,   382
Accumulations. *See* Perpetuities and
  accumulations
Agricultural holdings,   182, 249, 266,
  311 et seq, 402 et seq. *See also* Land
  Charges; Tenancies
    compensation,   407 et seq
    definition,   311
    'farm business tenancy',   182, 266,
     402 et seq, 603
    landlord, remedies of,   314 et seq
    lettings, restrictions on,   312, 313
    rent,
     arrears of,   314
     review,   406
    tenant, removal of fixtures by,   313,
     405
Aircraft,
  flying over property,   289

Business tenants. *See also* Tenancies
  security of tenure for,   177 et seq,
  349

Charging orders,   273–274, 287
Charities. *See* Land; Registration
Civil partnership,   609 et seq
  definition,   609
  disputes,   610, 611
  home rights,   476 et seq, 496, 515,
  582 et seq
    occupation orders,   479 et seq,
    487, 498
  non-molestation orders,   489–491
  property improvement,   609
Commonhold,   570 et seq
  association,   581
  'common parts',   578
    charge over,   579
  'commonhold unit',   573
  community statement,   574, 580
    use and maintenance,   574

Commonhold (*contd.*)
  definition,   570, 571, 602
  extinguished lease,   573
  home rights,   582
  leasing,   575–576
  limitation period,   277
  mortgages,   580
  registration,   570–572, 601
Commons,
  inclosure of,   149
  public, rights of, over,   148
  registration of,   197 et seq, 540
Consumer credit,
  agreements,   232
    reopening,   233
  early payment,   232
  extortionate bargains,   232–234
Contracts,   94 et seq. *See also* Land
  misrepresentation in,   201–202
  requirements as to,   363
  restricted,   345
Conversion,
  doctrine of, abolition,   460
  perpetual leasehold, of,   10
  premises into flats,   300
Conveyances,   94 et seq. *See also*
  Covenants; Legal estates; Mortgages
  all estate clause implied in,   98
  conditions not implied in,   96
  covenants,
    benefit of,   101
    burden of,   101
    implied in,   96, 99, 156, 397 et seq
  definition,   152, 225
  execution of by court,   288
  general words, implied in,   97
  himself, to,   99
  minors, to,   472
  personal representative, by,   161
  requirements as to,   95–96, 362
  technicalities, abolition of,   96
  vesting orders as,   89
Covenants,   413 et seq. *See also*
  Conveyances; Mortgages

Covenants (*contd.*)
  assignment,
    after,   415–417, 419, 424 et seq
    against,   167, 183, 242, 324–326, 334, 605
    in breach of,   419
    liability after,   424 et seq
  benefit of,   101, 396, 414, 430
  breach of, relief of under-lessees, 170
  burden of,   101, 414, 430, 434
  enforcement of,   88, 172, 182, 422
  guarantee of performance of,   422
  himself, with,   103
  implied,   156, 304
    construction of,   103
    disposition, on,   393 et seq
    lease, validity of,   395
    title, for,   393 et seq
  joint,   102, 421
  land, binding,   101
  lease, in, waiver of,   138
  liability,   429–431
    apportionment,   417–419
    restriction on,   424–429, 431
  management companies, with, 420
  release from,   416 et seq
  repair, to,   166, 172–174, 182, 304–307, 606
    access for,   335
    specific performance,   308, 309
  restrictive,
    discharge of,   103
    notice of,   151
    power to modify,   103
    registration,   540
  reversion, running with,   133, 434
  saving,   88
  tenancies, in,   413 et seq

Deeds,   362
  construction of,   97
  conveyance by,   95
  description of,   96
  execution of,   362
  receipts, in,   99
Defective premises,   215, 606
Discrimination,
  on grounds of,
    disability,   435 et seq
    race,   241 et seq
    sex,   243

Easements,
  benefit of land, for,   148
  legal,   148
  notice of,   151
  party wall,   452
Enfranchisement. *See* Leaseholds
Equitable interests,   84 et seq, 129 et seq, 155
  conveyances overrreaching,   85
  creation and disposition of,   87
  dealings with,   130
  enforcement of,   21, 87
  entailed interests, creation of,   129
  executory limitations, restrictions on,   130
  heirs, taking by,   129
  limitation period,   282
  manner of giving effect to,   87
  registration,   558
  waste, right to commit,   130
Eviction,
  damages for unlawful,   340
  protection from,   262 et seq, 340 et seq
    exclusions,   264

Fire,
  insurance money, application of,   1, 122
  liability for,   1
Freeholds,
  mortgages of,   106, 108

Gender recognition,   607–608

Harassment,
  occupier, of,   262
Husband and wife. *See also* Matrimonial proceedings
  home rights,   476 et seq
    occupation orders,   479 et seq, 487, 498
    rights to,   295, 476 et seq, 582
  housekeeping allowances,   188
  non-molestation orders,   489–491
  rights of,   94

Incorporeal hereditaments,
  provisions apply to,   152
Injunctions,   282, 287
  anti-social behaviour,   520
  unlawful use,   521

Joint tenants,
    corporations holding property as,   9
    rights of,   93
    settled land,   93
    survivor, sale by,   196

Land,
    charity, disposition of,   384, 460,
      473
    commonhold,   570 et seq
    contracts for disposition of,   363
    covenants binding,   101
    definitions,   70, 82, 152, 225, 283,
      560
    disposition of,
      registered,   536 et seq, 562–564
      registered social landlord, by,
        505 et seq
      voidable,   147
    interests in,
      creation by parol,   95
      merger of,   148
    neighbouring, access to,   379 et seq,
      451
    notices affecting,   400
    possession, person in,   90
    registration of,   527 et seq
    third parties, taking by,   96
    time limit for recovery of,   275, 277,
      284
Land charges,   217 et seq
    access orders,   382
    agricultural holdings,   226
    contracts affected by,   210
    definitions,   225
    effect of,   220, 224
    knowledge of,   210 et seq
    local,   235 et seq
      evidence of,   240
      financial,   238
      general,   237
      mortgages,   240
      non-registration of,   238, 240
      register, appropriate,   237
      registering authorities,   236
      solicitors, protection of,   240
      what are,   235–236
    overreaching, powers of,   224
    purchasers, protection of,   220
    register of,   217, 218
      annuities,   217, 225
      deeds of arrangement,   217, 223
      pending actions,   217, 221, 223,
      382

Land charges, register of (*contd.*)
      writs,   217, 222, 223
    registered land, matters
      affecting,   225
    registration of,   150, 220, 223, 399,
      429, 479
      effective, date of,   224
    searches,   223
      official,   223
    solicitors, protection of,   224
    undisclosed,   211
Landlord. *See also* Covenants; Rent;
  Tenancies
    covenants, release from,   416 et seq
    duty of care, repairs,   215
    re-entry, right of,   415, 430, 597
    registered social,   503 et seq
      disposal of land by,   505 et seq
      repair, failure to,   508
      tenant's right to acquire,
        506–508
    repairing obligations of,   304
Leases. *See* Leaseholds
Leaseholds. *See also* Covenants;
  Tenancies
    commonhold,   575–576
    conversion of perpetually
      renewable,   10–12, 45
    covenant, waiver of,   138
    decorative repairs, relief,   137
    definition,   309
    disposition of, covenants implied
      on,   393
    enlargement of,   141
    flats,
      conversion into,   300
      enfranchisement,   386 et seq
      new leases of,   391 et seq
    forfeiture, relief against,   135, 287,
      291, 429, 510, 597–598
    insurance,   595
    invalid,   140
    licences,
      assign, to,   135, 242, 324
      effect of,   134
    lives, for,   138
    long,   596 et seq
      enfranchisement of,   203 et seq,
        386 et seq
      enlargement of,   141
      extension of,   203 et seq
      rent,   596
      special provisions,   586–587, 595
      tenancy, meaning,   208

Leaseholds (*contd.*)
  mortgages of,   107, 109
  overriding,   426–428
  perpetually renewable,   10–12, 45
  powers to grant,   89
  reversion,
    acquisition at under value,   147
    covenants running with,   133, 414
    et seq
    extinguishment of,   132
  reversionary,   138
  right to manage,   584 et seq, 603 et
  seq
    claim to,   588
    long leases,   586–587
    management functions,   591–593
    qualifying tenants,   586
  secure tenant, right to buy,   298 et
  seq
    exceptions,   299, 300
  severance, apportionment on,   132
  shared ownership,   247
  surrender of,   139
  valuation tribunals,   600
Legal estates,   84 et seq
  conversion,   155
  conveyance of, subject to interests,
  165
  definition,   153, 163
  dispositions of,   89
  infant, vested in,   156
  mentally disordered persons, vested
  in,   91
  pre-emption, rights of,   148
  reservation of,   98
  saving of,   88
  term of years,
    absolute, definition,   154
    satisfaction of,   88
Light. *See also* Prescription
  notice, registration of,   184–185
  party wall,   452
Limitation of actions,   90, 275 et seq,
  555 et seq
Local land charges. *See* Land charges

Matrimonial home. *See* Husband and
  wife
Matrimonial proceedings,
  property adjustment orders,   230,
  295, 496, 515
  sale, order for,   231
Merger,
  estates, of,   148

Misrepresentation,
  contracts in,   201–202
  damages for,   201
Mortgages,   106 et seq
  cesser of,   128
  charges by way of,   108, 128
  commonhold,   580
  contracts for land affected by,   210
  consolidation of,   112
  covenants implied in,   128
  death, on,   161
  definition,   153
  discharge,   128, 129
  documents,   113
  equitable,   111
  freeholds, of,   106, 108
  insurance money, application
    of,   122
  joint,   125
  leaseholds, of,   107, 109
  leases, surrender of,   117
  leasing powers,   114
  limitation period,   276, 277
  matrimonial home,   491–492
  mortgagee,
    powers of,   119, 121–122
    receipt of,   122, 126
  mortgagor, bankruptcy of,   124
  possession, actions for,   113, 114,
  213, 228, 492
  property subject to, sale of,   108 et
  seq, 121–122, 354
  puisne, priorities between,   114
  realisation of,   108, 109
    equitable charges,   111
  receiver, appointment of,   123, 124
  redemption of,   92, 111, 128, 284
  registered land, of,   546
  sale,
    application of proceeds of,   121
    conveyance on,   121
  statutory,   128–129
  tacking and further advances,   112,
  545
  transfer of,   113, 126
  trusts affecting, notice of,   125
  undivided shares, as to,   120

Occupier,
  harassment of,   262
  protected intending,   269 et seq

Party structures,   94, 156, 445 et seq

Party structures (*contd.*)
  disputes, 449, 452
  notices, 448–449
  walls, 445 et seq
    definition, 457
    repair, 446
Perpetuities and accumulations, 145
  et seq, 189 et seq
  appointment, powers of, 192
  double possibility, abolition of, 145
  income, accumulation, restrictions
    on, 146–147, 194, 195
  options, 193
  parenthood, presumptions as
    to, 189
  perpetuity,
    period, power to specify, 189
    rule, restrictions on, 145
  remoteness,
    avoidance of, 191, 193
    uncertainty as to, 190
  rentcharges, 194
  reverter, possibilities of, 194
  spouse, surviving, 192
Personal representatives,
  conveyance by, 17, 161
  definition, 153, 163
  devolution on, 158
  indemnities to, 61
  powers of, 77 et seq, 192, 400, 468,
  525
Powers,
  appointment, of, 144, 195
  attorney, of, 106 et seq, 470
  disclaimer of, 143
  execution of, 144
  release of, 143
Prescription, 2–4, 90. *See also* Light
  common, rights of, 198
  infant, claim against, 4
  profits a prendre, 2
  light, use of, 3
  way, rights of, 2
Public Trustee,
  estate vesting in, 159, 399

Real estate,
  administration of, 158 et seq
  devolution of, 158
Receivers, 123, 287, 470
Registration, 197 et seq, 527 et seq.
  See also Land; Land charges
  access orders, 382
  actual notice, as, 150

Registration (*contd.*)
  adjudication, 557–558
  adverse possession, 555, 565
  bankruptcy, 553
  bona vacantia, 553
  boundaries, 548
  cautions against, 534 et seq, 553
    effect, 535
    register of, 536
    right to lodge, 534
  charges, 539, 545 et seq, 563
    local land, 547, 561
    overriding statutory, 546
    tacking and further advances,
    545
  commonhold, 570–572, 601
  commons, of, 197 et seq, 540
  conclusiveness, 547
  duty to apply for, 530
  failure to comply with, 530
  effective date of, 552
  estoppel, proprietary, 558
  first, 528 et seq, 534, 561
  home rights, 477
  incorporeal hereditaments, 554
  land, dispositions of, 536 et seq,
  542, 646 et seq
    effect, 538, 539, 564
    when required, 537
  Land Registry, 556
  legal estates, 528
  notice, 539, 553
    constitutes, 150
    unilateral, 541
  pending actions, 554
  pre-emption, right of, 558
  priority protection, 551
  'proprietor in possession', 560
  restrictions, 542 et seq, 553
    application for, 543, 544
    effect, 542
    obligatory, 544
  settlements, 540, 554, 561
  title, of, 527 et seq
    freehold estates, 531, 532
    leasehold estates, 532, 533, 561
    upgrading, 548–549
Rent,
  Acts, phasing out, 342 et seq
  definition, 154
  limitation period, 277
  'low', 208, 246
  non-payment of,
    proceedings for, 7–8, 291 et seq

Rent, non-payment of (*contd.*)
    relief,   135, 287, 597
    notifying due,   596
Rented accommodation. *See* Tenancies
Rentcharge,   106 et seq
    definition,   171, 283
    enforcement of,   194
Reverter of sites,   318 et seq
    charity land,   319–327
Right to buy. *See* Leaseholds

Security of tenure. *See* Tenancies
Settled land,   13 et seq, 52. *See also*
Settlement
    charities,   460
    definitions,   14, 70, 459–460
    disposition of, restrictions on,   24
    improvement of,   54 et seq, 73 et
       seq, 374
    incumbrances affecting,   48, 52
    insurance,   56
    limitation period,   276
    maintenance,   56
    minority, during,   62, 81
    protection of,   59
    purchasers of,   67–69, 78
    registration of,   540, 554, 561
    restoration of interest in,   27
    undivided shares,   32
    what is,   14
Settlement,   13 et seq. *See also*
Settled land; Statutory owner; Tenant for
life
    assent, vesting by,   17
    capital money,
       application of,   50 et seq, 55, 175,
          372, 374, 410
       definition,   70
       investment of,   50 et seq
       repayment of,   56, 374
    compound,   30
    court, questions to,   59
    discharge, on termination of,   23
    estate owner, enforcement
      against,   21
    infant, how affected,   29, 62
    land, of,   14, 18, 19
      contracts for,   19
      duration,   14
      inter vivos,   15
    married woman, how affected,   28
    ownership, change of,   16
    personal representatives, assent
      by,   17

Settlement (*contd.*)
    trust instrument, what is,   15, 18
    trust of land in place of,   459,
      472–474
    trustees,
      application of money by,   54
      appointment of,   31, 79, 81, 90
      continuance of,   30
      infant, appointment of,   90
      notice to,   61
      number of,   59, 78
      powers of,   27, 63, 69, 77 et seq
      protection of,   60
      receipts of,   60
      reimbursement of,   61
      who are,   30
    vesting deeds,
      contents of,   15, 72
      definition,   72
      effect of,   20
      instrument, disposition prior
        to,   20
      orders, power to make,   20
    what constitutes,   13
    will, by,   16
Statutory owner. *See also* Settlement
    death of,   16
    definition,   72, 154, 164
    notice to trustees by,   60
    powers of, exercise of,   69
Survivorship,
    presumption of,   148

Tenancies. *See also* Agricultural holdings;
Covenants; Leaseholds; Rent
    agricultural,   182, 249, 266, 310 et
      seq, 342, 350, 360, 402 et seq, 497,
      498, 597, 602
    alternative accommodation,   252,
      259, 358
    assured,   266 et seq, 327, 346, 349 et
      seq, 497, 506
      accommodation
        shared,   328
        suitable alternative,   358
      assignment of,   334
      demotion,   332
      periodic,   365
      non-shorthold,   359
      possession, grounds for,   333, 353
      et seq
      security of tenure,   329
    assured shorthold,   335 et seq
      demotion,   338

Tenancies, assured shorthold (*contd.*)
  possession, recovery of, 338
  statement of terms, 336
asylum-seekers, 353
board, with, 248
business use, 177, 251, 266, 309,
  349, 350
consent,
  duty to approve, 325, 326
  duty to give, 324, 326
  refusal of, 183, 242
continuation of, 178
  rent, 179
demoted, 297, 332, 338, 517 et seq
  assignment, 519
  duration, 518
  succession to, 519
holiday, 249, 351
housing association, 250, 267, 343,
  353
housing co-operative, 251
human habitation, fitness for, 302
  et seq
introductory, 362, 511 et seq
  assignment, 516
  succession to, 515
land with dwelling-house, 248, 251,
  328
landlord, resident, 249, 351
licensed premises, 249, 350
local authority, 250, 296, 352
long, security of tenure, 365–366
low rents, at, 246, 349
new,
  duration of, 180
  terms of, 180–182
possession,
  grounds for, 252, 253 et seq, 333,
    353 et seq, 372
  orders for, 263, 333, 514, 518
  recovery of, 338
premiums, 252–253
protected, 244 et seq, 266, 342, 353,
  497
quit, notice to, 265
re-entry, right of, 415, 430, 597
regulated, 251, 255, 267
renewal of, 180
secure, 296 et seq, 326, 353, 497
  right to buy, 298 et seq
security of tenure, 177, 252, 297,
  329, 365–366
  demotion, 297

Tenancies, security of tenure (*contd.*)
  exclusions, 182
service charges, 308 et seq, 424,
  510
shared ownership, 247
statutory, 244–245, 252, 253, 266,
  309, 342, 498
  periodic, 331, 355
  terms and conditions, 245
students, 248, 351
termination of, 179, 510
transfer of, 347, 491, 496, 499
  compensation, 499
Tenant for life. *See also* Settlement
absolute owners with powers of, 26
conveyance, completion by, 49
dealings with, 47
death of, 16
definition, 72, 154, 164
married woman, exercise of powers
  by, 28
notice to trustees by, 61
others with powers of, 25
parted with interest, where, 28
powers of, 25, 26, 33 et seq, 66, 67,
  69
  assignment of, 63
  charges, 53, 69
  completion, of, 49
  compromise, to, 43, 46
  consents, to give, 44
  contracts, to enter into, 58, 63
  dispositions, on, 38
  exchange, 47, 69
  exercise of, 63, 65
  general, 46, 175
  heirlooms, to sell or buy, 47
  improvements,
    concurrence in, 56
    maintenance of, 56–57
  incumbrances, as to, 48, 52
  lease,
    acceptance by, 40
    to, 34–37, 44, 45, 47, 69
  mansion, dispose of, 46
  minerals, 38
  mortgage, to, 48, 69
  options, to grant, 39
  public purposes, to grant for, 41
  rentcharge, creation of, 56
  rents, to apportion, 44
  restrictions,
    to impose, 38

Tenants for life, powers of, restrictions
(*contd.*)
    to release,   43
    sell and exchange, to   33–34, 46,
      47, 58, 69
    small dwellings, for,   43
    streets, dedication   for,   42
    surrenders, to accept,   39
    timber, to cut,   46, 58, 62
    water rights, to grant,   41
  surrender by,   65
  trustee, as,   66
  waste, right to commit,   57, 130
  who is,   24
Tenants in common,
  dispositions to,   93
Things in action,   129
Title,
  extinction of,   276
  implied covenants for,   393
  register of,   527
  statutory period of,   210
Town and country planning,   367 et
 seq
  conservation areas,   373
  'development',   367, 409
    orders,   370
  listed buildings,   373
  'new development',   367
  obligations,   371
  permission,
    application for, 370 et seq
    granting,   369
    when required,   369
  possession, rights of, overriding   372
Treasure,   440 et seq
  definition,   440–441
  finder, duty of,   442
  inquests,   442–443
  ownership,   441, 442
  rewards,   443
Trespasser,
  entry as,   269–272
Trust for sale,   475
  definition,   155
  implied, trust of land,   460
  intestate, death of,   160
  reverter, right of,   318
  sale, postponement of,   460
Trustees. *See also* Settlement; Trust for
 sale; Trust of land
  appointment of,   31, 79, 81, 90, 91,
   469–471

Trustees (*contd.*)
  duty of care,   524, 525
  infant, appointment of,   90
  number of,   59, 78
  personal representatives, as,   92,
   468
  powers of,   27, 63, 69, 81, 193, 461,
   593 et seq
    acquisition of land,   524–525
    delegation,   462–464
    general,   77 et seq, 175
    sale,   77–78, 193
  purchase from,   91
  vesting of property in,   79, 80
Trusts of land,   32, 318, 459 et seq
  beneficiaries,
    consultation with,   464
    definition,   471
    occupy, right to,   465
  consents,   464
  definition,   459
  limitation period,   276
  minors,   472
  mortgaged property,   92
  orders, court,   466
  purchasers, protection of,   91, 467
  registration,   540
  sale,
    postponement of,   460
    proceeds of,   468
    trusts for,   460
  settlements, in place of,   459,
   472–474
  trustees,
    appointment,   79, 91, 469–471
    delegation by,   462–464
    powers of,   91, 461 et seq
    retirement,   469

Violence,
  domestic,   476 et seq
  entry by,   268

Water,
  abstraction of,   375 et seq
Will,   5–6
  construction of,   97
  devise,
    effect,   5
    property included in,   5–6
  general gift, effect,   6
  property, disposal of by,   5–6, 96
  settlement by,   16

Revision Aids

Designed for the undergraduate, the 101 Questions & Answers series and the Suggested Solutions series are for all those who have a positive commitment to passing their law examinations. Each series covers a different examinable topic and comprises a selection of answers to examination questions and, in the case of the 101 Questions and Answers, interrograms. The majority of questions represent examination 'bankers' and are supported by full-length essay solutions. These titles will undoubtedly assist you with your research and further your understanding of the subject in question.

101 Questions & Answers Series

Only £7.95 Published December 2003

Constitutional Law
ISBN: 1 85836 522 8

Law of Contract
ISBN: 1 85836 517 1

Criminal Law
ISBN: 1 85836 432 9

Law of Tort
ISBN: 1 85836 516 3

Land Law
ISBN: 1 85836 515 5

Suggested Solutions to Past Examination Questions 2001–2002 Series

Only £6.95 Published December 2003

Company Law
ISBN: 1 85836 519 8

Evidence
ISBN: 1 85836 521 X

Employment Law
ISBN: 1 85836 520 1

Family Law
ISBN: 1 85836 525 2

European Union Law
ISBN: 1 85836 524 4

For further information or to place an order, please contact:

Mail Order
Old Bailey Press at Holborn College
Woolwich Road
Charlton
London
SE7 8LN

Telephone: 020 8317 6039
Fax: 020 8317 6004
Website: www.oldbaileypress.co.uk
E-Mail: mailorder@oldbaileypress.co.uk

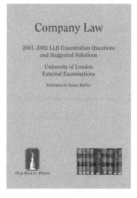

Unannotated Cracknell's Statutes for Use in Examinations

New Editions of Cracknell's Statutes

Only £11.95   Due 2005

Cracknell's Statutes provide a comprehensive series of essential statutory provisions for each subject. Amendments are consolidated, avoiding the need to cross-refer to amending legislation. Unannotated, they are suitable for use in examinations, and provide the precise wording of vital Acts of Parliament for the diligent student.

Company Law
ISBN: 1 85836 563 5

Equity and Trusts
ISBN: 1 85836 589 9

Constitutional & Administrative Law
ISBN: 1 85836 584 8

European Union Legislation
ISBN: 1 85836 590 2

Contract, Tort and Remedies
ISBN: 1 85836 583 X

Family Law
ISBN: 1 85836 566 X

Criminal Law
ISBN: 1 85836 586 4

Land: The Law of Real Property
ISBN: 1 85836 585 6

Employment Law
ISBN: 1 85836 587 2

Law of International Trade
ISBN: 1 85836 582 1

English Legal System
ISBN: 1 85836 588 0

Medical Law
ISBN: 1 85836 567 8

Revenue Law
ISBN: 1 85836 569 4

For further information or to place an order, please contact:

Customer Services
Old Bailey Press at Holborn College
Woolwich Road, Charlton
London, SE7 8LN
Telephone: 020 8317 6039
Fax: 020 8317 6004
Website: www.oldbaileypress.co.uk
E-Mail: customerservices@oldbaileypress.co.uk

Old Bailey Press

The Old Bailey Press Integrated Student Law Library is tailor-made to help you at every stage of your studies, from the preliminaries of each subject through to the final examination. The series of Textbooks, Revision WorkBooks, 150 Leading Cases and Cracknell's Statutes are interrelated to provide you with a comprehensive set of study materials.

You can buy Old Bailey Press books from your University Bookshop, your local Bookshop, directly using this form, or you can order a free catalogue of our titles from the address shown overleaf.

The following subjects each have a Textbook, 150 Leading Cases, Revision WorkBook and Cracknell's Statutes unless otherwise stated.

Administrative Law
Commercial Law
Company Law
Conflict of Laws
Constitutional Law
Conveyancing (Textbook and 150 Leading Cases)
Criminal Law
Criminology (Textbook and Sourcebook)
Employment Law (Textbook and Cracknell's Statutes)
English and European Legal Systems
Equity and Trusts
Evidence
Family Law
Jurisprudence: The Philosophy of Law (Textbook, Sourcebook and
    Revision WorkBook)
Land: The Law of Real Property
Law of International Trade
Law of the European Union
Legal Skills and System
    (Textbook)
Obligations: Contract Law
Obligations: The Law of Tort
Public International Law
Revenue Law (Textbook,
    Revision WorkBook and
    Cracknell's Statutes)
Succession (Textbook, Revision
    WorkBook and Cracknell's
    Statutes)

Mail order prices:	
Textbook	£15.95
150 Leading Cases	£12.95
Revision WorkBook	£10.95
Cracknell's Statutes	£11.95
Suggested Solutions 1999–2000	£6.95
Suggested Solutions 2000–2001	£6.95
Suggested Solutions 2001–2002	£6.95
101 Questions and Answers	£7.95
Law Update 2004	£10.95
Law Update 2005	£10.95

Please note details and prices are subject to alteration.

To complete your order, please fill in the form below:

Module	Books required	Quantity	Price	Cost
		Postage		
		TOTAL		

For the UK and Europe, add £4.95 for the first book ordered, then add £1.00 for each subsequent book ordered for postage and packing.
For the rest of the world, add 50% for airmail.

ORDERING

By telephone to Customer Services at 020 8317 6039, with your credit card to hand.

By fax to 020 8317 6004 (giving your credit card details).

Website: www.oldbaileypress.co.uk
E-Mail: customerservices@oldbaileypress.co.uk

By post to: Customer Services, Old Bailey Press at Holborn College, Woolwich Road, Charlton, London, SE7 8LN.

When ordering by post, please enclose full payment by cheque or banker's draft, or complete the credit card details below. You may also order a free catalogue of our complete range of titles from this address.

We aim to despatch your books within 3 working days of receiving your order. All parts of the form must be completed.

Name

Address

Postcode

E-Mail
Telephone

Total value of order, including postage: £ ....

I enclose a cheque/banker's draft for the above sum, or

charge my   ☐ Access/Mastercard   ☐ Visa   ☐ American Express

Cardholder: ....

Card number

☐☐☐☐ ☐☐☐☐ ☐☐☐☐ ☐☐☐☐

Expiry date   ☐☐☐☐

Signature: ....Date: ....